CPA excel

CPA Review

Financial Accounting and Reporting 2

Allen H. Bizzell, Ph.D., CPA
Ervin L. Black, Ph.D.
Charles J. Davis, Ph.D., CPA
Donald R. Deis Jr., Ph.D., CPA, CFE
Pam Smith, Ph.D., CPA, MBA

EFFICIENT LEARNING SYSTEMS ™

PO Box 4223 Sedona, AZ 86340-4223
888.884.5669 N.America   928.204.1066 International

www.cpaexcel.com

Edward Foley, Chairman and Founder
Rahul Srivastava, CEO and President
Nigel Snow, VP Content Development
Gun Granath, Editor

Efficient Learning Systems, Inc.
1120 W. SR 89A, Suite D9
Sedona, AZ 86336 U.S.A.
www.cpaexcel.com

ISBN 978-1-4802316-0-3
Edition 7.8

Printed in the United States of America

ABOUT THE CPAexcel™ CPA EXAM REVIEW COURSES
OUR AUTHORS

CPAexcel™ content is authored by a team of accounting professors and CPA exam experts from top accounting colleges such as the University of Texas at Austin (frequently ranked the #1 accounting school in the country), California State University at Sacramento, Northern Illinois University, and University of North Alabama.

Professor Allen H. Bizzell
CPAexcel Author, Mentor and Video Lecturer
Ph.D., CPA
Former Associate Dean and Accounting Faculty, University of Texas (Retired)
Associate Professor, Department of Accounting, Texas State University (Retired)

Professor Ervin L. Black
CPAexcel Author and Video Lecturer
Ph.D.
Brigham Young University - Lecturer in international accounting and financial accounting.

Professor Gregory Carnes
CPAexcel Author and Video Lecturer
Ph.D., CPA
Raburn Eminent Scholar of Accounting, University of North Alabama
Former Dean, College of Business, Lipscomb University
Former Chair, Department of Accountancy, Northern Illinois University

Professor B. Douglas Clinton
CPAexcel Author and Video Lecturer
Ph.D., CPA, CMA
Alta Via Consulting Professor of Management Accountancy, Department of Accountancy, Northern Illinois University

Professor Charles J. Davis
CPAexcel Author, Mentor and Video Lecturer
Ph.D., CPA
Professor of Accounting, Department of Accounting, College of Business Administration, California State University - Sacramento

Professor Donald R. Deis Jr.
CPAexcel Author and Video Lecturer
Ph.D., CPA, MBA
Ennis & Virginia Joslin Endowed Chair in Accounting, College of Business, Texas A&M University - Corpus Christi
Former Director of the School of Accountancy, University of Missouri - Columbia
Former Professor and Director of the Accounting Ph.D. Program, Louisiana State University - Baton Rouge

Professor Marianne M. Jennings
CPAexcel Author and Video Lecturer
J.D.
Professor of Legal and Ethical Studies, W.P. Carey School of Business, Arizona State University

Robert A. Prentice
CPAexcel Business Law Co-Author
Ed and Molly Smith Centennial Professor In Business Law and Distinguished Teaching Professor, J.D.
McCombs School of Business, University of Texas - Austin

Professor Pam Smith
CPAexcel Author and Video Lecturer
Ph.D., MBA, CPA
KPMG Professor of Accountancy, Department of Accountancy, Northern Illinois University

Professor Dan Stone
CPAexcel Author and Video Lecturer
Ph.D., MPA
Gatton Endowed Chair, Von Allmen School of Accountancy and the Department of Management, University of Kentucky

Professor Donald Tidrick
CPAexcel Author and Video Lecturer
Ph.D., CPA, CMA, CIA
Deloitte Professor of Accountancy, Northern Illinois University, Former Associate Chairman of the Department of Accounting, Director of the Professional Program in Accounting and Director of the CPA Review Course, University of Texas at Austin, 1991 - 2000

CPAexcel's BITE-SIZED LESSONS^{SM} AND EFFICIENT LEARNING SYSTEM™

A key reason why CPAexcel students pass the CPA exam at rates almost twice that for all other students is that they study using CPAexcel's bite-sized lessons^{SM} and Efficient Learning System.

Bite-Sized Lessons:
CPAexcel's course materials are broken down into many lessons each one of which covers a single topic that can often be learned in about 30 minutes. The course materials available in each bite-sized lesson are shown below in an image of a typical "Lesson Overview" panel displayed alongside a part of the Table of Contents for that section of the course materials. Each of the learning resources listed in the Lesson Overview are linked to that particular learning resource for that lesson.

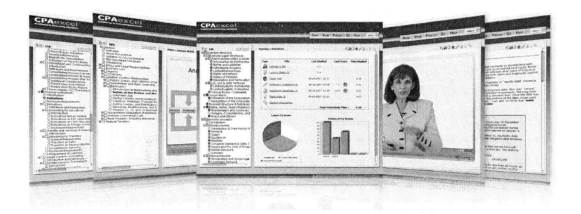

Students may use each lesson's learning resources in any desired sequence. Typically, a student will first watch and listen to the Video Lecture and then either review the Study Text or go directly to the Proficiency Questions to test and reinforce his or her knowledge of the lesson content. Then he or she might test his or her knowledge on Past Exam Questions. Note that each of the learning resources are just one click away from each other, enabling the student to easily access all the resources needed to quickly master that bite-sized topic before moving to the next topic.

Compared to other review courses, CPAexcel's bite-sized lessons are a much more efficient way to master the large body of knowledge required to pass the CPA exam. They are a key contributor to the exam success of CPAexcel's students.

Efficient Learning System:
CPAexcel's software-driven Efficient Learning System tightly-integrates the use of all CPAexcel's learning functions including bite-sized lessons. Key benefits to students are:
- Significant increases in knowledge gained and retained per hour of study
- Increased student focus and motivation
- Automatic progress measurement, tracking, and reporting
- Two-click access to fellow students and professors worldwide
- Exact replication of the formats and software functions used in the CPA exam itself
- 24/7/365 courseware access from any computer anywhere, with synchronization of scores
- Online and offline personalized updates with automatic alerts

Free Demonstration:
Free demonstrations of CPAexcel are available at http://www.cpaexcel.com/demo_reg.jsp

Table of Contents

Legend:

The following icons indicate specific types of content within the study text of this book.

 Exam Tip

 Study Tip

 Example

 Definition

 Note

 Question

Financial Accounting and Reporting

Welcome

I. **Business Enterprise Accounting and Reporting**

A. Business enterprise accounting and reporting relates to for-profit enterprises in the Financial Accounting and Reporting (FAR) section of the CPA exam. The CPA exam focuses on the accounting and reporting represented on the four major financial statements: balance sheet, income statement, statement of cash flows and the statement of changes in equity. A very large amount of information is presented in FAR, but it all basically boils down to three functions:

1. Recognition;

2. Measurement;

3. Disclosure.

B. One of the most important threads running through the CPA Exam is the framework of concepts from which the FASB develops GAAP. This framework provides the theoretical underpinnings for all GAAP. The framework concepts are:

1. Primary qualitative characteristics - relevance and faithful representation;

2. Enhancing qualitative characteristics - comparability, verification, timeliness and understandability;

3. Assumptions - entity, going concern, time period and unit of measure;

4. Principles - historical cost, revenue recognition, matching and full disclosure;

5. Constraints - materiality and cost benefit.

    Each of these concepts is covered in the material.

C. If you really understand these concepts, you then have a basis for figuring out specific questions in areas you may not have studied completely. Trust your training and your gut instinct when answering the questions. Basing your response on the framework will serve you well.

D. All of the areas and topics in the AICPA Content Specifications for FAR are covered in the Study Text. Generally, the topics are presented in the Study Text in the same sequence as they are presented in the Content Specification. However, in a few cases, the order of presentation for some items is different than in the specifications.

1. The Content Specifications provide a complete list of matters subject to being tested on the exam, but the topics are not intended to be presented in a logical sequence for learning purposes.

2. Therefore, a few topics have been rearranged in the Study Text to present them in a more logical sequence for learning purposes.

E. In covering the material, you should spend more time on the areas most difficult for you. These may come from the following list of topics which are common on the exam:

1. Inventories;

2. Revenue recognition;

3. Financial instruments, including Investments, Bonds and Derivatives;

4. Stock options and Earnings per Share (EPS);

5. Pensions;

6. Leases;

7. Income tax accounting;

8. Statement of cash flows;

9. Accounting changes.

10. Business combinations;

11. Consolidated financial statements.

F. For each topic, outline the main GAAP (what is recognized and when, how much, and are there additional important disclosures). Concentrate on journal entries. If you know how to record the relevant journal entries and understand how they affect the financial statements, you are 85% there.

G. Don't ignore topics you feel are really challenging. You learned it once, so you can refresh your mind more easily than you think. Remember Dollar Value LIFO for example - if you have covered this in your classes, you can "relearn" it quickly.

H. Significant differences between U.S. GAAP and International Financial Reporting Standards (IFRS) will be tested. Review the significant differences that are presented at the end of all relevant lessons of the Study Text. Focus on differences related to recognition and measurement.

I. Finally, when you study and review, don't just read passively. There is so much to remember as you study:

1. Continually assess whether you understand the material;

2. Take notes in your own words on aspects that you find difficult to remember;

3. For the more complex material, jot down the main procedures and reasons for the procedure;

4. Periodically go back over your notes and you will find that the amount of material that seems most challenging begins to dwindle.

J. We are confident that you will succeed if you spend sufficient quality time studying the material and practicing the questions. Please let us know if you feel there are areas where the material needs improving. Thank you.

~ Professors Charles Davis, Pam Smith and Allen Bizzell

II. Governmental and Not-for-Profit Enterprises

A. The governmental and not-for-profit (GNP) topics are traditionally covered in a governmental accounting course and represent about twenty percent of the material in FAR. If you took a governmental accounting course, you should find the questions to be fairly easy. Do not worry if you did not take such a course because the questions lean toward basic governmental and nonprofit accounting and financial reporting, which can be learned with a modest amount of effort.

B. The governmental accounting and reporting topics in the new exam are very similar to those covered in the old exam.

1. Governmental accounting concepts

  a. Measurement focus and basis of accounting

  b. Fund accounting concepts and applications

  c. Budgetary accounting

 2. Financial Statements

  a. Government-wide financial statements

  b. Fund-level financial statements

 3. Financial reporting entity

 4. Typical items and specific types of transactions and events

  a. Net assets

  b. Fund balances

  c. Capital assets and infrastructure assets

  d. General long-term liabilities

  e. Interfund activity

  f. Nonexchange transactions (e.g., property taxes)

  g. Expenditures

  h. Encumbrances

C. The not-for-profit (nongovernmental) accounting and reporting topics on the new exam are also similar to the topics covered on the old exam.

 1. Financial statements

 2. Typical items and specific types of transactions and events

  a. Contributions

  b. Restrictions

  c. Net Assets

  d. Expenses including functional expenses

  e. Investments

D. It is important to remember that the Governmental Accounting Standards Board (GASB) establishes accounting and reporting standards for state and local governmental entities. The Financial Accounting Standards Board (FASB) establishes accounting and reporting standards for not-for-profit (nongovernmental) entities. Be on the lookout for questions related to hospitals or universities since governmental hospitals and universities follow GASB standards while nongovernmental (not-for-profit) hospitals and universities follow FASB standards. It is possible that you will see task-based questions that will require you to search the FASB standards to answer not-for-profit questions.

E. In the governmental area, it is very important to have a good understanding of each of the types of funds used. You must know the basis of accounting for each fund type and the purpose of each fund. You should also have a good understanding of both government-wide financial statements (GASB Statement No. 34) and fund-level financial statements. If you took a governmental accounting course in the past, be careful with questions about fund balance since GASB Statement No. 54 completely changed all of the categories of fund balance.

F. In the not-for-profit area, you should expect questions about when to recognize a contribution as revenue and how to account for contributions that have restrictions related to purpose or time.

G. With practice, you should be able to master GNP questions. In my governmental accounting classes, I give a pre-test on the first day with 20 typical GNP CPA exam-style questions and a post-test at the end. Since GNP accounting is "different," the pre-test result is usually less than 20% correct. The post-test is usually 85 to 90% correct. You should see similar results.

Professor Donald Deis

Financial Accounting Professors

Dr. Allen Bizzell has been involved with the CPA Exam for almost 30 years as a researcher, developer of exam-related materials, and review course instructor. He has conducted numerous CPA Exam-related studies, including several analyses of CPA Exam Candidates' Characteristics and Performance for the Texas State Board of Public Accountancy. He has developed CPA review materials and taught review courses at both the national and local levels. Included in his innovative review materials is the use of simple network diagrams to depict the relationships between related accounting concepts/topics and the appropriate treatment for each. These diagrams are powerful tools for not only understanding accounting materials, but also for retaining the knowledge needed to pass the CPA Exam.

Several publishers have approached Dr. Bizzell to develop financial accounting textbooks incorporating his instructional methodology. According to Dr. Bizzell, he has not done so because the traditional textbook does not lend itself to using all the elements of the methodology. He believes, "The CPAexcel approach is the first to provide the capabilities to capture and deliver to the user the benefits of the methodology."

Dr. Ervin L. Black completed his Ph.D. at the University of Washington in 1995 and has held faculty positions at Brigham Young University, University of Washington, University of Wyoming, and University of Arkansas. Dr. Black teaches undergraduate and graduate courses in international accounting and financial accounting. He has also taught CPA review courses for the past 12 years. Professor Black's research is primarily in the financial accounting and international accounting areas, with emphasis on examining the usefulness of firm financial characteristics in different settings. His research has been published in academic and practitioner journals and cited in the Wall Street Journal, Fortune and The Financial Times. Professor Black is active in the International and Financial Reporting Sections of the American Accounting Association. He is also an associate editor of the Journal of International Accounting Research. Prior to his academic career he worked for seven years in private industry as a financial analyst and corporate treasurer.

Dr. Charles Davis is currently Professor of Accounting in the College of Business Administration, California State University, Sacramento. His main teaching interest is financial reporting. He has taught in several educational and professional development programs including calculus for MBA students, CPA review courses, seminars for international groups from Russia, Turkmenistan, Latvia, and technical lectures in financial reporting for accounting professionals.

Prof. Davis's work has been published in several domestic and international academic and professional journals in the area of accounting and health care finance. In addition, Dr. Davis is a co-author of *Intermediate Accounting*, published by McGraw-Hill (2002), a mainstream accounting text used by many universities in the U.S. and internationally. Prof. Davis has also written several online accounting educational packages and has reviewed twelve academic accounting texts.

Prof. Davis has been involved in many consulting engagements in the area of financial reporting, real estate feasibility, EDP auditing and accounting systems, and has "Big Eight" accounting experience (now the "Big Four"). He is the recipient of teaching awards from California State University, Sacramento and the University of Illinois.

Dr. Donald R. Deis Jr. is the Ennis & Virginia Joslin Endowed Chair in Accounting within the College of Business at Texas A&M University - Corpus Christi. Prior to joining TAMUCC, Dr. Deis was the Joseph A. Silvoso Distinguished Director of the School of Accountancy at the University of Missouri-Columbia, which is one of the top 20 accounting programs in the country, and was Ernst&Young Endowed Research Professor and Director of the Accounting Ph.D. Program at Louisiana State University-Baton Rouge. His primary research focus is on the quality of audits provided by public accounting firms, fraud, corporate governance and the privatization of government services. He is a recipient of the George F. Fair Excellence in Teaching and MBA Association Professor of the Year awards (LSU).

Dr. Pam Smith is KPMG Professor of Accountancy at Northern Illinois University. She has won awards voted on by her students (Executive MBA Golden Apple) and by her peers (Illinois CPA Society's 2008 Educator of the Year). As faculty advisor, Pam sparked the creation of an honor pledge and code of conduct. She is co-author of NIU's *Building Ethical Leaders* handbook and a developer of the college's BELIEF initiative (Building Ethical Leaders using an Integrated Ethics Framework), both of which have been integrated across the college. Because of her research in accounting for derivatives and hedging, she was called as an expert witness in the Enron trial. Pam and her husband are licensed handlers of their certified therapy dog, Shelby, who provides emotional therapy to seniors and special needs children.

Specific Transactions, Events and Disclosures

Accounting Changes and Error Corrections

Types of Changes and Accounting Approaches

This is the first of several lessons addressing accounting changes. This lesson provides a description of the types of changes, and of the accounting approaches that apply to them.

After studying this lesson, you should be able to:

1. *Identify the types of accounting changes allowed by GAAP.*

2. *Note the available accounting approaches.*

3. *Choose the appropriate accounting approach for a given accounting change.*

4. *List items which do not qualify as accounting principle changes.*

5. *Contrast the basic aspects of the two available accounting approaches.*

6. *Distinguish direct and indirect effects of accounting principle changes.*

I. **Background and Summary**

   A. **Accounting Changes and Error Corrections --** GAAP specifies how to account for changes in accounting. The four items addressed:

      1. Accounting principle changes (example: change from FIFO to weighted-average method);

      2. Accounting estimate changes (example: change the useful life of a plant asset);

      3. Changes in reporting entity (example: change in the composition of the subsidiary group in a consolidated enterprise);

      4. Corrections of errors in prior financial statements (example: discover that an item expensed in a prior year should have been capitalized and amortized).

   B. Error corrections are not considered an accounting change but the procedures for recording are the same as for accounting principle changes and thus are covered in this set of lessons.

II. **Accounting Approaches are Specified for Accounting Changes and Errors**

   A. Retrospective - application of a principle to prior periods as if that principle had always been used. The procedure records the effect of the change on prior years as an adjustment to the beginning balance in retained earnings for the year of change rather than in income; prior year financial statements reported comparatively with the current year statements are adjusted to reflect the new method. The result is that the financial statements of all periods presented reflect the same (new) accounting principle. Retrospective application enhances comparability (a quality from the conceptual framework) across the financial statements of different years reported comparatively. Therefore the term "retrospective application" implies that the company applied the new standard it adopted to all periods shown unless it was impracticable to determine the cumulative effect or the period-specific change. When there is retrospective application the entity must disclose the effects on income and income taxes.

   B. Prospective - apply the change to current and future periods only; prior year statements are unaffected.

   C. Restatement is the term reserved specifically for error changes. Restatement requires correcting the comparative financial information presented along with correcting the opening retained earnings balance. The entity must disclose the nature of the error and the effect on current and prior periods.

III. Summary of Accounting -- The following summarizes the types of items found in the accounting changes area, and the associated accounting approach.

Accounting Change or Item	Accounting Approach
Accounting principle change	Retrospective
Accounting principle change - determining prior year effects impracticable	Prospective
Accounting estimate change*	Prospective
Change in reporting entity	Retrospective
Correction of accounting error	Restatement**

*includes changes in depreciation, amortization and depletion methods which are treated as a change in estimate effected by a change in accounting principle

**this is the same accounting procedure as retrospective but the difference in terminology highlights the distinction between a voluntary accounting principle change and the correction of an error, called a "prior period adjustment."

IV. Accounting For Principle Changes - Retrospective Application

Definition:
A Change in Accounting Principle: A change from one generally accepted accounting principle to another when there are at least two acceptable principles, or when the current principle used is no longer generally accepted. A change in the method of **applying** a principle is also considered a change in accounting principle.

Example:
Changing inventory cost flow assumption (LIFO to FIFO); changing the accounting for long-term construction contracts (completed contract to percentage of completion), change in method of applying LCM to inventory (individual, group, aggregate).

A. Changes in depreciation method, amortization method, and depletion method are treated as **estimate changes**.

B. The following are **not accounting principle changes**:

   1. Initial adoption of a new principle to new events for the first time or for events that were immaterial in their effect in the past;

Example:
Capitalizing interest for the first time because in the past the firm was not involved in construction activities to a significant extent. This is not an accounting principle change.

   2. Adoption or modification of a principle for transactions that are clearly different in substance from those in the past;

3. A change in method that is a planned procedure as part of the normal application of a method (example: the change to the straight-line method late in the life of an asset depreciated on the double-declining balance method);

4. The change from a principle that is not generally accepted to one that is accepted (treat as an error correction).

C. **Retrospective Application --** The following steps are performed to implement retrospective application of an accounting principle change.

1. The cumulative effect of the change on periods before those presented is reflected in the carrying amounts of affected assets and liabilities as of the beginning of the earliest period presented, along with an offsetting adjustment to the opening balance of retained earnings for that period.

2. The financial statements for prior periods presented comparatively are recast to reflect the period-specific effects of applying the new principle. Each account affected by the change is adjusted as if the new method had been used in those periods.

3. Through a journal entry, the beginning balance of retained earnings in the year of the change is adjusted to reflect the use of the new principle through that date. The amount of this cumulative effect is generally not the same amount as that for step 1 above because different periods are covered in each.

Example:
In 20x5, a firm changes from the weighted-average (WA) method of accounting for inventory to FIFO. The 20x3 and 20x4 reports reissued comparatively with 20x5 will now reflect the FIFO method even though in those prior years the WA had been used. The journal entry to record the change will adjust beginning 20x5 inventory and retained earnings to the amounts that would have been in those accounts at that date had FIFO always been used (this is the cumulative effect recorded in the entry - through 1/1/x5). In the retained earnings statement, the beginning balance in retained earnings for 20x3 will be adjusted for the effects of the change on income for all years before 20x3 (this is the cumulative effect reported in the retained earnings statement - through 1/1/x3). The two cumulative effect amounts cover different numbers of years.

D. **Justification for Principle Change --** An accounting principle change can be made only if the change is required by a new pronouncement, or if the entity can justify the use of an allowable new principle on the basis that it is preferable in terms of financial reporting. The allowable new principle must improve financial reporting given the environment of the firm. Common justifications include changing business conditions, and better matching of revenues and expenses.

1. **Caution:** When new accounting standards are adopted, retrospective application may not be required, even though the standard may require that a new accounting principle or method be applied. In such cases, the transitional guidance of the new standard is to be followed.

E. **Direct and Indirect Effects --** Retrospective application of a change in accounting principle is limited to the direct effects of the change and related tax effects. *Direct effects* are those recognized changes in assets or liabilities necessary to effect the change (for example, the change to inventory due to change in cost flow assumption). Related effects on deferred tax accounts, or an impairment adjustment resulting from applying LCM valuation to the new inventory balance are also examples of direct effects.

1. *Indirect effects* are changes in current or future cash flows resulting from making a change in accounting principle applied retrospectively. Such changes are recognized in the period of change. Prior period financial statements are not adjusted although a description of the effects, amounts and per share amounts are disclosed in the footnotes.

> **Example:**
> A change in nondiscretionary profit-sharing plan resulting from a principle change affecting earnings causes the firm to increase profit-sharing payments in the current period as a result of restating prior period income. The payments are recognized in the current year, not retrospectively.

2. Litigation settlements from lawsuits initiated in previous years but paid or received in the current year are also not treated retrospectively. They are considered an event of the period of settlement and included in that period's earnings.

F. **Disclosures for Principle Changes --** Disclosures in the year of change and also the interim period of change include the following. Subsequent financial statements need not repeat these disclosures.

1. Nature and reason for the change including why the new change is preferable (a change caused by the adoption of a new standard is sufficient justification).

2. Method of applying the change.

3. For current and prior periods retrospectively adjusted, the effect of the change on income from continuing operations and net income, and all other affected line items (for income statement, balance sheet and statement of cash flows), and any affected per share amounts. A firm may provide only the line item information, or may disclose the entire statements as adjusted, in the notes.

4. The cumulative effect on retained earnings (or other relevant equity accounts) as of the beginning of the earliest period presented.

5. If it was not practicable to apply the retrospective method to all periods, the reasons why and a description of the alternative method used report the change.

6. Summaries of financial results (such as major financial statement subtotals for the previous ten years) as reported in the notes are also retrospectively adjusted for the change.

Retrospective Application

This lesson provides detailed guidance on how to account for accounting principle changes.

After studying this lesson, you should be able to:

1. *Record the journal entry for an accounting principle change.*

2. *Discuss how prior year financial statements are recast for reporting in the year of change.*

3. *Prepare the comparative retained earnings statements for an accounting principle change.*

4. *Explain the modifications to the procedures when it is impracticable to determine prior year effects.*

I. **Accounting Principle Change - Retrospective Application**

A. A firm changed its method of inventory valuation from WA (weighted-average) to FIFO in 20x8 and reports the previous two years' financial statements comparatively with 20x8. The change was made for financial reporting purposes only. Management believes that the FIFO method more accurately portrays the movement of goods and provides a better matching of revenues and expenses. The income tax rate is 40%. Net income for 20x8 as computed under WA would have been $12,000. The retained earnings balance at the beginning of 20x6 was $42,000. The firm has not declared dividends during the last four years.

	Ending inventory balances		Income recomputed under FIFO
	WA	**FIFO**	
20x8	$56,000	$68,000	$14,400
20x7	42,000	50,000	12,800
20x6	30,000	34,000	10,200
20x5	25,000	27,000	

B. *Journal entry to record the principle change:*

1/1/x8		
Inventory ($50,000 - $42,000)	8,000	
Cumulative effect of accounting change (.60 x $8,000)		4,800
Deferred income tax liability		3,200

C. **The Cumulative Effect --** Is closed to retained earnings. It does not appear in the income statement. The $8,000 amount is the difference in total pretax income for the firm from its beginning to 12/31/x7 between WA and FIFO. If the firm had been on FIFO for those years, then cost of goods sold for those years would have been $8,000 less because FIFO ends that period with $8,000 more inventory.

1. The accounting change increases income for financial reporting in years before 20x8. Therefore, income tax expense has increased for those years causing the deferred tax liability to increase as well through the beginning of 20x8.

D. The 20x8 journal involving inventory and cost of goods sold will reflect the FIFO method.

E. *Comparative statements:*

1. The income statements and balance sheets for 20x7 and 20x6 will now report cost of sales, income, inventory, and any other related account based on the FIFO method.

2. 20x8 statements reflect the application of the FIFO method.

3. The retained earnings statement reports the effect of the change on income for all years before 20x6. The income amounts reported in the statement reflect the FIFO method.

F. *Retained Earnings Statements*

	20x8	20x7	20x6
Retained earnings, January 1			$42,000
			1,200*
	$66,200	$53,400	$43,200
Net income	14,400	12,800	10,200
Retained earnings, December 31	$80,600	$66,200	$53,400

*post-tax difference in beginning 20x6 inventory amounts ($27,000 - $25,000) x .6 = $1,200. Note that the $1,200 amount is the *reported* cumulative effect and is different from the $4,800 amount *recorded*. The income amounts shown for 20x6 and 20x7 are the updated amounts reflecting FIFO and thus update the retained earnings balances subsequent to the 1/1/x6 retained earnings balance. Ultimately, by 1/1/x8, a $4,800 increase is reflected in the retained earnings balances reported.

II. **Inability to Determine Prior Year Effects --** It is not always possible to apply a method retrospectively because required information is not available. In such cases, the usual procedures are not applied.

Example:
The change to LIFO requires the firm to apply LIFO all the way back to the beginning of the firm (or a point at which there was no inventory). The procedure requires the identification of cost layers for any prior year for which inventory increased in physical amount. This information may be difficult or impossible to obtain. Purchase price information may no longer be available. Even more challenging would be to apply LIFO retrospectively in a manufacturing context where possibly hundreds of different items are integrated into many different products.

A. **Impracticability Exception --** The retrospective approach is not to be applied if any of the following applies:

1. After making a reasonable effort to apply the principle to prior periods, the entity is unable to do so;

2. Assumptions about management's intent in prior periods are required and such assumptions cannot be independently substantiated;

3. Retrospective application requires estimates of amounts based on information that was unavailable in the prior periods or on circumstances that did not exist in the prior periods.

B. Two Impracticability Cases

1. When it is impracticable to determine the period-specific effects of the change for one or more prior periods presented, the change is applied as of the beginning of the earliest period for which retrospective application is practicable (which may be the current period).

2. When the cumulative effect as of the beginning of the current period cannot be determined, then the change is made prospectively as of the earliest date possible.

Example:
A firm changes from FIFO to LIFO in 20x4, but the cumulative effect for prior years cannot be determined. However, records enable the firm to apply LIFO beginning in 20x1. The FIFO ending inventory balance for 20x0 is used as the beginning LIFO balance for 20x1. LIFO is applied from that point. No cumulative effect is recorded.

III. Change in Reporting Entity - Retrospective Application

A. Change in Reporting Entity -- A change in reporting entity results in financial statements of a different reporting entity. A change in reporting entity is limited mainly to:

1. Presenting consolidated or combined financial statements in place of financial statements of individual entities;

2. Changing the set of subsidiaries that make up a consolidated group;

3. Changing the entities included in combined financial statements;

4. Change from cost or fair value method for accounting for an investment to the equity method for investment.

B. A business combination accounted for by the purchase method, or the consolidation of a variable interest entity is not a change in reporting entity.

C. Retrospective Method -- The retrospective method is applied (not considered a restatement of prior financial statements). Prior financial statements are recast as if the new entity existed in those prior periods.

> **Note:**
> A change from cost or fair value method accounting for an investment to equity method is a retrospective change in accounting. A change from equity method to cost or fair value method is accounted for prospectively.

D. Disclosures Required for Current Period -- (subsequent financial statements need not repeat these disclosures).

1. Nature of the change and reason for it;

2. Effect of the change on income from continuing operations, net income, other comprehensive income, and related per share amounts.

Prospective Application

This lesson takes a closer look at accounting for estimate changes, including changes in depreciation, amortization, and depletion methods.

After studying this lesson, you should be able to:

1. *Identify accounting estimate changes.*

2. *Prepare the appropriate reporting for estimate changes.*

3. *Account for changes in depreciation, amortization and depletion methods.*

I. **Accounting for Estimate Changes - Prospective Application**

> **Definition:**
> *A Change in Accounting Estimate*: derived from new information and is a change that causes the carrying amount of an asset or liability to change, or that changes the subsequent accounting for an asset or liability. Estimate changes are the most frequent type of accounting change.

> **Example:**
> Most areas within financial accounting are subject to estimation. Bad debts, warranties, depreciation, pension accounting, lower of cost or market, asset impairment, and many others are examples.

A. Recall that this category of accounting change - **estimate changes** - now also includes changing a method of depreciation, amortization, or depletion. Such a principle change cannot be distinguished from a change in estimate, because the method change reflects a change in the expected pattern of benefits to be received from the asset in the future. Therefore, a change in depreciation method is considered to be a change in estimate effected by a change in accounting principle.

1. In general, when a change in principle cannot be distinguished from a change in estimate, the change is treated as a change in estimate (prospectively). For example, a cost that has been capitalized and amortized in the past is now expensed immediately because future benefits are no longer probable. The change to immediate expensing is treated as a change in estimate (no future periods are expected to benefit).

B. **Prospective Application --** Changes in accounting estimate are accounted for in the current and future periods (if affected). Prior period statements are not affected in anyway nor are there disclosures with respect to prior statements. The new information prompting the change was not known until the current year and is not relevant to prior periods.

1. There is no "cumulative effect" account for estimate changes;

2. For estimate changes affecting only the current period, the new estimate is used and the usual accounting procedure applies;

3. For changes affecting current and future periods, the book value of the relevant account at the beginning of the current year is used as the basis for applying the new estimate;

4. For changes in method of depreciation, amortization, or depletion, the book value at the beginning of the current period is used as the basis for expense recognition over the

asset's remaining useful life, along with new estimates of salvage value and useful life if necessary. The new method is applied as of the beginning of the period of change.

C. **Disclosures for Estimate Changes** -- For the current period, the following are required:

1. Effect of the change on income from continuing operations, net income, and related per share amounts for the period of change for estimate changes affecting current and future periods;

2. For estimate changes affecting only the period of change, the above disclosures are required only if material.

D. **Numerical Example - Change in Estimate of Useful Life** -- In 20x8, a firm using the sum-of-years-digits (SYD) method of depreciation changed the total useful life of a plant asset (cost $19,000; residual value $4,000) from ten years to five years. The revised estimate of residual value is $1,000. The asset was purchased 1/1/x5.

Example:
Original SYD = 1 + 2 + ... + 9 + 10 = 55

Revised SYD = 1 + 2 = 3 (only two years remain in revised useful life at 1/1/x8)

Book value at 1/1/x8 = $19,000 - ($19,000 - $4,000)[(10+9+8)/55] = $11,636

Depreciation for 20x8 = ($11,636 - $1,000)/[(2/3)] = $7,091

Journal entry for depreciation, 12/31/x8

Depreciation expense	7,091	
Accumulated depreciation		7,091

If the estimates were not changed, depreciation in 20x8 would have been: ($19,000 - $4,000)(7/55) = $1,909. The increase in depreciation is $7,091 ? $1,909 = $5,182. Assume a 30% tax rate. The decrease in income for the current year due to the estimate change is .70($5,182) = $3,627.

Footnote: During the current year, the useful life and salvage value of equipment were reduced resulting in a decrease in current year income of $3,627.

E. **Numerical Example - Change in Depreciation Method** -- In 20x6, management changes from the double-declining balance method (DDB) to the straight-line method (SL) to reflect new information suggesting that the asset will provide more uniform benefits and for a longer period of time than originally expected. The affected asset was purchased at the beginning of 20x5 for $22,000. Original estimates were: 5-year total useful life; $2,000 residual value. As of the beginning of 20x6, the revised estimates are: 9-year total useful life; $200 residual value.

See the following example.

Example:
Book value at 1/1/x6 = $22,000 - $22,000(2/5) = $13,200

Depreciation for 20x6 = ($13,200 - $200)/(9 - 1) = $1,625

(at the beginning of 20x6, eight years remain in the asset's useful life)

Journal entry for depreciation, 12/31/x6

Depreciation expense	1,625	
Accumulated depreciation		1,625

The same entry would be recorded for the remaining seven years of the asset's life after 20x6 unless additional estimate or method changes were made.

Accounting Errors - Restatement

The last lesson on accounting changes considers errors affecting income of prior periods.

After studying this lesson, you should be able to:

1. *Identify when an error has occurred, and if it affects income of prior periods. Record a prior period adjustment from given information.*

2. *Record a prior period adjustment from given information.*

3. *Describe how statements of prior periods are restated for an error correction.*

4. *Determine when a prior period adjustment is recorded in a journal entry, and when it is reported in the retained earnings statement.*

I. **Correction of Error In Prior Financial Statements - Restatement**

A. **Error in prior period financial statements --** An error in a prior period financial statement is caused when information existed at the time the statements were prepared enabling correct reporting, but a misstatement was made causing erroneous recognition, measurement, or disclosure. The presumption is that the correct reporting could have been accomplished in the past. Errors made in the current year but discovered before the closing process are corrected without special procedures.

   1. Recall that the change from an inappropriate accounting principle to one that is generally accepted is considered an error correction.

   2. Changes in estimates that reflect negligence or that were made in bad faith are also considered error corrections.

B. **Restatement of prior financial statements --** Although not an accounting change, an error correction uses the same accounting procedures as accounting principle changes and is addressed by the same accounting standard. However, the term "restatement" is used rather than "retrospective application" to distinguish voluntary principle changes from restatements due to errors and to reduce potential confusion between the two.

C. The procedure for **error corrections** is the same as for retrospective application except for the use of the term "restatement."

   1. The effect of the error correction on periods before those presented is reflected in the affected real accounts as of the beginning of the earliest period presented, including an adjustment to the opening balance of retained earnings (prior period adjustment) for that period, for the effect of the change on all periods before that date;

   2. The financial statements for prior periods presented comparatively are recast to reflect the effect of the error correction;

   3. Through a journal entry, the beginning balance of retained earnings in the year of the correction is adjusted to reflect the correct accounting through that date (prior period adjustment).

D. **Numerical example --** In 20x8, a firm discovered that in 20x5, a cash advance of $600,000 received from a client as a prepayment for advertising services was credited to revenue. The contract called for the firm to provide services evenly over the 5 years ending 12/31/x9. Net income for 20x7 was $300,000 and for 20x8 was $400,000 before the error correction. The retained earnings (RE) balance 1/1/x7 was $800,000. 20x8 and 20x7 are shown comparatively in 20x8 annual report. No dividends were paid in either year. Ignore income tax effects.

Example:
1. *Journal entry to record the error correction:*

1/1/x8:

Prior period adjustment	240,000	
Unearned revenue		240,000

The prior period adjustment is closed to retained earnings.

2. Analysis of error:

(annual revenue = $120,000 = ($600,000/5))

Amount of revenue recorded through 1/1/x8:	$600,000
Correct amount of revenue earned through 1/1/x8:	
$120,000(3 years)	360,000
Overstatement of RE at 1/1/x8	$240,000
(this is the prior period adjustment through 1/1/x8)	
Amount of revenue recorded through 1/1/x7:	$600,000
Correct amount of revenue earned through 1/1/x7:	
$120,000(2 years)	240,000
Overstatement of RE at 1/1/x7	$360,000
(this is the prior period adjustment through 1/1/x7)	

3. Corrected net income amounts:

20x8: $400,000 + $120,000 = $520,000 (correct)

20x7: $300,000 + $120,000 = $420,000 (correct)

4. *Journal entry 12/31/x8:*

Unearned revenue	120,000	
Revenue		120,000

5. *Comparative statements:* The 20x7 statements will be recast to show the corrected amounts of unearned revenue, revenue, and other affected accounts.

6. *Retained Earnings Statements*

	20x8	20x7
Retained earnings, January 1		$800,000
Prior period adjustment, error correction		(360,000)
Retained earnings, January 1, as corrected	$ 860,000	440,000
Net income	520,000	420,000
E 12/31	$1,380,000	$860,000

Footnote: The firm discovered an error in recognizing revenue recorded in 20x5 and has restated the financials for 20x7 and 20x8. The error understated income for 20x7 previously reported by $120,000.

7. The amount of the prior period adjustment to the beginning balance of retained earnings for each year shown is to be reported. For consistency with accounting principle changes, this example reports the adjustment only for the earliest year reported in the retained earnings statement. Firms may report the other amounts in the footnotes.

E. **Disclosures for error corrections --** Disclosures in the period of correction include the following. Subsequent financial statements need not repeat these disclosures.

    1. A statement that previous financial statements were restated, and the nature of the error;

    2. Effect of the correction on each financial statement line item and related per share amounts for each prior period presented;

    3. The total cumulative effect of the change on retained earnings as of the beginning of the first period presented;

    4. Pre and post-tax effects of the correction on net income for each prior period presented.

II. **Counter-Balancing Errors --** Many accounting errors counterbalance or "self-correct" after a certain period of time if they are not corrected. These errors require no entry to correct retained earnings or other current account balance after the error counterbalances. However, prior year financial statements remain in error.

 Example:
A. In counting its ending inventory for the 20x3 accounting year, one row of merchandise in the warehouse was counted twice. The result of this error is that ending inventory for 20x3 was overstated by $5,000. The error was detected on December 28, 20x7. Ignore income tax considerations.

20x3 effects:

*ending inventory is overstated $5,000

*cost of goods sold is understated $5,000

*net income is overstated $5,000

*ending retained earnings is overstated $5,000

20x4 effects:

*beginning inventory is overstated $5,000

*cost of goods sold is overstated $5,000

*net income is understated $5,000

*ending retained earnings is now correct because the income effects for 20x3 and 20x4 cancel each other

The error was detected on December 28, 20x7. At that time, the balance in retained earnings was correct, and no correcting entry is needed. Most likely, neither the 20x3 nor 20x4 statements will be reissued comparatively with those of 20x7 - no prior year financial statements require restatement.

B. However, now assume the same error was discovered in 20x4 instead. Beginning retained earnings is overstated $5,000, and beginning inventory for 20x4 is overstated. The following entry is required and illustrates a prior period adjustment:

As of 1/1/x4:

Prior period adjustment	5,000	
Inventory		5,000

Although this is a counterbalancing error, if it is discovered before it has a chance to counterbalance, an error-correcting entry is needed.

III. U.S. GAAP - IFRS Differences

A. One of the early convergence efforts between the IASB and FASB occurred in the area of accounting changes. However, minor differences continue. The terminology between the two standards is somewhat different. For example, the term "accounting policies" is used for international standards; the term "accounting principles" or "accounting methods" is used in the U.S. Also, the disclosure requirements are more detailed for U.S .reporting.

Major Differences

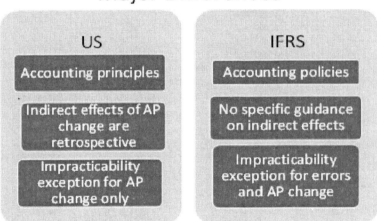

B. International standards do not address the accounting for the indirect effects of an accounting principle change.

  1. Indirect effects of a change in accounting principle is any changes to current or future cash flows of an entity that result from making a change in accounting principle that is applied retrospectively. An example of an indirect effect is a change in a nondiscretionary profit sharing or royalty payment that is based on a reported amount such as revenue or net income. (ASC 250-10-55-6)

C. The change to or from LIFO is not an issue for international reporting because LIFO is not permitted.

D. International standards allow for the impracticability exception for errors as well as for accounting principle changes. U.S. standards allow this exception only for accounting principle changes.

  1. For international reporting, the error is corrected by restating the financial statements for the earliest period practicable, which may result in the reporting of the correction in a year other than the year in which the error occurred. For U.S. reporting, the presumption is that if an error is discovered, it can be corrected as of the date it occurred.

E. Occasionally, a new international standard is adopted with a delayed effective date. If the firm does not elect early adoption, the following must be disclosed:

1. Nature of the future change;

2. Date by which the standard is required to be adopted;

3. Planned date of adoption;

4. Estimate of the effect the new standard will have on the firm's financial position or a statement explaining why such an estimate cannot be made.

Asset Retirement and Environmental Obligations

This lesson provides information on the accounting for asset retirement and environmental obligations.

After studying this lesson, you should be able to:

1. *Identify how asset retirement obligations are measured.*

2. *Explain how asset retirement obligations are accreted over time.*

3. *Identify when to accrue an environmental obligation.*

I. **ASC 410-20 Asset Retirement Obligations** -- ASC 410-20 addresses the accounting and reporting for asset retirement obligations (AROs) and requires firms to capitalize future asset retirement costs in the underlying asset account, and also in an ARO liability. Such future costs include the cost of dismantling an asset, removal, site reclamation, nuclear decommissioning and closing mines. The costs are incurred at the end of the asset's life but are capitalized when they become estimable, often at the beginning of the asset's useful life. The rationale for capitalizing such costs to the asset is that the retirement activities are integral to the operation of the asset.

II. **Scope and Initial Measurement**

A. Fair value is used to measure the ARO and the amount is to be recognized at the time the cost becomes reasonably estimable. The fair value is the amount the firm would be reasonably expected to pay today to cover the future costs, and is the present value of all future payments expected to retire the asset. This amount is debited to the asset and credited to the ARO. The obligation must stem from a legal obligation--one that the firm is required to settle as a result of a law or contract.

B. If a present value technique is used to measure fair value, then the probability-weighted estimates of future cash flows are discounted using a credit-adjusted risk-free rate. The probability-weighted cash flows incorporates risks and uncertainties regarding the future obligation.

C. The amount capitalized does not qualify as an expenditure for the purpose of capitalizing interest.

D. U.S. accounting concepts identify a liability as a probable future economic sacrifice arising from present obligations. "Probable" in this definition is more easily met than in ASC 450-20 Loss Contingencies. In other words, when the liability is incurred and is estimable, the ARO is recognized.

E. ASC 410-20 applies to all *legal* obligations associated with the retirement of a tangible noncurrent asset but does not apply to environmental remediation liabilities arising from improper use of an asset because such costs are not an integral part of the cost basis of the asset (see next section on environmental obligations).

III. **Subsequent Recognition and Measurement**

A. After the asset and ARO are increased by the initial fair value (present value) of future payments to retire the asset, (1) total depreciation or depletion expense over the asset's life is thus automatically increased by the amount capitalized initially, and (2) the ARO is increased each year due to the passage of time causing the firm to also record "accretion expense." The annual accretion expense and corresponding increase in ARO is found by multiplying the interest rate used in capitalizing the initial amount, by the beginning balance in the ARO. The annual expense is considered an operating expense but is not included in "interest expense" for the purpose of interest capitalization.

B. Thus, the ARO gradually increases over time (to the final amount expected to be paid) while the net book value of the asset declines through the depreciation or depletion process. Only the initial fair value (present value) is capitalized to the asset. Only that initial amount is subject to depreciation or depletion.

 Example: Example of ARO: A firm opened a mine on January 1, 20x3 with a total capitalized cost of $4,000,000 (acquisition, exploration, and development). In addition, the firm is legally required to close the mine for the safety of the surrounding community, and to reclaim the land for environmental purposes. Operations are expected to cease at the end of 20x7, at which time the closing and reclamation costs will be incurred.

Based on current bids by independent contractors, the following range of closing and reclamation costs are generated:

Closing and reclamation costs	Probability assessment	Expected Cash Flow
$200,000	.20	$40,000
300,000	.50	150,000
400,000	.30	120,000
		310,000

The risk-free rate of interest on 1/1/x3 is 3%. The firm adds 4% to reflect the effect of its credit standing. Therefore, the credit-adjusted risk-free rate of return is 7%. In addition, the firm assumes annual inflation of 2% over the five-year period of operating the mine. Assume SL depletion although the units of production method would normally be used. Also assume the firm immediately sells ore as it is removed from the site.

Amount capitalized to mine and ARO:

Expected cost to close mine and reclaim land, 1/1/x3	$310,000
Effect of inflation (future value of single payment, 2%, 5 years)	x 1.10408
Expected future cost to close mine and reclaim land, 12/31/x7	$342,265
Present value factor (present value of single payment, 7%, 5 years)	x .71299
Present value (fair value) of cost to close mine and reclaim land	$244,032

1/1/x3

Developed mine (noncurrent asset, depletable resource)	244,032	
Asset retirement obligation (ARO-a liability)		244,032

(The total capitalized cost of the developed mine is now $4,244,032, the sum of the initial capitalized cost, and the amount capitalized for closing the mine and reclaiming the land.)

12/31/x3

Depletion expense (to cost of goods sold)	848,806	
Accumulated depletion (contra to Developed Mine)		848,806

$4,244,032/5 = $848,806

(Note that annual depletion expense includes $244,032/5 = $48,806 of depletion on the capitalized closing and reclamation cost)

Accretion expense $244,032(.07)	17,082	
ARO		17,082

(The $17,082 amount is the increase in the ARO liability due to the passage of time. The initial amount recorded in the ARO grows to its future value; the increase each year is the cost associated with that increase.)

12/31/x4

Depletion expense (to cost of goods sold)	848,806	
Accumulated depletion (contra to Developed Mine)		848,806

Accretion expense ($244,032 + $17,082)(.07)	18,278	
ARO		18,278

After the 12/31/x7 entries (the last year), the accumulated depletion balance equals the balance in the Developed Mine account. The resulting zero net book value is removed from the accounts. Also, the balance in the ARO account is $342,265. Assume that the actual cost to close the mine and reclaim the land is $360,000:

ARO	342,265	
Loss on Settlement of ARO	17,735	
Cash		360,000

IV. ASC 410-30 Environmental Obligations

A. ASC 410-30 addresses the accounting and reporting for environmental obligations. Unlike the ARO's an environmental obligation is not associated directly with an asset. An environmental obligation stems from a legal action in violation of one of various Environmental Protection Acts (i.e., Clean Air Act). An environmental liability must be accrued when the liabilities are both probable and reasonably estimable. Frequently the company would accrue an environmental liability when it has been named the potentially responsible party (PRP) for the environmental remediation.

Business Combinations

Introduction to Business Combinations

This lesson addresses accounting requirements when control is acquired and, therefore, a business combination has occurred. This lesson also discusses that one of the elements in determining the correct accounting to use for a business combination is the legal form that the combination takes. When a business combination occurs, the operating results of two or more entities are combined. This lesson considers the determination of combined operating results of entities included in a business combination as of the date of the business combination and at the end of subsequent periods.

After studying this lesson you should be able to :

1. *Define "business combination."*

2. *Provide a frame of reference for understanding the accounting for business combinations.*

3. *Present a model that depicts the issues relevant to accounting for business combinations.*

4. *Describe the accounting elements (accounts) and entries determined by the legal form of combination.*

5. *Account for stock issuance costs.*

6. *Understand what constitutes the consolidated income of affiliated entities:*

   as of the date of the business combination,

   as of the end of the period of the combination, and

   for periods subsequent to the period of the combination.

I. **Definition --** *A business combination:* is a **transaction or an event** where an acquirer obtains **control** of a **business**:

A. A **transaction** means that there was an exchange of consideration between two parties. Sometimes an **event** occurs where one party may gain control over another party without an exchange transaction or outright purchase.

   1. For example, in the diagram below Co A is a 40% owner with veto rights and Co B is a 60% owner of Co C. The veto rights require that Co A be in agreement with any major decisions made by Co B. Since Co A has veto rights Co B does not control Co C. However, if Co A's veto rights expire, then Co B now controls Co C.

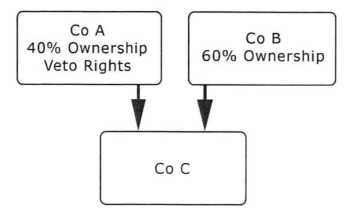

B. **Control** is currently defined as voting control and is essentially greater than 50% voting interest.

C. A business is defined as "an integrated set of activities and assets that is capable of being conducted and managed for the purpose of providing a return..." This definition means that the set of activities and assets does not need to be profitable to be considered a business. A startup company that has yet to generate profits would be considered a business.

II. Considerations

A. The accounting for recording a business combination depends on the legal (or statutory) form that the combination takes and the application of the acquisition method of accounting. The alternative legal forms of a business combination are: (1) merger, (2) consolidation, and (3) acquisition; each is described and illustrated below.

B. The acquisition method of accounting must be used to record all business combinations for which the acquisition date is on or after the first annual reporting period beginning on or after December 15, 2008. (Prior to that date, a business combination would be accounted for using either the purchase method or the pooling of interests method. The pooling of interests method was allowed for combinations initiated before June 30, 2001.)

C. The following lessons cover accounting for a business combination under the alternative legal forms and the requirements of the acquisition method of accounting. In addition, lessons identify the circumstance under which a business combination will result in the need to prepare consolidated financial statements and the alternative methods that an investor might use to carry an investment on its books prior to consolidation.

D. Since a primary means of accomplishing a business combination is the acquisition by one entity (investor/parent) of the common stock of another entity (investee) so as to gain control of the investee/subsidiary, the current topic of "Business Combinations" is an extension of the prior topic dealing with investments in equity securities and also the next topic dealing with consolidated financial statements. Those relationships can be illustrated as:

1. **Investments in Equity Securities** may result in

2. **Business Combinations**, which will likely require preparation of

3. **Consolidated Financial Statements** for the "combined" businesses.

E. The lessons in this section deal with the second of those related issues, accounting for business combinations.

III. Business Combination Overview

A. The diagram below summarizes the alternative issues and treatments in accounting for business combinations. Specifically, this diagram, is used to show (1) the relationships between the legal forms of business combinations, (2) the use of the acquisition method of accounting to record those combinations, (3) whether or not consolidated financial statements will be required, and (4) the accounting methods the parent may use to carry its investment in the subsidiary on its (parent's) books prior to preparing consolidated financial statements.

B. The lessons in this section (Business Combinations) describe and illustrate the accounting treatments for the alternatives depicted in this model. One of the fundamental differences in treatments derives from differences in the legal form of a business combination, as shown in the second column (from the left) in the model. The next lesson describes the different legal forms of business combinations and the accounting consequences of those different forms.

C. This overview should be used as a frame of reference as you study the lessons in this Business Combinations section.

INVESTMENT MADE CONTROLLING INTEREST IS ACQUIRED	LEGAL FORM OF COMBINATION	ACCOUNTING TREATMENT	ELIGIBILITY FOR CONSOLIDATION	CARRY ON BOOKS AT	REPORT AT
		ACQUISITION (Purchase)	N/A	N/A	SINGLE ENTITY
>50% VOTING STOCK Or GROUP OF ASSETS that constitute a Business	MERGER OR CONSOLIDATION / ACQUISITION			COST	CONSOLIDATED STATEMENTS
		ACQUISITION (Purchase)	YES	EQUITY	
			NO (Lack Control)	COST OR EQUITY	COST OR EQUITY

IV. Introduction to Legal Forms of Business Combinations -- The legal form of a business combination is concerned with the legal (or statutory) means by which businesses are combined or come under common control. While the legal form of a combination is distinct from the accounting treatment of the combination, the legal form will determine certain aspects of accounting for a combination.

A. Legal Forms of Business Combinations -- The three legal forms of business combinations are merger, consolidation and acquisition.

1. **Merger --** One preexisting entity acquires either a group of assets that constitute a business or controlling equity interest of another preexisting entity and "collapses" the acquired assets or entity into the acquiring entity.

   a. Graphic Illustration – see the following example.

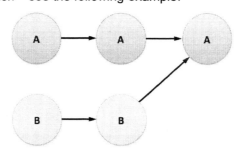

   a. Note; only one entity (A) survives. (B) (a group of assets or another entity) ceases to exist separate from (A).

2. **Consolidation --** A new entity consolidates the net assets or the equity interests of two (or more) preexisting entities.

   a. Graphic Illustration

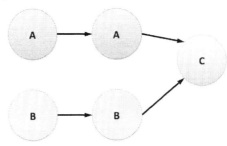

   a. Note, that only one entity (new C) exists; it consolidated the net assets or equity interests of (A) and (B) into it. (A) and (B) cease to exist as legal entities.

2. **Acquisition** -- One preexisting entity acquires controlling equity interest of another preexisting entity, but both continue to exist and operate as separate legal entities.

   a. Graphic Illustration

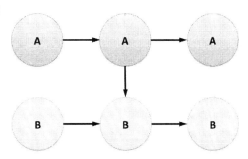

   b. Note, that both entities survive, with (A) owning controlling interest in (B). Both (A) and (B) continue to exist and operate as separate legal entities.

B. **For Accounting Purposes** -- Because both a merger and a consolidation result in only one entity surviving, they can be treated alike.

C. **Merger/Consolidation** -- In a merger or consolidation, one entity (the acquirer) buys either a group of assets that constitute a business or controlling interest (typically > 50% of the common stock) of one or more target companies (the acquiree) and the group of assets or the assets and liabilities of the acquired entity become a part of the acquiring entity.

   1. The acquirer records (picks-up) the group of assets or the assets and liabilities of the acquiree(s) onto its book. (The acquired entity/entities will no longer exist.)

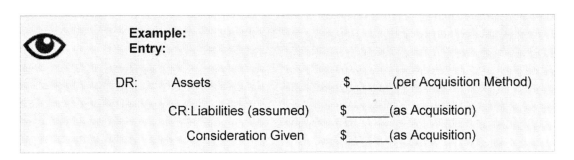

Example:
Entry:

DR: Assets $_____(per Acquisition Method)

CR:Liabilities (assumed) $_____(as Acquisition)

Consideration Given $_____(as Acquisition)

   1. The legal form - merger or combination - determines the kinds of accounts (i.e., various assets and liabilities) used to record the combination.

   2. The acquisition method of accounting determines the values to be used in the combination entry. (Determination of those values is covered in detail in later lessons.)

   3. Since after a merger or consolidation only one entity exists, a merger or consolidation does not result in the need to prepare Consolidated Financial Statements.

D. **Acquisition** -- In an acquisition, one entity (the acquirer) buys controlling interest (> 50%) of the voting stock of a target entity (the acquiree) and both entities (acquiring and acquired entities) continue as separate legal and accounting entities.

   1. The acquirer records its ownership of the stock of the acquiree as a Long-Term Investment.

   a. The acquirer does **not** record (pick up) on its books the assets and liabilities of the acquiree.

   b. The assets and liabilities of the acquiree stay on that entity's (separate) books.

> **Example:**
> **Entry:**
>
> DR: Investment in subsidiary $_____(Per Acquisition Method)
>
>   CR: Consideration Given $_____(As Acquisition)

    a. The legal form - acquisition - determines the kind of asset (Investment!) used to record the combination.

    b. The acquisition method of accounting determines the values to be used in the combination entry. (Determination of those values is covered in detail in later lessons.)

    c. Since after an acquisition two entities exist, one controlled by the other, an acquisition usually **does** require preparation of Consolidated Financial Statements, those of the acquirer together with those of the acquiree(s).

E. Income Determination at Date of Combination

    1. Only the acquirer's (acquiring firm's) operating results (income/loss) up to the date of combination enter into determination of consolidated net income **as of the date of the combination**.

    2. The acquiree's (acquired firm's) operating results (income/loss) up to the date of combination are part of what the acquirer purchases when it acquires the acquiree (i.e., makes its "Investment" in the acquiree), and are not part of consolidated net income as of the date of combination.

        a. The acquiree's operating results up to the date of the combination will be closed (or treated as closed) to its retained earnings.

        b. The acquiree's retained earnings as of the date of the combination is part of the equity "paid for" by the acquirer when it makes its investment.

        c. The acquiree's retained earnings as of the date of the combination will be part of the acquiree's equity eliminated against the acquirer's investment account in the consolidating process. (The consolidating process is covered as the next major topic.)

V. Income Determination at the End of the Year of Combination and Subsequent Years

    A. Income at the End of the Period (e.g., year) of Combination: The acquirer's operating results (income/loss) for the entire year **plus** the acquiree's operating results (income/loss) **after the date of the combination** enter into the determination of consolidated income for the year of combination.

    B. Income for Periods (e.g., years) Subsequent to Combination: In periods subsequent to the period in which the combination occurs, both the acquirer's and the acquiree's operating results (income/loss) for the entire reporting period enter into the determination of consolidated net income or loss.

VI. Summary of Determining Income/Loss Associated with a Business Combination -- The following timeline graphic summarizes what operating results are included or excluded in determining consolidated income or loss following a business combination. The timeline should be read from left to right.

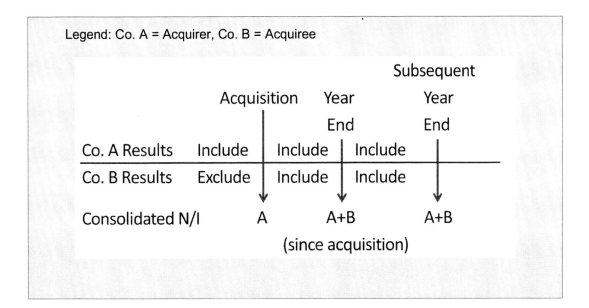

Acquisition Method of Accounting

Introduction to Acquisition Method of Accounting

Application of the acquisition method of accounting to a business combination involves several requirements: (1) Identifying the acquirer, (2) Determining the acquisition date and measurement period, (3) Determining the cost of the acquisition, (4) Recognizing and measuring the assets acquired, liabilities assumed, and noncontrolling interest in the acquiree, and (5) Recognizing and measuring any goodwill or bargain purchase amount. This lesson covers the first and second of those requirements. Subsequent lessons cover the remaining acquisition requirements and related issues.

After studying this lesson you should be able to :

1. *Identify the requirements (steps) for applying the acquisition method of accounting to a business combination.*

2. *Identify the nature of the acquirer.*

3. *Provide guidelines for determining the acquiring entity (acquirer) in a business combination.*

4. *Define and determine the acquisition date and the measurement period.*

5. *Describe the effects of changes made to accounts and amounts during the measurement period.*

I. Historical Perspective

A. Prior to 2001, Accounting Principles Board Opinion #16, "Business Combinations," permitted the use of two different methods to account for business combinations: (1) the purchase method and (2) the pooling-of-interests method. The method used in a particular case depended on the facts and circumstances of the combination. FASB #141, "Business Combinations," which became effective in 2001, eliminated the pooling-of-interests method as an acceptable method of accounting for business combinations. Between 2001 and 2009 only the purchase method was used to account for new business combinations.

B. In 2002, as part of their on-going convergence project, the FASB and the International Accounting Standards Board (IASB) agreed to work together to reconsider standards for applying the purchase method of accounting for business combinations. The objective of that joint undertaking was to develop "a common and comprehensive standard for accounting for business combinations that could be used for both domestic and international financial reporting." That joint effort resulted in ACS 805 issued in December, 2007, and IFRS #3 issued in January, 2008. While the requirements of those pronouncements resulted in a high degree of convergence between U.S. GAAP and the international standard for business combinations, some differences still remain. Those differences are in the areas of scope (especially as relates to not-for-profit organizations); the definition of control; how fair value, contingencies, employee benefit obligations, noncontrolling interest (FASB requires the use of fair value; IASB permits either fair value or proportionate share of acquiree's net assets) and goodwill are measured; and certain disclosure requirements.

II. Current Standard

A. The topic of business combinations is part of ASC 805 in the codification of accounting standards. ASC 805 (FAS 141R) requires the use of the acquisition method of accounting for business combinations, which is a variation of the purchase method of accounting, and applies to all transactions or events in which an entity obtains control of one or more businesses (including a group of assets that constitute a business) except the following:

1. The formation of a joint venture.

2. The acquisition of an asset or group of assets that does not constitute a business.

3. A combination between entities under common control.

4. A combination between not-for-profit organizations.

5. The acquisition of a for-profit entity by a not-for-profit organization.

B. ASC 805 specifies how the acquiring entity (acquirer) in a business combination should:

1. Recognize and measure the identifiable assets acquired, the liabilities assumed, and any noncontrolling interest in the acquired business.

2. Recognize and measure goodwill or a bargain purchase amount.

3. Disclose information about a business combination to enable financial statement users to evaluate the business combination.

III. Applying the Acquisition Method

A. Recording a business combination using the acquisition method of accounting involves the following steps:

1. Identifying the acquiring entity (the acquirer).

2. Determining the acquisition date and measurement period.

3. Determining the cost of the acquisition.

4. Recognizing and measuring the identifiable assets acquired, the liabilities assumed and any noncontrolling interest in the acquired business (the acquiree).

5. Recognizing and measuring goodwill or a gain from a bargain purchase, if any.

IV. The First Step in Applying the Acquisition Method -- Identifying the Acquiring Entity.

A. **Use of the acquisition method --** Use of the acquisition method requires identifying the acquiring entity (i.e., the acquirer).

1. The acquirer is the entity that obtains control of a business.

2. A business (for the purposes of this FASB) is an integrated set of activities and assets that is capable of being conducted and managed through the use of inputs and processes for the purpose of providing economic benefits to owners, members or participants.

3. A business may be a group of assets/net assets (which constitute a business as defined in B, above) or a separate legal entity.

B. **Determining the Acquirer --** The acquirer should be determined based on the facts and the circumstances of the combination.

1. In a combination effected primarily through the distribution of cash or other assets or by incurring liabilities (or a combination thereof) to obtain control of a group of assets or a separate entity, the entity that distributes assets or incurs liabilities is generally the acquiring entity.

2. As a general rule, ownership by one entity (investor), directly or indirectly, of more than 50 percent of the outstanding voting shares of another entity (investee) establishes the investor as the acquiring entity.

3. In a combination effected through an exchange of equity interest (e.g., common stock for common stock), the entity that issues (new) equity interest is generally the acquiring entity; however, all pertinent facts and circumstances should be considered, including:

    a. The relative voting rights in the combined entity after the combination - If all else is equal, the acquiring entity is the combining entity whose owners as a group have the larger portion of the voting rights in the combined entity;

    b. The existence of a large minority voting interest when no other owner(s) have a significant voting interest - If all else is equal, the acquiring entity is the combining entity whose owner(s) hold the largest minority voting interest in the combined entity;

    c. The composition of the governing body of the combined entity - If all else is equal, the acquiring entity is the combining entity whose owner(s) have the ability to select or remove a voting majority of the governing body of the combined entity;

    d. The composition of the senior management of the combined entity - If all else is equal, the acquiring entity is the combining entity whose former management dominates that of the combined entity;

    e. The terms of the equity exchange - If all else is equal, the acquiring entity is the combining entity that pays a premium over the precombination fair value of the equity interest of the other combining entity(ies).

4. The acquirer usually is the combining entity whose relative size (for example, measured in assets, revenues or earnings) is significantly larger than that of the other combining entity(ies).

5. A new entity formed to effect a business combination is not necessarily the acquirer.

    a. If the new entity transfers cash or other assets or incurs liabilities to effect a business combination, the new entity is likely the acquirer.

    b. If a new entity is formed to issue equity interest to effect a business combination, one of the pre-existing combining entities must be determined to be the acquiring entity based on available evidence, including taking into account the guidance in C. and D., above.

6. If more than two entities are in the combination, in addition to the guidance in C. and D., above, consideration should be given to which combining entity initiated the combination and the relative assets, revenues and earnings of the combining entities.

7. The acquirer of a variable interest entity is the primary beneficiary of the variable interest entity.

    a. Simply put, a variable interest entity is one in which contractual, ownership or other pecuniary interests in the entity change with changes in the fair value of the entity's net assets, excluding the variable interest.

    b. An entity will consolidate a variable interest entity when it has an investment or other interest that will absorb a majority of the investee entity's expected losses, receive a majority of the entity's expected residual returns, or both.

    c. The entity that consolidates a variable interest entity is the primary beneficiary of that entity.

V. The Second Step in Applying the Acquisition method -- Determining the Acquisition Date and Measurement Period.

  A. The Acquisition Date -- The acquisition date is the date on which the acquirer obtains control of the acquiree (i.e., business).

    1. It is normally the date on which the acquirer legally transfers consideration for, and acquires the assets and assumes the liabilities of, the acquiree.

    2. It is also called the "closing date" for the combination.

    3. The acquisition date can be before or after the closing date, if by agreement or otherwise the acquirer gains control of the acquiree at an earlier or later date.

4. An acquirer should consider all pertinent facts and circumstances in determining the acquisition date.

B. **Measurement Period** -- If the initial accounting for a business combination is not complete by the end of the reporting period in which the combination occurs, the acquirer will report provisional amounts in its financial statements for items for which the accounting is incomplete and adjust those amounts during the measurement period.

1. The **measurement period** is the period after the acquisition date during which the acquirer may adjust any provisional amounts.

2. The measurement period provides the acquirer reasonable time (usually one year) to obtain information needed to identify and measure, **as of the acquisition date**, the following:

   a. Identifiable assets, liabilities and noncontrolling interest in the acquiree;

   b. Consideration transferred to obtain the acquiree;

   c. Any precombination interest held in the acquiree;

   d. Any goodwill or bargain purchase gain.

3. During the measurement period new information about facts **that existed at the acquisition date** that would have affected the recognition of assets or liabilities, or that would have affected the measurement of amounts recognized, will be used to retrospectively adjust the provisional accounts and amounts.

   a. The recognition of additional identifiable assets or asset amounts will result in a decrease in the amount of (provisional) goodwill, if any.

   b. The recognition of additional identifiable liabilities or liability amounts will result in an increase in the amount of (provisional) goodwill, if any.

   c. Adjustments to provisional accounts and/or amounts must be reflected in comparative information for prior period financial statements.

4. The measurement period ends when the acquirer obtains information it was seeking about facts **that existed at the acquisition date** or learns that no additional information is available.

   a. In no case should the measurement period exceed one year from the acquisition date.

   b. After the measurement period, accounting for the business combination should be changed only to correct an error (following the provisions of ASC 250, "Accounting Changes and Error Corrections").

Determining the Cost of the Business Acquired

Application of the acquisition method of accounting to a business combination involves the following requirements: (1) Identifying the acquirer, (2) Determining the acquisition date and measurement period, (3) Determining the cost of the acquired business, (4) Recognizing and measuring the assets acquired, liabilities assumed, and noncontrolling interest in the acquiree, and (5) Recognizing and measuring any goodwill or bargain purchase amount. This lesson covers the third of these requirements, determining the cost of the acquired business. Subsequent lessons cover the remaining requirements and related issues.

After studying this lesson, you should be able to:

1. *Identify the ways that an acquirer may gain control of a business.*

2. *Identify and measure the elements of consideration that may be used to carry out a combination.*

3. *Describe the appropriate treatment when control is obtained without transferring consideration.*

4. *Describe how costs of carrying out a business combination should be treated.*

I. **The Third Step in Applying the Acquisition Method --** Determining the Cost of an Acquired Business.

II. **An Acquirer May Obtain Control of a Business in Two Ways**

A. By transferring consideration to either another entity or its owner(s):

1. To obtain a group of assets that constitute a business, or

2. To gain control of another entity.

B. Without transferring consideration; for example, by contract or through the lapse of the minority veto rights of others.

III. **Obtaining Control by Transferring Consideration**

A. The consideration used by the acquirer may take a number of forms, including:

1. Transferring cash, cash equivalents, or other assets;

2. Incurring liabilities;

3. Issuing equity interests, including common and preferred stock, options and warrants.;

4. A combination of transferring assets, incurring liabilities or issuing equity.

B. The consideration used to effect a business combination generally must be measured at fair value (see exception in D., below).

C. If any assets or liabilities transferred by the acquirer (except as noted in D., below) have a carrying value before transfer that is different than fair value at acquisition, the assets or liabilities must be adjusted (remeasured) to fair value at the date of the combination and the related gains or losses recognized in current income by the acquirer.

See the following example.

Example: P, Inc. acquires a group of assets that constitute a business from S, Inc. As payment for the group of assets, P transfers cash and land to S. The land had been acquired by P 12 years ago for $126,000. It had a fair value of $150,000 at the time of the business acquisition. Prior to transferring the land to S, P should make an entry to revalue the land to fair value and recognize a gain.

DR: Land $24,000

CR: Gain on Land Revaluation $24,000

(Fair value $150,000 - Carrying value $126,000 = $24,000 gain.)

The land, with a new carrying value of $150,000, would then be transferred to Sill as part of the consideration for the acquired business.

D. An exception to the requirement that assets and liabilities to be transferred as consideration in a business combination be remeasured to fair value applies when the transferred assets or liabilities remain under the control of the acquirer.

1. In that case, the assets or liabilities are not adjusted to fair value, but are transferred at carrying value and no gain or loss is recognized.

Example: P, Inc. gained control of S, Inc. by acquiring more than 50% of S's voting common stock. As a part of its acquisition of S's stock, P transferred land with a carrying value of $126,000 and a fair value of $150,000 to S for 10,000 shares of S's common stock. Because it has controlling interest in S, P also retains control of the land transferred to S. Therefore, the land should be transferred at the carrying value, $126,000, not fair value, and no gain (or loss) will be recognized.

E. Contingent consideration as cost elements

1. The consideration transferred by the acquirer to acquire a business may include a contingent element.

2. Contingent consideration is either:

   a. An obligation of the acquirer to transfer additional assets or equity interest to the former owner(s) of the acquired business as part of the consideration if future events occur or conditions are met, or

   b. A right of the acquirer to a return of previously transferred consideration if specific conditions are met.

3. Contingent consideration should be recognized on the acquisition date at fair value as part of the consideration transferred in exchange for the acquired business.

   a. An obligation to pay contingent consideration should be recognized as either a liability or as equity (according to the provisions of ASC 480, "Distinguishing Liabilities from Equity").

   b. A right to the return of previously transferred consideration should be recognized as an asset.

4. Changes in the fair value of contingent consideration after the acquisition date that result from new information about facts and circumstances **that existed at the acquisition date** should be accounted for as measurement period adjustments (and, therefore, as adjustments to the cost of the acquired business).

5. Changes in the fair value of contingent consideration **resulting from occurrences after the acquisition date** - including meeting earning targets, reaching a specified share market price, or reaching research and development milestones - are not measurement period adjustments and do not enter into the cost of the business combination.

   a. Changes resulting from occurrences after the acquisition date related to contingent consideration classified as equity are not remeasured; subsequent settlement should be accounted for as an equity adjustment.

   b. Changes resulting from occurrences after the acquisition date related to contingent consideration classified as assets or liabilities are remeasured to fair value at each balance sheet date until the contingency is resolved, with changes recognized in current income.

F. Acquirer's share-based payment awards as cost elements.

  1. An acquirer may exchange its share-based payment awards for awards held by the acquiree's employees as part of a business combination.

    a. For example, in a merger the acquirer may exchange its stock options (options to acquire its stock) for the stock options in the acquiree held by the acquiree's employees at the date of the merger.

    b. Such an exchange would be a modification of share-based payment awards under ASC 718 "Stock Compensation" and would be treated as the exchange of the original award for a new award.

  2. The treatment of the exchange of share-based awards in a business combination depends on whether or not the acquirer is obligated to make the exchange or does so at its own discretion.

  3. An acquirer may be obligated to exchange share-based awards because of:

    a. The terms of the acquisition agreement;

    b. The terms of the acquiree's awards;

    c. Applicable laws or regulations.

  4. If the acquirer is obligated to exchange awards:

    a. The portion (all or part) of the replacement awards (measured in accord with the provisions of ASC 718) that relates to precombination services based on conditions of the acquiree's awards will be part of the consideration transferred in the business combination.

    b. The portion (all or part) of the replacement awards (measured in accord with the provisions of ASC 718) that relates to post-combination services (the amount not allocated to precombination services) will be treated as compensation expense in post-combination financial statements.

  5. If the acquirer elects to replace acquiree share-based awards, even though it is not obligated to do so, all of the value of the awards (measured in accord with the provisions of ASC 718) will be treated as compensation expense in post-combination financial statements.

IV. Obtaining Control Without Transferring Consideration

A. An entity (acquirer) may acquire control of another entity (acquiree) without transferring any consideration. Examples include:

  1. An entity (acquiree) reacquires a sufficient number of its own outstanding shares from selected investors so that another investor (acquirer) obtains control with its existing ownership.

2. Minority veto rights lapse that previously kept a majority owner (acquirer) from controlling the investee (acquiree).

3. Two entities agree to combine by contract alone; neither entity owns controlling equity interest in the other entity.

B. When a business combination occurs as a result of a contract between entities:

1. One of the combining entities must be identified as the acquirer and, therefore, the other entity is the acquiree.

2. The equity interests in the acquiree held by parties other than the acquirer are noncontrolling interest in the post-combination financial statements of the acquirer, even if all (100%) of the equity interest in the acquiree is attributable to the noncontrolling interest (i.e., the entity designated as the acquirer has no equity interest in the acquiree).

V. Treatment of Acquisition-Related Costs

A. Acquisition-related costs are costs the acquirer incurs to carry out the acquisition (of a group of assets that constitute a business or an entity).

B. Acquisition costs include:

1. Finder's fees;

2. Advising, legal, accounting, valuation (appraisal) and other professional and consulting fees;

3. General administrative costs, including the cost of an internal acquisitions department;

4. Cost of registering and issuing debt and equity securities in connection with an acquisition.

C. Acquisition-related costs (except as noted in D, below) should be expensed in the period in which the costs are incurred and the services are received; these costs are not included as part of the cost of an acquired business.

D. The cost of issuing debt and equity securities for the purposes of a business combination are not treated as cost of the acquired business, but should be accounted for as provided for by other applicable GAAP. While current GAAP is not uniform with respect to treatment of issuance costs, generally, the following would apply:

1. Debt issuance costs (legal, printing, etc.) may be either recognized as a deferred asset and amortized over the life of the debt, or expensed when incurred;

2. Equity issuance costs (legal, printing, registering, etc.) reduce the proceeds from the securities issued and, in effect, reduce Additional Paid-in Capital.

VI. Summary -- In summary, the cost of an acquired business is the sum of

A. Fair value of assets transferred by the acquirer;

B. Fair value of liabilities incurred by the acquirer;

C. Fair value of equity interest issued by the acquirer;

D. Fair value of contingent consideration (net) obligations of the acquirer;

E. Fair value of share-based payment awards for precombination services that the acquirer is obligated to provide.

Recognizing/Measuring Assets, Liabilities and Noncontrolling Interest

Application of the acquisition method of accounting to a business combination involves the following requirements: (1) Identifying the acquirer, (2) Determining the acquisition date and measurement period, (3) Determining the cost of the acquisition, (4) Recognizing and measuring the assets acquired, liabilities assumed, and noncontrolling interest in the acquiree, and (5) Recognizing and measuring any goodwill or bargain purchase amount. This lesson covers the fourth of these requirements, recognizing and measuring the assets acquired, liabilities assumed, and noncontrolling interest in the acquiree. Subsequent lessons cover the remaining requirement and related issues.

After studying this lesson, you should be able to:

1. *Identify and measure items that should be recognized as assets or liabilities in a business combination.*

2. *Identify and measure items that are exceptions to the general recognition and measurement guidelines.*

3. *Describe the requirements when a business is acquired in stages.*

4. *Describe how noncontrolling interest in an acquiree is recognized and measured.*

5. *Identify the differences between U.S. GAAP and IFRS that relate to this lesson.*

I. **The Fourth Step in Applying the Acquisition Method** -- Recognizing and Measuring Assets Acquired, Liabilities Assumed. and Noncontrolling Interest in an Acquiree.

II. **Recognition** -- At the acquisition date, the acquirer must recognize (distinct from goodwill, if any) the identifiable assets acquired, liabilities assumed and any noncontrolling interest in the acquiree.

   A. Identifiable assets and liabilities must meet the definition of assets and liabilities in FASB Conceptual Framework, "Elements of Financial Statements."

      1. Rights or obligations that do not exist at the date of acquisition, even if expected to exist in the future, are not recognized as assets or liabilities acquired.

      2. Benefits received or obligations that occur, but do not exist, at the date of acquisition are recognized as post combination items as called for by the provisions of other appropriate GAAP. They are not part of the business acquisition. For example:

         a. Cost expected to be incurred to exit an acquired activity;

         b. Cost expected to be incurred in terminating or relocating employees of the acquiree.

   B. To qualify for recognition as part of the business combination, the assets and liabilities must be part of what the acquirer and acquiree exchanged in the business combination, not the subject matter of any separate transaction.

      1. A precombination transaction or arrangement that primarily benefits the acquirer or the subsequent combined entity, rather than the acquiree or the former owner(s), is likely to be a separate transaction.

      2. The following would be separate transactions, not a part of the combination transaction:

     a. A transaction that settles a preexisting relationship between the acquirer and the acquiree;

     b. A transaction that compensates employees or former owner(s) of the acquiree for future services;

     c. A transaction that reimburses the acquiree or its former owner(s) for paying the acquirer's acquisition-related costs.

C. The acquirer may recognize assets and/or liabilities not previously recognized by the acquiree; for example, an internally developed brand name, patent or other asset for which costs were expensed by the acquiree would be recognized as identifiable assets by the acquirer.

D. An intangible asset (separate from goodwill) is identifiable and would be recognized by the acquirer if it either:

     1. Is capable of being separated from the acquiree and sold, transferred, leased, rented or exchanged (for example, customer lists); or

     2. Arises from contractual or other legal rights.

E. Goodwill on the books of the acquired entity prior to a business combination would not be recognized by the acquirer in recording the combination. Any goodwill attributable to the acquiree would be separately determined by the acquirer. (See the next lesson "Recognizing and Measuring Goodwill or Bargain Purchase.")

III. Classification and Designation -- At the acquisition date, the acquirer must classify or designate the identifiable assets acquired and liabilities assumed so as to subsequently apply GAAP requirements.

A. Classification or designation will be made on the basis of related contractual terms, economic conditions, operating and accounting policies, and other relevant conditions that exist at the acquisition date.

B. Example of items that need classification or designation include:

     1. Investments in debt and equity securities as being held-to-maturity, trading or available-for-sale;

     2. Derivatives as to whether they are hedging instruments or not, and if so, the particulars;

     3. Embedded derivatives as to whether they will be treated as separate from the host instrument;

     4. Long-term assets as to whether they will be used or held for sale.

C. Leases (lease contracts) and insurance/reinsurance contracts should continue to be classified as established at inception of the contract (unless subsequent modifications of the contract have warranted reclassification).

IV. Measuring (Recording) at Fair Value -- At the acquisition date, identifiable assets, liabilities and any noncontrolling interest in the acquiree should be measured (recorded) at fair value at that date.

A. Fair value for identifiable assets and liabilities acquired should be determined using the guidelines and techniques established in FASB #157, "Fair Value Measurement."

B. Fair value for each identifiable asset and liability, or group of related assets or related liabilities, should be determined based on its specific attributes, including condition, location, highest and best use, etc.

C. Subject to the requirements of ASC 820, the following may be a basis for determining fair value of certain assets acquired and liabilities assumed:

1. Marketable securities - quoted prices in active markets;

2. Receivables - present value of amounts to be received;

3. Inventories (finished goods and merchandise) - estimated selling price less the cost of disposal and a reasonable profit;

4. Inventories (work-in-process) - estimated selling price less costs to complete, cost of disposal, and a reasonable profit.;

5. Inventories (raw materials) - current replacement cost;

6. Plant and equipment held for use - current replacement cost;

7. Plant and equipment held for disposal - fair value (based on market or cost valuation) less cost of disposal;

8. Intangible assets - estimated fair value (based on market, income or cost valuation);

9. Land and natural resources - fair value (based on market, income or cost valuation);

10. Accounts and notes payable, long-term debt and other liabilities - present values of amounts to be paid determined using appropriate current interest rates.

V. **Exceptions** -- Certain exceptions to the general recognition and/or measurement principles apply to specific identifiable assets and liabilities; those exceptions include:

A. **Contingencies** -- (Recognition principle exception - to ASC 450):

1. A contingency is an existing condition involving uncertainty as to possible gain or loss that will be resolved when one or more future events occur or fail to occur.

2. Contingencies related to existing contracts ("contractual contingencies" - e.g., warranty obligation) should be recognized and measured at fair value.

3. Contingencies not related to existing contracts ("noncontractual contingencies" - e.g., a lawsuit) should be recognized and measured at fair value only if it is more likely than not as of the acquisition date that the contingency will give rise to an asset or a liability.

B. **Income tax issues** -- (Recognition and measurement principles exceptions):

1. The acquirer will recognize and measure a deferred tax asset or liability related to assets acquired and liabilities assumed in a business combination as provided by the provisions of ASC 740.

2. The acquirer will account for the potential tax effects of temporary differences, carry forwards and income tax uncertainties of an acquiree at the acquisition date, or that will result from the acquisition, as provided for by the provisions of ASC 740, Tax Provisions.

C. **Employee benefits** -- (Recognition and measurement principles exceptions). The acquirer will recognize and measure a liability (or asset, if any) related to the acquiree's employee benefit arrangements in accord with applicable GAAP.

D. **Indemnification provisions** -- (Recognition and measurement principles exceptions):

1. An indemnification provision in a business combination would establish a seller's guarantee that limits the acquirer's liability for the outcome of an uncertainty related to an identifiable asset or liability.

2. The acquirer normally should recognize the indemnification benefit as an asset (indemnification asset) at the time and using the same measurement basis as the indemnified asset or liability.

E. Reacquisition rights -- (Measurement principle exception):

1. Prior to a business combination, the acquirer may have granted the acquiree the right to use an asset of the acquirer; for example, the right to use the acquirer's trade name as part of a franchise agreement.

2. If, as part of the business combination, the acquirer reacquires that right, it should be recognized by the acquirer as an intangible asset and measured on the basis of the remaining contractual term of the contract that granted the right.

3. Subsequent to the business combination, the intangible asset "reacquired right" should be amortized over the remaining period of the contract that granted the right.

F. Share-based payment awards -- (Measurement principle exception):

1. An acquirer may grant its share-based payment awards (e.g., employee stock options) for awards held by the acquiree's employees.

2. The liability or equity recognized as a result of such awards should be measured in accord with the provisions of ASC 718.

G. Assets held for sale -- (Measurement principle exception):

1. Long-term assets acquired by the acquirer which it classifies as held for sale at the acquisition date should be measured in accord with the provisions of ASC 360.

2. Basically, ASC 360 requires that assets held for sale be measured at fair value less cost to dispose.

VI. Fair Value of Previously Held Equity -- Fair value of acquirer's previously held equity interest in acquiree, if any.

A. At the acquisition date, the acquirer must measure (determine) the fair value of its previously held equity interest in the acquiree, if any.

1. An acquirer would have an equity interest in the acquiree prior to the acquisition date if the business combination was achieved in stages (also called a step acquisition).

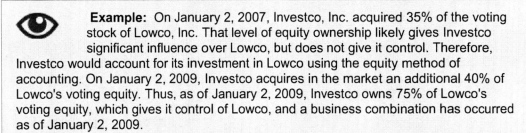

Example: On January 2, 2007, Investco, Inc. acquired 35% of the voting stock of Lowco, Inc. That level of equity ownership likely gives Investco significant influence over Lowco, but does not give it control. Therefore, Investco would account for its investment in Lowco using the equity method of accounting. On January 2, 2009, Investco acquires in the market an additional 40% of Lowco's voting equity. Thus, as of January 2, 2009, Investco owns 75% of Lowco's voting equity, which gives it control of Lowco, and a business combination has occurred as of January 2, 2009.

In this example, Investco would need to determine the fair value of its 35% ownership of Lowco as of January 2, 2009, the date of the business combination.

B. Any difference between the fair value of the acquirer's precombination equity interest in the acquiree and the carrying value of that interest on the acquirer's books would be recognized by the acquirer as a gain or loss in income of the period of the combination.

1. If the acquirer had accounted for its precombination equity ownership using the equity method of accounting (as in the Example above), the carrying amount of the investment using that method would be used in determining any gain or loss related to the previously held equity interest.

Example:
On January 2, 2007, Investco, Inc. acquired 35% of the voting stock of Lowco, Inc. for $150,000. Because its investment gave Investco significant influence over Lowco, it used the equity method to account for its investment. On January 2, 2009, Investco acquired in the market an additional 40% of Lowco's voting stock, which resulted in a business combination. At that time, Investco's investment in the 35% of Lowco acquired in January, 2007, had a carrying value of $185,000 and a market value of $200,000. As a part of its acquisition accounting for the business combination, Investco must revalue its 35% precombination investment in Lowco to fair value at the date of the business combination and recognize a gain.

Entry:

DR: Investment in Lowco, Inc. $15,000

CR: Gain on Investment Revaluation $15,000

(Fair value = $200,000 - Carrying value $185,000 = $15,000 gain.)

The fair value of Investco's precombination investment in Lowco ($200,000) would be included as a part of the cost of Investco's acquisition of Lowco.

If the acquirer had accounted for its precombination equity ownership as an available-for-sale investment, any amount recognized in prior periods in other comprehensive income would be removed from accumulated other comprehensive income and included in calculating the gain or loss as of the date of the combination.

C. The fair value of the equity owned prior to the acquisition date (i.e., the business combination) would become part of the "cost" of the investment in the acquiree.

VII. Fair Value of Noncontrolling Interest

A. At the acquisition date, the acquirer must measure (determine) the fair value of the noncontrolling interest in the acquiree.

1. A noncontrolling interest in an acquiree occurs when the acquirer obtains less than 100% of the equity interest of the acquiree.

2. The percent of equity interest not owned either directly or indirectly by the acquirer is the noncontrolling interest (formerly called "minority interest") and must be measured at fair value at the acquisition date.

B. The value assigned to the noncontrolling interest should not be based simply on the noncontrolling interest's proportional interest in the identifiable assets acquired, liabilities assumed and share of goodwill, but rather on the separately determined fair value of the noncontrolling interest in the acquiree.

1. If an active market price for the equity shares of the acquiree is available, the acquisition date fair value of the noncontrolling interest would be based on the market value of the equity shares not held by the acquirer.

2. If an active market price for the equity shares of the acquiree is not available, the acquirer would use some other valuation technique to value the equity shares not held by the acquirer.

C. The fair value of the acquirer's interest on a per-share basis may be different than the fair value of the noncontrolling interest on a per-share basis, due mainly to a "control premium" associated with the acquirer's ownership.

Recognizing/Measuring Goodwill or Bargain Purchase Amount

Application of the acquisition method of accounting to a business combination involves the following requirements: (1) Identifying the acquirer, (2) Determining the acquisition date and measurement period, (3) Determining the cost of the acquisition, (4) Recognizing and measuring the assets acquired, liabilities assumed, and noncontrolling interest in the acquiree, and (5) Recognizing and measuring any goodwill or bargain purchase amount. This lesson covers the last of these requirements, recognizing and measuring goodwill or a bargain purchase amount in a business combination. Subsequent lessons cover post-combination issues.

After studying this lesson, you should be able to:

1. *Describe how to determine whether or not goodwill or a bargain purchase amount exists.*

2. *Determine the amount of any goodwill or bargain purchase amount.*

3. *Understand certain special circumstances that may be relevant to determining goodwill or a bargain purchase amount.*

4. *Identify the differences between U.S. GAAP and IFRS related to this lesson.*

I. **The Fifth and Final Step in Applying the Acquisition Method --** Recognizing and Measuring Goodwill or a Gain from a Bargain Purchase, if any.

II. **At the Acquisition Date --** The acquirer must recognize and measure any goodwill or gain from a bargain purchase that resulted from the business combination.

III. **Amount of Gain --** The amount of that goodwill or bargain purchase gain, if any is determined using

   A. The "Investment value" of the acquired business, and

   B. The fair value of the net of identifiable assets acquired and liabilities assumed in the business combination.

IV. **"Investment Value" --** The "Investment value" is the sum of the following elements (The term "investment value" is not used in the FASB, but has been adopted here to include the sum of A. and B., as follows):

   A. The consideration transferred (cost) to effect the business combination (as detailed in the earlier lesson "Determining the Cost of an Acquired Business"), including the fair value of the following:

   1. Assets transferred;

   2. Liabilities incurred;

   3. Equity interest issued;

   4. Contingent consideration (at acquisition date);

   5. Required share-based payment awards to employees for precombination services;

   6. Precombination equity of the acquiree held by the acquirer (if the combination was achieved in stages or steps).

B. The fair value of the noncontrolling interest in the acquiree, if any (as detailed in the prior lesson "Recognizing and Measuring Assets Acquired, Liabilities Assumed and Noncontrolling Interest in an Acquiree").

> "Investment Value" = Costs (in A., above) + FV of NCI.

V. Measured at Fair Value -- The identifiable assets acquired, the liabilities assumed and any noncontrolling interest in the acquiree as of the acquisition date generally would be measured at fair value (with certain exceptions as noted in the prior lesson "Recognizing/Measuring Assets, Liabilities and Noncontrolling Interest").

VI. Goodwill -- Goodwill results when the investment value (see IV., above) is **greater** than the net fair value of assets assumed and liabilities incurred at the date of the business combination (see IV., above).

A. Simply put, goodwill (if it exists) is the excess of the fair value of the investment in the acquiree (including the fair value of the claim of the noncontrolling interest) over the fair value (or other required measure) of the identifiable net assets of the acquired business.

Example:

1. On January 2, 2009, Investco, Inc. acquired all of the outstanding common stock of Lowco, Inc. in the market for $1,000,000 cash and merged the assets acquired and liabilities assumed into Investco. At that date the fair values of Lowco's identifiable assets and liabilities were:

Accounts Receivable	$ 200,000
Inventories	400,000
Property, Plant and Equipment	800,000
Other Identifiable Assets	200,000
TOTAL ASSETS	$1,600,000
Accounts Payable	300,000
Other Current Liabilities	200,000
Long-term Liabilities	200,000
TOTAL LIABILITIES	$ 700,000
FAIR VALUE OF NET ASSETS	$ 900,000

2. Goodwill calculation:

Investment value = $1,000,000 - Fair value of net assets = $900,000 = $100,000 Goodwill.

B. Post-combination treatment of goodwill provides that:

1. Goodwill is not amortized;

2. Goodwill is assessed at least annually for impairment, as provided by ASC 350.

VII. Bargain Purchase -- A bargain purchase results when the investment value (see IV., above) is **less** than the net fair value of assets assumed and liabilities incurred as of the date of the business combination (see V., above).

A. Simply put, a bargain purchase (if it exists) is the excess of the fair value (or other required measure) of the net assets of the acquired business over the fair value of the investment in the acquiree (including the fair value of the claim of noncontrolling interest).

B. A bargain purchase may result from the following reasons, among others:

    1. The business combination occurs when the owner(s) of the acquired entity are under compulsion to carry out the sale (i.e., a "forced" sale), resulting in a bargain purchase by the acquirer;

    2. The valuation of assets acquired and/or liabilities assumed is constrained by the exceptions to the use of fair value, as detailed in the prior lesson "Recognizing/Measuring Assets, Liabilities and Noncontrolling Interest."

C. If the acquirer determines that the fair value (or other required measure) of the net assets of the acquiree is greater than the investment in the acquiree (an apparent bargain purchase), before recognizing a gain from a bargain purchase the acquirer must fully reassess whether all assets acquired and liabilities assumed have been identified and properly measured according to the provisions of ASC 805, including the measurement of:

    1. Identifiable assets acquired and liabilities assumed;

    2. Acquirer's precombination equity interest in the acquiree;

    3. Noncontrolling interest in the acquiree;

    4. Consideration transferred.

D. If, after reassessment, the acquirer still concludes that a bargain purchase exists, the amount of that bargain purchase shall be recognized as a gain in earnings as of the date of the business combination.

Example: **1.** On January 2, 2009, Investco, Inc. acquired all of the outstanding common stock of Lowco, Inc. in the market for $850,000 cash and merged the assets acquired and liabilities assumed into Investco. At that date, the fair values of Lowco's identifiable assets and liabilities were:

Accounts Receivable	$ 200,000
Inventories	400,000
Property, Plant and Equipment	800,000
Other Identifiable Assets	200,000
TOTAL ASSETS	$1,600,000
Accounts Payable	300,000
Other Current Liabilities	200,000
Long-term Liabilities	200,000
TOTAL LIABILITIES	$ 700,000
FAIR VALUE OF NET ASSETS	$ 900,000

2. Bargain purchase calculation:

Fair value of net assets = $900,000 - Investment value = $850,000 = $50,000 Bargain purchase amount. This amount would be recognized as a gain in the period of the business combination.

(Note: See the entry for this Example in the subsequent lesson, "Recording Business Combinations.")

3. The gain is attributable only to the acquirer.

VIII. Special Circumstances -- Special circumstances may affect the determination and measurement of goodwill or a bargain purchase amount. These include:

A. If the business combination is carried out solely through the exchange of equity (e.g., acquirer's common stock for acquiree's common stock), the fair value of the acquiree's equity interest at the acquisition date may be a more reliable measure of fair value than the acquirer's equity interest and, if so, the amount of goodwill or bargain purchase should be based on the acquiree's equity interest instead of the equity interest transferred by the acquirer;

B. If no consideration is transferred in carrying out the business combination, goodwill or a bargain purchase amount should be determined using a valuation technique, instead of the value of the consideration transferred.

Post-Acquisition Issues

Prior presented the steps required in the application of the acquisition method of accounting to a business combination. Following the combination, most items recognized in a combination will be measured and accounted for following the requirements of GAAP for those specific items. However, some items recognized in a combination have specific post-combination requirements. This lesson is concerned with those items.

After studying this lesson, you should be able to:

1. *Know the items recognized in a business combination that require specific post-combination treatment.*

2. *Understand how to measure and account for items that require specific post-combination treatment.*

3. *Understand the differences between U.S. GAAP and IFRS in the post-combination treatment of certain items recognized in a business combination.*

I. **Conventional Treatment** -- Once the business combination has been recorded using the acquisition method of accounting, the acquirer generally will measure and account for assets acquired, liabilities assumed or incurred, and equity issued in the combination in accord with the provisions of established GAAP for those items.

II. **Specific Treatment** -- However, certain items acquired or issued in carrying out a combination require specific treatment as provided by ASC 805; those items are:

A. **Assets and liabilities arising from contingencies**

1. An asset or liability arising from a contingency recognized at the time of a business combination should be accounted for based on subsequent information about the contingency.

2. Until new information about the possible outcome of a contingency is received, the acquirer will continue to report the contingency at its fair value at the date of the combination.

3. When new information about the possible outcome of a contingency is received, the acquirer will measure and report the item according to the following rule:

   a. If the contingency is a **liability**, it will be measured and reported at the **higher** of:

      i. Its acquisition-date fair value, or

      ii. The amount that would be recognized if the requirements of ASC 450 were followed.

   b. If the contingency is an **asset**, it will be measured and reported at the **lower** of:

      i. Its acquisition-date fair value, or

      ii. The best estimate of its future settlement amount.

4. A contingency recognized in a business combination will be derecognized only when the contingency is settled or expires.

B. **Indemnification assets**

1. An indemnification asset recognized in a business combination should be measured and reported on the same basis as the liability or asset that is indemnified, subject to any contractual limitations.

2. An indemnification assets recognized in a business combination will be derecognized only when it is settled or expires.

C. Contingent consideration

1. Contingent consideration recognized in a business combination should be measured and reported at fair value.

2. Changes in information about the fair value of contingent consideration as it existed at the date of the business combination are measurement period adjustments and change the cost of the investment.

3. Changes in the fair value of contingent consideration that results from events after the business combination (including reaching a specific share price, meeting an earnings target, etc.) are not measurement period adjustments and do not change the cost of the investment; these changes should be accounted for as follows:

    a. Contingent consideration classified as equity is not remeasured and its subsequent settlement is accounted for within (by adjusting) equity;

    b. Contingent consideration classified as an asset or liability is remeasured at each reporting date and recognized in earnings (unless the contingent consideration is a hedging arrangement, in which case the changes in value are recognized in other comprehensive income).

Disclosure Requirements - Acquisition Method

When a business combination has been carried out, considerable disclosure is required of the acquirer. Disclosures are required not only for the period in which the combination occurs, but also in subsequent period during the measurement period. This lesson identifies the most significant disclosures when a business combination occurs

After studying this lesson, you should be able to:

1. *Know the required disclosures that enable financial statement users to evaluate: a) The nature and financial effects of a business combination; b) The financial effects of adjustments related to business combinations.*

I. **Business Combination Disclosure Requirements** -- The acquirer in a business combination is required to disclose considerable information related both directly to the combination and to certain post-combination effects. The following summarizes those disclosure requirements.

A. Required information that enables users of the acquirer's financial statements to evaluate the nature and financial effects of a business combination that occurs either: (1) During the current reporting period, or (2) After the reporting period, but before the financial statements for that period are released, including the following:

1. The name and a description of the acquiree, the acquisition date, and the percentage voting equity interest acquired (if any);

2. The primary reasons for the business combination and a description of how the acquirer obtained control of the acquiree;

3. A quantitative description of the factors that make up the goodwill recognized (if any), such as expected synergies from combining operations, intangible assets that do not qualify for separate recognition (e.g., an assembled workforce), and other factors;

4. The acquisition-date fair value of the total consideration transferred and the acquisition-date fair value of **each major class** of consideration transferred;

5. For contingent consideration and indemnification assets the following:

    a. The amount recognized as of the acquisition date;

    b. A description of the arrangement and the basis for determining the amount of payment;

    c. An estimate of the (undiscounted) range of outcomes or, if a range cannot be estimated, that fact and the reasons why a range cannot be estimated;

    d. If the maximum amount of payment is unlimited, disclosure of that fact.

6. For most receivables, disclosure for **each major class** of receivable the fair value, the gross contractual amounts receivable, and the best estimate as of the acquisition date of the contractual cash flows not expected to be collected;

7. The amount recognized at the acquisition-date for **each major class** of assets acquired and liabilities assumed;

8. For assets and liabilities arising from contingencies, the amount recognized or why no amount was recognized, the nature of recognized and unrecognized contingencies, and an estimate of the (undiscounted) range of outcomes or, if a range cannot be estimated, that fact and the reasons why a range cannot be estimated;

9. The total amount of goodwill that is expected to be deductible for tax purposes;

10. The amount of goodwill assigned to each reportable segment (if segment information is required);

11. For any transactions between the acquirer and acquiree (or its former owners) that are recognized separately from the acquisition of assets and assumption of liabilities in the business combination the following:

    a. A description of each transaction;

    b. How the acquirer accounted for each transaction;

    c. The amounts recognized for each transaction and the line item(s) in the financial statements where each amount is recognized, including those amounts recognized as expenses and, separately, issuance costs not recognized as expenses.

12. For a bargain purchase, the amount of gain recognized, the line item in the income statement where the gain is recognized, and a description of why the transaction resulted in a gain;

13. For business combinations in which the acquirer owns less than 100% of the equity interest of the acquiree at the acquisition date, the fair value of the noncontrolling interest at the acquisition date and the valuation techniques and inputs used to measure that fair value;

14. For a business combination achieved in stages, the fair value of the equity interest held by the acquirer immediately prior to the combination, the amount of any gain or loss resulting from remeasuring the interest to fair value at the date of the combination, and the line item in the income statement where the gain or loss is recognized;

15. For public business enterprises (basically, publicly traded entities), the following:

    a. The amount of revenue and earnings of the acquiree occurring since the acquisition date that is included in consolidated statements for the period;

    b. The revenue and earnings of the combined entity for the current reporting period as though the acquisition date for all business combinations that occurred during the period had been at the beginning of the annual reporting period (this would be "supplemental pro forma information");

    c. For comparative statements, the revenue and earnings of the combined entity for the comparable prior reporting period(s) as though the acquisition date for all business combinations that occurred during the current year had occurred as of the beginning of the comparable prior annual reporting period(s) (this would be "supplemental pro forma information");

    d. For any of the above information that is impracticable to provide, disclosure of that fact and the reasons why the disclosure is impracticable.

B. Required information that enables users of the acquirer's financial statements to evaluate the financial effects of adjustments recognized in the current reporting period that relate to business combinations that occurred in the current or prior reporting periods, including the following:

1. If the initial accounting for a business combination is incomplete for particular assets, liabilities, noncontrolling interests, or items of consideration, and only provisional amounts have been recognized, the following information:

    a. The reasons why the initial accounting is incomplete;

    b. The assets, liabilities, equity interests, or items of consideration for which the initial accounting is incomplete;

    c. The nature and amount of any measurement period adjustments recognized during the reporting period.

2. For contingent consideration assets or liabilities that remain unsettled, the following should be provided in each reporting period:

   a. Any changes in the recognized amounts, including any differences arising as a result of settlement;

   b. Any changes in the (undiscounted) range of outcomes and the reasons for those changes;

   c. The disclosures required by ASC 820, "Fair Value Measurement" which deal with how fair value was determined.

3. Reconciliation of the carrying amount of goodwill at the beginning and end of the reporting period.

C. Any additional information necessary to meet the objectives set forth in A. and B., above.

Recording Business Combinations

Previous lessons have identified and illustrated the legal forms of business - merger, consolidation, and acquisition, Those lessons have described the requirements of the acquisition method of accounting for a business combination. This lesson is concerned with the entries that will be made in recording a business combination under the alternative legal forms.

After studying this lesson, you should be able to:

1. *Recall the nature of the various legal forms of business and understand the effects of the alternative legal forms on the accounting entry.*

2. *Make the entry to record a merger/consolidation under the following circumstances:*

    - *When there is goodwill and the acquirer has no precombination ownership of the acquiree.*

    - *When there is goodwill and the acquirer has precombination ownership of the acquiree.*

    - *When there is a bargain purchase and the acquirer has no precombination ownership of the acquiree.*

    - *When there is a bargain purchase and the acquirer has precombination ownership of the acquiree.*

3. *Make the entry to record an acquisition, both when the acquirer has no precombination ownership of the acquiree and when the acquirer has precombination ownership of the acquiree.*

I. **Legal Form and Acquisition Accounting** -- The legal form of a business combination determines the accounts that the acquirer will use in recording a business combination; the acquisition method of accounting determines the amounts at which those accounts will be recorded, and is required regardless of the legal form.

II. **Recording a Legal Merger or Legal Consolidation**

   A. Recall the characteristics of a legal merger and legal consolidation:

   1. **Legal Merger** -- One preexisting entity (acquirer) acquires either a group of assets that constitutes a business or controlling interest in the stock of another preexisting entity (acquiree) and merges the acquired assets or other entity (assets and liabilities) into the acquirer entity.

   2. **Legal Consolidation** -- A new entity is created to consolidate two or more preexisting entities.

      a. The preexisting entities cease to exist as legal entities.

      b. Under the acquisition method of accounting, if only equity interest is issued by the new entity, one of the preexisting entities must be determined to be the acquirer, not the new legal entity.

   3. **In either legal form** -- Only one entity remains after the business combination.

   B. The basic entry by the acquirer to record a legal merger (or group of assets that constitute a business) or a legal consolidation using the acquisition method of accounting is:

1. Entry:

> DR: Assets acquired (at FMV)
>
> CR: Liabilities assumed (at FMV)   } = A - L = Net Assets
>
> Consideration Paid (at FMV)

2. Assets acquired and recognized may be:

   a. Tangible (e.g., equipment) or intangible (e.g., patent);

   b. Severable - separately "sellable" (e.g., investments) or nonseverable (e.g., trademark).

3. Assets recognized would NOT include preexisting goodwill of the acquiree.

4. Assets acquired and liabilities assumed by the acquirer would be measured at fair value, with the following exceptions:

   a. Acquired income tax-related items, including deferred tax asset or deferred tax liability related to assets acquired or liabilities assumed, and tax effects of temporary differences, carry forwards, and tax uncertainties, would be measured under the provisions of FASB #109 and FASB Interpretation #48;

   b. Employee benefit liabilities (or assets), using the provisions of other applicable FASBs;

   c. Indemnification asset, using the same measurement basis as the indemnified asset or liability;

   d. Reacquisition rights, using the remaining contractual term of the contract that granted the right;

   e. Share-based employee payment awards, using the provisions of ASC 718;

   f. Assets held for sale, using the provisions of ASC 360.

5. Consideration used by the acquirer could include the following and would be measured at fair value (except when transferred assets (or liabilities) remain under the control of the acquirer - then, they would be measured at carrying value to the acquirer):

   a. Cash and cash equivalents transferred;

   b. Other assets transferred;

   c. Liabilities incurred;

   d. Equity interest issued, including common and preferred stock, options and warrants;

   e. Any combination of the above forms of consideration.

C. **Goodwill** -- Would be recognized if the investment value in the acquiree is greater than the fair value of the net assets of the acquiree at the acquisition date.

   1. Investment value in the acquiree is the sum of the fair value of consideration transferred to effect the combination + the fair value of any precombination equity owned by the acquirer + the fair value of the noncontrolling interest in the acquiree, if any.

   2. The fair value of the acquiree's net assets is the difference between the acquiree's total assets at fair value and total liabilities at fair value:

> Total assets (@ FV) - Total liabilities (@ FV) = FV of Net Assets

3. If Investment Value > Fair Value of Net Assets, Goodwill is recognized.

 Example:
No precombination ownership of the acquiree by the acquirer.

a. Facts: On January 2, 20x9, Investco, Inc. acquired all of the outstanding common stock of Lowco, Inc. in the market for $1,000,000 cash and merged the assets acquired and liabilities assumed into Investco. At that date the fair values of Lowco's identifiable assets and liabilities were:

Accounts Receivable	$ 200,000
Inventories	400,000
Property, Plant and Equipment	800,000
Other Identifiable Assets	200,000
TOTAL ASSETS	$1,600,000
Accounts Payable	300,000
Other Current Liabilities	200,000
Long-term Liabilities	200,000
TOTAL LIABILITIES	$ 700,000
FAIR VALUE OF NET ASSETS	$ 900,000

b. Goodwill calculation:

Investment value = $1,000,000 - Fair value of net assets = $900,000 = $100,000 Goodwill.

c. Entry:

DR: Accounts Receivable	$ 200,000	
Inventories	400,000	
Property, Plant and Equipment	800,000	
Other Identifiable Assets	200,000	
Goodwill	100,000	
CR: Accounts Payable		$ 300,000
Other Current Liabilities		200,000
Long-term Liabilities		200,000
Cash		1,000,000

See the following example.

Example:
With precombination ownership of the acquiree by the acquirer

a. Facts: (The following accounts and amounts are taken from a disclosure illustration in ASC 805; the other facts are assumed.)

On January 2, 20x8, Topco, Inc. acquired 15% of the voting equity of Noco, Inc. for $1,200 and subsequently treated the investment as available for sale. On June 30, 20x9, Topco, Inc. acquired the remaining 85% of Noco, using the following consideration:

Cash	$ 8,300
Common Stock (1,000 shares x $4)	4,000
Contingent Consideration Obligation	1,000
Total Consideration at Combination	$13,300

At that date, the fair value of Topco's original 15% was $2,000. Topco incurred $1,250 of acquisition-related costs. Topco's common stock is $1.00 par, with a market value of $4.00 per share at the acquisition date

The fair values and other appropriate values assigned to Noco's identifiable assets and liabilities were:

Financial assets	$ 3,500
Inventory	1,000
Property, plant and equipment	10,000
Identifiable intangible assets	3,300
Total Assets	$17,800
Financial liabilities	$ 4,000
Liability arising from a contingency	1,000
Total Liabilities	$ 5,000

b. Goodwill calculation:

Investment value:

Acquirer's Consideration at Combination	$13,300
Acquirer's Precombination Equity @ FV	2,000
Total Investment Value	$15,300
Fair Value of Net Assets ($17,800 - $5,000)	$12,800
Goodwill = Investment Value > FV of NA	$ 2,500

c. Entry:

DR:	Financial assets*	$ 3,500	
	Inventory*	1,000	
	Property, plant and equipment*	10,000	
	Identifiable intangible assets*	3,300	
	Goodwill****	2,500	
	CR: Financial liabilities*		4,000
	Liability arising from contingency*		1,000
	Contingent Consideration Obligation**		1,000
	Cash**		8,300
	Investment - Available for Sale***		2,000
	Common Stock ($1 par)**		1,000
	Additional Paid-in Capital**		3,000

* =   Identifiable assets and liabilities acquired.

** =   Consideration Transferred at combination.

*** =   Precombination Investment in Noco at fair value - now part of the cost of the assets and liabilities acquired.

**** = Computed Goodwill

d. Comments on Entry:

1) The acquirer would have to classify or designate the assets acquired and liabilities assumed to subsequently apply the appropriate GAAP. For example, if any financial assets are investments, the acquirer would need to classify as held-to-maturity, held-for-trading, or available for sale.
2) Since the precombination investment in Noco was classified as available-for-sale, the difference between the cost ($1,200) and the fair value at the date of combination ($2,000), or $800, would be removed from Accumulated Other Comprehensive Income and recognized by Noco as a realized gain.
3) Goodwill recognized by Topco will not be amortized, but will be assessed at least annually for impairment.
4) The $1,250 cost incurred to carry out the combination is not part of the consideration used to acquire Noco, but would be expensed by Topco when incurred.

D. A Bargain Purchase -- Would be recognized if the fair value of the net assets of the acquiree at the acquisition date is greater than the investment value in the acquiree.

    1. Investment value in the acquiree is the sum of the fair value of consideration transferred to effect the combination + the fair value of any precombination equity owned by the acquirer + the fair value of the noncontrolling interest in the acquiree, if any.

    2. The fair value of the acquiree's net assets is the difference between the acquiree's total assets at fair value and total liabilities at fair value:

Total assets (@ FV) - Total liabilities (@ FV) = FV of Net Assets

3. If Fair Value of Net Assets > Investment Value, a Bargain Purchase Gain is recognized.

 Example:
No precombination ownership of the acquiree by the acquirer

a. Facts: On January 2, 20x9, Investco, Inc. acquired all of the outstanding common stock of Lowco, Inc. in the market for $850,000 cash and merged the assets acquired and liabilities assumed into Investco. At that date the fair values of Lowco's identifiable assets and liabilities were:

Accounts Receivable	$ 200,000
Inventories	400,000
Property, Plant and Equipment	800,000
Other Identifiable Assets	200,000
TOTAL ASSETS	$1,600,000
Accounts Payable	300,000
Other Current Liabilities	200,000
Long-term Liabilities	200,000
TOTAL LIABILITIES	$ 700,000
FAIR VALUE OF NET ASSETS	$ 900,000

b. Bargain purchase calculation: Fair value of net assets = $900,000 - Investment value = $850,000 = $50,000 Bargain purchase amount. This amount would be recognized as a gain in the period of the business combination.

c. Entry:

DR: Accounts Receivable	$ 200,000	
Inventories	400,000	
Property, Plant and Equipment	800,000	
Other Identifiable Assets	200,000	
CR: Accounts Payable		$300,000
Other Current Liabilities		200,000
Long-term Liabilities		200,000
Cash		850,000
Bargain Purchase Gain		50,000

See the following example.

Example:
With precombination ownership of the acquiree by the acquirer

a. Facts: (The following accounts and amounts are taken from a disclosure illustration in ASC 805; the other facts are assumed.)

On January 2, 20x8, Topco, Inc. acquired 15% of the voting equity of Noco, Inc. for $1,200 and subsequently treated the investment as available for sale. On June 30, 20x9, Topco, Inc. acquired the remaining 85% of Noco, using the following consideration:

Cash	$ 5,000
Common Stock (1,000 shares x $4)	4,000
Contingent Consideration Obligation	1,000
Total Consideration at Combination	$10,000

At that date, the fair value of Topco's original 15% was $2,000. Topco incurred $1,250 of acquisition-related costs. Topco's common stock is $1.00 par, with a market value of $4.00 per share at the acquisition date.

The fair values and other appropriate values assigned to Noco's identifiable assets and liabilities were:

Financial assets	$ 3,500
Inventory	1,000
Property, plant and equipment	10,000
Identifiable intangible assets	3,300
Total Assets	$ 17,800

Financial liabilities	$ 4,000
Liability arising from a contingency	1,000
Total Liabilities	$ 5,000

b. Bargain purchase calculation:

Investment value:

Acquirer's Consideration at Combination	$10,000
Acquirer's Precombination Equity @ FV	2,000
Total Investment Value	$12,000

Fair Value of Net Assets ($17,800 - $5,000)	$12,800

Bargain Purchase Gain:

FV of NA > Investment Value	$ 800

c. Entry:

DR: Financial assets*	$ 3,500	
Inventory*	1,000	
Property, Plant and Equipment*	10,000	
Identifiable intangible assets*	3,300	
CR: Financial liabilities*		4,000
Liability arising from contingency*		1,000
Contingent Consideration Obligation**		1,000
Cash**		5,000
Investment - Available for Sale***		2,000
Common Stock ($1 par)**		1,000
Additional Paid-in Capital**		3,000
Bargain Purchase Gain****		800

* =   Identifiable assets and liabilities acquired.

** =   Consideration Transferred at combination.

*** =   Precombination Investment in Noco at fair value - now part of the cost of the assets and liabilities acquired.

**** =   Computed Bargain Purchase Gain

d. Comments on Entry:

1) The acquirer would have to classify or designate the assets acquired and liabilities assumed to subsequently apply the appropriate GAAP. For example, if any financial assets are investments, the acquirer would need to classify as held-to-maturity, held-for-trading, or available for sale.

2) Since the precombination investment in Noco was classified as available-for-sale, the difference between the cost ($1,200) and the fair value at the date of combination ($2,000), or $800, would be removed from Accumulated Other Comprehensive Income and recognized by Noco as a realized gain.

3) The bargain purchase gain will be recognized by Topco in its earnings for the period of the business combination.

4) The $1,250 cost incurred to carry out the combination is not part of the consideration used to acquire Noco, but would be expensed by Topco when incurred.

III. Recording a Legal Acquisition.

A. Recall the characteristics of a legal acquisition:

1. One preexisting entity (acquirer) acquires controlling interest in the voting stock of another preexisting entity (acquiree) and both entities continue to exist and operate as separate legal entities;

2. Example: Company P acquires more than 50% of the voting stock of Company S and Company P does not merge Company S into Company P; rather, Company S continues to exist as a separate corporation with Company P holding the majority of its voting stock;

3. In this legal form, both entities continue to exist, operate and maintain separate accounting records, but one entity has controlling interest in the other entity;

4. Since the controlling entity may not have 100% ownership of the acquired entity's voting stock, there can be other shareholders with an interest in the acquired entity; those shareholders are the noncontrolling interest (formerly called "minority interest").

B. The basic entry by the acquirer to record a legal acquisition using the acquisition method of accounting is:

1. Entry:

> DR: Investment in Subsidiary X (at FMV of Consideration Paid)
> CR: Consideration Paid (at FMV)

2. Consideration used by the acquirer could include the following and would be measured at fair value (except when transferred assets (or liabilities) remain under the control of the acquirer - then, they would be measured at carrying value to the acquirer):

   a. Cash and cash equivalents transferred;

   b. Other assets transferred;

   c. Liabilities incurred;

   d. Equity interest issued, including common and preferred stock, options and warrants;

   e. Any combination of the above forms of consideration.

3. As a result of the acquisition and related entry:

   a. A Parent-Subsidiary relationship is established;

   b. The firms operate and maintain accounting books and records as separate entities;

   c. The parent carries "Investment in Subsidiary" on its books using the Cost, Equity, or other method.

4. The subsidiary will be reported in the consolidated statements of the parent, unless the parent lacks effective control of the subsidiary. (The consolidating process, including when a parent lacks effective control over a subsidiary, is covered in later lessons.)

   See the following examples.

Example:
No precombination ownership of the acquiree by the acquirer and no noncontrolling ownership

1. Facts: On January 2, 20x9, Investco, Inc. acquired all of the outstanding common stock of Lowco, Inc. in the market for $1,000,000 cash in a legal acquisition.

2. Entry:

DR: Investment in Lowco, Inc. (Subsidiary) $1,000,000

       CR: Cash $1,000,000

3. At that date, Investco also would have to determine the following information:

    a. The book values of Lowco's assets and liabilities.

    b. The fair value of Lowco's assets and liabilities.

    c. Any goodwill or bargain purchase amount implicit in the relationship between its investment and the fair value of Lowco's net assets.

4. The information determined and "captured" in 3, above, will be the basis for the preparation of consolidated financial statements; the preparation of those statements will include, among other things:

    a. Revaluing Lowco's assets and liabilities to fair value as of the date of the business combination.

    b. Recognizing any goodwill or bargain purchase amount implicit in the business combination.

Example:
With precombination ownership of the acquiree by the acquirer and a noncontrolling interest

1. Facts: (The following accounts and amounts are taken from a disclosure illustration in ASC 805; the other facts are assumed.)

On January 2, 20x8, Topco, Inc. acquired 15% of the voting equity of Noco, Inc. for $1,200 and subsequently treated the investment as available for sale. On June 30, 20x9, Topco, Inc. acquired an additional 65% of Noco, using the following consideration:

Cash	$ 5,000
Common Stock (1,000 shares x $4)	4,000
Contingent Consideration Obligation	1,000
Total Consideration at Combination	$10,000

At that date, the fair value of Topco's original 15% was $2,000. Topco incurred $1,250 cost of acquisition-related costs. The remaining 20% ownership in Noco is the noncontrolling interest. Topco's common stock is $1.00 par, with a market value of $4.00 per share at the acquisition date.

2. Entry:

DR:	Investment in Noco, Inc. (Subsidiary)	$12,000
	CR: Contingent Consideration Obligation	1,000
	Cash	5,000
	Investment - Available for Sale	2,000
	Common Stock ($1 par)	1,000
	Additional Paid-in Capital	3,000

3. Comments on Entry:

   a. Since the precombination investment in Noco was classified as available-for-sale, the difference between the cost ($1,200) and the fair value at the date of combination ($2,000), or $800, would be removed from Accumulated Other Comprehensive Income and recognized by Noco as a realized gain.

   b. The $1,250 cost incurred to carry out the combination is not part of the consideration used to acquire Noco, but would be expensed by Topco when incurred.

4. At that date, Topco would also have to determine the following information:

   a. The book values of Noco's assets and liabilities.

   b. The fair value of Noco's assets and liabilities.

   c. The fair value of the 20% noncontrolling interest.

   d. Any goodwill or bargain purchase amount implicit in the relationship between the investment value in Noco (Topco's consideration transferred - $10,000, plus its precombination investment at fair value - $2,000, plus the fair value of the noncontrolling interest) and the fair value of Noco's net assets.

5. The information determined and "captured" in 4, above, will be the basis for the preparation of consolidated financial statements; the preparation of those statements will include, among other things:

   a. Revaluing Noco's assets and liabilities to fair value as of the date of the business combination.

   b. Recognizing the fair value of the noncontrolling interest in Noco as an equity item.

   c. Recognizing any goodwill or bargain purchase amount implicit in the business combination.

6. On Topco's books, it will carry its investment in its subsidiary Noco as an asset using the cost method, the equity method, or some other method; that investment will be eliminated in the consolidating process and consolidated financial statements will be issued for Topco and Noco.

Variable Interest Entities (VIEs)

Consolidated financial statements may be required in certain other circumstances where one entity has control over another entity through means other than equity ownership. This control usually occurs through a variable interest in another entity. This lesson identifies a variable interest entity (VIE) and when the VIE should be consolidated financial statement with the primary beneficiary.

After studying this lesson, you should be able to:

1. *Understand the concept of variable-interest entities (VIEs) and when VIEs must be consolidated.*

2. *Identify a primary beneficiary and when the VIE should be consolidated.*

I. **Eligibility for Consolidated Financial Statements** -- Whether or not an entity (e.g., an investee), in which another entity (e.g., an investor) has an interest, must be consolidated or not, depends on the nature of the relationship between entities. GAAP establishes a two-step (or two-tier) process for determining whether or not the relationship requires an entity be consolidated with another entity. The entity being considered for consolidation must be assessed to determine (1) if it is a variable-interest entity (VIE) and, if so, the primary beneficiary of the VIE, and (2) if the entity is not a VIE, whether or not an investor has equity ownership that enables it to exercise control of the investee.

II. **Variable-Interest Entity Assessment** -- Each entity that is considered for consolidation must first be evaluated to determine if it is a variable-interest entity (VIE) and, if it is, which other entity is its primary beneficiary.

    A. A VIE is a legal entity which by design either:

        1. Cannot finance its activities without additional subordinated financial support (i.e., its expected losses exceed its total equity investment at risk), or

        2. Its equity holders, as a group, do not have the direct or indirect ability to make decisions about the VIE's activities.

    B. Structurally, a VIE may be a legal trust, partnership, joint venture, limited company or corporation.

        1. Typically, a VIE is established by another entity or entities (the sponsors) to carry out a well-defined, limited business purpose, with the sponsor(s) - also the variable-interest holders - providing most resources to the VIE, often in the form of loans or loan guarantees.

        2. The activities of and decision-making in a VIE are governed largely by the agreement that establishes the entity and generally resides with the variable-interest holders; non-sponsor equity owners may play little role in the operation of the entity.

        3. The risks and rewards associated with the VIE are largely attributable to the variable-interest holders, not the equity owners who may bear little risk and receive only a small rate of return.

        4. The value of the VIE to the variable-interest holders depends on (varies with) the success of the VIE; the variable-interest holders' interest increases if the net asset value of the VIE increases or decreases if the net asset value of the VIE decreases.

    C. In summary, even though the equity investors in a VIE are its legal owners, because of contractual or other arrangements they play little role in the operation of the entity and carry little risk or receive little benefit from ownership; those risks and benefits accrue to the variable-interest holders (usually also the sponsors). Thus, a VIE is an entity in which another entity has a controlling interest achieved by a means other than holding a majority of the voting rights.

D. An entity with a variable interest in a VIE must qualitatively assess whether or not it is the primary beneficiary of the VIE; if so, it is deemed to have a controlling financial interest in the VIE.

E. An entity will be considered the primary beneficiary of a VIE if it meets both of the following conditions:

   1. It has the power to direct activities of the VIE that most significantly impact the VIEs economic performance (called the power criterion), and

   2. It has the obligation to absorb losses from or right to receive benefits of the VIE that potentially could be significant to the VIE (called the losses/benefits or risks/rewards criterion).

F. Only one entity (e.g., sponsor), if any, will be the primary beneficiary of a VIE.

G. An entity that is determined to be the primary beneficiary of a VIE (and therefore has a controlling financial interest) will consolidate the financial statements of the VIE.

H. An entity that is determined to be the primary beneficiary of a VIE and, therefore, consolidates its financial statements, must assess whether or not it continues to be the primary beneficiary on an on-going basis.

III: Voting Interest Assessment -- If an entity being considered for consolidation (e.g., an investee) is not a variable-interest entity, it would be assessed to determine whether or not an investor has majority ownership of its voting securities and, if so, that nothing prevents the investor from exercising its control of the operating and financial activities of the investee.

A. Controlling ownership of an investee by an investor results from a business combination carried out in the form of a legal acquisition.

   1. A business combination carried out as a legal merger or legal consolidation results in only one remaining firm. Financial statements are prepared for that single firm; there are no sets of financial statements to consolidate.

   2. A business combination carried out as a legal acquisition results in one legal entity (the parent) having majority ownership, either directly or indirectly, of the other legal entity (the subsidiary). Each firm is a separate legal (and accounting) entity, but under the common control of the parent shareholder.

   3. In form, the parent and subsidiary are separate legal entities; in substance, they are a single "economic entity." If the parent can exercise its majority ownership to control the operating and financial activities of the subsidiary, consolidated parent-subsidiary financial statements must be the primary form of financial reporting for the entities.

B. A majority owned (> 50% of voting stock, controlled either directly or indirectly) subsidiary must be consolidated with its parent unless the parent lacks the ability to exercise its majority ownership to control the operating and financial activities of the subsidiary (i.e., the parent lacks effective control of the subsidiary).

   1. Effective control may be lacking due to:

      a. Foreign subsidiary being largely controlled by the foreign government through:

         i. Prohibition on paying dividends;

         ii. Control of day-to-day operations.

      b. Domestic subsidiary in bankruptcy and under the control of the courts.

C. Unless a parent lacks effective control of a subsidiary, the subsidiary's financial statements must be consolidated with parent's financial statements for public reporting.

D. If a majority owned subsidiary is not consolidated because the investor lacks effective control (for one of the reasons given above), the subsidiary is an "unconsolidated subsidiary."

    1. An unconsolidated subsidiary would be reported as an "Investment" asset by the parent.

    2. The parent would account for its investment in an unconsolidated subsidiary using either fair value or the equity method, depending on the extent of influence that it can exercise over the investee.

IFRS - Business Combinations

The accounting standard on Business Combinations was a joint project of the FASB and IFRS. Therefore, there are very few differences between U.S. GAAP and IFRS. The major differences arise from the implementation of acquisition method accounting.

After studying this lesson you should be able to :

1. *Identify the major differences in the application of acquisition method accounting under IFRS versus U.S. GAAP.*

I. IFRS Business Combinations

A. The most significant differences in the application of the acquisition method of accounting between U.S. GAAP and IFRS are related to the differences in the accounting for the acquired item. Below is a table of the major differences. Each difference is discussed further in the study text.

U.S. GAAP	IFRS
Contingent assets and liabilities can be recognized if criterion are met	Contingent assets are not recognized
Goodwill allocation is to the reporting units	Goodwill is allocated to the cash generating units
Goodwill impairment testing has a qualitative 'pre-step' and then, if needed, a 2 step approach	Goodwill impairment testing is a one-step test
Must disclose pro-forma information for current and prior periods presented	Must disclose pro-forma information only for current period
Not required to disclose assumptions related to acquired contingencies	Required to disclose assumptions related to acquired contingencies

B. **Contingency Recognition and Measurement**

1. There are significant differences between U.S. GAAP and IFRS in accounting for contingencies acquired in a business combination.

    a. Under U.S. GAAP, both contingent assets and contingent liabilities are recognized. A distinction is made between contingencies that are contractual (e.g., a warranty obligation) and those that are not contractual (e.g., an unsettled law suit). Contractual contingencies are recognized at fair value if that value can be determined during the measurement period. Noncontractual contingencies are recognized only if it is more likely than not that they qualify as an asset or liability.

    b. Under IFRS, contingent assets are not recognized. Contingent liabilities are recognized if they:

        i. Are a present obligation that arises from a past event, and

        ii. Fair value can be measured reliably.

2. Subsequent to recognition, the treatments between U.S. GAAP and IFRS differ, as follows:

    a. Under U.S. GAAP, recognized contingent assets and liabilities will continue to be reported at their acquisition-date fair value until new information about the outcome of the contingency becomes known. When new information about the outcome becomes known, the contingency will be remeasured using criteria based on whether the contingency is an asset or liability (as described in II. B., above).

    b. Under IFRS, recognized contingent liabilities subsequently are remeasured at the higher of the amount initially recognized or the best estimate of the amount required to settle the contingent liability. Since contingent assets are not recognized under IFRS, no subsequent treatment applies.

C. Goodwill Allocation -- Both U.S. GAAP and IFRS require that recognized goodwill be allocated to component units of the entity, but there is a difference in the specification of those component units.

    1. Under U.S. GAAP, goodwill must be allocated to the **reporting units** of the entity. A reporting unit is an operating segment of the entity that:

        a. constitutes a business;

        b. constitutes a business;

        c. has operating results regularly reviewed by management.

    2. The difference between U.S. GAAP and IFRS in the allocation of goodwill is likely to result in the allocation of goodwill to more units under IFRS than under GAAP, which may result in more frequent goodwill impairment.

    3. Under both U.S. GAAP and IFRS goodwill must be tested for impairment at the unit level (reporting unit under U.S. GAAP; cash-generating unit under IFRS).

    4. Goodwill Impairment -- Both U.S. GAAP and IFRS require that recognized goodwill be tested for impairment at least annually, but there are differences in the testing methodology that can create differences in loss recognition.

        a. Under U.S. GAAP, goodwill may be tested for impairment using one of two general approaches:

            i. The first general approach begins by conducting a qualitative assessment to determine if it is more likely than not (i.e., a likelihood of greater than 50%) that the fair value of the reporting unit has declined below its carrying value. If it is determined to be more likely than not that fair value is less than carrying value, then the first of a two-step process must be followed to make a quantitative determination of whether or not an impairment has occurred and, if so, measure the amount of the related loss. If it is determined in the qualitative assessment that it is NOT more likely than not that the fair value of the reporting unit is less than its carrying value, then no further assessment for impairment is required.

            ii. The second general approach, which is an alternative to the first described above, is to skip the qualitative assessment and carry out the two-step quantitative process to determine if goodwill is impaired and, if so, to measure that impairment loss.

        b. Under IFRS, goodwill is tested for impairment using a one-step approach, measured as the excess of the carrying amount (CV) of the cash-generating unit over the recoverable amount (RA) of the cash-generating unit. If CV > RA, adjust goodwill and recognize a loss in operating results.

        c. Goodwill impairment testing and measurement is covered in detail in the lesson "Goodwill" in the Intangible Assets - Goodwill and Other topic lesson.

D. Disclosure Requirements -- There are differences in disclosure requirements between the standards. The most significant of their disclosure differences are identified here.

1. Pro-Forma Disclosures -- Under U.S. GAAP, public business enterprises (basically, publicly traded entities) are required to disclose certain supplemental pro-forma information, including revenue and earnings information. This pro-forma information must be disclosed for the current and prior periods presented. Similar disclosures are not required for other (nonpublic) entities. Under IFRS, however, all acquirers are required to provide pro-forma information, but only for the period of the combination, not for prior periods presented. The pro-forma disclosures required by IFRS include:

   a. The amount of revenue and profit or loss of the acquiree since the acquisition date included in the consolidated statement of comprehensive income for the reporting period;

   b. The revenue and profit or loss of the combined entity for the current reporting period through the acquisition date for all business combinations that occurred during the year as if they had been as of the beginning of the annual reporting period.

2. Acquired Contingencies -- Under U.S. GAAP, when contingent assets or contingent liabilities are acquired in a business combination, the acquirer is not required to disclose the major assumptions made about the future events or the amount of any expected reimbursement used in valuing the contingencies. Under IFRS, the acquirer is required to disclose major assumptions made about future events and the amount of expected reimbursement, if any, used in valuing the contingencies.

3. Goodwill -- Under U.S. GAAP (ASC 280), public business enterprise acquirers that recognize goodwill must disclose the amount of the goodwill allocated to each reportable segment as of the acquisition date. Under IFRS (No. 3), acquirers are not required to disclose the amount of goodwill allocated to each cash-generating unit (comparable to a reportable segment under U.S. GAAP); however, other IFRS (IAS No. 36) requires disclosure by all entities (not just public business enterprises) of goodwill for each cash-generating unit as of each balance sheet date.

Consolidated Financial Statements

Introduction to Consolidated Financial Statements

This lesson presents the criteria for consolidated financial statements, the exceptions to those criteria, and an overview to the consolidating process.

After studying this lesson you should be able to :

1. Identify the alternative accounting methods that a parent may use to carry an investment in a subsidiary on its books.

2. Describe the effects of the alternative accounting methods on the consolidating process and on the consolidated statements.

3. Describe when consolidated financial statements are required under U.S. GAAP (and when they are not appropriate) .

4. Describe the information needed in order to prepare consolidated financial statements.

5. Describe where the consolidating process is carried out.

6. List the basic sequence of steps used in carrying out the consolidating process.

7. Identify the specific circumstances that affect how the consolidating process is carried out.

I. Background

A. Consolidated financial statements are required when one entity has effective control over another entity.

    1. Controlling interest is usually present when an entity (investor/parent) has a greater than 50% ownership (directly or indirectly) of another entity (investee/subsidiary) and therefore can direct the activities of the investee/subsidiary; or

    2. Control is also evident when an entity (variable-interest holder) is the principal beneficiary of a variable-interest entity.

B. In either of the foregoing cases, the entities are separate legal entities, but are under common economic control.

    1. The shareholders of the parent entity control that entity which, in turn, has control of the subsidiary entity.

    2. The shareholders of the variable-interest holder entity control that entity which, in turn, has control of the variable-interest entity.

C. Because the entities are under common economic control, GAAP requires consolidated financial statements.

    1. Consolidated financial statements present the financial information of two or more separate legal entities, usually a parent company and one or more if its subsidiaries, as though they were a single economic entity (remember the economic entity concept from the conceptual framework?!).

    2. The **consolidating process** is the sequence of steps or activities carried out in order to combine the financial information of two or more entities. The consolidating process results in consolidated financial statements.

D. The process of presenting consolidated financial statements can be represented graphically in the following way:

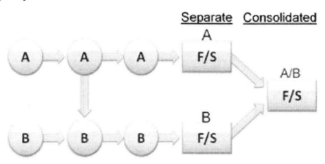

II. Justification -- The preparation and presentation of consolidated financial statements is justified based on:

    A. The presumption that consolidated statements are more meaningful than separate financial statements.

        1. "There is a presumption that consolidated statements are more meaningful than separate statements and that they are usually necessary for a fair presentation when one of the entities in the group directly or indirectly has a controlling financial interest in the other entities" (ASC 810-10-1).

    B. The supposition that economic substance (common controlling interest) take precedence over legal form (separate legal entities).

III. Exceptions -- There are certain limited exceptions to when an entity must consolidate another entity. Those exceptions include:

    A. If an investor/parent has majority ownership of an investee/subsidiary (> 50% of the voting stock of the investee), but is prevented from exercising that majority ownership to control the financial and operating policies or activities of the subsidiary, it will not consolidate the subsidiary. Effective control may be lacking (even for a majority owned subsidiary) when it is:

        1. A foreign subsidiary largely controlled by the foreign government through prohibition on paying dividends, control of day-to-day operations, or other impediments to control.

        2. A domestic subsidiary in bankruptcy and under the control of the courts.

    B. Certain entities are precluded from consolidating controlled entities by industry-specific guidelines, including:

        1. Registered investment companies.

        2. Brokers/dealers in securities.

    C. A variable-interest (investment) or subsidiary (unconsolidated subsidiary) that is not included in consolidated statements would be reported as an "Investment" by the interest-holder/investor.

        1. The variable-interest investment would be measured as the entity's claim to the net asset value of the variable-interest entity.

        2. The unconsolidated subsidiary investment would be measured using either fair value or the equity method of accounting, depending on the extent of influence that can be exercise over the subsidiary by the parent.

IV. Parent's Accounting for a Subsidiary to be Consolidated

    A. A Parent records a subsidiary **on its books** as an "Investment" (in Subsidiary).

B. Subsequently, a Parent may carry an "Investment" in a subsidiary that will be consolidated **on its books** using:

   1. Cost Method;

   2. Equity Method;

   3. Any other method it chooses.

V. A Parent Must Report Entities under its Control in Consolidated Statements

   A. The method a Parent uses to carry an "Investment" in a subsidiary on its books (cost, equity, or other) **will affect only** the consolidating process (entries).

   B. The method a Parent uses to carry an "Investment" in a subsidiary on its books (cost, equity, or other) **will not affect** final resulting Consolidated Statements.

   C. Consolidating Process Illustrated -- The following illustrates the use of alternative methods by a parent to carry its investment in a subsidiary (the cost method and the equity method) and the effects of those different methods on the consolidating process (different) and on the final consolidated statements (the same).

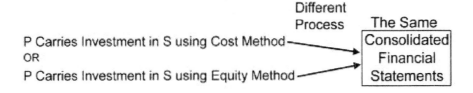

VI. Information Requirements -- In order to consolidate the financial statements of two or more entities, certain specific information is needed, including:

   A. Financial statements (or adjusted trial balances) of the separate affiliated entities to be consolidated.

   B. Data as of the date of a business combination (i.e., acquisition date):

      1. Book values of assets acquired and liabilities assumed as of the acquisition date.

      2. Fair values of assets acquired and liabilities assumed as of the acquisition date.

      3. Fair value of any noncontrolling interest in the acquired entity as of the acquisition date.

      4. Fair value of any equity interest in the acquired entity owned by the parent prior to the acquisition date.

   C. Intercompany (i.e., between the companies being consolidated) transaction data (for the operating period) and intercompany balances (as of period end).

VII. Consolidating Process

   A. The consolidating process is carried out on a consolidating worksheet, not on the books of any entity.

      1. The basic information for the worksheet comes from the account balances of the separate entities.

      2. The consolidating process is primarily concerned with adjusting and eliminating those balances to develop information that would report the separate entities as though they were a single entity.

      3. The consolidating process and the results of that process are not recorded on the books of any of the affiliated entities.

      4. The result of the consolidating process is the full set of consolidated financial statements.

B. The basic sequence of steps in carrying out the consolidating process are (each of these requirements is covered in detail in the following lessons):

   1. Record Trial Balances -- Record account titles and balances of the separate entities on the consolidating worksheet from the adjusted trial balances, separate statements, or other sources.

   2. Record Adjusting Entries -- Develop and post to the worksheet consolidating adjusting entries, if any.

   3. Record Eliminating Entries -- Develop and post to the worksheet consolidating eliminating entries; these entries are likely to include:

   a. Investment eliminating entry (always required);

   b. Intercompany receivables/payables elimination(s);

   c. Intercompany revenue/expense elimination(s);

   d. Intercompany profit elimination(s).

   4. Complete consolidating worksheet.

   5. Prepare formal consolidated financial statements from worksheet.

VIII. Factors Effecting the Consolidation Process -- While the general process is the same for carrying out all consolidating processes, the specific adjustments, eliminations and related amounts depend on the specific circumstances. The following alternatives will affect the specific adjustments and eliminations made during the consolidating process:

A. Whether the consolidating process is being carried out at the date of the business combination or at a subsequent date.

B. Whether the parent owns 100% (all) of the voting stock of a subsidiary or less than 100% of the voting stock.

C. Whether on its books the parent carries its investment in a subsidiary using the cost or equity method of accounting.

D. Whether transactions between the affiliated entities (parent and its subsidiaries) originate with the parent or with a subsidiary.

Consolidating Process

Consolidation at Acquisition

*This lesson discusses the preparation of consolidated financial statements immediately following a business combination or following an operating period that occurs after the combination. This lesson describes and illustrates the specific requirements of the consolidating process carried out **immediately following the acquisition** of a subsidiary by a parent.*

After studying this lesson, you should be able to:

1. *Describe the characteristics of consolidated financial statements immediately following a business combination.*

2. *Prepare consolidated financial statements immediately following a business combination, including:*

    • *Calculate consolidated balances on the consolidated balance sheet.*

    • *Understand consolidating investment eliminating entries.*

    • *Understand intercompany receivable/payable eliminating entries.*

3. *Describe the effects that the method a parent uses to carry an investment (on its books) in a subsidiary has on the investment balance that must be eliminated in the consolidating process.*

I. **Business Combinations --** A business combination must be accounted for using the acquisition method of accounting. Immediately following an acquisition the consolidated balance sheet will be different from the Parent's (acquiring entity's) financial statements. If an income statement, statement of cash flows, or statement of retained earnings were prepared at the date of acquisition, it would represent information of the Parent company only because there will not yet have been any activity including the subsidiary.

II. **Consolidated Balance Sheet --** At the date of the combination, a consolidated balance sheet will "combine" the assets, liabilities, and shareholder claims (majority and noncontrolling, if any) of the Parent and its newly acquired Subsidiary(ies).

III. **Consolidated Income Statement/Retained Earnings Statement/Cash Flow Statement --** At the date of combination, a consolidated income statement, statement of retained earnings, or statement of cash flow would be the same as the statements of the Parent entity.

   A. Under the acquisition method of accounting for the combination, the operating results of the acquired entity up to the date of the combination is part of what the Parent paid for in the cost of the investment in the Subsidiary.

   B. There has not yet been an operating period (and operating results) during which the Subsidiary was controlled by the Parent. Therefore, the consolidated income statement, retained earnings statement, and cash flow statement will be the same as the parent's at the date of the combination.

IV. **Carrying Investment in Subsidiary --** At the date of combination, the method the Parent will use to account for the investment in the subsidiary (cost, equity or other) is not a consideration - there is no "carrying" period yet.

V. **Overview --** The following example will depict the information needed to answer questions regarding the date of acquisition.

Example:
P (Passing) purchased 100% of S (Score) for $200,000 on January 1, 2002. The book value equals the fair market value of all of S's assets and liabilities except for equipment, which had a FMV of $100,000 (the carrying value was $80,000). Any excess purchase price is attributed to goodwill. P owes S $10,000 and S has a receivable from P of $10,000.

The decomposition of the purchase price is:

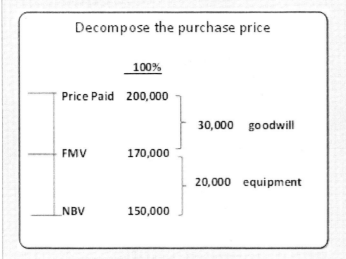

Below are the balance sheets of P and S immediately after the acquisition. The far right-hand columns represent the *consolidated entity* as of **January 1, 2002** (the date of the acquisition).

	Passing		Score		ELIM	CONSOLIDATED	
	Debit	Credit	Debit	Credit		Debit	Credit
Current assets	80,000		30,000			100,000[1]	
Inventory	150,000		350,000			500,000	
Equipment (net)	430,000		80,000			530,000[2]	
Investment in Score	200,000					0	
Goodwill						30,000	
Current liabilities		150,000		110,000			250,000[3]
Long-term debt		460,000		200,000			660,000
Common Stock		200,000		140,000			200,000[4]
Retained Earnings		50,000		10,000			50,000[4]
Totals	810,000	810,000	460,000	460,000		1,160,000	1,160,000

[1]**P's current assets**	80,000
S's current assets	30,000
Less interco AR	(10,000)
Consolidated current assets	100,000

[2]P's equipment	430,000
S's equipment	80,000
Plus FMV adjust	20,000
Consolidated equipment	530,000
[3]P's current liabilities	150,000
S's current liabilities	110,000
Less interco AP	(10,000)
Consolidated current liabilities	250,000

[4]Only P's

VI. Focus on the end result (the consolidated balances) for most of the CPA exam questions. If you need to complete an entire consolidating worksheet, knowing how to derive the ending balances will help you get to consolidated totals. If you want a refresher on the process of consolidation (or have never studied consolidation in your course work) then you will want to review the following description of the steps to consolidation.

VII. **Process Steps to Follow --** The steps to be followed in deriving consolidated financial statements from the separate trial balances or statements of the separate companies are:

A. **Record Trial Balances --** Record Account Titles and Balances on Worksheet from Trial Balance, separate financial statements, or other sources of the separate companies that are to be consolidated. (In simulations on recent CPA Exams this data has been provided in the form of a preprinted worksheet.)

B. **Adjusting Entries --** Identify and record consolidating **adjusting** entries required, if any:

1. **Adjusting entries --** Are needed if one company (to be consolidated) has recorded a transaction with another company (to be consolidated), but the receiving company has not recorded the transaction. In such a case, the transaction is "in-transit" to the receiving company.

2. **Examples are**

a. Payment of Accounts Payable by one company at year-end, but not yet received/recognized by the other company;

b. Dividend Declared by one company (e.g., Sub) at year-end, but not yet recognized by the receiving company (e.g., Parent).

3. **Rule --** The rule for handling "in-transit" intercompany transactions is to make an adjusting entry on the consolidating worksheet to complete the transaction as though it had been received by the receiving company (i.e., as though the transaction were completed on both sets of books).

a. **Example --** At the time P acquired S, S had recorded a payment of $5,000 to P on an Accounts Payable; the payment was still in transit (i.e., P had not yet received the payment). What entry would be made **on the consolidating worksheet immediately after the combination** as an adjusting entry?

DR: Cash	$5,000	
CR: Accounts Receivable		$5,000

4. **Posting of Adjusting Entries** -- The effects of adjusting entries are eventually posted to the appropriate separate company books as a result of actual completion of the in-transit transaction.

C. **Eliminating Entries** -- Identify and Record Balance Sheet Eliminating Entries: The common balance sheet eliminating entries at the date of combination are:

1. **Investment Elimination Entry** -- All consolidations **require** an Investment Elimination Entry to eliminate Investment in Sub account (brought on to the consolidating worksheet (W/S) by the Parent) against the Sub's Shareholders' Equity (brought on to the W/S by the Sub).

   a. **Avoids Double Counting** -- This elimination avoids "double counting" that would otherwise result on the Consolidated B/S, i.e., counting the asset "Investment" (from the Parent) and the assets and liabilities (from the Sub) to which the Investment gives the Parent a claim.

   b. **Entry when Parent owns 100% of Subsidiary** -- Sample investment elimination (on the consolidating worksheet) when there is no noncontrolling interest (formerly "minority interest") in the subsidiary:

   > DR: Common Stock (of Sub)
   >
   >   Additional Paid-in Cap (of Sub)
   >
   >   Retained Earnings (of Sub)
   >
   >   Identifiable Assets (of Sub to FV, as needed)
   >
   >   Goodwill (if Investment cost > FV of Sub's NA)
   >
   > CR: Identifiable Liabilities (of Sub to FV, as needed)
   >
   >   Investment in Sub (from Parent's books)

      i. In the sample entry, Identifiable Assets (Liabilities) would be debited (credited) if the fair value of Identifiable Assets (Liabilities) is greater than the book value of Identifiable Assets (Liabilities) at the acquisition date.

         1. This debit or credit would be to specific assets or liabilities (for example: Inventory, Equipment, Land, or Accounts Payable, etc.) to adjust them to fair value (on the worksheet) at the date of the business combination.

         2. If depreciable assets are increased (debited), at the date of acquisition no assessment of impairment is required. (But, at the end of every subsequent period, additional depreciation expense must be taken on the consolidating worksheet).

         3. If the identifiable assets or liabilities had a fair value less than book value, the specific assets or liabilities would be written down to fair value (on the worksheet).

      ii. In the sample entry, Goodwill would be debited if the Investment value is greater than the FV of net Identifiable assets.

         1. Recall from a prior lesson that "investment value" is the fair value of consideration paid by the acquirer (parent) to acquire the subsidiary plus the fair value of the noncontrolling interest at the acquisition date.

         2. If Goodwill is recognized (debited), at the date of acquisition no assessment of impairment is required. (But, at the end of every subsequent period goodwill must be assessed for impairment; it is not amortized.)

   iii. Allocation assuming fair value exceed book value of the net identifiable assets at the date of acquisition and that the investment value exceed the fair value of the net (identifiable) assets.

  c. **Entry when Parent owns less than 100% of Subsidiary --** Sample investment elimination entry (on the consolidating worksheet) when there is a noncontrolling interest in the Subsidiary.

   i. Sub's Shareholder Equity not owned by the Parent (either directly or indirectly) belongs to the Noncontrolling Interest.

   ii. It is **the noncontrolling interest(minority) claim** to consolidate net assets attributable to the subsidiary, which includes the Sub's net assets at fair value and the full fair value of any goodwill recognized on the acquisition.

   iii. **Sample entry**

DR: Common Stock (of Sub)

 Add'l Paid-in Cap (of Sub)

 Retained Earnings (of Sub)

 Identifiable Assets (of Sub to FV, as needed)

 Goodwill (if Investment value > FV of Sub's NA)

 CR:Identifiable Liabilities (of Sub to FV, as needed)

  Investment in Sub (from Parent's books)

  Noncontrolling Interest (% claim to consolidated net assets attributable to the subsidiary)

---

   iv. **The Noncontrolling Interest Account --** Will show on the Consolidated Balance Sheet as a separate item within Shareholders' Equity.

2. **Intercompany Receivables/Payables Eliminations --** Receivables and payables between companies being consolidated must be eliminated to the extent the amounts are intercompany (between the companies).

  a. **Examples** and the amount to eliminate are:

   i. **Accounts Receivable/Account Payable (100%) --** All intercompany receivables and payables between the affiliated firms that exist at the date of the combination must be eliminated.

    1. **Illustration Facts --** Assume that at the date Company P acquired controlling interest of Company S in a legal acquisition, Company S owed Company P $10,000 for services it had received from Company P. Therefore, the separate companies would bring onto the consolidating worksheet the following balances:

Company P / Receivable from S = $ 10,000

Company S / Payable to Company P = $ 10,000

---

    2. **Eliminating Entry --** On the consolidating worksheet the following eliminating entry would be made:

DR: Payable to P	$10,000	
CR:Receivable from S		$10,000

3. **Consequence** -- As a consequence of the eliminating entry, on the consolidating worksheet (and the consolidated financial statements) there will be no receivable/payable between Companies P and S shown; it is as though they are a single entry.

ii. **Interest** -- Interest Receivable/Interest Payable (100%): If an intercompany receivable/payable was for interest, an entry similar to the one above would be made for 100% of the intercompany balance.

iii. **Dividends** -- Dividends Receivable/Dividends Payable (Intercompany %): Dividends Receivable and Dividends Payable between the affiliated firms that exist at the date of the combination must be eliminated.

1. **Illustration Facts** -- Assume that at the date Company P acquired controlling interest of Company S in a legal acquisition, Company S had a $100,000 dividends payable balance on its books and that Company P owned 5% of Company S just prior to acquiring controlling interest. As a consequence, 5% of Company S's dividends payable is a dividends receivable to Company P. The separate companies would bring onto the consolidating worksheet the following balances:

Company P / Dividends Receivable (from Co. S) = $5,000

Company S / Dividends Payable = $100,000

2. **Eliminating Entry** -- On the consolidating worksheet the following eliminating entry would be made:

DR: Dividends Payable	$5,000	
CR:Dividends Receivable		$5,000

3. **Consequence** -- As a consequence of the eliminating entry, on the consolidating worksheet (and the consolidated financial statements) Company P's dividends receivable will have been eliminated and Company S's dividends payable will have been reduced to $95,000, the amount due to non-affiliates. Note that only the intercompany (between P and S) portion of the dividend is eliminated.

iv. **Bonds** -- Investment in Bonds/Bonds Payable (Intercompany %): Bonds issued by one affiliate (Bonds Payable) and held by another affiliate (Investment in Bonds) at the date of the combination must be eliminated against each other.

1. **Illustration Facts** -- Assume that at the date Company P acquired controlling interest of Company S in a legal acquisition, Company P already held $100,000 of Company S's bonds which it had acquired at par ($100,000). Company S had total bonds payable of $1,000,000. Therefore, the separate companies would bring onto the consolidating worksheet the following balances:

Company P / Investment in S Bonds = $100,000

Company S / Bonds Payable (at par) = $1,000,000

2. **Eliminating Entry** -- On the consolidating worksheet the following eliminating entry would be made:

DR: Bonds Payable	$100,000	
CR: Investment in Bonds		$100,000

3. **Consequence** -- As a consequence of the eliminating entry, on the consolidating worksheet (and the consolidated financial statements) Company P's investment in Company S's bonds will have been eliminated and Company S's bonds payable will have been reduced to $900,000, the amount due to non-affiliates. Note that only the intercompany (between P and S) portion of the bonds is eliminated.

4. **Other Eliminations** -- If either the investment in bonds or the bonds payable accounts had a related premium or discount, these amounts would have been eliminated as well and would have resulted in a gain or loss depending on the nature of the premium or discount (debit or credit). (Eliminating intercompany bonds with premiums or discounts is covered in the following section dealing with the consolidating process following the date of acquisition.)

VIII. **Complete Worksheet** -- After the separate company account balances and the adjusting and eliminating entries have been posted to the worksheet, it can be complete, mostly by "adding" across and down.

IX. **Formal Consolidated Statements** -- Prepare Formal Consolidated Statements: Once the worksheet is completed, it is the basis for preparing the formal consolidated financial statements.

Consolidation Subsequent to Acquisition

On its books, a parent may carry an investment in a subsidiary to be consolidated using any accounting method it desires because the investment will be eliminated in the consolidating process. The method a parent uses will affect the entries for the investment eliminating entry made on the worksheet in the consolidating process, but will not affect the final consolidated statements - they will be the same regardless of the method used by the parent to carry the investment on its books. While the parent can use any method it chooses to carry the investment, the two traditional methods are the cost method and the equity method. (Those are the only methods assumed on the CPA Exam.) This lesson covers the consolidating process when the parent uses the cost method.

After studying this lesson, you should be able to:

1. *Describe the characteristics of the cost method of accounting for an investment.*

2. *Describe the necessary treatment of the consolidating worksheet when a parent uses the cost method to account for an investment in a subsidiary.*

3. *Record the adjusting (reciprocity) entry and the investment-eliminating entry on the consolidating worksheet when a parent uses the cost method to account for an investment in a subsidiary.*

4. *Record other eliminating entries that may be necessary on the consolidating worksheet as a direct result of the investment-eliminating entry.*

I. **Consolidation After Acquisition --** After the date of acquisition, the Parent Company (P) will account for its Investment in S using either the equity method or cost method. Remember that P's stand alone financial statements are not GAAP compliant because P must consolidate all subsidiaries under its control. In order to consolidate P and S, you must first understand how P accounted for the Investment in S, because upon consolidation the Investment in S is eliminated.

II. **If P uses the Equity Method --** If the equity method is used to carry the investment in the subsidiary, the parent:

A. **DOES** adjust on its books the carrying value of its investment in the subsidiary to reflect:

1. The parent's share of the subsidiary's income or loss.

> DR: Investment in Subsidiary
>   CR: Income from Equity Investment

2. The parent's share of dividends declared by the subsidiary.

> DR: Dividends Receivable/Cash
>   CR: Investment in Subsidiary

3. The amortization (e.g., "depreciation") of any difference between the FV of identifiable assets (but not goodwill) and the book value of those assets. Example entry (assuming FV > BV):

> DR: Income from Equity Investment
>
> CR: Investment in Subsidiary

4. This entry reduces the income recognized from the Subsidiary (and the related investment increase) by the amount of "depreciation" the parent must recognize on its fair value greater than book value. Below are the T-accounts on P's books with respect to the equity method accounting for S.

Equity Method Accounting			
Investment in S		**Income from Equity Investment in S**	
Initial investment	P's share of S's dividends	Depr/amortization of purchase price differential	P's % share of S's NI
P's % share of S's NI	Depr/amortization of purchase price differential		
Ending Balance			Ending Balance

Example:

P (Passing) purchased 100% of S (Score) for $200,000 on January 1, 20X2. On that date the book value equaled the fair market value of all of S's assets and liabilities except for equipment, which had a FMV of $100,000. Any additional excess purchase price is attributed to goodwill. The equipment has a remaining life of four years.

Below we show the decomposition of the price paid for S and reconstruct the T-accounts for the equity method accounting recorded by P. Understanding the components of the purchase price and the equity method accounting aids understanding of the consolidation.

The decomposition of the purchase price is as follows:

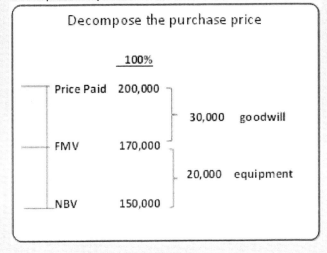

T- Account

Equity Method Accounting

Investment in S		Income from Investment in S	
Cost 200,000	0 dividends		50,000 - P's share of S's NI
		Depr of equip 5,000	
P's % S's NI 50,000	5,000 depr equip		
Ending Balance 245,000			45,000

The consolidating worksheet presents the trail balance of P and S and the Consolidated balances as follows. The consolidating worksheet does not reflect the eliminating entries in the consolidation process. Rather our focus is on the end result after consolidation. The footnotes below show how certain balances were derived.

	Passing		Score		ELIM	CONSOLIDATED	
	Debit	Credit	Debit	Credit		Debit	Credit
Current assets	80,000		30,000			**110,000**	
Inventory	150,000		350,000			**500,000**	
Equipment (net)	430,000		80,000			**525,000**[1]	
Investment in Score	245,000					**0**	
Goodwill	0		0			**30,000**[2]	
Current liabilities		150,000		110,000			**260,000**[3]
Long-term debt		255,000		150,000			**405,000**
Common Stock		200,000		140,000			**200,000**[4]
Retained Earnings		50,000		10,000			**50,000**
Sales		500,000		75,000			**575,000**
Income from S		45,000					**0**
Expenses	295,000		25,000			**325,000**[3]	
Totals	1,200,000	1,200,000	485,000	485,000		**1,490,000**	**1,490,000**

[1]**P's Equipment**	430,000
S's Equipment	80,000
FMV adjustment	20,000
Depr of FMV adj	(5,000)
Total	525,000

[2]Goodwill	30,000
Impairment	0
Total	30,000
[3]P's Expenses	295,000
S's Expenses	25,000
Depr of FMV adj	5,000
Total	325,000

[4]Only P's

NOTE: Push down accounting would require that S record the fair market revaluations on the general ledger on the date of acquisition. Push down accounting is required for SEC Registrants with 100% owned subsidiaries. Push down accounting essentially "pushes down" the revaluations on to the general ledger of S so that the revaluations are not allocated during the consolidation process. In the example above, the push down accounting entry made by S would be:

Equipment   20,000
Goodwill   30,000
   Revaluation Capital (an equity account) 50,000

Upon consolidation the revaluation capital account would be eliminated.

III. **If P uses the Cost Method to account for the Investment in S --** In this case the parent:

   A. **DOES NOT adjust** on its books **the carrying value of its investment in the subsidiary** to reflect:

   1. The parent's share of the subsidiary's income or loss;

   2. The parent's share of dividends **declared by** the subsidiary;

   3. The "depreciation"/amortization of any difference between the fair value of the subsidiary's identifiable net assets and the book value of the subsidiary's identifiable net assets.

   B. **DOES** recognize its share of dividends declared by the subsidiary **as dividend income**. (not as an adjustment to the investment account)

   1. **Example entry**

   | DR: Dividends Receivable/Cash |
   | CR:Dividend Income |

IV. **Investment Elimination --** The Investment elimination entry is made to eliminate the adjusted Investment account (as of the beginning of year) against the subsidiary Shareholders' Equity (as of the beginning of year).

   A. Sample entry assuming the Parent owns 100% of the Subsidiary:

DR: C/S (of Sub)

   Additional Paid-in Capital (of Sub)

   R/E (of Sub including change since acquisition)

   Identifiable Assets (of Sub to FV at acquisition, as needed)

   Goodwill (If Investment > FV of Sub's NA at acquisition)

   CR:Identifiable Liabilities (of Sub to FV at acquisition, as needed)

   Investment in Subsidiary

B. The effects of this entry on the worksheet are to:

    1. Eliminate the investment account of the parent (as of the beginning of the year) against the shareholder equity accounts of the subsidiary (as of the beginning of the year);

    2. Adjust identifiable assets and liabilities of the subsidiary to fair value as of the date of the business combination;

    3. Recognize goodwill, if any, as of the date of the business combination. Goodwill would be recognized at the original amount by which the investment value > FV of identifiable net assets acquired.

V. **Fair Value of Subsidiary's Identifiable Assets/Liabilities Different than Book Value --** When the fair value of the subsidiary's identifiable assets and/or liabilities are different than the book value at the date of acquisition, depreciation/amortization must be recognized on the worksheet for any amount of Identifiable Assets recognized by the Investment elimination (above).

   A. Recall that the extent to which the parent's investment (and the fair value of noncontrolling interest, if any) as of the acquisition date is greater than the book value of subsidiary's identifiable net assets at the acquisition date is not identified on the separate books.

    1. Any difference is implicit in the acquisition date difference between the Investment on the parent's books (plus the noncontrolling interest, if any) and the Shareholders' Equity on the Sub's books (which is also the book value of the Sub's net assets).

    2. It is only when the two values (P's Investment + any noncontrolling interest and S's Shareholders' Equity) are brought together in the Investment elimination entry on the worksheet that the difference becomes explicit. The Sub's identifiable assets and liabilities are adjusted to fair value on the worksheet and, if the investment value is different than the resulting net asset value, goodwill (or a bargain purchase gain) is recognized. Any adjustment (increase or decrease) to depreciable or amortizable assets on the worksheet will result in the need for an adjustment (increase or decrease) to depreciation or amortization expense on the worksheet.

   B. When the Sub's assets are written up to fair value (in the investment elimination entry, for example) it is as though the Parent and noncontrolling interest, if any, paid more for the assets than the Subsidiary paid for them. Therefore, additional depreciation or amortization must be taken.

   C. **Sample entry on Worksheet (at end of 1st period) --** assuming depreciable and amortizable assets were written up as part of the investment eliminating entry:

> DR: Depreciation Expense
>
> Amortization Expense
>
> CR:Accumulated Depreciation
>
> Intangible Assets (Not Goodwill!)

D. Sample entry on Worksheet (at end of subsequent periods) -- assuming depreciable and amortizable assets were written up as part of the investment eliminating entry:

> DR: Retained Earnings P - Beginning*
>
> Depreciation Expense**
>
> Amortization Expense**
>
> CR:Accumulated Depreciation***
>
> Intangible Assets (Not Goodwill!)***
>
> * For expense recognized in prior year(s) on consolidating worksheet(s)
>
> ** For current year expense
>
> *** For cumulative prior and current amounts

E. If at acquisition the fair value of the subsidiary's identifiable net assets was greater than the parent's investment (plus the fair value of the noncontrolling interest, if any), a bargain purchase would have resulted.

   1. In this case, the bargain purchase amount would have been recognized by the parent as a gain in the period of the business combination.

   2. At the end of the period of the business combination, the bargain purchase gain would have been closed to the parent's Retained Earnings, and would be included in that Retained Earnings in all subsequent periods.

Consolidation Less than 100% Ownership

In many instances the Parent company purchases less than 100% of the Subsidiary. When P owns more than 50% of S, P will consolidate S to create consolidated statements. The percentage of S not owned by P is reflected in the consolidated financial statements as Noncontrolling Interest (NCI). On the balance sheet NCI is presented in the equity section of the consolidated balance sheet. On the income statement NCI is presented as Income to NCI - a reduction of consolidated net income.

After studying this lesson, you should be able to:

1. *Allocate the purchase price for a less than 100% acquisition.*

2. *Calculate the components of the balance sheet and income statement that would be represented on the consolidated statements with a less than 100% acquisition.*

3. *Calculate the amount of income to the noncontrolling interest that would be represented on the consolidated income statement.*

4. *Calculate the amount of equity attributed to the noncontrolling interest on the consolidated balance sheet.*

I. **Noncontrolling Interest (NCI) --** If the Parent does not own 100% of the Subsidiary, the Noncontrolling Interest must be determined and recognized in the consolidated statements.

   A. **Consolidated Income Statement**

      1. For each operating period, the noncontrolling interest percentage claim to consolidated net income will be shown as a separate line item on the consolidated income statement. This account is usually shown as "Income to Noncontrolling Interest."

      2. The noncontrolling interest claim to consolidated net income is the noncontrolling interest percentage share of the subsidiary's reported net income, plus (minus) its percentage share of depreciation/amortization expense on fair value in excess of (less than) book value and its percentage share of any other revenues/expenses or gains/losses attributable to the subsidiary recognized on the consolidating worksheet.

   B. **Consolidated Balance Sheet**

      1. On each consolidated balance sheet, the noncontrolling interest will be recognized as a separate line item (e.g., Noncontrolling Interest Equity) in the Shareholders' Equity section.

      2. The amount of the noncontrolling equity interest is the noncontrolling percentage claim to the subsidiary's book value at the acquisition date, plus (minus) its claim to the unamortized difference between fair values and book values at acquisition, plus its claim to goodwill recognized at acquisition, minus its share of any goodwill/impairment /losses.

II. **Determining NCI Equity**

   A. Determining the value of the NCI Equity reported by the consolidated entity can be done via calculation. NCI Equity is represented on the consolidated financial statements and is created during the consolidation process. This account does not exist on the individual financial statements of P or S. The CPA Exam frequently will ask you to provide the value of the NCI Equity or the Income that should be allocated to the NCI. Here we show you how to calculate theses values, it is also important because the calculation shows the conceptual relationship between S's NBV and the amount of S's NBV that is allocated to the noncontrolling interest.

NCI Equity is the NBV of S that is allocated to the noncontrolling interest and is represented on the consolidated balance sheet.

B. First determine the NBV of S as of the date of consolidation. Add to S's NBV the 100% purchase price differential less 100% of any depreciation/amortization or goodwill impairment. Multiply the S's adjusted NBV by the NCI % to arrive at NCI Equity. NCI Equity represents the amount of S's NBV allocated to the non-controlling shareholders of S including any FMV adjustments from the date of acquisition.

Calculation of NCI Equity	End of Year
S's Net Book Value	$
Plus 100% of the differential	
Less: Goodwill impairment loss	
Less: Depreciation / amortization of differential	$
S's adjusted NBV	$
NCI % ownership of S	%
NCI Equity	$

III. Determining Income to NCI

A. The portion of S's net income that is allocated to the NCI is created during the consolidation process and can be calculated. 100% of S's revenues and expenses are represented on the consolidated income statement. The NCI portion of S's net income that is not available for distribution to the shareholders of P must be subtracted out of total net income.

B. To calculate income to the NCI, start with S's net income and adjust it for the depreciation and/or amortization of the purchase price differential from the date of acquisition. You will also subtract any goodwill impairment loss that occurred during the current year. Once you have S's net income adjusted for the amounts related to the purchase price differential, multiply by the NCI percentage ownership and this will give you the amount of income to the NCI.

Calculation of Income to NCI	End of Year
S's Net Income	$
Less: Depreciation / amortization of differential	$
Less: Goodwill impairment loss	$
S's adjusted Net Income	$
NCI % ownership of S	%
Income to Noncontrolling Interest	$

See the following example.

Example:

P (Passing) purchased 80% of S (Score) for $200,000 on January 1, 20X2. On that date the full value of the Noncontrolling interest is $50,000. The book value equaled the fair market value of all of S's assets and liabilities except for equipment, which had a FMV of $100,000 (the carrying value of the equipment is $80,000). Any additional excess purchase price is attributed to goodwill. The equipment has a remaining life of four years. During 20X2 S reported net income of $50,000 and did not pay dividends.

Below is the decomposition of the value of S allocated between the controlling and noncontrolling interest. In addition we have reconstructed the T-accounts for the equity method accounting that would have been recorded by P during the year. Understanding the components of the equity method accounting, and tying the ending balances of these T-accounts to the consolidation worksheet, is useful in understanding the consolidations process.

The decomposition of the purchase pice is:

	100%	80%	20%
Total	250	200	50
Goodwill	80	64	16
FMV	170	136	34
Equip.	20	16	4 (4 yr. life)
BV	150	120	30

Below are the equity method accounts:

Equity Method Accounting

Investment in S		Income from Equity Investment
Cost 200,000	0 dividends	40,000 P's share of S's NI
	Depr of equip 4,000	
P's % of S's NI 40,000	4,000 depr equip	
Ending Bal 236,000		36,000

Below is the consolidation worksheet with the trial balance of P and S on December 31, 20X2. The *consolidated entity* as of **December 31, 20X2** is presented in the final two columns. The focus here is **not** the consolidation process. That is, the focus is not on completion of eliminating entries. The focus is on the ending balances reported by the consolidated entity. The footnotes below the worksheet show the computations to derive the ending balances.

	Passing		Score		Eliminati on	CONSOLIDATED	
	Debit	Credit	Debit	Credit		Debit	Credit
Current assets	80,000		30,000			**110,000**	
Inventory	150,000		350,000			**500,000**	
Equipment (net)	430,000		80,000			**525,000[1]**	
Investment in S	236,000					**0**	
Goodwill	0	0				**80,000[2]**	
Current liabilities		150,000		110,000			**260,000[3]**
Long-term debt		260,000		150,000			**410,000**
NCI Equity	0	0				**59,000[3]**	
Common Stock		200,000		140,000			**200,000[4]**
Retained Earnings		50,000		10,000			**50,000**
Sales		500,000		75,000			**575,000**
Income from S		36,000					**0**
Expenses	300,000		25,000			**330,000[5]**	
Income to NCI	0	0				**9,000[4]**	
Totals	1,196,000	1,196,000	485,000	485,000		**1,554,000**	**1,554,000**

1. Equipment

P's equipment	430,000
S's equipment	80,000
FMV adjustment	20,000
Depreciation	(5,000)
Total	525,000

2. Goodwill

Beg. balance	80,000
Impairment	(0)
Total	80,000

3. NCI Equity

Book Value of S*	200,000
FMV adjustment	100,000
Depreciation	(5,000)

Total	295,000
NCI %	x .20
NCI Equity	59,000

*Note: S's ending Net Book Value (NBV) is beginning NBV plus Net Income less Dividends. In this example beginning NBV $150,000 (140,000 CS + 10,000 RE) plus NI (75,000 Sales - 25,000 Expenses) = Ending NBV $200,000.

4. Income to NCI

S's NI	50,000
FMV Depreciation	(5,000)
	45,000
NCI %	x .20
Income to NCI	9,000

5. Expenses

P's expenses	300,000
S's expenses	25,000
Depreciation	5,000
Total	330,000

Intercompany (I/C) Transactions and Balances

I/C Transactions and Balances - Introduction

Transactions between entities that are to be consolidated are referred to as "intercompany transactions," or "transactions between affiliated companies." To the extent the entities being consolidated have intercompany transactions, or account balances that resulted from intercompany transactions, those transactions or balances have to be eliminated in the consolidating process. This lesson provides an overview of the elimination of intercompany transactions in the consolidating process.

After studying this lesson, you should be able to:

1. *Describe the conceptual basis for the elimination of intercompany transactions.*

2. *Identify the primary types of intercompany transactions and balances that will need to be eliminated in preparing consolidated financial statements.*

3. *Record the entries required on the consolidating worksheet to eliminate intercompany receivables/payables and revenues/expenses.*

4. *Describe how intercompany receivables/payables and intercompany revenues/expenses come about.*

I. **Conceptual Basis**

    A. From the perspective of the **separate legal entities**, transactions between them, and the related gains/losses and changes in account balances, should be recognized on their separate books. Even if the Parent owns less than 100% of the subsidiary (but more than 50% as required for consolidation) – the entire amount of the intercompany transaction must be eliminated.

    B. For **consolidated financial statements** purposes the separate entities are treated as a single economic entity. As a consequence, only transactions with non-affiliates should be recognized in consolidating financial statements.

    C. The results of transactions with other entities to be included in the consolidated financial statements must be eliminated, including the results of:

        1. Transactions between a parent and its subsidiaries;

        2. Transactions between affiliated subsidiaries.

    D. The kinds of transactions (and their related consequences) that must be eliminated, and those not to be eliminated, can be illustrated as follows:

PS Consolidation

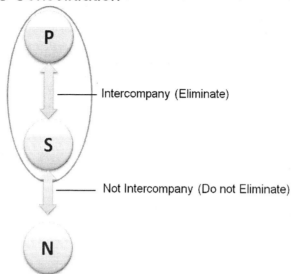

Intercompany (Eliminate)

Not Intercompany (Do not Eliminate)

II. Intercompany Items

A. The primary types of intercompany transactions and related intercompany balances are:

   1. Receivable/payables;

   2. Revenues/expenses;

   3. Inventory;

   4. Fixed assets;

   5. Bonds.

III. I/C Receivables and Payables

A. Recall that intercompany receivables and payables result from one affiliated company providing goods or services to another affiliated company and permitting the buying affiliated to "charge" the amount owed.

> **Example:**
> Assume that during the period Company P, the parent company, provided services to its subsidiary, Company S, and that Company S owed Company P $10,000 for those services at the end of the period. Each company would bring the following account balances onto the consolidating worksheet:
>
> Company P / Receivable from S = $10,000 (DR)
>
> Company S / Payable to P = $10,000 (CR)
>
> On the consolidating worksheet the following eliminating entry would be required so that no intercompany receivable or payable will show on the consolidated financial statements:
>
> DR: Payable to P $10,000
>
> CR: Receivable from S $10,000

B. Typical intercompany accounts receivable/accounts payable and the amount of each to eliminate are:

1. (Trade) Accounts Receivable/Accounts Payable (100%): The full amount of the intercompany receivable and intercompany payable must be eliminated;

2. Loan Receivable/Loan Payable;

3. Interest Receivable/Interest Receivable (100%);

4. Dividends Receivable (100%)/Dividends Payable (Intercompany %): Note that only the intercompany amount of the dividends payable must be eliminated. Any dividend payable to noncontrolling shareholders will not be eliminated.

IV. I/C Revenues and Expenses

A. Recall that intercompany revenues and expenses result from one affiliated company providing services for a fee to another affiliated company.

> **Example:**
> Assume that during the period Company P, the parent company, provided services to its subsidiary, Company S for $10,000. Each company would bring the following account balances onto the consolidating worksheet:
>
> Company P / I/C Revenue (from S) = $10,000 (DR)
>
> Company S / I/C Expense (to P) = $10,000 (CR)
>
> On the consolidating worksheet the following eliminating entry would be required so that no intercompany revenue or expense will show on the consolidated financial statements:
>
> DR: I/C Revenue (from S) $10,000
>
>   CR: I/C Expense (to P) $10,000

B. The full amount (100%) of intercompany revenues and expenses must be eliminated, even if the original transaction occurred at no profit to the "selling" affiliate.

C. Typical intercompany revenues and expenses and the amount of each to eliminate are:

1. Management Services Expense/Management Services Revenue (100%);

2. Interest Expense/Interest Revenue (100%).

Intercompany (I/C) Inventory Transactions

When one affiliated entity sells inventory (finished goods, raw materials, etc.) to another affiliated entity, an intercompany inventory transaction has occurred. Intercompany transactions need to be eliminated and the account balances adjusted to the values as if the transaction did not occur. This lesson identifies the accounts that will be affected, and describes and illustrates the eliminations that are needed on the consolidating worksheet.

After studying this lesson, you should be able to:

1. *Identify the accounts affected by intercompany inventory transactions.*

2. *Record intercompany bond eliminations on a consolidating worksheet under the various circumstances identified above.*

3. *Analyze facts and calculate the amounts needed to be eliminated for intercompany inventory transactions under various circumstances, including:*

   - when intercompany inventory transactions occur at cost,

   - when intercompany inventory transactions occur at more (or less) than cost,

   - when intercompany balances are in ending inventory and/or in beginning inventory,

   - when intercompany sales are made by a parent (to a subsidiary) or by a subsidiary (to a parent), and

   - when intercompany sales by a subsidiary are from a 100% owned subsidiary or less than 100% owned subsidiary.

I. Objective

A. **ALL** intercompany transactions **must be removed (eliminated)** as if the transaction never occurred. You cannot have a transaction with YOURSELF! Transactions of the consolidated entity are ONLY those with outside third parties.

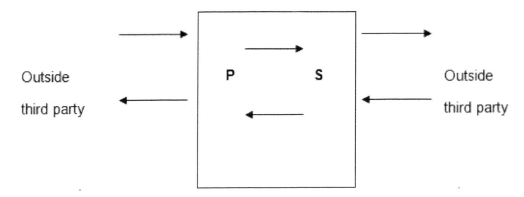

II. Terms and Concepts

A. **Intercompany transactions** -- include buying, selling, and transfers. They also include the profits or losses and the outstanding balances that result from these transactions.

1. A **downstream** transaction is when the parent sells to the subsidiary. Any intercompany profit that results from the sale will be on the books of the parent.

2. An **upstream** transaction is when the subsidiary sells to the parent. Any intercompany profit that results from the sale will be on the books of the subsidiary.

3. A transaction may also be between two subsidiaries with a common parent, or any other combination of tiering the transaction.

III. **Accounts Affected** -- Intercompany Inventory Transactions affect the following accounts:

A. **Sales/Cost of Goods Sold** -- The level of sales and cost of goods sold (COGS)(of the selling affiliate) are overstated because for consolidated purposes it is as though no sale occurred and, therefore, the effects of the sale should be eliminated.

B. **Inventory** -- Any intercompany profit (or loss) in the ending inventory of the buying affiliate overstates (or understates) the carrying value of that inventory for consolidated purposes and should be eliminated.

IV. Tool to use to help you organize information and answer questions:

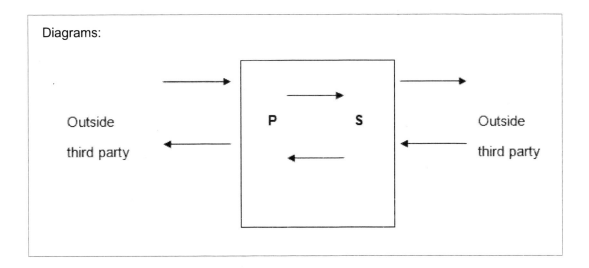

	Should be	What is		Difference
		P	S	
Sales				
CGS				
Inventory				

V. **Example application using tools**

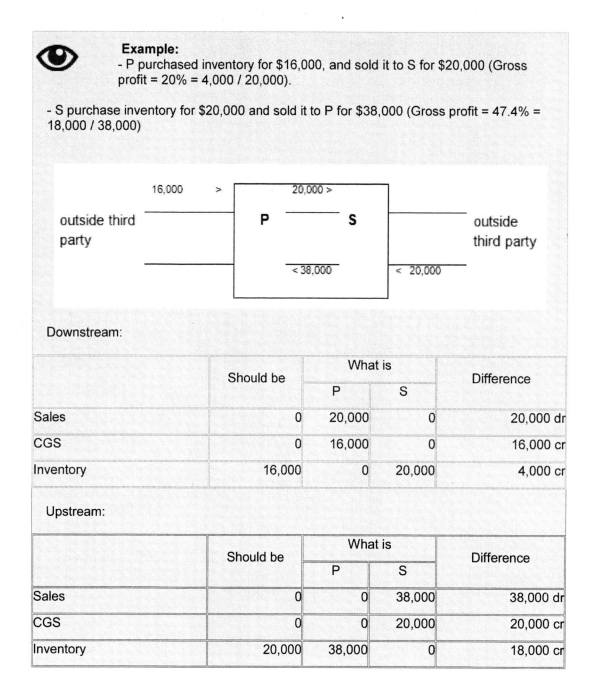

Example:
- P purchased inventory for $16,000, and sold it to S for $20,000 (Gross profit = 20% = 4,000 / 20,000).

- S purchase inventory for $20,000 and sold it to P for $38,000 (Gross profit = 47.4% = 18,000 / 38,000)

Downstream:

	Should be	What is		Difference
		P	S	
Sales	0	20,000	0	20,000 dr
CGS	0	16,000	0	16,000 cr
Inventory	16,000	0	20,000	4,000 cr

Upstream:

	Should be	What is		Difference
		P	S	
Sales	0	0	38,000	38,000 dr
CGS	0	0	20,000	20,000 cr
Inventory	20,000	38,000	0	18,000 cr

A. The following sections of this lesson present a step-by-step walk through of the elimination of intercompany inventory transactions. Use the method/technique that works best for you!

VI. Elimination of Intercompany Sales/COGS

A. For **consolidated purposes**, sales by one affiliate to another affiliate will overstate sales and cost of goods sold brought onto the worksheet by the selling affiliate and, if the inventory was sold between the affiliates at a profit, overstate inventory (or purchases) brought onto the worksheet by the buying affiliate.

   1. Sales and cost of goods sold (or purchases) for consolidated purposes should consist only of the effects of sales to and purchases from non-affiliates.

   2. Even though they may have no effect on consolidated net income (because the sale was at cost to the selling affiliate), intercompany sales and cost of goods sold (or purchases)

overstate the absolute amount of sales and cost of goods sold (or purchases) for consolidated purposes and, therefore, must be eliminated against each other to prevent incorrect values for ratios and other analytical purposes.

B. **Illustration - I/C Sale with NO Profit** -- Assume Company P sold inventory that cost it $8,000 to its 100% owned subsidiary, Company S, for $8,000 cash (P to S = a downstream sale). Entries made by the respective companies on their books would be:

Company P

DR: Cash	$8,000	
CR: Sales		$8,000
DR: COGS	$8,000	
CR: Inventory		$8,000

Company S

DR: Inventory	$8,000	
CR: Cash		$8,000

1. Because Company P sold the goods at its cost, there is no intercompany profit in the sales, cost of goods sold or in the inventory held by Company S.

2. All of the resulting balances are brought on to the consolidating worksheet by the separate companies at year-end.

C. **Eliminating Entry** -- Even though the intercompany sale resulted in no net profit or loss, on the consolidating worksheet, the following eliminating entry would be made to eliminate (only) the intercompany sale/COGS. (The eliminating entry for intercompany profit and profit in ending inventory will be illustrated in the following subsection.)

	Should be	What is		Difference
		P	S	
Sales	0	8,000	0	8,000 dr
CGS	0	8,000	0	8,000 cr
Inventory	8,000	0	8,000	0

DR: Sales	$8,000	
CR: COGS		$8,000

1. This elimination is a reversal of the original intercompany sale and COGS.

2. As a consequence of this eliminating entry, on the consolidating worksheet (and consolidated financial statements) no sales or COGS results from transactions between the affiliated companies; it is as though they never occurred.

3. The same kind of eliminating entry (i.e., same DR and CR at the amount of intercompany sale) would be made if all of the intercompany inventory had been resold by the buying affiliate to nonaffiliates during the period of intercompany sale.

VII. IC Sales with Profit/Loss -- Elimination of intercompany inventory profit (or loss) in ending inventory:

   A. Ending Inventory Value -- Profit (or loss) recognized on an intercompany sale that is related to inventory **that has not been resold** (to a non-affiliate) by the buying affiliate, will also overstate (or understate) the carrying value of the remaining intercompany ending inventory (as brought onto the worksheet by the buying affiliate).

   B. Illustration Facts -- Assume Company P sold inventory that cost it $8,000 to its 100% owned subsidiary, Company S, for $12,000 cash (P to S = a downstream sale). Entries made by the respective companies on their books would be:

Company P		
DR: Cash	$12,000	
CR: Sales		$12,000
DR: COGS	$ 8,000	
CR: Inventory		$ 8,000
Company S		
DR: Inventory	$12,000	
CR: Cash		$12,000

   1. Because Company P sold the goods to Company S at more than its (P's) cost, the inventory carrying value to Company S includes an intercompany profit that must be eliminated for consolidated purposes.

   2. All of the resulting balances are brought on to the consolidating worksheet by the separate companies at year-end.

   C. Eliminating Entry -- On the consolidating worksheet the following eliminating entries (or combined entry) would be made to simultaneously eliminate the intercompany sales, intercompany cost of goods sold, and intercompany profit in ending inventory (i.e., intercompany inventory not resold.

   1. Illustration #1 -- Assume from the example that 100% (all) of the intercompany inventory is still in the buying affiliate's inventory (on-hand) at year end:

Company P Sales Price (to Co. S)	$12,000
Company P COGS (from non-affiliate)	8,000
Intercompany Profit (all on-hand)	$ 4,000

   2. Entries to eliminate intercompany sales/COGS and profit in ending inventory:

DR: Sales (I/S)	$12,000	
CR: COGS (I/S)		$12,000
DR: COGS (I/S)	$4,000	
CR: Inventory (B/S)		$4,000

a. In the first entry, the debit to sales and credit to COGS have the effect of eliminating (reversing) the intercompany amounts brought onto the worksheet by the selling affiliate.

b. In the second entry, the debit to COGS (an I/S account) reduces consolidated net income by $4,000 (the unrealized profit in intercompany inventory) and the credit to Inventory eliminates the intercompany profit of $4,000 from ending inventory brought onto the worksheet by the buying affiliate.

c. The two eliminating entries shown above could be (and often are) combined into a single entry, as follows:

	Should be	What is		Difference
		P	S	
Sales	0	12,000	0	12,000 dr
CGS	0	8,000	0	8,000 cr
Inventory	8,000	0	12,000	4,000 cr

DR: Sales (I/S)	$12,000	
CR: COGS (Inventory - I/S)		$8,000
CR: Inventory (B/S)		$4,000

d. As a consequence of the eliminating entries (or entry), no intercompany sales, or COGS is recognized from the intercompany transaction and the inventory would be reported at its cost from a non-affiliate, $8,000.

3. **Illustration #2 --** Assume from the example above that 50% (half) of the intercompany inventory has been resold and, therefore, only 50% is still in the buying affiliates inventory (on-hand) at year end. S sold the inventory for $10,000:

Company P Sales Price (to Co. S)	$12,000
Company P COGS (from non-affiliate)	8,000
Total Intercompany Profit	$ 4,000
% of Intercompany Inventory On-hand	x .50
Intercompany Profit to Eliminate	$ 2,000

4. Entries to eliminate intercompany sale/COGS and profit in ending inventory:

DR: Sales (I/S)	$12,000	
CR: COGS (Inventory - I/S)		$12,000
DR: COGS (I/S)	$2,000	
CR: Inventory (B/S)		$2,000

a. In the first entry, the debit to sales and credit to COGS have the effects of eliminating (reversing) the intercompany amounts brought onto the worksheet by the selling affiliate.

b. In the second entry, the debit to COGS (an I/S account) reduces consolidated net income by $2,000 (the unrealized profit in ending inventory) and the credit to Inventory eliminates from the remaining ending inventory the intercompany profit of $2,000 brought onto the worksheet by the buying affiliate.

c. No intercompany profit eliminating entry is required for the goods that have already been resold and therefore, are not in ending inventory.

d. The two eliminating entries present above could be (and often are) combined into a single entry:

	Should be	What is		Difference
		P	S	
Sales	10,000	12,000	10,000	12,000 dr
CGS	4,000	8,000	6,000	10,000 cr
Inventory	4,000	0	6,000	2,000 cr

DR: Sales (I/S)	$12,000	
CR: COGS (I/S)(+$2,000 - $12,000)		$10,000
CR: Inventory (B/S)		$2,000

Note: S's selling price to an outside third party will always be the amount reported on the consolidated statements. So if you are not given the selling price to the third party - it doesn't matter - because the selling price you want to eliminate is just the price from P to S.

e. The correctness of the above entries can be confirmed by looking at the resulting balances on the consolidating worksheet after the eliminating entries are recorded:

   i. Intercompany sales are $0 (zero).

   ii. Cost of goods sold is : DR. $8,000 (P) + $6,000 (S) + $2,000 (E) - CR. $12,000 (E) = $4,000, the cost from a nonaffiliated of 1/2 the inventory now sold (1/2 x $8,000 = $4,000).

   1. The $8,000 in COGS is the cost to P from a nonaffiliated recognized when it sold the inventory to S.

   2. The $6,000 in COGS is 1/2 the $12,000 cost to S of the inventory acquired from P and recognized as COGS when it sold 1/2 the goods to nonaffiliates.

   3. The $2,000 and $12,000 are the eliminating entries (E) posted to COGS.

VIII. **Sale by Subsidiary to Parent** -- Intercompany Inventory Sale by Subsidiary to Parent: The prior illustrations assumed that the sale was made by the parent company to a subsidiary -- a downstream sale. If a subsidiary sells to its parent, the transaction is an upstream sale. The intercompany elimination for upstream sales depends, in part, on the parent's percentage ownership of the subsidiary.

A. **Parent owns 100% of the subsidiary**

   1. **Eliminate Sales/COGS** -- All of the intercompany sale/COGS would be eliminated as above. It is a mere reversal of the original intercompany sale and cost of goods sold.

   2. **Profit Elimination** -- All the intercompany profit and profit in ending inventory carrying value would be eliminated as above and would reduce the parent's claim to net income and asset (inventory) carrying value, since there are no noncontrolling claims to the subsidiary.

B. **Parent owns *less than* 100% of the subsidiary – If you have a worksheet without Income Statement –** If the elimination occurs on a consolidating worksheet that does not include an income statement (i.e., only a balance sheet is provided), the elimination would be allocated on the worksheet between the parent and the noncontrolling shareholders' interest in proportion to their respective ownership percentages.

   1. **Eliminate Sale/COGS --** All of the intercompany sale/COGS would be eliminated as above. It is a mere reversal of the original intercompany sale and cost of goods sold.

   2. **Profit Elimination --** All of the intercompany profit and the profit in ending inventory would be eliminated, but the profit elimination would be allocated between the parent and the noncontrolling shareholders' interest in proportion to their respective ownership percentages as part of the allocation of net income.

      a. **Worksheet with Income Statement --** If the elimination occurs on a consolidating worksheet that includes an income statement, the elimination would be the same as presented above to eliminate intercompany profit in ending inventory:

DR: COGS (I/S)

   CR: Inventory (B/S)

---

      i. Eliminating Entry on Worksheet with Balance Sheet only. Assume that P owns 80% and noncontrolling interest owns 20% of the subsidiary.

DR: Retained Earnings - P	$3,200.	
Noncontrolling Interest	800	
CR: Inventory (B/S)		$4,000

---

      ii. The debits reduce Company P's consolidated retained earnings ($3,200) and noncontrolling interest ($800); the credit eliminates the profit in ending inventory ($4,000), all on the consolidated balance sheet.

C. **Illustration Facts --** Assume Company P owns 80% of its subsidiary, Company S. Company S sold inventory that cost it $8,000 to Company P for $12,000 cash (an upstream sale). All of the inventory is still held by Company P at year-end. The elimination of intercompany profit in ending inventory would be allocated as follows:

Parent	.80 X $4,000 =	$3,200
Noncontrolling Interest	.20 X $4,000 =	800
Total Profit Eliminated		$ 4,000

D. Eliminating Entry on Worksheet with Balance Sheet only:

DR: Retained Earnings - P	$3,200	
Noncontrolling Interest	800	
CR: Inventory (B/S)		$4,000

E. The debits reduce Company P's consolidated retained earnings ($3,200) and noncontrolling interest ($800); the credit eliminates the profit in ending inventory ($4,000), all on the consolidated balance sheet.

IX. Eliminate Profit/Loss in Beginning Inventory -- Elimination of intercompany inventory profit (or loss) in beginning inventory:

A. Profit/Loss Remain -- Because the intercompany inventory profit (or loss) eliminated from ending inventory (illustrated above) occurs ONLY on the consolidating worksheet, the intercompany profit (or loss) will remain:

1. On the books of the selling affiliate as an element of profit (or loss) closed to its retained earnings;

2. On the books of the buying affiliate as an overstatement (or understatement) of its beginning inventory for the subsequent period.

B. Eliminate on Worksheet -- The intercompany profit (or loss) in retained earnings and beginning inventory will be brought onto the consolidating worksheet of the subsequent period by the selling and buying affiliate, respectively, and must be eliminated on the worksheet.

C. Eliminating Entry -- On the subsequent consolidating worksheet, the following eliminating entry would be made to simultaneously eliminate the intercompany profit in (beginning) retained earnings (of the selling affiliate) and the overstatement of the beginning inventory (of the buying affiliate):

DR: Retained Earnings
CR: Inventory - Beginning (I/S)

1. If a loss in intercompany inventory had been eliminated in the prior period, the debit and credit would be reversed.

2. The amount of intercompany profit (or loss) in retained earnings and beginning inventory to be eliminated is the same amount as eliminated in the ending inventory of the prior period.

3. The debit to retained earnings eliminates the intercompany profit recognized in the prior period on the books of the selling affiliate and brought on to the worksheet of the current period in its (selling affiliates) retained earnings; the credit to beginning inventory as reported on the worksheet income statement eliminates the intercompany profit in the beginning inventory shown on the books of the buying affiliate and brought on to the worksheet of the current period.

4. The credit to beginning inventory on the consolidating worksheet causes a reduction in beginning inventory in the income statement section of the worksheet that reduces cost of goods sold as follows (using assumed amounts, including intercompany profit in beginning inventory of $20,000):

		Without Elimination		With Elimination
	Begin Inventory	$120,000	<------->	$100,000
+	Purchases	100,000		100,000
=	Available for Sale	$220,000		$200,000
-	Ending Inventory	50,000		50,000
=	Cost of Goods Sold	$170,000		$150,000

a. The credit to beginning inventory in the income statement section (and the resulting reduction in cost of goods sold) causes the intercompany profit eliminated (deferred) in the prior period **to be treated as though it is confirmed (recognized) in the subsequent period**.

b. If the intercompany inventory on hand at the beginning of the period is not sold to a non-affiliate as of the end of the period, the related intercompany profit will be eliminated (deferred) again as part of the elimination of intercompany profit in ending inventory of that period.

Intercompany (I/C) Fixed Asset Transactions

When one affiliated entity sells fixed assets to another affiliated entity, an intercompany fixed asset transaction has occurred. This transaction needs to be eliminated and the account balances brought to the balances as if the transaction had not occurred. This lesson identifies the accounts that will be affected and illustrates the adjustments or eliminations that will be needed on the consolidating worksheet.

After studying this lesson you should be able to :

1. *Analyze facts and calculate the amounts needed to be eliminated for intercompany fixed asset transactions under various circumstances, including:*

    - *For the effects of intercompany fixed asset transactions in the period of the transfer and on post-transfer depreciation expense and accumulated depreciation,*

    - *When intercompany fixed asset sales are made by a parent (to a subsidiary) or by a subsidiary (to a parent), and*

    - *When intercompany fixed asset sales by a subsidiary are from a 100% owned subsidiary or less than 100% owned subsidiary.*

2. *Record intercompany fixed-asset eliminations on a consolidating worksheet under the various circumstances identified above.*

3. *Identify the accounts affected by intercompany fixed-asset transactions.*

I. **Objective**

A. **ALL** intercompany transactions **must be removed (eliminated)** as if the transaction never occurred. You can not have a transaction with YOURSELF! Transactions of the consolidated entity are ONLY those with outside third parties.

B. Transfer of a depreciable or nondepreciable asset between parent and subsidiary for anything other than original cost must be stated on the consolidated trial balance as if the transfer had not occurred.

II. **Accounts Affected** -- Intercompany Fixed Asset Transactions affect the following accounts:

A. **Fixed Asset** -- Any gain (or loss) recognized by the selling affiliate will cause the cost to the buying affiliate to overstate (or understate) the carrying value of the asset for consolidated purposes and must be corrected so that the asset is reported at original cost from a non-affiliate.

B. **Accumulated Depreciation** -- The sale of the fixed asset will cause the selling affiliate to write off its accumulated depreciation (on the asset sold) which will understate accumulated depreciation for consolidated purposes; the accumulated depreciation should be reinstated.

C. **Depreciation Expense/Accumulated Depreciation** -- Any gain (or loss) included in the cost to the buying affiliate will cause subsequent depreciation taken by the buying affiliate and brought onto the consolidating worksheet to overstate (or understate) depreciation expense and accumulated depreciation for consolidated purposes in each subsequent period; these elements must be adjusted.

D. Tool to use to help you organize information and answer questions:

1. Diagrams:

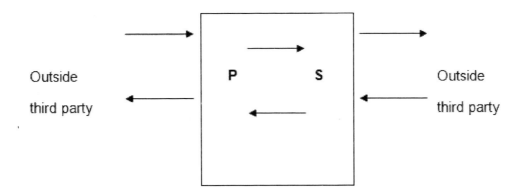

2. Tables to organize data:

	Should be	What is	Difference
Equipment			
Accum Depr			
Depr expense			
Gain on sale			

E. Nondepreciable assets

1. Suppose on December 31, P sold land to S for $150,000, the land originally cost P $130,000. S still holds the land.

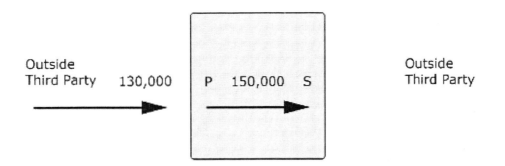

2. To understand the transaction, it helps to first evaluate the journal entries each company made at the date of the sale. Here are the entries that P and S would have made on December 31.

On P's books			On S's books		
Cash	150,000		Land	150,000	
Land		130,000	Cash		150,000
Gain on sale		20,000			

3. To help keep straight what the consolidated amount should be, prepare a table that compares the original asset basis to the intercompany asset basis.

	Should be	What is	Difference
Land	130,000	150,000	20,000 cr
Gain on sale	0	20,000	20,000 dr

4. If this transaction had never occurred, Land "Should be" $130,000 on the consolidated financial, therefore $130,000 is in the "Should be" column. Because of the intercompany transaction, the Land "Is" recorded on S's books at $150,000. P recorded a gain as a result of this transaction - and there should be no gain because from the consolidated perspective you cannot have a transaction with yourself! To adjust the asset to $130,000 the eliminating entry is a credit land for $20,000 and a debit to Gain on sale.

5. In the years subsequent to the intercompany sale, the Land will be adjusted each year on the consolidating worksheet. The offset to the adjustment of the Land will be to Retained Earnings. The gain in the year of sale would have been closed to the seller's Retained Earnings (in this case P's Retained Earnings). During the consolidation process, the following eliminating entry would be made each year that the land is still held by the buyer (in this case S).

DR:	Retained Earnings	20,000	
	CR: Land		20,000

III. Depreciable assets

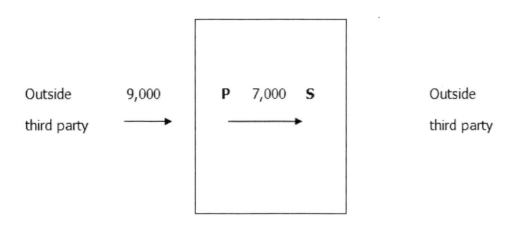

A. Now suppose on December 31, P sold equipment to S for $7,000, the equipment originally cost $9,000. The equipment had an original life of 10 years and P held the equipment for 3 years before the sale to S.

B. To understand the transaction, it helps to first evaluate the journal entries each company made at the date of the sale. Here are the entries that P and S would have made on December 31.

Original cost to P	9,000	NBV	6,300
Less AD (900 x 3yrs)	(2,700)	Selling Price	7,000
NBV	6,300	Gain on Sale	700

On P's books		On S's books	
Depr exp	900	Accum Depr	900
Cash	7,000	Equip	7,000
Accum Depr	2,700	Cash	7,000
Equip	9,000		
Gain on sale	700		

	Should be	What is	Difference
Equipment	9,000	7,000	2,000 dr
Accum Depr	2,700	0	2,700 cr
Depr expense	900	900	0
Gain on sale	0	700	700 dr

1. The eliminating entry in year 1 is the "difference" column:

Equipment	2,000	
Gain on Sale	700	
Accumulated Depreciation		2,700

2. The table for year 2 would appear as follows:

	Should be	What is	Difference
Equipment	9,000	7,000	2,000 dr
Accum Depr	3,600	1,000	2,600 cr
Depr expense	900	1,000	100 cr
Retained Earnings	-	-	700 dr

Note: The intercompany gain on the date of sale, divided by the remaining useful live of the asset, will always equal the difference in deprecation taken by the buyer and seller (this holds true only if the useful life of the asset remains unchanged). This calculation will serve as a check figure for the "Should be - Is - Difference" table.

IV. Summary of Intercompany Sales of Depreciable Assets

A. Downstream (P sells to S):

	Calculation of CNI, CI, NCI	Calculation of NCI Equity	Consolidating Entries
Year of sale	1. Adjust P's independent NI for CY gain or loss 2. Adjust P's independent NI for CY depreciation adjustment (if sale is not at EOY)	N/A	Eliminate intercompany gain or loss, adjust asset basis, accum depreciation, and depreciation expense
Years after sale	Adjust P s independent NI for CY depreciation adjustment	N/A	Eliminate prior year intercompany gain or loss through Investment in S, adjust asset basis, accum depreciation, and depreciation expense

B. Upstream (S sells to P)

	Calculation of CNI, CI, NCI	Calculation of NCI Equity	Consolidating Entries
Year of sale	1. Adjust S's independent NI for CY gain or loss 2. Adjust S's independent NI for CY depreciation adjustment (if sale is not at EOY)	1. Adjust S's NBV for CY gain or loss 2. Adjust S's NBV for CY depreciation adjustment (if sale is not at EOY)	Eliminate intercompany gain or loss, adjust asset basis, accum depreciation, and depreciation expense
Years after sale	Adjust S's independent NI for CY depreciation adjustment	1. Adjust S's NBV for PY gain or loss 2. Adjust S's NBV for PY PLUS CY depreciation adjustment	Eliminate prior year intercompany gain or loss through **Invest in S and NCI Equity**, adjust asset basis, accum depreciation, and depreciation expense

C. The following sections of this lesson present a step-by-step walk through of the elimination of intercompany inventory transactions. Use the method/technique that works best for you!

V. Elimination of Intercompany Gain (or Loss) and Reinstatement of Accumulated Depreciation -- In Year of Intercompany Transactions

A. Illustration Facts -- Assume that on January 2, 20X1 Company P sold a depreciable fixed asset to its 100% owned subsidiary, Company S, for $30,000 cash (P to S = a downstream sale). At the time of the sale, the asset had the following values on Company P's books:

Original Cost	$40,000
Accumulated Depreciation	15,000
Net Book Value	$25,000

1. The asset net book value had an original expected life of 8 years, no expected residual value, and is being depreciated using the straight-line method. Entries made by the respective companies on their books to record the intercompany sale would be:

Company P

DR: Cash $30,000

      Accumulated Depreciation   15,000

      CR:Fixed Asset $40,000

        Gain on Sale   5,000

Company S

DR: Fixed Asset $30,000

      CR:Cash $30,000

2. All of the resulting balances are brought onto the consolidating worksheet by the separate companies at year-end.

B. **Eliminating Entry** -- On the consolidating worksheet, the following eliminating entry would be made to simultaneously eliminate the intercompany gain, reinstate the carrying value of the asset to its cost to the parent from a nonaffiliate, and reinstate the accumulated depreciation: (The eliminating entry for overstated depreciation expense and accumulated depreciation taken by the purchasing subsidiary will be illustrated in the following section.)

DR: Fixed Asset $10,000

      Gain on Sale   5,000

      CR:Accumulated Depreciation $15,000

1. This eliminating entry on the consolidating worksheet will:

   a. Reestablish the fixed asset to its original cost from a non-affiliate -- $40,000;

   b. Eliminate the gain of $5,000 brought onto the consolidating worksheet by the selling affiliate -- Company P;

   c. Reestablish the accumulated depreciation as of the date of the intercompany sale to the amount based on original cost -- $15,000.

2. As a consequence of this eliminating entry, on the consolidating worksheet (and consolidated financial statements) the intercompany gain will have been eliminated and the fixed asset and related accumulated depreciation will be reported at amounts based on original cost from a non-affiliate.

VI. **Elimination of Overstated (or Understated) Depreciation Expense and Accumulated Depreciation**

A. **Illustration Facts** -- (continued from above): Company S would record on its books the depreciable fixed asset purchased from its Parent at $30,000. It elects to continue to use straight-line depreciation with no expected residual value over the remaining 5 years of the asset life. Therefore, each year Company S would record depreciation expense of $6,000 ($30,000/5yrs.) as follows:

DR: Depreciation Expense $6,000

      CR: Accumulated Depreciation $6,000

1. These amounts would be brought onto the consolidating worksheet by Company S.

B. Analysis of Facts -- On the books of the selling affiliate (prior to the intercompany sale) the asset had a book value of $25,000 (cost $40,000 - accumulated depreciation $15,000 = $25,000) which would have been depreciated at the rate of $5,000 per year ($25,000/5 yrs.).

    1. Because the purchase price to the buying affiliate included a $5,000 intercompany profit (Cost $30,000 - BV $25,000 = $5,000) the buying affiliate will recognize depreciation expense on its books (and brought onto the worksheet) of $6,000 per year ($30,000/5 yrs.).

    2. The extra $1,000 per year is attributable to the intercompany profit ($5,000) depreciated over 5 years. In summary, an analysis for each year shows:

Depreciation after the intercompany transaction	=	$6,000
Depreciation based on original cost	=	5,000
Excess depreciation expenses (per year)	=	$1,000

    3. The excess depreciation expense (and related accumulated depreciation) must be eliminated on the consolidating worksheet.

C. Eliminating Entry -- On the consolidating worksheet the following eliminating entry would be made to reduce the depreciation expense and the related accumulated depreciation:

DR: Accumulated Depreciation	$1,000	
CR:Depreciation Expense		$1,000

    1. This eliminating entry on the consolidating worksheet will:

        a. Reduce the depreciation expense recognized to the amount ($5,000) based on the original cost from a non-affiliate;

        b. Reduce the accumulated depreciation to the amount ($5,000, for the first year) based on the original cost from a non-affiliate.

    2. As a consequence of the eliminating entry, (net) depreciation expense for consolidated purposes will be $5,000 ($6,000 - $1,000) and accumulated depreciation will be $20,000 ($15,000 reinstated as part of the gain elimination above + $5,000 net depreciation recognized for the current period). The correctness of the accumulated depreciation is confirmed by:

Original cost $40,000/8 years life = $5,000 per year X 4 years since acquisition of the asset = $20,000.

VII. Elimination in Years Subsequent to Intercompany Transaction -- Elimination of Intercompany Gain (or Loss) and Adjustment of Asset and Accumulated Depreciation - In Years Subsequent to Intercompany Transaction:

A. Effects/Eliminations -- Because the elimination made at the end of one period is recorded only on the consolidating worksheet (and not on the entity books), in years subsequent to the intercompany sale the following affects and eliminations apply:

    1. The gain (or loss) on the sale of fixed assets recognized by the selling affiliate will have been closed through net income to retained earnings. Therefore, the unconfirmed portion of the gain (or loss) will have to be eliminated from retained earnings brought onto the worksheet by the selling affiliate.

2. The cost of the asset as recorded by the buying affiliate will continue to misstate the cost from a non-affiliate. Therefore, the asset value brought onto the worksheet by the buying affiliate will have to be adjusted to its cost from a non-affiliate; the amount of the adjustment will remain the same and will have to be made for as long as the asset remains on the books of the buying affiliate.

3. The accumulated depreciation on the buying affiliate's books will continue to be misstated (by a decreasing amount) until the asset is fully depreciated because it does not include the accumulated depreciation written off by the selling affiliate. Therefore, accumulated depreciation related to the intercompany fixed asset will have to be adjusted each period until the asset is fully depreciated.

B. **Correct Depreciation Expense --** Because the buying affiliate has the asset on its books at its cost from the selling affiliate, the annual depreciation expense (and related accumulated depreciation) recognized will be misstated for consolidated purposes because it will include depreciation on the intercompany gain (or loss). Therefore, the depreciation expense for the period brought onto the consolidating worksheet by the buying affiliate will have to be corrected to eliminate the depreciation related to the intercompany gain or loss.

C. **Illustration Facts --** (continued from above): As a result of entries made on the books of the affiliated companies P and S during the prior period in which the intercompany fixed asset transaction occurred and the depreciation expense taken for the current period, the following account balances will be brought onto the worksheet at the end of the second period:

Company P (Selling Affiliate)	
Retained Earnings (Original Intercompany Gain)	$ 5,000
Company S (Buying Affiliate)	
Fixed Assets	$30,000
Accumulated Depreciation ($30,000/5 yrs. = $6,000 X 2 yrs)	$12,000
Depreciation Expense (current year only)	$ 6,000

1. Each of these account balances is analyzed below.

D. **Analysis of Facts --** The following should be noted about the account balances (above) brought onto the consolidated worksheet:

1. Retained earnings of the selling affiliate contains the $5,000 intercompany gain recognized on the sale of the asset to the buying affiliate. At the end of the second period $1,000 of the intercompany gain will have been confirmed as a result of the depreciation on the intercompany gain taken during the first period. Therefore, the unconfirmed intercompany gain in retained earnings to be eliminated on the consolidating worksheet at the end of the second year is $4,000.

2. Fixed assets of the buying affiliate are reported at its cost, $30,000. The original cost from a non-affiliate was $40,000. Therefore, the fixed assets will have to be written up $10,000 on the consolidating worksheet. This write up of $10,000 will increase the assets' reported value for consolidated purposes to $40,000, its original cost from a non-affiliate.

3. Accumulated depreciation of the buying affiliate, $12,000, consists of two years depreciation on the intercompany asset at $6,000 per year ($30,000 cost/5 year remaining life = $6,000). The $12,000 includes $2,000 of depreciation expense related to the intercompany gain, $1,000 each for the prior year and the current year end which have the following affects:

a. The depreciation of the gain related to the prior period ($1,000) reduces the amount of accumulated depreciation written off by the selling affiliate. Recall that Company P, the selling affiliate, wrote off $15,000 in accumulated depreciation when it sold the fixed asset to the buying affiliate.

b. The $1,000 in excess depreciation taken by the buying affiliate (on the $5,000 gain) during the prior period reinstates $1,000 of the $15,000 written off by the selling affiliate. Thus, at the end of the second year only $14,000 needs to be reinstated.

c. The depreciation of the gain related to the current period ($1,000) must be reversed in order to report depreciation expense for the current period at $5,000. (See next item.)

4. Depreciation expense for the current period of $6,000 ($30,000/5 years) will have been recognized by the buying affiliate on its books and brought onto the consolidating worksheet. That $6,000 includes $1,000 depreciation ($5,000 gain/5 years) on the gain recognized by the selling affiliate and must be eliminated for consolidated purposes. Therefore, depreciation expense (and related accumulated depreciation) brought to the worksheet by the buying affiliate must be reversed by $1,000.

E. **Eliminating Entries** -- On the consolidating worksheet at the end of the second period the following entries would be made:

1. To simultaneously eliminate the unconfirmed gain in retained earnings, reinstate the carrying value of the asset to its original cost to the parent and reinstate the accumulated depreciation:

DR: Retained Earnings	$4,000	
Fixed Asset	10,000	
CR:Accumulated Depreciation		$14,000

2. To reduce the depreciation expense and related accumulated depreciation for the current period:

DR: Accumulated Depreciation	$1,000	
CR: Depreciation Expense		$1,000

3. The two entries could be made as a single entry:

DR: Retained Earnings	$4,000	
Fixed Asset	10,000	
CR:Accumulated Depreciation		$13,000
Depreciation Expense		1,000

4. The effects of the eliminated entries (or entry) for consolidating purposes will be to:

a. Reestablish the fixed asset to its original cost from a non-affiliate -- $40,000.

b. Eliminate the unconfirmed intercompany gain in retained earnings -- $4,000.

c. Reduce depreciation expense recognized for the period to the amount based on original cost from a non-affiliate -- $5,000.

d. Reestablish accumulated depreciation to the amount based on depreciation of original cost -- $25,000 -- as follows:

Brought onto worksheet	$12,000
Reinstatement on worksheet	13,000
Total Accumulated Depreciation	$25,000

    e. Proof:

Written off by selling affiliate	$15,000
Two years additional depreciation	10,000
(Cost $40,000/8 years) X 5 years =	$25,000

5. **Remaining Three Year Period** -- The eliminating entries made above will continue to be made as part of the consolidating process for the remaining three year estimated life of the fixed asset:

    a. The following elements of the eliminations will not change during the three-year period:

        i. The amount of addition to fixed asset remains $10,000;

        ii. The amount of depreciation expense eliminated remains $1,000.

    b. The following elements of the elimination will change:

        i. The amount of unconfirmed intercompany profit in retained earnings to be eliminated will decrease by $1,000 each year;

        ii. The amount of accumulated depreciation to be reinstated will decrease by $1,000 each year.

    c. The eliminating entries for each of the remaining three years would be:

		Year 6	Year 7	Year 8
DR:	Retained Earnings	$ 3,000	$ 2,000	$ 1,000
	Fixed Asset	10,000	10,000	10,000
	CR:Accumulated Depre.	$12,000	$11,000	$10,000
	Depreciation Exp.	1,000	1,000	1,000

    d. If the asset is retained beyond the 8th year, the following eliminating entry will be required until the asset is disposed:

DR:	Fixed Asset	$10,000
	CR: Accumulated Depreciation	$10,000

VIII. Sale By Subsidiary to Parent -- Intercompany Fixed Asset by Subsidiary to Parent: The prior illustration assumed that the sale was made by the parent company to a subsidiary - a downstream sale. If a subsidiary sells to its parent the transaction is an upstream sale. The intercompany elimination for upstream sales depends, in part, on the parent's percentage ownership of the subsidiary.

A. Parent owns 100% of the subsidiary

1. The worksheet eliminating entries made when the parent **owns 100%** of a subsidiary which sells fixed assets to the parent are the same as those made when the parent sells fixed assets to the subsidiary; there is no noncontrolling interest in the subsidiary.

2. All of the intercompany gain (or loss), net asset adjustment and subsequent depreciation expense adjustment would affect the parent's claim to net income and net asset carrying value.

B. Parent owns less than 100% of the subsidiary

1. The worksheet eliminating entries made when the parent **owns less than 100%** of a subsidiary that sells fixed assets to the parent are the same as those made when the parent sells fixed assets to the subsidiary, but the gain (or loss) eliminated, the net asset adjustment and the subsequent depreciation expense adjustment would be allocated between the parent and the noncontrolling shareholders' interest in proportion to their respective ownership percentages. Those entries are repeated below as a means of review and to show the allocations necessary when a less than 100% owned subsidiary sells fixed assets to its parent.

2. **Worksheet with Income Statement --** If the elimination occurs on a consolidating worksheet that includes an income statement, the eliminations assuming an intercompany gain would be:

   a. **For Period of Intercompany Sale**

DR: Fixed Asset
Gain on Sale
CR: Accumulated Depreciation

   b. To reestablish the fixed asset to its original cost, eliminate the intercompany gain, and reestablish accumulated depreciation written off by the selling affiliate. The debit to the gain will reduce the amount of income that will be allocated between the parent and the noncontrolling shareholders (interest) in proportion to their respective ownership percentages.

DR: Accumulated Depreciation
CR: Depreciation Expense

   c. To eliminate the depreciation expense (and related accumulated depreciation) taken by the buying affiliate on the intercompany gain. The credit to depreciation expense will increase the amount of income taht will be allocated between the parent and the noncontrolling shareholders' interest in proportion to their respective ownership percentages.

   d. **For Periods Subsequent to Intercompany Sale**

DR: Fixed Assets
Retained Earnings - S
CR: Accumulated Depreciation

   e. To reestablish the fixed asset to its original cost, eliminate the unconfirmed portion of the intercompany gain in retained earnings and reestablish accumulated depreciation to the amount based on depreciation of original cost. The debit to fixed asset will remain constant; the debit to retained earnings and the credit to accumulated depreciation will decrease each year as a portion of the intercompany gain is confirmed.

f. The debit to retained earnings of S, the selling affiliate, will reduce the sub's retained earnings by the amount of the **un**confirmed profit.

DR: Accumulated Depreciation

    CR: Depreciation Expense

g. To eliminate the depreciation expense (and related accumulated depreciation) taken by the buying affiliate on the intercompany gain. The credit to depreciation expense will increase income that will be allocated between the parent and noncontrolling interest.

3. **Worksheet without Income Statement --** If the elimination occurs on a consolidating worksheet that does not include an income statement (i.e., only a balance sheet is provided), the eliminations would be allocated on the worksheet between the parent and the noncontrolling shareholders' interest in proportion to their respective ownership percentages. The eliminating entries each year, assuming a gain, would be:

DR: Fixed Assets

    Retained Earnings - S

    CR: Accumulated Depreciation

DR: Accumulated Depreciation

    CR: Retained Earnings - P

a. The debit to retained earnings of S replaces a debit to gain because there is only a balance sheet. Otherwise, the purpose and effect of each debit and credit is the same as previously described.

Intercompany (I/C) Bond Transactions

When one affiliated entity owns the bonds issued by another affiliated entity an intercompany bond transaction has occurred and those bonds are intercompany bonds. Such transactions will result in the need to adjust and/or eliminate a number of account balances brought on to the consolidating worksheet by the separate entities. This lesson identifies the accounts that will be affected, and illustrates the adjustments or eliminations that will be needed on the consolidating worksheet.

After studying this lesson you should be able to :

1. *Identify the accounts affected by intercompany bond transactions.*

2. *Analyze facts and calculate the amounts needed to be eliminated for intercompany bond transactions under various circumstances, including:*

   - *When intercompany bonds have premiums or discounts associated with either the intercompany bond investment or bond liability.*

   - *When intercompany bonds are issued by a parent (and held by a subsidiary) or issued by a subsidiary (and held by a parent).*

   - *When intercompany bonds are issued by a subsidiary that is a 100% owned subsidiary or less than 100% owned subsidiary.*

3. *Record intercompany bond eliminations on a consolidating worksheet under the various circumstances identified above.*

> **Note:** Intercompany bond transactions are sometimes tested on the CPA exam; however, these transactions are tested less frequently. You should review and be familiar with how I/C Bond transactions are eliminated and the impact of the consolidated balance sheet only AFTER you are comfortable with I/C Inventory and I/C Fixed Asset transactions.

I. **Intercompany Bonds --** Occur when one affiliate owns the bonds issued by another affiliate.

II. **Intercompany Bonds May Result from**

   A. Bonds issued by one company are held by another company at the time the two companies become affiliated as a result of a business combination.

   B. One affiliate acquires the bonds issued by another affiliate (after the two companies are already affiliated as a result of a business combination).

III. **Intercompany Bond Consequences**

   A. When one affiliate acquires the bonds of another affiliate, for consolidated purposes it is as though the bonds have been retired; they have been constructively retired for consolidated purposes.

   B. Therefore, on the consolidating worksheet the bonds payable (and related accounts) brought on by the issuing company must be eliminated against the investment in bonds (and related accounts) brought on by the buying affiliate.

IV. **Accounts Affected --** Intercompany bonds affect the following accounts brought onto the consolidating worksheet by the separate companies:

   A. **Bonds Payable --** To the extent the bonds are held by an affiliate, the bonds have been constructively retired and the liability must be eliminated against the investment in the bonds held by an affiliate (in III. C., below);

B. Premium or Discount on Bonds Payable -- Any premium (issue price > face value of bonds) or discount (issue price < face value) related to bonds payable that are constructively retired must also be eliminated;

   1. Since the face value of the bonds payable will be exactly eliminated against the face value of the bond investment, any premium or discount on bonds payable that is eliminated will result in a gain or loss on constructive retirement.

     a. Elimination of a Premium on Bonds Payable = Gain (on constructive retirement);

     b. Elimination of a Discount on Bonds Payable = Loss (on constructive retirement).

C. Investment in Bonds -- Any investment in the bonds of an affiliate has been constructively retired and the asset must be eliminated against the owned portion of the bonds payable of the affiliate (in III. A., above);

D. Premium or Discount on Investment in Bonds -- Any premium (cost > face value of bonds) or discount (cost < face value) on the bond investment being eliminated also must be eliminated. Since the face value of the bond investment will be exactly eliminated against the face value of the bonds liability, any premium or discount on the bond investment that is eliminated will result in a loss or gain on constructive retirement:

   1. Elimination of a Premium on Investment in Bonds = Loss (on constructive retirement);

   2. Elimination of a Discount on Investment in Bonds = Gain (on constructive retirement).

E. Interest Income/Interest Expense -- Any interest income recognized by the affiliate with the investment in intercompany bonds and the interest expense related to the intercompany bonds recognized by the issuing affiliate must be eliminated. Since for consolidated purposes the bonds are considered retired at the time they became intercompany, no subsequent interest income or interest expense can be recognized for consolidated purposes;

F. Interest Receivable/Interest Payable -- Any intercompany interest receivables and interest payable resulting from intercompany bonds must be eliminated against each other.

V. Elimination of Intercompany Bonds and Related Premiums/Discounts - At Date Bonds become Intercompany

A. Illustration Facts -- Assume that on January 1, 20x1 Company P had the following account balances related to its 10% bonds.

Bonds Payable (face amount)	$100,000
Premium on Bonds Payable	3,000

B. The bonds have a three year remaining life and pay interest annually on December 31.

C. On January 1, 20x1 P's subsidiary, Company S, acquired all of P's bonds in the market for $106,000 ($100,000 face amount plus a $6,000 premium). Entries and related account balances on the books of the respective companies would be:

Company P (account balances)	
Bonds Payable	$100,000
Premium on Bonds Payable	3,000
Carrying Value	$103,000

<u>Company S (entry)</u>

Investment in P Bonds (face)	$100,000*	
Premium on Investment in P Bonds	6,000*	
Cash		$106,000

* These two debits likely would be combined in practice.

D. **Analysis of Intercompany Bond Facts** -- At the time Company S acquired its parent's bonds, the bonds became intercompany and for consolidated purposes will be treated as if they are retired.

   1. The constructive retirement of the bond investment ($100,000) against the bond liability ($100,000) will necessitate the elimination of the related premiums on the investment and on the liability.

   2. The elimination of the related premiums will result in recognition of a $3,000 loss on constructive retirement for consolidated purposes, calculated as:

Premium on Bonds Payable (Credit)	= $3,000	Gain
Premium on Investment Bonds (Debit)	= <u>$6,000</u>	Loss
Net Loss on Constructive Retirement	= $3,000	Loss

E. **Eliminating Entry** -- If an eliminating entry was made on a consolidating worksheet immediately following the intercompany bond transaction, the entry would be:

DR: Bonds Payable	$100,000	
Premium on Bonds Payable	3,000	
Loss (on Constructive Retirement)	3,000	
CR: Investment in Bonds Payable		$100,000
Premium on Investment in Bonds		6,000

   1. The loss (or gain) is attributable to the company that issued the bonds, Company P in this illustration.

VI. **Book Transactions Subsequent to Intercompany Bonds Relationship** -- Although the intercompany bonds are constructively retired and eliminated for consolidated purposes, the bond liability and the bond investment will continue to exist on the books of the separate companies.

   A. As a consequence, the companies will make the following entries on their separate books for each of the three years' remaining life of the bonds:

   See the following example.

<u>Company P</u>

Interest Expense	$10,000	
Interest Payable/Cash		$10,000

(Annual interest @ $100,000 X .10)

Premium on Bonds Payable	$ 1,000	
Interest Expense		$ 1,000

(Annual amortization @ $3,000/3 years)

<u>Company S</u>

Interest Receivable/Cash	$10,000	
Interest Income		$10,000

(Annual interest @ $100,000 X .10)

Interest Income	$ 2,000	
Premium on Investment in bonds		$ 2,000

(Annual amortization @ $6,000/3 years)

B. Although the above bond related entries will be recorded on the books of the separate companies, for consolidated purposes the bonds were constructively retired at the date the bonds became intercompany-owned.

C. Therefore, the effects of the bond related entries that apply after the bonds become intercompany must be eliminated for consolidated purposes.

VII. **Elimination - Year End --** Elimination of Intercompany Bonds and Related Accounts -- **At End of Year of Intercompany Bond Transaction**.

A. **Illustration Facts --** (continued from above): As a result of the transactions described above, at the end of 20X1, (the year in which the bonds became intercompany), the following account balances would exist on the books of the separate companies and be brought onto the consolidating worksheet:

Company P	
Bonds Payable (face amount)	$100,000 (CR)
Premium on Bonds Payable ($3,000-$1,000)	2,000 (CR)
Interest Expense ($10,000 - $1,000)	9,000 (DR)
Company S	
Investment in P Bonds (face amount)	$100,000 (DR)
Premium on Bonds Investment ($6,000-$2,000)	4,000 (DR)
Interest Income ($10,000 - $2,000)	8,000 (CR)

B. Eliminating Entry -- The following eliminating entry would be made on the consolidating worksheet at the end of the period in which the bonds become intercompany bonds:

DR: Bonds Payable	$100,000	
Premium on Bonds Payable	2,000	
Interest Income	8,000	
Loss on Constructive Retirement	3,000	
CR: Investment in P Bonds		$100,000
Premium on Bond Investment		4,000
Interest Expense		9,000

C. Recall, this eliminating entry is required because for consolidated purposes the bonds must be treated as though they were retired at the time they became intercompany. Therefore, all subsequent balances and effects must be eliminated. The eliminating entry accomplishes the following:

1. Eliminates the intercompany liability and investment ($100,000);

2. Eliminates the non-amortized premiums on the liability ($2,000) and on the investment ($4,000);

3. Eliminates the net interest income recognized by Company S, the owner of the bonds (interest received $10,000 minus $2,000 premium amortization = $8,000);

4. Eliminates the net interest expense recognized by Company P, the issuing affiliate (interest paid $10,000 minus $1,000 premium amortization = $9,000);

5. Recognizes for consolidated purposes the $3,000 loss on the constructive retirement of the bonds.

VIII. Elimination - Subsequent Years -- Elimination of Intercompany Bonds and Related Accounts **-- In Years Subsequent to Intercompany Transaction**.

A. Gain/Loss

1. The gain or loss on constructive retirement of intercompany bonds is determined as the net amount of premium(s) and/or discount(s) related to the bonds when they become intercompany and is recognized at the date (in the period) in which the bonds become intercompany.

2. However, as shown above, the separate companies will continue to carry on their books and amortize the premium and/or discount. At the end of each period, the effects of such amortization will be to recognize on the separate company books a portion (by the amount being amortized for the period) of the gain or loss already recognized for consolidated purposes (at the time the bonds became intercompany).

3. Therefore, in subsequent periods the amount needed to be recognized in eliminating entries for consolidated purposes that has not been recognized on the separate books will decrease each period. When the premium and/or discount related to intercompany bonds is fully amortized on the separate books (i.e., at maturity), the separate books will have recognized the total gain or loss recognized for consolidated purposes when the bonds became intercompany.

B. Illustration Facts -- (continued from above): The following illustration shows the effects on the separate company books of amortizing the premiums from the facts in the above illustration:

	I/C Date 1/1/X1	X1 Amortize Net Income Affect +/-	Balance 12/31/X1	X2 Amortize Net Income Affect +/-	Balance 12/31/X2
Co. P Prem. on B/P (CR)	$3,000	(+1,000)	2,000	(+1,000)	1,000
Co. S Prem. on B/I (DR)	$6,000	(-2,000)	4,000	(-2,000)	2,000
Net (DR)	$3,000	(-1,000)	2,000	(-1,000)	1,000
Consolidated Loss	$3,000				

1. **Net Value** -- Note that the net value of the premiums at the date the bonds became intercompany, $3,000, is the amount of loss recognized at that time for consolidated purposes.

2. **Subsequent Year** -- Each subsequent year the amortization taken on the books of the separate companies causes $1,000 (net) of the $3,000 to be recognized on the books of the companies. The books are "catching up" a portion of the $3,000 already recognized for consolidated purposes.

3. Therefore, in subsequent periods the amount of gain or loss needed to be recognized for consolidated purposes will decrease.

4. **Account Balances** -- As a result of transactions by the separate companies during 20X1 and 20X2 (including the closing of accounts at the end of 20X1), at the end of 20X2 the following account balances would exist on the books of the separate companies and be brought onto the consolidating worksheet:

Company P	
Bonds Payable (face amount)	$100,000 (CR)
Premium on Bonds Payable	1,000 (CR)
Interest Expense ($10,000 - $1,000)	9,000 (DR)
Company S	
Investment in P Bonds (face amount)	$100,000 (DR)
Premium on Bonds Investment ($6,000 - $2,000 - $2,000)	2,000 (DR)
Interest Income ($10,000 - $2,000)	8,000 (CR)

C. **Eliminating Entry** -- The following eliminating entry would be made on the consolidating worksheet at the end of 20X2, the period after the one in which the bonds became intercompany bonds:

DR: Bonds Payable	$100,000	
Premium on Bonds Payable	1,000	
Interest Income	8,000	
Retained Earnings - P	2,000	
CR: Investment in P Bonds		$100,000
Premium on Bond Investment		2,000
Interest Expense		9,000

D. This entry is the same as for the prior year except:

1. The amount of the premiums has decreased by the amounts of amortization taken in the second year;

2. The debit to Retained Earnings replaces the debit to Loss because the loss occurred in the prior period for consolidated purposes. The amount of the debit to Retained Earnings ($2,000) is $1,000 less than the debit to the loss in the prior period ($3,000) because $1,000 of the loss -- the net amortization for the first period -- has now been closed to retained earnings on the separate books;

3. A similar entry would be made on the consolidating worksheet at the end of 20X3, except the premiums will have been fully eliminated on the separate books (thus, no eliminating entry will be required for them) and the debit to retained earnings will be $1,000, the amount not yet recognized in the retained earnings of the separate companies through amortization of the premiums.

IX. Bonds Issued by Subsidiary -- Intercompany Bond Issued by a Subsidiary: The prior illustration assumed that the bonds were issued by the parent and acquired by a subsidiary. If a subsidiary issues bonds, which are subsequently acquired by the parent, the consolidating eliminations will depend, in part, on the parent's percentage ownership of the subsidiary.

A. Parent owns 100% of the subsidiary

1. The worksheet eliminating entries made when the parent owns 100% of a subsidiary, which has its bonds reacquired by its parent, are the same as those made when the parent was the issuer.

2. The gain or loss on constructive retirement will be attributable to the issuing subsidiary, but the full amount will effect the parent's claim to net income since there is no noncontrolling interest in the subsidiary.

3. The eliminating entry in years subsequent to the bonds becoming intercompany will debit (loss) or credit (gain) the retained earnings of the subsidiary, rather than the parent, but the consolidated income and retained earnings effects will be the same.

B. Parent owns < 100% of the subsidiary

1. The worksheet eliminating entries made when the parent owns < 100% of a subsidiary, which has its bonds reacquired by its parent, are essentially the same as those made when the parent was the issuer, but the gain or loss on constructive retirement would be allocated between the parent and the noncontrolling shareholders' interest in proportion to their respective ownership on the consolidated income statement and balance sheet. Those entries are repeated below as a means of review and to show the allocations necessary when the subsidiary issues the bonds.

2. **Worksheet with Income Statement --** If the elimination occurs on a consolidating worksheet that includes an income statement, the elimination assuming a discount on the bond issue, a premium on the bond investment, and a net loss on the constructive retirement would be:

a. **For Period of Intercompany Bond Transaction**

DR: Bonds Payable

Loss on Constructive Retirement

CR: Investment in Intercompany Bonds

Discount on Bonds Payable

Premium on Investment in Bonds

b. To eliminate the intercompany bond liability and bond investment, related premium and discount, and recognize the resulting loss on constructive retirement. Since the loss is attributable to the issuer, the subsidiary's net income will be reduced which will reduce its contribution to consolidated net income. The amount of the loss attributable to noncontrolling shareholders will be allocated to that interest when the share of consolidated net income attributable to noncontrolling interest is allocated to those shareholders on the consolidated income statement.

c. **For Periods Subsequent to the Intercompany Bond Transaction**

DR: Bonds Payable

Retained Earnings - S

CR: Investment in Intercompany Bonds

Discount on Bonds Payable

Premium on Investment in Bonds

d. This entry is the same as that made in the period following the intercompany bond transaction, except that retained earnings of the subsidiary is debited rather than loss because the loss occurred in a prior period. The debit will reduce retained earnings of the subsidiary, which will be allocated between the parent and the noncontrolling shareholders' interest in proportion to their respective ownership percentages.

3. **Worksheet without Income Statement --** If the elimination occurs on a consolidating worksheet that does not include an income statement (i.e., only a balance sheet is provided) the eliminations would be allocated on the worksheet between the parent and the noncontrolling shareholders' interest in proportion to their respective ownership percentages. The eliminating entry each year, assuming a discount on the bond issue, a premium on the bonds investment, and a net loss on constructive retirement, would be:

DR: Bonds Payable

Retained Earnings - S

CR: Investment in Intercompany Bonds

Discount on Bonds Payable   ·

Premium on Investment in Bonds

4. This debit to retained earnings of S replaces a debit to loss because there is only a balance sheet. Otherwise, the purpose and effect of each debit and credit is the same as previously described.

IFRS – Consolidations

This lesson presents the significant differences in the accounting for consolidations under IFRS versus U.S. GAAP.

After studying this lesson you should be able to:

    I. *Identify the major differences in the accounting for consolidations under IFRS versus US GAAP.*

I. Consolidations U.S. GAAP - IFRS Differences

U.S. GAAP	IFRS
Control defined as <50% ownership	Control can be obtained with >50% ownership in certain circumstances i.e., potential rights, right to appoint key personnel, or decision making rights
Defines variable interest entities	Does not define variable interest entities, but does have similar concept with special purpose entities
Accounting policies do not have to align	Accounting policies have to align
Accounting periods can be up to three months apart	Accounting periods should have the same end date, if not adjust for transactions during gap period .
Noncontrolling interest is assigned their percentage of goodwill from the acquisition premium (purchase price differential)	Parent has a choice at acquisition whether or not to either assign goodwill to NCI

  A. Control Concept Differences

      1. U.S. GAAP -- Under U.S. GAAP, generally, the entity (investor) that owns, directly or indirectly, greater than 50% of the voting shares of another entity (investee) is considered to have control of that entity and, generally, would be required to consolidate the investee. If the investee entity is a variable interest entity, the controlling entity is the one that is the primary beneficiary of the variable interest entity. (Simply put, a variable interest entity [VIE] is an investee in which the investor holds controlling interest that is not based on holding a majority of the voting rights in the entity. They are a form of special purpose entity [SPE]. Both VIEs and SPEs are covered in a later lesson.)

      2. IFRS

          a. Under IFRS No. 10, like under U.S. GAAP, the ability of one entity (investor) to control another entity (investee) requires that the controlled entity be consolidated with the investor. However, under IFRS the definition and determination of control specifies that control can be achieved even when less than 50% of the voting rights are held by an investor.

          b. Under IFRS, one entity (investor) controls another entity (investee) when the investor has:

      i. Power over an investee through existing rights that give it the ability to direct the activities that significantly affect the investee's returns; and

      ii. Exposure, or rights, to variable returns from its involvement with the investee; and

      iii. The ability to use its power over the investee to affect the amount of the investor's return.

  c. Under IFRS, power over an investee arises from rights of the investor, which may include:

      i. Voting rights (the critical criteria under U.S. GAAP);

      ii. Potential voting rights (e.g., convertible instruments, stock options, etc.);

      iii. Rights to appoint key personnel of the investee;

      iv. Decision-making rights under a management agreement.

  d. Under IFRS, an exposure, or a right, to variable returns from its involvement with an investee, which may be either positive, negative or both, might include, for example:

      i. Dividends;

      ii. Remuneration;

      iii. Other returns or benefits not available to other stakeholders (e.g., economies of scale, cost savings, access to scarce resources or proprietary information, synergies, etc.).

3. Thus, under IFRS, the standard for determining control is broader than under U.S. GAAP. The IFRS standard applies regardless of the form of the investee entity, including to structured entities (what would be designated as SPEs or VIEs under U.S. GAAP) and the determination that control exists may occur in a greater number of relational circumstances than under U.S. GAAP. For example, under IFRS control may be deemed to exist in the following circumstances (which would not be considered control for consolidation purposes under U.S. GAAP):

  a. An investor has control over more than 50% of the voting rights by virtue of an agreement with other investors;

  b. An investor has the ability to govern the financial and operating policies of the entity under a statute or an agreement;

  c. An investor can appoint or remove the majority of the members of the board of directors;

  d. An investor can cast the majority of votes at a meeting of the board of directors.

B. Variable-Interest Entities/Special-Purpose Entities -- IFRS does not address variable-interest entities or control of such entities, but it does address special-purpose entities, a similar entity concept.

  1. A special-purpose entity (SPE), as the term implies, is a separate legal entity (or other entity) established to fulfill a narrow, specific or temporary purpose, generally with the intent of isolating the establishing firm from risk and assigning responsibility for risk through the use of agreements and other instruments.

  2. Most, but not all, special-purpose entities will be variable-interest entities. Therefore, they have the same general characteristics as VIEs and, under IFRS, are treated similar to the treatment of VIEs under U.S. GAAP.

3. IFRS establishes that an entity may control a special-purpose entity (SPE), even when it owns little or none of the SPE's equity.

4. Under IFRS, the determination of control would be based on an analysis of all the relevant facts and circumstances, including the design of the entity and the risk and reward relationship between the entities.

5. Where the substance of the relationship indicates that an entity controls an SPE, the SPE should be consolidated by the controlling entity.

Note: In rare circumstances, under IFRS an investor may have the ability to control another entity with 50% or less of its voting ownership when it has significant ownership and other ownership is widely dispersed and not organized. Such a determination would have to be made on a case-by-case basis taking into account all relevant facts and circumstances.

C. Accounting Policy and Period Requirements

1. **Accounting Policy Requirement --** Under U.S. GAAP, a parent and its subsidiaries do not have to follow the same accounting policies in order to be consolidated. Different accounting policies can be used by different affiliated entities as long as all policies used are U.S. GAAP. Under IFRS, however, consolidated statements have to be prepared using the same accounting policies by all affiliated entities for like transactions and events. Thus, under IFRS, if a subsidiary used an accounting policy different than that employed by the parent, for consolidating purposes the subsidiary's accounts affected by the different policy would have to be adjusted prior to consolidation.

2. **Accounting Period Requirement --** Under U.S. GAAP, the fiscal reporting period of a parent and its subsidiaries may be up to 3 months different. Significant transactions or events that occur during the gap require only disclosure in the consolidated statements; no adjustment to accounts or amounts is required. Under IFRS, however, the financial information of a parent and its subsidiaries should be as of the same period-ending date, unless it is impracticable to do so. In any case, the difference between the parent ending date and the subsidiary ending date cannot be more than 3 months. Further, significant transactions or events that occur during the gap must be reflected in adjustments to the accounts/amounts used for consolidating purposes.

D. Noncontrolling Interest Valuation

1. One of the most significant differences between U.S. GAAP and IFRS in accounting for business combinations is in the possible measurement of noncontrolling interest (NCI) because of the goodwill allocated to NCI.

    a. U.S. GAAP requires that any noncontrolling interest be measured at full fair value, including the goodwill attributable to the noncontrolling interest.

    b. IFRS gives the acquirer a choice between two options for measuring noncontrolling interest in the acquiree; those options are to measure noncontrolling interest using either:

        i. Full fair value of the NCI, including goodwill attributable to noncontrolling interest, or

        ii. Proportional share of fair value of the fair value, excluding goodwill attributable to the noncontrolling interest.

    c. Example of allocation of Full Fair Value vs. Proportional Share of Noncontrolling Interest (NCI)

i. (Note: The primary purpose of these examples is to illustrate the difference between allocating goodwill to NCI. Eliminating entries are given to show how the different measures result in different amounts of goodwill and noncontrolling interest. The preparation of eliminating entries is covered in detail in other sections on consolidated statements.)

Example:

Facts: Torco, Inc., acquired 70% of Teeco, Inc. for $900 cash. The fair value of the 30% noncontrolling interest was determined to be $400. Therefore, the total fair value of Teeco at the date of the business combination is $900 + $400 = $1,300. The fair value of Teeco's identifiable net assets is $1,000.

1) Full Fair Value calculation - which is U.S. GAAP and one (of two) options under IFRS

Total Fair Value ($900 + $400)	$1,300
Fair Value of Identifiable Net Assets (given)	1,000
Total Goodwill	$ 300
Goodwill Allocated to Torco $900 - (.70 x $1,000) = $900 - $700 =	(200)
Goodwill Allocated to NCI	100
Total Noncontrolling Interest (given)	400

	100%	Parent share 70%	NCI share 30%
Total (FV of entity)	1,300	900	400
Goodwill	300	200	100
FMV net assets	1,000	700	300

Entries:
Investment

DR: Investment in Sub Teeco	$ 900	
CR: Cash		$ 900

Investment Elimination (Summary)

DR: Teeco Shareholder' Equity/Net Assets	$1,000	
Goodwill	300	
CR: Investment in Sub Teeco		$ 900
Noncontrolling Interest		400

2) Proportional Share of Fair Value calculation - which is not U.S. GAAP, but is one (of two) options under IFRS

Total Fair Value ($900 + $400)		$1,300
Fair Value of Identifiable Net Assets (given)		1,000
Goodwill Recognized - Torco only $900 - (.70 x $1,000) = $900 - $700 =		200
Goodwill Allocated to NCI		-0-
Goodwill Allocated to Torco		(200)
Total Noncontrolling Interest (given)		300

	100%	Parent share 70%	NCI share 30%
Total (FV of entity)	1,300	900	400
Goodwill		200	0
FMV net assets	1,000	700	300

Entries:
Investment

DR: Investment in Sub Teeco $ 900
      CR: Cash $ 900

Investment Elimination (Summary)

DR: Investment in Sub Teeco $1,000
      Goodwill   200
      CR: Investment in Sub Teeco $ 900
         Noncontrolling Interest   300

Comments on Noncontrolling Interest Valuation

1) Under IFRS, the acquirer can elect to allocate the proportional share goodwill on a business combination-by-business combination basis; it does not have to use the same basis for all combinations.

2) The net effect of the alternative valuations of NCI is in the amount of goodwill recognized. Under the full fair value approach, the goodwill attributable to the NCI is derived and allocated to NCI. Under the proportional share of fair value approach, only the goodwill paid for by the acquirer is recognized; no goodwill is derived for or allocated to NCI.

Combined Financial Statements

Combined Financial Statements

Sometimes there is a need to aggregate the financial information of two or more affiliated entities, but the preparation of consolidated financial statements is not appropriate because none of the affiliated entities controls (is the parent) of the other firms. In such circumstances, the preparation of combined financial statements may be appropriate. This lesson is concerned with the concept and preparation of combined financial statements.

After studying this lesson, you should be able to:

1. *Identify when combined financial statements are appropriate.*

2. *Describe how combined financial statements are prepared.*

I. **Basis for Combined Financial Statements --** Like consolidated financial statements, combined financial statements are the product of bringing together the financial statements of two or more related firms. However, the circumstances when combined financial statements (as opposed to consolidated financial statements) would be appropriate, as well as the process of combining financial statements (as opposed to consolidating financial statements), are somewhat different.

   A. Consolidated financial statements are justified only when the controlling financial interest of the firms being consolidated rests directly or indirectly with one of the firms (a "parent") to be included in the consolidation.

   B. There are circumstances when there is not a parent company, or when a parent does not have effective control of subsidiaries, but bringing together (combining) the financial statements of two or more related firms would be more meaningful than their separate financial statements.

   C. Combined financial statements (as distinguished from consolidated statements) would be appropriate when:

      1. Common Control: One individual (not a corporation) owns a controlling interest in two or more businesses that have related operations;

      2. Common Management: Two or more businesses are under common management;

      3. Unconsolidated Subsidiaries: A parent lacks effective control over two or more subsidiaries (unconsolidated subsidiaries) for which it wishes to show summary results.

II. **Process for Combining Financial Statements --** The process of preparing combined financial statements is similar to the process of consolidating financial statements.

   A. **Intercompany Items --** Intercompany transactions and balances (i.e., between the companies being combined) are eliminated, including:

      1. Intercompany receivables and payables;

      2. Intercompany revenues and expenses;

      3. Intercompany gains and losses;

      4. Intercompany ownership and related equity - The carrying value of an investment in a company to be combined is eliminated against an equal amount of equity of that company; thus, there are no differences (between the debit and credit) to be allocated.

   B. Any other "unusual" matters would be treated in the same manner as in consolidated financial statements, including:

      1. Minority ownership in any combined company;

2. Foreign operations;

3. Income taxes;

4. Different fiscal periods.

C. Unlike consolidated financial statements, the resulting combined financial statements do not represent the financial position, results of operations or cash flows of a single controlling entity, but rather the aggregate results of the combined companies after eliminating intercompany account activity and balances.

Financial Instruments

Financial Instruments Introduction

This lesson begins a set of lessons (a new study unit) that covers financial instruments, including derivatives and the use of financial instruments and other contracts for speculation and hedging purposes. Specifically, this lesson introduces the material by defining financial instruments, giving common examples of financial instruments that are (financial) assets and (financial) liabilities, and providing an overview of the other lessons covering financial instruments and related matters.

After studying this lesson, you should be able to:

1. *Define and describe financial instruments.*

2. *Identify asset and liability accounts that are financial instruments.*

I. **Introduction** -- The term "financial instruments" includes a diverse variety of items found in contemporary business activity. Some of these items (instruments) are common, well understood and have long established accounting treatments. Other financial instruments are not so common nor are they well understood, and often challenge accounting principles. Those challenges are further complicated by the on-going development of even more exotic financial instruments.

II. **Financial Instruments**

A. **Defined** -- Financial instruments are defined (in ASC 825) as any of the following:

1. **Cash** -- (including foreign currency and demand deposits).

2. **Evidence of an ownership interest in an entity** -- (including investments in common and preferred stock, warrants and options to purchase stock, and partnership and limited liability company interest).

3. **Contracts that result in an exchange of cash or ownership interest in an entity and that both**

a. **Imposes on one entity a contractual obligation or duty (liability)**

i. To deliver cash (e.g., trade accounts payable, loan obligations, bonds payable, etc.) or another financial instrument (e.g., a note payable in U.S. treasury bonds) to a **second entity**, or

ii. To exchange financial instruments on potentially unfavorable terms with a **second entity**.

b. **Conveys to a second entity a contractual right (asset)**

i. To receive cash (e.g., accounts receivable, investment in bonds, etc.) or another financial instrument from the **first entity**, or

ii. To exchange financial instruments on potentially favorable terms with the **first entity**.

4. Derivatives are a special form of financial instrument, which will be defined and described in a subsequent lesson.

B. **Common Examples** -- Many of the items covered in prior lessons were financial instruments, either financial assets or financial liabilities. Those items (accounts), as well as other financial assets and financial liabilities, would include:

1. **Financial Assets**

a. Cash and cash equivalents;

      b. Accounts receivable;

      c. Investments in debt (notes, bonds, etc.) and equity securities (common and preferred stock, etc.);

      d. Interest in partnerships, limited liability entities, and joint ventures;

      e. Option contracts (w/favorable terms);

      f. Futures and forward contracts (w/favorable terms);

      g. Swap contracts (w/favorable terms);

   2. Financial Liabilities

      a. Accounts payable;

      b. Notes and bonds payable;

      c. Option contracts (w/unfavorable terms);

      d. Futures and forward contracts (w/unfavorable terms);

      e. Swap contracts (w/unfavorable terms).

III. Categories -- While many asset and liability items (accounts) are financial instruments, only a few of those items are designated as comprising a financial instrument "category."

   A. Specifically, the following are designated as categories of investments (financial assets):

      1. Held-to-maturity;

      2. Held-for-trading;

      3. Available-for-sale.

   B. Each of these categories (in A., above) requires a specific accounting treatment.

   C. Other financial assets and financial liabilities, including those listed above (in II., B. 1., and 2.) are subject to one or more accounting treatments that are specified for each item (depending on the nature, use, and other characteristics of the specific financial item); accounting treatments are not specified for categories into which the items are classified.

IV. Transaction Costs -- The treatment of cost associated with acquiring a financial asset or incurring a financial liability depends on the nature and treatment of the particular financial instrument:

   A. For all financial instruments (assets or liabilities) to be measured at fair value, the transaction costs associated with acquiring or incurring the item are excluded from the cost of the financial instrument.

   B. Except for certain costs associated with the purchase of (investment in) debt and lending activities, transaction costs directly attributable to the financial item are expensed when incurred.

   C. Costs associated with debt issuance (incurring financial liabilities) are treated as deferred charges.

V. Impairment Assessment -- Financial assets must be assessed for impairment and, if it is determined that fair value is less than carrying value and the decline is other than temporary, the asset must be written down and (generally) a loss recognized in current income.

   A. If the financial asset is classified as available-for-sale, it must be assessed for impairment because, even though it is carried at fair value, changes in fair value are not reported through income; an impairment loss must be reported through income.

B. If the financial asset is a debt security, then the treatment of the loss depends on whether or not the entity expects to dispose of the security before its carrying amount is recovered.

    1. If the entity does not expect to hold the debt security until recovery of its carrying amount, the loss is recognized in current income.

    2. If the entity expects to hold the debt security until recovery of its carrying amount, the loss must be separated into two components:

        a. Any portion of loss in fair value attributable to credit standing of the issuer is recognized in income.

        b. Any other loss in fair value is recognized in other comprehensive income, net of tax.

VI. Preview -- The following lessons dealing with financial instruments cover:

    A. The required and recommended disclosures that apply to all financial instruments, including derivatives.

    B. The definition of derivatives, as a special form of financial instrument, and the measurement requirements, which apply to all derivatives.

    C. The different accounting requirements, which apply depending on the specific purpose for which a derivative instrument is held. Four possible purposes are identified for accounting:

        1. To speculate;

        2. As a fair value hedge;

        3. As a cash flow hedge;

        4. As a foreign currency hedge.

    D. The use of derivatives (or other contracts) for each of the above purposes (C.1. - C.4.) has certain criteria that must be met, and each purpose requires a somewhat different accounting treatment.

        1. The criteria and accounting treatments for each of the first three accounting purposes of derivatives (C.1. - C.3., above) are covered in detail in the immediate following lessons.

        2. Accounting for derivatives used as foreign currency hedges (C.4., above) is summarized in this "Financial Instruments" subsection, but is considered in detail in the subsection "Foreign Currency Accounting."

    E. The last set of lessons in this "Financial Instruments" subsection deal with the "Transfer and Servicing of Financial Assets" and "Extinguishment of Liabilities."

IFRS - Financial Instruments

While there are many similarities between U.S. GAAP and IFRS in accounting for financial instruments, there are also notable differences. This lesson identifies the most significant differences between U.S. GAAP and current IFRS accounting requirements for financial instruments.

After studying this lesson, you should be able to:

1. *Identify significant areas of difference between U.S. GAAP and IFRS in accounting for financial instruments.*

2. *Describe the measurement and recognition differences between U.S. GAAP and IFRS in accounting for financial instruments.*

I. **Introduction**

A. Currently, IFRS for financial instruments is provided primarily by International Accounting Standard (IAS) No. 32, Financial Instruments: Presentation, IAS No. 39, Financial Instruments: Recognition and Measurement, and IAS No. 7, Financial Instruments: Disclosures.

B. In November, 2009, the IASB issued IFRS No. 9, Financial Instruments, to replace, in part, IAS No. 39. IFRS No. 9 replaces IAS No. 39 only as it relates to classification and measurement of financial assets. On-going IASB projects will address the additional financial instrument topics of financial liabilities, derecognition of financial instruments, impairment, and hedge accounting.

C. IFRS No. 9 has an effective date of January 1, 2015, with earlier adoption permitted. Therefore, between 2009 and 2015 two sets of international standards (IFRS) may be used in practice to account for financial assets.

D. We are of the view that it is highly unlikely that the AICPA will test two forms of IFRS and that the most recent standards will be the focus on the CPA exam. We suspect that the differences in U.S. GAAP and IFRS will be a lightly tested area until 2015.

E. Below is a table with a high level summary of the significant differences between U.S. GAAP and IFRS.

U.S. GAAP	IFRS
Does not define financial assets and liabilities separately	Defines financial assets and liabilities separately. The definition of financial liabilities may likely classify certain preferred shares as liabilities not equity.
No specific category for "loans and receivables"	Identifies a specific category for "loans and receivables"
Impairment testing is completed relative to fair value	Impairment testing is completed relative to the recoverable amount

II. **Financial Instruments Definition** -- IFRS defines financial assets and financial liabilities separately, and in a more descriptive manner than the definition provided by U.S. GAAP.

A. Financial assets are defined as comprising:

1. Cash;

2. Rights to receive cash or another financial asset;

3. A contract to exchange financial instruments on potentially favorable terms;

4. Equity instruments in another entity;

5. A non-derivative contract to receive a variable number of the entity's own equity instruments;

6. Certain complex derivatives involving an entity's own instruments.

B. Financial liabilities are defined as financial instruments that require the issuer to deliver cash or another financial asset or to exchange instruments on potentially unfavorable terms.

1. Under this definition, preferred shares with a commitment to pay dividends and redeemable preferred shares likely would be financial liabilities, not equity items. Under U.S. GAAP these items would most likely be equity.

2. Compound financial instruments that contain both a liability and an equity element (e.g., convertible debt) would be split, with the debt element accounted for as a financial liability and the equity element treated as equity.

III. **Financial Instruments Categories** -- Like U.S. GAAP, IFRS requires that financial instruments be classified into categories and prescribes a specific accounting treatment for each category. The categories under IFRS are somewhat different from, and more specific than, those under U.S. GAAP.

A. **The categories for financial assets** -- (financial assets must "fit" into one of these categories)

1. Financial assets at fair value through profit or loss, which includes:

a. Assets held for trading - instruments acquired to generate profit from short-term fluctuations in price or dealer's margin;

b. All derivatives (that are assets), including contracts that contain an embedded derivative;

c. Financial assets designated irrevocably into this category upon initial recognition (i.e., the fair value option);

d. Circumstances that make this designation appropriate because it eliminates an accounting mismatch (e.g., a liability at fair value, but a related asset would otherwise be measured at other than fair value).

2. **Loans and receivables**

a. Comprised of non-derivative financial assets with fixed or determinable payments that are not quoted in an active market.

b. Does not include held-for-trading assets or other assets designated at fair value through profit or loss, assets classified as available for sale, or instruments for which the holder may not recover substantially all of its investment (which must be classified as available-for-sale).

c. U.S. GAAP does not specifically identify a comparable category.

3. **Instruments held to maturity (other than loans and receivables)**

a. Comprised only of assets with fixed or determinable payments and fixed maturity for which the entity has the positive intent and ability to hold until maturity.

b. This category generally may not be used by an entity for two years following the sale of more than an insignificant amount of assets classified as held to maturity at time of sale; that time period is called the "taint" period. While U.S. GAAP does not specify a taint period, the SEC uses a two-year period; during that period a firm that has sold more than an insignificant amount of held-to-maturity securities may not use that category for other securities.

    4. Instruments available-for-sale

        a. Comprised of all financial assets not falling into one of the categories above (a., b., or c.).

B. The categories for financial liabilities are:

    1. Financial liabilities at fair value through profit or loss, which includes:

        a. Liabilities held for trading;

        b. All derivatives (that are liabilities);

        c. Financial liabilities designated irrevocably in this category upon initial recognition (i.e., the fair value option).

    2. Other financial liabilities.

IV. Financial Instruments - Measurement and Recognition -- The measurement and recognition requirements under IFRS for financial assets and liabilities are very similar to those requirements under U.S. GAAP, except that requirements for the loan and receivables category are specified. The requirements are:

A. Assets at fair value through profit or loss are remeasured to fair value at each reporting date with gains and losses recognized in income;

B. Loans and receivables (assets) are measured at amortized cost, with related interest and amortization recognized in income;

C. Held-to-maturity financial assets are measured at amortized cost, with related interest and amortization recognized in income;

D. Available-for-sale assets are measured at fair value at each reporting date with gains and losses recognized in comprehensive income until disposed of, at which time the accumulated gains/losses are recognized in income;

E. Liabilities at fair value through profit or loss are remeasured to fair value at each reporting date with gains and losses recognized in income;

F. Other financial liabilities are measured at amortized cost, with related amortization recognized in income.

V. Financial Asset Impairment -- Under IFRS, financial assets must be reviewed for impairment.

A. When there is objective evidence that a financial asset is impaired, its recoverable amount (not its fair value, as under U.S. GAAP) must be determined.

B. The difference between recoverable amount and carrying value is the impairment loss.

C. Impairment losses are recognized in income.

    1. Unlike U.S. GAAP, the treatment of impairment losses on debt securities does not depend on whether or not the entity expects to dispose of the security before recovery of its carrying amount.

    2. Like U.S. GAAP, instruments categorized as available-for-sale must be assessed for impairment and any loss recognized in income (not other comprehensive income).

Financial Instruments Disclosures

This lesson identifies and describes the financial statement disclosures required and recommended for all financial instruments, including derivatives. Requirements include fair value disclosures and concentration of credit risk disclosures; market risk-related disclosures are recommended, but not required.

After studying this lesson, you should be able to:

1. *Identify the kinds of disclosures required and the kinds of disclosures recommended (but not required) for all financial instruments.*

2. *Describe the specific information that must be disclosed to satisfy disclosure requirements.*

3. *Describe the kinds of information that might be disclosed when disclosures are recommended, but not required.*

I. **Fair Value and Related Disclosure Requirements That Apply to All Financial Instruments**

A. **The following must be disclosed for all financial instruments, whether recognized or not recognized in the balance sheet (except as noted in D, below), for which it is practicable to estimate fair value.**

   1. **Fair Value**;

   2. **Related carrying amount**;

   3. **Whether the instrument/amount is an asset or liability**.

B. **"Practicable to estimate"** -- Means that fair value estimates can be made without incurring excessive costs; it is a cost/benefit assessment. If it is not practicable to estimate fair value, the following must be disclosed:

   1. The reasons why it is not practicable to estimate fair value, and

   2. Information pertinent to estimating fair value, such as carrying amount, effective interest rate, and maturity.

C. **Fair value** -- Should be determined in accordance with the definition and requirements of ASC 820, "Fair Value Measurement."

   1. Fair value is the price that would be received to sell an asset or paid to transfer a liability in an orderly transaction between market participants at the measurement date.

   2. Quoted market prices in an active market provide the most reliable evidence of fair value.

D. Disclosures about fair value **are not required** for the following financial items:

   1. Employer's and plan's obligations for pension benefits, post-retirement benefits, post-employment benefits, employee stock option and stock purchase plans, and other forms of deferred compensation arrangements;

   2. Substantially extinguished debt;

   3. Insurance contracts (other than financial guarantee insurance contracts) and certain investments made by insurance entities;

   4. Lease contracts;

   5. Warranty obligations and rights;

   6. Unconditional purchase contracts;

   7. Investments accounted for under the equity method;

8. Noncontrolling interest in a consolidated subsidiary.

9. Equity instruments issued and classified in shareholders' equity.

E. No fair value disclosure is required for trade accounts receivable or trade accounts payable when their carrying amounts approximate fair value.

F. **Fair values of different financial instruments -- May not be netted**, even if they are of the same class or otherwise related.

G. **Required disclosures -- May be in either the body of the financial statements or in the footnotes**. If in the footnotes, one note must show fair values and carrying amounts for all financial instruments.

II. **Concentration of Credit Risk Disclosure Requirement That Apply to All Financial Instruments**

A. **All entities must disclose all significant concentrations of credit risks arising from all financial instruments --** (With limited exceptions) Whether from a single party or a group of parties engaged in similar activities and that have similar economic characteristics.

B. **Credit risk --** Is the possibility of loss from the failure of another party (or parties) to perform according to the terms of a contract.

C. **Concentrations of credit risk --** Occurs when an entity has contracts of material value with one or more parties in the same industry or region or having similar economic characteristics (e.g., receivables from a group of highly leveraged entities).

D. **The following must be disclosed --** About each significant concentration of credit risk:

1. **Information about the common activity, region, or economic characteristic that identifies the concentration**;

2. **The maximum amount of loss due to the credit risk** (measured as the gross fair value of the financial instruments) that would occur if the other parties failed completely to perform according to the terms of the contract and assuming any collateral was of no value;

3. **The entity's policy of requiring collateral or other security to support financial instruments subject to credit risk**, a brief description of any collateral, and information about the entity's access to the collateral;

4. **The entity's policy of entering into master netting arrangements to reduce the credit risk associated with financial instruments**, a brief description of any such arrangements, and the extent to which such arrangements would reduce the entity's maximum risk of loss.

III. **Market Risk Disclosure Recommendations**

A. **Market risk disclosures for financial instruments are NOT required**, but are encouraged.

B. **Market risk** is the possibility of loss from changes in market value due to changes in economic circumstances, not necessarily due to the failure of another party.

C. **Entities are encouraged to disclose quantitative information about the market risk of financial instruments**, including the following possible disclosures:

1. More details about current position and related period activity;

2. Hypothetical effects on income of different changes in market prices;

3. An analysis of interest rate repricing or maturity dates;

4. Duration of financial instruments;

5. The entity's value at risk from derivatives.

IV. Other Disclosures

A. Qualitative Disclosures

1. Except for disclosures related to concentrations of credit risk, GAAP does not require substantive qualitative disclosures about financial instruments.

2. Under SEC requirements, SEC registrants are required to provide qualitative disclosures about:

   a. Market risk;

   b. Interest rate risk;

   c. Foreign currency risk;

   d. Commodity price risk;

   e. Similar risks.

3. The SEC qualitative disclosures are provided in management's discussion and analysis, and not in the financial statements or notes thereto.

B. Quantitative Disclosures

1. Except for disclosures related to concentrations of credit risk, required quantitative disclosures about financial instruments under GAAP are nominal.

2. Under SEC requirements, SEC registrants are required to provide quantitative disclosures only about financial instrument market risk , and those disclosures are in management's discussion and analysis, not in the financial statements or notes thereto.

C. Class Disclosures -- Under SEC requirements, SEC registrants are required to provide separate presentation in the balance sheet of financial instruments by class; however, there is no comparable requirement under GAAP for entities that are not SEC registrants.

Derivatives and Hedging

Derivatives Introduction

This lesson defines derivatives and provides guidance on recognition and measurement. Specifically, it identifies the elements necessary for a financial instrument to be a derivative, gives examples of common derivatives and items that are not derivatives, and explains the concept of embedded derivatives. The general recognition requirement applicable to all derivatives is also presented.

After studying this lesson you should be able to:

1. *Define and describe derivatives.*

2. *Identify common derivatives and contracts that are not derivatives for accounting purposes.*

3. *Determine when a contract includes a derivative embedded in it.*

4. *Describe the general recognition requirement applicable to all derivatives.*

I. **Definitions**

   A. **A "derivative" -- Is a financial instrument (or other contract) with all three of the following elements**

      1. **It has one or more** *underlyings*, **and one or more** *notional amounts* **--** (or payment provisions if -> then), and

      2. **It requires no initial net investment --** Or one that is smaller than would be required for other types of similar contracts, and

      3. **Its terms require or permit a net settlement --** i.e., it can be settled for cash or an asset readily convertible to cash in lieu of physical delivery of the subject matter of the contract.

   B. **An "underlying" is a specified price, rate, or other variable --** e.g., a stock price or index, a commodity price or index, an interest rate or index, a foreign exchange rate or index, etc.

   C. **A "notional amount" is a specified unit of measure --** e.g., shares of stock, pounds or bushels of a commodity, number of currency units, etc.

   D. **The value or settlement amount -- of a derivative is the amount determined by the multiplication (or other arithmetic calculation) of the notional amount and the underlying.** For example, shares of stock times the price per share.

II. **Derivative Examples --** The following contracts are examples of common derivatives.

   A. **Option contracts --** e.g., a stock option that requires the maker to deliver shares of stock at a later time in exchange for a fixed - option - price. The value of the option contract is a function of market price of the stock (compared to the option or strike price) and the number of shares.

   B. **Futures contracts --** Made through a clearinghouse (e.g., to deliver or receive a commodity or foreign currency in the future at a price set at the present).

   C. **Forward contracts --** Not made through a clearinghouse (e.g., like a futures contract, but made directly between contracting parties).

   D. **Swap contracts --** (e.g., an agreement to exchange currencies, debt securities, etc. For example, swap fixed rate debt for variable rate debt).

   E. **Contracts with characteristics comparable --** With those in the above listed contracts should be accounted for as derivative contracts.

III. **Items Not Derivatives** -- The following contracts are not derivatives for accounting purposes:

    A. Normal purchases and sales contracts (for something other than a financial instrument);

    B. Regular security trades;

    C. Traditional life insurance and property and casualty insurance contracts;

    D. Investments in life insurance;

    E. Contracts indexed to a company's own stock;

    F. Contracts issued in connection with stock-based compensation arrangements;

    G. Contracts to enter into a business combination at a future date;

    H. Other contracts as listed in FASB #133 (as amended).

IV. **Recognition and Measurement** -- **All derivative instruments must be *recognized as either an asset* (contractual right) *or a liability* (contractual obligation) and *measured at fair value.***

    A. The measurement of derivatives at (changing) fair values will result in gains and losses.

    B. The accounting treatment of the resulting gains and losses depends on whether or not the derivative has been designated (and qualifies) as a hedge and, if so, the purpose of the hedge.

V. **Embedded Derivative Instruments**

    A. A host contract (debt instrument, lease or equity instrument) may have a derivative "embedded" into the contract.

        1. An embedded derivative exists when the host contract contains a term or component that behaves like a derivative.

        2. The instrument containing both the host contract and the embedded derivative is called a hybrid instrument.

    B. An embedded derivative should be separated from the host contract (the hybrid contract should be bifurcated) and accounted for as a separate derivative instrument if, and only if, it meets all of the following requirements:

        1. The economic characteristics and risks of the embedded derivative are not clearly and closely related to the characteristics and risks of the host contract (Example: debt instrument that is convertible into a fixed number of the debtor's common stock; changes in the fair value of the debt element and the potential equity interest are not clearly and closely related);

        2. The hybrid instrument (host contact with derivative instrument) is not itself remeasured to fair value with changes reported in current income as they occur;

        3. As a separate instrument, the embedded instrument would meet the requirements of a derivative instrument.

    C. If a single host-contract contains more than one embedded derivative that meets the requirements to be accounted for as a separate derivative instrument, those embedded derivatives must be bundled together and treated as a single, compound embedded derivative which is accounted for separately.

    D. When an embedded derivative is separated from its host contract, the carrying value of the host contract (before bifurcation) is allocated between the embedded derivative and the host contract as follows:

        1. The derivative is initially recorded at its fair value.

2. The difference between the carrying value of the hybrid contract and the fair value of the derivative element is the initial value of the remaining host contract.

E. The host contract, without the embedded derivative, will be accounted for based on GAAP applicable to that type of instrument.

VI. Accounting for Derivatives Not Designated for Hedge Accounting

A. In this case, the derivative (contract) is not intended to hedge (offset) a separate risk or does not meet the accounting requirements to qualify as a hedge. For example, the derivative (e.g., a stock option contract) may have been entered into for speculative purposes (i.e., to make a profit).

B. **Initial Recognition**

1. An acquired contract that is a derivative instrument is initially measured and recorded at the then-current fair value.

2. Sample entry, assuming the acquisition of a derivative asset with value at the date of acquisition:

DR: Investment in Derivative
     CR: Cash (or other compensation)

C. **Subsequent Measurement and Recognition --** Changes in the fair value of these derivatives result in:

1. **Adjusting the carrying value of the derivative instrument to current fair value** (i.e., increase or decrease an asset or a liability); and

2. **Recognizing the related gain or loss in current income**.

D. Below is a brief description of the value components of options. Options have both intrinsic value (strike price - market price) and time value (option value - intrinsic value). Option can also be "in-the-money" or "out-of-the-money."

1. **Options:**

   a. Call - right to buy --- A call is in-the-money when the strike price less than the spot price

   b. Put - right to sell --- A put is in-the-money when the strike price is greater than the spot

   c. Assume: stock with a $30 market value has an at-the-money option with a strike price of $30 (market = strike so the entire option value at the time of purchase is time value - this is an "at-the-money" option) and this option sells for $2 and is good for 60 days.

	Market price $35	Market price $25
Call (right to buy)	In-the-money	Out-of-the-money
Put (right to sell)	Out-of-the-money	In-the-money

   d. Option value = Intrinsic value + time value. In the table below assume that the option prices is quoted to be $8 per option.

   e. Intrinsic value = In the money (ITM) value

   See the following table.

	Option value = (quoted value)	Intrinsic Value + (ITM value)	Time value (quoted value - ITM)
Call (right to buy)	8	5 (35 Market - 30 Strike)	3
	8	0 (25 Market - 30 Strike)	8
Put (right to sell)	8	0 (35 Market - 30 Strike)	8
	8	5 (25 Market - 30 Strike)	3

  f. The accounting for the intrinsic value and time value can be different depending on how the derivative is used. Time value is associated with the time value of money or the anticipated passage of time - where intrinsic value is value associated with the amount of benefit that is associated with the derivative terms relative to the market price.

 2. Futures and Forwards

  a. Time value for futures and forwards is most commonly calculated as the time value of money.

E. The following simplified example illustrates the accounting for a derivative held for speculative purposes (i.e., to make a profit).

> **Example:**
> On December 1, 2010, Echo, Inc. purchased options to buy (a call option) 1,000 shares of Levy, Inc. in 60 days at a strike price of $45 per share when Levy's stock was selling for $43 per share in the market. Echo's purchase of the options was based on its intent to earn a profit on expected short-term increases in the market price of Levy's stock. On December 31, 2010, Echo's stock was selling in the market for $46 per share.
>
> Because the options have a strike price of $45 per share, Echo can purchase 1,000 shares of Levy from the option counterparty for $45 per share, even though the stock is selling in the market for $46 per share. Thus, on December 31 the options have a fair value of $1,000 (1,000 options x ($46 - $45) = $1,000).
>
> 1. Echo would make the following entry as of December 31, 2010:
>
>   DR: Stock Options (market price > strike price) $1,000
>
>   CR: Gain on Stock Options $1,000
>
> 2. The gain would be recognized in current income.

VII. Hedging

A. Hedging is a risk management strategy -- Which involves using offsetting (or counter) transactions or positions so that a loss on one transaction or position would be offset (at least in part) by a gain on another transaction or position (and vice versa).

1. You would "hedge a bet" by offsetting a possible loss (from betting on one team to win) by also betting on the other team to win.

2. You would hedge against a possible loss in inventory value by entering into a contract to sell comparable inventory at a fixed price (set now) for future delivery.

B. For accounting purposes, derivative financial instruments that meet certain criteria may be used as hedges of the risks associated with certain economic undertakings and account balances.

C. For accounting purposes, nonderivative financial instruments may not be used to hedge an asset, liability, unrecognized firm commitment, or forecasted transaction, except that a nonderivative instrument denominated in a foreign currency may be used to hedge the foreign currency exposure of an unrecognized firm commitment to be settled in a foreign currency or a net investment in a foreign operation. (Certain concepts used in this item are developed in the immediate following lessons dealing with hedging.)

Hedging Introduction

This lesson makes the distinction between hedging and hedge accounting. There are three broad categories of hedge accounting. This lesson identifies those categories and the documentation required in order to get hedge accounting. In addition, this lesson describes the elements in a hedging relationship, the general kinds of risk that may be hedged, the specific risk components that may be hedged for accounting purposes, and the items and instruments that cannot be used for accounting hedges .

After studying this lesson, you should be able to:

1. *Identify the possible uses of derivatives for accounting purposes.*

2. *Identify and describe the basic elements of a hedge relationship.*

3. *Identify the basic kinds of hedges for accounting purposes.*

4. *Identify the specific kinds of risks that can be hedged for accounting purposes.*

5. *Identify items and instruments that cannot be used for accounting hedges.*

I. **Hedging**

   A. Hedging means that the entity utilizes a derivative financial instrument to offset the risk related to a transaction, item or event:

      1. **Natural or economic hedges --** A derivative can be used as a natural hedge with no special hedge accounting treatment. In a natural hedge, both the underlying risk and the derivative instrument are marked-to-market value through earnings. The changes in the value of the hedged risk and derivative offset - to the extent these match, there is no impact on net income.

      2. **Hedge accounting --** If certain conditions are met, a derivative may be specifically designated as a hedging instrument and special hedge accounting can be used. The gain (loss) on the derivative (the hedging instrument) is used to match the loss (gain) on the hedged item.

II. **Formal Documentation Requirements**

   A. In order to qualify for the special hedge accounting, there must be formal documentation of the hedged item (or hedgeable risk), the hedging instrument, how effectiveness will be assessed, and how ineffectiveness will be measured.

   B. The formal documentation must be made with enough specificity and clarity that an independent third party could understand and identity the hedging relationship and reperform the effectiveness tests and measurement of ineffectiveness. All documentation must be contemporaneous - that is the documentation must be completed at the time the hedge is created. The following items must be documented:

      1. The risk management objective and strategy:

         a. The nature of the risk being hedged;

         b. How the hedging instrument (derivative) is expected to reduce the risk exposure.

      2. The hedging relationship:

         a. Hedged risk, hedged item, and hedging instrument.

      3. How effectiveness will be assessed and the method to measure ineffectiveness.

III. **Hedge Elements --** Hedging involves two basic elements; those elements are:

A. **Hedged item** -- The recognized asset, recognized liability, commitment, or planned transaction that is at risk of loss; it is the possible loss on the hedged item that is hedged.

B. **Hedging instrument** -- The contract or other arrangement that is entered into to mitigate or eliminate the risk of loss associated with the hedged item.

IV. Types of Hedge Accounting

    A. Hedge accounting essential falls into to two broad categories:

        1. **Fair value risk** -- The risk of loss due to changes in fair value.

        2. **Cash flow risk** -- The risk of loss due to changes in cash flows.

    B. Risks identified as foreign currency risks or net investment in foreign operations risks embody specific forms of fair value and/or cash flow risks, some with unique accounting treatment.

V. Items Eligible for Hedge Accounting -- For accounting purposes, there are risks that can be designated as the hedged item.

    A. For financial assets and financial liabilities the following risks can be hedged:

        1. Commodity price risk;

        2. Interest rate risk, where the interest rate being hedged is a benchmark rate;

        3. Foreign exchange risk;

        4. Credit risk (except not for investments in available-for-sale securities).

VI. Items Not Eligible for Hedge Accounting -- For accounting purposes, a number of items (recognized assets/liabilities, commitments, planned transactions, etc.) are specifically excluded from being designated as a hedged item. Those include, among other, the following:

    A. An investment accounted for using the equity method of accounting;

    B. A firm commitment to carry out a business combination;

    C. A noncontrolling interest in a subsidiary;

    D. Transactions between entities included in consolidated statements, except for foreign-currency-denominated forecasted intra-entity transactions;

    E. Transactions with shareholders as shareholders (e.g., projected purchase of treasury stock or payment of dividends);

    F. The risk of changes in fair value of held-to-maturity securities due to changes in interest rates (interest rate risk);

    G. Part of the term (or life) of a hedged item (e.g., cannot hedge the first five years of a 10-year fixed rate bond investment).

VII. Summary of Hedged Item and Fair Value Versus Cash Flow Hedge Accounting

    See the following example.

Item	Fair Value Hedge	Cash Flow Hedge
A recognized asset or liability	Hedges the risk of changes in the fair value of the hedged item	Hedges the risk related to the cash flows of the hedged item
Firm commitment	Hedges the risk related to the fair value changes of the commitment. The firm commitment is recognized as an asset or liability if hedged.	Not applicable
Forecasted transaction	Not applicable	Hedges the cash flows related to a forecasted transaction. The forecasted transaction must be specifically identifiable, probable, and with a party external to the reporting entity.
Foreign currency	1. Hedge of unrecognized firm commitment, denominated in a foreign currency.[3] 2. Hedge of available-for-sale securities, denominated in a foreign currency.	3. Hedge of a net investment in foreign operations: include changes in fair value as other comprehensive income. 4. Hedge of foreign currency denominated forecasted transactions.
Gain or loss on hedged item	Included in net income [1]	Ineffective portion in net income Effective portion in other comprehensive income [2]
Gain or loss on hedging instrument	Included in net income [1]	Ineffective portion in net income Effective portion in other comprehensive income[2]

[1] Gains and losses on hedged asset/liability and the hedging instrument shall be recognized in current earnings. To the extent that the hedge is effective, the gains and losses will offset. To the extent the hedge is ineffective, the effect will show in current earnings as a gain or loss with no offset.

[2] The effective portion of the hedge is reported in other comprehensive income (check to make sure of linking of hedged asset/liability and hedging instrument; i.e., that value of both are valued from same index or rate). The ineffective portion is reported in earnings immediately.

[3] A foreign currency denominated firm commitment has two risks: 1) the risk associated with the change in the price of the item associated with the firm commitment (a fixed price risk - therefore a fair value hedge) and 2) the risk associated with the change in the exchange rate for the value of the foreign currency (a floating price risk - therefore a cash flow hedge). This distinction is discussed further in the lesson in the foreign currency section on hedging firm commitments.

VIII. Two Common Transactions to Which Hedge Accounting is Applied

A. Forecasted transaction

1. A transaction that is expected to occur for which there is no firm commitment. Because no transaction or event has yet occurred, when the transaction or event does occur, it will be at the prevailing market price. (ASC 815)

2. The forecasted transaction must be:

   a. Specifically identifiable, probable to occur (ASC 450), with an external party, and does not involve future assets/liabilities that will be remeasured thru earnings.

3. Accounting for a forecasted transaction - unhedged:

   a. A forecasted item is recorded at the market value on the day the forecasted transaction occurs.

Example:

Assume that on May 1, the company anticipates the purchase of 1,000 barrels (bbls) of fuel oil in six months (November 1). The quantity of the fuel oil is what is normally used in the course of business. The company has not selected a specific vendor or set a price. The spot price of fuel oil on May 1 is $70 bbl and the spot price on November 1 is $85 bbl. No entry would be made at the forecast date or at any time during the forecast period. An entry is made on November 1 when the fuel oil is actually purchased. The entries would be:

Date	May 1	November 1	
Price	($70 bbl)	($85 bbl)	
Entry	No entry	Fuel Oil	$85,000
		Cash	$85,000

4. **Risk - cash flows --** The cash flows on November 1 are uncertain and have variability and are dependent on the price on November 1.

5. Benefits of a forecasted transaction:

   a. Flexibility with respect to vendor, price, quantity, quality, delivery specifics;

   b. Allows the company to complete due diligence on potential vendors;

   c. Allows the company to "shop around" on the days prior to the purchase;

   d. Increased possibility for price concessions in the days prior to the purchase (i.e., discounts and incentives);

   e. Prices may decrease and the purchase price will be lower.

6. Limitations of a forecasted transaction:

   a. Prices may increase;

   b. Shortage of supply and cannot obtain the fuel oil (or must obtain substandard quality);

   c. No opportunity to build a relationship with a single vendor.

B. **Firm commitment**

1. An agreement with an unrelated party that is binding on both parties and usually legally enforceable. The agreement usually specifies all significant terms (including quantity to be exchanged, fixed price, timing of the transaction) and includes a disincentive for nonperformance that is sufficiently large enough to make performance probable. (ASC 815)

2. Accounting for a firm commitment - unhedged:

   a. A firm commitment is also known as a purchase (or sales) commitment and is recorded at the commitment price on the date specified in the firm commitment.

Example:
Assume that on May 1, the company enters into a firm commitment with a specific vendor to purchase 1,000 barrels (bbls) of fuel oil in six months. The firm commitment specifies the quantity, quality, price and delivery terms. The firm commitment price agreed to on May 1 is $70 bbl with delivery on November 1. The spot price of fuel oil on May 1 is $70 bbl and the spot price on November 1 is $85 bbl. No entry would be made on the date of the firm commitment (May 1) or at any time during the firm commitment period. An entry is made on November 1 when the fuel oil is actually purchased and the fuel oil would be recorded at the firm commitment price. The entries are as follows:

Date	May 1	November 1	
Price	($70 bbl)	($85 bbl)	
Entry	No entry	Fuel Oil	$70,000
		Cash	$70,000

3. **Risk - fair value --** The fair value of the $70,000 contract goes up if the price goes up to $85 (because you can get the oil cheaper than the market price). The fair value of the contract goes down if the price goes down to $65 (because you have to pay a price higher than the market price).

4. Benefits of a firm commitment:

    a. Certainty with respect to vendor, price, quantity, quality, delivery specifics;

    b. Permits better budgeting;

    c. Allows the company to develop a relationship with a specific vendor;

    d. Increases the likelihood of obtaining the product if there is a shortage;

    e. Mitigates the risk of prices increasing.

5. Limitations of a firm commitment:

    a. Prices may decrease;

    b. Vendor may go bankrupt;

    c. Less opportunity to build relationships with other vendors;

    d. Cannot take advantage of last minute discounts.

IX. **Exclusions --** For accounting purposes, a number of instruments (contracts, options, etc.) are specifically excluded from being used as a hedging instrument. Those include, among other, the following:

A. A nonderivative instrument (e.g., U.S. Treasury note), except as permitted in certain intra-company cases for:

    1. Hedging changes in the fair value of an unrecognized firm commitment attributable to foreign currency exchange rates, or

    2. Hedging the foreign currency exposure of a net investment in a foreign operation.

B. Components of a compound derivative instrument used for different risks.

C. A hybrid financial instrument if:

    1. It is irrevocably elected to be measured in its entirety at fair value under the fair value option, or

    2. It has an embedded derivative that cannot be reliably identified and measured.

Fair Value Hedges

This lesson covers the accounting for fair value hedges. As the name implies, the purpose of this hedge is to offset changes in the fair value of the hedged item. This lesson will define fair value hedges, the requirements that must be met in order for a derivative to be treated as a fair value hedge, and the accounting treatment of derivatives and related hedged items in a fair value hedge.

After studying this lesson, you should be able to:

1. *Define a fair value hedge.*

2. *Describe the criteria that must be met for a derivative to qualify as a fair value hedge.*

3. *Describe the accounting for derivatives used as fair value hedges and for the related hedged item.*

4. *Record entries related to fair value hedges.*

5. *Describe the accounting when the requirements for a fair value hedge are no longer satisfied.*

I. **Accounting for Fair Value Hedges**

> **Definition:**
> *Fair Value Hedge:* The hedge of an exposure to changes in fair value of a (recognized) asset, liability, or an unrecognized firm commitment due to a particular risk. A fair value hedge converts a fixed price to a floating price.

1. For example, the use of a futures contract to hedge the fair value of a recognized asset or liability such as inventory.

2. A derivative can also be used to hedge the fair value of an **"unrecognized firm commitment"**. A firm commitment exists when an entity enters into a contract to buy or sell (i.e., a purchase commitment).

    a. Unhedged firm commitments are not recognized because the purchase has not yet occurred. Once the firm commitment is designated as the hedged item, the changes in the fair value of the firm commitment are recognized.

    b. A firm commitment to purchase an item is at a fixed price. The changes in the market price relative to the firm commitment price will increase or decrease the fair value of the firm commitment contract.

        i. For example: Assume a company has a firm commitment to purchase fuel oil at $60 barrel. If the market price of the fuel oil rises to $65 a barrel, the fair value of the firm commitment contract has increased because the company can buy the fuel oil at a price less than the market price. If the price of the fuel oil declines to $50 a barrel, then the fair value of the firm commitment contract will decrease because the company is locked into a price that is higher than the market price.

B. A derivative may be used to create a fair value hedge only if both the hedging instrument (the derivative) and the hedged item (asset, liability, or firm commitment) meet **certain criteria**, including:

1. At inception of the hedge there must be **formal documentation** of (1) the hedging relationship, (2) the objective and strategy for undertaking the hedge, (3) identification of

the hedging instrument and the hedged item, (4) the nature of the risk being hedged, (5) how effectiveness of the hedge will be assessed, and (6) when a firm commitment is the hedged item, how the related asset or liability will be recognized.

2. Both at inception of the hedge and on an ongoing basis, the hedge must be expected to be **highly effective** in offsetting changes in fair value of the hedged item, **with an assessment** of effectiveness required **when financial statements are prepared and at least every 3 months**.

3. The hedged item (1) is specifically identified as a recognized asset, liability, or firm commitment (or portion thereof), (2) presents exposure to changes in fair value that could affect reported income, (3) is not accounted for at fair value with changes reported in income, (4) not an investment accounted for using the equity method, (5) not a noncontrolling interest or an equity interest in a consolidated subsidiary and (6) if a debt security classified as held-to-maturity, the risk being hedged is the creditworthiness of the obligor (not the interest rate because the investor intends to hold to maturity).

C. **Additional Qualifications**

1. If the hedged item is interest rate risk, only a benchmark interest rate may be hedged. Only two interest rates are considered to be benchmark interest rates:

    a. Direct U.S. Treasury obligations.

    b. London Interbank Offer Rate (LIBOR)

2. If the hedged item is a nonfinancial asset or liability, the risk being hedged is the risk of change in the fair value of the entire hedged asset or liability, not a portion of the asset or liability.

D. **Changes** -- Changes in fair value of both the derivative qualifying as a fair value hedge (hedging instrument) and the asset, liability, or firm commitment being hedged (hedged item) are accounted for by:

1. **Adjusting the carrying amount of both the derivative and the hedged item to fair value**.

    a. If the hedged item is a firm commitment, a new asset or liability will have to be recognized on the balance sheet when the initial adjustment occurs.

    b. The amount of the adjustment to the hedged item becomes a part of the carrying amount of the item and is accounted for as such.

2. **Recognizing gains and losses from revaluing both the derivative and the hedged item** *in current income*.

    a. If the hedged item is normally adjusted through "other comprehensive income" (i.e., an available-for-sale investment), the change in fair value, if hedged, must be recognized in current income.

    b. To the extent the gain or loss on the hedging instrument offsets the loss or gain on the hedged item, the hedge is "effective." To the extent the gain or loss on the hedging instrument is more or less than that on the hedged item, the hedge is "ineffective" and will result in a net effect (gain or loss) on current income.

E. If the criteria for fair value hedges are no longer met, the derivative may no longer be accounted for as a hedge.

1. If the hedged item was an unrecognized firm commitment, the asset or liability created to account for its change in value must be written off and a corresponding gain or loss recognized in current income.

F. Hedged assets and liabilities should continue to be assessed for impairment.

G. **A hedge of a recognized asset or liability --** can be EITHER A CASH FLOW HEDGE OR A FAIR VALUE HEDGE.

    1. To qualify as a cash flow hedge, the hedging instrument must completely offset the variability in (dollar) cash flows associated with the receivable or payable.

    2. If the instrument does not qualify as a cash flow hedge, or if management so designates, the hedging instrument will be a fair value hedge.

H. **Accounting Treatment --** The accounting for the hedge of a recognized asset or liability would depend on the designated purpose of the hedge - whether to hedge cash flow or to hedge fair value.

    1. If to hedge cash flow, the treatment would include:

        a. Adjusting the hedged item (receivable or payable) to fair value each balance sheet date using the spot exchange rate and recognizing the change in fair value as a foreign currency gain or loss in current income.

        b. Adjusting the hedging instrument to fair value each balance sheet date using the forward exchange rate and recognizing the change in fair value as follows:

            i. To the extent the change in fair value of the hedging instrument and the change in the fair value of the hedged item are different there will be a net effect in current income.

            See the following example.

Example:

Assume that the company enters into a firm commitment with a supplier of cotton on January 1 to buy 1,000,000 tons of cotton on March 31 for $42/ton. The terms and conditions of the firm commitment meet all the required criteria. In order to protect against the risk of prices decreasing in the first quarter, the company enters into a futures contract on January 1 to sell cotton on March 31 for $42/ton. The futures contract is purchased "at-the-money" and a margin account is established with the broker. Therefore, there is no cash outlay for the purchase of the futures contract. The example below ignores the time value of money (the ineffective portion of the hedge). The table below shows the entries that would be made at the date the transaction is initiated (January 1), at an interim date (February 28 is an assumed date), and the settlement date (March 31).

	Jan 1, 20X9	Feb 28, 20X9	Mar 31, 20X9
Spot Price per ton	$40	$38	$37
Futures rate per ton	$42	$41	$37
Entries with Broker for Futures Contract	none	Futures Contract 1,000,000 Gain/loss (I/S) 1,000,000 ($41 - $42) x 1,000,000	Futures Contract 4,000,000 Gain/loss (I/S) 4,000,000 ($37 - $41) x 1,000,000 Cash 5,000,000 Futures Contract 5,000,000
Entries for Firm Commitment with Supplier	none	Gain/loss (I/S) 1,000,000 Firm Commitment 1,000,000 ($41 - $42) x 1,000,000	Gain/loss (I/S) 4,000,000 Firm Commitment 4,000,000 ($37 - $41) x 1,000,000 Inventory – cotton 37,000,000 Firm Commitment 5,000,000 Cash 42,000,000
Impact on Balance Sheet	none	Increase assets 1,000,000 Increase liabilities 1,000,000	Decrease assets 1,000,000 Decrease liabilities 1,000,000
Impact on Income Statement	none	none	none

After production and sale of the end product, the inventory is reduced and cost of goods sold is recorded. Assume that the product is sold on June 1, 20X9. The following entries would be made on June 1.

Cost of goods sold	37,000,000	
Inventory		37,000,000
(to record CGS)		

I. Items to note:

1. The firm commitment is recognized and marked-to-market using the changes in the futures rate.

2. The futures contract is marked-to-market using the changes in the futures rate.

3. The gains and losses perfectly off set each other. If there were any ineffectiveness, it would be a residual amount reflected in earnings.

4. The value of the inventory is reduced for the amount of deferred gains or losses in the firm commitment account.

5. The fair value hedge converted the fixed price of the firm commitment ($42/ton) to a floating price on March 31 ($42/ton paid less $5/ton received from the futures contract = $37/ton which was the March 31 spot price).

Cash Flow Hedges

This lesson covers the accounting for a cash flow hedge. As the name of the use implies, the purpose of this hedge is to reduce the variability related to uncertain future cash flows. This lesson defines cash flow hedges, the requirements that must be met in order for cash flow hedge accounting, and the accounting for the derivative and related hedged item.

After studying this lesson, you should be able to:

1. *Define a cash flow hedge.*

2. *Describe the criteria that must be met for a derivative to qualify as a cash flow hedge.*

3. *Describe the accounting for derivatives used as cash flow hedges and for the related hedged item.*

4. *Record entries related to cash flow hedges.*

5. *Describe the accounting when the requirements for a cash flow hedge are no longer satisfied.*

I. Accounting for Cash Flow Hedges

> **Definition:**
> *Cash Flow Hedge*: The hedge of an exposure to variability (changes) in the cash flow associated with a (recognized) asset, liability, or a forecasted transaction due to a particular risk. A cash flow hedge converts a floating price to a fixed price.

1. For example, the use of an interest-rate swap to hedge the cash outflow from variable-rate debt, or the use of a futures contract to hedge the cash inflow from a forecasted sale.

2. A **"forecasted transaction"** is a planned or expected transaction with a third party, but for which there is not yet a firm commitment and there are not yet any established rights or obligations associated with the planned transaction.

B. A derivative may be accounted for as a cash flow hedge only if both the hedging instrument (the derivative) and the hedged item (asset, liability, or forecasted transaction) meet **certain criteria**, including:

1. At inception of the hedge, there must be **formal documentation** of (1) the hedging relationship, (2) the objective and strategy for undertaking the hedge, (3) identification of the hedging instrument and the hedged item, (4) the nature of the risk being hedged, and (5) how effectiveness of the hedge will be assessed.

2. Both at inception of the hedge and on an ongoing basis, the hedge must be expected to **be highly effective** in offsetting change in cash flow of the hedged item, with an assessment of effectiveness required when financial statements are prepared and at least every 3 months.

3. A forecasted transaction can be hedged only if it is (1) specifically identified as a single transaction or group of individual transactions with the same risk exposure, (2) probable of occurring, (3) with an external party (except for certain intercompany hedges), (4) capable of affecting cash flows that would affect earnings, and (5) not for the acquisition

of an asset or the incurrence of a liability, which is accounted for at fair value with the change reported in current income.

C. Additional Qualifications

1. If the hedged item is the cash flow from a forecasted transaction related to an investment classified as held-to-maturity, the risk being hedged is the risk of changes in cash flow attributable to credit risk, foreign exchange risk, or both.

2. If the hedged item is the cash flow from a forecasted transaction, it cannot involve:

    a. A business combination;

    b. A parent's equity interest in a subsidiary;

    c. An entity's own equity instruments.

D. Changes in fair value of derivatives qualifying as cash flow hedges (hedging instrument) are accounted for by

1. Determining for each period the change in (1) the fair value of the derivative (hedging instrument) and (2) the present value of the cash flows associated with the asset, liability, or forecasted transaction being hedged (hedged item).

2. Determine for each period (1) the cumulative change in the fair value of the derivative and (2) the cumulative change in the present value of the cash flows associated with the hedged item.

3. Recognize the change in the fair value of the derivative for the period (write up or write down the derivative).

4. Recognize as an item of "Other Comprehensive Income" an amount equal to the (cumulative) change in the present value of cash flows associated with the hedged item. This is the **"effective portion" of the hedge**; the extent to which the change in the value of the hedge offsets the change in value of the hedged item.

5. Recognize as a gain or loss in current income the amount by which the (cumulative) change in the derivative is different from the (cumulative) change in the present value of the cash flows associated with the hedged item. This is the **"ineffective portion" of the hedge**; the extent to which the hedge is more or less than the change in value of the hedged item.

    See the following example.

> **Example:** The following two period example illustrates the process for determining and recording (1) the change in the fair value of a derivative that hedges the cash flow of a hedged item (asset, liability, or forecasted transaction), (2) the effective portion of the gain or loss on the hedge, and (3) the ineffective portion of the gain or loss on the hedge.
>
> Assume Alpha Company anticipates selling inventory (say, silver) to a third party two years in the future. To protect the cash value of that sale against future declines, Alpha enters into a futures contract to sell that inventory at a (futures) price set now. The relevant values, analysis, and entries are as follows:

	HEDGING INSTRUMENT		HEDGED ITEM PV of Expected			
	Derivative Fair Value		Cash Flows		Hedge Allocation	
End of Period	Period Change	Cumulative Change	Period Change	Cumulative Change	Effective Portion	Ineffective Portion
1	$150	$150	$(148)	$(148)	$148	$2 (Gain)
2	147	297	(151)	(299)	149	2 (Loss)

Period 1 Entry: DR: Futures Contract (Derivative) $150

    CR: Other Comprehensive Income $148

        Gain on Cash Value Hedge   2

Period 2 Entry: DR: Futures Contract $147

    Loss on Cash Value Hedge   2

    CR: Other Comprehensive Income $149

E. The effective portion of cash flow hedges (deferred gains/losses) are reported as a component of **"Other Comprehensive Income"** in the Statement of Comprehensive Income for the period and in **"Accumulated Other Comprehensive Income"** in the Balance Sheet **until the period(s) in which the hedged item affects income**. For example:

 1. The effective portion of a hedge of a forecasted sale (example above) would be reclassified to (and recognized in) income in the period of the sale.

 2. The effective portion of a hedge of a forecasted purchase of a depreciable asset would be reclassified to (and recognized in) income over the periods depreciation expense is taken on the asset.

F. If the criteria for cash flow hedges are no longer met, the derivative may no longer be accounted for as a hedge.

 1. The deferred gain or loss remaining in accumulated other comprehensive income should continue to be reclassified to (and recognized in) income in the period(s) in which the hedged items affect income.

 2. If a hedged forecasted transactions is no longer expected to occur, the deferred gain or loss in accumulated other comprehensive income should be reclassified to (and recognized in) income immediately.

G. Assets and liabilities for which related cash flows have been hedged should continue to be assessed for impairment.

 1. If an impairment loss is recognized, any deferred gain in accumulated other comprehensive income should be reclassified (recognized) to offset the loss.

H. A hedge of a recognized asset or liability can be EITHER A CASH FLOW HEDGE OR A FAIR VALUE HEDGE.

    1. To qualify as a cash flow hedge, the hedging instrument must completely offset the variability in (dollar) cash flows associated with the receivable or payable.

    2. If the instrument does not qualify as a cash flow hedge, or if management so designates, the hedging instrument will be a fair value hedge.

I. Accounting Treatment -- The accounting for the hedge of a recognized asset or liability would depend on the designated purpose of the hedge - whether to hedge cash flow or to hedge fair value.

    1. If to hedge cash flow, the treatment would include:

        a. Adjusting the hedged item (receivable or payable) to fair value each balance sheet date using the spot exchange rate and recognizing the change in fair value as a foreign currency gain or loss in current income.

        b. Adjusting the hedging instrument to fair value each balance sheet date using the forward exchange rate and recognizing the change in fair value as follows:

            i. An amount up to the amount equal to the gain or loss recognized on the hedged item is recognized as a foreign currency loss or gain in current income to offset the gain or loss on the hedged item.

            ii. An amount up to an amount equal to the current period amortization of any premium or discount on the hedging instrument is recognized in current income (income or expense).

            iii. The balance, if any, is recognized in other comprehensive income for the current period.

    See the following example.

Example:

Cash Flow hedge of a forecasted transaction: Assume at the beginning of the year the company anticipates the production needs and will need 1,000,000 tons of cotton at the end of each quarter. In order to protect against the risk of prices increasing in the first quarter, the company enters into a futures contract on January 1 to buy cotton on March 31 for $42/ton. The futures contract is purchased "at-the-money" and a margin account is established with the broker. Therefore, there is no cash outlay for the purchase of the futures contract. This example ignores the time value of money (the ineffective portion of the hedge).

	Jan 1, 20X9	Feb 28, 20X9	Mar 31, 20X9
Spot Price per ton	$40	$46	$44
Futures rate per ton	$42	$45	$44

Entries with Broker for Futures Contract	none	Futures Contract 3,000,000
		  G/L on Futures (OCI) 3,000,000*
		  ($42-$45) x 1,000,000
			G/L on Futures (OCI) 1,000,000*
			  Futures Contract
			  1,000,000
			  ($45 - $44) x 1,000,000
			
			Cash 2,000,000
			  Futures Contract
			  2,000,000
			  ($42 - $44) x 1,000,000

Entries for Forecasted Transaction with Supplier	none	none	Inventory – cotton 44,000,000
			  Cash
			  44,000,000
			  ($44 x 1,000,000)

Impact on Balance Sheet	none	Increase assets 3,000,000 Increase equity 3,000,000	Decrease assets 1,000,000 Decrease equity 1,000,000
Impact on Income Statement	none	none	none

* The unrealized gain or loss in OCI remains in that account until the inventory is sold. After production and sale of the end product, the inventory is reduced and cost of goods sold is recorded. Cost of goods sold is then adjusted for the cumulated gain or loss in OCI. Assume that the product is sold on June 1, 20X9. The following entries would be made on June 1.

Cost of goods sold 44,000,000   Gain/loss on futures (OCI) 2,000,000

 Inventory   44,000,000   Cost of goods sold   2,000,000

  (to record CGS)   (to close OCI into CGS)

II. Items to note:

A. The forecasted transaction is not recognized until the item is purchased.

B. The futures contract is marked-to-market using the changes in the futures rate.

C. The gains and losses on the futures contract are deferred into OCI until the item that is hedged effects earnings.

D. The value of the cost of goods sold is reduced for the amount of deferred gains or losses once the inventory is sold.

E. The cash flow hedge converted the floating price of the forecasted transaction (unknown) to a fixed price on Jan 1 ($42/ ton the price of the futures contract). Total cash paid on March 31 is $42/ton (the spot price) = $44/ton (the spot price paid) less the cash received on the futures contract $2/ton.

Foreign Currency Hedges

This lesson covers the final use of derivatives for accounting purposes - as a hedge of amounts denominated (to be settled) in a foreign currency. As the name of the use implies, the purpose of these derivatives is to offset changes in the dollar value of expected transactions, commitments, transactions and balances measured in a foreign currency. This lesson identifies and describes the alternative foreign currency hedges; lessons included in the "Foreign Currency Accounting" topic cover these hedges in detail.

After studying this lesson, you should be able to:

1. *Define a foreign currency hedge.*

2. *Identify and describe the specific kinds of foreign currency items that may be hedged.*

3. *Describe the differences between U.S. GAAP and IFRS for this lesson.*

I. **Accounting for Derivatives that Qualify as Foreign Currency Hedges and Other Eligible Contracts used as Foreign Currency Hedges** -- (This is a summary introduction; the full details of such hedges are covered in the lessons dealing with "Foreign Currency Hedging.")

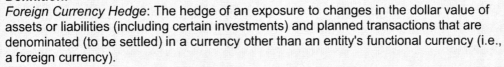

> **Definition:**
> *Foreign Currency Hedge*: The hedge of an exposure to changes in the dollar value of assets or liabilities (including certain investments) and planned transactions that are denominated (to be settled) in a currency other than an entity's functional currency (i.e., a foreign currency).

A. An entity may **hedge foreign currency exposure of** the following kinds:

1. **Forecasted foreign-currency-denominated transactions --** (including inter-company transactions). The risk being hedged is the risk that exchange rate changes will have on the **cash flow** from non-firm but planned transactions to be settled in a foreign currency. For example, the dollar value of royalty revenue **forecasted to be received** in a foreign currency from a foreign entity, including a related entity.

2. **Unrecognized foreign-currency-denominated firm commitments --** The risk being hedged is the risk that exchange rate changes will have on the **fair value** or_**cash flow** of firm commitments for a future sale or purchase to be settled in a foreign currency. For example, a commitment (contract) to purchase custom-built equipment from a foreign manufacturer with payment to be made in a foreign currency.

3. **Foreign-currency-denominated recognized assets --** (e.g., receivables) **or liabilities** (e.g., payables). The risk being hedged is the **fair value** or **cash flow**, measured in dollars of:

   a. An already booked asset or liability to be settled in a foreign currency (fair value or cash flow hedge), or

   b. A forecasted functional-currency-equivalent cash flow associated with a recognized asset or liability (cash flow hedge), or

   c. An investment denominated in a foreign currency.

4. **Investments in available-for-sale securities --** The risk being hedged is the risk that exchange rate changes will have on the

> **Note:**
> The dollar value of or cash flows from such assets and liabilities may change as a result of changes in the foreign exchange rate between recognition and settlement of the asset or liability.

fair value of investments in available-for-sale securities (debt or equity) denominated in a foreign currency.

5. **Net investments in foreign operations --** The risk being hedged is the risk that exchange rate changes will have on the **fair (economic) value** of financial statements converted from a foreign currency to the functional currency. In this case, the accounting for the hedging instrument (derivative) must be treated like the accounting for the translation adjustment for the associated foreign investment.

B. The accounting treatments for these foreign currency-hedging purposes generally are consistent with the fair value and cash flow hedge treatments described in earlier lessons and are discussed in detail in the subsequent material on "Foreign Currency Accounting."

Effectiveness and Disclosure

In order to qualify for hedge accounting, the company must document how it will assess hedge effectiveness and measure hedge ineffectiveness. In addition, this lesson presents the disclosure requirements associated with hedging.

After studying this lesson, you should be able to:

1. *Identify and describe how effectiveness is assessed when hedging is used.*

2. *Describe the ways by which ineffectiveness can be measured.*

3. *Describe the treatment of ineffectiveness resulting from the use of hedging.*

4. *Describe the short-cut method of effectiveness assessment.*

5. *Describe the most significant disclosures required when hedging is used.*

I. **Effectiveness**

   A. There are two terms associated with "effectiveness." **Assessing hedge effectiveness** is the necessary criteria in order to get hedge accounting. To qualify for hedge accounting, the hedging instrument must be highly effective, both at inception of the hedge and on an on-going basis, in offsetting changes in the fair value or the cash flows of the hedge item. This correlation must be between 80 - 125% in order for the hedge to qualify for hedge accounting.

   B. If the hedge is determined to be effective, and hedge accounting is permitted. Then the ineffective portion of the hedge needs to be measured - **measuring ineffectiveness**. The measurement of the ineffectiveness is important because in hedge accounting the ineffective portion of the hedge is accounted for separate from the effective portion of the hedge.

II. **Assessing hedge effectiveness** -- Hedge effectiveness is assessed in two stages.

   A. **Prospective consideration** -- A forward-looking assessment of the entity's expectations that a planned hedging relationship will be highly effective over future periods in achieving offsetting changes in fair value or cash flows.

      1. The prospective assessment should consider all reasonable possible changes in fair value and/or cash flows of both the hedged item and the hedging instrument.

      2. The prospective assessment can be based on:

         a. Regression analysis or other statistical analysis of past changes in fair value or cash flows.

         b. Qualitative assessment of the extent to which the critical terms (e.g., nominal amounts, expiration date, etc.) of the hedging instrument and the hedged item match.

      3. Generally, the prospective assessment involves a probability-weighted analysis of the possible changes in fair value and/or cash flows.

   B. **Retrospective evaluation** -- When a relationship between an instrument and an item qualifies as a hedge for accounting purposes, the relationship must continue to be assessed for effectiveness and measured for ineffectiveness whenever financial statements are reported, and at least every three months.

      1. A single method of evaluating effectiveness or measuring ineffectiveness is not specified by GAAP.

      2. The retrospective evaluation can be accomplished using a number of approaches, including:

a. A dollar-offset approach - an assessment based on how well the dollar change in the hedging instrument actually has offset the dollar change in the hedged item, with the assessment performed either on a period-by-period basis or on a cumulative basis.

b. Regression analysis or other statistical analysis.

c. Qualitative assessment.

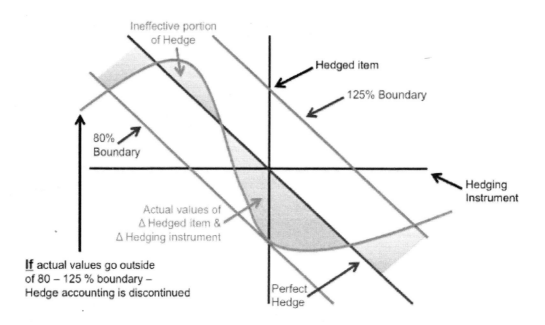

III. Effectiveness testing

A. In order to qualify for hedge accounting, the hedge must be "highly effective." Highly effective means the correlation between the hedged item and the hedging instrument must be between 80 and 125%. In the graph above the boundaries of 80 - 125% indicated that the plotted changes in the value of the hedged item and the hedging instrument need to fall within these boundaries. As long as the change in the hedged item and hedging instrument is between the boundaries of 80% and 125% the hedge is permitted. If the change is outside of this range (shown at either end of the curve) hedge accounting is no longer permitted.

> **Note:**
> It is becoming very difficult to qualify for the short cut method and therefore it is becoming more and more rare in practice.

B. Effectiveness is the change in the fair value of the derivative divided by the change in the value of the hedged item.

$$\underline{\Delta \text{ FV derivative}} = 80 - 125\%$$
$$\Delta \text{ FV hedged risk}$$

C. Effectiveness of the hedge must be assessed as highly effective throughout its life with a review at least every three months (i.e., that hedging instrument gain or loss covers hedged item's loss or gain).

D. Measuring ineffectiveness -- The straight line through the axis of the above graph represents a "perfect hedge" where changes in the value of the hedged item and hedging instrument offset each other perfectly. Since very few circumstances will result in a perfect hedge, the ineffective part of the hedge must be measured and reported on the income statement. Ineffectiveness is the distance measured on the curved line to the straight line within the 80 - 12% boundaries. This area is designated with hatch marks to show what amount of the hedge is ineffective.

1. **Measuring ineffectiveness treatment** -- Ineffectiveness, as measured by the extent to which there is not an exact offset in the hedging relationship, must be included in earnings in the period of the ineffectiveness.

2. **Time value**

   a. In establishing its effectiveness assessment policy, an entity must specify whether or not all or a part of the time value of the hedging instrument will be included in the assessment.

   b. Any element of time value that is excluded from effectiveness assessment must be included in earnings in the period of change.

3. **Short-cut method**

   a. The short-cut method is a simplified way to assess and measure hedge effectiveness/ineffectiveness.

   b. The short-cut method applies only to hedging relationships of interest rate risk that involves a recognized interest-bearing financial asset or liability (hedged item) and an interest rate swap (hedging instrument).

   c. The short-cut method assumes that (and is possible because) the change in value of the interest-rate swap is a perfect proxy for the change in the value of the interest-bearing financial instrument.

   d. The short-cut method can be used by an entity only if all aspects of the hedging relationship exactly match (e.g., nominal amount, expiration date, etc.) and other criteria are met.

   e. If all of the criteria are met, an entity may assume no ineffectiveness in the hedging relationship and does not have to carry out an effectiveness assessment.

IV. Disclosure Requirements

A. An entity that issues or holds derivatives (or other contracts used for hedging) must disclose (mostly in the footnotes) a considerable amount of information in both annual and interim financial statements, including:

1. **General Disclosure Requirements**

   a. Its objectives for issuing or holding the derivatives (or other contracts), the context needed to understand those objectives, and its strategies for achieving those objectives.

   b. Information must distinguish between instruments used for risk management (hedging) and those used for other purposes (e.g., profit).

   c. Information must be disclosed in the context of each instrument's underlying risk exposure, including, for example: interest rate risk, credit risk, foreign currency exchange risk, overall price risk, etc.

   d. Information must distinguish between instruments designated as fair value hedges, cash flow hedges, hedges of foreign currency exposure of net investments in foreign operations, and any other derivatives.

    e. Information that would enable users to understand the volume of its derivative activities.

    f. Quantitative disclosures must be presented in tabular format.

    g. If information on derivatives is disclosed in multiple footnotes, the derivative-related footnotes must be cross referenced.

B. **Balance Sheet Related Disclosures --** The following specific balance sheet-related disclosures are required:

    1. The location (line item) and fair value amounts of derivative instruments.

    2. Fair value must be presented as a gross (not net) amount.

    3. Fair value amounts must be shown separately as assets and liabilities, and segregated between those derivatives that are hedges and those that are not.

    4. For derivatives used as hedges, the fair value amounts must be presented separately for each type of hedge contract (e.g., interest rate contract, foreign currency contract, commodity contract, etc.).

    5. The amounts reclassified from Accumulated Other Comprehensive Income to current income.

C. **Income Statement Related Disclosures --** The following specific income statement-related disclosures are required:

    1. The location (line item) and amounts of gains/losses on derivative instruments.

    2. Gains/losses must be presented separately for:

        a. Derivatives designated as fair value hedges and for the related hedged item.

        b. Derivatives designated as cash flow hedges and net investment hedges, separating the effective and ineffective portions.

        c. Derivatives not functioning as hedges.

        d. Amounts reclassified from Accumulated Other Comprehensive Income to current income.

        e. Amounts recognized from hedged firm commitments that no longer qualify for hedge treatment.

D. **Cash Flow Specific Disclosures --** For derivatives designated as cash flow hedges and for the related hedged item the following specific disclosures are required:

    1. A description of transactions or other events that will result in the reclassification (recognition) of accumulated other comprehensive income into income and an estimate of the amount to be reclassified during the next 12 months.

    2. The maximum length of time over which the entity is hedging cash flows for forecasted transactions.

    3. The gain/loss recognized in earnings from hedged forecasted transactions that no longer qualify for hedge treatment.

E. **Credit-Risk-Related Contingent Features Specific Disclosures**

    1. Credit-risk-related contingent features are provisions in a derivative (or other instrument) that trigger immediate settlement (or other consequences) if a specific event or condition occurs or fails to occur. For example, an interest rate swap may provide for immediate settlement if an entity's credit rating is downgraded.

    2. For derivatives that contain credit-risk-related contingent features the following specific disclosures are required:

    a. The existence and nature of credit-risk-related contingent features and the circumstances in which the features could be triggered for derivatives that are liabilities.

    b. The aggregate fair value amounts of derivatives that contain credit-risk-related contingent features that are liabilities.

    c. The aggregate fair value of assets (1) that are already posted as collateral, (2) additional assets that would be required as collateral and/or (3) needed to settle the instrument immediately if the contingent feature is triggered.

V. Note on Derivatives and Hedging Disclosures -- The required disclosures related to the issuing and/or holding of derivatives and the use of derivatives (and other instruments) for hedging purposes are extensive, detailed, and continuously changing (usually resulting in more disclosures). The disclosures identified and described above are those that are most significant and, therefore, most likely to occur on the CPA exam.

IFRS - Hedging

There are many similarities between U.S. GAAP and IFRS in the accounting for derivatives and hedging. This lesson identifies and describes the major differences between U.S. GAAP and IFRS with respect to hedge accounting.

After studying this lesson you should be able to :

1. *Identify significant areas of difference between U.S. GAAP and IFRS in accounting for derivatives.*

2. *Identify the significant areas of difference between U.S. GAAP and IFRS in hedge accounting.*

I.   U.S. GAAP - IFRS Differences

U.S. GAAP	IFRS
Definition of derivative includes identifying a notional amount	Definition of a derivative does not include a notional amount
Normal purchase / sales contracts not considered a derivative if documented	Normal purchase / sales contracts not considered a derivative and no formal documentation necessary
Embedded derivatives assessed throughout life of contract	Embedded derivatives assessed only at initiation of contract
Embedded derivatives within a single host separated and bundled as one derivative	Embedded derivatives within a single host separated as multiple derivatives

A.   Definition -- The definition of a derivative under IFRS is different from the definition under U.S. GAAP. Like U.S. GAAP, the IFRS definition establishes a derivative as a financial instrument whose value changes with changes in an underlying and one that requires a minimal or no initial net investment. Unlike U.S. GAAP, the IFRS definition does not:

1.   Include reference to a "notional" concept or element.

2.   Specify that net settlement is required or permitted, only that the contract will be settled at a future date.

B.   Documentation -- Under both U.S. GAAP and IFRS, normal purchase and sales contracts are not considered derivatives. U.S. GAAP requires that a financial instrument that is a normal purchase or sale be formally documented to establish that it is not a derivative; IFRS does not require such formal documentation.

C.   Embedded Derivatives

1.   **Recognition --** Under IFRS an embedded derivative is separated from the host contract only if

    a.   the entire (hybrid) contract is not measured at fair value with changes recognized in profit or loss, and

    b.   the economic characteristics and risks of the embedded derivative are not "closely related" to those of the host contract.

Note:
While this recognition standard is similar to that under U.S. GAAP, application of the separate standards can sometimes result in differences in the recognition of embedded derivative as separate instruments.

2. **Assessment** -- Under U.S. GAAP, the assessment of whether or not there is an embedded derivative that must be separated from the host contract and accounted for as a separate derivative generally must occur throughout the life of the contract. Under IFRS, however, that assessment generally occurs only when the reporting party becomes a party to the contract.

3. **Multiple Embedded Derivatives** -- Under U.S. GAAP when a single host contract contains more than one embedded derivative that meets the requirements to be accounted for as a separate derivative instrument, those embedded derivatives must be bundled together and treated as a single, compound embedded derivative. Under IFRS, however, when a single host contract contains more than one embedded derivative with different underlying risk exposure that are readily separable and are independent of each other, the embedded derivative elements must be accounted for separately.

4. **Measurement** -- There are no significant differences between U.S. GAAP and IFRS with respect to the measurement of derivative instruments; however, there are differences with respect to the use of derivatives for hedging purposes. Those differences will be covered in the appropriate lessons on hedging.

II. **Hedging: U.S. GAAP - IFRS Differences**

The table below summarizes the significant differences with respect to hedge accounting

U.S. GAAP	IFRS
Risk associated with business combination cannot be hedged	Foreign exchange risk associated with business combination can be hedged
Part term hedges not permitted	Part term hedges are permitted
Very limited when non-derivative items can be used as hedging instruments	Non-derivative items can be used as hedging instruments
Only benchmark rates can be hedged	Interest rate does not need to be the benchmark rate
The short-cut method is permitted	The short-cut method is not permitted

A. Under IFRS, unlike under U.S. GAAP, a forecasted (planned) business combination that is subject to foreign exchange risk can be hedged.

B. Under IFRS, hedging part of the term (or life) of a hedged item is permitted; part-term hedges are not permitted under U.S. GAAP.

C. Under IFRS, nonderivative financial instruments can be used as hedging instruments for hedging any kind of item; under U.S. GAAP, nonderivative instruments can be used only in very limited circumstances.

III. **Fair Value Hedges: U.S. GAAP - IFRS Differences** -- Under IFRS, the risks associated with financial items that can be hedged are less restrictive than under U.S. GAAP.

A. Generally, any financial item can be hedged as long as effectiveness can be measured. In addition, under IFRS hedge effectiveness is required only at each reporting date, which may not be as often as every three months.

B. Unlike U.S. GAAP, under IFRS a hedged interest rate does not have to be a benchmark rate.

C. Unlike U.S. GAAP, IFRS permits fair value hedging of a portion of a specified risk and/or for a portion of a time period unit maturity.

IV. Cash Flow Hedges: U.S. GAAP - IFRS Differences

A. Under IFRS, the gain or loss on the hedge of a forecasted transaction of a nonfinancial asset or liability (e.g., inventory, equipment, etc.) may be used, at the option of the entity, to adjust the basis of the hedged item; under U.S. GAAP, that gain or loss must be deferred through other comprehensive income until the hedged item affects income.

B. Under U.S. GAAP, for consolidated purposes, foreign currency risk can be hedged with internal derivatives (between entities to be consolidated) provided comparable derivatives are entered into (by the intercompany counterparty) with an unrelated third party so that net basis hedging is accomplished. Under IFRS, for consolidated purposes only instruments with parties external to the reporting entity can be designated as hedging instruments.

V. Foreign Currency Hedges: U.S. GAAP - IFRS Differences

A. Under IFRS, the kinds of intercompany transactions subject to hedging of foreign currency exchange risk are more limited than under U.S. GAAP. Generally, only intercompany monetary items and certain intercompany forecasted purchases and sales can be hedged under IFRS. Thus, for example, forecasted or recognized intercompany royalties cannot be hedged under IFRS.

VI. Effectiveness: U.S. GAAP - IFRS Differences

A. Under IFRS, an assessment of hedge effectiveness is required only on a reporting date; there is no requirement, as under U.S. GAAP, that an assessment be conducted at least every three months.

B. Under IFRS, qualitative assessment of effectiveness (i.e., using the extent to which critical terms of the hedging instrument and the hedged item match) can be used only in limited circumstances in carrying out prospective assessment; such assessment may not be used to assume perfect effectiveness in retrospective assessment.

C. Under IFRS, the short-cut method for assessing effectiveness is not permitted. U.S. GAAP and IFRS generally have the same disclosure requirement - both require extensive disclosures.

Transfer and Servicing of Financial Assets

Introduction to Transfer and Servicing of Financial Assets

There are many different forms of financial asset transfers. Financial assets are commonly transferred between parties under various arrangements, including factoring, securitization, lending and others. When the transferor has no continuing involvement with the transferred financial assets or with the transferee, the accounting is quite simple. However, in some cases, there is some kind of continuing involvement. For example, the transferring party may continue to service the transferred asset; in other cases, another party may acquire the servicing responsibility. These more complex types of transactions raise issues concerning whether the transaction should be considered a sale (all or partial) or a secured borrowing. This lesson introduces the transferring and servicing of financial assets. Specifically, it defines what constitutes a transfer of a financial asset and gives common examples of transfers. It also identifies and defines basic concepts that underlie accounting for these transactions .

After studying this lesson, you should be able to:

1. *Define the transfer of a financial asset.*

2. *Identify examples of common financial asset transfers.*

3. *Describe the basic concepts that underlie accounting for the transfer and servicing of assets.*

4. *Describe the criteria that must be met for surrender of control of a financial asset to have occurred.*

I. Overview

> **Definition:**
> *Transfer of Financial Assets*: The conveyance of a noncash financial asset by an entity other than the issuer (the transferor) of the financial asset to an entity other than the issuer (the transferee) of the financial asset.

A. **Types of Transfers** -- Transfers of financial assets may take many forms, including:

1. **Factoring** -- A means of discounting accounts receivable on a non-recourse basis by the outright sale of the receivables to a factor (the transferee).

2. **Transferring receivables with recourse** -- A means of discounting accounts receivable by the sale of the receivables with the seller (transferor) providing the buyer (transferee) full or limited recourse in the form of an obligation to make payments to the transferee or repurchase receivables under certain circumstances.

3. **Securities lending transactions** -- These are generally initiated by a financial institution such as a broker-dealer that needs specific securities to cover a short sale or a customer's failure to deliver securities sold. Transferees (borrowers) of securities are generally required to provide collateral to the transferor (lender) of the securities.

4. **Securitizations** -- An originator of a securitization (the transferor) transfers a portfolio of financial assets (e.g., a group of mortgage loans, automobile loans, credit card receivables, etc.) to a special purpose entity (commonly a trust).

5. **Repurchase agreements** -- An agreement under which one party (a transferor) transfers securities to another party (a transferee) in exchange for cash and concurrently agrees to repurchase the securities at a future date for the original cash plus interest.

6. **Loan participation** -- A bank transfers a portion of a large loan to one or more other banks that participate in the lending.

7. **Banker's acceptances** -- A bank agrees to pay a client's liability to a vendor upon presentation of documents that evidence delivery and acceptance of goods purchased from the vendor. One of the documents presented is the client's draft. Once the draft is approved by the bank, it becomes a negotiable instrument that can be transferred between entities.

II. **Underlying Concepts** -- Three basic concepts underlie accounting for both the transfer of financial assets and the servicing of those assets:

   A. **Control Determination Concept** -- Whether or not the party transferring a financial asset has surrendered (or has retained) control over the asset transferred or any portion thereof.

   B. **Financial-component Concept** -- Financial assets and liabilities can be disaggregated (separated) into components that become separate assets and/or liabilities.

   C. **Participating Interest Concept** -- A specific ownership relationship between an entity (commonly the transferor) with an interest in a financial asset and other entities that have an ownership interest in the financial asset. An ownership interest in an individual financial asset constitutes a participating interest if it has the following characteristics:

   1. There is a proportional (pro rata) ownership interest in an **entire** financial asset.

   2. All cash flows received from the entire financial asset are divided proportionately among the participating interest holders in proportion to their share of ownership.

   3. Cash flows are allocated such that:

      a. The rights of each participating interest holder have the same priority.

      b. No participating interest holder's interest is subordinated to the interest of another participating interest holder.

      c. The priority does not change, even in the event of bankruptcy of any party.

      d. Participating interest holders have no recourse to the transferor (which may continue to be a participating interest holder), except for standard representations and warranties, ongoing servicing obligations, and contractual obligations to share any set-off benefits.

   4. No party has the right to pledge or exchange the entire financial asset unless all participating interest holders agree.

III. **Criteria for Surrender of Control**

   A. In order to determine the appropriate application of accounting rules to the transfer of assets (or portion thereof) it must be determined if the transferred asset has been surrendered. The following three conditions must ALL be met before control is deemed to have been surrendered.

   1. The transferred asset must have been legally isolated from the transferor, all of the entities included in the transferor's financial statements (i.e., consolidated affiliates), and the transferor's creditors, even in case of bankruptcy or other receivership.

   2. The transferee has the right to pledge or exchange assets, such that no condition exists that constrains the transferee from exercising that right and it provides more than a trivial benefit to the transferor.

   3. The transferor does not maintain control over transferred assets under either a repurchase agreement or a return of assets requirement.

Accounting for Transfers

General Accounting Requirements for the Transfers of Assets - Sales and Secured Borrowing

Whether or not a transfer of a financial asset or portion of a financial asset qualifies as a sale depends on the nature of the asset transferred and whether or not control over the transferred asset has been surrendered. This lesson addresses the determination of when a transfer should be recognized as a sale and when a transfer is not recognized as a sale, but rather as a secured borrowing with a pledge of collateral. Also included in this lesson is the accounting treatment for both transfers recognized as sales and secured borrowing.

After studying this lesson, you should be able to:

1. *Identify the circumstances when a transfer of a financial asset as a sale or a secured borrowing for accounting purposes .*

2. *Describe the basic accounting guidelines that apply to the transfer of a financial asset as either a sale or a secured borrowing.*

3. *Describe the accounting treatment when the transfer of a financial asset meets the requirements for a 1) sale and 2) secured borrowing.*

I. **Background** -- The transfer of a financial asset occurs when a party (other than the issuer) conveys a noncash financial asset to another party (other than the issuer of the financial instrument). Examples include, among others:

   A. Selling accounts, notes, or other receivables (with and without recourse);

   B. Securitizing assets;

   C. Using assets as collateral.

II. **General Requirements**

   A. In any transfer of a financial asset (or portion thereof) the following general requirements apply:

      1. Sale - surrender of control of entire asset

         a. If the criteria for surrender of control are met, and the financial asset has not been divided into components prior to transfer, the transfer is accounted for as a sale; the asset will be derecognized by the transferor.

      2. Secured borrowing - surrender of control of entire asset NOT met

         a. If the entire asset is transferred, but the criteria for surrender of control have not been met, then this is treated as a secured borrowing.

      3. Surrender of control of component

         a. Sale - If the criteria for surrender of control are met, and the financial asset has been divided into components prior to transfer, the transfer can be accounted for as a sale only if all of the components involve participating interest (as previously defined in an earlier lesson).

         b. Secured borrowing - If the criteria for surrender of control are not met or components of the transferred asset do not involve participating interest, the transfer is accounted for as a secured borrowing with pledge of collateral; the asset will not be derecognized by the transferor.

B. **Accounting Guidelines** -- Whether treated as a sale or secured borrowing, the transferor should:

    1. Derecognize a financial asset (or portion thereof) for which the transfer qualifies as a sale.

    2. Continue to carry in its balance sheet any retained interest in the transferred asset. Such retained interest may include, for example:

        a. The entire asset in the case of a secured borrowing.

        b. Components of the transferred asset over which the transferor has not relinquished control in the case of a sale (e.g., portion of the asset not transferred).

            i. In this case, the carrying amount of the asset before the transfer would be allocated between the portion transferred and the portion retained based on relative fair values at the date of transfer.

    3. Recognize any assets or liabilities that result from the transfer (e.g., servicing rights, repurchase obligations, options, etc.).

C. **Accounting Symmetry** -- Accounting for the transfer of financial assets should be accounted for symmetrically by the transferor (e.g., seller) and the transferee (e.g., buyer).

III. Transfers as Sales

A. **Criteria for Sale Accounting**

    1. In order to treat the transfer of a financial asset as a sale, the following must exist:

        a. The criteria for surrender of control must be met.

        b. The transfer must be of:

            i. An entire financial asset, or

            ii. A group of entire financial assets, or

            iii. A participating interest in an entire financial asset.

    2. If those conditions are satisfied, the transfer is accounted for as a sale by the transferor and as a purchase by the transferee.

B. **Transferor Accounting** -- Accounting for the sale of financial assets by the transferor requires:

    1. **Writing off** -- (derecognizing) the carrying value of all assets (or portions thereof) sold.

    2. **Writing on** -- (recognizing) all assets obtained and liabilities incurred (as proceeds of the sale).

        a. **Assets obtained** -- Might include, for example, cash, options, swaps, servicing assets, etc. (but does not include any interest in the transferred asset); these serve to increase the proceeds.

        b. **Liabilities incurred** -- Might include, for example, forward commitments, options, servicing net obligations, etc.; these serve to decrease the proceeds.

    3. **Measuring** -- All assets and liabilities at fair value.

    4. **Recognizing** -- In current earnings, any gain or loss on the sale as the difference between the net proceeds received and the carrying value of the asset sold.

C. **Transferee Accounting** -- Accounting for the purchase of financial assets by the transferee requires:

1. **Writing on all assets** -- Obtained (including any participating interest) and any liabilities incurred.

2. **Measuring all assets and liabilities at fair value** -- The price paid.

D. **Illustration - Accounting For a Sale of Financial Assets with No Retained Interest --** This illustration assumes the transfer qualifies as a sale and that the transferor has no retained interest in the assets transferred; the entire asset is sold. Therefore, no allocation of the transferor's carrying value is required.

1. **Facts** -- Company A (transferor) transfers to Company B (transferee) loans receivable with a carrying value (on A's books) of $1,000. Company A assumes a limited recourse obligation to repurchase delinquent loans. In addition, Company A agrees to provide Company B a return at a variable rate of interest, even though the loans are fixed rate (effectively, this is an interest rate swap). The transfer qualifies as a sale and the terms of the sale contract provide:

   a. Co. A receives from Co. B cash of $1,050 and a benefit from the interest rate swap with a fair value of $40;

   b. Co. A assumes a limited recourse obligation (liability) to repurchase delinquent loans that has a fair value of $60;

   c. Co. A retains no servicing responsibilities for, or other interest in, the loans.

2. **Sale Proceeds and Gain Calculated**

Cash Received	$1,050
Interest Rate Swap	40
Obligation Assumed	(60)
Net Proceeds	$1,030
Carrying Value	1,000
Gain on Sale	$30

3. **Sale Recorded By Transferor**

DR: Cash	$1,050	
Interest Rate Swap	40	
CR: Loans Receivable		$1,000
Repurchase Obligation		60
Gain on Sale		30

4. **Purchase Recorded by Transferee**

DR: Loans Receivable	$1,030	
Sell Back Right	60	
CR: Cash		$1050
Interest Rate Swap		40

5. Generally, debt, equity and derivative instruments recognized in a transfer of financial assets will be accounted for according to the GAAP applicable to that type of item.

E. Illustration - Accounting for a Sale of Financial Assets with a Retained Interest

1. This illustration assumes the transfer qualifies as a sale and that the transferor retains a partial interest in the asset transferred. The carrying value of the asset before the transfer must be allocated between the portion sold and the portion retained based on relative fair value of each portion.

2. **Facts --** Company X transfers to Company Y for $660 a 60-percent interest in loans receivable with a carrying value (on X's books) of $1000 and a fair value of $1100. The transfer qualifies as a sale; no other rights or obligations are involved.

3. Allocation of carrying value ($1000)

	Fair Value	%of FV		Carrying Value		Allocated Cost
60% Sold	$660	60	X	$1,000	=	$600
40% Retained	$440	40	X	1000	=	400
Totals	$1,100	100				$1,000

4. **Gain Calculated**

Proceeds	$660
Loan Allocated Carrying Value (9/10 sold)	600
Gain on Sale	$60

5. **Sale Recorded By Transferor**

DR: Cash	$660	
CR: Loans Receivable (.60)		$600
Gain on Sale		60

6. **Purchase Recorded By Transferee**

DR: Loans Receivable	$660	
CR: Cash		$660

IV. Transfers as Secured Borrowing

A. The Appropriate Accounting for the Transfer of Noncash Collateral -- By the transferor (debtor) and the transferee (secured party) depends on

1. Whether the secured party has the right to sell or repledge the collateral, and

2. Whether the debtor has defaulted.

B. Accounting for Transferred Collateral by the Transferor

1. **Initial Recognition --** Upon transfer, the transferor initially will recognize asset(s) received from the transferee and a liability to the transferee.

2. **Subsequent Recognition**

a. If the transferor (debtor) has not defaulted under the terms of the contract, the transferor will continue to carry the collateral on its books as an asset (and the transferee will not recognize the pledged asset).

b. However, if the transferee has the right to sell or repledge the collateral, the transferor must reclassify and report the pledged asset separate from other assets in its Balance Sheet (e.g., "Security Pledged to Creditors").

c. If the transferor (debtor) has defaulted under the terms of the contract and is no longer entitled to redeem the pledged asset, the transferor will write off (derecognize) the pledged asset (and the transferee will recognize the asset).

C. Accounting for Transferred Collateral by the Transferee

1. **Initial Recognition** -- Upon transfer, the transferee initially will recognize a receivable from the transferor and a reduction in the asset(s) transferred to the transferor.

2. **Subsequent Recognition**

   a. If the transferor has not defaulted under the terms of the contract, the transferee will not recognize the pledged asset.

   b. If the transferee has the right to sell the asset and exercises that right, the transferee will recognize the following journal entry:

DR: Cash Proceeds From Sale	$XX	
CR: Pledged Collateral Liability		$XX

   c. If the transferor has defaulted under the terms of the contract, the transferee will

   i. Recognize the collateral as its asset, at fair value or

   ii. Derecognize its liability to the transferor, if the collateral has been sold.

D. COMPREHENSIVE EXAMPLE PROBLEM

Sale of Receivables With, and Without Recourse AND Secured Borrowing:

WITHOUT RECOURSE:

PineTop Company needs cash, so it decides that $100,000 of receivables are factored (sold without recourse), to a finance company for $85,000. An allowance for bad debts equal to $3,000 had previously been established for these accounts. This amount will need to be written off along with the accounts receivables being sold. The finance company withholds 5% of the purchase price as protection against sales returns. The entry to record the sale of these receivables is as follows:

DR: Cash	$80,750	
Receivable from Factor	4,250	
Allowance for Bad Debts	3,000	
Loss from Factoring Receivables	12,000	
CR: Accounts Receivable		$100,000

To record the factoring of receivables:

Computations

Cash = *85,000 - (5% of $85,000) = $80,750

Receivable from Factor = 5% of $85,000 = $4,250

Factoring Loss = ($100,000 - $3,000) - $85,000 = $12,000

WITH RECOURSE:

Continuing the previous example, now assume that the receivables are sold with recourse and the recourse obligation has an estimated fair value of $5,000. In this instance, the loss to be recognized on the transaction would be $17,000 and is computed as follows:

Cash Received	$	85,000
Estimated Value of Recourse Obligation		(5,000)
Net Proceeds	$	80,000
Book Value of the Receivables (100,000 - 3,000)	$	97,000
Net Proceeds to be received		(80,000)
Loss on Sale of Receivables	$	17,000

The entry to record the sale of receivables with recourse would be:

DR: Cash	$80,750	
Receivable from Factor	4,250	
Allowance for Bad Debts	3,000	
Loss on Sale of Receivables	17,000	
CR: Accounts Receivable		$100,000
Recourse Obligation		5,000

SECURED BORROWING:

Continuing the previous example, now assume that the accounts receivable are NOT sold, but instead PineTop Company decides they want to borrow money using the receivables as collateral. This would be a secured borrowing. PineTop Company will collect the receivables. PineTop assigns the $100,000 of receivables to the financing company (LakeShores) as collateral for a $60,000, 6% note. PineTop does not notify its accounts receivables' debtors and will continue to collect the assigned receivables. LakeShores assesses a 1% finance charge on assigned receivables in addition to the interest on the note. PineTop will make monthly payments to LakeShores with cash collected on assigned receivables. The journal entries through the first monthly payment are the following for both PineTop and LakeShores:

Issuance of note and assignment of specific receivables:

PineTop			LakeShores		
Cash	59,400		Notes Receivable	60,000	
Finance Charge	600		Finance Revenue		600
Notes Payable		60,000	Cash		59,400

Collections of assigned accounts during 1st month of $50,000, less sales returns of $2,000:

Cash	48,000	(No Entry)
Sales Returns	2,000	
Accounts Receivable	50,000	

Paid LakeShores amounts owed for 1st month collections plus accrued interest on note:

Interest Expense	300	Cash	48,300
(60,000 x .06/12)			
Notes Payable	48,000	Interest Revenue	300
Cash	48,300	Notes Receivable	48,000

NOTE: Eventually the note would be paid from the proceeds at a later month from the collections of the receivables.

Accounting for Servicing of Financial Assets

By their nature, financial assets require servicing. In some cases, the requirements are nominal - performing accounting functions, for example. In other cases, a variety of functions may be required - billing, collecting, making payments, etc. Certain of these service functions can be contractually separated. When that occurs, a separate asset or liability will be recognized. This lesson describes the accounting for such assets and liabilities, and illustrates the required accounting.

After studying this lesson, you should be able to:

1. *Describe what constitutes a servicing function for accounting purposes.*

2. *Describe when a servicing asset or servicing liability exists.*

3. *Describe how to measure a servicing asset or servicing liability upon initial recognition.*

4. *Describe how servicing assets and servicing liabilities are measured subsequent to recognition.*

5. *Record the entries to be made by both the transferor and transferee to recognize and subsequently measure servicing assets.*

I. **Servicing Function -- Servicing Function**

A. The servicing of financial assets is inherent in all financial assets and includes such functions as:

1. Collecting principle, interest, escrow amounts and fees, etc.;

2. Paying taxes, insurance and other obligations; and

3. Performing accounting and other services.

B. These service functions become a distinct asset or liability only when contractually separated from the underlying asset. This separation can occur either:

1. As a result of sale (or securitization) of the assets with a servicing right retained by the seller; or

2. As a result of a separate purchase of the servicing right.

II. **General Requirements**

A. Any contract to service financial assets **must be separately recognized** as either a servicing asset or a servicing liability, depending on whether a net revenue or net loss is expected from the contract.

1. A **servicing asset** results when estimated future revenues are expected to exceed estimated costs of servicing the assets, as reflected by its fair value.

2. A **servicing liability** results when estimated future revenues are not expected to be as much as expected costs of servicing the assets, as reflected by its fair value.

B. A servicing contract, either an asset or a liability, will be **initially measured at fair value**, regardless of whether the service contract is retained in a sale of financial assets or separately purchased.

C. **Subsequent measurement of recognized servicing assets and servicing liabilities --** However obtained, should be done using one of the following methods:

1. Amortized in proportion to and over the period of estimated net income or net loss and assess the asset or liability for impairment or increased obligation based on fair value, or

2. Adjusted to fair value at each reporting date with gains or losses recognized in current income (the fair value option).

III. **Illustration - Accounting for Servicing of Financial Assets** -- This illustration assumes the sale of a financial asset (receivables) and that the transferor has no retained interest in the asset, but that the transferor will continue to service the receivables.

A. **Facts** -- Offshore Company has $100,000 of loans receivable that yield 10% annual interest income and have a remaining life of nine years. Offshore sells the $100,000 loan principle to Scholes Company. Offshore will continue to service the loans, for which it will receive 2% to the interest. At the date of transfer, the fair value of the loans is $100,000 and the fair value to the servicing rights is $8,000. The terms of contract provide:

1. Offshore receives from Scholes $100,000 cash;

2. Scholes receives the loans receivable and the right to receive interest income of 8%;

3. Offshore will continue to service the loans and receive the remaining 2% interest income not sold with a fair value of $9,000 as compensation.

B. **Proceeds Calculated**

Cash Proceeds	$100,000
Servicing Asset (FV)	9,000
Total Proceeds	$109,000

C. **Gain Calculated**

Proceeds	$109,000
Loans Carrying Value	100,000
Gain on Sale	$9,000

1. Since Offshore sold the entire asset (loans receivable) there is no issue of participating interest and there is no need to allocate the carrying value.

2. The servicing right is recognized as a new asset (separate from the carrying value of the loans receivable) that is initially measured at fair value.

D. **Sale recorded by Offshore (the transferor)**

Servicing Asset	9,000	
Cash	$100,000	
Loans Receivable		$100,000
Gain on Sale		9,000

E. **Purchase recorded by Scholes (the transferee)**

Loans Receivable	$100,000	
Cash		$100,000

F. Amortization of Servicing Asset

1. If the estimated net servicing income is expected to be earned evenly over the nine year life of the loans, Offshores could amortize one-ninth of the servicing asset each year, as follows:

Servicing Asset Amortization Expense	$1,000
Servicing Asset	1,000
($9,000/9 years = $1,000 per year)	

G. As an alternative, Offshores could elect to subsequently measure the servicing asset at fair value each period (the fair value option).

Disclosure Requirements for Transfer of Assets

Significant disclosures are required of entities that engage in the transfer and/or servicing of financial assets. This lesson summarizes the most important of those requirements.

After studying this lesson, you should be able to:

1. *Describe the objectives of required disclosures.*

2. *Describe the most significant disclosure that must be made by:*

   - *Transferors of financial assets.*

   - *Transferees of financial assets.*

   - *Entities with servicing assets or liabilities.*

3. *Understand the definitions of common terms related to the transfer of assets.*

I. **GAAP Requirements** -- GAAP requires significant disclosures by entities that engage in the transfer and/or servicing of financial assets. The following only summarizes those requirements. (ASC 860-10-50, 860-20-50, 860-30-50 and 860-50-50 provide detailed disclosure requirements.)

II. **General Disclosure Objectives** -- Disclosures are intended to provide information that enables users to understand, among other things:

   A. The transferor's continuing involvement with transferred assets.

   B. The nature of restrictions on assets reported in the balance sheet that relates to transferred assets and the carrying amounts of those assets.

   C. How servicing assets and liabilities are reported.

   D. How transferred assets accounted for as sales when the transferor has continuing involvement with the transferred asset, or when the transfer is accounted for as a secured borrowing, affect the transferor's balance sheet, income statement, and cash flows.

   E. Fair value disclosures related to the measurement of fair values for financial assets or liabilities that have been transferred. These include assumptions used in the determination of fair values determined by the general guidelines under the Fair Value Hierarchy.

III. **The Transferor of Financial Assets Must Disclose**

   A. For any assets pledged as collateral that are not separately disclosed in the Balance Sheet, the carrying amount and classification of those assets.

   B. For securitized financial assets accounted for as a sale, for each major type information about:

   1. Accounting policies;

   2. Characteristics of the securitizations and the gain or loss on assets securitized;

   3. Key assumption used in measuring (and remeasuring) fair value at securitization (and subsequently) and sensitivity of those measures to changes in key assumptions.

IV. **The Transferee of Financial Assets Must Disclose**

   A. Its policy for requiring collateral or other security.

   B. For collateral that it is permitted to sell or repledge:

1. Information about the sources and uses of the collateral;

2. The fair value of such collateral;

3. The portion of such collateral that has been sold or repledged.

V. Entities with Servicing Assets or Liabilities Must Disclose

A. Management's basis for determining the classes of servicing assets and liabilities, a description of the risks inherent in those assets and liabilities, and instruments used to mitigate the income statement effects of changes in fair value.

B. The valuation technique, methodology, and key assumptions used in estimating fair value.

C. The amount of fees recognized in income during the period.

D. Details of activity in servicing asset or servicing liability accounts, and in any impairment valuation allowance account, during the period.

VI. For All Entities Engaged in the Transfer or Servicing of Financial Assets -- If it is not practicable to estimate the fair value of certain assets obtained or liabilities incurred during the period, a description of those items and why it is not practicable to estimate fair value.

VII. COMMON TERMS

A. It is important that to gain an understanding of some commonly used terms when studying this section of FAR relating to the Transfer of Financial Assets. These are some of those common terms with their descriptions/definitions:

1. **Interest only strip** -- contractual right to receive some or all of the interest due on an interest bearing financial asset such as a bond or mortgage loan.

2. **Cleanup call** -- option held by the servicer to purchase transferred financial assets when the amount of outstanding assets falls below a certain level.

3. **Securitization** -- process by which financial assets are transformed into securities.

4. **Wash Sales** -- process where the same financial asset is purchased soon after the sale of the asset.

5. **Factoring** -- arrangements to discount accounts receivable on a nonrecourse notification basis.

Accounting for Extinguishment of Liabilities

This lesson covers the extinguishment (derecognition) of liabilities. Specifically, it identifies the conditions under which a debt may be written off the books of the debtor.

After studying this lesson, you should be able to:

1. *Describe the conditions under which a liability will be derecognized (written off).*

2. *Describe the accounting requirements when a debtor becomes a guarantor.*

I. **Conditions for Derecognizing a Liability** -- A debtor should write off (derecognize) a liability if, and only if, it is extinguished by either of the following conditions:

   A. The **debtor pays the creditor** and is relieved of its obligation for the liability.

      1. Paying the creditor could be in the form of cash, other financial assets, goods, or services.

      2. If satisfaction of the debt is in conjunction with the debtor's reacquisition of its outstanding debt securities, it does not matter whether the securities are canceled or held as "treasury" instruments by the (former) debtor.

   B. The **debtor is legally released** from being the primary obligator under the liability either by the creditor or by law/courts.

      1. If a creditor releases a debtor from primary obligation on the condition that a **third party assumes the obligation** and the original debtor becomes secondarily liable, that release extinguishes the original debtor's liability and the original debtor becomes a guarantor.

      2. As a **guarantor**, the original debtor will account for the guarantee obligation just as though it had never had primary obligation for the liability, including:

         a. Recognize any resulting obligation, giving due regard to the likelihood that the new obligator will default;

         b. Measuring any recognized obligations at fair value;

         c. Using any recognized obligations as an adjustment to any gain or loss on extinguishment.

II. **Accounting for Extinguishment of Liabilities**

   A. Determining and Recording Gains or Losses

      1. Debt reacquisition items that must be accounted for include:

         a. Debt issuance costs;

         b. Any unamortized discount/premium;

         c. Difference between debt's face value and reacquisition amount.

      GAIN/LOSS = Reacquisition Price - Net Carrying Amount

      2. Reacquisition price is usually shown as a % of debt's face value:

Example:
$100,000 at 103 or $100,000 at 96

Reacquisition Price = $100,000 x 103% = $103,000

OR $100,000 x 96% = $ 96,000

Net Carrying Amount =   Face Value of Debt

                        + Unamortized Premium OR

                        Unamortized Discount

III. COMPREHENSIVE EXAMPLE -- Early Extinguishment of Debt

Example: Assume that $100,000 of bonds due in five years are issued on January 1, 20X1 at a discount for $92,500. The issuer uses straight-line amortization of the $7,500 discount. Two years later on January 1, 20X3 the entire issue is redeemed at $102 and canceled.

Gain/Loss Computation:

Reacquisition Price = $100,000 x 102% = $102,000

Bond carrying value = Face Value - Unamortized Discount*

                    = 100,000 - 4,500*

                    = $95,500

LOSS   = $102,000 - $95,500 = $6,500

Original discount of $7,500/15 years = $1,500 discount amortized/yr.

2 years amortization = 2 x 1,500 = $3,000

Unamortized discount = $7,500 - $3,000 = $4,500

This is a loss because more was paid to reacquire the bonds than the carrying value of the bond.

Journal entry to cancel the bonds:

Bonds Payable	100,000	
Loss on extinguishment of bonds	6,500	
Discount on bonds payable		4,500
Cash		102,000

IV. In-Substance Defeasance

A. In-Substance Defeasance is an arrangement in which a company places secured securities in an irrevocable trust and pledges them for future principal and interest payments on its long-term debt. The company retains the obligation on the debt, therefore there is no liability extinguishment.

U.S. GAAP - IFRS Differences - Transfer of Financial Assets

This lesson covers differences between U.S. GAAP and IFRS that deal with the transfer of financial assets. Under U.S. GAAP the key accounting issue with the transfer of financial assets is whether the transfer should be recorded as a sale, with the asset removed from the books of the transferor, or whether the transfer should be accounted for as a secured loan with the asset remaining on the books of the transferor. The IASB uses the term "derecognition" to signify the removal of the asset from the books of the transferor.

After studying this lesson you should be able to :

1. *Understand IFRS differences for the following:*

   - *Requirements for the sale/derecognition of the asset,*
   - *Servicing Rights,*
   - *Disclosures,*
   - *Extinguishment of Liabilities.*

2. *Understand the difference between U.S. GAAP and IFRS concerning general accounting guidelines related to the transfer of risks and rewards as it relates to financial assets.*

I. **Transfers of Risks and Rewards Relating to Financial Assets** -- Under IFRS, financial assets are derecognized when the entity loses control of the contractual benefits that comprise the financial asset. Loss of control focuses on the transfer of risks and rewards associated with the financial asset. The general guidelines state that:

A. Derecognize financial asset when all risks and rewards have been transferred.

   1. Do not derecognize if all risks and rewards have been substantially retained.

B. If substantially all risks and rewards are neither transferred nor retained, entity determines whether it has retained control.

   1. If not, derecognize transferred asset and recognize asset or liability for any right or obligation created or retained.

   2. If so, continue to recognize asset to extent of involvement.

C. Financial asset derecognized when both

   1. Asset has been transferred outside transferor's consolidated group, and

   2. Transferor has transferred substantially all risks and rewards of ownership.

D. If substantially all risks and rewards have been neither retained nor transferred, control assessment made:

   1. Transferee has unilateral ability to sell transferred asset = Control deemed transferred.

   2. Transferee does not have ability to sell transferred asset = Control deemed retained - partial derecognition may be required .

II. **Requirements for Sale/Derecognition of Financial Assets**

A. Under IFRS, (IAS No. 39) a financial asset would be derecognized in full (i.e., written off) when both of the following conditions have been met:

> **Note:**
> Under U.S. GAAP, there is a third requirement: derecognition of a financial asset is not permitted if the contractual rights to the assets cash flows are retained.

   1. The financial asset has been transferred outside the consolidated group of the transferor, which may be achieved when:

      a. An entity transfers to an entity outside its consolidated group the contractual rights to receive cash flows of the financial asset, or

      b. An entity retains the rights to receive the cash flows, but assumes a related obligation to pass the cash flows to a recipient outside its consolidated group.

   2. The transferor has transferred substantially all of the risks and rewards of ownership of the financial asset.

B. When an asset has been transferred and substantially all of the risks and rewards have been neither retained nor transferred, an assessment of control is necessary.

   1. If the transferor determines that the transferee has the unilateral ability to sell the transferred asset, control is deemed to have been transferred.

   2. If the transferor determines that the transferee does not have the ability to sell the transferred asset, control is deemed to be retained by the transferor and the transferred asset may require partial derecognition (also called "continuing involvement"). Under continuing involvement, the transferor continues to recognize the asset to the extent it has exposure to changes in the value of the transferred asset.

C. Under U.S. GAAP, for affiliated entities, the determination of whether or not the transfer of a financial asset is considered a sale is made prior to determining whether or not an affiliated entity will be consolidated. Under IFRS, the consolidation of affiliates occurs before the determination of whether or not a transfer of a financial asset is considered a sale. Said another way, under U.S. GAAP, derecognition of financial assets is assessed at the entity level, while under IFRS it is assessed at the consolidated level.

III. **Secured Borrowing --** There are no significant differences between U.S. GAAP and IFRS related to the portion of this lesson related to secured borrowing.

IV. **Servicing Rights**

A. Unlike U.S. GAAP, IFRS considers servicing rights retained in the transfer of a financial asset as a retained interest in the transferred asset, not as a new separate asset (as under U.S. GAAP). Therefore, in such a case, under IFRS the servicing asset would be recognized based on its allocated portion of the carrying value of the entire financial asset before transfer. That carrying value would be allocated to the transferred asset and the retained servicing right based on their relative fair values at the date of transfer.

B. Under IFRS, separate servicing rights are not considered a financial instrument and there is no specific guidance on treatment of the servicing rights subsequent to recognition. Under U.S. GAAP, servicing rights (as assets or liabilities) are considered financial instruments and may be measured at amortized cost or, at the option of an entity, at fair value.

V. **Disclosures --** The disclosure requirements of both U.S. GAAP and IFRS related to the transfer and/or servicing of financial assets are extensive and detailed. Generally, however, both sets of requirements have the same objectives and require the same significant disclosures.

VI. **Extinguishment of Liabilities**

A. Under IFRS, a liability is considered extinguished when a specific obligation is discharged, canceled, or expires, or when the responsibility for the liability (or part thereof) is transferred to another party.

B. Like U.S. GAAP, under IFRS merely segregating assets to be used for retirement of an obligation (in-substance defeasance) would not be recognized as extinguishing the obligation.

Contingencies, Commitments, and Guarantees
(Provisions)

Contingent Liability Principles

This lesson introduces an important type of liability and the underlying principles for recognition.

After studying this lesson, you should be able to:

1. *Define "contingent" liability.*

2. *Explain when they are recognized in the accounts, and when they are footnoted only.*

3. *Record the journal entries for a regular warranty, a common type of contingent liability.*

4. *Determine the amount to recognize for a contingent liability when only a range of values can be estimated.*

I. Introduction

Definition:
A Contingency: An existing condition (at the balance sheet date) involving uncertainty as to a possible gain or loss that will be resolved when a future event occurs or fails to occur. Resolution of the uncertainty may confirm an increase in assets (or reduction in a liability), or the incurrence of a liability or an asset impairment.

A. Remember that all liabilities must be the result of a past event. The same holds for a contingent liability. As of the balance sheet date, there must have been a transaction or event implying that a liability may have been incurred (or asset impaired). However, a future event also plays an important role in the recognition of a contingent liability. A contingent liability is not definite as of the balance sheet date.

   1. For example, a firm is a defendant in a lawsuit. The suit is not resolved as of the balance sheet date. The firm does have a definite liability at year-end, but is contingently liable. The outcome of the suit in the following year will result in either a definite liability or no liability at all. Contingent liabilities are generally disclosed and possibly recognized, as discussed below.

   2. General risks and contingencies such as the possibility of a strike or casualty are not recognized or disclosed because no event or transaction has occurred as of the balance sheet date to substantiate that a liability has been incurred. A firm cannot accrue future casualty losses for example.

B. The accounting for contingencies is dependent on the probability of the future event occurring, and whether the amount of the gain or loss is estimable. This lesson considers only contingent liabilities. Other contingencies such as uncollectible accounts receivable and asset impairments are discussed elsewhere.

II. Probability of Future Event

A. In accounting for contingencies, a determination must be made related to the probability of occurrence of the future event (which will resolve the contingency) and the possibility of estimation.

B. In assessing the probability of occurrence, professional judgment is employed to classify the probability into one of three categories. These categories are described below.

1. **Probable** -- Based on professional judgment, the probability of occurrence is considered very high or a near certainty.

2. **Reasonably Possible** -- Based on professional judgment, the probability of occurrence is neither very high nor remote. In other words, when probability of occurrence is considered along a spectrum of possibilities, the probability of occurrence is not at either end of the spectrum, but is in the large middle section of the spectrum.

3. **Remote** -- Based on professional judgment, the probability of occurrence is considered to be very low, or as the title implies, remote.

C. **Reasonable Estimate of Amount** -- Based on professional judgment and experience, a determination is made about the possibility of estimating the amount of the contingency. Either the amount of resulting gain or loss is reasonably estimable, or it is not. In addition, firms may be able to estimate a possible range of amounts for the gain or loss, but be unable to assign any amount in the range a higher probability of occurring than any other amount.

D. **The loss contingency is probable and can be reasonably estimated at the balance sheet date** -- GAAP requires that if a contingent loss is both *probable* and *estimable*, then an estimated loss and estimated liability will be recognized - actually recorded in the accounts in the amount estimated. The guiding theoretical considerations here are conservatism and the definition of a liability. Because the loss (asset decrease or liability increase) will most likely occur in the future and because the firm can estimate the amount, there is no reason to postpone the loss and liability recognition until it actually occurs. The general definition of a liability is essentially met when the contingent liability is probable and estimable.

Example:
Recognized contingent liability. A large retailer offers warranties on its products. The firm estimates that total warranty costs will amount to 2% of sales for the year. Warranty claims are expected to occur on an even basis over the two years following sale. Sales were $1,000,000 for the year. There is no beginning warranty liability account balance for the year and there have been warranty claims totaling $6,000 during the year. This is a probable and estimable contingent liability. The actual loss or expense is contingent on a future event: customers making warranty claims. But a past transaction has occurred indicating it is probable that services will have to be provided in the future and the amount is estimable. Therefore, the loss or expense, and liability are recognized in the year of sale with the following adjusting entry.

Warranty Expense	20,000
Warranty Liability	20,000

The fact that the warranty liability is a contingent liability does not change the fact that it must be recorded in the accounts. Note the entire estimated amount is recorded in the year of sale. The pattern of claims is not a factor in the recognition of the expense. When claims are actually made, the warranty liability is reduced and cash, inventory, and other assets are reduced:

Warranty Liability	6,000
Cash, Parts Inventory, etc.	6,000

Firms must disclose the accounting policy with respect to warranty accounting, and disclose a schedule of the changes in the warranty liability for the period (increases due to expense, decreases due to claim service).

If the estimate of claims significantly overstates the actual claims cost, then the adjusting entry at the end of the year uses a smaller percentage to compensate. The opposite is true as well. There is no retroactive adjustment; rather the estimate is changed for the current and future periods to reflect the actual level of claims.

If the firm is able to estimate a range of possible losses, with no amount in the range having a higher probability of occurring than any other amount, the amount recognized in the accounts is the **lowest** amount in the range. Use of the lowest amount is the least conservative alternative. The footnotes should describe the entire range, however.

In all other cases (other than probable and estimable), no accrual of the loss is required. Footnote disclosure is required unless the probability of occurrence is remote.

Note: The **range** of possible values issue appears on the CPA exam from time to time. The candidate must remember that conservatism plays an important role in recognizing contingent liabilities, but when only a range of possible values is known, an exception is made: the lowest rather than the highest amount is used for reporting purposes. If a range of values were given but one value in the range has a higher probability assigned to it than any other, the value with the higher probability is used for reporting.

E. **The loss contingency is probable and cannot be reasonably estimated --** In this situation, the loss contingency should be disclosed in the footnotes to the financial statements.

F. **The loss contingency is reasonably possible --** In this situation, whether the loss can be reasonably estimated or not, the loss contingency is disclosed in the footnotes to the financial statements.

G. **The loss contingency is remote --** In this situation, whether the loss can be reasonably estimated or not, the loss contingency can be disclosed in the footnotes to the financial statements. Please note that footnote disclosure is permitted but not required.

Examples of Contingent Liabilities

This lesson provides additional examples of recognized contingent liabilities, and addresses unasserted claims, gain contingencies and guarantees.

After studying this lesson, you should be able to:

Chapter 1 :Record a variety of recognized contingent liabilities.

Chapter 2 :Determine when an unasserted claim is recognized in the accounts.

Chapter 3 :State the appropriate reporting of gain contingencies.

Chapter 4 :Explain the reporting of guarantees.

I. Examples of Contingent Liabilities

Example: A. Recognized contingent litigation liability

The Lion Company was sued during the last quarter of 20x7 because of an accident involving a vehicle owned and operated by the company. After discussing the case with the company's legal representatives, it was decided that the company would probably lose the case, **and** the amount of damages could be reasonably estimated at $50,000.

Entry:

Estimated Loss from Pending Lawsuit	$50,000	
Estimated Liability from Pending Lawsuit		$50,000

Had the firm believed that the loss was only reasonably possible, the above entry would not be made. The lawsuit and possible loss would be discussed in the footnotes. Only a small percentage of contingent lawsuit losses are recognized.

B. Recognized contingent premium liability

The Wolf Company offered to its customers a premium - a special coffee cup free of charge (cost per cup: $ .75) with the return of 20 coupons. One coupon is placed in each can of coffee when packed. The company estimated, on the basis of past experience that only 70% of the coupons will be redeemed. The following additional data is available for two years.

	Year 1	Year 2
Number of Coffee Cups Purchased	6,000	4,000
Number of Cans of Coffee Sold	100,000	200,000
Number of Coupons Redeemed	40,000	120,000

Entries:

Record the Purchase of Cups:

Year 1: Premium Inventory	$4,500	
Cash ($.75 x 6,000)		$4,500
Year 2: Premium Inventory	$3,000	
Cash		$3,000

Record the Estimated Premium Expense and Liability:

Year 1: Estimated Premium Expense $2,625

        Estimated Premium Liability $2,625

        $2,625 = (100,000/20) x $.75 x .70

Year 2: Estimated Premium Expense $5,250

        Estimated Premium Liability $5,250

        $5,250 = (200,000/20) x $.75 x .70

This is another example of a recognized contingent liability. Because it is probable and estimable, it is recorded like any other recognized liability.

Record the Redemption of the Coupons:

Year 1: Estimated Premium Liability $1,500

        Premium Inventory $1,500

        $1,500 = (40,000/20) x $.75 = 1,500

Year 2: Estimated Premium Liability $4,500

        Premium Inventory $4,500

        $4,500 = (120,000/20) x $.75 = 4,500

II. Unasserted Claims and Assessments

A. Entities may be subject to future claims and assessments not yet filed as of the balance sheet date. Examples include possible IRS actions against the entity for violations of the tax law, EPA claims against the entity for environmental violations, and other events that have occurred as of the balance sheet date.

B. If, at the balance sheet date, it is not probable that a claim or assessment will occur or if the outcome is not expected to be unfavorable to the entity, then no recognition or disclosure is required.

C. If it is probable that a claim or assessment will occur, and there is at least a reasonable probability that the outcome will be unfavorable to the entity, then the claim or assessment is treated as a contingency, even though no claim or assessment has been filed. The event before the balance sheet that would trigger the claim or assessment (such as a previous year's tax return filing or environmental violation) must have occurred, before the entity recognizes or discloses the contingency.

    1. If the amount is estimable, the contingent liability is recognized.

    2. Otherwise, it is footnoted only.

III. Contingencies Acquired in Business Combinations

A. In mergers and acquisitions, the acquiring firm may acquire contingencies of the acquired firm. The amounts ascribed to contingencies, as is the case for any other identifiable asset or liability, affects the valuation of recorded goodwill on the acquisition. The amount recognized for this type of contingent liability is somewhat different than that discussed above.

B. At acquisition, if the contingency is contractual (e.g., a regular warranty), then contingent liability is recognized by the acquirer at fair value.

C. At acquisition, if the contingency is not contractual and has more than a 50% probability of becoming a definite liability when a future event occurs or does not occur, then the liability is recognized at fair value. Otherwise, there is no recognition.

D. After acquisition, as new information is obtained, the contingency is reported at the greater of acquisition date fair value, and the amount that would be recognized under normal contingency rules. Any changes in the reported liability are recognized as gains or losses.

IV. Gain Contingencies

A. The gain contingency is probable -- In this situation, whether the gain can be reasonably estimated or not, the gain contingency is disclosed in the footnotes to the financial statements. Probable and estimable gain contingencies, in contrast with loss contingencies, are not recognized in the accounts. Conservatism dictates that the future event must first occur before recognizing the gain and asset increase (or liability decrease).

B. The gain contingency is reasonably possible -- In this situation, whether the gain can be reasonably estimated or not, the gain contingency is disclosed in the footnotes to the financial statements.

C. The gain contingency is remote -- In this situation, whether the gain can be reasonably estimated or not, footnote disclosure of the gain contingency is not recommended.

V. Guarantees

A. Entities may guarantee a future payment based on a future event. An example is the guarantee of the debt of an affiliate to help the affiliate obtain a loan. Others include the guarantee of a line of credit and guarantees to repurchase receivables that have been sold or assigned.

B. There are two parts to the guarantee.

1. The first part is the obligation of the guarantor to be ready to comply with the guarantee if the triggering event occurs (for example, default by the debtor whose debt is guaranteed by the guarantor). The guarantor recognizes this liability at fair value initially even if there is no expectation of payment. The debit depends on the nature of the guarantee.

 Example:
If the guarantee is for the debt of a customer incurred to buy the products of the entity guaranteeing the customer's debt, the debit is a reduction in the profit on the sale. In a stand-alone guarantee to an unrelated party without consideration, the debit is to an expense. For a lessee guarantee of residual value in an operating lease, the debit is to prepaid rent.

---

2. The second part is the uncertain contingent obligation - the contingent liability. This part is subject to the usual principles regarding contingent liabilities. When a contingent liability is recognized, the amount recorded is the greater of the initial fair value for part 1 above, and the amount to be recognized as a contingency. Subsequent measurement is not addressed by GAAP although recognition of the change in value is presumed with a corresponding change in earnings.

C. The guarantor is required to disclose the following:

1. The nature of the guarantee, the term of the guarantee, how the guarantee came into existence, and the triggering event;

2. The maximum future amount payable under the guarantee;

3. The carrying amount of the liability;

4. A description of recourse provisions or available collateral enabling the guarantor to recover the amounts paid under the guarantee, if any.

IFRS - Contingencies

The last lesson on contingent liabilities addresses international accounting standards.

After studying this lesson, you should be able to:

1. *Define* **"provisions"** *and* **"contingent liability"** *under international accounting standards.*

2. *Determine when provisions are recognized under international accounting standards.*

3. *Describe the similarities and differences in reporting between U.S. and international accounting standards.*

4. *Define* **"more likely than not"** *under international accounting standards.*

I. Contingencies

A. There are a few differences in IFRS and U.S. GAAP for the recognition and measurement of contingencies. The main difference is in terminology. The term "contingent liability" under U.S. GAAP refers to both recognized and unrecognized uncertain obligations. Under IFRS a recognized contingent obligation is referred to as a "provision" and an unrecognized contingent obligation is referred to as a "contingent liability."

B. Another terminology difference is "probable" versus "more likely than not." In U.S. GAAP the term "probable" is interpreted to mean "likely to occur." This distinction is usually a legal opinion made by attorneys. In IFRS, "more likely than not" is interpreted to mean <50%. US GAAP is a higher threshold for accrual because likely to occur would mean more than 70% or so probability of occurrence - where "more likely than not" is a threshold of more than 50% likelihood of occurrence.

C. The table below summarizes the main terminology differences.

	IFRS	U.S. GAAP
Accrued contingent obligation reported on the balance sheet	Provision	Contingent liability
Contingent obligation disclosed in the footnotes	Contingent liability	Contingent liability
Threshold for accrual of the contingent obligation	More likely than not <50%	Probable

II. Liability - Definition under IFRS --
The IFRS definition for liabilities: "present obligations arising from past events, the settlement of which is expected to result in an outflow from the entity of resources embodying economic benefits."

A. There are two general sources of present obligations or liabilities:

1. Legal obligations that derive from a contract, legislation or other legal process.

2. Constructive obligations deriving from the entity's established practices, published policies or other statements that create a valid expectation on the part of other parties that the entity will discharge those responsibilities.

B. Among all the possible types of liabilities, the focus in this section is on estimated liabilities. These include accruals and "provisions." Accruals are much less uncertain than provisions. Examples of accruals include utilities payable and wages payable. Examples of provisions include income taxes payable, property taxes payable and compensated absences liabilities. Under IFRS, accruals and provisions are reported separately.

III. Provisions -- A provision is a liability that is uncertain in terms of timing and amount but is not of uncertain existence. A provision is recognized if the entity has a present obligation (either legal or constructive) as a result of an obligating event that will result in an outflow that is more likely than not. In order to recognize the provision, you must be able to reliably estimate the amount.

   A. Note that except for the 50% threshold, an item meeting the above requirements would qualify as a recognized contingent liability under US standards. However, for US contingent liabilities, there also must be a probable outflow of benefits, where "probable" means much higher than the 50% threshold for international standards. As a result, international standards recognize many more liabilities (as provisions) compared with recognized contingent liabilities under US standards.

   B. If the outflow of benefits is not "more likely than not " but reasonably possible, then the entity discloses the possible obligation and refers to it as a contingent liability.

   C. If the outflow of benefits is "more likely than not " but not estimable, then the entity discloses the possible obligation and refers to it as a contingent liability.

   D. If the outflow of benefits is only remotely possible, there is no recognition or disclosure.

   E. In comparing the two sets of standards in this area, examples of provisions under international standards include (1) income taxes payable, property taxes payable and compensated absences liability; and also (2) warranty liability and premium liability. The first group refers to estimated liabilities under US standards and the second group refers to recognized contingent liabilities under US standards. Thus provisions include but are not limited to US recognized contingent liabilities.

IV. Measuring Provisions

   A. Provisions are measured at the best estimate of the amount required to settle the obligation at the balance sheet date.

   B. Discounting is required if there is a material difference between the expected amount paid, and its present value. This is contrary to US standards which, in most cases, do not apply discounting. Changes in the present value over periods are recognized as a borrowing cost.

   1. Present value measurement can be applied using either of the following techniques:

      a. The traditional present value technique applies the risk adjusted rate directly to estimates of cash flows. If the cash flows are contractual, this technique may be appropriate.

      b. The expected present value technique applies the risk-free rate to multiple cash flow projections each with an associated probability of outcome. If the cash flows are considerably uncertain and there is a wide range of possible amounts, this technique may be appropriate.

Note:
If a range of equally likely amounts is possible for a provision, international standards require recognition of the midpoint of the range (U.S. standards use the lowest amount in the range).

V. Disclosures for Contingent Liabilities under International Standards Include -- (1) an estimate of the financial effect, (2) information about the uncertainties relating to the amount and timing of the outflow of benefits, and (3) the possibility of any reimbursement or recourse for the entity.

VI. Gain Contingencies - Assets

   A. A disclosable contingent asset under international standards is one that is possible or probable (> 50%) but less than "virtually certain," arising from past events and whose existence will be confirmed by the occurrence or non-occurrence of a future uncertain event not wholly in the control of the entity. Contingent assets arise from unplanned or unexpected events that give rise to the possibility of an inflow of economic benefits to the entity.

1. An example is a claim against an insurance company that an entity is pursuing legally. If later the receipt of benefits from the insurance company becomes virtually certain (much higher than probable), then it is recognized - it is no longer contingent at that point. **This is in contrast with U.S. standards, which require realization before recognition.**

B. If the probability of receipt of benefits is remote, no disclosure is warranted.

Earnings Per Share

Introduction to Earnings Per Share

This is the first of three lessons on Earnings Per Share (EPS). This lesson provides the basic and diluted EPS calculations as well as the disclosure requirements.

After studying this lesson, you should be able to:

1. *Complete a calculation of basic EPS.*

2. *Complete a calculation of diluted EPS.*

3. *Identify the disclosure requirements for EPS.*

I. **Earnings Per Share --** There are two EPS figures that firms disclose: basic and diluted. Basic EPS is the EPS based only on actual transactions for the year. Diluted EPS is a "worst-case" figure reflecting the potential dilution of stock options and convertible securities. EPS allows comparisons of performance for firms of any size.

II. **EPS Background**

    A. EPS is computed only for common stock. It represents the amount of earnings on a per-share basis. If EPS were $4, this means that $4 of dividends could have been paid, on average, to each share of common stock outstanding during the year, from earnings in that year. It does not mean the firm is obligated to pay that much, or that it will pay that much. Also, actual common stock dividends paid do not reduce EPS.

    B. There are **two different EPS figures**, each of which is reported for several intermediate subtotals in addition to net income.

> **Definitions:**
> *Basic EPS (BEPS)*: Includes only actual common shares outstanding.
>
> *Diluted EPS (DEPS)*: Includes securities that may become common stock in the future, such as convertible stock and stock options, in addition to actual shares of common outstanding.

       1. The securities that may become common stock in the future are called potential common stock (PCS) or potentially dilutive securities. If a firm has no PCS then only BEPS is reported.

    C. **Disclosure of EPS --** SFAS #128 provides guidance on the disclosure of earnings per share information on the face of the income statement. This guidance is provided for companies with a simple capital structure and for those companies with a complex capital structure.

       1. **Simple Capital Structure --** A simple capital structure is one in which the corporation only has common stock outstanding or one in which the corporation has common stock and nonconvertible preferred stock outstanding.

          a. **Formula --** If the corporation only has common stock outstanding, the Basic Earnings per Share (BEPS) is calculated by the formula shown below.

> BEPS = (net income) / (weighted average common shares outstanding)

          b. **Formula --** If the company has common stock and nonconvertible preferred stock outstanding, the Basic Earnings per Share is calculated by the formulas shown below.

BEPS = (net income available to common) / (weighted average common shares outstanding)

BEPS = (net income - preferred stock dividend) / (weighted average common shares outstanding)

2. **Complex Capital Structure**

   a. A complex capital structure typically includes common stock, along with equity contracts and convertible securities. These securities may become common stock in the future and thus must be included in an EPS figure so that users can assess the impact of these potential changes on EPS.

   b. A company with a complex capital structure is required to disclose the Basic Earnings per Share and the Diluted Earnings per Share. This is called dual EPS reporting.

   Note:
   The potential common stock may affect both the numerator and denominator.

   i. **Formula --** The Diluted Earnings per Share is calculated by the formula shown below, which includes the effects of potential common stock (PCS).

DEPS = (net income available to common adjusted for effects of PCS) / (weighted average common shares plus shares issuable from PCS)

Example:
A convertible bond is a PCS. Under certain conditions, discussed below, they are assumed converted into common stock. If they were actually converted, no interest would be paid and net income (numerator of DEPS) would increase. Likewise, the common shares from conversion would have been outstanding, thus increasing the denominator of DEPS.

III. Disclosure Requirements

A. EPS amounts (all after tax) must be disclosed for the following line items in the income statement:

	Simple Capital Structure (No PCS)	Complex Capital Structure (PCS Present)
On the face of the Income Statement		
1. Income from continuing operations	BEPS	BEPS and DEPS
2. Net income	BEPS	BEPS and DEPS
Either on the face of the Income Statement or in Footnotes		
3. Discontinued operations	BEPS	BEPS and DEPS
4. Extraordinary items	BEPS	BEPS and DEPS

B. BEPS and DEPS for the first two amounts must be shown with equal prominence. The terms basic EPS and diluted EPS are not required terms. Earnings per share, and earnings per share-assuming dilution, are also acceptable.

C. Elaboration

1. As the previous table shows, the maximum EPS disclosures in a simple capital structure is 4 BEPS amounts and in a complex capital structure the maximum disclosure is 4 BEPS and 4 DEPS (or 8 total EPS amounts).

2. Financial statement users wishing to compute EPS for intermediate subtotals such as income before extraordinary items may do so with the required disclosures.

3. If BEPS and DEPS are equal, both are reported so that users know there are PCS but there was no material dilutive effect.

IV. Basic EPS - A Closer Look

A. Effect of Preferred Stock (numerator of BEPS)

> BEPS = (net income available to common) / weighted average shares outstanding
>
> BEPS = (net income - preferred stock dividends) / weighted average shares outstanding

B. Preferred Stock Cumulative/Not

1. The amount of preferred stock dividends subtracted in the numerator of BEPS depends on whether the preferred stock is cumulative or not, and if not, on the amount declared in the period.

2. **Amount Subtracted Table** -- Amount of Preferred Dividend Subtracted in EPS Numerator:

Study Tip:
Most Preferred Stock is Cumulative.

	Cumulative Preferred	Noncumulative Preferred
Current period dividends Declared	1 full year's dividends	Amount declared
Current period dividends Not declared	1 full year's dividends	None

3. "Cumulative" means that if a year's preferred dividend is not paid (skipped), no other dividends may be paid before the skipped dividends (dividends in arrears) are paid. Whether or not dividends are declared on cumulative preferred stock, one full year's dividends is subtracted from the numerator of BEPS because no common dividends can be paid on these earnings before the preferred dividends are declared. This also means that in a year in which dividends in arrears from a previous year are paid in addition to the current year dividend, still only one year is subtracted from the current year BEPS numerator because BEPS in the previous year has already been reduced by the skipped dividends.

4. **Noncumulative Preferred Stock** -- Receives dividends only if declared. Skipped dividends are never paid.

5. **Tax Effect** -- There is no tax effect to consider for preferred stock dividends because dividends paid are not deductible for tax purposes.

6. **Examples** -- A firm has had 1,000 shares of 7%, $100 preferred stock outstanding for several years. The annual dividend on the preferred is $7,000 = .07($100)(1,000). Year 4 is the current year.

a. The preferred stock is cumulative and there are no dividends in arrears. $7,000 is subtracted from income in computing BEPS whether or not the dividend is declared in Year 4. Even if only a partial dividend (say $4,000) is paid, the full $7,000 is subtracted.

b. The preferred stock is cumulative and there are two years' dividends in arrears. $7,000 is subtracted from income in computing BEPS whether or not the dividend is declared, and regardless of the amount declared.

c. The preferred stock is noncumulative. No dividends are declared in Year 4. There is no subtraction in computing Year 4 BEPS.

Note:
In all these cases, it is the amount of dividends declared that matters, not the amount paid.

d. The preferred stock is noncumulative and $2,000 of dividends is declared in Year 4. Subtract $2,000 only.

e. The preferred stock is noncumulative, three years' dividends have been skipped, and $2,000 of dividends is declared in Year 4. Subtract $2,000 only.

Basic Earnings Per Share

This is the second of three lessons on Earnings Per Share (EPS). This lesson explains the calculation of weighted average shares outstanding.

After studying this lesson, you should be able to:

1. *Complete a calculation of weighted average shares outstanding with stock issuance, repurchase, dividends and splits.*

I. **Weighted Average (WA) Computation (denominator of BEPS)**

    A. The denominator of BEPS is the weighted average (WA) shares outstanding during the period (not the number outstanding at the end of the period unless there has been no change in the number of shares outstanding all year). Treasury shares purchased during the period reduce the WA. The reason for weighting the shares is that shares outstanding a longer portion of the year represent capital investment that has been working longer for the firm than shares outstanding a shorter portion of the year. The numerator of EPS is income, an amount representing the entire year. The income earned on the capital investment must be related to the period for which the investment was used by the firm.

    B. The calculation weights each change in shares for the portion of the period the new shares are outstanding (add), or for the period the shares were not outstanding as in the case of a purchase of treasury shares (subtract).

	# Shares
Shares outstanding January 1	2,000
Issue shares April 1	1,200
Purchase shares for treasury October 1	400
Issue shares December 1	120
Issue shares December 31	200

The WA shares outstanding (denominator of BEPS) =

2,000(12/12) + 1,200(9/12) - 400(3/12) + 120(1/12) = 2,810

        1. **Explanation** -- The April 1 issuance caused 1,200 shares to be issued. These shares were outstanding 9 months. This is equivalent to 900 shares being outstanding the entire year. The shares issued December 31 were not outstanding for any period of time during the year and are not included in the WA. If the firm had no preferred stock and net income was $5,620 for the period, BEPS would be $2.00 ($5,620/2,810).

II. **Share Adjustments** -- Stock dividends and splits are adjustments to the number of shares outstanding for all investors holding stocks.

    A. **Two for One Stock Split** -- A 10% stock dividend gives an investor holding 1,000 shares an additional 100 shares. Each investor maintains the percentage of the firm previously owned. There are 10% more shares outstanding but each share is worth proportionately less. A two-for-one stock split doubles the number of shares outstanding but the value of each share is halved. These are not substantive changes in shares outstanding the way a new stock issuance is. They bring no resources into the firm.

B. General Rule WA Calculation -- All stock dividends and splits are assumed to have been outstanding since the inception of the firm. Apply the percentage of the stock dividend or the factor in a split (factor = 3 in a three-for-one split) to all changes in outstanding stock occurring before the stock dividend or split.

Example: Assume the data from the previous example, with the addition of a stock split and dividend:

Shares outstanding January 1	2,000
Issue shares April 1	1,200
Two-for-One stock split May 1	
Purchase shares for treasury October 1	400
30% stock dividend November 1	
Issue shares December 1	120
Issue shares December 31	200

The WA shares outstanding (denominator of BEPS) =

$$\{[2,000(12/12) + 1,200(9/12)]2 - 400(3/12)\}1.30 + 120(1/12)$$

$$= 7,420$$

The factor of 2 for the two-for-one split is applied to the shares outstanding at the beginning of the year and the April 1 issuance. The 30% stock dividend is likewise applied to all changes before it. The factor used is 1.30 because the 30% stock dividend increases the shares already outstanding on that date by 30%.

C. Adjust for EPS -- If a stock dividend or split occurs between the balance sheet date and issuance of the balance sheet, all share amounts are adjusted for EPS purposes.

III. Contingent Shares

A. Are shares issuable for little or no cash consideration upon satisfaction of certain conditions. They are considered outstanding as of the date the conditions have been met.

B. Weighting Fraction Period -- The weighting is for the fraction of the period the conditions were met.

Example:
If 2,400 shares are issuable contingent on a particular performance measure that is met by the firm on August 1, then even though the shares may not be issued until the next period, 1,000 shares are included in the WA for BEPS for the current period (2,400 x 5/12).

C. Contingency -- If the contingency is a future earnings level, no contingent shares are included in the WA of BEPS because the contingency cannot be met until a future period. The same holds for a current period earnings level because the contingency cannot be met until the last day of the year.

IV. Illustration BEPS Reporting

> 👁 **Example:**
> All amounts after-tax: Common Stock:
>
> | | | |
> |---|---|---|
> | Income from continuing operations | $40,000 | Shares outstanding Jan.1: 10,000 |
> | Discontinued operations (net) | (10,000) | Issued 2,000 shares May 1 |
> | Extraordinary gain | 12,000 | Issued 20% stock dividend June 14 |
> | | | Purchased 1,000 treasury shares July 1 |
> | Net income | $42,000 | |
>
> The firm has 1,000 shares of 4%, $100 par cumulative preferred stock. No dividends were declared on the preferred stock in this year.
>
> WA shares = [10,000 + 2,000(8/12)]1.2 - 1,000(6/12) = 13,100. This value is used for all EPS figures.
>
> Annual preferred dividend requirement: 1,000($100)(.04) = $4,000
>
> **Presentation of EPS:**
>
> | | |
> |---|---|
> | Income from continuing operations: ($40,000 - $4,000)/13,100 | $2.75 |
> | Discontinued operations: ($10,000/13,100) | (.76) |
> | Extraordinary gain ($12,000/13,100) | .92 |
> | Net income ($42,000 - $4,000)/13,100 (rounded) | $2.91 |

Note: Only income from continuing operations and net income subtract the preferred dividends from the numerator. The other EPS amounts are not income amounts but rather individual components on a per-share basis (for example, extraordinary items). If the firm chooses to report intermediate income figures such as income before extraordinary items per share, these intermediate income figures subtract the preferred dividends.

V. Additional Example -- The following example is provided for additional practice. You should verify the calculations for practice.

Example:

This example shows an alternative way to compute the weighted average shares. The Simple Company is located in Knoxville, Tennessee and has an accounting year that ends on December 31 of each year. A modified income statement for the 20x7 accounting year is presented below.

Income from Continuing Operations	$1,500,000
Extraordinary Gain (less Income Tax Expense of $90,000)	210,000
Net Income	$1,710,000

The tax rate for 20x7 was 30%.

The capital structure of the Simple Company includes common stock and nonconvertible, cumulative, preferred stock. Relevant information related to these securities is shown below.

Common Stock, Par Value of $1

Common Shares Outstanding on January 1, 20x7	270,000	Shares
Sold Common Shares on September 1, 20x7	18,000	Shares
Common Shares Outstanding on December 31, 20x7	288,000	Shares

Non-Convertible, Cumulative, 6% Preferred Stock, Par Value of $20

Preferred Shares Outstanding throughout the year 7,500 Shares

Requirement: Determine the earnings per-share disclosure for the 20x7 accounting year.

Preferred Stock Dividend: 7,500 X $20 X 6% = $9,000

Weighted Average of Common Shares Outstanding:

Shares		Months	
270,000	x	8	2,160,000
288,000	x	4	1,152,000
		12	3,312,000

3,312,000/12 = 276,000 Shares*

Basic Earnings Per Share Calculation:

Income from Continuing Operations	($1,500,000 - $9,000)/276,000	=	$5.40
Extraordinary Gain	$210,000/276,000	=	0.76
Net Income	($1,710,000 - $9,000)/276,000	=	$6.16

=*This agrees with the calculation method shown in the previous discussion: 270,000 + 18,000(4/12) = 276,000

Diluted Earnings Per Share

This is the third of three lessons on Earnings Per Share (EPS). This lesson presents how to incorporate potentially dilutive securities into the diluted EPS calculation.

After studying this lesson, you should be able to:

1. *Calculate the potentially dilutive effect of convertible preferred stock on basic EPS.*

2. *Calculate the potentially dilutive effect of stock options and warrants using the "treasure stock method" on basic EPS.*

3. *Calculate the potentially dilutive effect of multiple dilutive securities on basic EPS.*

I. **Diluted EPS --** is conceptually different from BEPS. It is an imaginary calculation based on events that have not happened as of the balance sheet date. The FASB believes that requiring a second EPS number reflecting the effects of securities that may become common stock in the future enhances the value of per-share disclosures.

II. **Background**

> **Definition:**
> *Diluted EPS (DEPS)*: Reflects the maximum dilution or **lowest value of EPS** that is possible given the firm's outstanding securities at the balance sheet date.

   A. **Effect PCS into BEPS --** DEPS incorporates the effect of potential common stock (PCS)- securities that can become common stock in the future, into BEPS. There may be both numerator and denominator effects. BEPS is used as the benchmark value into which the numerator and denominator changes stemming from PCS are incorporated. Thus, DEPS equals BEPS adjusted by the effects of PCS.

III. **How Potential Common Stock Affects EPS**

> **Note:** An important thing to remember is that PCS is not common stock at the balance sheet date. They are assumed to be exercised (stock options and warrants) or converted (convertible preferred stock and bonds) as of the beginning of the year (or date of issuance if later). Upon assumed exercise or conversion, the numerator and denominator effects are computed, and are considered for incorporation into EPS.

> **Example:**
> A firm has 10, 8%, $1,000 convertible bonds outstanding the entire period. Each bond is convertible into 20 shares of common stock. The tax rate is 30%. At the beginning of the period, the bonds are assumed converted. The result is that interest of $560 after tax would not have been paid (10)($1,000)(.08)(1 - .30). That is the numerator effect. The denominator effect is the 200 shares of common stock that would be issued on conversion (10)(20).

IV. **Dilution and Antidilution**

   A. **Diluted PCS --** Only dilutive PCS are incorporated into DEPS.

1. **Explanation --** This means when we add the numerator effect of a PCS to the numerator of BEPS, and the denominator effect to the denominator of BEPS, the result is a lower EPS number. A dilutive PCS means that DEPS is lower than BEPS as a result of assumed conversion or exercise of the PCS.

B. **An antidilutive PCS** (one that increases EPS when it is added into BEPS) is ignored for purposes of computing DEPS.

C. **Control Number --** For purposes of testing for dilution and antidilution, the control number is income from continuing operations.

> **Example:**
> **1.** BEPS = $1,000/2,000 = $.50. A potential common stock is assumed converted and the numerator and denominator effects are $200 and 500, respectively. DEPS = ($1,000 + $200)/(2,000 + 500) = $.48. The numerator and denominator effects are added to the numerator and denominator of BEPS. In this case, the PCS is dilutive because DEPS is lower than BEPS. BEPS would be reported at $.50 and DEPS would be reported at $.48.
>
> **2.** BEPS = $1,000/2,000 = $.50. A potential common stock is assumed converted and the numerator and denominator effects are $200 and 300, respectively. DEPS = ($1,000 + $200)/(2,000 + 300) = $.52. In this case, the PCS is antidilutive because DEPS is higher than BEPS. The PCS is not entered into BEPS. BEPS = DEPS in this case.
>
> **3.** Income from continuing operations is $1,200 and the WA shares outstanding is 2,400. An extraordinary loss of $200 is also reported, resulting in net income of $1,000. The firm has a PCS with no numerator effect but a denominator effect of 200 (200 shares issuable on exercise).
>
> | | BEPS | DEPS |
> |---|---|---|
> | Income from continuing operations | | |
> | $1,200/2,400 = | $.50 | |
> | $1,200/2,600 = | | $.462 |
> | Extraordinary loss | | |
> | $200/2,400 = | (.083) | |
> | $200/2,600 = | | (.077) |
> | Net income | | |
> | $1,000/2,400 = | $.417 | |
> | $1,000/2,600 = | | $.385 |
>
> The EPS amounts above would be reported as shown. However, the result for the extraordinary loss is antidilutive because the DEPS result (negative .077) is larger (less negative) than for BEPS (negative .083). Because the result is dilutive for income from continuing operations (the control number), all EPS amounts use the same denominator.
>
> Conversely, if income from continuing operations is negative and including the denominator effect of a PCS in the calculation of DEPS for that income figure causes it to be less negative (larger), then no PCS is assumed converted for any income amount. BEPS = DEPS in this case, for all amounts to be shown on a per-share basis.

V. **Treasury Stock Method --** Incorporating stock options and warrants into DEPS

A. To enter stock options and warrants (which are PCS) into DEPS, a three-step process is used called the treasury stock method.

Example:
Assume a firm's BEPS = $1,200/700 = $1.71. The firm has 2,000 stock options outstanding the entire year. The exercise price is $30. The average market price of common stock for the period is $40.

1. Assume exercise of the options. Shares issued on exercise = 2,000

2. Purchase treasury shares with the proceeds from exercise: 2,000($30)/$40 = number of treasury shares purchased = (1,500)

3. Incremental shares = denominator effect = 500

Step b. divides the total proceeds from exercise [$60,000 = 2,000($30)] by the average price per stock the firm would be required to pay for its own shares ($40). The result is that the firm would buy back 1,500 of its own shares. The net number of new shares outstanding as a result of the treasury stock method is 500. DEPS = $1,200/(700 + 500) = $1.00. DEPS is less than BEPS. Therefore the options are dilutive and are entered into DEPS.

The purpose of assuming the purchase of treasury stock is to reduce the total dilution from exercise. Otherwise, the denominator effect would be 2,000, not 500. There is no numerator effect.

B. **Antidilutive Options --** Options are antidilutive when the option price exceeds the market price. In the above example, if the average market price were $25, the three steps would produce a negative number, causing DEPS to increase. The easy way to remember this is that no one would exercise such a stock option and pay more than market price.

VI. **If-Converted Method --** Incorporating convertible securities into DEPS.

   A. To enter convertible securities (which are PCS) into DEPS, the if-converted method is used.

   B. **Convertible Assumed Converted --** The convertible is assumed converted as of the beginning of the period or date of issuance, whichever is later. The numerator and denominator effects are computed and entered into DEPS. If DEPS decreases, the PCS is dilutive and the security is included in the computation of DEPS.

Example:
(Convertible bonds) BEPS for a firm is $3,000/1,000 = $3.00. The firm also has 10, 8%, $1,000 convertible bonds outstanding the entire period. Each bond is convertible into 20 shares of common stock. The tax rate is 30%. At the beginning of the period, the bonds are assumed converted under the if-converted method. The numerator effect is the interest of $560 after tax that would not have been paid (10)($1,000)(.08)(1 - .30). The denominator effect is the 200 shares of common stock that would be issued on conversion (10)(20). DEPS = ($3,000 + $560)/(1,000 + 200) = $2.97. DEPS is less than BEPS. Therefore, the bonds are dilutive and are entered into DEPS.

   C. **Interest Expense --** If the bonds were sold at a discount or premium, interest expense will reflect periodic amortization. The interest expense recognized should be added back (after tax), not the cash interest paid, because earnings was reduced by the expense.

   D. **Issued Mid-Year --** If the bonds were issued at midyear, the numerator and denominator effects each would be multiplied by 1/2, resulting in smaller increases to the BEPS numerator and denominator.

E. No Tax Effect -- Convertible preferred stock is handled the same way as convertible bonds except there is no tax effect.

 Example:
Net income is $3,400 and WA shares are 700. The annual preferred dividend claim on convertible preferred stock is $400 and if converted, 100 common shares would be issued. In computing BEPS, convertible preferred stock is treated just like nonconvertible preferred stock.

BEPS = ($3,400 - $400)/700 = $4.29

The numerator effect is the dividends that would not be paid if the convertible preferred stock were converted. The denominator effect is the common shares issued on conversion.

DEPS = ($3,400 - $400 + $400)/(700 + 100) = $4.25

The $400 of dividends is added back (after being subtracted in calculating BEPS) in calculating DEPS. DEPS is less than BEPS. Therefore, the convertible preferred stock is dilutive and is entered into DEPS.

VII. The Dilution/Antidilution Method -- when there is more than one PCS

A. Two or More PCS -- The previous examples have used only one PCS. What happens if there are two or more? Which one is entered into BEPS first? The solution is to incorporate the PCS into DEPS in order of most dilutive first, then the next dilutive PCS and so forth. The PCS with the most dilutive potential is the one with the lowest ratio of numerator effect/denominator effect (N/D).

B. Process -- The process is to enter the PCS with the lowest N/D into DEPS first. Then compare the next lowest N/D with the resulting DEPS. Continue to add PCS into DEPS until a PCS is encountered with a higher N/D than the previous DEPS figure, or until all PCS are entered. Use income from continuing operations as the control number.

Example: Data for Year 5:

Income from continuing operations	$26,000
Extraordinary gain after tax	12,000
Net income	$38,000

Common stock shares outstanding all period: 10,000

BEPS for income from continuing operations = $26,000/10,000= $2.60

Potential common stock outstanding all period:	Numerator Effect	Denominator Effect	Numerator/ Denominator (N/D)
Warrants	$ 0	2,000	$ 0
Convertible bonds issue A	3,000	1,000	3.00
Convertible bonds issue B	2,000	1,500	1.33

The warrants are considered first because the ratio of its numerator effect to denominator effect (N/D) is the lowest of the three.

Income from continuing operations is used as the control number. The warrants are entered into DEPS for income from continuing operations because its N/D of $0 is less than BEPS. The tentative DEPS = ($26,000 + $0)/(10,000 + 2,000) = $2.17.

The convertible bonds issue B is the next to consider because it has the second lowest N/D. Its ratio is $1.33 which is less than the tentative DEPS of $2.17 and thus is entered into DEPS. The new tentative DEPS = ($26,000 + $0 + $2,000)/(10,000 + 2,000 + 1,500) = $2.07.

The convertible bonds issue A is not entered into DEPS because its N/D exceeds the previous tentative DEPS of $2.07. Thus, the final DEPS for income from continuing operations is $2.07. This process thus determines the denominator for all DEPS numbers.

The complete EPS presentation for this firm:

	BEPS	DEPS
Income from continuing operations	$2.60	$2.07
Extraordinary gain		
$12,000/10,000	1.20	
$12,000/(10,000 + 2,000 + 1,500)		.89
Net income		
$38,000/10,000	$3.80	
($38,000+ $0 + $2,000)/(10,000 + 2,000 + 1,500)		$2.96

VIII. Additional Examples -- This section provides an example Income Statement and analysis of the stock options. You should verify the calculations for practice.

Example:
The Complex Company is located in Knoxville, Tennessee and has an accounting year that ends on December 31. A modified income statement for the 20x7 accounting year is presented below.

Income from Continuing Operations	$1,500,000
Extraordinary Gain (less Income Tax Expense of $90,000)	$210,000
Net Income	$1,710,000

The tax rate for 20x7 was 30%.

The capital structure of the Complex Company includes common stock, nonconvertible, cumulative, preferred stock, and stock options. Relevant information related to these securities is shown below.

Common Stock, Par Value of $1

Common Shares Outstanding on January 1, 20x7	270,000 Shares
Sold Common Shares on September 1, 20x7	18,000 Shares
Common Shares Outstanding on December 31, 20x7	288,000 Shares

Non-Convertible, Cumulative, 6% Preferred Stock, Par Value of $20

Preferred Shares Outstanding throughout the year	7,500 Shares

Stock Options - The options represent 6,000 shares. The option price is $20. The average market price for the 20x7 accounting year is $25. The stock options were outstanding for the entire 20x7 accounting year.

Requirement: Determine the earnings per share disclosure for the 20x7 accounting year.

Solution: Preferred Stock Dividend:
7,500 X $20 X 6% = $9,000

Weighted Average of Common Shares Outstanding:

Shares		Months	
270,000	x	8	2,160,000
288,000	x	4	1,152,000
		12	3,312,000

3,312,000 /12 = 276,000 Shares

*This agrees with the calculation method shown in the previous discussion: 270,000 + 18,000(4/12) = 276,000

Analysis of Stock Options - Treasury Stock Method:

1. Since the average market price is greater than the option price, the stock options are dilutive.

2. To determine the impact of the stock options on the Diluted Earnings per Share Calculation, the treasury stock method is applied.

Step 1: The Stock Options are assumed exercised and 6,000 new shares are issued at $20 per share.

Step 2: The cash from the exercise of the stock options, $120,000, is used to purchase treasury stock at the average market price for the period (6,000 x $20 = $120,000). The number of treasury shares would be 4,800 shares ($120,000/25 = 4,800).

Under step 1, 6,000 new shares would be issued, and under step 2, 4,800 shares would be acquired. The net increase in shares outstanding would be 1,200 shares, the denominator effect.

Effect of the Stock Options:

Adjustment to the Numerator:	$0.00
Adjustment to the Denominator	1,200 shares
N/D Ratio $0/1,200:	$0.00

Basic Earnings Per Share Calculation:

Income from Continuing Operations

($1,500,000 - $9,000)/276,000 = $5.40

Extraordinary Gain

$210,000/276,000 = $0.76

Net Income

($1,710,000 - $9,000)/276,000 = $6.16

Diluted Earnings Per Share Calculation:

Income from Continuing Operations

($1,500,000 - $9,000)/(276,000 + 1,200) = $5.38

Extraordinary Gain

($210,000/276,000 + 1,200) =   0.76

Net Income

($1,710,000 - $9,000)/(276,000 + 1,200) = $6.14

Example:
This example has both nonconvertible preferred and convertible preferred.

Background/Requirement
The Complex Company is located in Knoxville, Tennessee and has an accounting year that ends on December 31. A modified income statement for the 20x7 accounting year is presented below.

Income from Continuing Operations	$1,500,000
Extraordinary Gain (less Income Tax Expense of $90,000)	$210,000
Net Income	$1,710,000

The tax rate for 20x7 was 30%.

The capital structure of the Complex Company includes common stock, nonconvertible and convertible, cumulative, preferred stock. Relevant information related to these securities is shown below.

Common Stock, Par Value of $1

Common Shares Outstanding on January 1, 20x7	270,000 Shares
Sold Common Shares on September 1, 20x7	18,000 Shares
Common Shares Outstanding on December 31, 20x7	288,000 Shares

Non-Convertible, Cumulative, 6% Preferred Stock, Par Value of $20

Preferred Shares Outstanding throughout the year	7,500 Shares

Cumulative, Convertible 4% Preferred Stock, Par Value of $10

Preferred Shares Outstanding throughout the year	5,000 Shares

The preferred stock is convertible at the rate of 5 common shares for one preferred share.

Requirement: Determine the earnings per share disclosure for the 20x7 accounting year.

Solution: Preferred Stock Dividend on Non-Convertible Preferred Stock:

7,500 X $20 X 6% = $9,000

Weighted Average of Common Shares Outstanding:

Cumulative, Convertible 4% Preferred Stock, Par Value of $10

Preferred Shares Outstanding throughout the year	5,000 Shares

Shares		Months	
270,000	x	8	2,160,000
288,000	x	4	1,152,000
		12	3,312,000

3,312,000   /12 = 276,000 Shares

*This agrees with the calculation method shown in the previous discussion: 270,000 + 18,000(4/12) = 276,000

Analysis of the Convertible Preferred Shares -- If Converted Method:

To analyze the impact of the convertible preferred shares on the Diluted Earnings per Share Calculation, the If Converted Method is applied.

Convertible Preferred Stock Dividend:	5,000 X $10 X 4% =	$2,000

Common Shares That Would be Issued Upon Conversion:

	5,000 X 5 =	25,000	Shares
Adjustment to the Numerator		$2,000	
Adjustment to the Denominator		25,000	Shares
N/D Ratio	$2,000/25,000 Shares =	$0.08	

Basic Earnings Per Share Calculation:

Income from Continuing Operations	($1,500,000 - $9,000 - $2,000)/276,000 =	$5.39
Extraordinary Gain	$210,000/276,000 =	.76
Net Income	($1,710,000 - $9,000 - $2,000)/276,000 =	$6.16

Diluted Earnings Per Share Calculation:

Note: Since the N/D ratio of the convertible preferred shares is less than the basic earnings per share for income from continuing operations, the convertible preferred shares will have a dilutive effect.

Income from Continuing Operations	($1,500,000 - $9,000)/(276,000 + 25,000) =	$4.95
Extraordinary Gain	($210,000)/301,000 =	.70
Net Income	($1,710,000 - $9,000)/(276,000 + 25,000) =	$5.65

Example: This example shows the EPS disclosure for an accounting year. Example: The Complex Company is located in Knoxville, Tennessee and has an accounting year that ends on December 31. A modified income statement for the 20x7 accounting year is presented below.

Income from Continuing Operations	$1,500,000
Extraordinary Gain (less Income Tax Expense of $90,000)	210,000
Net Income	$1,710,000

The tax rate for 20x7 was 30%.

The capital structure of the Complex Company includes common stock, nonconvertible, cumulative, preferred stock, and convertible bonds. Relevant information related to these securities is shown below.

Common Stock, Par Value of $1

Common Shares Outstanding on January 1, 20x7	270,000	Shares
Sold Common Shares on September 1, 20x7	18,000	Shares
Common Shares Outstanding on December 31, 20x7	288,000	Shares

Non-Convertible, Cumulative, 6% Preferred Stock, Par Value of $20

Preferred Shares Outstanding throughout the year   7,500   Shares

6% Convertible Bonds Payable

Total Face Value of Outstanding Bonds $1,000,000

The bonds were outstanding throughout the year

The bonds are convertible to common shares at the rate of 50

shares for each $1,000 bond.

Requirement: Determine the earnings per share disclosure for the 20x7 accounting year.
Solution:
Preferred Stock Dividend on Non-Convertible Preferred Stock: 7,500 X $20 X 6% = $9,000

Weighted Average of Common Shares Outstanding:

Shares		Months	
270,000	x	8	2,160,000
288,000	x	4	1,152,000
		12	3,312,000
			3,312,000/12 = 276,000 Shares

*This agrees with the calculation method shown in the previous discussion: 270,000 + 18,000(4/12) = 276,000

Analysis of the Convertible Bonds - If Converted Method:
To analyze the impact of the convertible bonds on the Diluted Earnings per Share Calculation, the If Converted Method is applied.

Bond Interest Expense

$1,000,000 X 6% = $60,000

Bond Interest Expense, Net of Tax

$60,000 (1-.30) = $42,000

Common Shares That Would be Issued Upon Conversion:

(1,000,000/$1,000) X 50 Shares = 50,000

Adjustment to the Numerator	$42,000	
Adjustment to the Denominator	50,000	Shares
N/D	$42,000/50,000 Shares	= $0.84

Basic Earnings Per Share Calculation:

Income from Continuing Operations	($1,500,000 - $9,000)/276,000 =	5.40
Extraordinary Gain	$210,000/276,000 =	.76
Net Income	($1,710,000 - $9,000)/276,000 =	$6.16

Diluted Earnings Per Share Calculation:

Note: Since the N/D ratio of the convertible bonds is less than the basic earnings per share for income from continuing operations, the convertible bonds will have a dilutive effect.

Income from Continuing Operations

	($1,500,000 - $9,000 + $42,000)/(276,000 + 50,000) =	$4.70
Extraordinary Gain	$210,000/326,000 =	.64
Net Income	$1,710,000 - 9,000 + 42,000)/326,000 =	$5.35

Example:

Note: In the last three examples (Complex Company), if the firm had all three potential common stock securities at the same time (stock options, convertible preferred shares, and convertible bonds payable), the equity contracts and convertible securities would be ranked in order of N/D ratio, from lowest to highest. Based on the data from the previous examples this rank ordering is shown below.

Security	N/D
Stock Options	$0.00 = $0/1,200
Convertible Preferred Shares	$0.08 = $2,000/25,000
Convertible Bonds	$0.84 = $42,000/50,000

The calculation of DEPS for income from continuing operations is as follows (all EPS figures are for income from continuing operations):

BEPS = ($1,500,000 - $9,000 - $2,000)/276,000 = $5.39

First, enter the stock options into DEPS because the N/D ratio of $0.00 is less than $5.39. The tentative DEPS figure = ($1,500,000 - $9,000 - $2,000)/(276,000 + 1,200) = $5.37.

Second, enter the convertible preferred into DEPS because the N/D ratio of $.08 is less than $5.37. The tentative DEPS figure = ($1,500,000 - $9,000 - $2,000 + $2,000)/(276,000 + 1,200 + 25,000) = $4.93.

Lastly, enter the convertible bonds into DEPS because the N/D ratio of $.84 is less than $4.93. The tentative DEPS figure = ($1,500,000 - $9,000 - $2,000 + $2,000 + $42,000)/(276,000 + 1,200 + 25,000 + 50,000) = $4.35.

This is the reported amount for DEPS for income from continuing operations.

Earnings Per Share and IFRS

This lesson presents the significant differences in the accounting for Earnings Per Share (EPS) under IFRS versus U.S. GAAP.

After studying this lesson, you should be able to:

1. *Identify the major differences in the accounting for EPS under IFRS versus U.S. GAAP.*

I. EPS and IFRS

A. There are a few significant differences in the accounting for EPS under IFRS than according to U.S. GAAP. The table below summarizes these differences.

IFRS	U.S. GAAP
There are no extraordinary items, so no EPS for extraordinary items	Must show EPS for extraordinary items
For diluted EPS dilution potential of ordinary shares determined independently each period	For diluted EPS dilution potential of ordinary shares determined cumulatively year to date
Basic and diluted EPS can be shown on alternative earnings measures	Basic and diluted EPS are not allowed for alternative earnings measures

B. **No EPS for extraordinary items** -- Under IFRS extraordinary items are not presented on the income statement.

C. **Potentially dilutive securities** -- The number of potentially dilutive securities is determined independently for each reporting period. Therefore the number of potentially dilutive securities in the annual or year-to-date report may not equal the potentially dilutive securities in the interim period.

D. **Alternative measures of earnings** -- IFRS permits presentation in the footnotes EPS information based on alternative measures of earnings. U.S. GAAP does not allow this reporting and the SEC restrict the use of non-GAAP measures.

Exit or Disposal Activities and Discontinued Operations

This lesson presents the accounting and reporting for exit or disposal activities and discontinued operations.

After studying this lesson, you should be able to:

1. *Calculate the gain or loss on the disposal or involuntary conversion of a plant asset.*

2. *Complete the journal entry to record the disposal or involuntary conversion of a plant asset.*

3. *Define what is meant by a "component of an entity."*

4. *Calculate the gain or loss on a discontinued operation.*

5. *Complete the financial statement presentation of a discontinued operation.*

I. Exit or Disposal Activity

A. A company may voluntarily sell, dispose or abandon plant assets. In the case of fire, flood or other event, the plant asset may be destroyed involuntarily. In either case, the asset must be depreciated up to the date of the disposal. So the first thing that must be done in recording an exit or disposal activity is to record depreciation.

B. Sale of a plant asset requires removing the asset and accumulated depreciation, recording the receipt of cash and recognition of the gain or loss on the sale. When the cash received from the sale exceeds the assets net book value (asset cost - accumulated depreciation), then a gain is recognized. When the cash received is less than the assets net book value, then a loss is recognized. The gain or loss on the disposal of an asset is reported on the income statement with other items from customary business activities.

 Example: Assume Shelby Company purchased a plant asset for $20,000 with a 10-year life on January 1, 20x0. On July 1, 20x8, Shelby Company sold the plant asset for $5,000. The entries for the sale of the plant asset are as follows:

Depreciation expense	$1,000
Accumulated depreciation	$1,000

(to record 6 months of depreciation in the year of sale - (20,000/10 yrs) x 6/12)

Cash	$5,000
Accumulated depreciation	$17,000*
Plant Asset	$20,000
Gain on sale of plant asset	$2,000

(to record the gain on the sale of the plant asset)
*((20,000/10 yrs) x 8.5 years held) = 17,000)

C. If the asset is abandoned or there is an involuntary conversion because the asset is destroyed, then no cash is received and the gain or loss equals the net book value of the asset on the date of the abandonment or conversion. The loss on abandonment or conversion is an ordinary loss and part of continuing operations on the income statement. The next section presents the accounting and reporting for discontinued operations.

II. Discontinued Operations

A. **Comparative financial statements** -- The income of a discontinued segment, and any gain or loss from its disposal, are separated from income from continuing operations, for **all periods presented**, even though in previous periods the income from the segment was part of continuing operations. This requirement enhances the consistency of comparative financial statements. Discontinued operations are shown below income from continuing operations in the income statement, and above extraordinary items. Earnings per share is presented for discontinued operations on the face of the income statement.

B. **Reporting Example** -- The example below is simplified to convey the basic reporting. The estimated disposal loss, is not shown in this example but appears in a later more complete example.

> **Example:**
> The income of Old, a reporting unit of Car, Inc., is $20 and $5 for years 6 and 7. Total Car income is $100 each year. In year 7 Old is discontinued and put up for sale. Year 7's comparative income statement shows the change in reporting for year 6.
>
> | | Year 6 | Year 7 |
> |---|---|---|
> | Income from continuing operations | $80 | $95 |
> | Discontinued operation | $20 | $5 |
> | Net income | $100 | $100 |
>
> The year 6 income statement published in year 6 included Old's income of $20 in income from continuing operations because in that year Old was part of the continuing operations of Car, Inc. However, in year 7, that is no longer the case and Old's results are separated from income from continuing operations for both years presented.

III. Scope

A. ASC 420-45 addresses the identification of discontinued operations (DOP) as a "component of an entity" with operations and cash flows that can be distinguished from the rest of the entity for operational and financial reporting purposes. If a distinguishable component of an entity will be eliminated from the ongoing operations of the entity in a disposal transaction, then that component is reported as a DOP. After the elimination of the component, the firm will have no more significant involvement in the operation of the component.

B. Any component of an entity that either has been disposed of (by sale, abandonment, or in a distribution to owners) or is classified as held for sale is separated for DOP reporting.

C. Once the component has been identified, separate DOP reporting is required if both of these criteria are met: (1) operations and cash flows have or will be eliminated as a result of the disposal transaction, and (2) there will be no continuing involvement in the operations of the component after disposal.

D. DOP reporting primarily affects the income statement, but the assets of the component are also reported separately for balance sheet purposes until disposal actually takes place.

IV. Two Values to Report -- The following two amounts are separately disclosed and computed in the income statement below income from continuing operations:

A. Income -- Of the discontinued segment for the portion of the year to disposal (or if disposal occurs in a later year, income for the entire year).

B. Gain or loss -- On disposal of the segment.

    1. This amount equals the net proceeds from sale of the component less book value of the component's net assets. Net proceeds are equal to the gross amount received on sale less the cost to dispose of the assets. Thus, the cost to dispose increases a loss and decreases a gain.

 Example: Disposal loss or gain calculation:

Component data:

Assets net of applicable depreciation	$400
Liabilities	$150
Amount received on sale	$220
Cost to sell	$20

Book value of net assets = $400 - $150 = $250. Proceeds = $220 - $20 = $200. Loss on disposal = $250 - $200 = $50.

C. All items reported for discontinued operations are net of tax (after tax).

D. The measurements for the DOP disposal loss is the same as for individual impaired assets held for disposal (impairment is covered in a different lesson). The only difference is the location on the income statement the gain or loss is reported. The gain or loss recognized for individual assets is included in income from continuing operations whereas the gain or loss from DOP is reported as *discontinued operations* below income from continuing operations (along with extraordinary items).

E. Gain on Disposal -- Actual gains on disposal (when the decision to discontinue the component and the disposal occur in the same period) are recognized but estimated gains are not. A gain occurs when the net proceeds from the sale of the component exceed the BV (book value) of the net assets of the component.

F. Loss on Disposal -- When the BV of the net assets of the component exceeds the component's fair value less cost of disposal at year-end, then the component assets are written down to fair value less cost of disposal. The latter amount (fair value less cost of disposal) is estimated at the end of the year, and the loss is recognized even though disposal or sale has not taken place.

G. If the disposal takes place in the year the decision is made, then the disposal loss reported is the actual amount.

H. If the actual disposal loss is different from the estimated loss recognized previously, then in the period of disposal the difference is recognized as a gain or loss.

 Example:
If the previously recognized estimated loss was $40,000 and the actual loss in the year of disposal was $30,000, then in the year of disposal a $10,000 gain is recognized and reported in the DOP section of the income statement.

I.   The disposal loss or gain is a separate line item in the DOP section of the income statement in addition to the separate operating income of the component during the period. Alternatively, the two amounts can be netted with footnote disclosure showing them both. The assets are separated from the others in the BS when disposal takes place after the decision to eliminate the component.

> **Example:**
> In year 3, a firm decided to sell a component that qualifies for separate DOP reporting. The component's operating income was $60 in year 2 and negative $20 in year 3 (operating loss). For simplicity, assume the firm shows only two years comparatively. At the end of year 3 the BV of the component's net assets is $400. The fair value of the component is $250, and the firm expects to incur $20 of direct incremental cost to dispose of the component in year 4. Income from continuing operations for year 2 reported in year 2 was $300. Income from continuing operations in year 3 is $320. The firm has no extraordinary items. All amounts are after-tax.
>
> The latter portion of the comparative income statement:
>
> | | Year 3 | Year 2 |
> |---|---|---|
> | Income from continuing operations | $320 | $240 |
> | Income from DOP | (20) | 60 |
> | Loss on disposal of DOP | (170)* | (190) |
> | Net income | $130 | $300 |
>
> * $170 = $400 BV - ($250 fair value - $20 cost to sell)
>
> All amounts shown above are after tax.
>
> **Note** that income from continuing operations for year 2 reported in the year 2 income statement was $300. For comparative purposes, the components year 2 income is separated from income from continuing operations. The assets of this component are also reported on a separate line on the balance sheet.

J.   After the disposal of a component is completed, there may be adjustments to amounts previously reported in the DOP section of the income statement. These adjustments might stem from resolution of contingencies, settlement of pension obligations, and others that occur after disposal. Such adjustments are reported in the DOP section of the income statement in the year they occur.

V.   Discontinued Operations and IFRS

A.   IFRS identifies a component of an entity similarly to U.S. GAAP: "operations and cash flows that can be clearly distinguished, operationally and for financial reporting purposes, from the rest of the entity." (IFRS 5 para 31)

B.   IFRS identifies a discontinued operation as a component of an entity that either has been disposed of or is classified as held for sale and:

1.   Represents a separate major line of business; or

2.   Geographical area; or

3.   Part of a coordinated plan to dispose of a separate major line of business, geographical area; or

4.   Subsidiary acquired with the intent to resell.

Extraordinary and Unusual Items

This lesson presents the accounting and reporting for extraordinary items.

After studying this lesson, you should be able to:

1. *Define an extraordinary item.*

2. *Identify the accounting and reporting for an extraordinary item.*

3. *Identify the differences in U.S. GAAP and IFRS for accounting for extraordinary items.*

> **Definition:**
> *Extraordinary Item*: Extraordinary gains and losses are those that meet two criteria. Both criteria must be met for an item to be extraordinary. (1) The gain or loss is unusual in nature. (2) The gain or loss is infrequent in occurrence.

I. **Classification of Extraordinary Items --** In classifying a gain or loss as extraordinary, the environment in which the business is operated must be considered. In particular, the environment must be considered from three different perspectives, which are described below:

    A. **General Business Environment --** The general business environment must be considered in classifying gains or losses. When a business enterprise is operated in today's economic climate, there are certain risks that must be assumed by the business entity. For example, if merchandise or services are provided to customers on a credit basis, there is a risk associated with bad debts. Therefore, the incurrence of bad debt expense is not considered an extraordinary loss.

    B. **Specific Industry Environment --** When operating a business in a particular industry group, there are certain risks that are assumed by business entities. For example, if a business is operated in an industry in which the labor force is unionized, there is a risk associated with that environmental factor. Therefore, a strike loss incurred by companies in that industry is not considered an extraordinary loss.

    C. **Geographic Environment --** When operating a business entity, the geographic environment presents some risks as well. Usually these risks are associated with so called natural disasters or catastrophes. For example, in certain regions of the country, an earthquake might not be unusual or infrequent, while in other parts of the country, an earthquake loss is considered extraordinary. Likewise, losses related to hurricane damage or tornado damage might not be unusual or infrequent in certain parts of the country, but these losses are extraordinary in other parts of the country. In addition, the size of the storm-related loss should be considered. For example, the major earthquakes that hit the San Francisco and Los Angeles areas in recent years would result in a classification of extraordinary. Likewise, there have been some hurricane losses in Florida and tornado losses in Texas in recent years that would be considered extraordinary due to the size of the loss.

II. **Items Identified as Extraordinary --** ASC 225-55-3 identifies the following as extraordinary:

    A. A large portion of a tobacco manufacturer's crops are destroyed by a hail storm. Severe damage from hail storms in the locality where the manufacturer grows tobacco is rare;

    B. An earthquake destroys one of the oil refineries owned by a large multinational oil entity.

III. **Items that are NOT Extraordinary**

    A. write-downs of inventory and other assets;

    B. discontinued operations gains and losses;

C. accounting changes;

D. investment losses and gains;

E. effects of a strike.

IV. Reporting Extraordinary Items

A. As with all three items below income from continuing operations, extraordinary items are disclosed net of tax. Earnings per share for extraordinary items is presented on the face of the income statement.

Example:
Assume the tax rate is 30%. A firm has a $100,000 pretax casualty loss that is considered unusual and infrequent.

Income from continuing operations	xx
Discontinued operations	xx
Extraordinary casualty loss, net of $30,000 tax savings	(70,000)

B. Please review the Tiger Company Illustrations, (in the section on single-step format and multiple-step format, for an example related to the presentation of extraordinary items on the income statement.)

V. Unusual "OR" Infrequent Items

A. Recall from a previous section in this module that if a material item meets only one of the criteria for extraordinary items, it is separately disclosed as an item included in income from continuing operations on a pretax basis.

B. Comparison of unusual *or* infrequent items with extraordinary items (unusual *and* infrequent):

	Unusual or infrequent item	Extraordinary item
Location in Income Statement	Above income from continuing operations	Below income from continuing operations
Tax basis of reporting:	Pretax basis	After-tax basis

VI. Extraordinary Items and IFRS

A. IFRS does not permit the presentation of extraordinary items.

Foreign Currency Denominated Transactions

Introduction and Definitions

This lesson begins a series of lessons covering foreign currency denominated transactions. The first set of lessons discusses the accounting for foreign currency denominated transactions; the second set of lessons deal with foreign currency conversion. This lesson distinguishes between foreign currency transactions and foreign currency translation and gives examples of each. In addition, currency exchange rates and the alternative ways those rates may be expressed are presented.

After studying this lesson, you should be able to:

1. *Define and describe foreign currency conversion.*

2. *Display your understanding of changes in exchange rates.*

3. *Define direct quote, indirect quote, spot rates and forward rates.*

4. *Describe how to account for changes in currency exchange rates at the following dates:*

   - *When transaction is initiated; and*

   - *the Balance Sheet date; and*

   - *settlement date.*

5. *Define and describe foreign currency denominated transaction.*

I. Foreign Currency Denominated Transactions

Definition:
Foreign Currency Transactions: Transactions of a domestic entity denominated in (to be settled in) a foreign currency, but to be recorded on the domestic entity's books in the domestic currency.

Example:
A U.S company buys goods from a Japanese company and agrees to pay for the goods with yen, rather than dollars. In this case, the transaction is denominated in yen, but the amount recorded on the books of the U.S. entity is measured in U.S. dollars; therefore, the transaction amount must be converted from yen to dollars.

II. Foreign Currency Translation

Definition:
Foreign Currency Translation: Financial statements denominated in (expressed in terms of) a foreign currency, but to be reported in the financial statements expressed in the domestic currency.

See the following example.

> **Example:**
> A U.S. company has a French subsidiary that maintains its books and prepares its financial statements in Euros. In this case, the financial statements are denominated in Euros, but must be converted to dollars in order to be consolidated by the U.S. parent.

III. Terms and Definitions

A. **Direct quote** -- This is a direct exchange rate and it measures how much domestic currency must be exchanged to receive one unit of a foreign currency. $1.25 = 1 €.

B. **Indirect quote** -- This is an indirect exchange rates and it measures how many units of foreign currency may be purchased with one unit of domestic currency. $1.00 = .80 €. The indirect quote is the reciprocal of the direct quote (1 ??? / $1.25 = .80 €).

C. **Spot rate** -- The number of units of a currency that would be exchanged for one unit of another currency on a given date.

D. **Forward rate** -- The number of units of one currency that would be exchanged for units of another currency at a specified future point in time.

KEY CONCEPTS

1. A foreign currency transaction is when a transaction is denominated in a currency other than the domestic currency.

2. An unsettled foreign currency transaction creates a payable or receivable in a foreign currency.

3. This payable or receivable presents a risk because of the changes in the exchange rates before settlement.

IV. Strengthening or Weakening of Currencies

A. A strengthening or weakening dollar means that the dollar buys more or less of the foreign currency. It also means we receive less or more of the foreign currency owed to us.

B. If we have a payable denominated in the € and the dollar strengthens, since we have to pay a fixed amount of €s, and they are now worth fewer dollars, we have experienced a gain on the liability. The gains or losses arising from transactions denominated in a foreign currency are foreign currency transaction gains or losses.

C. The following chart illustrates the relationship between fluctuations in exchange rates and exchange gains and losses.

	Accounts Receivable Denominated in Foreign Currency	Accounts Payable Denominated in Foreign Currency
Domestic Currency **Weakens**	Exchange Gain	Exchange Loss
Domestic Currency **Strengthens**	Exchange Loss	Exchange Gain

Example:
IF THE DOLLAR WEAKENS:

	from	to
indirect	$1.00 = 0.80 €	$1.00 = 0.625 €
direct	$1.25 = 1 €	$1.60 = 1 €

It will take more U.S. dollars to acquire one unit of foreign currency (€ = foreign currency unit).

Imports become more expensive to the U.S.

U.S. exports become less expensive to the foreign country.

IF THE DOLLAR STRENGTHENS:

	from	to
indirect	$1.00 = 0.80 €	$1.00 = 0.909 €
direct	$1.25 = 1 €	$1.10 = 1 €

It will take fewer U.S. dollars to acquire one unit of foreign currency.

Imports become less expensive to the U.S.

U.S. exports become more expensive to the foreign country.

V. General Principles/Rules

A. Transaction terms provide that the transaction will be settled (by a domestic entity) in a foreign currency.

B. The domestic entity will ultimately pay or receive a foreign currency.

VI. General Rules

A. Measure and Record transaction on books in terms of the Functional Currency.

Example:
For a U.S. entity, the transaction must be measured and recorded in dollars.

B. Convert Foreign Currency Units (FC units) to Functional Currency Units ($) using spot exchange rate at date of transaction.

C. Recognize the effects of exchange rate changes:

1. On accounts denominated in a foreign currency (e.g., Receivables/ Payables);

2. In the period in which the exchange rate changes;

3. As adjustment to account balance, and as exchange loss or gain.

VII. Application at Date of Transaction

A. Determine FC units to settle transaction.

B. Translate (convert) FC units to reporting currency (U.S. Dollars) by:

> # FC Units multiplied by Spot Exchange Rate = Dollar amount to Settle.

C. Record transaction at Dollar amount to Settle.

VIII. Application at Balance Sheet Date

A. Determine (New) Dollar amount to Settle currently by

> #FC Units multiplied by Balance Sheet Date Spot Exchange Rate = Dollar amount at balance sheet date

B. Determine Difference between Recorded Dollar amount to Settle and New (current) Dollar amount at Balance Sheet Date.

C. Record Difference as

    1. Adjustment to Recorded Receivable/Payable;

    2. Exchange Loss or Gain.

D. Report Exchange Loss or Gain in Current Period Income Statement as component of Income from Continuing Operations.

IX. Application at Settlement Date

A. Determine (New) Dollar amount to Settle currently by

> #FC Units multiplied by Settlement Date Spot Exchange Rate = dollar amount to settle.

B. Determine Difference between Recorded Dollar amount to Settle and New (current) Dollar amount to Settle at settlement date.

C. Record Difference as

    1. Adjustment to Recorded Receivable/Payable;

    2. Exchange Loss or Gain.

D. Report Exchange Loss or Gain in Current Period Income Statement as component of Income from Continuing Operations.

E. Record Settlement of Adjusted Receivable/Payable account balance.

X. Summary

A. Below is a summary of the accounting for foreign currency denominated transactions (described above) in table form:

At Date Transaction Initiated	At Balance Sheet Date, If Before Settlement Date	At Date Transaction is Settled
Translate Transaction into Dollars using Current Spot Exchange Rate:	Determine Dollar Amount to Settle Transaction at Balance Sheet Date (Settlement Amount):	Determine Dollar Amount to Settle Transaction (Settlement Amount).
(#FC units X ER/Spot = $ Value)	(#FC units X ER/Spot = $ Value)	(#FC units X ER/Spot = $ Value)
Record Asset, Liability, Revenue, Expense, Loss and/or Gain on Transaction at Dollar Amount.	Determine Difference Between Recorded Amount and Settlement Amount.	Determine Difference Between Recorded Amount and Settlement Amount.
	Record Difference As:	Record Difference As:
	-- Adjustment to Recorded Account Balance (Receivable/Payable), and	-- Adjustment to Recorded Account Balance (Receivable/Payable), and
	-- Loss or Gain for the Period.	-- Loss or Gain for the Period.
	Report Loss or Gain in Current Period Income Statement as Component of Income from Continuing Operations.	Record Settlement of Adjusted Account Balance.
		Report Loss or Gain in Current Period Income Statement as Component of Income from Continuing Operations.

Import Transactions

when a domestic entity (assume U.S. entity) imports (purchases) an item from a foreign entity and the settlement of the transaction is in the foreign currency, the transaction is denominated in the foreign currency, but reported in the U.S. dollar equivalent of that foreign currency. This lesson illustrates a foreign currency denominated import transaction at initiation of the transaction, adjustment for changes in exchange rates at the balance sheet date, and settlement of the transaction .

After studying this lesson, you should be able to:

1. *Record the entries for foreign currency denominated import transactions :*

   - calculate the effect of the changes in the exchange rates and related gains and losses and

   - record the entries for the initial transaction, interim balance sheet date, and the settlement date.

I. Simple Illustration - Purchase (Import) Transaction Denominated in Foreign Currency

Assume: On October 1, 20X2 we entered into a transaction to purchase goods payable in a Foreign Currency (FC) on January 31, 20X3. The purchase was for 1 FC worth of merchandise.

The exchange rates are as follows:

Transaction date:	October 1	$2.00 = 1 FC (direct quotation)
Balance sheet date:	December 31	$1.00 = 1 FC
Settlement date:	January 31	$1.50 = 1 FC

October 1: The entry to record the purchase.

Inventory	$2	
Accounts Payable (FC)		$2

December 31: The FC is worth $1. The change in the exchange rate is recorded.

Accounts Payable (FC)	$1	
Foreign currency transaction G/L (IS)		$1

Note: Foreign currency transaction gain/loss (G/L could be a debit (loss) or credit (gain) depending on the changes in the exchange rates. Also, this account is recognized in earnings on the Income Statement (IS).

January 31: The FC is worth $1.5. Below are the following entries to: 1) record the change in the exchange rate, 2) the purchase of the FC, and 3) settle the transaction.

1. Foreign currency transaction G/L (IS)	$.50	
Accounts Payable (FC)		$.50
2. Investment in FC	$1.50	
Cash		$1.50
3. Accounts Payable (FC)	$1.50	
Investment in FC		$1.50

II. Illustration: Purchase (Import) Transaction Denominated in Foreign Currency

Assume: On November 15 a U.S. Co. purchases equipment from Foreign Co. for 500,000 units of Foreign currency (500,000 FC) with the full amount payable on January 31.

The exchange rates are as follows:

November 15   1 FC = $.75 (direct quotation)

December 31   1 FC = $.74

January 31   1 FC = $.76

November 1: The entry to record the purchase (500,000 x .75 = 375,000).

Inventory	$375,000	
Accounts Payable (FC)		$375,000

December 31: The change in the exchange rate is recorded. It will now take fewer dollars to settle the obligation in FC. (500,000 x (.75 - .74)) = 5,000

Accounts Payable (FC)	$5,000	
Foreign currency transaction G/L (IS)		$5,000

January 31: It will now take more dollars to settle the obligation in FC. Below are the following entries to: 1) record the change in the exchange rate from December 31 to January 31 (500,000 x (.74 - .76) = 10,000), 2) the purchase of the FC (500,000 x .76 = 380,000), and 3) settle the Accounts Payable in FC.

1. Foreign currency transaction G/L (IS)	$10,000	
Accounts Payable (FC)		$10,000
2. Investment in FC	$380,000	
Cash		$380,000
3. Accounts Payable (FC)	$380,000	
Investment in FC		$380,000

Complete a T-account for the Account Payable in Foreign Currency (FC) as a double check to make sure you have recorded everything properly:

Accounts Payable FC

		375,000 (500,000 X .75)	Nov 1
Dec 31 MTM	5,000		
		370,000 (500,000 X .74)	Dec 31
		10,000 MTM	Jan 1
		380,000 (500,000 X .76)	Jan 31
Jan 31 Payment	380,000		
		0 Ending Balance	

Now try to work through the above problem using indirect exchange rates. With indirect exchange rates you divide the foreign currency amount by the exchange rate. Using the rates below you will get the exact same journal entries and T-accounts shown above.

The exchange rates are as follows:

November 15   1.333333 FC = $1 (direct quotation)

December 31   1.351351 FC = $1

January 31   1.315789 FC = $1

Export Transactions

When a domestic entity (assume U.S. entity) exports (sells) an item to a foreign entity and the settlement of the transaction is in the foreign currency, the transaction is denominated in the foreign currency but reported in the U.S. dollar equivalent of that foreign currency. This lesson illustrates a foreign currency denominated export transaction At initiation of the transaction, adjustment for changes in exchange rates at the balance sheet date, and settlement of the transaction .

After studying this lesson, you should be able to:

1. *Record the entries for foreign currency denominated export transactions :*

   - *calculate the effect of the changes in the exchange rates and related gains and losses and*

   - *record the entries for the initial transaction, interim balance sheet date, and the settlement date.*

I. Simple Illustration - Sale (Export) Transaction Denominated in Foreign Currency

Assume: On October 1, 20X2 we agreed to sell goods with the receivable to be paid in Euro on February 1, 20X3, for 1 FC worth of merchandise.

The exchange rates are as follows:

Transaction date:	October 1	$2.00 = 1 FC
Balance sheet date:	December 31	$1.00 = 1 FC
Settlement date:	February 1	$3 = 1 FC

October 1: The entry to record the sale at the current exchange rate.

Accounts Receivable (FC)	$2	
Sales		$2

December 31: The entry to record the change in the exchange rate. (We will now receive only $1 worth of FC instead of $2).

Foreign currency transaction G/L (IS)	$1	
Accounts Receivable (FC)		$1

Note: Foreign currency transaction gain/loss (G/L could be a debit (loss) or credit (gain) depending on the changes in the exchange rates. Also, this account is recognized in earnings on the Income Statement (IS).

February 1: The FC is now worth $3. Below are the following entries to: 1) record the change in the exchange rate, 2) the receipt of FCs, and 3) convert the FCs to dollars.

1. Accounts Receivable (FC)	$2	
Foreign currency transaction G/L (IS)		$2
2. Investment in FC	$3	
Accounts receivable (FC)		$3
3. Cash	$3	
Investment in FC		$3

II. Illustration: Sale (Export) Transaction Denominated in Foreign Currency

Assume: On December 15 a U.S. Co. sells goods to a Foreign Co. for 500,000 units of Foreign Currency (500,000 FC) with the full amount payable on January 15.

The exchange rates are as follows:

December 15	1 FC = $.75 (direct quotation)
December 31	1 FC = $.72
January 15	1 FC = $.74

December 15: The entry to record the sale (500,000 x .75 = 375,000).

Accounts Receivable (FC)	$375,000	
Sales		$375,000

December 31: The change in the exchange rate is recorded. When 1 FC is received, it is worth fewer dollars. (500,000 x (.75 - .72)) = 15,000

Foreign currency transaction G/L (IS)	$15,000	
Accounts Receivable (FC)		$15,000

January 31: When 1 FC is received it is worth more dollars. Below are the following entries to: 1) record the change in the exchange rate (500,000 x (.72 - .74) = 10,000), 2) the receipt of the FC to settle the account receivable (500,000 x .74 = 370,000), and 3) convert the FC to dollars.

1. Accounts Receivable (FC)	$10,000	
Foreign currency transaction G/L (IS)		$10,000
2. Investment in FC	$370,000	
Accounts Receivable (FC)		$370,000
3. Cash	$370,000	
Investment in FC		$370,000

Complete a T-account for the Account Receivable in Foreign Currency (FC) as a double check to make sure you have recorded everything properly:

Accounts Receivable FC

Dec 15	(500,000 x .75)	375,000				
			15,000	MTM	Dec 31	
Dec 31	(500,000 x .72)	360,000				
Jan 31	MTM	10,000				
Jan 31	(500,000 x .74)	370,000				
			370,000	Collection	Jan 31	
		0				

Now try to work through the above problem using indirect exchange rates. With indirect exchange rates you divide the foreign currency amount by the exchange rate. Using the rates below you will get the exact same journal entries and T-accounts shown above.

The exchange rates are as follows:

        December 15   1.333333 FC = $1 (direct quotation)

        December 31   1.388888 FC = $1

        January 15   1.351351 FC = $1

Foreign Investment

In a foreign currency investment transaction, a U.S. entity (domestic entity) makes an investment through a foreign market (or other investment mechanism) with both the purchase price and eventual sales proceeds carried out (denominated) in a foreign currency. Such an investment will result in two elements of gain and/or loss: (1) the gain or loss on the change in market value, and (2) the gain or loss on any change in exchange rate between the dollar and the foreign currency. This lesson illustrates a foreign currency investment made in one fiscal period and sold in a subsequent fiscal period.

After studying this lesson you should be able to :

1. *Apply the accounting requirements for foreign currency operating transactions to foreign investments when the transaction is initiated and settled in different periods, including:*

   - *determining changing settlement amounts and allocating related gains and losses between:*

     1. *investment gains/losses, and exchange gains/losses.*

2. *Record entries for the initial transaction, at a subsequent Balance Sheet date and at the settlement date.*

I. **Illustration: Investment in the equity securities of a foreign entity --** When an entity invests in an equity security of a foreign entity there are two changes in value that need to be accounted for: 1) the change in the exchange rates related to the foreign investment and 2) changes in the value of the market price of the foreign investment. Gains or losses related to changes in the exchange rates are a foreign currency gain / loss that is reported in earnings on the income statement. Gains or losses related to changes in the market price of the equity security are reported in earnings if the security is classified as trading or in other comprehensive income if the security is classified as available-for-sale.

Assume: On November 1, 20X1 a U.S. Co. purchases shares of Foreign Co. Equity Securities for 1,500,000€. The U.S. Co. intends to sell the securities within 1 year.

The exchange rates and market value of the security are as follows:

Transaction date:	November 1, 20X1	$.90 = 1 €	1,500,000€ market value
Balance sheet date:	December 31, 20x1	$.95 = 1 €	1,500,000€ market value
Settlement date:	June 1, 20X2	$.94 = 1 €	1,600,000€ market value

November 1: The entry to record the purchase of the equity security at the current exchange rate(1,500,000€ x .90 = $1,350,000).

Investment in securities - trading (€)	$1,350,000	
Cash		$1,350,000

December 31: The entry to record the change in the exchange rate (1,500,000€ x (.90 - .95) = $75,000)).

Investment in securities - trading (€)	$75,000	
Foreign currency G/L (IS)		$75,000

June 1: The entry to record the exchange rate(1,500,000 € x (.95 – 94) = $15,000).

Foreign currency G/L (IS)	$15,000	
Investment in securities - trading (€)		$15,000

June 1: The entry to record the change in the market price of the security (1,500,000 - 1,600,000€ x (.94) = $94,000) and record the sale of the securities (1,600,000€ x .94 = $1,504,000).

Investment securities - trading	$94,000	
Gain on trading securities		$94,000
Cash	$1,504,000	
Investment securities - trading		$1,504,000

Complete a T-account for the Investment securities - Trading as a double check to make sure you have recorded everything properly:

Investment Securities - Trading

(1,500,000 X .90)	1,350,000		
(1,500,000 x (.90 - 95))	75,000		
(1,500,000 X .95)	1,425,000		
(1,600,000 - 1,500,000 x .94)	94,000	15,000	(1,500,000 x (.95 - .94))
(1,600,000 x .94)	1,504,000		

Foreign Currency Hedges

Introduction to Forward and Option Contracts

The objective of this lesson is to provide an overview of the accounting for forward and option contracts to buy or sell a foreign currency. This lesson defines forward and option and gives examples of each .

After studying this lesson, you should be able to:

1. *Define terms related to forward and option contracts, including:*

   - *Forward contracts,*

   - *Foreign currency forward exchange contracts, and*

   - *Foreign currency option contracts.*

2. *Describe and compute the value of a forward and option contract, including:*

   - *At inception of the contract,*
   - *At subsequent Balance Sheet dates and*
   - *At settlement of the contract.*

3. *Record the entries to account for both forward exchange contract and forward option contracts.*

I. Definitions

A. Forward Contract

> **Definition:**
> *Forward Contracts*: Agreements (contracts) to buy or sell (or which give the right to buy or sell) a specified commodity in the future at a price (rate) determined at the time the forward contract is executed.

B. For accounting purposes -- the most important types of forward contracts are:

1. Foreign Currency Forward Exchange Contracts (FXFC).

> **Definition:**
> *Foreign Currency Forward Exchange Contracts (FXFC)*: An agreement to buy or sell a specified amount of a foreign currency at a specified future date at a specified (forward) rate.

   a. Under an FXFC contract, the obligation to buy or sell is firm; the exchange must occur.

   b. This contract is an "exchange" because the contract provides for trading (exchanging) one currency for another currency.

Example:
A U.S. entity enters into a FXFC to pay a predetermined price in U.S. dollars for a predetermined quantity of Euros.

2. Foreign Currency Option Contracts (FCO).

Definition:
Foreign Currency Option Contracts (FCO): An agreement that gives the right (option) to buy (call option) or sell (put option) a specified amount of a foreign currency at a specified (forward) rate during or at the end of a specified time period.

a. Under an FCO contract, the party holding the option has the right (option) to buy or sell, but does not have to exercise that option. The exchange will occur at the option of the option holder.

Example:
A U.S. entity acquires an option (right) to buy Euros, but does not have to buy the Euros.

b. If the option is exercised, there is an exchange of currencies.

c. FCO contracts are significantly more costly to execute than FXFC contracts because the option must be purchased by paying an option premium to the counterparty for the right to buy or sell the currency.

d. The benefit of a FCO (over a FXFC) is that if changes in the exchange rate do not warrant it, the contract does not have to be exercised; therefore, only the option premium (cost) is incurred.

II. The Accounting Treatment

A. Derivative instruments -- Both foreign currency forward exchange contracts and foreign currency option contracts are derivative instruments.

1. All derivative instruments are adjusted to and reported at fair value.

2. Changing fair value of derivatives result in gains and losses.

3. When derivatives are used for hedging purposes, gains and losses on those derivatives serve to offset losses or gains on the hedged item.

B. Determining Fair Value of Forward Exchange Contracts

1. A forward exchange contract requires the parties to the contract to exchange currencies at the maturity of the contract (or to otherwise settle the contract).

2. The fair value of a forward exchange contract is determined by **changes** in the forward (exchange) rate during the life of the contract, discounted to its present value.

3. Changes in the forward rate can result in an increase in fair value (a gain) or a decrease in fair value (a loss).

4. At the inception of a forward contract, it typically has no value (there has been no **change** in the forward rate); changes in value (and gains or losses) occur as the forward rate changes.

5. Illustration.

a. Facts: On November 2, 2009, Usco, Inc. enters into a forward exchange contract to sell 10,000 Euros (€) in 90 days. The relevant direct exchange rates are:

	Spot Rates	Forward Rates (To January 31, 2010)
November 2, 2009	$1.20	$1.25
December 31, 2009	1.22	1.23
January 31, 2010	1.24	1.24

b. November 2 - Contract Initiated:

    i. The contract amount is 10,000€ x $1.25 = $12,500, and since that is based on the quoted rate at that date, it has no intrinsic value - anyone could obtain a 90-day forward contract at $1.25.

    ii. Entry: No entry required; no payment was made and the contract has no value.

c. December 31 - Balance Sheet Date:

    i. The forward rate at December 31 is $1.23, a decrease of .02 per Euro. Thus, the contract amount is now 10,000€ x $1.23 = $12,300, a change (decrease) of $200. Since Usco has a contract that enables it to sell 10,000€ for $1.25 each and 10,000€ could be sold now (December 31) for only $1.23 each, the $200 change is the nominal value of the contract - the value of Usco's right to sell 10,000€ at $1.25 each. The fair value (and amount of gain) is the present value of the $200. That would be determined by discounting the $200 for 1 month (31 days in January) at the appropriate discount rate (for example, the firm's incremental borrowing rate).

    ii. If the appropriate discount rate is 12%, or 1% per month, the present value of $200 due in one month (January 1 - 31) would be $200 x .99 = $198, the fair value of the contract asset on December 31. The entry would be:

DR: Forward Contract	$198	
CR: Gain on Forward Contract		$198

    1. If the contract was entered into for speculative purposes (i.e., to make a profit), the gain would be recognized in current (2009) income.

    2. If the contract was entered into as a qualifying hedge, the treatment of the gain would depend on the nature of the hedge (see subsequent lessons).

d. January 31 - Settlement Date:

e. The forward rate is the spot rate, $1.24 (the forward and spot rate converge upon the maturity of the forward contract), an increase of .01 per Euro since December 31. Thus, the current amount to , an increase of .01 per Euro since December 31. Thus, the current amount to satisfy the contract is 10,000€ x $1.24 = $12,400, the amount that would be paid to acquire 10,000€ to satisfy the contract (and the amount that would be received if the Euros were sold on the current spot market). As provided by its forward contract, however, Usco will received 10,000€ x $1.25 = $12,500, not $12,400. Thus, its entry would be:

DR: Cash (sell 10,000€ x $1.25)	$12,500	
Loss on Forward contract	98	
CR: Cash (buy 10,000€ x $1.24)		$12,400
Forward Contract (booked 12/31)		198

   f. The net effect over the life of the contract is a $198 gain in 2009 and a $98 loss in 2010, for a net gain of $100, which is the difference between the dollar cost of buying 10,000€ at $1.24 = $12,400 and the dollar amount received from reselling the Euros under the forward contract, 10,000€ at $1.25 = $12,500.

C. Determining Fair Value of Forward Exchange Option Contracts

   1. A forward exchange option contract gives the holder of the contract the right to buy (call option) or sell (put option) a foreign currency, but does not require the holder to do so.

   2. The determination of the fair value of a forward exchange option contract depends on the market in which the option is traded, if any.

   3. Alternatives for determining forward exchange option fair value:

      a. Exchange-traded options: Market price quoted on exchange = fair value.

      b. Over-the-counter options: Price quoted from option dealer = fair value.

      c. Not traded in active market: Option pricing model (e.g., modified Black-Scholes option price model) = fair value.

   4. At the inception of a forward option contract, the buyer will pay a premium (option premium) to the counter party for the right to buy from or sell to the counterparty according to the terms of the contract; the amount of the premium would be a function of the intrinsic value of the option and the "time value" factor.

      a. Intrinsic value: The difference between the current spot rate for the currency and the strike price - the price at which exercise of the option would result in a gain.

      b. Time value: The "value" assigned to the probability that the relationship between the changing spot price and the strike price will increase the value of the option during its life.

   5. Illustration.

      a. **Facts:** On November 2, 2009, Usco, Inc. enters into a call option contract to buy 10,000 Euros (€) in 90 days with a strike price of $1.21. The exchange rates and option premiums for the option period are:

	Spot Rate	Forward Rates (to January 31, 2010)	Option Premium
November 2, 2009	$1.20	$1.25	$200
December 31, 2009	1.22	1.23	350
January 31, 2010	1.24	1.24	300

      b. November 2 - Contract Initiated:

         i. Usco paid a premium of $200 for the contract; that is its fair value at that date.

Entry:

      DR: Foreign Currency Option $200

         CR: Cash $200

      c. December 31 - Balance Sheet Date:

         i. The option premium, as quoted by option sellers for a contract with comparable terms, has increased from $200 to $350, an increase (gain) of $150.

Entry:

DR: Foreign Currency Option $150

CR: Foreign Currency Option Gain $150

If the contract was entered into for speculative purposes (i.e., to make a profit), the gain would be recognized in current (2009) income.

If the contract was entered into as a qualified hedge, the treatment of the gain would depend on the nature of the hedge (see subsequent lessons).

    d. January 31 - Settlement Date:

        i. The option premium is $300, the intrinsic value of the option at that date, computed as 10,000€ x ($1.24 - $1.21) = 10,000€ x .03 = $300. At the settlement date, there is no time value associated with the contract; it has only intrinsic value.

Entry:

DR: Foreign Currency (Euros) $12,400

    Loss on Foreign Currency Option 50

CR: Cash (10,000€ x $1.21) $12,100

    Foreign Currency Option 350

    e. The net effect over the life of the contract is a $150 gain in 2009 and a $50 loss in 2010, or a net gain of $100. Thus, the difference between the cost of Euros if purchased January 31 of $12,400 (10,000€ x $1.24) and the cost of the Euros purchased under the option contract of $12,100 (10,000€ x $1.21) of $300 is reflected in the $200 cost of the option and a net gain of $100.

D. Both foreign currency forward exchange contracts and foreign currency option contracts are referred to as "Forward Contracts" in these lessons.

Natural (Economic) Hedge

This lesson illustrates a natural or economic hedge that is not accounted for using hedge accounting. This lesson illustrates the hedge of a purchase and sale denominated in a foreign currency .

After studying this lesson, you should be able to:

1. *Define hedging.*

2. *Describe how a forward exchange contract can be used to hedge a receivable denominated in a foreign currency.*

3. *Record entries associated with a foreign currency receivable, the hedging of that receivable, and the settlement of both the receivable and the hedging instrument.*

I. Hedging Definition

Definition:
Hedging: A risk management strategy, which generally involves offsetting or counter transactions so that a loss on one transaction would be offset (at least in part) by a gain on the other transaction.

A. You would "hedge a bet" by offsetting a possible loss from betting on one team (to win) by betting on the other team to win.

B. You would hedge against a possible loss in the dollar value of a foreign currency to be received in the future by selling that foreign currency now at a specified rate for delivery when you receive it in the future (a forward contract).

II. See the Following Simple Illustration

	November 2	December 31	January 31
Spot rates	$2.00 = 1 €	$3.00 = 1 €	$2.80 = 1 €
Forward rates	$2.10 = 1 €	$3.20 = 1 €	$2.80 = 1 €

Entries with the Broker
 	
At forward rates
	AR – Broker (€) $2.10
	  AP – Broker ($) $2.10
	
	Record the forward contract with the broker. We will pay the broker $2.10 on 1/31 and he will give us 1 €.
		AR – Broker (€) $1.10
		  G/L on FX (IS) $1.10
		
		    ($2.10 - $3.20)
		
		Record the gain on the forward contract with the Broker. The € due from the Broker is now worth more dollars.
			G/L on FX (IS) $ .40
			  AR – Broker (€) $ .40
			    ($3.20 - $2.80)
			
			AP – Broker ($) $2.10
			  Cash $2.10
			
			Investment in € $2.80
			  AR – Broker (€)
			    $2.80
			
			Record the settlement with the Broker.

Entries with the Spain Company
 	
At spot rates
	Inventory $2.00
	  AP – Spain Co (€) $2.00
	
	Record the commitment to pay 1 € to Spain Co. which will cost us $2.
		Gain/Loss on FX (IS) $1.00
		  AP - Spain Co (€) $1.00
		    ($2.00 - $3.00)
		
		Record the loss from the weakening dollar.
			AP – Spain Co (€) $ .20
			  G/L on FX (IS) $ .20
			    ($3.00 - $2.80)
			
			AP - Spain Co (€) $2.80
			  Investment in € $2.80
			
			Record the settlement of our AP with the Spain Company.

A. Purchase Denominated in Foreign Currency with Natural Hedge

1. Pumped Up Company purchased equipment from Switzerland for 140,000 francs on December 16, 20X7, with payment due on February 14, 20X8. On December 16, 20X7, Pumped Up also acquired a 60-day forward contract to purchase francs at a forward rate of SFr 1 = $.67. On December 31, 20X7, the forward rate for an exchange on February 14, 20X8, is SFr 1 = $.695. The spot rates were:

December 16, 20X7	1 SFr = $.68
December 31, 20X7	1 SFr = .70
February 14, 20X8	1 SFr = .69

	December 16	December 31	February 14
Spot rate	$.68	$.70	$.69
Forward Rate	$.67	$.695	$.69

Entries with the Company
 	
The hedged item
 	
Changes in the spot
	Equip 95,200
	   AP (SFr) 95,200
	(140,000 SFr * .68)
		Fx G/L (IS) 2,800
		   AP (SFr) 2,800
		(140,000 * (.68-.70))
			AP (SFr) 1,400
			   Fx G/L (IS) 1,400
			(140,000 * (.70-.69))
			
			AP (SFr) 96,600
			   Invest in (SFr) 96,600
			   (Pay Swiss Co.)
			   (.69 * 140,000)

Entries with the Broker
 	
The hedging instrument
 	
Changes in the forward
	AR (SFr) 93,800
	   AP ($) 93,800
	(140,000 SFr * .67)
		AR (SFr) 3,500
		   Fx G/L (IS) 3,500
		(140,000 * (.67-.695))
			Fx G/L (IS) 700
			   AR (SFr) 700
			(140,000 * (.695-.69))
			
			AP ($) 93,800
			   Cash 93,800
			   (Pay Broker)
			   (.67 * 140,000)
			
			Invest in (SFr) 96,600
			   AR (SFr) 96,600
			Receive SFr (.69 * 140,000)

Accounts Receivable Sfr		Accounts Payable Sfr	
(140,000 x .68) 93,800			95,200 (140,000 x .67)
3,500			2,800
(140,000 x .695) 97,300	700	1,400	98,000 (140,000 x .70)
(140,000 x .69) 96,600			96,600 (140,000 x .69)

III. Sale Denominated in Foreign Currency with Natural Hedge

A. Alman Company sold pharmaceuticals to a Swedish company for 200,000 kronor (SKr) on April 20, with settlement to be in 60 days. On the same date, Alman entered into a 60-day forward contract to sell 200,000 SKr at a forward rate of 1 SKr = $.167 in order to manage its exposed foreign currency receivable. The forward rate on May 31 was 1 SKr = $.168. The forward contract is not designated as a hedge. The spot rates were:

April 20	SKr 1 = $.170
May 31	SKr 1 = .172
June 19	SKr 1 = .165

	April 20	May 31	June 19
Spot rate SKr	.170	.172	.165
Forward Rate	.167	.168	-

Entries with the Company
 	
The hedged item
 	
Changes in the spot
	AR (SKr) 34,000
	    Sales 34,000
	
	(200,000 * .17)
		AR (SKr) 400
		    FX G/L (IS) 400
		
		((.170-.172) * 200,000)
			Fx G/L (IS) 1,400
			    AR(SKr) 1,400
			
			((.172 - .165) * 200,000)
			
			Invest in SKr 33,000
			    AR (SKr) 33,000
			
			(Receive SKr)
			(.165*200,000)

Entries with the Broker
 	
The hedging instrument
 	
Changes in the forward
	AR $ 33,400
	    AP(SKr) 33,400
	
	(200,000 * .167)
		Fx (G/L) (IS) 200
		    AP (SKr) 200
		
		((.167 - .168) * 200,000)
			AP(SKr) 600
			    Fx G/L (IS) 600
			
			((.168 - .165) * 200,000)
			
			AP (SKr) 33,000
			    Invest in SKr 33,000
			    (Pay Broker)
			
			Cash 33,400
			    AR 33,400
			    (Receive $)

Accounts Receivable SKr		Accounts Payable SKr	
(200,000 x .17) 34,000			33,400 (200,000 x .167)
400			200
(200,000 x .172) 34,400	700	600	33,600 (200,000 x .168)
(200,000 x .165) 33,000			33,000 (200,000 x .165)

IV. Hedging Costs

A. **Hedging minimizes or prevents losses** -- From exchange rate changes (per se), but usually involves some costs of doing so, including:

1. Fees or other charges imposed by the other party to the forward contract, and

2. Differences between spot rates and forward rates at the date the forward contract is initiated.

Hedging Forecasted Transactions and Firm Commitment

When forward currency forward exchange contracts are used for hedging, GAAP defines the kinds of risks that may be hedged for accounting purposes. This lesson identifies those types of risks and provides discussion of the hedge of a foreign currency denominated forecasted transaction and firm commitment.

After studying this lesson, you should be able to:

1. *Describe the criteria and accounting treatment for the hedge of a foreign currency denominated transaction.*

2. *Describe the criteria and accounting treatment for the hedge of a foreign currency denominated transaction.*

3. *Identify and describe the items that can be hedged for accounting purposes.*

I. **Purpose of Hedging --** GAAP identifies the following types/purposes of using forward contracts for hedging purposes when the item hedged is denominated in a foreign currency:

   A. **Forecasted Transaction --** Hedge a forecasted transaction denominated in a foreign currency; to offset the risk of exchange rate changes on non-firm, but budgeted (planned) transactions to be denominated in a foreign currency.

   B. **Unrecognized, Firm Commitment --** Hedge an unrecognized, but firm commitment denominated in a foreign currency; to offset the risk of exchange rate changes on firm commitments for a future purchase or sale to be denominated in a foreign currency.

   C. **Recognized Assets or Liabilities --** Hedge recognized (exposed) assets (e.g., receivables) or liabilities (e.g., payables); to offset the risk of exchange rate changes on already booked assets and liabilities denominated in a foreign currency.

   D. **Available-for-Sale Investment --** Hedge an investment in available-for-sale securities; to offset the risk of exchange rate changes on this class of investments denominated in a foreign currency.

   E. **Net Investment in Foreign Operation --** Hedge a net investment in a foreign operation (e.g., subsidiary); to offset the risk of exchange rate changes on an investment in a foreign operation (e.g., translated value of financial statements expressed in a foreign currency).

II. **Relationships**

   A. The first three types of hedges listed above can occur as a sequence of events (hedges). In sequence of occurrences, these hedges are of:

   1. A forecasted transaction, which may become;

   2. An identifiable foreign currency commitment, which results in a recorded transaction that creates;

   3. A recognized asset (receivable) or liability (payable).

      See the following example.

> **Example:**
> A US entity may include in its annual budget the purchase of a major piece of equipment from a foreign entity to be paid in the foreign currency (a forecasted transaction);
>
> During the budget period, the US entity enters into a contract with a foreign entity to construct the equipment (an identifiable firm commitment);
>
> Upon receiving the equipment, the US entity records the asset and the payable to the foreign entity (a recognized liability).

B. The **purpose**, **criteria**, and **accounting treatment** for each of the five types of hedges and for speculation are presented in the following lessons.

III. Hedging Forecasted Transactions

A. **Purpose** -- To offset the risk of exchange rate changes on non-firm, but budgeted (planned) foreign currency transactions (e.g., purchase or sale) between the time the transaction is planned and when it becomes firm or is executed.

> **Example:**
> **1.** Hedge import or export transactions (denominated in a foreign currency) which are included in a firm's annual budget (i.e., planned).
> **2.** Hedge dividends from a foreign subsidiary that are budgeted for the coming year.

B. **Designation**

1. **Criteria for designation** -- Use of a forward contract, either an exchange contract or an option contract, to hedge a forecasted transaction requires that (these requirements generally apply to all hedges):

    a. The forecasted transaction must be identified, probable of occurring and present an exposure to foreign currency price changes.

    b. Use of a forward contract to hedge must be consistent with company risk management policy, designated and documented in advance as intended as a hedge, and be highly effective as a hedge.

2. **Nature of Designation** -- A hedge of a forecasted transaction is a CASH FLOW HEDGE; the hedge is to offset changes in cash flow associated with the forecasted transaction.

3. **Accounting Treatment**

    a. The **change in the fair value** of the forward exchange contract, measured as the change in the forward exchange rate, should be recognized as an increase or decrease in the contract carrying value with a corresponding loss or gain recognized.

    b. To the extent the change in the value of the forward contract (the hedge) is effective in offsetting a decrease (loss) or an increase (gain) in the expected cash flow of the forecasted transaction, the gain or the loss should be deferred and reported as a component of "other comprehensive income."

    c. To the extent the change in the value of the forward contract (the hedge) is ineffective in offsetting the change in the expected cash flow of the forecasted transaction (i.e., to the extent the changes in the forward contract and the expected cash flow are different), that amount of loss or gain should be reported in current income.

d. **Illustration --** Assume for a period the following changes occurred in the present value (PV) of a forecasted cash flow and the fair value (FV) of a forward contract designated as a hedge of the forecasted cash flow:

Decrease in PV of expected cash flow of forecasted transaction	$48,000
Increase in FV of forward contract	$50,000
Increase in FV > Decrease in PV	$ 2,000

Related Entry (at B/S date):

DR: Forward Contract	$50,000	
CR: Other Comprehensive Income		$48,000
Gain on Cash Flow Hedge		2,000

e. Amounts (losses and gains) deferred in "other comprehensive income" should be recognized in net income in the period(s) in which the related forecasted transaction(s) affect net income.

IV. Hedging Firm Commitments

A. **Purpose --** To offset the risk of exchange rate changes on a firm commitment for a future purchase or sale denominated in a foreign currency; a contract has been entered into, but the related transaction has not been recorded under GAAP. The risk of an exchange rate change on the contract is the same as if the purchase or sale were recorded.

> **Example:**
> Hedge the obligation incurred when a purchase order is placed with a foreign entity to manufacture and deliver equipment with payment to be made in a specified amount of foreign currency. The buying party has a contractual obligation to "take and pay" on delivery of the equipment, but under GAAP will not record the obligation until the equipment is delivered.

B. **Risk of Exchange Rate Changes --** Since the contract is to pay a specified amount of foreign currency, the party is at risk of exchange rate changes between the date of the contract (purchase order) and the date the purchase and obligation to pay (accounts payable) are recorded.

C. **Designation**

1. **Criteria for Designation --** Use of a forward contract, either an exchange contract or an option contract, to hedge a firm commitment requires that:

   a. The commitment being hedged **must be firm**, be identified, and present exposure to foreign currency prices changes.

   b. The forward contract must be designated and effective as a hedge of a commitment and be in an amount that does not exceed the amount of the commitment. (To the extent the amount of the forward contract exceeds the amount of the commitment, the forward contract is treated as speculation, not a hedge.)

2. **Nature of Designation --** A hedge of a firm commitment can be either a FAIR VALUE HEDGE (the hedge is to offset changes in (dollar) fair value of the firm commitment); or a

CASH FLOW HEDGE (the hedge is to offset changes in expected cash flow associated with settling the firm commitment).

3. **Accounting Treatment (assuming a FAIR VALUE HEDGE)**

   a. The change in fair value of the forward contract (the hedging instrument), measured as the change in the forward exchange rate, should be recognized as an increase or decrease in the carrying value of the forward contract with a corresponding gain or loss recognized in net income.

   b. The change in fair value of the firm commitment (the hedged item), measured as the change in the forward exchange rate, should be recognized as in increase or decrease in the carrying value of the firm commitment with a corresponding gain or loss recognized in net income. (Note: This treatment requires recognizing an asset or liability for the firm commitment that otherwise would not be recognized under GAAP.)

   c. To the extent the gain or loss on the forward contract does not exactly offset the loss or gain on the firm commitment (i.e., the de facto ineffectiveness of the hedge), there will be a net gain or loss reported in current net income.

4. **Accounting Treatment (assuming a CASH FLOW HEDGE)**

   a. The change in the fair value of the forward exchange contract, measured as the change in the forward exchange rate, should be recognized as an increase or decrease in the contract carrying value with a corresponding loss or gain recognized.

   b. To the extent the change in the value of the forward contract (the hedging instrument) is effective in offsetting a decrease (loss) or an increase (gain) in the expected cash flow of the firm commitment, the gain or the loss should be deferred and reported as a component of "other comprehensive income."

   c. To the extent the change in the value of the forward contract (the hedging instrument) is ineffective in offsetting the change in the expected cash flow of the firm commitment (i.e., to the extent the changes in the forward contract and the expected cash flow are different), that amount of loss or gain should be reported in current income.

5. These treatments as fair value hedge or cash flow hedge are the same as described and illustrated for fair value and cash flow hedges in the financial instruments topic.

Hedging Recognized Asset/Liabilities, Available-for-Sale, and Foreign Operations

This lesson covers the hedge accounting for a foreign currency denominated asset or liability, an available for sale security, and an investment in foreign operations .

After studying this lesson, you should be able to:

1. *Describe the hedge accounting of a hedge of a foreign currency denominated asset or liability .*

2. *Describe the hedge accounting of a hedge of a foreign currency denominated available for sale security .*

3. *Describe the hedge accounting of a hedge of an investment in foreign operations .*

I. **Hedging Foreign Currency Denominated Asset or Liability** -- To offset the risk of exchange rate changes on an existing (already booked) asset or liability.

> **Example:**
> Hedge the risk of exchange rate changes reducing the dollar value of a receivable denominated (to be received) in a foreign currency, or the risk of exchange rate changes increasing the dollars required to settle a payable denominated (to be paid) in a foreign currency. For example, a receivable denominated in a foreign currency will result in collection of a fixed number of foreign currency units, but the dollar value of those units will vary with changes in the exchange rate between that foreign currency and the dollar. A U.S. company could enter into a forward contract now to sell those foreign currency units when received in the future and thus hedge the receivable.

A. **Criteria for Designation** -- Use of a forward contract, either an exchange contract or an option contract, to hedge a recognized asset or liability requires that:

1. The asset or liability is denominated in a foreign currency and has already been booked (recognized).

2. The gain or loss on the hedged asset or liability must be recognized in earnings.

B. **Nature of Designation** -- A hedge of a recognized asset or liability can be EITHER A CASH FLOW HEDGE OR A FAIR VALUE HEDGE.

1. To qualify as a cash flow hedge, the hedging instrument must completely offset the variability in (dollar) cash flows associated with the receivable or payable.

2. If the instrument does not qualify as a cash flow hedge, or if management so designates, the hedging instrument will be a fair value hedge.

C. **Accounting Treatment** -- The accounting for the hedge of a recognized asset or liability would depend on the designated purpose of the hedge - whether to hedge cash flow or to hedge fair value.

1. If to hedge cash flow, the treatment would include:

a. Adjusting the hedged item (receivable or payable) to fair value each balance sheet date using the spot exchange rate and recognizing the change in fair value as a foreign currency gain or loss in current income.

    b. Adjusting the hedging instrument to fair value each balance sheet date using the forward exchange rate and recognizing the change in fair value as follows:

        i. An amount up to the amount equal to the gain or loss recognized on the hedged item is recognized as a foreign currency loss or gain in current income to offset the gain or loss on the hedged item.

        ii. An amount up to an amount equal to the current period amortization of any premium or discount on the hedging instrument is recognized in current income (income or expense).

        iii. The balance, if any, is recognized in other comprehensive income for the current period.

  2. If to hedge fair value, the treatment would include:

    a. Adjusting the hedged item (receivable or payable) to fair value each balance sheet date using the spot exchange rate and recognizing the change in fair value as a gain or loss in current income.

    b. Adjusting the hedging instrument to fair value each balance sheet date using the forward exchange rate and recognizing the change in fair value as a gain or loss in current income.

    c. To the extent the change in fair value of the hedging instrument and the change in the fair value of the hedged item are different there will be a net effect in current income.

D. Alternate Accounting Treatment -- A firm can mitigate the risk of exchange rate changes on recognized accounts receivable and accounts payable denominated in a foreign currency without using hedge accounting. See the lesson "Natural (Economic) Hedge" for an illustration of this type of hedge.

II. Hedging Foreign Currency Denominated Available-for-Sale Security -- To offset the risk of exchange rate changes on an investment in securities (debt or equity) that are held available-for-sale.

> **Example:**
> Hedge the risk of exchange rate changes on the (dollar) fair value of an investment in debt or equity securities held available-for-sale that will be settled in (sold for) a foreign currency.

A. Criteria for Designation -- Use of a forward contract, either an exchange contract or an option contract, to hedge an available-for-sale investment requires that:

  1. The securities being hedged must be identified and must not be traded in the investor's currency.

  2. The forward contract must be designated and highly effective as a hedge of the investment, and in an amount that does not exceed the amount of the investment being hedged. (To the extent the amount of the forward contract exceeds the investment, the forward contract is treated as speculation, not a hedge.)

B. Nature of Designation -- A Hedge Of An Investment Available-For-Sale Is A FAIR VALUE HEDGE; the hedge is to offset changes in (dollar) fair value of an investment.

  1. Accounting Treatment

    a. The change in fair value of the forward contract (the hedge), measured as the change in the forward exchange rate, should be recognized as an increase or decrease in the carrying value of the forward contract with a corresponding gain or loss in net income.

b. The change in fair value of the investment (the hedged item), measured as the change in market value, should be recognized as an increase or decrease in the carrying value of the investment with a corresponding gain or loss in net income.

> **Note:**
> This treatment requires recognizing changes in the fair value of available-for-sale investments in net income, not in other comprehensive income as otherwise would be required under GAAP.

c. To the extent the gain or loss on the forward contract does not exactly offset the loss or gain on the investment (i.e., the de facto ineffectiveness of the hedge), there will be a net gain or loss reported in current net income.

III. **Hedging Foreign Investment in Foreign Operations** -- To offset the risk of exchange rate changes on the translation (conversion) of the financial statements of a foreign operation, (branch, investee or subsidiary) from the foreign currency to dollars.

> **Example:**
> Hedge the risk that the dollar value of an investment in a foreign subsidiary will fluctuate as a result of exchange rate changes. Translation (conversion from foreign currency units to dollars) of accounts on the financial statements of the foreign subsidiary requires use of changing exchange rates, which subject the investment carried by the parent to fluctuate solely as a result of exchange rate changes.
>
> The U.S. parent could (1) borrow in the foreign currency of the subsidiary (a liability) to offset (hedge) the effects of changes in the exchange rate on conversion of the financial statements (a net asset), (2) acquire a foreign currency call option to offset (hedge) the effects of changes in exchange rate on the conversion of the financial statements (a net asset).

A. **Criteria for Designation** -- Use of a hedge instrument (e.g., borrowing or derivative contract) to hedge a net investment in a foreign operation requires that the contract be designated as a hedge of the net investment and be highly effective as an economic (fair value) hedge.

B. **Nature of Designation** -- A hedge of a net investment in a foreign operation is accounted for like a cash flow hedge with the effective portion recorded in Other Comprehensive Income.

C. **Accounting Treatment**

1. The change in fair value (in dollars) of both the hedging instrument (e.g., a borrowing) and the change in the translated value of the balance sheet of the foreign entity (hedged item) should be determined.

2. To the extent the change in fair value (in dollars) of the hedging instrument is equal to, or less than, the change in the translated balance sheet, both changes enter into the cumulative translation adjustment (an item of other comprehensive income) as offsets to each other.

3. To the extent the change in fair value (in dollars) of the hedging instrument is greater than the change in the translated balance sheet, the excess (of change in the hedging instrument) is recognized as a gain and reported in current net income.

Speculation and Summary

Forward contracts can be used for speculative purposes. In this case, there is no existing obligation (to pay or receive a foreign currency) being hedged, rather the forward contract is entered into to make money. This lesson also presents a summary of the use of forward contracts and the accounting treatment for such contracts .

After studying this lesson, you should be able to:

1. *Describe the accounting treatment of a forward contract used for speculation.*

I. Purpose

A. To make a gain as a result of exchange rate changes either by buying foreign currency for future delivery at a price lower than its value when delivered or by selling foreign currency for future delivery at a price higher than it can be bought at the delivery date. In this case, there is no existing obligation or other conversion being hedged, rather the forward contract is entered into to make a profit (i.e., for speculative purposes).

> **Example:**
> A U.S. entity enters into a forward contract to purchase Euros in 180 days at a rate (forward rate) existing now in the belief that the existing forward rate is less than the spot rate will be in 180 days. To the extent the forward contract rate is less than the spot rate on the date the contract expires, the entity would make a gain. (Of course, if the spot rate at expiration is less than the forward contract rate, the entity would incur a loss.)

B. Any derivative that does not meet the requirements to qualify as a hedging instrument would be treated as held for speculative purposes.

II. Criteria for, and Nature of, Designation -- When a forward contract is used for speculation, there is no separate risk being hedged. The forward contract, and the resulting loss or gain stand alone. They are not intended to offset any existing exposure.

III. Accounting Treatment

A. The forward exchange contract is measured (valued) and recorded at the forward exchange rate (quoted now) for exchanges that will occur at the maturity date of the contract.

B. If a balance sheet date occurs between initiation of the contract and maturity (settlement) of the contract, the contract must be revalued (at the balance sheet date) by using the forward exchange rate quoted at that time for the maturity date of the contract. Any change between the balance sheet date value of the contract and the already recorded value of the contract, will be recognized as a gain or loss in net income for the period.

C. At the settlement date (maturity date of the contract), the contract must be revalued by using the spot (current) exchange rate for the maturity date of the contract. Any change between the settlement date value of the contract and the already recorded value of the contract, will be recognized as a gain or loss in net income for the current period.

D. In summary, all gains and losses on derivative instruments held for speculative purposes or treated as for speculative purposes are recognized in current income.

IV. Summary of Foreign Currency Hedges

A. Summary of Accounting for Forward Exchange Contracts by Purpose of Contracts

HEDGE OF:	Type of Hedge	Basic Approach	Treat Gain/Loss	Comments
Forecasted Transaction: to offset risk of exchange rate changes on planned (forecasted) transaction	Cash Flow	Adjust Forward Contract to Fair Value	Effective portion deferred in "Other Comprehensive Income;" Ineffective portion recognize in Current Income	Only derivative instruments qualify. Deferred gain/loss recognized when forecasted transaction affects income.
Unrecognized Firm Commitment: to offset risk of exchange rate changes on a firm commitment	Cash Flow OR Fair Value	Adjust carrying value to Fair Value for both Forward Contract and Firm Commitment (recognize asset or liability)	Cash Flow: Effective Portion deferred in "Other Comprehensive Income," Ineffective portion in Current Income Fair Value: Recognize in current income for both forward contract and firm commitment; any difference will affect net income	Either derivative instruments or non-derivative financial instruments may be used.
Recognized Asset or Liability: to offset risk of exchange rate changes on booked assets or liabilities	Cash Flow OR Fair Value	Adjust carrying value to Fair Value for both Forward Contract and Recognized Asset or Liability	Cash Flow: Effective portion in "Other Comprehensive Income;" Ineffective portion in Current Income. Fair Value Recognize in current income for both forward contract and recognized asset or liability; any difference will affect net income.	Gain/Loss on Hedged Item must be recognized in earnings.
Investment in Available-For-Sale Securities: to offset risk of exchange rate changes on investment	Fair Value	Adjust carrying value to Fair Value for Forward Contract and Investment	Recognize both forward contract and investment change in FV in current income; any difference will affect current net income	Only derivative instruments qualify. Gain/Loss is not recognized in "Other Comprehensive Income."
Net Investment in Foreign Operation: to offset risk of exchange rate changes on conversion of financial statements	Fair Value	Adjust carrying value of Forward Contract to Fair Value	Recognize as adjustment to Translation Adjustment; Gain in excess of Translation Adjustment to Net Income of current period	Either derivative instruments or non-derivative financial instruments may be used. Adjustment offsets gain/loss on translation of foreign financial statements.
SPECULATION: Entered into for profit; Not hedging an exposure to currency risk	(None)	Adjust carrying value of Forward Contract to Fair Value	Recognize in current net income	Not offsetting any obligation or other translation.

Conversion of Foreign Financial Statements

Introduction to Conversion of Foreign Financial Statements

This lesson begins a series of lessons covering foreign currency conversion. Conversion is the process expressing of financial statements expressed in one (foreign) currency to a (domestic) currency. There are two methods of conversion: translation and remeasurement. The key criteria for determining the method of conversion is to determine the entities function currency. This lesson describes the nature of foreign currency conversion and how to determine the functional currency .

After studying this lesson, you should be able to:

1. *Identify* and define currency concept relevant to foreign currency conversion, including: a) recording currency; b) reporting currency; and c) functional currency

2. Determine which currency is the functional currency of an entity .

I. **Conversion -- The conversion of financial statements from one currency to another currency, involves two major steps:**

   A. Determining the functional currency of the entity that prepared the original financial statements, and

   B. Applying the correct conversion process based on the functional currency of the entity that prepared the original financial statements.

   C. Foreign currency conversion occurs when a domestic (U.S.) entity must convert financial statements denominated (expressed) in a foreign currency into their domestic (dollar) equivalents.

II. **Sources of Financial Statements --** The financial statements denominated in the foreign currency could be those of a branch, joint venture, partnership, equity investee or subsidiary of the domestic entity.

III. **Conversion Needed --** The conversion could be needed in order to:

   A. Apply equity method by U.S. Investor;

   B. Combine with other Entities;

   C. Consolidate with U.S. Parent (and other subs).

IV. **Conversion Objectives --** The objectives of Foreign Currency Conversion are:

   A. To provide information that is generally compatible with the expected economic effects of rate changes on an enterprise's cash flows and equity, and

   B. To reflect in consolidated statements the financial results and relationships of the individual consolidated entities as measured in their functional primary currencies in conformity with U.S. GAAP.

V. **Currency Concepts --** The following currency concepts are relevant to Foreign Currency Translation:

   A. **Recording Currency --** The currency in which the foreign entity's books of account are maintained.

   B. **Reporting Currency --** The currency in which the final (e.g., consolidated) financial statements are expressed.

C. **Functional Currency** -- The currency of the primary economic environment in which an entity operates and generates net cash flows.

VI. **Conversion Methodology** -- The specific translation methodology to use to convert financial statements expressed in a foreign currency into domestic (dollar) equivalents depends on the Functional Currency of the foreign entity. The Functional Currency of the foreign entity can be:

A. **The Recording Currency** -- The foreign entity's local foreign currency.

B. **The Reporting Currency** -- The currency of the final reporting entity (the dollar for a U.S. entity).

C. **Another Foreign Currency** -- A foreign currency other than the Recording Currency.

VII. **Determining Functional Currency** -- Generally, the Functional Currency of the foreign entity will be determined according to the following guidelines:

A. **Functional Currency = (Local, foreign) Recording Currency** -- If operations of the foreign entity are relatively self-contained and integrated within the country in which it is located.

1. **EXCEPTION** -- If the local economy is highly inflationary (i.e., cumulative inflation of 100% or more over a three-year period) the Functional Currency = Reporting Currency (the $ if a U.S. subsidiary).

B. **Functional Currency = U.S. Reporting Currency**

1. If operations are a direct and integral component or extension of a U.S. entity's (e.g., Parent's) operations, or

2. When the foreign entity is located in a country with a highly inflationary economy, defined as cumulative inflation of 100% or more over a three-year period.

C. **Functional Currency = Another Foreign Currency** -- (other than local foreign Recording Currency or the Reporting Currency) If the foreign entity generates most of its cash flows in the currency of another foreign country or if required by law or contract.

VIII. **Role of Functional Currency** -- The functional currency of the entity issuing financial statements to be converted to another currency will determine the method to be used to convert the financial statements. Two methods are possible:

A. Translation;

B. Remeasurement.

Conversion Using Translation

This lesson identifies the exchange rates to use when the translation method of conversion is used and how to treat the resulting translation adjustment .

After studying this lesson, you should be able to:

1. *Describe the sequence of requirements when financial statements are converted using translation.*

2. *Identify the exchange rates to use for converting different financial statement accounts using translation.*

3. *Describe how the translation adjustment amount is treated when financial statements are converted using translation.*

4. *Apply the translation method in converting financial statements from one currency to another currency.*

5. *Describe and apply the reporting of the translation adjustment in a set of converted financial statements.*

I. **Translation Process -- Local Recording Currency = Functional Currency --** Use Translation to convert from foreign currency to reporting currency (the $):

    A. Convert Accounts from Foreign Currency Units (FCU) to Dollars using a current exchange rate (CR) - also called spot rate.

        1. **Example --** Conversion: FCU X CR = $

    B. **Current Exchange Rates (CR) to use**

        1. **Revenues, Expenses, Gains, and Losses --** Use exchange rate at dates on which earned or incurred; however, a weighted average rate for the period can be used.

        2. **Assets and Liabilities --** Use Spot rate at Balance Sheet date (except paid-in-capital and retained earnings, see below).

        3. **Paid-In Capital --** Use Historic Rate in existence when Paid-In Capital arose (but not earlier than investment in foreign entity).

        4. **Retained Earnings --** Calculated as Beginning R/E (end of prior period) + Translated N/I - Dividends declared converted at spot rate at date of declaration = Ending R/E ($).

II. **Translation Adjustment --** The amount needed to make the Balance Sheet (expressed in Dollars) balance is the amount of the Translation Adjustment.

    A. Under **Translation** (method of converting) the Translation Adjustment does NOT enter into determination of Net Income, but is treated as "Other Comprehensive Income" for reporting purposes.

    B. "Accumulated Other Comprehensive Income" (including the Accumulated Translation Adjustment) is reported as an item in Shareholders' Equity in the translated ($) Balance Sheet.

III. **Illustration (simple) of Translation (Local Foreign Currency is the functional currency):**

Example:
Assume a U.S. entity has a Mexican subsidiary, which maintains its accounting records and prepares its financial statements in the local currency, the Mexican peso (MP).

Relevant exchange rates are:
Historic rate when Sub was established:

1MP = $.0950

Average rate for the current period 20x8:

1 MP = $.1000

Spot rate at date of dividend declaration:

1 MP = $.1010

Spot rate at end of current period 12/31/x8:

1 MP = $.1020

IV. **Translation** -- Of the (simple) financial statements from MP to U.S. dollars would occur as follows:

Foreign Sub Statements

For the Year Ended 12/31/x8		Translation Process	
Statement of Net Income and Comprehensive Income (20x8)	MP	Rate for Translation	US$
Sales	100,000	$.1000	$10,000
COGS	(50,000)	.1000	(5,000)
Depreciation	(10,000)	.1000	(1,000)
Other Expenses	(5,000)	.1000	(500)
Net Income	35,000		$ 3,500
Net Income	======		
Other (Items of) Comprehensive Income: (from B/S below) Translation Adjustment			680
Comprehensive Income			4,180
Retained Earnings (20x8)			
Beginning R/E	60,000	(End 20x7)	$ 5,700
Add: N/I (20x8)	35,000	(Above)	3,500
Deduct: Dividends 20x8	(20,000)	.1010	(2,020)
Ending R/E	75,000		$ 7,180
	======		======

Balance Sheet (12/31/x8)

Cash and Accounts Receivable	20,000	.1020	$ 2,040
Inventory	80,000	.1020	8,160
Fixed Assets	25,000	.1020	2,250
Total Assets	125,000		12,750
	======		======
Liabilities	20,000	.1020	2,040
Common Stock	30,000	.0950	2,850
Retained Earnings	75,000	(Above)	7,180
Subtotals	125,000		12,070
Accumulated Other Comprehensive Income		(To Balance)	680
Total Liability + Equity	125,000		$12,750
	======		======

A. Items to Note in above Illustration:

1. All revenue (sales) and expense items were assumed to have occurred evenly throughout the year.

2. Beginning Retained Earnings is the dollar value at the end of the prior year.

3. Dividends are translated at the exchange rate in effect on the date of declaration.

4. Common stock is translated at the exchange rate in effect the day the stock was issued (since parent created the sub).

5. The translated Balance Sheet does not balance (Assets = $12,750; liabilities + Equity = $12,070) until the translation adjustment is included. The amount of the translation adjustment is the amount needed to make the Balance Sheet balance ($680). The $680 is "plugged."

6. The Translation Adjustment is reported in the Shareholders' Equity Section of the Balance Sheet and as an item of Other Comprehensive Income in reporting Comprehensive Income.

Conversion Using Remeasurement

If the final reporting currency is the functional currency, rather than the local foreign currency, the foreign financial statements will be converted using remeasurement, instead of translation. Similarly, if another foreign currency (other than the recording currency) is the functional currency, the foreign financial statements will have to be remeasured to the functional currency, and then translated to the reporting currency. This lesson identifies the exchange rates to be used when the remeasurement method of conversion is used and how to treat any resulting remeasurement adjustment.

After studying this lesson, you should be able to:

1. *Describe the sequence of requirements when converting financial statements using remeasurement.*

2. *Identify the exchange rates to use for converting different financial statement accounts using remeasurement.*

3. *Describe how the translation adjustment amount is treated when financial statements are converted using remeasurement.*

4. *Apply the remeasurement method in converting financial statements from one currency to another currency.*

5. *Describe and apply the reporting of the remeasurement translation adjustment in a set of converted financial statements.*

I. **Remeasurement Process - U.S. Dollar = Functional Currency --** Use Remeasurement to convert from foreign currency to reporting currency (the $):

   A. Convert Accounts from Foreign Currency Units (FCU) to Dollars using (Temporal Method):

   1. For Monetary Items - Current Exchange Rate (CR).

   2. For Non-Monetary Items - Historical Exchange Rate (HR), i.e., exchange rate in existence when account item arose. Monetary items are those where value is fixed by contract (examples: cash, accounts receivable, accounts payable, bonds and notes etc.)

   Examples

   FCU of Monetary x CR = $

   FCU of Non-Monetary x HR = $

   B. **Historic Exchange Rate --** Basically, use historic exchange rate for nonmonetary items:

   1. **Past Price Valuation --** Assets and liabilities valued at past prices (not for assets and liabilities measured at amounts promised).

      a. **Examples**

         i. Securities Carried at Cost, if any;

         ii. Inventories Carried at Cost;

         iii. Prepaid Costs;

         iv. Fixed Assets/Accumulated Depreciation;

         v. Intangibles (Goodwill, etc.);

      vi. Deferred Revenue;

      vii. Paid-In Capital.

   2. Historic Rate Conversion -- Revenue and expenses related to assets and liabilities converted at Historic Rate (only).

     a. Examples

       i. COGS (when Inventory at cost);

       ii. Depreciation;

       iii. Amortization of Intangibles (Not GW!).

II. Use Current Exchange Rates for

   A. All other (Monetary) Assets and Liabilities;

   B. All other Revenue, Expense, Gain and Loss Items.

III. Remeasurement Adjustment -- Amount needed to make the trial balance debit and credits (expressed in Dollars) balance is amount of Remeasurement Adjustment:

   A. The Remeasurement Adjustment is reported as a Gain or Loss in the Income from Continuing Operations section of the Income Statement (expressed in Dollars).

   B. The remeasurement adjustment "flows thru" the Income Statement to Retained Earnings.

IV. Illustration (Simple) of Remeasurement (Reporting Currency is the Functional Currency)

Example:
Assume a U.S. entity has a Mexican subsidiary, which maintains its accounting records and prepares its financial statements in the local currency, the Mexican peso (MP). Because the Mexican subsidiary is a sales unit that purchases its inventory for its U.S. parent, it is basically an extension of its parent, not independent of it. Therefore, its functional currency is the U.S. dollar.

Relevant exchange rates are:

Historic rate when Sub was established:

1 MP = $.0950

Historic rate when Sub Fixed Assets were acquired:

1 MP = $.0975

Average rate for the current period 20x8:

1 MP = $.1000

Spot rate at date dividend declared:

1 MP = $.1010

Spot rate at end of current period 12/1/x8:

1 MP = $.1020

V. Remeasurement Illustration

Remeasurement Illustration

For the Year Ended 12/31/x8		Translation Process	
Income Statement (20x8)	MP	Rate for Translation	US$
Sales	100,000	$.1000	$10,000
COGS	(50,000)	.1000	(5,000)
Depreciation Expense	(10,000)	.0975	(975)
Other Expenses	(5,000)	.1000	(500)
Preliminary Net Income	35,000		$ 3,525
Translation Adjustment			
Gain			383
Net Income			3,908
			======
Retained Earnings (20x8)			
Beginning R/E	60,000	(End 20x7)	$ 5,700
Add: Preliminary N/I (20x8)	35,000	(Above)	3,525
Deduct: Dividends 20x8	(20,000)	.1010	(2,020)
Preliminary End R/E	75,000		$ 7,205
	======		
Add: Adjustment to NI			
(Translation Gain)			383
Ending R/E (Final)			$ 7,588
			======
Balance Sheet (12/31/x8)			
Cash and Accounts Receivable	20,000	.1020	$ 2,040
Inventory (at cost)	80,000	.1000	8,000
Fixed Assets	25,000	.0975	2,438
Total Assets	125,000		12,478
	======		======
Liabilities	20,000	.1020	2,040
Common Stock	30,000	.0950	2,850
Preliminary R/E	75,000	(Above)	7,205
Preliminary Subtotals	125,000		12,095
	======		======
Deduct: Preliminary R/E			7,205
Add: Final R/E			7,588
Total Liability + Equity			$12,478

Calculation of Cumulative Translation Adjustment (to be carried to Preliminary Net Income)

Total Assets	$12,478
Subtotal L + C	12,095
Adjustment to NI	$ 383("Flows Thru" to Retained Earnings)

A. Items to Note in previous Illustration:

1. Revenues (sales) are assumed to have occurred evenly throughout the year.

2. All inventory sold during the year and remaining on hand at year-end is assumed to have been acquired from the parent evenly throughout the year.

3. Fixed assets and Depreciation expense are translated at the exchange rate in effect when the fixed assets were acquired.

4. Dividends are translated at the exchange rate in effect on the date of declaration.

5. Common stock is translated at the exchange rate in effect the day the stock was issued (since the parent created the Sub).

6. The preliminary translated Balance Sheet does not balance (assets = $12,478; Preliminary Liabilities + Equity = $12,095). The difference ($383) is not reported as a Translation Adjustment in Shareholders' Equity.

7. The amount needed to balance the Balance Sheet ($383) is recognized as a Translation Adjustment Gain in the Income from Continuing Operations section of the Income Statement, which increases Net Income which, in turn, increases Ending Retained Earnings resulting in balancing the Balance Sheet.

8. Since the translation adjustment is recognized in net income, it is not shown as an item of Other Comprehensive Income.

Remeasurement, then Translation

Under special circumstances, both the remeasurement and the translation methods of converting foreign currency financial statements will be required. This lesson identifies when that would be necessary and the accounting treatment, including the handling of the remeasurement and translation adjustments.

After studying this lesson, you should be able to:

1. *Describe when both the remeasurement and translation forms of conversion of financial statements will be required.*

2. *Describe the application of the remeasurement and translation processes in combination when they are both required.*

I. **Remeasurement, then Translation --** A foreign currency other than the recording currency = Functional Currency.

    A. In this case, both remeasurement and translation will be required:

        1. **Remeasure --** (as previously described) From Recording Currency to Functional Currency (which is another foreign currency), then

        2. **Translate --** (as previously described) From Functional Currency to U.S. $ Reporting Currency.

II. **The Translation Adjustments --** Resulting from each of the conversion processes will be reported as follows:

    A. **Remeasurement** (Translation) **Adjustment** - In Income Statement.

    B. **Translation** (Translation) **Adjustment** - In Other Comprehensive Income for reporting purposes and, subsequently, in Accumulated Other Comprehensive Income in the Shareholders' Equity section of the Balance Sheet.

> **Example:**
> A subsidiary of a company in the United States is in England. The subsidiary functions in the Euro. The local currency is the British Pound, the functional currency is the Euro, and the reporting currency is the US Dollar.
>
> The financial statements would be *remeasured* from British Pound to Euro and then *translated* from Euro to the US Dollar.

Impairment

This lesson presents the accounting and reporting for impairment of long-lived assets.

After studying this lesson, you should be able to:

1. *Describe the two steps in the test for impairment of assets held in use.*

2. *Describe the impairment test for assets held for disposal.*

3. *Identify the major differences between U.S. GAAP and IFRS in accounting for impairment.*

I. **Introduction - Asset Categories**

    A. Assets subject to impairment fall into one of three categories:

        1. Assets in use;

        2. Assets held for disposal (sale); and

        3. Assets to be disposed of other than by sale (by spin-off to shareholders, by exchange for other assets, or by abandonment).

    B. The most important category for exam purposes is the first, assets in use.

II. **Assets in Use**

    A. **Assets in Use** -- Are written down to fair value if their recoverable cost is less than book value. The amount of the impairment loss recognized is the difference between book value and fair value. Note that the determination of impairment is a step separate from the measurement of the loss; both use different values.

        1. **Fair Value (FV)** -- The price that would be acceptable to the firm and another party for the transfer of the asset. **Present value** is used when no active market exists for the asset.

        2. **Recoverable Cost (RC)** -- Is the sum of expected future net cash inflows from use and ultimate disposal. Costs of maintaining the asset are included in the computation of RC, reducing it. RC is a nominal sum, not a present value. RC is based on how the firm currently uses the asset; the expected remaining useful life is used in computing RC. RC is the net increase in cash expected from using and disposing of the asset over its remaining life. RC always exceeds FV because RC is not a discounted amount.

    B. **Test for Impairment**

        1. If book value (BV) > RC then the asset is impaired because book value will not be recovered. If BV is $100 and RC is $70, then there is no accounting justification for reporting the asset of $100.

        2. If BV <= RC, then the asset is not impaired and no impairment loss is recognized. In this case, the book value is recoverable.

        3. Assets should be evaluated for impairment when certain indications are present, rather than on a regular basis. Significant declines in FV, changes in legal climate or physical nature of the asset are examples of signals that suggest an impairment may have occurred.

    C. **Measurement of Impairment Loss**

        1. An impaired asset is written down to FV. The loss equals: BV - FV

2. Note that the *test* for impairment uses BV and RC, while the *measurement* of the loss uses BV and FV.

D. **Examples**

 Example:
1. An asset with a book value of $100 has a recoverable cost of $120 and a fair value of $75.

Test for Impairment: BV of $100 < RC of $120. The asset is not impaired because the book value is recoverable. There is no loss computation; there is no impairment loss.

2. An asset with a book value of $100 has a recoverable cost of $90 and a fair value of $75.

Test for Impairment: BV of $100 > RC of $90. The asset is impaired because the book value is not fully recoverable.

Loss Measurement: Loss = BV of $100 - FV of $75 = $25. The asset is written down to $75. The loss is a component of income from continuing operations (not extraordinary).

The entry to record the loss of $25:

Impairment loss   25

   Asset or Accumulated depreciation   25

Accounting after recognizing the $25 loss.

a. The new BV of the asset is the FV of 75 and is used as the cost for future depreciation. The new depreciable cost is $75 less any residual value.

b. An impairment loss on an asset in use cannot be recovered; there are no upward revaluation or gains recognized if FV increases.

c. Additional impairments are possible.

E. **Asset Groups --** Many, if not most, assets do not function independently, but are rather part of a working group. For purposes of the **test for impairment**, assets are grouped at the *lowest* possible organizational level at which cash flows can be identified. The 3 amounts (BV, FV, RC) are measured at this level. One intended effect of this rule on grouping at the LOWEST level rather than a higher one is to decrease the incidence of merging assets with impairment losses with those for which FV > BV in which case there would be fewer or no impairment losses recognized.

III. **Assets Held for Disposal --** Recoverable cost is not used for assets held for disposal. Rather, the test for impairment and the loss computation both use the same values (BV, and FV less cost to sell).

A. **Decision to Dispose**

1. If the decision to dispose of an asset and the ultimate disposal occur in the **same period**, the actual gain or loss on disposal is recognized in income from continuing operations. The disposal loss or gain equals the difference between FV and BV (if BV > FV, then a loss occurs; if BV < FV, then a gain occurs). Depreciation should be recognized to the date of the disposal unless the firm uses a convention for fractional year depreciation. The accumulated depreciation account is removed along with the asset's original cost.

2. If the decision to dispose **precedes** the period of disposal, an estimated loss is recorded if it is probable and estimable. Estimated gains are not recognized.

B. Held For Sale Criteria

1. There are 6 criteria for determining when an asset is considered held for sale. All 6 must be met for the accounting provisions to apply. Otherwise, the asset is considered in use.

   a. Management commits to a plan to sell the asset or group of assets;

   b. The asset must be available for immediate sale in its present condition subject only to terms that are usual and customary for such sales. This criterion does not preclude a firm from using the asset while it is held for sale nor does it require a binding agreement for future sale;

   c. An active program to locate a buyer has been initiated;

   d. The sale is expected to take place within one year. In limited cases, the one-year rule is waived for circumstances beyond the firm's control (for example, due to a new regulation or law, environmental remediation, or deteriorating market);

   e. The asset is being actively marketed for sale at a price that is reasonable in relation to its current value;

   f. Sale of the asset must be probable.

2. If the 6 criteria are not met at the balance sheet date but are met before issuance, treat the asset as held for use in those statements. If an asset held for sale fails to meet all 6 criteria at a later date, it is reclassified as held for use.

3. An asset held for sale is impaired if its BV exceeds its fair value less cost to sell at the end of the reporting period.

C. Held For Sale Accounting

1. The asset is written down to (fair value - cost to sell) - here the test for impairment and the measurement of the loss are the same. The term 'recoverable cost' is not used for assets for sale. If sale is expected beyond one year, the cost to sell is discounted.

2. Only direct incremental costs are used in the computation of cost to sell.

3. The impairment loss recorded equals the difference between the asset's BV and its (FV - cost to sell). The estimated cost to sell increases the loss. The loss is not extraordinary.

4. The asset is removed from plant assets because it is no longer in use.

5. Depreciation is no longer recognized on the asset.

6. The results of operating the asset during the holding period are recognized in period of occurrence - estimated future operating losses or gains are not recognized until they actually occur. Note that although these assets are held for disposal, they may require maintenance and other cash expenditures. These are expensed as incurred.

7. The asset can be written up or down if held for another period - gains are limited to the amount of the initial impairment loss (BV cannot exceed the amount immediately before recording the initial impairment loss).

   See the following example.

Example:
A plant asset (cost $100,000; accumulated depreciation $40,000) has a current fair value of $30,000 at the end of Year 4. Management has decided to sell the asset as soon as possible during the next reporting period. The estimated direct cost to sell is $5,000. The six criteria of FAS 144 are met.

End of Year 4

Asset held for disposal	25,000*
Accumulated depreciation	40,000
Loss on asset held for disposal	35,000**
Plant asset	100,000

* $30,000 fair value - $5,000

** $60,000 old book value - $25,000 new book value. The loss of $35,000 is the impairment loss.

At the end of Year 5, the asset remains unsold. Fair value is now $20,000 and the estimated cost to sell is $12,000.

End of Year 5

New book value = $8,000 = ($20,000 - $12,000).

Loss on asset held for disposal 17,000 *

Asset held for disposal 17,000

* $25,000 book value at end of 20x4 - $8,000 new book value

Limit on Gains: Assume instead that at the end of 20x5 the fair value had risen to $70,000 and estimated cost to sell remained at $5,000. The difference between fair value and estimated cost to sell has increased from $25,000 to $65,000, an increase of $40,000. This amount exceeds the previous loss of $35,000. The maximum gain allowed is $35,000, the amount of the previous loss. Therefore, the asset would be written back up to $60,000 (the book value immediately before the initial impairment), and a gain of $35,000 would be recognized.

IV. Assets To Be Disposed Of Other Than By Sale

A. This category includes disposal by abandonment, by exchange for a similar asset, and by distribution to shareholders as a spin-off. Note that dissimilar asset exchange is not included in this category because that transaction is considered a sale - the culmination of an earnings process.

B. **Accounting** -- Continue to classify the asset as held for use until disposal occurs, and continue to depreciate the asset. Apply the impairment standards for assets in use. Compute recoverable cost as for assets in use. These assets are treated as such because even though the plan is to dispose of the asset, the firm will derive the remaining utility of the asset (if any) from operations rather than via disposal. For exchanges and spin-offs, an additional impairment is recorded at disposal if BV > FV.

C. These assets are not treated as assets for sale because there is no accounting income generated from a similar asset exchange, spin-off, or abandonment.

V. Impairment and IFRS

A. Under IFRS impairment is testing is at the "cash generating unit" rather than at the reporting unit level. The cash generating unit is the smallest identifiable group of assets that generates cash inflows.

B. IFRS impairment testing is one step and compares the carrying value with the recoverable amount that is the greater of:

    1. Net selling price - market value less disposal cost;

    2. Value in use - discounted future cash flows.

C. Reversals of impairment are permitted.

    1. If there is impairment on a revalued asset, the impairment loss is charged to the revaluation reserve first.

D. There are a few differences with the treatment of goodwill at the cash generating unit.

    1. Goodwill is allocated to the cash generating unit;

    2. The carrying amount of goodwill is grossed up if there are minority interests;

    3. Any impairment loss is allocated to goodwill first.

Impairment and IFRS

This lesson presents the significant differences in the accounting for impairment under IFRS versus U.S. GAAP.

After studying this lesson you should be able to:

1. *Identify the major differences in the accounting for impairment under IFRS versus U.S. GAAP.*

I. Impairment and IFRS

A. Under IFRS a financial asset is impaired when its carrying value exceeds the present value of the future cash flows discounted at the financial asset's original effective interest rate. Impairment applies only to those assets carried at cost or amortized cost. Assets carried at fair value with the unrealized gains and losses recording in income do not create an impairment loss because the impairment is already captured in the fair value. If the asset is carried at fair value through other comprehensive income, then any impairment would require reclassification of the impairment loss from OCI to earnings.

B. An entity must complete a review of its assets at each balance sheet date to determine if there is evidence that impairment may exist. IAS 39 provides a list of factors to consider in this review. Examples of these observable factors are:

- Significant financial difficulty of the issuer;

- Breach of contract such as default or delinquency in payments;

- Concessions granted to the borrower because of legal or financial reasons that otherwise would not have been considered;

- Bankruptcy of the borrower becomes a probability.

C. If there is objective evidence that impairment may exist, the entity should measure and record the impairment loss.

> The impairment loss exists when the recoverable amount is less than the carrying amount.

Major Differences	
IFRS	**U.S. GAAP**
One-step process	Two-step process
Recoverable amount is the higher of - Fair value less cost to sell or - Value in use	Undiscounted cash flows from use establish recoverability (step one) Fair value is used for the impairment calculation (step two)
Discounting required in evaluation stage	No discounting of cash flows in step one
Impairment losses can be reversed if circumstances change (except for Goodwill)	No reversals permitted

Example:

1. Shelby Company is assessing Asset A for impairment and has determined the following:

Carrying amount:	$42,000
Future undiscounted cash flows:	$45,000
Discounted cash flows:	$40,000
Fair value:	$37,000
Fair value less cost to sell:	$35,000

U.S. GAAP (ASC 360)

Future cash flows $45,000 > Carrying amount $42,000 --> therefore NO impairment

IFRS (IAS 36)

Recoverable amount the great of FV less cost to sell or value in use --> $35,000 or **$40,000**

Recoverable amount $40,000 < Carrying amount $42,000 --> there IS impairment

Impairment loss: write down to the recoverable amount. $42,000 - $40,000 = $2,000

2. Shelby Company is assessing Asset A for impairment and has determined the following:

Carrying amount:	$50,000
Future undiscounted cash flows:	$45,000
Discounted cash flows:	$40,000
Fair value:	$37,000
Fair value less cost to sell:	$35,000

U.S. GAAP (ASC 360)

Future cash flows $45,000 < Carrying amount $50,000 --> there IS impairment

Impairment loss = write down to fair value. $50,000 - $37,000 = $13,000

IFRS (IAS 36)

Recoverable amount the great of FV less cost to sell or value in use --> $35,000 or **$40,000**

Recoverable amount $40,000 < Carrying amount $50,000 --> there IS impairment

Impairment loss = write down to the recoverable amount. $50,000 - $40,000 = $10,000

Interim Financial Reporting

Interim Reporting Principles

The first of two lessons about interim reporting develops the basic principles and provides guidance on specific reporting topics.

After studying this lesson, you should be able to:

1. *Explain the underlying approach to interim reporting.*

2. *List examples of applying that underlying approach.*

3. *Note exceptions to the underlying approach.*

4. *Compute income tax expense for interim periods.*

5. *Describe the application of the lower-of-cost-or-market procedure for interim periods.*

I. **Background and General Approach to Interim Reporting** – Why interim reporting? TIMELINESS is one of our enhancing characteristics of accounting information.

   A. Interim reports are not audited although for SEC registrants the reports are reviewed - a more limited procedure relative to an audit. As such, interim reports must be analyzed with more caution, compared with annual reports. Interim reports tend to be less accurate, subject to greater estimation error due to the shorter period involved, and are less complete. However, they improve the timeliness (time period assumption) of financial reporting.

   B. The general reporting philosophy for interim reports is that interim periods are to be viewed as an integral part of the annual period, rather than as a separate or discrete period. This principle guides many of the specific accounting principles. For example, materiality is determined with reference to annual reports, not to amounts in interim reports.

   C. In general, firms must use the same accounting methods (e.g., LIFO, straight-line depreciation) for interim reporting as they do for annual reporting.

   D. **Interim Relates to Annual --** When investors read an interim report, they are interested in evaluating the interim period as it relates to the annual period.

      1. Thus, when more than one interim period is affected by an expenditure for example, the related expense is recognized in the periods benefited rather than recognized in the period cash was paid.

      2. There are exceptions to this principle, however. Although the integral view is required by GAAP, the "discrete" view - considering each interim reporting period as a separate period - is applied in several situations. The following material first highlights items that reflect the discrete view. The later items exemplify the integral view.

   E. **Interim Period Length --** Interim periods can be of any length less than a year; they are not limited to three-month periods (quarterly periods) although for SEC registrants, the quarterly report (10-Q) is the focus of interim reporting. Revenues earned and realizable in an interim period are recognized in that interim period.

   F. The following table summarizes the general rule for recognition during interim periods.

Item	General Rule	Exceptions
Revenues	Same basis as annual reports	None
Cost of Goods Sold	Same basis as annual reports	1.Gross profit method may be used to estimate CGS and ending inventory for each interim period. 2. Liquidation of LIFO base-period Inventory, if expected to be replaced by year end, should be charged to CGS at expected replacement cost. 3. Temporary declines in inventory market value not recognized, but must recognize other than temporary declines in interim period of decline 4. Planned manufacturing variances should be deferred if expected to be absorbed by year-end.
All Other Costs and Expenses	Same basis as annual reports	Expenditures which clearly benefit more than one interim period may be allocated among periods benefited, e.g., annual repairs, property taxes
Income Taxes	Estimate annual effective tax rate	None
Discontinued Operations	Recognized in interim period as incurred	None
Extraordinary Items	Recognized in interim period as incurred; materiality is evaluated based upon expected annual results	None

II. **Revenue Recognition** -- Revenues are recognized in each interim period, as they would be in an annual period. Revenues earned and realizable in an interim period are recognized in that interim period.

    A. A firm uses the percentage of completion method on long-term contracts. The profit recognized each quarter is based on the percentage of completion at the end of each quarter. If a loss is anticipated in quarter 3, the entire contract loss is recognized in quarter 3.

    B. Earnings Per Share (EPS) is reported under the discrete view. Each quarterly EPS amount reflects only the events of that quarter. The assumptions and computations leading to the quarterly EPS amount reflect the circumstances within each interim period separately, rather than estimations of year-end circumstances. For example, shares issued in the third quarter affect reported EPS for the third and fourth quarter only, not the first two quarters.

III. **Expense Recognition**

    A. The general rule for expense recognition is:

        1. If the cost or expense has no relationship to other quarters, recognize the entire expense in the quarter in which the cost was incurred (the discrete view).

            a. Examples

                i. Extraordinary items net of applicable tax;

                ii. Discontinued operations net of applicable tax (if a component qualifying for discontinued operations reporting is considered held for sale in a particular quarter, the usual discontinued operations reporting is required for that quarter with later adjustments to any gain or loss recognized in those later quarters);

      iii. Gains and losses on disposals of plant assets;

      iv. Unusual or infrequent losses and expenses. (Recall for annual reporting, these items must be separately reported as a component of income from continuing operations - the same applies for interim reporting.)

   b. These items have no relationship to interim periods other than the one in which they occurred.

   c. Arbitrary allocation of these items to other quarters is not permitted.

2. If the cost or expense benefits other quarters or interim periods, allocate the cost to those other quarters and recognize the appropriate amount of expense in those quarters (the integral view).

   a. Examples

      i. Depreciation;

      ii. Property tax expense;

      iii. Rent expense if prepaid for longer than one interim period;

      iv. Advertising expense if expenditures benefit more than one interim period;

      v. Bad debt expense if the firm uses an annual estimation procedure.

   b. These expenses are allocated to the interim periods benefited even though some may be paid in full in one interim period, because they benefit more than one interim period.

   c. Repairs and maintenance expenditures may be cyclical with significant expenditures in one quarter benefiting the entire year. If the expenditures are planned to cover an annual period (or longer), then each interim period should recognize only its portion of the total expenditure as expense.

B. Expenses directly related to revenue -- Expenses directly related to revenue (cost of goods sold, sales commissions) are recognized in the same period as the related revenue.

C. Income tax expense -- Firms face a graduated annual income tax rate. The final rate(s) applicable to annual income is not known until the end of the year.

   1. The income tax expense (which is computed only for income from continuing operations) for each interim period is computed as follows:

   a. The annual rate to be applied to income from continuing operations is reestimated each quarter (the rate does not consider the tax on discontinued operations and extraordinary items, which would be reported in the quarter these items were incurred, at the incremental rate at the time);

   b. That rate is applied to total interim income through the end of the current quarter, yielding total estimated tax to date;

   c. The income tax reported in previous quarters is subtracted from the results in the second step to yield the income tax expense for the current quarter;

   d. This procedure is a good example of the integral view of interim reporting -- the interim period is an integral part of an annual period.

   See the following example.

> **Example:**
> Income tax recognized for quarter 1 is $20,000, based on the annual rate that is expected to apply to the firm. At the end of quarter 2, the expected annual income tax rate is 30% and pretax income for the first two quarters is $130,000.
>
> Income tax expense to be recognized for quarter 2 only is $19,000 (.30 x $130,000 - $20,000).

IV. Declines in Inventory Application of the LCM Method to Interim Reports

A. **Temporary declines --** are those expected to reverse by year-end.

    1. These are not recognized as losses in the interim periods in which they occur. This treatment is consistent with the integral view of interim reporting.

    2. No loss is expected for the year, therefore, a temporary loss should not be recognized in a specific quarter.

    3. Later recoveries are not recorded because the previous loss was not recorded.

B. **Permanent declines --** (those not expected to reverse in the current year) are recognized as losses in the interim periods in which they occur.

    1. Later recoveries are recognized as gains to the extent of previous losses only.

    2. The inventory may not be marked up above cost.

C. **Related Questions**

> **Question:**
> An inventory loss (decline in inventory value below cost) is incurred in quarter 2 but is expected to be recovered by year-end. However, it was not actually recovered by the end of the year. In what interim periods is the loss recognized under LCM?
>
> **Answer:**
> The loss is recognized in quarter 4 because it was expected to be temporary as of the end of quarter 2 and no loss was recognized then.

> **Question:**
> An inventory loss occurred in the first quarter and was not expected to reverse in the current year. But the loss was recovered in the second quarter with the market price increase exceeding the decline from the first quarter. How should this be treated in the interim reports for quarters 1 and 2?
>
> **Answer:**
> Write the inventory down in quarter 1, recognize the loss, and then write it back up in quarter 2 but only to cost, recognizing a gain.

Interim Reporting – Details and IFRS

The second lesson on interim reporting addresses additional financial reporting topics, and international standards.

After studying this lesson, you should be able to:

1. *Describe the reporting of LIFO liquidations and cost accounting variances in interim reports.*

2. *Explain the application of interim reporting principles to accounting changes.*

3. *List the minimum reporting requirements for interim reports.*

4. *Note the underlying approach to interim reporting for international standards.*

5. *List differences in interim reporting under the two sets of standards for specific reporting topics.*

I. **LIFO Liquidation** -- If a firm uses LIFO for annual reporting, it must also use LIFO for interim reporting. When a LIFO layer is liquidated in a particular interim period (number of units purchased is less than number of units sold in the interim period), the accounting depends on whether the liquidation is expected to be restored by the end of the annual period.

   A. **Restoration Expected** -- If the liquidation is expected to be restored, then the interim period cost of goods sold should reflect the estimated cost of the replacement (this preserves the effect of LIFO for the interim period during which the liquidation took place). The firm recognizes an increase in cost of goods sold and recognizes a provision (liability) for the future purchase. This liability is extinguished in a later interim period when the inventory is replenished. As a result, overestimated earnings are avoided. Also, the ending inventory for the interim period reflects the restoration. This is another example of the integral view of interim reporting.

   B. **Restoration Not Expected** -- If the liquidation is not expected to be restored, then the interim period cost of goods sold should reflect the actual cost of the layer liquidated.

II. **Cost Accounting Variances** -- Purchase price variances, and volume variances expected to be absorbed by the end of the current year are deferred (not recognized in earnings) for the interim period.

   A. This is consistent with the integral view of interim reporting because there is no variance expected for the year.

   B. The reason for the deferral is that, from the point of view of the entire reporting year, there will be no volume variance.

   C. If the variances will not be absorbed (reversed) by other purchases of material or by increased production later in the year, they are recognized in the quarter of incurrence.

III. **Gross Margin Method for Inventory** -- The gross margin method (also called the gross profit method) is not allowed for annual reporting purposes, but can be used for interim reporting. This method uses the gross margin percentage to estimate cost of goods sold from purchase information. The estimated cost of goods sold then is used to estimate ending inventory for the quarter without having to count inventory. Footnote disclosure of the use of this method is required.

IV. Principle Changes

A. A change in accounting principle made in an interim period is reported in the same way as for annual statements. The retained earnings balance at the beginning of that interim period is adjusted to reflect the new principle, and the balances of previous interim periods reported comparatively with the interim period of change are retrospectively adjusted.

Example:
A new accounting principle is adopted in quarter 3. The beginning retained earnings balance for quarter 3 is adjusted to reflect the new method up to that point, and quarter 1 and 2 statements are retrospectively adjusted to reflect the new principle.

B. **Impracticability Exception** -- However, the impracticability exception for annual periods does not apply to prechange interim periods in the year the change was made. When it is impracticable to apply the retrospective method to prechange interim periods of the same fiscal year, then the change is made as of the beginning of the subsequent fiscal year.

C. For interim periods after an accounting principle change, the effect of the principle change on income from continuing operations and net income, and related per share amounts are shown.

Example:
If an accounting principle change is adopted in the second quarter, these disclosures are required for the last three quarters of the fiscal year.

V. Estimate Changes

A. A change in estimate is accounted for in the interim period in which the change in estimate is made. Earlier interim periods are not affected. If material, the effect of the change on net income for the interim period and subsequent periods is reported.

Example:
A change in property, plant, and equipment useful lives is made in quarter 3. The new estimate is applied as of the beginning of quarter 3. The effect of the change on earnings for quarter 3 is reported in quarter 3 results. The new estimate is also applied to quarter 4 and the effect of the change on quarter 4 earnings is reported.

VI. Interim Reports and Segment Reporting -- When a firm subject to the segmental disclosure requirements issues interim reports, the following interim information is required to be reported for each segment:

A. External revenues (other than from intersegment sales)

   1. Intersegment revenues;

   2. Segment profit or loss.

VII. Reporting Requirements

A. GAAP does not require interim reports. However, the SEC requires that registrants file the 10-Q report for each quarter. Also, quarterly reports are provided as supplemental information within the annual report.

B. If non-SEC registrants choose to report interim financial statements, there is no requirement that the statements be as complete as annual statements. As a result, there is considerable variation in the detail reported. The FASB encourages the reporting of an interim balance sheet and statement of cash flows. Larger firms tend to provide more complete information. When the fourth quarter interim report is not provided, the annual report should disclose significant events for that quarter, along with material adjustments at year-end including unusual or infrequent items, discontinued operations, and extraordinary items.

C. If an interim report is provided, the minimum required disclosures include information about:

    1. Sales and other revenue, unusual or infrequent items, discontinued operations, extraordinary items, net income;

    2. Seasonal revenues and expenses allowing users to assess the impact on both the interim period and annual period;

    3. Changes in estimated income tax expense;

    4. Contingencies;

    5. Fair value;

    6. Earnings per share;

    7. Changes in accounting principle and estimates;

    8. Significant cash flow changes.

D. **Cumulatives and Comparatives** -- At any interim period the financial statements would present the cumulative results as well as the comparative for the prior year.

    1. For example: reporting as of June /30 (Quarter 2):

        a. Income Statements (4):

            i. Income Statement for Quarter 2 (and PY Q 2)

            ii. Cumulative Income Statement for 1/1 -- 6/30 (and Comparatives for PY)

        b. Balance Sheets (3):

            i. Balance Sheet as of 6/30 (and Comparatives for PY)

            ii. Balance Sheet as of 12/31/Prior Year-end

        c. Statement of Cash Flows: (4)

            i. Statement of Cash Flows for Quarter II (and Comparatives for PY)

            ii. Cumulative Statement of Cash Flows for 1/1--6/30 (and Comparatives for PY

VIII. U.S. GAAP - IFRS Differences

A. Whereas the stated preference in U.S. reporting for interim statements is the integral view (with major exceptions), international standards have a stated preference for the discrete view, again with major exceptions. For example, assessments of materiality are made with reference to interim amounts (a lower threshold than for U.S. standards). However, neither reporting system is a pure approach.

B. One of the guiding interim reporting principles for international standards is that all recognized accounts for interim purposes must meet their IFRS definitions in the interim period. The same process for estimates, accruals, deferrals and allocations made at the end of an annual period apply to each interim period. This provision of the international standards reflects the preference for the discrete view, and is in contrast with U.S. standards.

    1. Assets -- For an expenditure in one interim period to be capitalized (and thus result in some expensing in a later interim period), the expenditure must meet the definition of an asset in the first interim period. Allocations of expenditures to more than one interim period as expense are not allowed, unless an asset exists at the end of the interim period. The balance sheet view prevails here rather than matching.

2. **Liabilities** -- Accrual of planned expenses at the end of an interim period before an expenditure is made (for example, planned maintenance to be paid for later in the same annual period) is not permitted unless the firm has a liability at the end of the interim period. Thus, international standards do not allow the allocation of accrued expenses between interim periods unless there is a liability at the end of an interim period.

> **Example:**
> A year-end bonus for management is not accrued in earlier interim periods unless there is a legal or constructive obligation for the bonus, and a reliable estimate of the amount can be made.

C. Revenues are recognized when earned and realizable. As a result, interest revenue is accrued in interim periods before receipt of cash, but dividend revenue is not because dividends are not mandatory - no liability exists on the part of the issuing firm until the dividends are declared.

   1. The cyclical nature of a revenue does not warrant deferral in an interim period simply because more sales revenue, for example, is recognized in one period and less is recognized in another.

D. Similar to U.S. standards, interim period income tax expense is computed on an annualized basis (integral view). For international standards, entities must estimate the average annual effective tax rate for the full fiscal year, and apply it to each quarter. Anticipated tax rate changes and the pattern of earnings must be taken into account. When the entity is subject to taxation from more than one jurisdiction, or is subject to more than one rate across categories of income, the entity is allowed to use a weighted average rate across jurisdictions and income categories provided that this process results in a reasonable approximation to the more exact calculation.

E. Specific examples of the discrete view applied in international standards.

   1. The deferral of manufacturing variances that are expected to be offset in a later interim period within the same annual period is not allowed.

   2. The deferral of a temporary market decline in inventory expected to be recovered in a later interim period within the same annual period is not allowed.

   3. Volume rebates and other anticipated changes in the costs of inventory to be purchased for the year can be anticipated (allocated over the year) only if the cost adjustments are contractual.

F. International reporting requirements. Neither U.S. nor international standards require interim financial statements. Depending on the country, securities regulators, governments or stock markets may require interim reports, however. In the U.S., quarterly reports are required for publicly traded firms. In other countries, semi-annual reporting is more common.

   1. If the entity (a) provides full interim statements as required by a securities regulator or other entity, or (b) voluntarily provides such statements described as complying with international standards, the statements must comply with IFRS.

   2. If full statements are not provided, the headings and subtotals should include those presented in the most recent annual statements. Basic and diluted EPS must be reported if the entity is subject to EPS requirements for its annual statements (publicly traded firms).

   3. International standards encourage publicly traded firms to provide semi-annual reports at a minimum. Firms are required to use the same accounting policies for interim reporting as they do for annual reports if they provide interim reports.

4. If a report is provided, the minimum reporting requirements include the following condensed financial statements: statement of comprehensive income, balance sheet, statement of cash flows, and statement of changes in equity.

5. The footnotes should include information about the following, if material

    a. Statement of accounting policies;

    b. Information about cyclical revenues and expenses;

    c. Unusual items;

    d. Changes in estimates;

    e. Changes in debt and equity securities;

    f. Dividends paid;

    g. Segment information;

    h. Subsequent events;

    i. Contingencies;

    j. Changes in composition of consolidated enterprises.

Leases

Background, Operating Leases

This is the first of several lessons addressing the accounting for leases. This lesson provides a big picture of the area and specific guidance on accounting for operating leases.

After studying this lesson, you should be able to:

1. *Distinguish between operating and capital leases and describe the general accounting for both types of lease on the lessor and lessee.*

2. *Articulate the general rationale for capitalizing a lease.*

3. *Compute annual rent expense and revenue for an operating lease with uneven periodic rentals.*

4. *Account for leasehold improvements in an operating lease.*

I.

Definitions:
Lease: A lease is a contract conveying the right to use property, plant, and equipment for a stated period of time.

Operating Lease: A lease that does not transfer the risks and rewards of ownership to the lessee. The lessee (renter) records rent expense; the lessor (owner) records rent revenue. The asset remains on the lessor's books.

Capital Lease: A lease that transfers the risks and rewards of ownership to the lessee. The lessee places the asset and a lease liability on its books and recognizes interest expense and depreciation over the lease term. The lessor removes the asset from its books, replaces it with a financial asset, and recognizes interest revenue over the lease term.

A. When a lease is capitalized by the lessee, the present value of the future lease payments is debited to the leased asset and credited to the lease liability accounts. For the lessor, the present value of lease payments is debited to the net financial asset (a receivable) created at inception (beginning of the lease).

B. A lease is capitalized when it meets the lease capitalization criteria (discussed later).

I. Theoretical Considerations

A. The theoretical considerations in accounting for leases are twofold. First, the overriding concern is to account for the economic substance of the transaction. Second, the objective of accounting for leases is to prevent off-balance sheet financing.

B. **Economic Substance Over Form --** In accounting for leases, a determination of the economic substance of the transaction must be made.

    1. If the transaction is a true rental arrangement, it should be accounted for as such. This type of lease is called an operating lease. That is, the lessee will not recognize any asset or liability related to the lease transaction. The lessee will simply record rent expense over the life of the lease contract. The lessor will retain the asset on its books and continue to depreciate the asset. The lessor will also recognize the lease payments as revenue over the term of the lease contract. This is an operating lease.

2. On the other hand, if the lease contract is in-substance a purchase agreement between the lessor and the lessee, the lessee will recognize the asset and, more importantly, the related liability. This type of lease is called a capital lease. Each payment made by the lessee will include principal and interest components, and the lessee will depreciate the asset. The lessor will record the sale of the asset and will record payments received by allocating those payments between the principal received and the interest received. Although the lessor continues to own the asset, it no longer appears on the lessor's books as a physical asset. The lessee never owns the leased asset during the lease term but will treat the arrangement as a financed purchase of an asset if it is in-substance a purchase agreement. This is a capital lease.

C. **Off-Balance Sheet Financing** -- A lease is a very effective approach used by companies to achieve "off-balance sheet financing," which means a firm has debt that does not appear on the balance sheet. If successful in the leasing context, that implies the company has successfully obtained the right to use an asset for the majority of its useful life without any recognition of the obligation related to the acquisition of the asset. In accounting for lease contracts, the primary objective, or goal, is to account for the substance of the transaction and prevent "off-balance sheet financing." The firm has committed to a long-term series of lease payments.

D. If the lease is noncancelable, the lessee fully intends to use the leased asset in its operations for the lease term, and the lease term is the substantial part of the useful life of the asset, then the full liability should be recorded, as well as the asset. Capital lease accounting significantly curtails the off-balance sheet financing nature of leasing.

1. The term "noncancelable" includes leases that are cancelable only due to a remote contingency, by permission by the lessor, by substitution of a new lease for the old with the same lessor, or requiring payment of a penalty amount that is so great that, at the inception, cancellation is considered unlikely.

E. The operating lease classification is still very popular. Lessees prefer them for accounting reasons because no liability is reported on the books. The key concept to remember is that rent expense and revenue are recognized on a straight-line basis, without regard to the schedule of rental payments.

II. Accounting for Operating Leases

A. Introduction

1. A lease is accounted for as an operating lease when the capitalization criteria are not met (discussed later). An operating lease is a lease that is not a capital lease.

2. Rental contracts often specify that the lessee must pay the first period's rent at the inception. In addition, a bonus or special payment may be required to secure the lease and the last period's rent may also be required to be paid at inception. Also, rent payments may not be of equal amount each year per the rental contract.

3. GAAP requires that the straight-line method of recognizing rent expense and revenue be applied unless another method more accurately reflects the pattern of use. The straight-line method allocates the total rentals, regardless of their timing, on an equal basis to each period. Thus, without regard to the rental schedule, the amount of rent revenue (lessor) and rent expense (lessee) to be recognized each year is:

> Annual rent expense or revenue = Total rentals over the lease term/number of years in lease term

4. The total rentals include any amounts that will be retained by the lessor as rent. They do not include damage or cleaning deposits. Free rental periods are automatically included

in the computation. For example, if the first year of a 10-year operating lease is rent-free, the numerator of the equation above reflects only 9 years of rent while the denominator includes 10 years. Each of the 10 years would recognize the same rent expense or revenue.

5. The rationale for the application of the straight-line method is the assumption that the asset will provide equal benefits to the lessee each year (matching concept). This is the usual assumption. Unless explicit information to the contrary is provided, assume the straight-line method.

6. In some cases, the annual (or monthly) rental begins at a relatively low amount and progressively increases. In the early years of the rental, the amount paid is less than the constant amount expensed per period. As a result, a liability (called deferred rent expense) is recorded for the difference. In later years, when the payment amounts exceed the constant expense amount, the liability is gradually extinguished.

7. Leasehold improvements are improvements made to a rental property that revert to the owner at the end of the lease term. These are typically structural changes that cannot be removed at the end of the rental period without damaging the rented property. The cost of leasehold improvements is capitalized by the lessee to a plant asset or an intangible asset and depreciated or amortized to expense over the shorter of (a) remaining term of the rental, and (b) useful life of the improvements. Typically, the remaining term is used for amortization, which is an expense separate from rent expense.

8. If the rental agreement includes an option to renew but renewal is uncertain, the renewal period is not used in the computation of annual rent expense or leasehold amortization expense. If the renewal period is likely, the renewal period is included.

9. The lessor reclassifies the leased asset from plant assets to another category such as "other assets" or "investment in leased assets" during the lease term. However, depreciation continues during the lease term because the asset is being used by the lessee.

See the following example.

Example:
Ace Co. signed a contract to rent office space from Deuce Co. for three years beginning January 1, Year 1. The rental contract called for annual rentals of $2,000 due at the beginning of each year. However, at inception Ace was required to pay a $600 bonus to obtain the space. Ace was also required to pay the third year's rent at inception. Both parties account for the lease as an operating lease.

Rent expense for Ace (revenue for Deuce) to be recognized each year is $2,200: = (3($2,000) + $600) / 3.

Entries:	Ace		Deuce	
January 1, Year 1				
	Prepaid Rent	4,600	Cash	4,600
	Cash	4,600	Unearned Rent	4,600*

*unearned rent is a liability; $4,600 = 2($2,000) + $600

December 31, Year 1				
	Rent Expense	2,200	Unearned Rent	2,200
	Prepaid Rent	2,200	Rent Revenue	2,200
January 1, Year 2				
	Prepaid Rent	2,000	Cash	2,000
	Cash	2,000	Unearned Rent	2,000
December 31, Year 2				
	Rent Expense	2,200	Unearned Rent	2,200
	Prepaid Rent	2,200	Rent Revenue	2,200
December 31, Year 3				
	Rent Expense	2,200	Unearned Rent	2,200
	Prepaid Rent	2,200	Rent Revenue	2,200

Example:
A firm rents office space beginning January 1, Year 1 for five years. The first year rental rate is $1,200 per year, and the rate for the last four years is $1,800 per year. As an added inducement, the first six-months of the first year are rent-free (a rent abatement). A refundable damage deposit of $800 is collected at inception. The firm accounts for the lease as an operating lease.

The annual rent expense to be recognized for each of the five years of the lease term is $1,560 = [(1/2)($1,200) + 4($1,800)]/5. Only one-half a year's rent is required to be paid for the first year. The damage deposit is not included in the rentals because it is to be refunded to the lessee. The lessee records a receivable for the deposit; the lessor records a payable.

Capital Lease Basics

The second lesson on lease accounting establishes the terminology and conceptual underpinnings for the remaining lessons on leases.

After studying this lesson, you should be able to:

1. *Define the important terms relevant to capital lease accounting including lease term, bargain purchase option, unguaranteed residual value, minimum lease payments and others.*

2. *List the items included in minimum lease payments for both parties to the lease.*

3. *Determine the applicable interest rate for both parties.*

4. *List and defend the four criteria for capitalizing a lease.*

5. *Note the additional two criteria for lessors.*

I. **Capital Lease Terminology**

A. The **lease term** is the period during which the lessee can reasonably be expected to continue leasing the asset. The lease term is the fixed noncancelable term of the lease plus periods covered by bargain renewal options plus all periods covered by renewal options during which there is a loan outstanding from the lessor to the lessee. The lease term cannot extend beyond the exercise date of a bargain purchase option, even if the lease specifies payments after the date of the bargain purchase option (those later payments would not be paid because the asset will be purchased before those payments).

B. The **bargain purchase option (BPO)** is an option whereby the lessee will have an opportunity in the future to purchase the asset at an amount that is significantly less than the asset's fair market value on that future date. The price is sufficiently low to reasonably assure exercise of the option by the lessee. If the lessee accepts the terms of the lease contract, the accounting for both parties assumes the purchase option will be exercised, in which case title transfers to the lessee. The exercise ends the lease term.

   1. The option is not really a bargain, however. The lessor expects the option to be taken and structures all of the payments, including the BPO, to provide the required rate of return. The BPO amount is really just another lease payment.

C. The **guaranteed residual value** clause is typically found in lease agreements in which there is no bargain purchase option or transfer of title. The guaranteed residual value is related to the condition of the property at the time that it reverts back to the lessor. If the lessee guarantees the residual value, the lessee is responsible for the condition of the asset at the conclusion of the lease term. If there is no guaranteed residual value in the lease agreement, the lessee is not responsible for the condition of the asset at the conclusion of the lease agreement. Third parties may also guarantee residual values.

   1. If the lessee guarantees a residual value, the expectation is that the title does not transfer to the lessee at the end of the lease term. The lessee will pay the lessor any shortfall between the amount guaranteed and the actual market value of the asset at the end of the lease term.

   2. An unguaranteed residual value is the expected salvage value of the leased asset at the end of the term that has not been guaranteed. The guarantee of residual value, or lack thereof, does not change the amount of the residual.

> **Example:**
> The estimated value of a leased asset at the end of the lease term is
> $3,000. With or without a guarantee, the value is expected to be $3,000.
> This is the same residual or salvage value discussed in the lessons on depreciation of
> plant assets, except that it is measured at the end of the lease term, which may be well
> before the end of the asset's economic life.

D. The **executory costs** include casualty insurance, maintenance, and property taxes. These costs are not capitalized by any party, but rather represent annual expenses associated with owning and maintaining the asset. They are not considered when determining whether the lease is a capital or operating lease, and they are not capitalized in a capital lease.

E. **Lessee Minimum Lease Payments --** The minimum lease payments for the lessee are all the payments the lessee is expected to make under the lease. The minimum lease payments of the lessee include all the rental payments that the lessee is obligated to make in connection with the leased property, excluding executory costs. The components of the lessee's minimum lease payments are listed below.

1. The annual lease payments;

2. Bargain purchase option;

3. If no Bargain Purchase Option exists, any residual value guaranteed by the lessee at the expiration of the lease term.

4. Any penalty payments the lessee is required to make for not renewing the lease term;

5. Excluded are payments required by the lessee for damage, extraordinary wear and tear, or excessive usage because they cannot be estimated. Rather, they are treated as expenses or losses in the period incurred.

F. **Lessor Minimum Lease Payments --** The minimum lease payments from the lessor's perspective are the same as those identified for the lessee with one additional element. The minimum lease payments also include any residual value guaranteed by a third party unrelated to either the lessee or the lessor. An unguaranteed residual is not included in the minimum lease payments of the lessor or lessee because it is a cash flow outside the lease arrangement.

G. The **implicit interest rate** is sometimes described as the lessor's required rate of interest. Mathematically, the implicit interest rate is the rate that equates the market value of the leased asset with the sum of the present value of the minimum lease payments (lessor's perspective) plus the present value of any unguaranteed residual value. This is the rate used by the lessor for all present value calculations in a capital lease, and for computing interest revenue.

1. This rate is the annual compounded rate of return to the lessor over the lease term. The unguaranteed residual value is included in the calculation because it is part of the value of the asset (as is the case with the salvage value for any plant asset).

   See the following example.

> **Example:**
> A lease requires 10 equal annual lease payments of $4,000 to be paid each January 1. The inception of the lease is January 1, Year 1. The market value of the asset leased is $27, 807. The unguaranteed residual value at the end of the lease term is $2,000. The lessor's implicit rate in the lease is 10%. The discounted cash flows, including the unguaranteed residual value, are related to the market value as shown in the equation:
>
> $27,807 = market value of asset = present value of the lease payments +
>
> present value of unguaranteed residual value
>
> $27,807 = $4,000(PV ann. due, I=10%, N=10) + $2,000(PV $1, I=10%, N=10)
>
> = $4,000(6.75902) + $2,000(.38554)
>
> If the cash flows are received as expected, the lessor will earn 10% on a compounded basis annually from its investment in the leased asset. All residual values at the end of the lease term are treated the same way in the above equation. It makes no difference in terms of the lessor's equation if the residual is guaranteed or not.

H. The **lessee's incremental borrowing rate** is the rate, at lease inception date, the lessee would have incurred to borrow the funds necessary to purchase the leased asset rather than lease it.

II. Capital Lease Criteria

A. The four criteria used to determine whether a lease is a capital lease follow. Both parties use these criteria. If one or more of the criteria is met, the lease is a capital lease for the lessee. The lessor also must meet two additional criteria. If none of the first four are met, the lease is an operating lease for both parties. The lessee is concerned only with the first four criteria.

> **Study Tip:**
> **Caution:** To facilitate the discussion, the lease capitalization criteria are referred to by number, but for the CPA exam, candidates should know the criteria by their descriptions as provided below.

B. In all cases, the lease must be noncancelable for it to be a capital lease. This is generally assumed, if not mentioned, in a problem.

   1. **Criterion 1 --** The lease agreement transfers ownership of the leased asset to the lessee at the conclusion of the lease term (Title transfer).

   2. **Criterion 2 --** The lease contains a bargain purchase option (BPO).

   3. **Criterion 3 --** The lease term is at least 75% of the remaining estimated economic life of the leased asset at inception (Term is 75% or more of useful life).

> **Example:**
> A lessor leases an asset with an original useful life when new of 20 years. After two years, the asset is leased for 12 years. The third criterion is not met because 12/18 = .67 which is less than .75. The remaining useful life at inception is 18 years. The lease term is less than 75% of the 18-year remaining useful life. If none of the other three criteria is met, the lease is an operating lease.

   4. **Criterion 4 --** The present value of minimum lease payments at the inception of the lease is at least 90% of the market value of the leased asset at that time (PV is 90% or more of market value). Review the definition of minimum lease payments. Criterion 4 is the reason that minimum lease payments were defined.

C. For criterion 4, the lessor uses the rate implicit in the lease to measure the present value. The lessee uses the lower of implicit interest rate, if the lessee knows the rate or can determine it, and the lessee's borrowing rate. The lower rate will cause the present value to be higher resulting in a better chance of the lessee fulfilling the fourth criterion and thus having a capital lease. The parties use these interest rates not only in measuring the present value for criterion 4, but also for capitalizing the minimum lease payments for recording purposes and for computing interest.

Example:
A lessor leases an asset with a market value of $100,000 for 10 years. Annual end-of-year lease payments are $15,000. The lessor's implicit rate and lessee's borrowing rate are 10%. The lease calls for no other payments by the lessee and the asset reverts to the lessor at the end of the lease term.

PV of minimum lease payments = $15,000(PV ord. ann., I=10%, N=10)

= $15,000 x 6.14457

= $92,169 > .90($100,000)

The fourth criterion is met for both parties because the present value of minimum lease payments for both lessor and lessee ($92,169) exceeds 90% of the market value of the asset. Thus, the lease is a capital lease.

Caution 1: The present value of minimum lease payments may be different for the lessor and lessee because: 1. Different cash flows may be included in their minimum lease payments; and   2. Their interest rates may be different.   **Caution 2:** When the lease term begins within the last 25% of the total useful life of the asset, criterion 3 and 4 no longer can be used to determine whether a lease is capitalized. In this case, title must transfer or a bargain purchase option must be present for a lease to be capitalized.

Example:
An asset's original useful life is 20 years. After 15 years of using the asset, a firm leases it to another firm for 4 years. Normally, this lease would qualify as a capital lease because the lease term is 80% of the remaining useful life at inception (4/5). But at inception, only 25% of the total useful life of the asset remains (5/20). Therefore, criterion 3 and criterion 4 can no longer be used for lease capitalization. Most of the asset's useful life is over. If this lease does not transfer title or include a bargain purchase option, then it is an operating lease.

III. **Rationale for Lease Capitalization**

A. The fundamental rationale for lease capitalization is that if most of the benefits and responsibilities of asset ownership are passed to the lessee, the lessee should record an asset and a lease liability equal to the present value of the minimum lease payments. The four criteria operationalize this concept.

B. If either of **criterion 1 or criterion 2** is met, the lease is essentially an installment purchase of the asset. There is little question that the lessee will obtain most of the benefits of the asset under such an agreement because in both cases, the lessee retains the asset at the end of the lease term.

C. If **criterion 3** is met, the lessee obtains at least 75% of the useful life of the asset. For many assets, this means the lessee will receive considerably more than 75% of the benefits of the asset because many assets are more productive earlier in their useful lives.

D. If **criterion 4** is met, the lessee is making payments with a present value of at least 90% of the market value of the asset. The lessee is essentially purchasing most of the asset's value. The lessee would not commit to such a stream of payments unless most of the asset's benefits were being purchased through the lease.

IV. **Two Additional Criteria for the Lessor** -- For the lease to be accounted for as a capital lease, the lessor must meet at least one of the first four criteria, and both of the next two, which apply only to the lessor:

A. **Criterion 5** -- There are no material cost uncertainties that would require unreimbursable costs to be incurred by the lessor.

 1. What this really means, is that there are no uncertainties that would call into question the capitalization of the lease payments by the lessor. For example, if the lessor guaranteed the asset against obsolescence (not usual in a capital lease), there would be significant uncertainty concerning the net amount of cash inflow per period to the lessor. If that were the case, the uncertain cash flows should not be capitalized, and the lease is accounted for as an operating lease by the lessor.

B. **Criterion 6** -- Collectibility of the minimum lease payments is reasonably assured.

 1. If collectibility of the lease payments is uncertain, there is no justification for capitalizing them into an asset account. Again, this means the lease is an operating lease for the lessor although it could be a capital lease for the lessee.

V. **Summary - Lease Capitalization Criteria**

A. To capitalize a lease:

 1. The lessee must meet one of criteria 1 - 4 (otherwise, the lease is an operating lease);

 2. The lessor must meet one of criteria 1 - 4, and both 5 and 6 (otherwise, the lease is an operating lease).

B. With the lessor using more criteria than the lessee, it is possible for a lease to be a capital lease for the lessee and an operating lease for the lessor. All that would be required is for the lessor to fail to meet either criteria 5 or 6.

C. Another possibility occurs with criterion 4. The lessor's implicit rate might be considerably lower than the lessee's borrowing rate and the lessee is unable to determine the lessor's rate. The present value of the minimum lease payments might then exceed 90% of the fair value of the property for the lessor, but not for the lessee. Also, the lessor may include payments such as the third party guarantee of residual value in minimum lease payments, whereas the lessee does not.

Note: When examining a lease agreement for the possible failure to meet criteria 5 and 6, the potential problem usually rests with criterion 6. For example, the prime interest rate at the inception of the lease is 7%, but the lessee's incremental borrowing rate is 13%. From that information, you should conclude the lessee is a poor credit risk and conclude the collectibility of lease payments is not assured.

For CPA exam purposes, assume criteria 1-4 are not met unless there is positive information indicating that one or more of the criteria is met. But for criteria 5 and 6, assume they are met unless there is negative information, as exemplified immediately above.

VI. Classification of Leases

A. A capital lease from the lessor's perspective will be further classified as a direct financing capital lease or a sales-type capital lease. No such classification exists for the lessee. Lessee capital lease accounting is unaffected by whether the lessor has a direct financing lease or a sales-type lease. The following is the breakdown of leases for both parties.

B. Lessee

  1. Operating;

  2. Capital.

C. Lessor

  1. Operating;

  2. Capital;

   a. Direct financing (defined later);

   b. Sales type (defined later).

Direct Financing Leases

This lease accounting lesson covers the specifics for recording a direct financing lease for both parties.

After studying this lesson, you should be able to:

1. *Identify a direct financing lease from given information.*

2. *Record the inception journal entry for both parties.*

3. *Prepare the journal entries for interest recognition for both parties over more than one period.*

I. **Direct Financing Capital Lease (DFL) Basics**

    A. A DFL is one of two types of capital leases for the lessor. The lessor derives only one type of income from a direct financing capital lease. Interest income is the sole type of income from this type of lease agreement.

    B. In a DFL, the book value of the lessor's asset is equal to its market value. There is no gross profit on the lease.

    C. The general entries for a DFL for both parties appear below. The numerical examples add additional aspects to the entries. The actual entries recorded by a firm are affected by the timing of the cash flows and whether the lease payment stream is an annuity due or an ordinary annuity.

    D. Lessor

At inception (assumes a new asset)	
Lease Receivable	sum of minimum lease payments + any unguaranteed residual
Unearned Interest revenue	total interest over term
Asset	market value = cost value

    1. The lessor typically uses the gross method. The net lease receivable balance is the difference between the Lease Receivable and Unearned Interest Revenue accounts and equals the present value of the lease payments using the lessor's implicit interest rate. The financial asset replaces the physical asset. The receivable is a noncurrent asset. Unearned Interest Revenue is contra to Lease Receivable. For a new asset, cost and book value are the same. If the asset is used, then the accumulated depreciation account is closed (debited). In this case, market value equals book value or carrying value.

    E. *Recognition of periodic interest revenue*

Cash	lease payment amount
Unearned Interest Revenue	equals interest revenue amount
Lease Receivable	lease payment amount
Interest Revenue	beginning net lease receivable X lessor's implicit interest rate

F. The lease payment amount includes principal and interest. The reduction in principal is the difference between the lease payment and the interest revenue amounts. The last lease payment closes the remaining balances in the lease receivable and unearned interest accounts. Caution: the lessor computes interest revenue based on the net lease receivable, even though the gross method is used for recording.

G. Lessee

> The entries for the lessee follow the same general principles for valuing all monetary noncurrent liabilities and for recognizing interest.
>
> *At inception*
>
> Leased Asset   present value of minimum lease payments
>
>   Lease Liability   present value of minimum lease payments

1. This is the entry that embodies the theory underlying capital leases. The lessee is capitalizing an asset it does not own and recording a significant liability based on a contract. The lessee typically uses the net method. The leased asset is included in plant assets. The lease liability is both a current and noncurrent liability. The present value is computed using the lower of implicit interest rate if the lessee knows the rate or can determine it, and the lessee's implicit rate. This is the same rate used by the lessee for criterion 4 for lease capitalization.

2. The amount recorded for the asset and liability cannot exceed the asset's market value. If the present value, as computed, exceeds the market value, the lease is recorded at the market value. A new (higher) interest rate, equating the present value of the lease payments and the market value, is used for computing interest.

H. *Recognition of Periodic Interest Expense*

> Interest Expense   beginning liability balance X interest rate
>
> Lease Liability   amount of liability reduction
>
>   Cash   lease payment amount

I. *Recognition of Periodic Depreciation*

> Depreciation expense   discussed later
>
>   Accumulated depreciation

1. In a later section, the computation of depreciation is discussed. The amount depends on whether title is transferred to the lessee at the end of the lease. Accumulated depreciation is contra to the leased asset. The computations are the same as discussed in previous lessons on depreciation.

II. Example - Direct Financing Lease.

A. On January 1, Year 1 Lessor leases equipment to Lessee. Data on the lease:

1. Equipment market value and Lessor's book value, $25,771 (asset is new);

2. Lessor's implicit rate and Lessee's implicit borrowing rate, 8%;

3. Lease payments due each December 31 through Year 3 (3-year lease term);

4. Useful life of equipment, 3 years (no residual value).

B. The annual lease payment (L) is computed as:

> $25,771 = L(PV ord.ann, I=8%, N=3)
>
> $25,771 = L(2.57710)
>
> L = $10,000

C. This example illustrates an ordinary annuity payment stream. Later examples illustrate an annuity due.

D. This is a capital lease for both parties because criterion 3 is met (lease term of 3 years = 100% of useful life at inception). Criterion 4 is also met (present value of minimum lease payments of $25,771 = 100% of market value at inception).

E. The entries for the first two years are shown for both parties.

F. **Lessor, inception**

> | 1/1/year 1 | Lease Receivable 3($10,000) | 30,000 | |
> |---|---|---|---|
> | | Unearned Interest ($30,000 - $25,771) | | 4,229 |
> | | Equipment | | 25,771 |
>
> The net lease receivable equals $25,771 ($30,000 - $4,229). If the net method were used in the entry above, the lease receivable would be recorded at $25,771 and no contra account (unearned revenue) would be used.

G. Recognition of interest and depreciation, year 1

> | 12/31/year 1 | Cash | 10,000 | |
> |---|---|---|---|
> | | Unearned Interest | 2,062 | |
> | | Lease Receivable | | 10,000 |
> | | Interest Revenue ($25,771 x .08) | | 2,062 |

H. The net lease receivable is now $17,833 [$25,771 - ($10,000 - $2,062)]. The reduction in principal is the lease payment less the interest revenue included in the lease payment. If the net method were used in the entry above, the lease receivable would be reduced by $7,938 ($10,000 - $2,062) and there would be no unearned interest account in the entry. Whether the gross or net method is used, interest revenue is always computed on the net lease receivable amount.

I. Recognition of interest, year 2

> | 12/31/year 2 | Cash | 10,000 | |
> |---|---|---|---|
> | | Unearned Interest | 1,427 | |
> | | Lease Receivable | | 10,000 |
> | | Interest Revenue ($17,833 x .08) | | 1,427 |

J. The Year 3 entry reduces the net lease receivable to zero.

K. Lessee inception and year 1 interest

1/1/year 1	Leased Asset	25,771	
	Lease Liability		25,771
12/31/year 1	Lease Liability	7,938	
	Interest Expense ($25,771 x .08)	2,062	
	Cash		10,000
	Depreciation Expense $25,771/3	8,590	
	Accumulated Depreciation		8,590

   1. There is no residual value and the useful life and lease term are the same. The leased asset's initial cost is allocated over the three year useful life. The amount recorded by the lessee in a capital lease for the leased asset and liability cannot exceed fair value. If the present value of the lease payments is greater than fair value, fair value is used for the recorded amount of both the asset and liability. This increases the interest rate used to compute periodic interest expense. This applies as well to the lessor. The amount recorded by the lessor as the net lease receivable (gross receipts less unearned interest) cannot exceed fair value.

L. Interest and depreciation recognition, year 2

12/31/year 2 Leased Liability	8,573	
Interest Expense ($25,771-$7,938)(.08)	1,427	
Cash		10,000
Depreciation Expense $25,771/3	8,590	
Accumulated Depreciation		8,590

M. The Year 3 entries reduce both the lease liability and net asset book value to zero.

Sales Type Leases, International

This lesson addresses the specifics for sales-type leases, and the main differences between U.S. and international standards regarding lease accounting.

After studying this lesson, you should be able to:

1. *Identify and define a sales-type lease from given information.*

2. *Prepare the inception journal entry for both parties.*

3. *Describe the differences in capital lease criteria between the two sets of standards.*

I. Sales-Type Capital Lease (STL) Basics

A. A STL is one of two types of capital leases for the lessor (the other being DFL) This distinction does not affect the lessee. The lessor derives two types of income from a sales-type capital lease: interest income or revenue, and dealer's gross profit, which is recognized at the inception of the lease agreement.

B. In a STL, the book value of the lessor's asset is not equal to (usually less than) its market value. There is gross profit (or loss) on the lease that is recorded at inception. The lessor need not be a manufacturer or dealer for a capital lease to be a STL for the lessor.

C. The general entries for a STL for both parties appear below. The numerical examples add additional aspects to the entries.

D. **Lessor --** *At inception:*

Lease Receivable	sum of minimum lease payments + any unguaranteed residual
Unearned Interest Revenue	total interest over term
Sales	market value = selling price
Cost of Goods Sold	cost of asset
Asset	cost of asset

1. These entries accomplish what the entry at inception did for the DFL above, but they also recognize dealer gross profit immediately. A sale is recorded, as is the cost of goods sold. The gross profit equals Sales (recorded at selling price) less Cost of Goods Sold. The net lease receivable (Lease Receivable less Unearned Interest Revenue) equals the market value of the asset, which also equals Sales. The above entry assumes a new asset. If the asset were used, accumulated depreciation would be debited (closed) and cost of goods sold would reflect the book value of the asset.

E. The lease payments are based on the market value, as they are in a DFL. Interest is also computed on the market value of the asset. The lessor is financing the lessee's purchase at the selling price, as would be the case in any sale arrangement.

F. The remaining entries for the lessor and lessee are the same as for a DFL.

II. Example - Sales-Type Capital Lease

A. Sales-Type Lease (same data as the previous DFL example except: cost and market value are not equal and the payments occur on the first of the year - annuity due). On January 1, Year 1 Lessor leases equipment to Lessee. Data on the lease:

    1. Equipment market value, $25,771 (asset is new);

    2. Lessor's book value (same as cost because asset is new), $20,000;

    3. Lessor's implicit rate and Lessee's implicit borrowing rate, 8%;

    4. Lease payments due each January 1 through Year 3 (3-year lease term;)

    5. Useful life of equipment, 3 years (no residual value).

B. The annual lease payment (L) is computed as:

$25,771 = L (PV ann. due, I=8%, N=3)

$25,771 = L (2.78326)

L = $9,259 (smaller than in the previous ordinary annuity example because the payments are made one year earlier reducing the total interest over the lease term)

C. This is a capital lease for both parties because criterion 3 is met (lease term of 3 years = 100% of useful life at inception). Criterion 4 is also met (present value of minimum lease payments of $25,771 = 100% of market value at inception).

D. The entries for the first two years are shown for both parties.

E. **Lessor inception**

1/1/year 1	Lease Receivable 3($9,259)	27,777	
	Unearned Interest ($27,777 - $25,771)		2,006
	Sales		25,771
	Cost of Goods Sold	20,000	
	Equipment		20,000
	Cash	9,259	
	Lease Receivable		9,259

    1. Gross profit of $5,771 ($25,771 - $20,000) is recognized at inception. Economically, the lease is an installment sale. There is no interest component to the first payment because it takes place at inception. The net lease receivable now equals $16,512 ($27,777 - $2,006 - $9,259).

F. Interest recognition, year 1

12/31/year 1	Unearned Interest ($16,512 x .08)	1,321	
	Interest Revenue		1,321

G. A year has passed and although no payment is due until the next day, the interest revenue for Year 1 must be accrued as recorded above. The entry for payment the next day is as follows:

1/1/year 2	Cash	9,259	
	Lease Receivable		9,259

H. The net lease receivable is now $8,574 ($16,512 + $1,321 - $9,259). The $1,321 reduction in unearned interest increases the net receivable and the cash payment reduces it.

I. Interest recognition, year 2

12/31/year 2	Unearned Interest ($8,574 x .08)	686	
	Interest Revenue		686

J. Lessee inception

1/1/year 1	Leased Asset	25,771	
	Lease Liability		25,771
1/1/year 1	Lease Liability	9,259	
	Cash		9,259

    1. The lease liability is now $16,512 ($25,771 - $9,259).

K. Interest and depreciation recognition, year 1, and payment at 1/1/year 2

12/31/year 1	Interest Expense ($16,512 x .08)	1,321	
	Lease Liability		1,321
	Depreciation Expense $25,771/3	8,590	
	Accumulated Depreciation		8,590
1/1/Year 2	Lease Liability	9,529	
	Cash		9,529

L. The lease liability is now $8,574 ($16,512 + $1,321 -$9,259).

M. Interest and depreciation recognition, year 2

12/31/year 2	Interest Expense ($8,574 x .08)	686	
	Lease Liability		686
	Depreciation Expense $25,771/3	8,590	
	Accumulated Depreciation		8,590

III. U.S. GAAP - IFRS Differences

A. Overall, international and U.S. accounting standards are similar in the leasing area but there are some significant differences in the details. International standards refer to capital leases as "finance" leases; to direct financing leases (DFLs) as regular finance leases; and to sales-type leases (STLs) as "manufacturer or dealer finance leases."

B. The classification of leases as capital leases is similar to U.S. standards although the details are somewhat different. A capital lease (finance lease for international standards) is one that transfers substantially all the risks and rewards of ownership to the lessee. Otherwise, it is an operating lease. The international standard does not define "substantially all" as compared with U.S. standards which use quantitative thresholds (75% and 90%).

C. The determination of whether a lease is a capital lease is based on two sets of conditions. Except for the first two below, judgment is required. If any one of the first five is met (with judgment required for 3-5), then the lease is a finance lease. Conditions 6-8 "could" point to a finance lease - the implication is that the evidence must be stronger for these last three criteria.

    1. Title transfer (same as U.S.);

    2. Bargain purchase option (same as U.S.);

    3. The term is for a major portion of the remaining life of the asset (U.S. uses 75% or more);

    4. The present value of minimum lease payments is substantially all of the fair value of the asset (U.S. uses 90% or more);

    5. The asset under lease is specialized or unique such that only the specific lessee can use it without major modification;

    6. If the lease is canceled, the lessee bears any loss of the lessor associated with cancellation;

    7. Gains and losses from changes in the fair value of the asset accrue to the lessee (for example, by reductions or increases in the lease payments);

    8. There is a bargain renewal option allowing the lessee to continue leasing the asset after the term for substantially less than fair rental at that time.

D. More than one indicator may be required for lease capitalization. The international standard stresses economic substance over legal form which requires professional judgment to be applied in many cases.

E. The lessee for international standards uses the lessor's implicit interest rate in all cases, unless the lessee is unable to determine that rate. In that case, the lessee's incremental borrowing rate is used. Recall that for U.S. standards, the lessee uses the lower of the two rates.

F. International standards do not formally use criteria 5 and 6 for lessors for lease capitalization. However, the standard does discuss the possibility that the two parties may account for the same lease differently, thus opening up the possibility that a lessor entity might use uncollectibility of payments or cost uncertainties as a reason for not capitalizing a lease.

Additional Aspects of Capital Leases

Several miscellaneous issues affecting lease accounting are covered here. These issues affect the journal entries and financial statement presentation of leases.

After studying this lesson, you should be able to:

1. *Determine the capitalizable amount for a lease when executory costs are given.*

2. *Describe residuals in a capital lease and how they may affect whether a lease is capitalized.*

3. *Modify the accounting for leases when the asset under lease involves land.*

4. *Account for initial direct costs depending on the classification of the lease.*

5. *Describe the accounting for contingent rentals.*

I. Executory Costs

A. These costs are flow-through costs and do not affect lease capitalization. They include property taxes, casualty insurance and maintenance. They are not capitalized because they do not contribute to the asset 's value beyond one year. However, if executory costs are included in the annual lease payment, they must be subtracted before computing the present value for determining the present value of the minimum lease payments and for determining the amounts to capitalize in the accounts.

> **Example:**
> If the total annual lease payment is $12,000 of which $2,000 is executory costs, only the $10,000 amount is used in the present value calculations and capitalization of the lease. The $2,000 amount is treated as an expense by the lessee. If the lessor pays all or a part of these costs (for example, because the property tax is paid by the legal owner), the lessee reimburses the lessor.

II. Unguaranteed Residual Value (End of Lease Term)

A. The **unguaranteed residual value** is an amount that is outside the lease agreement. It is not an expected payment to be made by the lessee, nor is it a payment the lessor expects to receive under the lease. Therefore, it is excluded from the minimum lease payments and not considered for Criterion 4. However, it is part of the value of the asset. The lessor includes it (at present value) in the net lease receivable. The Lease Receivable account will equal the amount of the unguaranteed residual (at nominal value) at the end of the lease term. Note: the unguaranteed residual value is the only case for either parties of a cash flow being included in only one, but not both, of the minimum lease payments and accounts.

B. When an unguaranteed residual value appears with a sales-type lease, the lessor must reduce both the amounts recorded for cost of goods sold and sales by the present value of the unguaranteed residual. Because there is no guarantee that the residual will be worth the amount estimated at inception, this reduction must be made to avoid overstating both cost of goods sold and sales of the current period. The gross margin is unaffected, however, and none of the other journal entries for the sales-type lease are affected.

III. Third Party Guarantee of Residual Value (End of Lease Term)

A. A **third party** (financial institution) may be enlisted to guarantee the residual value of a leased asset (for a fee). The lessee is not involved and therefore does not include the guarantee in its minimum lease payments or lease liability. The lessor does include the guarantee because it is a payment expected to be received under the lease.

B. This is another instance in which the lessee and lessor may classify the lease differently. If the third party guarantee is large enough, the lessor can reduce the annual lease payments to the point at which the present value of the lessee's minimum lease payments is less than 90% of the market value of the property. The lessor will continue to earn its implicit rate because of the guarantee. If no other lease capitalization criterion is met by the lessee, the lessee will account for the lease as an operating lease with the lessor treating the lease as a capital lease. One of the main reasons third party guarantees are used is to achieve this very result. The lessee keeps the lease off its balance sheet.

IV. Leases Involving Land

A. When land is the only asset under capital lease, criterion 3 and 4 do not apply. Only criterion 1 and criterion 2 are applicable for determining whether the lease is a capital lease, and depreciation expense is not recognized by the lessee if the lease is capitalized. If neither criterion 1 or 2 is met, then the lease is an operating lease.

B. Land and Building Leases

1. When the assets under lease are land and a building, the lessee records the two leases separately if criterion 1 or 2 is met because land is not depreciated. For recording purposes, the total present value is allocated to the assets on the basis of fair value. Again, the land leased asset is not depreciated if that lease is a capital lease. The lessor combines the assets into one lease receivable.

2. If neither criterion 1 or 2 is met, and the fair value of the land is less than 25% of the combined fair value, the assets are treated as one single asset for purposes of accounting for the capital lease by both parties. The single asset is depreciated even though land is a component of that single asset, if the lease is capitalized i.e. meets criteria 3 or 4.

3. If neither criterion 1 or 2 is met, and the fair value of the land is 25% or more of the combined value, the land lease is treated as an operating lease (because title will not transfer to the lessee) and the building lease as is an operating or capital lease, depending on whether the building lease meets the lease capitalization criteria.

V. U.S. GAAP - IFRS Differences -- For leases involving land, the land and building elements are treated separately unless the land is an immaterial part (U.S. uses a 25% threshold for materiality for the land portion). This is another example of U.S. standards using a quantitative or rule-based threshold while international standards use a principles-based determination.

VI. Initial Direct Costs

A. Initial direct costs of a lease effort are incurred by a lessor in negotiating and completing lease arrangements. Legal fees, costs of credit investigations, employee compensation related to initiating the lease, and any clerical costs are included. Initial direct costs are identified after a specific party is considered a potential lessee. They exclude advertising and solicitation costs and the costs of servicing leases.

B. Lessee accounting is unaffected by these costs.

C. Lessor accounting: The accounting treatment of initial direct costs is suggested by the type of lease to which they pertain.

1. Operating leases

a. Capitalize the initial direct costs and amortize to expense over the term of the lease in proportion to revenue recognized (usually the straight-line basis).

2. **Sales-type leases**

    a. Recognize the initial direct costs immediately as a selling expense. The costs are therefore matched against the sale recognized on the lease arrangement at inception.

3. **Direct financing leases**

    a. The initial direct costs are included in the lessor's gross receivable (investment in the lease). Cash and other assets are decreased (credited) as a result of the costs. The initial direct costs therefore are included in the base on which the annual payments are computed. The resulting interest rate is reduced causing total interest revenue over the lease term to be reduced by the amount of the initial direct costs, gradually over the lease term. There is no separate accounting for the initial direct costs in this case - their recognition is automatic by virtue of their inclusion in the receivable.

VII. Contingent Rentals

A. Contingent rentals are payments in addition to the regular periodic payments called for in the lease. Contingent rental payments are not required or known until a future event occurs and are based on performance by the lessee.

    1. For example, if the lessee earns revenues from the leased property beyond a certain amount, the lessee must pay an additional amount of rent. Note that regular periodic rentals that are set by the lease agreement to fluctuate over time are not contingent rentals and are treated as we have shown for other rental amounts.

B. For both operating and capital leases, and for both lessors and lessees, contingent rentals are recognized in income in the period the event causing the contingent payment occurs.

    1. For operating leases, they are recognized as they occur. They are not included in the computation of annual rent expense or revenue because they are not determinable at inception.

    2. For capital leases, they are not included in the minimum lease payments (they are not determinable at inception) and are not included in the capitalization process because they cannot be estimated.

Depreciation, BPO and Residuals

This lesson provides specific guidance for recording capital leases with bargain purchase options and residuals.

After studying this lesson, you should be able to:

1. *Compute the lease payment for a lease in different situations.*

2. *Explain the inception journal entry when there is a bargain purchase option, or one of three different types of residuals.*

3. *Describe how annual depreciation on a capital lease is affected when the lease meets different capitalization criteria.*

I. Clustering of Capitalization Criteria

A. The lease capitalization criterion or criteria met in a particular lease has a significant effect on the accounting. This lesson discusses these effects and later lessons provide examples.

B. If criteria 1 or 2 is met (title transfer and BPO), then the lessee retains the asset at the end of the lease term. There is no residual to the lessor at the end of the lease term - it is not used in the accounting.

C. If only one or both of criteria 3 or 4 are met (75% of term, 90% of market value), but not 1 or 2, then the asset reverts to the lessor. The lessor obtains the residual at the end of the term, which becomes important to the accounting. This residual can be (a) unguaranteed, (b) guaranteed by the lessee, or (c) guaranteed by a third party.

II. Lessor's Equation

A. The lessor's equation describes the relevant cash flows and residuals in the lease, and incorporates the interest rate implicit in the lease - the annual compounded rate of return to the lessor.

B. The equation is:

Market or fair value of the asset under lease at inception	=	Present value of annual lease payments	+	Z(present value of a single payment)

C. In calculating the present values, the lessor's implicit rate is used. The first present value can be either an ordinary annuity, or an annuity due. The second present value is always a single payment.

D. The amount "Z" in the equation can be the BPO or one of the three residuals noted above. A BPO and a residual would not occur in the same situation.

1. If criterion 2 is met, then Z is the amount of the BPO - the amount the lessee would pay to purchase the asset at the end of the lease term.

2. If only one or both of criteria 3 or 4 are met, but not 1 or 2, then Z is one of the three residuals at the end of the term: (a) unguaranteed, (b) guaranteed by the lessee, or (c) guaranteed by a third party.

E. Problems may require you to compute the amount of the annual lease payment, which you need for the journal entries. You will be given the fair value of the asset under lease, the book value or cost, and any amount Z. Insert the relevant values (do not use book value or cost - always use fair value), and solve for the ordinary lease payment. Remember that the lease payment is always based on fair value, not cost (in a DFL cost and fair value are equal).

> **Example:**
> An asset with a fair value of $60,000 and cost of $50,000 is leased for four years on 1/1/x1. The lease calls for equal annual lease payments each December 31 during the term. The useful life at inception is six years. The asset reverts to the lessor at the end of the term at which time it is expected to be worth $5,857. This is an unguaranteed residual. The lessor's implicit rate is 10%. The lessor's equation below shows how the annual lease payment (L) is determined.
>
> $$60,000 = L(pva, .10, 4) + 5,857(pv1, .10,4)$$
> $$60,000 = L(3.16987) + 5,857(.68301)$$
> $$60,000 = L(3.16987) + 4,000$$
> $$56,000 = L(3.16987)$$
> $$56,000/(3.16987) = L = 17,666$$
>
> Although the unguaranteed residual is not included in the minimum lease payments of either party, it is part of the return to the lessor. The larger the residual, the smaller the annual lease payment.

III. Depreciation of the Leased Asset by the Lessee

A. Knowing the criterion met by the lease is required for the correct lessee depreciation calculation in a capital lease. The lessee does not depreciate the lease in an operating lease. The lessor does not depreciate the asset in a capital lease.

B. Any acceptable depreciation method (straight-line, accelerated) can be used by the lessee.

C. The annual journal entry was shown previously and is:

> Depreciation expense*
>
>   Accumulated depreciation
>
> * The amount recognized for depreciation, assuming straight-line depreciation, equals:
> (leased asset balance at inception - residual value)/number of years

D. The values to use for the residual value and number of years in the above expression depend on the capitalization criteria met by the lease:

Criteria met by lease	Residual Value	Number of Years
1 or 2 (title transfer, BPO)	residual value at end of asset's useful life	useful life at inception
3 or 4 only (not 1 or 2)		
Unguaranteed residual	0	lease term
Lessee guarantee	lessee guarantee	lease term
Third party guarantee	0	lease term

1. For example, if the lease contains a BPO, the lessee is expected to use the asset for its entire economic life, beginning with the date of inception. If there is any residual at the end of that period, it is used in the depreciation calculations for that entire period.

2. If the lessee guarantees the residual value at the end of the lease term, that is the amount of the asset not used by the lessee and is the appropriate residual value to use for the lessee's annual depreciation. The asset reverts to the lessor at the end of term thus defining the period of use by the lessee.

IV. Amounts to Include in Minimum Lease Payments and Accounts

A. In a capital lease, the amounts to include in minimum lease payments for the lessor and lessee, and to include in the reported amounts, also depend on which criterion is met by the lease. Criterion 4 is often the critical one for capital leases - hence the importance of minimum lease payments.

B. The following summary table shows the inclusions for a BPO, the three residuals discussed above, and for executory costs and the annual lease payment. "No" means the item is not included in the attribute listed. A "yes" means it is included. The net account balance columns show whether to include the item in the accounts at present value (a net account is measured at present value). The related gross amount follows the same guide for the lessor. The table provides a "roadmap" for solving almost any capital lease journal entry problem you might encounter. Any amount included in the lessee's lease liability is also included in the leased asset account.

	Include in			
	Minimum Lease Payments		Net Account Balance	
Item	Lessee	Lessor	Lease Liability	Lease Receivable
Executory costs	No	No	No	No
Annual lease payment	Yes	Yes	Yes	Yes
Bargain purchase Option	Yes	Yes	Yes	Yes
Unguaranteed Residual	No	No	No	Yes
Lessee guarantee of Residual	Yes	Yes	Yes	Yes
3rd party guarantee of Residual	No	Yes	No	Yes

1. For example, a lease includes an unguaranteed residual. Neither party includes this amount in minimum lease payments because it is outside the lease. The unguaranteed residual thus does not contribute to capitalizing the lease. The lessee does not receive the residual, and the lease payments do not reflect it. Therefore, the lessee does not include it in the lease liability (or asset). But the unguaranteed residual is part of the asset's value. When the lessor removes the physical asset from its books at inception, it replaces it with a receivable. Part of that receivable is the residual value - the value the asset will be worth at the end of the term. The net lease receivable includes the unguaranteed residual at present value. The unguaranteed residual is the only example of an item excluded from minimum lease payments but included in the account balances, for a particular party.

2. The third party guarantee of residual does not involve the lessee - therefore it is excluded from the lessee's minimum lease payments and accounts. It is included in the lessor's minimum lease payments and accounts.

3. Executory costs are ignored for lease capitalization purposes, except to remember to subtract them if they are included in the lease payment before discounting the lease payments, determining whether criterion 4 is met, and recording the journal entries.

C. Later lessons provide several examples of using this roadmap and provide practice with more complex capital lease situations.

Capital Lease Examples 1

This lesson illustrates detailed accounting for a capital lease with a bargain purchase option.

After studying this lesson, you should be able to:

1. *Record all the journal entries for both parties to a capital lease with a bargain purchase option.*

2. *Modify your entries depending on whether the lease is a direct financing lease or sales type lease.*

3. *Classify the lease liability for a capital lease.*

I. **Overview** – This lesson provides examples of different lease situations and discussion of one additional aspect of capital lease accounting. The four two examples in this section are listed below. Remember to use the guide in the previous lesson for computing depreciation and determining amounts to include in minimum lease payments and the accounts for the lessee and lessor.

  A. DFL-BPO;

  B. STL-BPO.

II. **Direct Financing Lease with a BPO**

  A. On January 1, 20A, Lessor and Lessee signed a three-year lease that qualifies as a direct financing lease to the Lessor and a capital lease to the Lessee. The leased asset cost the lessor $100,000, and the negotiated lease price is also $100,000 (market value), making the lease a DFL. The estimated economic life of the asset is four years, and the estimated residual value of the asset at the end of four years is zero.

  B. The lessee has an option to purchase the asset for $10,000 on December 31, 20C. At that date, the estimated residual value is $15,000. The option is a BPO because the purchase option is for an amount significantly less than the estimated value.

  C. The lease requires three annual rentals of $33,809, payable each January 1. Lessor has an implicit interest rate of 10% on the cost of the asset. The calculation of the periodic rentals (L) is shown below. The BPO amount is included in the lessor's equation because it is an amount expected to be received. It should be considered just another lease payment.

100,000	= L(PV ann.due, N=3, I=10%) + 10,000(PV $1, N=3,I=10%)
100,000	= L(2.73554) + 10,000(.75131)
92,487	= L(2.73554)
L	= 33,809

  D. The lease is a capital lease for both parties because criterion 2 is met (BPO), criterion 3 is met (term = 75% of useful life at inception), and criterion 4 is met (PV of minimum lease payments is 100% of the market value of the asset). When no information is given concerning the lessee's interest rate, you can assume it is the same as the lessor's.

  E. **Selected Entries** -- You should verify the calculations for practice. Not all entries are shown. The unearned revenue account is the same account as unearned interest used previously. There is variation in the account names used in practice.

Lessor			Lessee		
January 1, 20A:					
Lease Receivable	111,427		Leased Property	100,000	
Asset		100,000	Lease Liability		100,000
Unearned Revenue		11,427			
111,427 = 3($33,809) + $10,000					
Cash	33,809		Lease Liability	33,809	
Lease Receivable		33,809	Cash		33,809
December 31, 20A:					
Unearned Revenue	6,619		Interest Expense	6,619	
Interest Revenue		6,619	Lease Liability		6,619
$6,619 = ($111,427 - $11,427 - $33,809) .10					
			Depreciation Expense	25,000	
			Acc.Depreciation		25,000
			(100,000/4)(Useful life is 4 years)		
January 1, 20B:					
Cash	33,809		Lease Liability	33,809	
Lease Receivable		33,809	Cash		33,809
December 31, 20C:					
Cash	10,000		Lease Liability	10,000	
Lease Receivable		10,000	Cash		10,000

1. The net lease receivable and lease liability balances equal the $10,000 BPO at the end of the lease term because the BPO was included in both at present value. By the end of the term, that amount had grown to its full nominal value. The net book value of the asset on the lessee's balance sheet is $25,000 after three years of depreciation. The lessee keeps the asset for its remaining year of useful life because of the BPO. The following amortization schedule provides information leading to the entries for the entire lease term.

F. **Amortization Schedule** – See the following example.

Date	Annual Lease Payments	10% Annual Interest	Decrease (Increase) in Net Receivable or Liability	Net Lease Receivable or Liability Balance
1/1/20A				100,000
1/1/20A	33,809		33,809	66,191
12/31/20A		6,619	(6,619)	72,810
1/1/20B	33,809		33,809	39,001
12/31/20B		3,900	(3,900)	42,901
1/1/20C	33,809		33,809	9,092
12/31/20C		908	(908)	10,000
12/31/20C	10,000		10,000	0
Totals	111,427	11,427	100,000	

III. Sales-Type Lease with a BPO

A. On January 1, 20A, Lessor and Lessee signed a three-year lease that qualifies as a sales-type lease to the Lessor and a capital lease to the Lessee. The leased asset cost the lessor $100,000 and the negotiated lease price is $120,000 (market value). The estimated economic life of the asset is four years and the estimated residual value of the asset at the end of four years is zero.

B. The lessee has an option to purchase the asset for $10,000 on December 31, 20C. At that date, the estimated residual value is $15,000.

C. The lease requires three annual rentals of $41,121, payable each January 1. Lessor has an implicit interest rate of 10% on the cost of the asset. The calculation of the periodic rentals (L) is shown below.

$$120,000 = L(\text{PV ann.due, N=3, I=10\%}) + 10,000(\text{PV \$1, N=3,I=10\%})$$

$$120,000 = L(2.73554) + 10,000(.75131)$$

$$112,487 = L(2.73554)$$

$$L = 41,121$$

D. The lease is a capital lease for both parties because criterion 2 is met (BPO), criterion 3 is met (term = 75% of useful life at inception), and criterion 4 is met (PV of minimum lease payments is 100% of the market value of the asset).

E. Selected Entries -- You should verify the calculations for practice, not all entries are shown in the following example.

Lessor			Lessee		
January 1, 20A:					
Lease Receivable	133,363				
Cost of Goods Sold	100,000		Leased Property	120,000	
Sales Revenue		120,000	Lease Liability		120,000
Unearned Revenue		13,363			
Asset		100,000			
$133,363 = 3(41,121) + 10,000$					
Cash	41,121		Lease Liability	41,121	
Lease Receivable		41,121	Cash		41,121
December 31, 20A:					
Unearned Revenue	7,888		Interest Expense	7,888	
Interest Revenue		7,888	Lease Liability		7,888
$7,888 = .10(\$133,363 - \$13,363 - \$41,121)$					
			Depreciation Expense	30,000	
			Acc.Depreciation		30,000
			($120,000/4 years)		
January 1, 20B:					
Cash	41,121		Lease Liability	41,121	
Lease Receivable		41,121	Cash		41,121
December 31, 20C:					
Cash	10,000		Lease Liability	10,000	
Lease Receivable		10,000	Cash		10,000

F. Amortization Schedule

Date	Annual Lease Payments	10% Annual Interest	Decrease (Increase) in Net Receivable or Liability	Net Lease Receivable or Liability Balance
1/1/20A				120,000
1/1/20A	41,121		41,121	78,879
12/31/20A		7,888	(7,888)	86,767
1/1/20B	41,121		41,121	45,646
12/31/20B		4,565	(4,565)	50,211
1/1/20C	41,121		41,121	9,090
12/31/20C		910	(910)	10,000
12/31/20C	10,000		10,000	0
Totals	133,363	13,363	120,000	

G. Classification of the total lease liability at the end of any year into current (CL) and noncurrent (NCL) portions is handled in one of two acceptable ways: (1) the CL is the present value of the next year's payment, or (2) the CL is the reduction of the total lease liability in the succeeding year. In either case, the NCL portion is the total lease liability less the CL portion.

Example:
In the above amortization schedule, the 12/31/20A total lease liability is $86,767. (1) Under the first approach, the CL portion is $41,121, which is the present value of the payment occurring one day after the 20A balance sheet date. The NCL portion is the rest, or $45,646 ($86,767 - $41,121). If the 20B lease payment were due 12/31/20B instead, the present value of $41,121 for one year would be the CL portion. (2) Under the second approach, the CL portion is the decrease in the total lease liability in 20B, or $36,556 ($86,767 - $50,211). The NCL portion is the rest, or $50,211 ($86,767 - $36,556). Note that the two approaches yield somewhat different results.

Capital Lease Examples 2

This lesson illustrates detailed accounting for a capital lease with a residual to the lessor.

After studying this lesson, you should be able to:

1. *Record all the journal entries for both parties to a capital lease with three different types of residuals.*

2. *Modify your entries depending on whether the lease is a direct financing lease or sales type lease.*

3. *Describe the accounting for the purchase of the asset under lease during the lease term.*

I. **Overview** – This lesson provides two more examples of different lease situations and a discussion of one additional aspect of capital lease accounting. The two examples in this section are

   A. DFL-Lessee guarantee of residual (and third-party guarantee of residual),

   B. STL-unguaranteed residual.

II. **Direct Financing Lease, Lessee Guarantee, Third-Party Guarantee**

   A. On January 1, 20A, Lessor and Lessee signed a three-year lease that qualifies as a direct financing lease to the Lessor and a capital lease to the Lessee. The leased asset cost the lessor $100,000, and the negotiated lease price is also $100,000 (market value). The estimated economic life of the asset is four years, and the estimated residual value of the asset at the end of four years is zero.

   B. Lessor retains ownership of the leased asset at the termination of the lease. On January 1, 20A, lessor and lessee estimated a residual value of $10,000 at the end of the three-year lease term. The terms of the lease agreement specify that the lessee will guarantee a minimum residual value of $10,000. If the actual residual value determined at the end of the lease term is less than $10,000, the lessee must pay the difference in cash.

   C. The lease requires three annual rentals of $33,809, payable each January 1. Lessor has an implicit interest rate of 10% on the cost of the asset. The calculation of the periodic rentals (L) is shown below. Note that this calculation is the same as for the DFL-BPO example. Both the BPO and guaranteed residual value provide the lessor with $10,000 at the end of the lease term. Thus, the lease payments should be the same for both situations. The amortization schedule is the same as well.

100,000	= L(PV ann.due, N=3, I=10%) + 10,000(PV $1, N=3,I=10%)
100,000	= L(2.73554) + 10,000(.75131)
92,487	= L(2.73554)
L	= 33,809

   D. The lessee includes the present value of the guarantee in the leased asset and liability because it is part of the cost of the asset. The lease is a capital lease for both parties because criterion 3 is met (term = 75% of useful life at inception) and criterion 4 is met (PV of minimum lease payments is 100% of the market value of the asset). The actual residual value at December 31, 20C is $9,000.

E. Selected Entries -- You should verify the calculations for practice, not all entries are shown.

Lessor			Lessee		
January 1, 20A:					
Lease Receivable	111,427		Leased Property	100,000	
Asset		100,000	Lease Liability		100,000
Unearned Revenue		11,427			
Cash	33,809		Lease Liability	33,809	
Lease Receivable		33,809	Cash		33,809
December 31, 20A:					
Unearned Revenue	6,619		Interest Expense	6,619	
Interest Revenue		6,619	Lease Liability		6,619
			Depreciation Expense	30,000	
			Acc.Depreciation		30,000
			(($100,000-$10,000)/3)		

1. The lessee guarantees the residual value. This is the portion of the value of the asset that will not be used by the lessee and thus is treated as a salvage value. The lessee will use the asset only 3 years.

January 1, 20B:					
Cash	33,809		Lease Liability	33,809	
Lease Receivable		33,809	Cash		33,809
December 31, 20C:					
Asset	9,000		Acc.Depreciation	90,000	
Cash	1,000		Lease Liability	10,000	
Lease Receivable		10,000	Leased Property		100,000
			Loss on Contract	1,000	
			Cash		1,000

2. The balance of the net lease receivable and the lease liability are $10,000 at the end of the lease term because both included the guaranteed residual at present value at inception. By the end of the lease term, that value has grown to its full nominal value. The asset is transferred to the lessor at market value. The lessee sustains a loss of $1,000 because the market value was less than the guaranteed amount.

F. Amortization Schedule – See the following example.

Date	Annual Lease Payments	10% Annual Interest	Decrease (Increase) in Net Receivable or Liability	Net Lease Receivable or Liability Balance
1/1/20A				100,000
1/1/20A	33,809		33,809	66,191
12/31/20A		6,619	(6,619)	72,810
1/1/20B	33,809		33,809	39,001
12/31/20B		3,900	(3,900)	42,901
1/1/20C	33,809		33,809	9,092
12/31/20C		908	(908)	10,000
12/31/20C	10,000		10,000	0
Totals	111,427	11,427	100,000	

G. Now assume, that instead of the lessee guaranteeing the residual, a third party provides the guarantee. There is no change in the lease payment or the accounting by the lessor because either way, the lessor will receive $10,000 at the end of the lease. But the lessee no longer includes the guarantee in its minimum lease payments and its account balances.

H. The lessee's present value of minimum lease payments = $92,487 = $33,809 (PV ann.due, N=3, I=10%) = $33,809(2.73554). This amount exceeds 90% of the fair value of the property ($100,000) so the lease continues to be a capital lease. Also, criterion 3 continues to be met. The lessee would record the leased asset and lease liability at $92,487 rather than $100,000. The payments are the same, but interest expense is somewhat smaller because of the smaller beginning lease liability. Finally, depreciation expense would be computed as $92,487/3 = $30,829. There is no residual value to deduct in this case.

III. Sales-Type Lease, Unguaranteed Residual

A. On January 1, 20A, Lessor and Lessee signed a three-year lease that qualifies as a sales-type lease to the Lessor and a capital lease to the Lessee. The leased asset cost the lessor $100,000 and the negotiated lease price is $120,000 (market value). The estimated economic life of the asset is four years and the estimated residual value of the asset at the end of four years is zero.

B. The lessor retains ownership of the leased asset at the termination of the lease. On January 1, 20A, lessor and lessee estimated a residual of $10,000, which is not guaranteed by the lessee or any other party.

C. The lease requires three annual rentals of $41,121, payable each January 1. Lessor has an implicit interest rate of 10% on the cost of the asset. The calculation of the periodic rentals (L) is shown below.

$$120,000 = L(PV\ ann.due, N=3, I=10\%) + 10,000(PV\ \$1, N=3, I=10\%)$$
$$120,000 = L(2.73554) + 10,000(.75131)$$
$$112,487 = L(2.73554)$$
$$L = 41,121$$

D. The present value of minimum lease payments is $112,487 ($41,121 x 2.73554), the amount excluding the unguaranteed residual value. The latter amount is not included in either party's minimum lease payments. However, it is included in the lessor's lease receivable.

E. The lease is a capital lease for both parties because criterion 3 is met (term = 75% of useful life at inception) and criterion 4 is met (PV of minimum lease payments is 94% of the market value of the asset -- $112,487/$120,000).

F. The actual residual value on December 31, 20C is $10,000.

G. Selected Entries -- You should verify the calculations for practice, not all entries are shown.

Lessor			Lessee		
January 1, 20A:					
Lease Receivable	133,363				
Cost of Goods Sold	92,487		Leased Property	112,487	
Sales Revenue		112,487	Lease Liability		112,487
Unearned Revenue		13,363			
Asset		100,000			

1. The present value of the unguaranteed residual is $7,513 ($10,000 x .75131). This amount must be subtracted from both cost of goods sold and sales. Cost of Goods Sold = $100,000 - $7,513, and Sales = $120,000 - $7,513. The lessee capitalizes only the lease payments.

Cash	41,121		Lease Liability	41,121	
Lease Receivable		41,121	Cash		41,121
December 31, 20A:					
Unearned Revenue	7,888		Interest Expense	7,137	
Interest Revenue		7,888	Lease Liability		7,137
			Depreciation Expense	37,496	
			Acc.Depreciation		37,496
			($112,487/3 years)		

2. The lessee will have the asset for three years. There is no residual value for the lessee. See the following example

January 1, 20B:				
Cash	41,121		Lease Liability	41,121
Lease Receivable		41,121	Cash	41,121
December 31, 20C:				
Asset	10,000		Acc.Depreciation	112,487
Lease Receivable		10,000	Leased Property	112,487

H. Lessor's Amortization Schedule

Date	Annual Lease Payments	10% Annual Interest	Decrease (Increase) in Net Receivable	Net Lease Receivable Balance
1/1/20A				120,000
1/1/20A	41,121		41,121	78,879
12/31/20A		7,888	(7,888)	86,767
1/1/20B	41,121		41,121	45,646
12/31/20B		4,565	(4,565)	50,211
1/1/20C	41,121		41,121	9,090
12/31/20C		910	(910)	10,000
12/31/20C	10,000	_____	10,000	0
Totals	133,363	13,363	120,000	

I. Lessee's Amortization Schedule

Lessee's Amortization Schedule -- In this case the lessee's amortization is based on a different starting value because the lessor included the unguaranteed residual in its net receivable but the lessee does not include it in the leased asset and liability.

Date	Annual Lease Payments	10% Annual Interest	Decrease (Increase) in Liability	Lease Liabilty Balance
1/1/20A				112,487
1/1/20A	41,121		41,121	71,366
12/31/20A		7,137	(7,137)	78,503
1/1/20B	41,121		41,121	37,382
12/31/20B		3,739	(3,739)	41,121
1/1/20C	41,121	_____	41,121	0
Totals	123,363	10,876	112,487	

J. Purchase of asset during lease term. In some capital leases that do not meet criteria 1 or 2, the lessee may have the option to purchase the asset during the lease term. The price may be a negotiated price, or the prices may be preset at inception, with the price decreasing over the term. This discussion applies to any capitalized lease.

1. At the purchase date, the lessee records interest expense and the increase in the lease liability from the last payment date through the purchase date, and also records depreciation since the most recent fiscal year-end. The lease liability, accumulated depreciation and leased asset accounts are closed, and cash is credited for the price. A new asset account is established and recorded at the updated book value of the leased asset at the time of purchase plus the excess of the purchase price over the updated book value of the lease liability. In other words, the lessee has paid more than the amount owed on the leased asset to purchase it - the excess is treated as an increase in the purchase cost. No loss is recognized. If the book value of the lease liability exceeds the purchase price, the difference is subtracted from the book value of the leased asset. No gain is recognized. The asset under lease is now being purchased; therefore no gain or loss is recognized. The lessee is in the same economic position with respect to the asset.

2. The lessor's accounting is somewhat different - a gain or loss is recognized immediately for the difference between the net receivable balance and the selling price of the asset. Interest revenue is first recognized to the point of sale to update the receivable balance. The entry for the sale closes the receivable and unearned interest revenue accounts.

3. Assume now that the lease in the current is example (STL-unguaranteed residual) allows the lessee to purchase the asset during the lease term. At 12/31/20A the lessee purchases the asset for $80,000, a negotiated price. Both parties first record the usual journal entries at that date. The net receivable balance at that date is $86,767 per the above amortization schedules (gross receivable balance is $92,242 = $133,363 - $41,121; unearned revenue balance is $5,475 =$92,242 - $86,767). The net lease liability is $78,503 per the above amortization schedule. The accumulated depreciation balance is $37,496. The book value of the asset is $74,991 ($112,487 - $37,496). The excess of the purchase price over the liability balance is $1,497 ($80,000 - $78,503).

Lessee entry:			
Equipment	76,488		$74,991 + $1,497
Accumulated depreciation	37,496		
Lease liability	78,503		
Leased property		112,487	
Cash		80,000	
Lessor entry:			
Cash	80,000		
Unearned revenue	5,475		
Loss on sale	6,767		$86,767 - $80,000
Lease receivable		92,242	

Sale Leasebacks and Disclosures

Lessee accounting for the sale of an asset and immediate leaseback is addressed in this lesson.

After studying this lesson, you should be able to:

1. *Explain why a firm would enter into a sales-leaseback transaction.*

2. *Compute the related gain or loss.*

3. *Account for three different levels of leaseback: major, minor, and in-between.*

4. *Modify your accounting depending on whether the lease is a capital or operating lease.*

5. *Identify when a loss is real or artificial.*

6. *Explain the basic attributes of a leveraged lease.*

7. *Note the general footnote disclosures for leases for both parties.*

I. Nature of the Transaction and Accounting Issues

A. A sale-leaseback transaction is actually two related transactions. The owner of property sells its asset and immediately leases it back. The asset is not physically moved. It is entirely a financial transaction. The seller-lessee is simply refinancing the asset but is no longer the owner. For the seller-lessee, leasing may be more attractive than financing the asset with other types of debt. The sale provides immediate cash, and the asset continues to be used as before.

B. The accounting issue for the seller-lessee is how to account for the gain or loss on the sale because often the sales price and payments under the leaseback are not independent. The seller-lessee lease is treated as a capital or operating lease depending on whether at least one of the usual four criteria are met. The accounting for the lessor-owner is not affected by sales-leasebacks - the usual procedures for lease accounting apply. Our coverage of sales-leasebacks therefore applies only to the seller-lessee.

    1. The recorded gain on the sale part of the transaction = selling price - book value.

    2. The recorded loss on the sale part of the transaction = book value - selling price.

    3. The recorded gain or loss is not always recognized in earnings immediately - in some cases it is deferred.

II. Accounting Situations

A. The accounting for a gain depends on the proportion of the asset value leased back. The accounting for a loss depends on whether the loss is real or artificial. The following situations are relevant. Remember that in each case only the sale entry is affected and any subsequent recognition of gain or loss. Accounting for the leaseback proceeds as previously discussed.

    1. Gain: major leaseback;

    2. Gain: minor leaseback;

    3. Gain: less than major, but more than minor leaseback;

    4. Losses: real and artificial;

B. Gain - Major Leaseback -- The gain is computed as always: the difference between the selling price and book value of the asset. However, the selling price may not be the same as fair value. The lessor pays the seller-lessee the selling price. If the price is greater than fair value, the difference will be returned to the lessor in the form of higher rentals. If the price is less than fair value, the rentals will be reduced. (In this case, acceptance of a lower selling price is in effect a prepayment of rent by the lessee.)

1. **Accounting --** If the present value of the minimum lease payments is $\geq$ 90% of the asset's fair value (major leaseback), then the gain is deferred (not immediately recognized in earnings) and amortized. In this case, the sale is not the dominant aspect of the transaction because the lessee retains most or all of the use of the asset. Because the lessee will continue to use the same asset, the gain should be recognized over the period the asset will be used. The seller has simply refinanced the asset and is in the same economic position as before the sale. In addition, an inflated selling price may be part of the cause of the gain.

2. **Capital lease --** If the lease is a capital lease, the gain is recorded in a contra-leased asset account and amortized as a reduction in depreciation expense in the same proportion as depreciation expense is recognized. The gain is thus recognized gradually over the lease term.

   a. If asset is retained by lessee at the end of the lease term, depreciation and amortization of the deferred gain continues to the end of the asset's life. If the asset reverts to the lessor, the lease term is used for the amortization period. If the asset is land, the amortization of the deferred gain is recognized as revenue because land is not depreciated.

3. **Operating lease --** If the lease is an operating lease, the gain is recorded in a liability account and amortized as a reduction in rent expense (there is no leased asset to depreciate). Again, the gain is recognized gradually over the lease term.

   See the following example.

Example: On 1/1/x1 QWEL Inc. sells an asset for its fair value of $25,771 (cost $40,000; accumulated depreciation $20,000) and leases it back under a 3-year noncancelable lease. The lease payments are based on the asset's fair value. The implicit rate of interest is 8%, remaining useful life of the asset is 3 years at lease inception, and the annual lease payments are due each Dec. 31 beginning 20x1. Assume the seller-lessee uses SL depreciation.

The annual lease payment (LP) for this ordinary annuity is computed as:

$25,771 = LP(pva, 8%,3)

$25,771 = LP(2.57710); LP = $10,000

This is a major leaseback because the present value of the minimum lease payments is 100% (> 90%) of fair value.

Journal entries for QWEL (seller-lessee):

1/1/x1

Cash	25,771	
Accumulated depreciation	20,000	
Asset		40,000
Deferred gain		5,771
Leased Asset	25,771	
Lease liability		25,771

A balance sheet at this point reports a net leased asset of $20,000 ($25,771 - $5,771 deferred gain) - the same value just before the sale-leaseback ($40,000 - $20,000).

12/31/x1

Interest expense (.08)25,771	2,062	
Lease liability	7,938	
Cash		10,000
Depreciation expense $25,771/3	8,590	
Accumulated depreciation		8,590
Deferred gain 5,771/3	1,924	
Depreciation expense		1,924

The reduction in depreciation expense has the same effect on earnings as recognizing an equivalent part of the gain each year during the term.
Had the lease instead been classified as an operating lease (for example, if at inception the asset is within its last 25% of original useful life and criterion 1- title transfer, and criterion 2 - bargain purchase option, are not met, then criterion 3 and 4 do not apply), the same entry above would be recorded for the sale, but the deferred gain account is classified as a liability. Each year, after recording rent expense, the following entry would be made:

Deferred gain	(total gain)/lease term
Rent expense	

C. Gain - Minor Leaseback -- In this situation, the two transactions (sale and leaseback) are considered separate because the lessee is not retaining most of the usefulness of the asset.

1. **Accounting --** If the present value of the minimum lease payments is ≤ 10% of the asset's fair market value (minor leaseback), then the sale and leaseback are considered unrelated. The gain is recognized immediately in the entry for sale, and the lease proceeds as usual.

 Example:

Fair value and selling price	$800,000
Carrying Value of Asset	600,000
Present Value of Lease Payments	72,000

$72,000/$800,000 < 10% of $800,000

Gain of $200,000 implied ($800,000 - $600,000)

The journal entry for sale recognizes the gain of $200,000 in earnings. The lease is recorded as an operating lease.

D. Gain - less than major but more than minor leaseback

1. This case has attributes of both the previous two and occurs when the present value of minimum lease payments is between 90% and 10% of fair value:

   a. (90% of fair value) > (present value of minimum lease payments) > (10% of fair value).

   b. **Accounting --** The lessee immediately recognizes the gain to the extent that it exceeds the present value of minimum lease payments. The amount of the gain up to the present value of minimum lease payments is deferred and amortized.

 Example:

Sales Price and fair value of asset	$900,000
Carrying Value of asset	300,000
Present Value of Lease Payments	450,000

The present value of minimum lease payments is 50% of fair value.

Gain of $600,000 is implied ($900,000 - $300,000)

Deferred gain, amortized over term or life, $450,000

Immediately recognized gain, $150,000

E. Losses - real and artificial -- The selling price of an asset in a sale-leaseback is not necessarily equal to fair value. For example, the lessee may accept a selling price below fair value in return for lower rentals during the lease term.

1. The recorded loss on sale is always the difference between selling price and book value (same for a gain). But the selling price may be set low to achieve a particular economic or reporting goal, even though the fair value exceeds book value. In this case, the loss is artificial.

2. In an outright sale of an asset, the selling price and fair value are equal. A real loss occurs when fair value is less than book value. If fair value exceeds book value, there is no real loss. Any recorded loss in this case (occurring because selling price is less than book value) is deferred and amortized.

3. In a sale-leaseback, the lessee immediately recognizes the loss to the extent that the fair value is less than book value (the real loss). Any loss in excess of that amount is deferred and amortized as in the case of gains discussed above. However, when a loss is amortized the opposite effect occurs: depreciation expense (capital lease) is increased, or rent expense (operating lease) is increased.

Example:
1. The selling price of an asset in a sale-leaseback is $10,000. Its fair value is $13,000, and its carrying value is $12,000. The recorded loss on sale is $2,000 ($12,000 carrying value - $10,000 selling price). But the firm really does not have a loss because fair value exceeds carrying value. This is an "artificial" loss. The loss will be made up through lower rentals on the leaseback side of the transaction. In this case, the entire loss is deferred and amortized as an increase in depreciation expense for a capital lease or rent expense for an operating lease.

2. Selling price $10,000; fair value $10,000; book value $12,000. Recorded loss is $2,000 (selling price less book value). Fair value is less than book value by that amount. Therefore, the entire loss is recognized immediately. The leaseback side of the transaction continues based on fair value, as usual.

3. Selling price $10,000; fair value $10,500; book value $12,000. Recorded loss is $2,000 (selling price less book value). Fair value is less than book value by $1,500. That amount of loss is recognized immediately. The remaining $500 is deferred and amortized.

III. U.S. GAAP - IFRS Differences

A. For operating leases in a sales leaseback arrangement, under international standards, if the selling price equals fair value, any gain or loss on the sale is recognized immediately rather than deferred and amortized as under U.S. standards.

1. If the selling price is less than fair value without lower than fair value rentals, the loss is also recognized immediately. But if the rentals are lower than fair value to compensate for the lower sales price, the loss is deferred and amortized in proportion to the payments.

2. If the selling price exceeds fair value, the excess is also deferred and amortized.

3. If the fair value is less than book value (which implies an impairment), the resulting loss is recognized immediately.

B. For finance (capital) leases, the gain is deferred and recognized over the lease term in all cases, even if the asset is acquired by the lessee at the end of the term (title transfer or BPO). U.S. standards, by contrast, distinguish among major, in-between, and minor leasebacks. In some cases, gains are immediately recognized.

IV. Leveraged Leases

A. The lessor in a leveraged lease borrows the cash from a third-party creditor to purchase the asset under lease, and then leases the asset to the lessee. Leveraged leases provide special tax benefits for the lessor including tax credits and an immediate deduction for the cost of the asset.

1. The FASB decided that the arrangement should be treated as an integrated set of transactions, rather than as separate transactions. Normal capital lease accounting would not convey the economic substance of the interrelationship among the lessor, third-party debt, and the lessee.

2. Only lessor accounting is affected; lessee accounting proceeds as usual.

B. The financing provided by the lessor's creditor must be nonrecourse financing (if the lessee fails to make the lease payments, the lessor must still honor its debt to the third party creditor). However, the creditor may require the loan to be secured by the asset under lease. The arrangement may also require that the lease payments be assigned to the creditor (lessee pays the creditor directly).

1. For favorable tax treatment, the lessor must maintain a certain minimum equity in the asset (less than 100% leveraged) but the amount of financing provided by the creditor must be substantial in relation to the fair value of the asset under lease (> 50%).

C. A leveraged lease must meet the requirement of a DFL (book value = fair value). There can be no dealer or manufacturer profit. However, the lessor does not account for the lease as a DFL. Rather, the gross investment in the lease begins with the amount that would be reported under a DFL, but that amount is reported net of the principal and interest payments due to the creditor, plus the tax benefits expected over the lease term, and plus or minus other items. Thus, the liability to the third-party creditor is offset against the lease receivable. The accounting provides for a declining net investment in the lease during the early years of the term with an increase during the later years.

V. Lease Disclosures

A. Lessees are required to disclose:

1. The gross amount of assets recorded under capital leases.

2. Future minimum lease payments in the aggregate and for each of the five succeeding years (capital leases).

3. Future minimum rentals in the aggregate and for each of the five succeeding years (operating leases).

4. General description of the lease arrangement, executory costs, contingent rentals, residual values, and other features.

5. Rent expense for operating leases.

B. Lessors are required to disclose:

1. The components of the net lease receivable (net investment in capital leases) including future minimum lease payments to be received, unguaranteed residual values, and unearned interest revenue.

2. Minimum future rentals on noncancelable operating leases in the aggregate and for each of the five succeeding fiscal years.

3. General description of the lease arrangement, executory costs, contingent rentals, residual values, and other features.

4. The cost and carrying amount of assets leased by others.

Distinguishing Liabilities from Equity

This lesson considers the theoretical question of whether a transaction yields a liability, equity, or both.

After studying this lesson, you should be able to:

1. *Discuss the basic issue.*

2. *Explain how mandatorily redeemable shares are classified.*

3. *Account for obligations to issue shares of a fixed dollar amount.*

4. *Record the journal entries for an obligation to issue a fixed number of shares.*

5. *Account for written put options.*

6. *Identify the main differences in this area between U.S. and international accounting standards.*

I. **Background** -- Although the definitions of "liability" and "equity" have been established for a long time, new transactions have developed that put these definitions to the test. The expectation is that new definitions will be forthcoming, along with affected specific accounting principles. Until then, the determination of whether an item is a liability or equity proceeds on a somewhat piecemeal basis. This lesson considers (1) transactions involving the firm's stock, and (2) compound financial instruments. Additional discussion of financial instruments as they affect liabilities and equity is found in lessons on derivatives.

II. **Adopted Standards** -- The FASB has adopted accounting standards that require certain items related to equity are to be reported as liabilities. These items obligate the firm to deliver assets of a fixed monetary value, either cash or equity shares, in the future, and include:

   A. Mandatorily redeemable shares;

   B. Certain stock appreciation rights (discussed in a previous lesson);

   C. Financial instruments obligating the issuing firm to issue stock worth a fixed value;

   D. Written put options and other financial instruments obligating the issuing firm to repurchase its own shares.

III. **Mandatorily Redeemable Shares** -- Mandatorily redeemable financial instruments are classified as liabilities if both of the following criteria are met. (1) They are obligations to repurchase the firm's equity shares or are indexed to such an obligation, and (2) They require or may require the issuer to settle the obligation by transferring assets. However, if the redemption is required only upon liquidation of the entity, then the classification is equity. An example of an instrument that is classified as debt is a written put option on the issuer's shares that is to be settled in cash. Mandatorily redeemable financial instruments are initially measured at fair value.

IV. **Obligations to Issue Shares of a Fixed Dollar Value**

   A. Firms may pay for services or goods by issuing stock after the goods or services are received. Recall that when shares are issued immediately upon receipt of goods or services, the expense or asset, and the stock issued, are measured at the more reliable of the fair values (good/service, or stock). When there is a period of time between receipt of consideration, and the issuance of stock, the stock price can change. The issue then arises, at the receipt of consideration: does the firm have a liability, or equity? The answer depends on whether the agreement specifies shares worth a fixed dollar amount, or a fixed number of shares.

B. Shares worth a fixed dollar amount (variable number of shares). When a firm agrees to issue shares in the future worth a fixed dollar amount, a liability rather than equity is recognized. The vendor is not at risk for fluctuations in the price of the stock to be received because shares worth the fixed amount will be received, regardless of the stock price.

> **Example:**
> A firm and a vendor agree that the firm will pay for service provided April 1, 20x2 with shares of the firm's $1 par common stock two months after that date. The value of shares to be issued is $10,000 - the parties agree that this is the fair valuation of the services.
>
> | 4/1/x2 | Service expense | 10,000 | | |
> |---|---|---|---|---|
> | | Liability for stock issuance (liability account) | | 10,000 | |
>
> On May 31, 20x2, the share price of the firm's stock is $40. The number of shares to be issued therefore is 250 ($10,000/$40).
>
> | 5/31/x2 | Liability for stock issuance | 10,000 | | |
> |---|---|---|---|---|
> | | Common stock | | 250 | 250($1) |
> | | Contributed cap. in excess of par-common | | 9,750 | 250($40 - $1) |

C. Fixed number of shares. By comparison, when the number of shares is fixed rather than the dollar amount, the issuing firm records an owner's equity account upon receipt of consideration. During the period between providing the goods or service, and receipt of stock, the vendor is at risk in the same way any other shareholder is at risk. If the stock price declines during this time, the value received by the vendor will also decline.

> **Example:**
> Using the information in the previous example, assume the two parties agree that the firm will issue 200 shares of $1 common stock two months after the service is provided. The market price of the stock on April 1, 20x2 is $50.
>
> | 4/1/x2 | Service expense | 10,000 | | |
> |---|---|---|---|---|
> | | Stock issuance obligation (OE account) | | 10,000 | |
> | 5/31/x2 | Stock issuance obligation | 10,000 | | |
> | | Common stock | | 200 | 200($1) |
> | | Contributed cap. in excess of par-common | | 9,800 | 250($50 - $1) |
>
> The fair value of the services was $10,000 on April 1. That amount determines the increase in contributed capital. The share price at the time of issuance is not relevant.

V. Written Put Options

A. As part of a share repurchase plan, firms may write an option allowing other entities to sell the firm's stock to the firm at a fixed price (option price) on a specific date or during a specified period. The purchaser (option holder) pays a fee for the option. The fee typically approximates the fair value of the option using an option-pricing model (the same type of model used to value employee stock options discussed in a previous lesson).

B. The purchaser of the option is betting that the firm's stock will decline in price. The firm is betting the price will stay above the option price.

C. The fair value of the option is reported as a liability. Changes in the option's fair value are recognized at each year-end before the exercise. An increase in the fair value represents a potential decrease in the share price because the option is more valuable. The option will be exercised if the share price during the exercise period is less than fixed option price. At exercise, the firm extinguishes the liability and pays the option price. If the option is not exercised (because the share price exceeds the option price during the exercise period), the liability is extinguished and a gain is recorded.

Example:

On January 1, 20x1, a firm wrote put options for 100 shares of its common stock.

Holders of the option will be able to sell the firm's stock back to the firm for $50 per share on December 31, 20x2. The estimated fair value of one option is $10. Journal entries for the firm follow:

1/1/x1	Cash	1,000		100($10)
	Put option liability		1,000	

On December 31, 20x1, the fair value of an option is re-estimated to be $12.50. The increase in fair value reflects an increased likelihood that the price of the firm's stock will be less than $50 on the exercise date.

12/31/x1	Loss on put option	250		100($12.50 - $10)
	Put option liability		250	

On December 31, 20x2, the price of the firm's stock is $45 per share. The option is exercised because the purchaser (option holder) will receive $50 per option when the shares are worth only $45. The purchaser can purchase a share of the stock for $45 on the market and sell it back to the firm for $50 - a gain of $5 per share. However, the purchaser has incurred a net loss of $500: $1,000 fee less the $500 gain on exercise [100($50 - $45)].

12/31/x2	Put option liability	1,250		
	Treasury stock	4,500		100($45) (fair value)
	Cash		5,000	100($50)
	Gain on put option		750	

The treasury stock is recorded at fair value. The $500 net gain to the firm over the two years is computed two ways:

1. $500 = $750 gain for 20x2 - $250 loss for 20x1 = $500

2. $500 = $1,000 fee - $500 (excess of $5,000 paid for stock - $4,500 fair value)

D. When the option is not exercised (stock price did not fall below the option price), the put option liability is closed and a gain is recognized. The overall gain to the firm is the fee. In this example, if the stock price were $55 on December 31, 20x2, the option would not be exercised and the firm would record the following journal entry:

12/31/x2 Put option liability	1,250	
Gain on put option		1,250

The firm's overall gain is $1,000 ($1,250 gain for 20x2 - $250 loss for 20x1).

VI. Compound Financial Instruments

A. At present, GAAP addresses this issue on an individual standard basis. The expectation is that this area will be revised based on a more general standard. Previous lessons addressed the following two items, for example.

    1. Convertible bonds are treated the same was as nonconvertible bonds at issuance and throughout the term - as debt. There is no separation of the debt and equity components. Only at conversion does the equity component surface. There is an exception - when convertible bonds can be settled in cash. This exception is consistent with the notion of a liability - the obligation to transfer assets in the future as a result of a past transaction.

    2. Bonds with detachable warrants separate the debt and equity components at issuance. This treatment is just the opposite that for most convertible bonds.

VII. U.S. GAAP - IFRS Differences

A. Whereas at present, U.S. standards address financial instruments on an individual basis, international standards apply more general concepts.

B. Under international standards, a financial instrument is classified as liability or equity, based on the substance of the transaction.

    1. If a financial instrument is an obligation to transfer cash or other financial assets, it is classified as a liability, regardless of form. It may be necessary to separate the liability and equity components as is the case with convertible bonds under international standards. The classification is made at issuance and continues until it is derecognized. When there is uncertainty as to measurement, the liability component is directly measured with the equity component treated as a residual.

C. More specifically, under international standards, an item is a liability if the firm has a contractual obligation to deliver cash or other financial asset to the holder, or to exchange another financial instrument with the holder under conditions that are potentially unfavorable to the issuer.

    1. Liability classification is required under these circumstances regardless of the consideration transferred to settle the obligation, and regardless of whether the issuer has restrictions on the ability to settle the obligation or regardless of the way the obligation is settled.

    2. For example, the instrument could be settled by issuing shares and yet be classified as a liability (the obligation to issue shares of a fixed dollar amount is an example). If the circumstances are not met, then the instrument is classified as equity, which implies that the instrument evidences a residual interest in the assets of an entity after deducting its liabilities.

Nonmonetary Exchange

Commercial Substance

This lesson presents the accounting for nonmonetary exchanges that have commercial substance.

After studying this lesson, you should be able to:

1. *Define a nonmonetary asset.*

2. *Define commercial substance.*

3. *Calculate the fair value of the asset received and the gain or loss in a nonmonetary exchange.*

I. Nonmonetary Assets

> **Definition:**
> A *nonmonetary asset*: Such an asset does not have a fixed nominal or stated value, as is the case with cash, accounts receivable, and other monetary assets.

A. Plant assets, inventories, and many investments are nonmonetary because their value changes with the market. The determination of the fair value and recorded value of nonmonetary assets presents a challenge when they are acquired in an exchange for other nonmonetary assets.

> **Note:**
> This topic is frequently tested on the exam.

1. What value should be used when recording the acquired asset?

2. Should gains or losses be recorded?

3. ASC 845 governs the accounting for this area.

B. When fair value is the appropriate valuation of the acquired asset, the preferred amount is the fair value of the assets given in exchange. However, if the fair of the asset acquired is more objectively determinable, then that amount should be used for its valuation.

C. Cash is frequently paid or received on exchange. When recording the journal entry for the exchange, the following common-sense relationships may help:

1. If cash is paid on the exchange (more common):

> fair value of acquired asset = fair value of asset exchanged + cash paid

2. If cash is received on the exchange (less common):

> fair value of acquired asset = fair value of asset exchanged - cash received

> **Example:**
> The fair value of a plant asset exchanged for another plant asset is $40,000. Cash of $6,000 is received on the exchange. The implied fair value of the asset acquired is $34,000 ($40,000 fair value of asset exchanged - $6,000 cash received).

D. However, fair value is not always the appropriate valuation for the acquired nonmonetary asset.

E. Gain or Loss -- The amount of the gain or loss on exchange is based solely on values pertaining to the asset exchanged. The book value of a plant asset is, for example, the difference between its cost and accumulated depreciation to date. The amount of gain or loss recorded, if any, is:

> gain = fair value of asset exchanged - book value of asset exchanged
>
> loss = book value of asset exchanged - fair value of asset exchanged

F. The asset exchanged should be tested for impairment before recording the exchange.

II. Caution on List Price -- The list price of the acquired asset should not be used for fair value-list prices are notoriously inflated. Any associated trade-in allowance is used only to determine the amount of cash to be paid: list price - trade-in allowance = cash paid on exchange. The trade-in allowance is not equal to the fair value of the asset exchanged.

> **Example:**
> The list price of a new machine is $32,000. An old machine is traded in for the new machine, and the seller gives the buyer a trade-in allowance of $18,000 for the old machine. The fair value of the old machine is $12,000.
>
> Cash to be paid on the exchange = list price - trade-in allowance
>
> = $32,000 - $18,000 = $14,000
>
> The fair value of the acquired asset equals:
>
> fair value of asset exchanged + Cash paid
>
> $12,000.00 + $14,000.00 = $26,000.00

III. ASC 845

A. ASC 845 requires that fair value be used to record a nonmonetary asset acquired in an exchange with another nonmonetary asset, with full recognition of gains and losses, unless any of the following apply:

1. The fair value of neither asset can be determined;

2. The exchange is made solely to facilitate sales to customers (for example, inventory is exchanged for other inventory in the same line of business to enable one of the firms to make a sale to an outside party);

3. The exchange **lacks commercial substance** - the cash flows of the firm are not expected to change significantly as a result of the exchange - which means:

   a. The cash flows from the acquired asset will not be significantly different from those of the asset exchanged in terms of amount, timing, or risk; or

   b. The use value of the acquired asset is not significantly different from that of the asset exchanged, in relation to the fair value of the assets exchanged;

B. Receipt or payment of cash to even the exchange does not necessarily imply that gains and losses should be recognized. For example, in situation 2 above, one firm may pay the other a certain amount of cash to even the exchange of inventory made to facilitate sales to customers. The cash flow does not cause the inventory to be valued at fair value.

C. If any of the above three criteria apply, then the accounting is simpler and based on book value, not fair value. No gain or loss is recorded (there are exceptions - see below), and the acquired asset is recorded at the book value of the asset exchanged plus cash paid on the exchange (or minus cash received on the exchange).

Example:
1. (Commercial Substance) A plant asset (cost $40,000; accumulated depreciation $13,000) is exchanged for another plant asset with a fair value of $30,000. Cash of $2,000 is also paid to even the exchange. The exchange is determined to have commercial substance.

The implied fair value of the asset exchanged is $28,000 ($30,000 fair value of acquired asset less $2,000 cash paid).

Journal entry for the exchange:

Plant asset	30,000	
Accumulated depreciation	13,000	
Plant asset		40,000
Cash		2,000
Gain on exchange		1,000

The acquired plant asset is valued at the sum of the $28,000 fair value of the asset exchanged and $2,000 cash paid. The $1,000 gain equals the difference between the exchanged asset's fair value of $28,000 and its book value of $27,000 ($40,000 - $13,000). A loss would have occurred if the book value had exceeded its fair value. Both losses and gains are recognized when there is commercial substance to the exchange.

2. (Lack of Commercial Substance) A plant asset (cost $40,000; accumulated depreciation $13,000) is exchanged for another plant asset with a fair value of $30,000. Cash of $2,000 is also paid to even the exchange. The exchange is determined to lack commercial substance. (Same data as previous example.)
Journal entry for the exchange:

Plant asset	29,000	
Accumulated depreciation	13,000	
Plant asset		40,000
Cash		2,000

The acquired asset is recorded at the sum of the $27,000 book value of the asset exchanged and $2,000 cash paid. No gain or loss is recognized. Another way to determine the debit to the new asset is to add subtract the unrecognized gain of $1,000 from the $30,000 fair value of the acquired asset.

IV. **Rationale for the Exception to Fair Value Recording**

A. If fair value is not available, the firm is forced into using book to record the acquired asset. If the exchange is made simply to facilitate the sale of goods to a customer, or if the exchange lacks commercial substance, then the firm is in essentially the same economic position after the exchange as before. Only the "identity" of the asset has changed. For example, exchanging an office building for a slightly different one leaves the firm in the same position. There is enough uncertainty inherent in fair values that it is considered more prudent to continue the accounting with the historically more reliable amounts (book value). Computationally, the exception also leaves future depreciation calculations unchanged.

B. Judgment is required for determining whether an exchange has commercial substance. The following characteristics of an exchange may indicate commercial substance:

1. The amount of cash paid or received on exchange is significant in relation to the fair value of the assets exchanged;

2. The functions of the assets exchanged are different. For example, exchanging land for equipment would imply at the very least a different timing and duration of cash flows.

No Commercial Substance

This lesson presents the accounting for nonmonetary exchanges that do not have commercial substance.

After studying this lesson, you should be able to:

1. *Calculate the fair value of the asset received and the gain or loss in a nonmonetary exchange with no commercial substance and cash is paid or received.*

I. **Accounting for an Exchange When There is No Commercial Substance**

   A. An exchange lacks of commercial substance whenever the cash flows to the firm are not expected to change significantly as a result of the exchange:

      1. The cash flows from the acquired asset will not be significantly different from those of the asset exchanged in terms of amount, timing, or risk; or

      2. The use value of the acquired asset is not significantly different from that of the asset exchanged, in relation to the fair value of the assets exchanged;

      3. When there is no commercial substance, the value of the asset acquired is the book value of the asset given.

   B. There are two exceptions to book value reporting when there is no commercial substance:

      1. When a loss is evident, it is recognized in full, and the acquired asset is recorded at market value. Cash can be paid or received on the exchange for this exception. Thus, losses are always recognized in full - an example of conservatism.

      2. When a gain is evident and cash is received (only), the gain is recognized in proportion to the amount of cash received, and the acquired asset is recorded at market value less the portion of the gain unrecognized. If the proportion represented by cash is 25% or more, then the entire gain is recognized, and the acquired asset is recorded at market value.

 Example:

1. No commercial substance, loss, cash paid

Cost of old asset, $40,000
Accumulated depreciation, $12,000
Fair value of new asset $30,000
Cash of $6,000 is paid to even the exchange

The implied fair value of the old asset is $24,000 ($30,000 fair value of new asset - $6,000 cash paid). A $4,000 loss is evident: $28,000 book value of old asset - $24,000 fair value of old asset. Losses are recognized in full and the new asset is recorded at fair value.

Plant asset	30,000	
Accumulated depreciation	12,000	
Loss	4,000	
Plant asset		40,000
Cash		6,000

---

2. No commercial substance, loss, cash received

Cost of old asset, $40,000

Accumulated depreciation, $12,000

Fair value of new asset $20,000

Cash of $3,000 is received to even the exchange

The implied fair value of the old asset is $23,000 ($20,000 fair value of new asset + $3,000 cash received). A $5,000 loss is evident: $28,000 book value of old asset - $23,000 fair value of old asset. Losses are recognized in full and the new asset is recorded at fair value.

Plant asset	20,000	
Accumulated depreciation	12,000	
Cash	3,000	
Loss	5,000	
Plant asset		40,000

3. No commercial substance, gain, cash received

Cost of old asset, $40,000

Accumulated depreciation, $30,000

Fair value of new asset $20,000

Cash of $3,000 is received to even the exchange

The implied fair value of the old asset is $23,000 ($20,000 fair value of new asset + $3,000 cash received). A $13,000 gain is evident: $23,000 fair value of old asset - $10,000 book value of old asset. Cash represents ($3,000/($3,000 + $20,000)) or 13% of the value of the transaction. 13% of the old asset has been "sold" for cash allowing 13% of the gain to be recognized: 13%(13,000) = $1,690. The unrecognized gain is $13,000 - $1,690 = $11,310. The new asset is recorded at fair value less the unrecorded gain = $20,000 - $11,310 = $8,690.

Plant asset	8,690	
Accumulated depreciation	30,000	
Cash	3,000	
Plant asset		40,000
Gain		1,690

4. No commercial substance, gain, cash received, proportion represented by cash > 25%

Cost of old asset, $40,000

Accumulated depreciation, $30,000

Fair value of new asset $20,000

Cash of $10,000 is received to even the exchange

The implied fair value of the old asset is $30,000 ($20,000 fair value of new asset + $10,000 cash received). A $20,000 gain is evident: $30,000 fair value of old asset - $10,000 book value of old asset = $20,000. Cash represents ($10,000/($10,000 + $20,000)) of the value of the transaction or 33% which is more than 25%. This firm has "sold" so much of its asset that the entire transaction is considered a monetary transaction. The entire gain is recognized and the new asset is recorded at fair value.

Plant asset	20,000	
Accumulated depreciation	30,000	
Cash	10,000	
Plant asset		40,000
Gain		20,000

II. Summary of All Cases for Nonmonetary Asset Exchanges

A. Fair value not determinable: recognize no loss or gain, and record the acquired asset at book value of old asset + cash paid or - cash received.

B. Losses (loss = book value of asset exchanged - fair value):

    1. Recognize loss in full, and record the acquired asset at fair value whether or not there is commercial substance. (Losses are always recognized in full.)

C. Gains (gain = fair value of asset exchanged - book value):

    1. If there is commercial substance, recognize gain in full, and record the acquired asset at fair value.

    2. If there is no commercial substance and cash is not received on the exchange, recognize no gain, and record the acquired asset at book value of asset exchanged + cash paid.

    3. If there is no commercial substance and cash is received on the exchange, recognize the gain in proportion to the cash received and record the asset acquired at fair value less the unrecognized portion of the gain.

        a. **Exception** -- if the proportion of cash received is 25% or more, account for the exchange as if there were commercial substance (recognize gain in full and record acquired asset at fair value).

Nonmonetary Exchanges and IFRS

This lesson presents the significant differences in the accounting for nonmonetary exchanges under IFRS versus U.S. GAAP.

After studying this lesson, you should be able to:

1. *Identify the major differences in the accounting for nonmonetary exchanges under IFRS versus U.S. GAAP.*

I. Nonmonetary Exchange and IFRS

A. There are a few significant differences in the accounting for nonmonetary exchange under IFRS than according to U.S. GAAP. The table below summarizes these differences.

IFRS	U.S. GAAP
Advertising revenue (gain) is recognized in barter transactions is determined by reference to a non-barter transaction	Advertising revenue (gain) is based on the services received or given, which ever can be most reliably measured
Assets transferred to the entity by the government are recognized as a government grant	U.S. GAAP does not address the accounting for government grants
There is no guidance when assets or resources are donated	Donated assets are recognized as an expense at fair value and the gain or loss is recognized on the donated asset

B. **Advertising revenue determined by reference to non-barter transaction --** Under IFRS, advertising revenue is determined by reference to a non-barter (another transaction in which cash is paid) transaction. U.S. GAAP permits measurement of the revenue by using the fair value of the advertising services given or received. IFRS assumes the value of these services is determinable only by referencing paid for services.

C. **Government grant transfers --** IFRS specifically addresses the accounting for assets transferred to the entity from a government. These transfers in general recognize an asset and income. U.S. GAAP does not specifically address this type of transaction.

D. **Donated assets --** IFRS does not specifically address the accounting when an asset or other resource is donated. U.S. GAAP requires that the fair value of the donated asset or service be recognized as an expense and a gain (or loss) is recognized on the revaluation of the donated item.

Related Parties and Related Party Transactions

This lesson presents the accounting and reporting for related party transactions.

After studying this lesson, you should be able to:

1. *Define related party.*

2. *Identify the key disclosures of related party transactions.*

I. **Related Party Transactions --** Parties are related if one of the transacting parties can significantly influence the policies of the other, or if both parties are subject to the influence of a third party. The usual "self-interest" profit maximization incentives are absent in such transactions. These transactions normally are not carried out at "arms-length."

  A. Examples of parties that may be related to the reporting firm include:

   1. Investees accounted for under the equity method;

   2. Affiliates of the firm;

   3. Pension trusts of the firm;

   4. Principal owners of the firm (owners of more than 10% of the voting stock);

   5. Immediate family members of principal owners of the firm.

  B. Many related party transactions occur in the normal course of business. The term "related" does not imply "inappropriate."

  C. Examples of related party transactions include:

   1. Sales of assets at unrealistically low amounts;

   2. Below-market interest rate loans;

   3. Transactions between parent and subsidiary;

   4. Transactions that appear to have no economic substance.

  D. **ASC 850 --** Related party transactions do not always result in accounting recognition. For example, a firm might receive services from a related party at no cost, and therefore not record a transaction. However, where material in dollar amount, the disclosures required by ASC 850 apply. ASC 850 is the governing pronouncement for related party transactions.

  E. One of the objectives of related party disclosures is to fully inform the financial statement user that these transactions exist.

  > ASC 850-10-05-5 "Transactions between related parties are considered to be related party transactions even though they may not be given accounting recognition. For example, an entity may receive services from a related party without charge and not record receipt of the services. While not providing accounting or measurement guidance for such transactions, this Topic requires their disclosure nonetheless."

  F. **Financial Reporting**

   1. Most disclosures requirements about related party transactions stem from SEC requirements laid out in Regulation S-X. These disclosures are aimed at revealing the economic substance behind related party transactions because their legal form often disguises the true financial nature of the arrangements.

2. Footnotes to the financial statements are required to include disclosures of material related party transactions. The required disclosures include:

   a. The nature of the relationship between the parties;

   b. A description of the transactions, and dollar amounts where relevant;

   c. The amounts due to or from related parties, and the terms of settlement.

G. **Additional Disclosures Required --** The primary purpose of the related disclosure requirement is related to the full disclosure principle. Absent disclosure about related party transactions, the assumption is that parties transacting with the reporting firm are independent of the reporting firm, and that such transactions are made at arm's-length. That assumption may not be not valid, when the parties are related. It is common for related party transactions to be structured to achieve certain prespecified results desired by both parties. The normal accounting for such transactions may not convey the economic substance of the transactions, because the parties are related. Hence the requirement for the additional disclosures regarding related parties.

II. **Related Parties and IFRS**

A. There are no significant differences between U.S. GAAP and IFRS (IAS 24).

Research and Development Costs

This lesson presents the accounting and reporting for research and development costs (R&D).

After studying this lesson, you should be able to:

1. *Identify what costs are considered research and what costs are considered development.*

2. *Identify the major difference in IFRS and U.S .GAAP with respect to R&D*

I. Details

A. Definitions

Definitions:
Research: The attempt to discover new knowledge aimed at the development of new products, services, processes, or techniques, or the significant improvement in an existing product.

Development: The translation of research findings or knowledge into a plan or design of a new product or significant improvement in an existing product or process whether intended for sale or use. Development includes formulation, design and testing of product alternatives, construction of prototypes, and operations of pilot plants.

1. Development does not include routine or periodic alterations to existing products, processes, or other ongoing operations. It also does not include market research.

> **Note:**
> The CPA exam frequently tests detailed knowledge of the definition and items included in R&D, and also what is not included in R&D.

B. Included in R&D are

1. Laboratory research;

2. Conceptual formulation and design of possible products or process alternatives;

3. Modification of the formulation or design of a product or process;

4. Design, construction, and testing of pre-production prototypes and models;

5. Design of tools, jigs, molds, and dies involving new technology;

6. Design of a pilot plant.

C. Excluded from R&D are

1. Engineering follow-through;

2. Quality control and routine testing;

3. Trouble-shooting;

4. Adaptation of an existing capability to a particular customer's needs;

5. Routine design of tools, jigs, molds and dies;

6. Legal work in connection with patent applications;

7. Software development costs.

II. Accounting for R&D

A. General Rule -- ASC 730 requires that research and development costs are expensed in the period incurred. Research and Development Costs include labor costs, materials costs, and overhead costs.

B. Fixed Assets -- In relation to the use of fixed assets in research and development activities, three specific situations need to be addressed.

> **Note:**
> This issue has appeared in CPA exam questions in the past. To some candidates, the treatment in the third situation below appears unusual because the fixed asset has a useful life of more than one year. ASC 730 views the purchase of such an asset as an irrevocable commitment of resources. Since the intent is to use the equipment only in the one R&D effort, and since it has no future value, conservatism and consistency with other R&D expenses would imply immediate expensing.

    1. Fixed Assets Used in Several Research and Development Projects -- These assets are capitalized and annual depreciation is included in the annual research and development costs. The debit is to R&D expense rather than to depreciation expense; the credit is to accumulated depreciation.

    2. Fixed Assets Used Temporarily in a Research and Development Project -- The depreciation related to the time frame of the project is included in the annual research and development costs.

    3. Fixed Assets Used in a Single Research and Development Project, the Asset has no Alternative Uses -- Even though the fixed asset has a useful life exceeding one year and the single R&D project will be in process for more than one year, the entire cost of the fixed asset is expensed as R&D immediately.

C. Patent Costs -- The internal costs of developing a patent are considered R&D and therefore are expensed. The result is that the only costs capitalized for internally developed patents are registration and legal costs. This contrasts with the cost of purchasing a patent from an outside party. The entire cost of such a patent is capitalized. The treatment appears somewhat inconsistent but stems from the reasoning that it is better to err on the side of conservatism when the benefits of R&D are so uncertain.

D. Purchased Services -- R&D services purchased from other firms are included in R&D. But if a firm performs R&D services for another firm, the costs are accumulated in an inventory account and expensed as cost of goods sold or cost of services provided at the conclusion of the contract.

E. R&D Examples – See the following example.

Example:

1. Maple Inc. does not have the expertise in a specific research area and contracted with Oak Co. to perform research on a new product design to be used by Maple. Maple will expense all of the payments made to Oak as R&D expense. However, Oak Co. will debit inventory for the cost of its research performed for Maple until the contract is completed, at which time contract revenue and expense is recognized. This is not R&D expense to Oak.

2. The following costs were incurred by a firm in the current year:

Materials, labor, and overhead cost incurred for:

Laboratory research	$40,000
Modification of the design of a product or process	10,000
Adaptation of an existing capability to a particular customer's needs	20,000

Purchase cost of fixed assets at beginning of year:

Equipment used the full year for lab research, annual depreciation $30,000;

    equipment has alternative non R&D uses, $300,000 cost

Equipment used the full year for lab research, annual depreciation $15,000;

    equipment has alternative R&D uses, $150,000 cost

Equipment used the full year for lab research, annual depreciation $25,000;

    equipment has no alternative use other than in one specific R&D effort, $250,000 cost

Total R&D expense for the year equals:

$345,000 = $40,000 + $10,000 + $30,000 + $15,000 + $250,000.

The $20,000 (adaptation of existing capability) is not R&D. The full cost of the third item of equipment is included in R&D for the current year because it has no alternative use (in other R&D or non-R&D uses).

III. Research and Development and IFRS

A. IFRS distinguishes between research and development, like U.S. GAAP. However, IFRS allows companies to capitalize development costs.

Risks and Uncertainties

This lesson addresses the required disclosures by firms of the risks and uncertainties they face.

After studying this lesson, you should be able to:

1. *Explain the scope of the required disclosures, and the kinds of risks and uncertainties that are not required to be disclosed.*

2. *Identify the four areas of required disclosure.*

3. *Describe the main disclosure requirements within the four areas.*

4. *Define and describe the four concentrations within the significant concentrations areas of disclosure.*

I. Background

A. Information about the risks and uncertainties faced by the firm enhances the ability of financial statement users to predict the future cash flows and operations of the firm. GAAP requires certain information about risks and uncertainties to be disclosed. The applicable accounting standard provides for selectivity whereby specified criteria are used to screen all the possible risks so that the required disclosures are limited to matters that materially affect a particular entity.

B. The disclosures are primarily concerned with risks and uncertainties that could materially affect financial statement amounts within one year of the balance sheet date (the near term).

C. The required disclosures involve the following four sources of risk and uncertainty. Each is discussed in more detail later in this lesson.

   1. Nature of the entity's operations;

   2. Use of estimates in financial statements;

   3. Certain significant estimates;

   4. Current vulnerability due to significant concentrations in certain aspects of operations.

D. The four areas are not mutually exclusive; rather there may be some overlap.

E. The requirements of the standard apply to annual and complete interim statements but not to condensed or summarized interim statements. The disclosure requirements only apply to the current year's statements in comparative financial statements.

F. The requirements apply only to those included in the standard and not to risks and uncertainties related to:

   1. Management or key personnel;

   2. Proposed changes in government regulations;

   3. Proposed changes in accounting principles;

   4. Deficiencies in internal control;

   5. Possible effects of acts of God, war, sudden catastrophe.

II. Nature of Operations

A. Different types of businesses have different risks. Knowledge of the firm's (1) products and services, (2) geographical locations and (3) principal markets will assist users in assessing risks concerning the firm's operations. For example, identification of competition and vulnerability to technological change are aided with this knowledge.

B. Financial statements and notes are required to include a description of the major products or services of the firm, and its principal markets and their locations. If the firm operates in more than one type of business, the relative importance of the operations in each business is disclosed, along with the basis of this determination (based on assets, revenues, or earnings for example).

C. These disclosures are not required to be on a quantified basis; relative importance can be described in such terms as major, intermediate, minor, and other similar ways.

III. Use of Estimates

A. The firm must communicate that: (1) use of estimates is inescapable in preparing financial statements that conform with GAAP, (2) the use of estimates results in approximate amounts, not certainty, and (3) estimates involve assumptions about future events.

B. The degree to which estimates can be relied upon is affected by many factors including whether the business and economic environment is stable or unstable at the time. This area of disclosure reminds users that they should not place an unwarranted degree of reliability on the reported amounts in financial statements.

IV. Certain Significant Estimates

A. When estimates used to value assets, liabilities or contingencies are subject to a reasonable possibility of material change, disclosures may be required. Disclosure about an estimate is required when information available before the financial statements are issued or are available to be issued indicates that the following two criteria are met:

1. It is at least reasonably possible that an estimate will change in the near term;

2. The effect of the change would be material.

   a. Materiality is based on the effect of using the new estimate on the financial statements.

B. The disclosures must include:

1. The nature of the uncertainty that may cause an estimate to change and a statement that it is at least reasonably possible that a change in an estimate will occur in the near term. If the estimate concerns a loss contingency, the disclosure must also include an estimate of the possible loss or range of loss, or state that such an estimate cannot be made.

2. The estimated effect of the change as of the date of the financial statements must be disclosed.

C. If the criteria above are not met because the firm uses a risk-reduction technique, the disclosures are encouraged but not required.

D. The following are examples of assets and liabilities, related revenues and expenses, and disclosures of gain or loss contingencies that may be particularly sensitive to change in the near term:

1. Inventory subject to obsolescence;

2. Equipment subject to technological obsolescence;

3. Deferred tax asset valuation allowances;

4. Capitalized software costs;

5. Environmental remediation obligations;

6. Litigation obligations;

7. Obligations for defined benefit pension plans and other postemployment benefits.

V. Significant Concentrations

A. Susceptibility to risk and uncertainty increases when diversification is lacking - when the firm has concentrations in various aspects of its business. Examples of concentrations include excessive reliance on one customer, having one product or service account for most of the firm's revenues, and reliance on one or a small number of suppliers.

B. The standard is concerned with "severe impacts" caused by concentrations. A severe impact is a significant financially disruptive effect on the normal functioning of the firm, where "severe" is greater than material but less than catastrophic. Bankruptcy is considered catastrophic for example.

C. The standard applies only to the following defined set of four concentrations, rather than all possible concentrations.

    1. Concentrations in the volume of business with a particular customer, supplier, lender, grantor or contributor. The loss of the relationship is an example of an event that could cause a severe impact. The standard states that it is always at least reasonably possible to lose such a customer, grantor or contributor although the impact may not be severe.

    2. Concentrations in revenue from specific products, services, or fund-raising sources. A price or demand change could cause a severe impact.

    3. Concentrations in specific sources (suppliers) of services, materials, labor, licenses or other rights used in operations. Loss of a key supplier or a patent are examples of events that could cause a severe impact.

    4. Concentrations in the market or geographic area of operations. The standard states that it is always at least reasonably possible that operations located outside the firm's home country will be disrupted in the near term.

D. Disclosure of a concentration is required if all of the following criteria are met. These concentrations are called "disclosable concentrations."

    1. The concentration exists at the balance sheet date;

    2. The entity is vulnerable to the risk of a near-term severe impact because of a concentration;

    3. It is at least reasonably possible that events capable of causing a severe impact will occur in the near term. (Note: reasonably estimable is less than probable.)

E. For disclosable concentrations (those meeting the above criteria), the following is to be disclosed:

    1. Information adequate to inform users about the nature of the risk associated with the concentration;

    2. For concentrations of labor (one of the four listed concentrations, see above) subject to collective bargaining agreements, the firm must disclose (a) the percentage of the labor force covered by the agreement, and (2) the percentage of the labor force covered the agreement that will expire within one year;

    3. For concentrations of operations located outside of the entity's home country (one of the four listed concentrations, see above), the firm also must disclose the carrying amounts of net assets and the geographic areas in which they are located.

VI. U.S. GAAP - IFRS Differences

A. International standards require some of the same disclosures regarding risks and uncertainties as for U.S. standards but the international requirements are less voluminous and the two sets of requirements are not exactly parallel.

B. Entities are encouraged (but not required) to present, outside the financial statements, a review by management describing the entity's financial performance and position, and the main uncertainties faced by the entity. This section of the standard does not provide detail regarding required disclosures in the risk and uncertainty area.

C. Entities are required to disclose judgments, other than those involving estimates, that management made in applying the firm's accounting policies.

D. Also required are disclosures about the assumptions made about the future, and major sources of estimation uncertainty that have a significant risk of requiring material adjustment to the carrying amounts of assets and liabilities within the coming year. An exception is assets and liabilities measured at fair value based on observed market prices because such changes are attributable to market forces.

    1. The above disclosures are to be presented in such a way that users of the statements understand the judgments made by management and about other sources of estimation uncertainty. Examples include:

        a. The nature of the assumption or other estimation uncertainty;

        b. The sensitivity of carrying amounts to assumptions and estimates, and an explanation for their sensitivity;

        c. How the uncertainty is expected to be resolved and the range of reasonably possible carrying values of the assets and liabilities affected, within the next year;

        d. If the uncertainty remains unresolved, a description of the changes made to past assumptions concerning the affected assets and liabilities.

    2. If it is impracticable to determine the effects of an assumption or another source of estimation uncertainty, the entity discloses that it is reasonably possible for outcomes to require a material adjustment to the carrying amount of the asset or liability affected.

Segment Reporting

The disclosure requirements for firms with different business segments are considered here.

After studying this lesson, you should be able to:

1. *Define an operating segment.*

2. *Explain how a reportable segment is identified using three quantitative tests.*

3. *Articulate the 75% rule for reporting.*

4. *List the major items to be disclosed for a reportable segment.*

5. *Apply the quantitative tests in an actual situation.*

I. Operating Segments

A. Financial statements provide highly aggregated information. For a firm that conducts activities in several different lines of business, users would benefit from disclosures that provide more disaggregated information. To that end, GAAP requires, under certain circumstances, that information be provided by major business segment.

B. Under GAAP, business segments are identified by employing a management approach. That is, segments are identified in the same manner that management segments the company for purposes of making operating decisions. These segments are referred to as operating segments.

> **Note:**
> The purpose of segment reporting is to assist the financial statement users' understanding of the entity's performance. Because segment reporting provides disaggregated information, it contains predictive value and confirmatory value to the financial statement user.

C. Operating segments must have three characteristics.

    1. The segment is involved in revenue producing and expense incurring activities.

    2. The operating results of the segment are reviewed by the company's chief operating decision maker on a regular basis.

    3. There is discrete financial information available for the segment.

D. Not all sub-units of a corporation are operating segments. The corporate headquarters would not be an operating segment for many firms for example.

II. Identification of Reportable Segments -- Quantitative Tests -- A
reportable segment is one that meets one or more of the following three quantitative tests. Not all operating segments are reportable segments. Disclosure is required only for reportable segments.

> **Note:**
> In the past, the quantitative tests have been the most frequently tested aspect of segment reporting.

A. The operating segment's revenue from all sources (internal and external) is 10% or more of the combined (internal and external) revenues of all of the company's reported operating segments.

B. The operating segment's operating profit or loss (absolute value) is 10% or more of the greater of the following two amounts (absolute value). Operating profit is pretax.

> **Note:**
> Each of the three criteria uses 10% or more as the cutoff percentage. The 10% cutoff is an example of a GAAP-imposed materiality threshold.

    1. The combined operating profit of all operating segments that did not report an operating loss;

    2. The combined loss of all operating segments that did report an operating loss.

  C. The operating segment's identifiable assets are 10% or more of the combined assets of all operating segments.

III. Aggregation of Two or More Segments

  A. For the quantitative tests, two or more segments can be aggregated provided this aggregation is consistent with the objective of segment reporting, and the segments are similar in each of the following areas:

    1. The nature of products and services;

    2. The nature of the production processes;

    3. Customer type or class;

    4. Distribution methods for products and services;

    5. The nature of the regulatory environment.

> **Example:**
> If a firm has three major department stores in various parts of the country, each of which meets the operating segment definition, the stores can be aggregated into a single reportable segment to avoid excessive reporting.

IV. Reportable Segments - the 75% Rule -- The total external revenue reported by reportable segments must be at least 75% of the company's total consolidated revenues. This is an overall materiality threshold for reporting.

  A. If this test is not met initially, more reportable operating segments must be identified, even if the additional segments do not meet one of the three quantitative tests.

  B. There is no stated limit on the number of reportable segments, but as a practical matter, if the number reaches ten, then the firm should assess whether adding more segments is worth the cost.

V. Reportable Segments - "All Other" Category -- All non-reportable segments are grouped into an "all other" category and their results are combined for reconciliation purposes.

VI. Reportable Segments - Required Disclosures -- The required disclosures for reportable segments include the following (note that operating segments that are not reportable segments are not subject to these reporting requirements). Note also that the information reported reflects the way the firm reports information internally, which may not always be in conformity with GAAP. However, this approach was considered to be more useful than a pure GAAP-based reporting model.

  A. Factors used to identify operating segments;

  B. General information about the products and services of the operating segments;

  C. Internal and external sales revenue;

  D. A measure of profit or loss, and total assets;

  E. The nature of differences between the measurement of segment quantitative information such as income and assets, and the measurement of the firm's reported quantitative information;

  F. Interest revenue;

  G. Interest expense;

  H. Depreciation, depletion, and amortization expense;

I. Other significant non-cash items;

J. Unusual or infrequent Items;

K. Extraordinary gains or losses;

L. Equity in net income of investees, in which the investment is accounted for under the equity method;

M. Income tax expense or benefit.

N. Reconciliation of the totals of segment revenues, reported profit or loss, assets, and other significant items to the total for the firm as a whole.

O. Capital expenditures.

VII. **Other Required Disclosures --** If the following information is not already provided through the required segment information, firms must separately disclose the following:

A. Revenues from external customers from each product and service or groups of similar products or services.

B. Revenues from the home country of the firm and from all foreign countries in total. If the revenues from one foreign country are material, then those revenues are to be disclosed separately.

C. The same disclosure as B above is required for long-lived assets other than financial instruments, long-term customer relationships with a financial institution, mortgage and other servicing rights, and deferred tax assets.

D. Major customers: If the revenue from a single customer amounts to 10% or more of the firm's revenues, this fact must be disclosed, including the amount of revenues from each such customer, and the operating segment or segments that earn that revenue. The identity of the customer need not be disclosed.

VIII. Comprehensive Example

 Example: The Smith Company has four operating segments which are identified below. Information related to the current accounting year is also shown below. The revenue column constitutes the firm's entire revenues.

Segment	Total Revenues	Operating Profit (Loss)	Identifiable Assets
Clothing	$200	$50	$100
Sports Equipment	$150	($60)	$90
Beverage	$50	($10)	$25
Furniture	$300	$150	$200
Totals	**$700**	**$130**	**$415**

Additional information: Revenues related to internal transactions totaled $20. Of this amount, $10 of revenues was recorded by the Clothing segment and $10 was reported by the Furniture segment.

Revenue test: 10% of $700 = $70

Reportable Segments: Clothing, Sports Equipment, and Furniture

Operating profit test: 10% of $200 = $20

Note: The combined operating profit for those segments with positive profit ($200) exceeded the absolute value of the combined operating loss for those segments with losses ($70). Therefore, $200 is used for the test.

Reportable Segments: Clothing, Sports Equipment, and Furniture.

Note that Sports Equipment has an operating loss but the absolute value of that loss exceeds the $20 test amount.

Identifiable asset test: 10% of $415 = $41.5

Reportable Segments: Clothing, Sports Equipment, and Furniture.

Clothing, Sports Equipment, and Furniture all meet at least one of the tests described above and are reportable segments. Only Beverages is not a reportable segment (but it is an operating segment). The results for each of the three quantitative tests are shown above for completeness but an operating segment need meet only one of the tests in order to qualify as an operating segment.

75% Test:

75% of $680 = $510. ($680 = $700 - $20 internal revenue). Consolidated revenues are computed by removing intersegment revenues.

(The $680 amount is the firm's external revenue.)

External Revenue of Clothing Segment	$190
External Revenue of Sports Equipment Segment	$150
External Revenue of Furniture Segment	$290
Total External Revenue	**$630**

The 75% Test is met collectively by the three reportable segments because $630 equals or exceeds $510. No additional reportable segments need be identified.

IX. U.S. GAAP - IFRS Differences

A. The international standard for segment reporting conforms in most respects with the corresponding U.S. standard adopted several years before the IASB's standard. One important difference is that, for reportable segments, the international standard requires disclosure of total liabilities if that information is provided to the firm's chief operating decision maker.

B. Liabilities are also included in the reconciliations of segment information with total firm data.

Computer Software Costs

This lesson presents the accounting and reporting for computer software costs.

After studying this lesson, you should be able to:

1. *Describe the accounting for software costs prior to and after technological feasibility.*

2. *Calculate the amortization of capitalized software costs.*

3. *Identify the major difference in IFRS and U.S. GAAP with respect to software costs.*

I. **Background**

   A. In the development of computer software, when does the research and development activity cease, and when is there sufficient probability that a product will be marketed?

   B. The costs incurred during research and development (R&D)of the software will be expensed, while the costs incurred subsequent to research and development activities will be capitalized.

   C. As per ASC 985, research and development activities continue until the technological feasibility of the software has been established. The difference between R&D and Software is the latter establishes a point after which development costs are capitalized to an intangible asset and subsequently amortized. In contrast, all R&D is expensed as incurred.

II. **Technological Feasibility**

   A. The critical point for software cost accounting is technological feasibility. The establishment of the technological feasibility of the software typically occurs when the program model or working model of the software is complete. The product is not yet ready to market, but the commitment is made at this point to continue with the product. There is sufficient reason, at this point, to allocate additional resources to the effort.

   B. The costs incurred subsequent to the establishment of the technological feasibility will be capitalized and amortized over the estimated economic life of the software.

III. **Breakdown of Software Costs and Their Accounting --** This listing of costs appears in the chronological order of incurrence with respect to a particular software product.

   A. **Research and development --** Costs incurred to establish technological feasibility (costs incurred before technological feasibility is established) *expense as incurred, as R&D expense.*

   1. The quest for technological feasibility is the activity in software development most similar to general R&D. During this period, the firm has not reached a decision on the feasibility of its product. Costs during this period include planning, designing, coding, and testing of programs.

   B. **Costs subsequent to establishing technological feasibility --** Through the completion of product masters: *capitalize as computer software costs (intangible asset) and amortize.*

   1. This second category of costs includes additional costs of coding, testing, debugging, and preparation of final product master and final documentation manual. It does not include duplication of product masters and manuals. This category ends when a product master is ready for duplication.

    2. This is the only category of software costs that is capitalized as an intangible asset and subsequently amortized.

C. Software production costs -- (Duplication of software and manuals) *Capitalize in inventory and expense through cost of goods sold as sales take place.*

D. Customer support and maintenance -- *Expense as incurred.*

E. Summary of Accounting Treatment of Software Costs

    1. Software development (coding and testing) before technological feasibility: dr. R&D expense;

    2. Software development (coding and testing) after technological feasibility to production of product masters: dr. Capitalized Software Development Costs;

    3. Duplication of product, packaging, etc.: dr. Inventory of product;

    4. Sell product: dr. Cost of Goods Sold;

    5. Customer service: dr. Expense.

IV. Amortization of Capitalized Computer Software Costs -- These are amortized using one of the two following methods, whichever results in a larger amortization amount. Each year the computation for both methods must be made to ensure the larger amount is recognized. The same method need not produce the larger amount each year. The amortization is an operating expense.

A. Revenue Method

> Amortization for current year = B x R
>
>   Where: B = book value of capitalized software costs at beginning of year
>
>   R = (current year revenue) / (current year revenue + estimated future revenue)

B. Straight-Line Method

> Amortization for current year = B/N
>
>   Where: B = book value of capitalized software costs at beginning of year
>
>   N = number of years remaining in product sales life at beginning of year

C. Cautions

    1. Remember to choose the higher of the two amounts each period. Also, the inputs to both methods change each year. The beginning book value changes, as does the estimate of future revenue and remaining years in the product life.

    2. After amortizing the capitalized costs for a particular year, the ending book value is compared with the net realizable value of the software (future estimated gross revenues less operating costs). If the ending book value exceeds the net realizable value, the book value is written down to net realizable value, with a loss recognized. The net realizable value becomes the beginning book value for the next period, for purposes of amortization. Write-ups are not allowed.

    See the following example.

Example:
The software costs incurred for a product developed for sale are:

Costs incurred to establish technological feasibility	$100,000
Costs incurred after establishment of technological feasibility and through the completion of product masters	200,000

Entries:
R&D Expense	100,000	
Cash, other accounts		100,000
Computer Software Costs (intangible asset)	200,000	
Cash, other accounts		200,000

(The product is marketed at the beginning of year 2 and is expected to have a 3-year sales life)

Revenue from software sales in year 2	$1,000,000
Estimate of revenue for years 3 and 4 (total)	3,000,000
Total current year and future estimated revenue	4,000,000

Amortization of computer software costs:

Revenue method amortization = $200,000($1,000,000/$4,000,000) = $50,000

Straight-line method amortization = $200,000/3 = $66,667

(higher of the two amounts)

Entry:
Amortization of Computer Software Costs	66,667	
Computer Software Costs		66,667

Book value of computer software costs at beginning of year $200,000 - $66,667 = $133,333

Revenue from software sales in year 3	$1,750,000
Estimate of revenue for year 4	500,000
Total current year and future estimated revenue	$2,250,000

Amortization of computer software costs:

Revenue method amortization = $133,333($1,750,000/$2,250,000) = $103,703

Straight-line method amortization = $133,333/2 = $66,667

Entry (at year-end):
Amortization of Computer Software Costs	103,703	
Computer Software Costs		103,703

The ending year 3 book value of computer software costs, reported in the balance sheet, is $29,630 ($133,333 - $103,703). This example shows that the same amortization method need not be used each year.

V. Software Costs and IFRS

A. IFRS does not specifically address internal software costs; therefore, the rules of research and development are applied. Under IFRS, software costs for research are expensed and those for development are capitalized. U.S. GAAP specifically addresses software costs and identifies the threshold of technological feasibility for capitalization.

Subsequent Events

This lesson presents the accounting and reporting for subsequent events.

After studying this lesson, you should be able to:

1. *Define a subsequent event.*

2. *Identify the key disclosures of subsequent events.*

I. **Subsequent Events**

A. **Definition and Examples**

> **Definition:**
> *Subsequent Events*: Subsequent events are also called "post balance sheet" events. Such events occur: *after* the date of the financial statements, but *before* the statements are issued or are available to be issued.

1. **Examples**

    a. Examples include uncollectibility of receivables, lawsuits, changes in corporate structure, issuances of debt and equity securities, major acquisitions, and significant gains and losses.

    b. Although the financial statement date is the "closing date" for reporting, users of financial statements typically read the disclosures as if they are current as of the date of issue. Furthermore, the full disclosure principle mandates that all relevant information be disclosed.

2. **Two Categories --** There are two categories of subsequent events, each requiring different accounting treatment:

    a. The condition leading to the subsequent event **existed** at the balance sheet date;

    b. The condition leading to the subsequent event **did not exist** at the balance sheet date-the condition arose after the balance sheet date.

B. **Subsequent events - *conditions existed* at the balance sheet date --** The financial statements for these events should reflect all information available up to the balance sheet date. This (first) category of subsequent events requires recognition in the financial statements and include all events that provide evidence about conditions existing at the balance sheet date including estimates used in the process of preparing the statements. Footnotes may be included to supplement and explain the recognition.

See the following example.

> **Example:**
> **1.** A major customer's financial situation has been deteriorating during the reporting year (20x4), with bankruptcy being declared early in 20x5. As a result, a receivable from that customer is deemed worthless after the 20x4 balance sheet date but before the issuance of the financial statements. The loss from the write-off of the receivable should be recognized in 20x4 income, and the 20x4 balance sheet should reflect the write-off because the condition leading to the bankruptcy existed at the balance sheet date.
>
> **2.** Information is discovered early in 20x5 indicating that the total useful life of certain plant assets will be significantly less than originally estimated due to obsolescence. This condition developed gradually during 20x4. The useful lives of the affected assets should be re-estimated and depreciation expense for 20x4 should reflect those revised estimates.

C. **Subsequent events - *conditions did not exist* at the balance sheet date --** This (second) category of subsequent event requires footnote disclosure (only) of events having material effects on the financial statements. The footnote disclosures include a description of the nature of the event and an estimate of the financial effect, or a statement that an estimate cannot be made. Recognition is inappropriate because the condition existed only after the balance sheet date

> **Example:**
> **1.** A major customer declared bankruptcy as a result of a casualty in early 20x5. As a result, a receivable from that customer is deemed worthless after the 20x4 balance sheet date but before the issuance of the financial statements. The loss from the worthless receivable is disclosed in the footnotes, but recognition is postponed until the 20x5 statements, because the casualty occurred after 20x4.
>
> **2.** A firm completes a large issuance of bonds early in 20x5, before the issuance of the 20x4 statements. The footnotes to the 20x4 statements should disclose the relevant information about the issuance, but recognition is postponed until the 20x5 statements.

D. **Period of evaluation for subsequent events**

   1. The period during which to evaluate subsequent events is the period between the balance sheet date, and either

      a. The date the financial statements are **issued** - when they are widely distributed (e.g., filed with the SEC) for general use, or

      b. The date the financial statements are **available to be issued** - when they are complete, comply with GAAP, and have all the approvals necessary for issuance.

   2. Entities (including publicly traded entities) that widely distribute their financial statements use the "issued" date. All other entities use the "available to be issued" date. These entities are not required to evaluate subsequent events after the point of availability.

E. **Related situations --** The recognition and disclosure requirements for subsequent events apply to both annual and interim financial statements but do not apply to subsequent events or transactions that are governed by other applicable GAAP.

   1. **Contingent Liabilities**

      a. This topic is addressed in detail in another section. The reporting principles for contingent liabilities are similar to those of subsequent events and in some cases overlap. However, for recognized contingencies (those that are probable and estimable as of the balance sheet date), the event confirming the loss, reduction in asset, or recognition of liability need not take place before the issuance of the financial statements.

b. For example, a firm recognizes warranty expense and a warranty liability at the end of 20x4 on sales recognized in 20x4 because warranty claims are probable and the amount to service the claims is estimable. The condition giving rise to the expense and liability existed at the balance sheet date (the obligation to service the claims and the probable nature of the claims) but the warranty claims need not occur before the issuance of the balance sheet in order for the liability to be recognized at the end of 20x4.

c. In addition, for contingent liabilities, the quality that distinguishes recognition from footnote disclosure only is the likelihood of the future event and whether the economic sacrifice is estimable. Thus, although the situation appears to be similar to subsequent events accounting, a specific accounting principle governs this accounting.

d. Gain contingencies are not recognized although it could be argued that the conditions giving rise to the gain existed before the balance sheet date.

2. **Refinancing Current Debt**

a. This topic is addressed in detail in another section. A firm can reclassify a current liability as non-current if it accomplishes one of the following after the balance sheet date but before the financial statements are issued:

   i. Issue stock to extinguish the debt;

   ii. Refinance the current liability with a non-current liability; or

   iii. Enter into an irrevocable agreement to refinance the current liability with a non-current liability.

b. The recognition (change in classification to non-current) takes place during the subsequent event period, but it can be argued that the decision was made to effect the reclassification after the balance sheet date. Thus, although the situation appears to be similar to subsequent events accounting, a specific accounting principle governs this accounting.

c. Stock dividends and splits after the balance sheet date are treated as if they occurred as of the balance sheet date. Although it could be argued that because the dividend or split should not be recognized because it took place after the balance sheet date, a specific accounting principle requires recognition.

II. **Subsequent Events and IFRS**

A. IFRS does not require adjustment to the balance sheet for share splits or reverse splits occurring after the reporting date, but before the financial statements are issued.

Not-for-Profit Accounting and Reporting

Introduction to Types of Not-For-Profit Entities and Standard Setting

This lesson presents a brief overview of the types of not-for-profit entities and the organizations that set accounting standards for these entities.

After studying this lesson, you should be able to:

1. *Describe the standard setting organization for each type of not-for-profit entity.*

2. *List the four main categories of not-for-profit organizations.*

I. **Background --** Not-for-profit (NFP) organizations comprise a wide variety of institutions, including some governmentally affiliated entities such as state universities and city and county hospitals. For many years, these organizations received little attention and guidance regarding their recording and reporting rules. As a result , standards were developed piecemeal by national industry associations (e.g., National Association of College & University Business Officers) and "industry" audit guides produced by the AICPA. When FASB was created, NFP organizations were included under its purview, but it was not until the release of Statements #116 and #117 twenty years later that accounting and reporting issues for NFP organizations were addressed in a meaningful, comprehensive manner.

II. **Categories of Not-for-Profit Organizations**

A. Historically, NFPOs have been grouped into the following four categories. Although accounting and reporting differences among the categories have been dramatically reduced, each category retains a few unique characteristics. The four categories are:

1. **Hospitals and Other Health Care Entities --** Includes both public and private hospitals, as well as nursing homes, home health agencies, continuing care retirement communities, health maintenance organizations, etc.;

2. **Colleges and Universities --** Includes both public and private four-year colleges and universities;

   a. **Exception --** Two-year institutions with taxing authority (i.e., most community colleges) are excluded from this category.

3. **Voluntary Health, and Welfare Organizations (VHWOs) --** These organizations promote research and education in a wide variety of social and health-related areas; they frequently offer free or low cost services to the general public or to special groups; they receive the majority of their funding from voluntary contributions from the general public and from grants; many of these organizations have local branches that are associated with national organizations with the same objectives;

   > **Example:**
   > Arthritis Foundation, United Way, American Cancer Society, Boy Scouts, Girl Scouts, etc. Almost all of these organizations are classified as "private" not-for-profit organizations.

4. **Other Nonprofit Organizations (ONPOs) --** These encompass a diverse group of organizations including social clubs, political parties, museums, fraternities, unions, athletic clubs, environmental action organizations, etc.; while the vast majority of these organizations are classified as "private," governmentally affiliated organizations are occasionally found within this category (public museums, historical sites, etc.)

III. Jurisdiction over Not-for-Profit Organizations

A. FASB -- Regulates the accounting and reporting practices for all "private" not-for-profit-organizations; GASB governs governmentally affiliated organizations.

B. "Private" NFPs -- Most not-for-profit organizations fall under this category; FAS 116 prescribes the rules for recognition of contributions and FAS 117 prescribes the external reporting requirements for all private NFP organizations;

    1. Traditional reporting practices (Fund model) are still expected to be used for internal reporting and still appear on the CPA exam.

C. "Public" (governmentally affiliated) NFPs -- These organizations are predominantly publicly funded hospitals and universities, although museums, parks, and landmarks can fall into this category as well.

    1. They use fund reporting in their independent statements, and for reporting purposes are usually combined with the primary government entity.

Financial Reporting

This lesson presents a summary of the primary financial statements for not-for-profit entities.

After studying this lesson, you should be able to:

1. *Describe the form and content of the statement of financial position.*

2. *Describe the form and content of the statement of activities.*

3. *Describe the form and content of the statement of cash flows.*

4. *Describe the form and content of the statement of functional expenses and know which type of not-for-profit should prepare this statement.*

I. **Statement #117 - Financial Statement Presentation --** This statement identifies a single set of statements that is to be prepared for all private NFP organizations. In these statements, **fund information is no longer presented**; assets and liabilities from all funds are combined and the Fund Balances are **translated to one of three classifications of Net Assets: Unrestricted Net Assets, Temporarily Restricted Net Assets, or Permanently Restricted Net Assets.**

   A. Three statements are required for all organizations:

   1. **Statement of Financial Position**;

   2. **Statement of Activity**;

   3. **Statement of Cash Flows**.

   B. An additional statement, the **Statement of Functional Expenses**, is required for Voluntary Health and Welfare organizations only.

II. **Statement of Financial Position**

   A. The Statement of Financial Position is required for all organizations. It differs from the "balance sheets" previously prepared by NFP organizations in that:

   1. It does not include any fund information but instead is presented **"for the organization as a whole;"**

   2. The term "Fund Balance" is replaced by **"Net Assets;"**

   3. Net Assets are broken down into three categories based on the nature of any **donor-imposed restrictions**:

      a. Unrestricted;

      b. Temporarily Restricted;

      c. Permanently Restricted.

   B. FAS 117 Statement of Financial Position

   See the following example.

Not-for-Profit Organization

Statements of Financial Position

June 30, 20x1 and 20x0

(in thousands)

	20x1	20x0
Assets:		
Cash and cash equivalents	$ 75	$ 460
Accounts and interest receivable	2,250	1,670
Inventories and prepaid expenses	610	1,000
Contributions receivable	3,025	2,700
Short-term investments	1,400	1,000
Assets restricted to investment		
in land, buildings, and equipment	5,210	4,560
Land, buildings, and equipment (Note A)	61,700	63,590
Long-term investments	217,950	203,500
Total assets	$292,220	$278,480
Liabilities and net assets:		
Accounts payable	$ 2,570	$ 1,050
Refundable advance		650
Grants payable	875	1,300
Notes payable		1,140
Annuity obligations	1,685	1,700
Long-term debt	5,500	6,500
Total liabilities	$ 10,630	$ 12,340
Net assets:		
Unrestricted (Note E)	$ 90,838	$ 78,940
Temporarily restricted (Note B)	48,732	50,200
Permanently restricted (Note C)	142,020	137,000
Total net assets	281,590	266,140
Total liabilities and net assets	$292,220	$278,480

III. Statement of Activity

A. The Statement of Activity is required for all organizations. The principal requirement of the statement is to provide the Change in Net Assets for each of the three classifications of Net Assets (Unrestricted, Temporarily Restricted and Permanently Restricted) and for the organization as a whole. This means that all revenue and expense amounts must be reported as belonging to one of these three classifications.

B. The Statement of Activity has four principal sections:

1. Revenues and Gains;

2. Net Assets Released from Restrictions;

3. Expenses and Losses;

4. Change in Net Assets (including reconciliation of beginning and ending Net Assets).

Note: The reporting of revenues and expenses on the Statement of Activities is heavily tested on the CPA exam. Be sure to memorize the format of this statement and understand how it is used. The areas of emphasis are classification of revenues, classification of expenses, timing of release of assets from restrictions, and evaluation of the effect on Temporarily Restricted Net Assets and restricted Net Assets when donor restricted monies are spent for their intended purpose.

C. Statement of Activity Format A

Format A

Not-for-Profit Organization

Statement of Activities

Year Ended June 30, 20x1

(in thousands)

Changes in unrestricted assets:

Revenues and gains:

Contributions	$ 8,500
Fees	5,400
Investment income on endowment	3,600
Other investment income	2,850
Net unrealized and realized gains on endowment	4,428
Net unrealized and realized gains on other investments	3,800
Other	150
Total unrestricted revenues and gains	28,728
Net assets released from restrictions (Note D)	15,220
Total unrestricted revenues, gains, and other support	43,948

Expenses and losses:

Program A	13,100
Program B	8,540
Program C	5,760
Management and general	2,420

Fund raising	2,150
Total expenses (Note G)	31,970
Fire loss	80
Total expenses and losses	32,050
Increase in unrestricted net assets	11,898
Changes in temporarily restricted net assets:	
Contributions	8,250
Investment income on annuity agreements	180
Investment income on endowment	2,400
Net unrealized and realized gains on endowment	2,952
Actuarial loss on annuity obligations	(30)
Net assets released from restrictions (Note D)	(15,220)
Decrease in temporarily restricted net assets	(1,468)
Changes in permanently restricted net assets:	
Contributions	280
Investment income on endowment	120
Net unrealized and realized gains on endowment (Note F)	4,620
Increase in permanently restricted net assets	5,020
Increase in net assets	15,450
Net assets at beginning of year	266,140
Net assets at end of year	$281,590

IV. Revenues and Gains Section

A. Note the following items in this section

1. Contribution revenue can be reported in all three classifications of net assets; this is also true of investment income and realized and unrealized gains on securities.

2. Exchange revenues (fees, dues, charges for services, etc.) can only be reported under Unrestricted Net Assets.

V. Expenses and Losses Section

A. Note the following items in this section

1. *All expenses are incurred from Unrestricted Net Assets.*

2. Expenses must be reported using **"functional classifications."** There are two primary ways to classifying the expenses.

3. **Programming Services --** Expenditures made to further the main mission of the organization. The line items listed under this category vary substantially from organization to organization but frequently include items such as Education, Outreach, Research, Clinical Care, etc.

4. **Supporting Services --** Expenditures made to provide the organizational infrastructure and to raise resources. Supporting services are always reported on two line items:

    a. **Management and General --** Administrative and support expenses such as the director's salary, office supplies, computer services;

    b. **Fund Raising --** Monies used to encourage contributions to the organization including advertisements, promotional literature and mailings, and "special events" such as galas, telethons, auctions, and other fund drives.

> **Note:** The separation of expenses into Program Services and Supporting Services classifications is extremely important as the percentage of revenues spent on Supporting Services is frequently used to measure the efficiency of a NFP organization. The examiners often include questions in which an expenditure is partially for a Program Service and partially for a Supporting Service (management and General or Fund Raising). In these instances, it is important to split the expenditure into the correct functional classifications.
>
> **Losses** are shown as line items after expenses and can occur in any classification of Net Assets.

VI. Net Assets Released from the Restrictions Section

A. Although contributions, which have restrictions on their use, are reported under Temporarily Restricted Net Assets, when the monies are expended for the intended purpose, the expense is reported under Unrestricted Net Assets, we need a mechanism to **reduce the amount of Temporarily Restricted Net Assets** and to **increase the amount of Unrestricted Net Assets** to cover the expenditure. This is the function of the section titled **"Net Assets Released from Restrictions."** Whenever the temporary restrictions placed on resources have been "satisfied," we transfer assets from Temporarily Restricted Net Assets into Unrestricted Net Assets.

B. We can move these resources in three instances, which correspond with the three types of restrictions placed on the resources:

1. **Satisfaction of Program Restrictions --** The resources have been spent for the intended operating purpose, which always results in the recognition of an expense;

2. **Satisfaction of Asset Acquisition Restrictions --** The resources have been spent for the intended capital purpose, which always results in the increase of an asset account;

3. **Satisfaction of Time Restrictions --** The time or event specified in the restriction on the resources has occurred; note that it is not necessary that the resources be spent.

C. Note the following on the Statement of Activities: 1) there is always an increase in Unrestricted Net Assets; 2) there is always a decrease in Temporarily Restricted Net Assets; and 3) there is never an entry under Permanently Restricted Net Assets.

Study Tip: Most questions in this area will ask for the "affect on net assets when monies restricted to a certain type of expenditure are actually expended for that purpose." Two separate transactions must be considered: the expense itself, which will reduce Unrestricted Net Assets, and the transfer of resources in the Net Assets Released from Restrictions Section, which increases Unrestricted Net Assets and decreases Temporarily Restricted Net Assets.

VII. Change in Net Assets

A. The "bottom line" of the Statement of Activity is entitled **"Change in Net Assets"** *not* "Net Income." The Change in Net Assets line item is always followed by the reconciliation of the ending balance in each of the three categories of Net Assets. That is:

+ Change in Net Assets

± Beginning Net Assets

= Ending Net Assets

B. Ending Net Assets totals on the Statement of Activity should reconcile to the Net Asset totals on the Statement of Financial Position.

VIII. Statement of Cash Flows

A. The Statement of Cash Flows is required for all organizations. Its format is identical to the Statement of Cash Flows required for for-profit organizations and consequently it is not heavily tested. The principal difference lies in the treatment of contributions that are restricted for long-term purposes - that is, resources that are subject to capital restrictions - which are reported in the Financing Activities section. Unrestricted contributions and contributions subject to Program or Time Restrictions are reported in the Operating Activities section.

B. The three classifications of cash flows and some examples of the items found in each section are shown below:

1. **Cash Flows from Operating Activities --** Includes **unrestricted contributions, unrestricted investment earnings, revenue restricted for operating purposes (Program Restrictions)**, revenue from exchange transactions, and **operating expenditures** (salaries, supplies, interest expense), including grants to other organizations;

2. **Cash Flows from Investing Activities --** Includes inflows from the sale of capital assets, marketable securities, etc., and outflows for the purchase of capital assets, etc.;

3. **Cash Flows from Financing Activities --** Include contributions and investment revenues restricted for long-term purposes (e.g., restrictions for acquisition of capital assets, endowments) as well as debt proceeds, debt repayment, lease payments, etc.

C. FAS 117 Statement of Cash Flows: See the following illustration.

Indirect Method

Not-for-Profit Organizations

Statement of Cash Flows

Year Ended June 30, 20x1

(in thousands)

Cash flows from operating activities:

Change in net assets	$ 15,450

Adjustments to reconcile change in net assets to net cash used by operating activities:

Depreciation	3,200
Fire loss	80
Actuarial loss on annuity obligations	30
Increase in accounts and interest receivable	(460)
Decrease in inventories and prepaid expenses	390
Increase in contributions receivable	(325)
Increase in accounts payable	1,520
Decrease in refundable advance	(650)
Decrease in grants payable	(425)
Contributions restricted for long-term investment	(2,740)
Interest and dividends restricted for long-term investment	(300)
Net unrealized and realized gains on long-term investments	(15,800)
Net cash used by operating activities	(30)

Cash flows from investing activities:

Insurance proceeds from fire loss on building	250
Purchase of equipment	(1,500)
Proceeds from sale of investments	76,100
Purchase of investments	(74,900)
Net cash used by investing activities	(50)

Cash flows from financing activities

Proceeds from contributions restricted for:

Investment in endowment	200
Investment in term endowment	70
Investment in plant	1,200
Investment subject to annuity agreements	200
	1,680

Other financing activities:	
Interest and dividends restricted for reinvestment	300
Payments of annuity obligations	(145)
Payments on notes payable	(1,140)
Payments on long-term debt	(1,000)
	(1,985)
Net cash used by financing activities	(305)
Net decrease in cash and cash equivalents	(385)
	======
Cash and cash equivalents at beginning of year	460
Cash and cash equivalents at end of year	$ 75

IX. Statement of Functional Expenses

A. The Statement of Functional Expenses is required *only for Voluntary Health and Welfare Organizations, but is recommended* for all NFP organizations. (This is the most frequently asked question about this statement!) The purpose of the Statement of Functional Expenses is to take the functional expense categories shown in the Statement of Activities (Program Services and Supporting Services) and break them down into "natural expense" categories (i.e. rent, utilities, salaries, depreciation, etc.).

B. FAS 117 Statement of Functional Expenses:

See the following example.

Statement of Functional Expenses

Illustrative VHWO/ONPO

Statement of Functional Expenses

For the Year Ended December 31, 20x1

	Program Services			Supporting Services			
	Research	Education	Total	Management and General	Fund Raising	Total	Total Expenses
Salaries	$16,000	$27,000	$43,000	$30,000	$15,000	$45,000	$88,000
Employee health and retirement benefits	1,289	3,340	4,629	4,648	1,284	5,932	10,561
Payroll taxes, etc.	644	1,670	2,314	2,324	642	2,966	5,280
Total salaries and related expenses	17,933	32,010	49,943	36,972	16,926	53,898	103,841
Professional fees & contract service payments	34,996	90,710	125,706	13,428	2,283	15,711	141,417
Supplies	4,852		4,852	9,296	6,000	15,296	20,148
Telephone and telegraph	1,245	1,670	2,915	7,747	5,965	13,712	16,627
Postage and shipping	1,192	1,670	2,862	6,714	8,015	14,729	17,391
Occupancy	10,000		10,000	15,494	7,707	23,201	33,201
Rental of equipment	322	835	1,157	1,549	4,567	6,116	7,273
Local transportation	966	2,305	3,471	11,879	8,563	20,442	23,913
Conferences, conventions, meetings	2,577	6,680	9,257	19,626	3,711	23,337	32,594
Printing & publications	1,289	3,340	4,629	7,231	18,268	25,499	30,128
Awards and grants	16,106	41,747	57,853				57,853
Interest				20,000		20,000	20,000
Meals					20,000	20,000	20,000
Gratuities					5,000	5,000	5,000
Miscellaneous	322	833	1,155	8,264	5,995	14,259	15,414
Total expenses before depreciation	91,800	182,000	273,800	113,000	271,200	246,200	545,000
Depreciation of buildings, improvements, and equipment	12,000	2,000	14,000	13,000	3,000	16,000	30,000
Total Expenses	103,800	184,000	287,800	171,200	116,000	287,200	575,000
Less: Expenses deducted directly from revenues					(25,000)	(25,000)	(25,000)
Total expenses reported by function	$103,800	$184,000	$287,800	$171,200	$91,000	$262,200	$550,000

Special Issues

This lesson describes some special issues pertaining to financial reporting for not-for-profit entities.

After studying this lesson, you should be able to:

1. *Describe the accounting and reporting of inexhaustible fixed assets (e.g., collections).*

2. *List three types of endowments that do not meet the requirements of a regular, "pure" endowment.*

I. "Inexhaustible" Fixed Assets

A. Inexhaustible fixed assets include works of art, cultural treasures, historical documents and property, etc. and are subject to special rules. In particular:

1. Inexhaustible fixed assets donated to the organization need **not be capitalized.** This means that, when such an asset is donated to the organization, we do not need to make an accounting entry to record the transaction and the value of the contribution and asset will not appear on the face of the financial statements. Further, if such an item is sold and the proceeds are used to purchase another inexhaustible fixed asset, those transactions also need not be recorded or reported on the face of the financial statements. Note that, although these transactions do not appear on the face of the financial statements, *they are disclosed in the notes.*

2. Depreciation on these inexhaustible fixed assets *need not* be recorded.

B. In order to use these procedures, the assets must fit the requirements of assets known as "collectibles" or "collections": Three conditions of the assets must be met. The assets must be:

1. Held for public exhibition, education, or research rather than financial gain;

2. Protected, kept unencumbered, cared for, and preserved;

3. Subject to a policy that requires proceeds from sales of collection items to be used to acquire other items for collections.

> **Example:** A local collector donates a Picasso painting to the Henderson Museum of Modern Art. Since Henderson already has several Picassos, it sells the painting and uses the proceeds to purchase a Calder mobile. The mobile will be displayed in Henderson's public galleries and will be well-protected.
>
> Because the art works meet the definition of a "collectible," Henderson need not record the donation of the Picasso or the subsequent sale and purchase of the Calder. Instead, these transactions are disclosed in the notes.

II. Investments

A. NFP organizations frequently hold significant amounts of investments. Statement #124 - Accounting for Certain Investments Held by Not-For-Profit Organizations addresses the accounting issues associated with these investments by NFP organizations. For the most part, accounting for these investments is handled in the same manner as it is for for-profit organizations. That is, NFP organizations must report (all) their marketable securities at fair value. Changes in market value are recognized on the Statement of Activities as unrealized gains and losses during the period of the change.

B. However, unlike for-profit organizations, NFP organizations do not break debt securities out into Trading, Available-for-Sale, and Held-to-Maturity categories. Because the Held-to-Maturity category is the only one that allows for valuation at other than market value, for NFP organizations, *debt securities* are *always* valued at fair value.

III. Endowments

A. Endowments are contributions to the organization from third parties for which the principal (corpus) must "remain intact in perpetuity." Earnings on the endowment may be **expendable-restricted** (expendable but only for specified purposes), **expendable-unrestricted** (expendable at any time, for any purpose) or **non-expendable**, depending on the stipulations of the donor. Endowments that have these characteristics are called "regular" endowments or "pure" endowments and are recorded as Permanently Restricted assets.

B. Other types of contributions are similar to regular endowments but fail to meet one of the regular endowment criteria.

   1. **Quasi-endowments --** Amounts set aside by the governing board of the organization, rather than outside sources, of which the principal must be retained and invested. Although these resources act like an endowment, they cannot be considered regular endowments as the restrictions on endowment resources must come from an external party. This type of endowment is know as a **quasi-endowment**. Quasi-endowments are not included in Permanently Restricted Net Assets but are **included with Unrestricted Net Assets**.

   2. **Term endowments --** Gifts and bequests from third parties which are to be retained and invested for a period of time or until a specific event occurs. However, after the criterion has been met, the full amount can be spent. The earnings on the invested amount are paid to a separate beneficiary (usually a spouse or a child) until the criterion is met. These contributions are known as **term endowments** and, because they can ultimately be spent, they are **classified as Temporarily Restricted Net Assets**.

> **Study Tip:**
> The examiners frequently try to confuse board designated funds with quasi-endowments. Candidates should pay particular attention to indications of how the principal is to be treated:
> If the principal can be spent, it is a board-designated fund;
> If only the earnings can be spent, it is a quasi-endowment.

   3. **Board designated funds --** Amounts set aside by the governing board of the organization to be spent for specific purposes; these funds are not endowments because the principal can be spent. Board-designated funds are frequently set apart from other unrestricted assets by establishing an account similar to a reservation of Retained Earnings. The account is normally titled "Unrestricted Net Assets Designated for _____" and is deducted from the total Unrestricted Net Assets.

> **Example:**
> Mantega Hospital received a $50,000 gift of securities that are to be retained and invested. The earnings may be used as Mantega wishes. Mantega's governing board designated, for special uses, $30,000 which had originated from unrestricted gifts. It set aside $80,000, the earnings from which are to be used to help fund charity care.
>
> Mantega reports $50,000 as a regular endowment (Permanently Restricted Net Assets); $30,000 is classified as a board designated fund (included in Unrestricted Net Assets); the remaining $80,000 is classified as a quasi-endowment (included in Unrestricted Net Assets).

IV. Earnings on Endowments

A. Earnings on endowments are reported as Endowment Income or Investment Income on the accrual basis. The income may be reported in any of the three classes of net assets depending on the restrictions on the use of the income:

1. If there are no restrictions on use, then report income under Unrestricted Net Assets.

2. If the income must be spent for specified purposes, or may not be spent until a specified time or event, report under Temporarily Restricted Net Assets;

3. If the income may not be spent, but must be used to increase or maintain the corpus, report under Permanently Restricted Net Assets.

> **Example:**
> Erica Gardner gives $100,000 to Borgans Children's Hospital to be used as a loan fund for families traveling to be with their children at the hospital. Interest charged on the loans (endowment earnings) is put back into the fund to increase the amount available to lend. The interest is reported under Permanently Restricted Net Assets.

Support, Revenues, Contributions, and Net Assets

This lesson describes contribution revenue recognition for not-for-profit entities.

After studying this lesson, you should be able to:

1. *Describe the four primary characteristics of a contribution.*

2. *Describe the difference between a condition and a restriction.*

3. *Describe the three categories of net assets.*

I. **Non-exchange Transactions --** "Contributions" are non-reciprocal receipts of assets or services. They are not "exchange" transactions, in which each party in the transaction gives up something of value. They are asymmetrical transactions in which one party relinquishes something of value to another party, but the other party provides nothing in return. The item of value may be cash, marketable securities, inventory, property, or even services (subject to limitations noted later). Statement #116-Accounting for Contributions Received and Contributions Made provides guidance on revenue recognition for non-exchange transactions.

II. **Contribution Recognition --** *All contributions are recognized as contribution revenue in the period in which the contribution is made, regardless of whether or not it is received in cash.* Donations other than cash are recorded at **fair value as of the date of the gift**.

III. **Pledges**

A. Promises to contribute ("pledges") may also be recognized as contributions as long as they are *unconditional. Conditional* promises to give are promises that depend on a specific event occurring in the future. They *cannot* be recognized as contributions until the uncertain future event has occurred. Conditional promises to give are recognized when the conditions are *substantially met* or when the *likelihood that the conditions will* **not** *be met is remote.*

> **Note:** The timing of the receipt of cash related to pledges is a frequent distractor in CPA exam questions. The examiners will give information about the pledge and about when the pledge was paid. The cash payment information should almost always be ignored. **Revenue recognition is not tied to the receipt of cash;** a pledge to contribute in the current period is recognized as revenue when the pledge is made, **not** when the cash is received (but see special rules for multi-year pledges below).

See the following example.

Example:
1. Simmons promises to give $1,000,000 to World Crisis Services to purchase food supplies for a drought-ridden country. Simmons also promises to give an additional $500,000 if the drought is not broken in six months. The $1,000,000 should be recognized as a Contribution since it is an unconditional promise. The $500,000 cannot be recognized as a Contribution since it is conditioned upon an uncertain future event.

2. Jesse Morgan pledges $10,000 to the McMillan School, a private not-for-profit elementary school that maintains a culturally diverse student body, as long as the average standardized tests scores for the student body are above 75% of the national average. The average standardized test scores for the McMillan School student body have always been above 85% in its 25-year history. Since the likelihood that the test average would fall below 75% for this year is remote, McMillan would recognize the promise to give immediately.

3. QuickCure Hospital receives pledges of $80,000 in November of the current year. It receives $50,000 cash related to the pledges in December and the remaining $30,000 in January. QuickCure's fiscal year runs from January 1 to December 31. QuickCure recognizes revenue of $80,000 in the current year.

B. Unconditional pledges -- *Are recognized as contribution revenue net* **of the estimated uncollectible pledges (allowance for uncollectible pledges).**

Example:
Little City Public Television recently held a fund drive and received $300,000 in pledges. Historically, the station has been unable to collect 30% of their pledges. Little City Public Television should recognize the contribution revenue of $210,000 ($300,000 - ($300,000 X 30%)).

The accounting entry for pledges is sometimes tested on the exam:

DR:	Pledges Receivable	$300,000	
	CR: Estimated Uncollectible Pledges		$ 90,000
	CR: Contribution Revenue		$210,000

IV. Revenue Classifications

A. All revenue must be reported in one of three categories based on the type of restrictions, if any, *placed by the donor* on its use. The three categories are:

Unrestricted	resources are available for expenditure *in the current period for any purpose*
Temporarily Restricted	resources are available for expenditure in the current period but only for **specified (operating) purposes**; these restrictions are known as **"program restrictions"**
	or
Temporarily Restricted	resources are available for expenditure in the current period only for **capital purposes**; these restrictions are known as **"asset acquisition"** or **"capital restrictions"**
	or
Temporarily Restricted	resources are available only after a specified time has elapsed or event has taken place: these restrictions are known as **"time restrictions"**
Permanently Restricted	resources are not available for expenditure at any time, although the earnings on the resources *may* be expended; permanently restricted assets are known as **"endowments"**

Note: Only revenue from non-exchange transactions (e.g. contributions) can be classified as Temporarily Restricted or Permanently Restricted because the restriction must be made by an external party (the donor); **revenue subject to internal restrictions**, such as might be made by the Board of Directors, **and revenue from exchange transactions** (i.e., dues, sales of goods, charges for services, etc.) are **always classified as Unrestricted**.

Example:
Animal Action recently received $100,000 in contributions. $30,000 of this amount was restricted by donors to covering the costs of a Spay/Neuter clinic. The director set aside an additional $50,000 of this amount to be used to build an addition to the animal shelter.

Animal Action reports $30,000 of the Contribution Revenue as Temporarily Restricted and reports $70,000 as Unrestricted. The $50,000 set aside by the director should be reported as designated resources within the Unrestricted category; it does not qualify for inclusion in the Temporarily Restricted category.

V. **Pledges Made Over Multiple Fiscal Periods** -- When revenue is to be received over multiple fiscal periods, as happens when contributions are pledged over several years (e.g., a pledge $10,000 per year for four years), special recognition rules apply:

   A. Recognize revenue at the *net present value* of the contribution;

   B. The portion of the pledge that is to be received in subsequent fiscal periods is considered **"temporarily restricted"** (time restricted - see below); the portion that is to be received in the current period is recognized as "unrestricted", assuming that no other restrictions are specified;

C. The net present value of the pledge is recalculated at the end of the period (or whenever the financial statements are prepared) and increases in net present value are booked as *contribution revenue*, **not interest**;

D. When the future payments are received the assets are reclassified to unrestricted net assets, assuming that there are no other restrictions on how the money may be spent, but **revenue is not recognized**. (It was recognized when the pledge was made.)

> **Example:**
> On January 1, Fly Free, a raptor preservation organization, received an unrestricted pledge of $10,000 per year for three years (the current year and the next two years).
>
> Assuming an interest rate of 10% and that the first payment is made immediately, the present value of the pledge is $27,355. Fly Free recognizes $10,000 Contribution Revenue in the Unrestricted category (the current year's payment) and $17,355 Contribution Revenue in the Temporarily Restricted category (the present value of the two remaining payments).
>
> At year-end, Fly Free recalculates the present value of the remaining pledge as $19,091. The difference of $1,736 ($19,091-$17,355) is recognized as Contribution Revenue in the Temporarily Restricted category.
>
> When the second year's payment of $10,000 is received, no additional revenue is recognized (cash increases and pledges decrease). The $10,000 will, however, be reclassified from Temporarily Restricted to Unrestricted since the "time restriction" has now been met (See FAS 117 - Statement of Activities for an explanation of how assets are "released from restriction").
>
> At the end of the second year, Fly Free recalculates the present value of the remaining pledge as $10,000. The difference of $909 ($10,000-$9,091) is recognized as Contribution Revenue in the Temporarily Restricted category.
>
> When the final payment of $10,000 is received, it will again be reclassified from Temporarily Restricted to Unrestricted. The total amount of Contribution Revenue recognized over the life of the pledge is $30,000 ($27,355 + $1,736 + $909).

VI. Donated Services

A. FASB allows NPF organizations to recognize the value of services that are donated to the organization, but only if certain conditions are met. Donated services are recognized if *either:*

  1. Non-financial assets are enhanced **OR**

  2. services requiring *a) special skills* are provided *b) by persons possessing those skills* and the services would *c) normally have been purchased* by the organization.

B. The entry to record the donated service recognizes the fair market value of the service as a *credit to contribution revenue* and as a *debit to either an asset* (if non-financial assets are enhanced) or as an expense (if services are provided) account.

  See the following example.

Example:
1. Non-Financial Assets are Enhanced: Prairie View Prep School is building an auditorium for their Fine Arts department. The parent of an eighth grade student is an architect and donates his services to design the auditorium. He normally charges $150,000 for this work, though the going market rate in the area for similar work is $100,000.

Since architectural fees are normally capitalized as part of the building cost, a non-financial asset has been enhanced. Prairie View can recognize the donated services at the fair market value of $100,000 with the following entry:

DR: Building	100,000	
CR: Contribution Revenue		100,000

2. Service Requiring Special Skills: Jennifer Rhodes, a professional deep-sea diver, has been hired by Sea Mammals R Us, an international sea mammal conservation group, to help record the activities of migrating whales. The original contract is for 5 days at $600 per day, however, the process requires an additional two days to complete and the contract is extended.

Rather than bill for the additional time, Jennifer contributes her time to the organization. Because Sea Mammals R Us would normally have had to purchase these services and because they are skilled services, they can recognize the value of the services with the following entry:

DR: Research Expenses (Diving Expense)	1,200	
CR: Contribution Revenue		1,200

3. Donated Services Not Recognized: Students at Central University have recently been accosted and robbed and/or threatened when crossing campus late at night. To combat this problem, student groups have banded together to offer escort services to students free of charge. The students estimate that a fair charge for such a service is approximately $10 per trip or $4,500 per month. The University has increased its campus police force in response to the problem and has decided against providing escort services to students.

Central is *not* able to recognize the value of these services because, even though this might arguably be classified as a "skilled" service, there is no indication that the students possess these skills and this is not a service that the university would normally provide.

Note: This is a consistently tested area on the exam. Most of the time the value of the services is recognized. Frequently, there are differences between rates charged and "standard" or "fair value" rates: Always record at fair value.

VII. Donated Fixed Assets

A. Donated fixed assets are **recorded at FMV** at date of donation. These assets are generally subject to depreciation.

B. **Classification of revenue from the donation --** Fixed assets are normally considered to be unrestricted so contribution revenue related to the donation is usually recognized as Unrestricted. If, however, there are restrictions on how the asset must be used or on how proceeds from the sale of the asset may be expended, it should be classified as Temporarily Restricted or even Permanently Restricted.

> **Example:**
> **1. Unrestricted Fixed Asset:** Newberry Cars donated a demonstration car to the McGrary Foundation, a not-for-profit organization. The car cost Newberry $15,000 and had a retail sales value of $22,000 when new. The car's current market value is $16,000. McGrary records the donation and reports Contribution Revenue of $16,000 under Unrestricted Net Assets.
>
> **2. Permanently Restricted Fixed Asset:** Mary Cochoran donates land to the Newport Home, a not-for-profit organization that provides temporary living accommodations for foster children, with the stipulation that the land be maintained by Newport Home in perpetuity and is used to provide recreational opportunities to the foster children. The land has a basis of $50,000 to Ms. Cochoran and a fair market value of $80,000. Newport Home records the donation and reports Contribution Revenue of $80,000 under Permanently Restricted Net Assets.

VIII. Contributions for Others

A. NFP organizations sometimes receive resources that are restricted by the donor to specific recipients. Depending on the degree of the restriction, these monies may represent Contribution Revenue to the NFP organization or they may actually be liabilities of the NFP organization. *Statement #136 - Transfers of Assets to a Not-For-Profit Organization That Raises or Holds Contributions for Others* addresses these recognition issues.

B. **What transactions are covered --** Statement #136 applies to transactions in which three entities are identified:

   1. A **donor** who has sent resources to;

   2. A **recipient** who is responsible for disbursing the money to;

   3. A **specified beneficiary**, who will ultimately be able to use the funds.

C. Statement #136 defines the instances in which the recipient can recognize revenue as follows:

   1. **Organization acts as a cash conduit/agent --** When the restrictions on the resources are such that the recipient has virtually no decision-making or monitoring responsibilities related to the disbursement of the money, and merely acts in an agency capacity then:

      a. Revenue should **not** be recognized; instead, a **liability** should offset the receipt of the cash *note: this is the point most frequently tested on the exam* ;

      b. The ultimate beneficiary recognizes a **receivable** in the amount of the transfer of assets;

      c. The donor recognizes a **receivable** instead of an expense.

   2. **Organization is granted variance power --** Though there may be detailed restrictions on how the.resources are to be distributed, the organization is granted the ability to set the restrictions aside and dispose of the resources as it sees fit (redirect or revoke):

      a. The organization should recognize **contribution revenue** as it now has significant decision-making authority;

      b. The donor recognizes an **expense** (charitable contribution).

   3. **Financially interrelated organizations --** When the recipient organization and the ultimate beneficiary organization are financially interrelated, then the

transfer should be recognized as **Contribution Revenue** by the recipient and the ultimate beneficiary must **recognize an interest in the net assets** of the recipient organization (similar to the equity method of accounting for a subsidiary). Financial interrelatedness exists when:

a. One entity has the ability to **influence** the operating and financial decisions of the other; *and*

b. One entity has an ongoing **economic interest** in the net assets of the other ("residual rights").

Health Care Organizations

This lesson describes basic accounting and financial reporting for health care organizations.

After studying this lesson, you should be able to:

1. *Describe how a government-run hospital is reported in the government's financial statements.*

2. *List the financial statements of a not-for-profit hospital.*

I. Unique Reporting Features for Hospitals

A. Hospitals Modify the Overall Format of the Statement of Activities -- To include an Operating sections and a Non-operating section. The general outline of the statement is:

> \+ Operating Revenues
>
> \- <u>Operating Expenses</u>
>
> = Operating Income
>
> +/- <u>Non-operating Gains & Losses</u>
>
> = Change in Net Assets
>
> \+ <u>Beginning Net Assets</u>
>
> = Ending Net Assets

B. Operating Section -- Several unique items of revenue are included in the Operating Section:

> \+ Net Patient Service Revenues
>
> \+ Other Operating Revenues
>
> \+ <u>Capitation Fees</u>
>
> = Total Operating Revenue

II. Patient Service Revenues

A. Patient Service Revenues -- These are gross charges for direct patient care. They include such things as room charges, doctors' fees, medicines, bandages, etc.; *ancillary revenues,* which are revenues for patient related services such as radiology, pathology, laboratory work, etc. - are also part of patient services revenues.

> **Note:**
> Net Patient Service Revenues are *not reduced by allowances for* **bad debt, which is an operating expense** for hospitals.

B. Charity Care -- When patients enter the hospital the *charity cases* are immediately identified and eliminated from the patient service revenue calculations. The amount of revenue as "donated" to charity cases is separately tracked and disclosed in the notes.

C. As paying patients begin to receive services, the charges for those services are *recorded in gross* (e.g. for the full amount). *Gross patient services revenues* are reduced by *contractual allowances* (price reductions allowed to third party payers such as insurance companies, Medicare, Medicaid, etc.). to determine Net Patient Service Revenues. **Net Patient Service Revenue** is the first line in the Statement of Activity. Gross Patient Service Revenues and Contractual Adjustments are displayed in the notes.

> \+ Gross Patient Service Revenues (*including Ancillary Revenues*)
>
> \- Less Contractual Adjustments
>
> = Net Patient Service Revenue

> **Example:**
> Daily charges for a semi-private room are $110. However, the hospital has an agreement with an HMO to accept $70 as full payment for the room. The hospital records Patient Service Revenue of $110, records a Contractual Allowance of $40, and reports Net Patient Service Revenues of $70 on the financial statements.

III. Other Operating Revenues

A. Other operating revenues include revenues from items related to the main operations of the hospital, but not directly related to patient care. Other operating revenues include:

1. Gift shop sales;

2. Parking garage receipts;

3. Cafeteria sales;

4. Tuition from classes offered by the hospital;

5. FMV of donated **materials and supplies;**

6. *Restricted* contributions;

7. Research grants.

> **Example:**
> Bay City Hospital recorded the following revenues:
>
> | | |
> |---|---|
> | Delivery room charges (only $15,000 is expected to be collected due to agreements with third party providers) | $20,000 |
> | Cafeteria sales | $3,000 |
> | Research grants | $10,000 |
> | Radiology charges | $2,000 |
> | Nursing fees | $12,000 |
> | Gift of medicines used for direct patient care | $1,000 |
>
> Bay City reports: Net Patient Service Revenues of $29,000 (15,000+2,000+12,000) and Other Operating Revenues of $14,000 (3,000+10,000+1,000).

> **Note:** Categorization of hospital revenue as Patient Service Revenue, Other Operating Revenue, or Non-Operating Gains has been a consistent area of emphasis on the exam. It is important to know how individual contributions and revenues fit into these categories. Less emphasis has been placed on the expense categories.

IV. Capitation Fee Revenues

    A. Capitation Fees are payments made to health care providers for comprehensive client coverage provided for a fixed fee (e.g., HMOs). Capitation fee revenues should be recognized during the period covered and estimated obligations related to patient care for this period should be accrued. Capitation Fees are shown as a separate line item in the operating section of the statement.

V. Operating Expenses

    A. Operating expenses include virtually all costs associated with running a hospital, including depreciation, bad debt expense and losses on disposal of fixed assets. However, expenses are not reported using natural expense categories (salary, supplies, rent, etc.); they are reported using the following functional categories:

        1. Nursing, Other Professional, General, Fiscal and Administrative.

VI. Non-operating Gains

    A. This category includes most **unrestricted** bequests and cash donations, most **donated services**, and **unrestricted** earnings on investments, including endowment income.

Example:
Belpark Hospital received the following contributions:

Contributions restricted for cancer research	$50,000
Unrestricted bequest	$25,000
Record-keeping services donated by current employees (these services would have been purchased)	$10,000
Bandages and ointments contributed by a supplier	$5,000
Government grant to fund research on birth defects	$20,000

Belpark reports Other Operating Revenue of $75,000 (50,000+5,000+20,000)

and Non-operating Gains of $35,000 (25,000+10,000).

VII. Contributions Other than Cash -- To properly report these donations, you must carefully evaluate the type and purpose of the contributions:

    A. Materials -- When goods and supplies normally purchased by the organization are donated, the items are **recorded as inventory or as an expense**, as appropriate, and the contribution is reported as **Other Operating Revenue.**

    B. Services -- Donated services may only be recorded if: 1) a non-financial asset is enhanced or 2) special skills are required and the service is provided by someone possessing those skills and the services would have otherwise have been purchased by the organization. If the service can be recognized, then it is necessary to look at the purpose of the service in order to report it:

        1. if the service relates to the main operating mission of the hospital (e.g. a doctor donates a surgical procedure), record it as an operating expense and as **Other Operating Revenue**;

2. if the service is of a support or administrative nature (e.g. a bookkeeper volunteers to enter transactions), record it as an operating expense and a **Non-Operating Gain**.

VIII. Statement Format -- The following format is commonly used to report hospital/health care entity activities.

Net Patient Service Revenues		**XXX**
Other Operating Revenue		<u>**XXX**</u>
Total Operating Revenues		XXX
Operating Expenses (by functional area)		
	Nursing	(XXX)
	Other professional	(XXX)
	General	(XXX)
	Fiscal	(XXX)
	Administrative	<u>(XXX)</u>
Total Operating Expenses		(XXX)
	Income from Operations	XXX
Non-operating Gains and Losses		
	Unrestricted Contributions	**XXX**
	Donated Services	**XXX**
	Endowment Income	<u>**XXX**</u>
Total Non-operating Gains and Losses		XXX
Excess (Deficiency) **of Revenues Over Expenses**		XXX

Colleges and Universities

This lesson describes basic accounting and financial reporting for colleges and universities.

After studying this lesson, you should be able to:

1. *List the financial statements for a not-for-profit college and university.*

2. *List the financial statements for a public (i.e., governmental) college and university.*

I. **Introduction** -- Colleges and universities use their own unique functional classifications for Revenues and Expenses.

    A. The following summary highlights the major sections of the statement. The following table shows a formal Statement of Activity for a college. Boldface titles indicate areas often used for exam questions.

Revenues:	
Tuition	XXX
Government Grants and Contracts	XXX
Private Gifts	XXX
Investment Income	XXX
Endowment Income	XXX
Auxiliary Enterprises	<u>XXX</u>
Total Revenues:	XXX
Expenditures	
Educational & General	
Instruction	(XXX)
Research	(XXX)
Scholarships & Fellowships	(XXX)
Academic Support	(XXX)
Student Services	(XXX)
Institutional Support	(XXX)
Plant Operation	<u>(XXX)</u>
Total Educational & General Expenditures	(XXX)
Auxiliary Enterprises	(XXX)
Total Expenditures	<u>XXX</u>
Net Increase(Decrease) in Fund Balance	XXX

II. Tuition Revenues

A. Shown at net of scholarship allowances and uncollectible amounts. Some scholarships and fellowships are reported as expenses.

> **Misconception:** Scholarship allowances and scholarships are not the same thing. Scholarship allowances are the difference between the stated tuition rate and the amount that is actually paid by the student and/or third parties making payments on behalf of the student. Scholarships are actual amounts paid to students by the college, rather than a reduction of charges. Tuition waivers given as a result of employment by the university - such as to graduate assistants - are reported as expenses. Tuition refunds (i.e., money returned to students because they *did not take* classes) **are** deducted from gross tuition revenues.

> **Example:**
> Students at Maplewood College register for classes for which the gross tuition is $1,000,000.
>
> The college grants scholarships totaling $250,000 to 50 students and waives tuition of $30,000 for college employees who are also taking classes.
>
> Refunds of $50,000 are given to students who drop classes before classes start.
>
> Maplewood reports Tuition Revenue of $950,000 (1,000,000-50,000) and reports $280,000 (250,000+30,000) as Scholarship and Fellowship Expense.

B. Tuition for **academic periods encompassing two fiscal periods** (common in summer semesters) should be recognized proportionately in the two fiscal years affected.

> **Example:**
> Blondell College's ten week summer session runs from June 1 until August 15. By the beginning of classes Blondell had received $500,000 for tuition charges. Another $200,000 was receivable on July 15.
>
> Blondell's fiscal year ends on June 30. The first four weeks of the summer semester occur in June.
>
> The College should recognize $280,000 in tuition revenue (4/10th) and $220,000 as deferred revenue in the fiscal year ended June 30. $420,000 ($220,000 deferred revenue from the first fiscal year and $200,000 collected in the second fiscal year) is subsequently recognized as Tuition Revenue for the second fiscal year. Expenditures are handled in a similar fashion.

C. Revenues for **auxiliary enterprises** are aggregated and reported as a single line item in the Revenues section. Expenditures for auxiliary enterprises are aggregated and reported as a single line item in the Expenditures section.

> **Definition:**
> *Auxiliary Enterprises*: Activities carried on by the educational institution but not related to the delivery of instruction. Examples include housing services, dining services, athletic programs, college stores, student unions, etc.

Governmental Accounting and Reporting

GASB Concept Statements

GASB Concept Statements

This lesson describes GASB's conceptual framework by covering GASB Concepts Statements released to date.

After studying this lesson you should be able to :

1. *Understand the unique characteristics of the governmental environment.*

2. *List the seven elements of financial statements.*

3. *List the hierarchy of communication methods to convey information to users of the general purpose external financial reports.*

4. *Understand the types of measures that can be used to report on service efforts and accomplishments.*

I. **Concepts Statement No. 1 --** *Objectives of Financial Reporting.* (Issued May 1987)

A. **Scope**

1. It establishes the objectives of general purpose external financial reporting by state and local governmental entities.

2. It applies to both governmental-type and business-type activities.

3. The statement does not establish financial reporting standards - it establishes the conceptual framework to be used by GASB in evaluating existing standards and establishing future standards.

4. General purpose external financial reporting includes general purpose financial statements, notes to the financial statements, required supplemental information, and other supplementary information.

5. This statement may not meet the needs of users of specific purpose financial reporting:

   a. Characteristics

      i. Used to meet the needs of specific users;

      ii. Presents financial information on a basis of accounting that differs from GAAP;

      iii. Presents financial information in a prescribed format; or

      iv. Reports on specified elements, accounts, or items taken from the general purpose financial statements.

   b. Examples

      i. Offering statements;

      ii. Budgets;

      iii. Reports to grantor agencies.

B. **Governmental Environment**

1. **Primary characteristics**

   a. Representative form of government and separation of powers.

   b. Federal system of government and the prevalence of intergovernmental revenues - intergovernmental revenues require state and local governments to be accountable to the governmental entity that provided the resources and to citizenry.

    c. The relationship of taxpayers to services received - governments impose taxes and provide services that may not have a direct relationship between the fees paid the services received:

        i. Taxpayers are involuntary resource providers - they cannot choose whether or not to pay taxes;

        ii. The amount of taxes paid by an individual seldom bears a proportional relationship to the cost or value of services received by the individual;

        iii. There is no "exchange" relationship between resources provided and services received;

        iv. Governments often have a monopoly on the services they provide.

2. Control aspects

    a. The budget is an expression of public policy and financial intent and as a method of providing control - the budget is

        i. An expression of public policy;

        ii. A financial plan;

        iii. A form of control having the force of law; and

        iv. It provides a basis for evaluating performance.

    b. The use of fund accounting for control purposes.

3. Other characteristics

    a. The dissimilarities between similarly designated governments;

    b. Significant investment in nonrevenue producing capital assets;

    c. The nature of the political process - balance the conflicting demands of different groups within the citizenry with the resources made available by the citizenry.

C. Users of financial reports

    1. The citizenry -- Those to whom government is primarily accountable (e.g., taxpayers, voters, service recipients, the media, advocate groups, public finance researchers);

    2. Legislative and oversight bodies -- Those who directly represent the citizens (e.g., state legislatures, county commissions, city councils, board of trustees, school boards);

    3. Investors and creditors -- Those who lend or participate in the lending process (e.g., institutional investors, underwriters, bond rating agencies, bond insurers, financial institutions).

D. Uses of financial reports

    1. Comparing actual financial reports with the legally adopted budget;

    2. Assessing financial condition and results of operations;

    3. Assisting in determining compliance with finance-related laws, rules, and regulators;

    4. Assisting in evaluating efficiency and effectiveness.

E. Purpose of financial reporting

    1. Accountability – This is based on the belief that the taxpayer has a "right to know" is accomplished by providing information to assist users in determining whether the government was operated within the legal constraints imposed by the citizenry.

2. Interperiod equity - This is a significant part of accountability by showing whether current-year revenues are sufficient to pay for current-year services or whether future taxpayers will be required to assume burdens for services previously provided.

F. Characteristics of information in financial reporting (TRUCCR "TRUCKER")

1. **T**imeliness

2. **R**elevance

3. **U**nderstandability

4. **C**omparability

5. **C**onsistency

6. **R**eliability

II. **Concepts Statement No. 2 --** *Service Efforts and Accomplishments Reporting* (Issued April 1994) and **Concepts Statement No. 5**. *Service Efforts and Accomplishments Reporting - an amendment of GASB Concepts Statement No. 2.* (Issued November 2008).

A. GASB believes that service effort and accomplishment (SEA) information assists users in assessing accountability and making better informed decisions. However, SEA is voluntary. In June 2010, GASB issue suggested guidelines for voluntary reporting of SEA performance information.

B. **Elements of SEA performance**

1. Measures of service efforts (inputs) - the amount of financial (e.g., cost of road maintenance) and nonfinancial resources (e.g., number of employee hours used in road maintenance) that are applied to a service.

2. Measures of service accomplishments (outputs and outcomes) - report what was provided or achieved with the resources used. There are two types of measures of accomplishments:

   a. **Output measures --** Quantity of service provided (e.g., miles of road repaired) or that meets a certain quality requirement (e.g., percentage of buses that meet a prescribed on-time standard).

   b. **Outcome measures --** Indicate the results that occur because of services provided including accomplishments as a result of the services provided (e.g., the clearance rate of serious crimes) and measures of public perception (e.g., residents' rating of their neighborhood's safety).

3. Measures that relate service efforts to service accomplishments (efficiency) - measure the resources used to achieve the level of output (e.g., the cost per lane-mile to resurface roads) or measure the resources used achieve a particular outcome (e.g., cost per lane-mile of road maintained in good condition).

4. GASB states that SEA performance information should focus on measures of service accomplishments (outputs and outcomes) and measures that relate service efforts and service accomplishments (efficiency).

C. **Characteristics of SEA Performance Information --** Should meet the same six characteristics for general purpose external financial reporting (i.e., GASB Concepts Statement No. 1) - timeliness, relevance, understandability, comparability, consistency, reliability (TRUCCR).

D. **Providing context for SEA Performance Information**

1. **Comparisons**

   a. With previous years;

      b. Entity established targets;

      c. Progress toward achievement of goals or objectives;

      d. With accepted norms and standards;

      e. With other parts of the entity;

      f. With other comparable jurisdictions.

   2. **Unintended effects --** Significant positive or negative indirect consequences;

   3. **Demand for services --** Competing demand for resources;

   4. **Factors that influence results --** External (e.g., extreme weather conditions) and internal (e.g., staff shortages);

   5. Narrative information.

III. Concepts Statement No. 3 -- *Communication Methods in General Purpose External Financial Reports that Contain Basic Financial Statements.* (Issued April 2005).

  A. Hierarchy of communication methods

   1. Recognition in basis financial statements;

   2. Disclosure in notes to basic financial statements

   3. Presentation as required supplementary information (RSI) - is *essential* for placing basic financial statements and notes to basic financial statements in an appropriate context. **RSI is required**.

   4. Presentation as supplementary information (SI) - is *useful* for placing basic financial statements and notes to basic financial statements in an appropriate context. **SI is** <u>not required</u>, but applicable GASB guidance should be followed when SI is presented.

IV. Concepts Statement No. 4 -- *Elements of Financial Statements.* (Issued June 2007).

  A. Five elements of the statement of financial position

   1. **Assets --** Resource with present service capacity that the government presently controls;

   2. **Liabilities --** Present obligations to sacrifice resources that the government has little or no discretion to avoid;

   3. **Deferred outflow of resources --** A consumption of net assets by the government that is applicable to a future reporting period;

   4. **Deferred inflow of resources --** An acquisition of net assets by the government that is applicable to a future reporting period;

   5. **Net position --** Is the residual of all other elements presented in the statement of financial position.

> **Note:**
> GASB issued an exposure draft, *Financial Reporting of Deferred Outflows of Resources, Deferred Inflows of Resources, and Net Position*, in November 2010.

  B. Two elements of resource flow statements

   1. **Outflow of resources --** Consumption of net assets by the government that is applicable to the reporting period;

   2. **Inflow of resources --** Acquisition of net assets by the government that is applicable to the reporting period.

> **Definition:**
> *Resource*: An item that can be drawn on to provide services to the citizenry.

C. Recognition of deferred inflows or resources and deferred outflows of resources is limited those instances identified and required by GASB in authoritative pronouncements.

> **Example:**
> GASB Statement No. 53, *Accounting and Financial Reporting for Derivative Instruments*, requires that changes in fair values of hedging derivative instruments be reported as either deferred inflows or deferred outflows of net assets.

Format and Content of Comprehensive Annual Financial Report

Introduction to Governmental and Not-for-Profit Organizations

After studying this lesson, you should be able to:

1. *Describe the characteristics that governments operate in that influence their accounting and financial reporting.*

2. *Describe the standard setting structure for governmental entities.*

3. *Describe the five levels of hierarchy of GAAP for state and local governments.*

I. **Exam Coverage --** The AICPA content specifications for accounting for governmental and not-for-profit organizations, including the approximate weighting of the questions, is shown below:

II. **Accounting and reporting for governmental entities (8%-12%)**

   A. Governmental accounting concepts

   1. Measurement focus and basis of accounting,

   2. Fund accounting concepts and application,

   3. Budgetary process.

   B. Format and content of governmental financial statements

   1. Government-wide financial statements,

   2. Governmental funds financial statements,

   3. Conversion from fund to government-wide financial statements,

   4. Proprietary fund financial statements,

   5. Fiduciary fund financial statements,

   6. Notes to financial statements,

   7. Required supplementary information, including management's discussion and analysis,

   8. Comprehensive annual financial report (CAFR).

   C. Financial reporting entity including blended and discrete component units

   D. Typical items and specific types of transactions and events: recognition, measurement, valuation and presentation in governmental entity financial statements in conformity with GAAP

   1. Net assets,

   2. Capital assets and infrastructure,

   3. Transfers,

   4. Other financing sources and uses,

   5. Fund balance,

   6. Non-exchange revenues,

      7. Expenditures,

      8. Special items,

      9. Encumbrances.

   E. Accounting and financial reporting for governmental not-for-profit organizations

III. Accounting and reporting for nongovernmental not-for-profit organizations (8%-12%)

   A. Objectives, elements and formats of financial statements

      1. Statement of financial position,

      2. Statement of activities,

      3. Statement of cash flows,

      4. Statement of functional expenses.

   B. Typical items and specific types of transactions and events: recognition, measurement, valuation and presentation

      1. Revenues and contributions,

      2. Restrictions on resources,

      3. Expenses, including depreciation and functional expenses,

      4. Investments.

IV. Characteristics and types of Governmental and Not-for-Profit Organizations -- Accounting and financial reporting for governments and other not-for-profit organizations is greatly influenced by the following unique characteristics of these organizations:

   A. Lack of a clear profit motive,

   B. Ownership is collective and nontransferable (i.e., cannot be sold or traded).

   C. Nonexchange transaction - financial resources contributed to the organization are often not in exchange for a direct or proportionate share of services (e.g., property taxes are paid to finance public schools regardless of the number of children the taxpayer has in school).

   D. Policy decisions are made by a vote of elected or appointed governing bodies.

   E. Policymaking is often open to the public and news media.

   F. The budget is an expression of the policies of the organization and success is frequently determined by the ability or inability to meet the budget.

   G. All the foregoing characteristics lead to an elaborate accounting and financial reporting structure.

V. Overview of fund accounting -- Because governmental and not-for-profit organizations do not try to generate income and are not "owned" by investors, standard financial accounting rules and financial statements are often not relevant to them.

VI. Who uses fund accounting?

   A. Fund accounting is used by governmental and non-profit organizations. Governmental and non-profit organizations include:

      1. **State and local governments (SLGs)** -- *General purpose governments* (cities, states, and counties), *limited or special purpose governments* (school districts, transit authorities, and municipal utility districts) and various *agencies and commissions* (e.g., employment commission, economic development commission, etc.). The Governmental Accounting Standards Board (GASB) establishes accounting and financial reporting standards for these entities.

2. **Not-for-profit organizations --** Colleges and universities, churches, museums, hospitals, private elementary and secondary schools, health and welfare organizations (i.e., the United Way, the March of Dimes, the Muscular Dystrophy Association, etc.). The Financial Accounting Standards Board (FASB) establishes accounting and financial reporting guidelines for these entities.

> **Note:**
> Although the federal government is a form of government, is not included in the state and local government category and, in general, is not tested on the CPA exam. The Financial Accounting Standards Advisory Board (FASAB) considers and recommends accounting principles for the federal government.

VII. Why use fund accounting?

A. Government and not-for-profit organizations differ from for-profit organizations in several fundamental ways:

1. Their **principal mission** is to provide goods and/or services to specified groups or individuals; not to provide a return for their investors.

2. Their **primary resources** are received through non-exchange transactions (taxes, fees, donations, etc.), making it difficult to match expenses with related revenues.

3. There are often **restrictions** on how resources can be expended.

4. There are **no individual "ownership" interests** (equities) in the organization.

B. Because of these factors, standard accrual accounting does not meet the needs of non-profit organizations.

VIII. How is fund accounting different from full accrual basis accounting?

A. To assist in managing and controlling not-for-profit organizations, specialized accounts have been created and some accounting rules and reports have been modified. These changes include:

1. The addition of *funds - separate accounting entities within the organization -* that are used to segregate resources according to restrictions on how the resources may be used;

2. Changes in the timing of revenue and expenditure recognition;

3. Inclusion of budgetary transactions in the accounting records;

4. Accounting recognition of outstanding purchase orders;

5. Specialized statements and reports.

B. Understanding these changes and the way they are applied to the various types of organizations is the essence of understanding fund accounting.

IX. Who makes the rules?

A. The governmental GAAP hierarchy is established by the AICPA's Auditing Standards Board Statement on Auditing Standard (SAS) No. 69 as amended by SAS Nos. 91 and 93 (AU 411). The principal sources of authority differ according to the type of organization.

1. **State and local governments --** The Governmental Accounting Standards Board (GASB) is the primary authority. Other authoritative sources for governmental entities include GASB's predecessor organization the National Council on Governmental Accounting (NCGA).

2. **Not-for-profit organizations --** The Financial Accounting Standards Board (FASB) is the primary source of standards. Other subordinate authoritative sources include AICPA Audit Guides and national associations related to for the various types of organizations (e.g., the American Hospital Association and the National Association for College and University Business Officers).

3. **Hybrid organizations (governmentally affiliated hospitals, universities, and museums)** -- GASB is the ultimate authority, although organizations may follow FASB guidelines when GASB pronouncements do not directly affect the item.

B. Because the accounting is very different for the two main types of organizations, each state, local government, and not-for-profit organization is studied independently.

Fund Accounting and Measurement Focus Basis of Accounting

This lesson describes fund accounting.

After studying this lesson, you should be able to:

1. *List the eleven types of funds used by governmental entities.*

2. *Describe the measurement focus basis of accounting for each type of fund.*

3. *Describe the primary purpose of each type of fund.*

I. **Governmental Accounting Concepts**

A. **Governmental entities use several unique accounting methods to provide organizational control**

1. **Funds --** Segregate resources according to restrictions on use. In the absence of a profit motive, **budgetary accounts** provide control over expenditures. Modification of revenue and expenditure recognition rules changes the flow of transactions through the accounting records to reflect better the nature of the non-exchange transactions that provide most of the resources for governmental expenditures.

B. **Fund Accounting --** Many resources received by government entities are restricted to use for specified purposes. Further, they are often required by law to be "separately accounted for." Governmental entities **use funds to segregate resources** by type of restriction.

> **Definition:**
> *A Fund* : A separate *fiscal* and *accounting* entity with a self-balancing set of accounts (i.e., assets, liabilities, and residual balances).

1. The accounting equation for a fund is:

Assets = Liabilities + Fund Balance

2. **Purpose of a fund --** Funds exist:

a. To improve management accountability and control;

b. To meet legal requirements.

3. **Types of Funds --** Governmental entities engage in non-exchange, exchange, and fiduciary transactions. These transactions are segregated into three fund categories:

a. **Governmental Funds --** Non-exchange revenues such as taxes, intergovernmental revenues, and grants provide resources for the majority of general government expenditures (i.e., expenditures for public health and safety, government infrastructure assets such as roads and bridges, government administration, etc.) These transactions are recorded in a group of funds collectively referred to as Governmental Funds.

b. **Proprietary Funds --** Governmental entities sometimes engage in activities in which they operate much like for-profit organizations. Public utilities, convention centers, motor pools, and airports are common examples of these activities. These activities result in exchange transactions, that is, charges to users for the goods and services that they receive. Most exchange transactions are recorded in a group of funds called Proprietary Funds.

   c. **Fiduciary Funds** -- Governmental entities frequently manage and/or process resources on behalf of other entities or individuals. Since these resources do not truly belong to the governmental entity, they are recorded separately in a group of funds called Fiduciary Funds.

C. Budgetary Accounting

   1. Because governmental entities do not try to earn a profit, they cannot rely on the profit motive – that is the need to have a positive net income - to control their spending. Instead, **several types of budgetary accounts are incorporated into the accounting records** to control revenues and expenditures and they are **subject to legal spending limits**. In budgetary accounting:

      a. **Formal DR/CR accounting entries** -- Are made at the beginning of the period to record estimated revenues and authorized expenditures (appropriations).

      b. These entries serve as a basis of comparison for actual revenues and expenditures.

      c. Unless there are changes in the budget, the budgetary accounts remain unaltered during the fiscal year.

      d. Since appropriations are usually valid for only one fiscal period, budgetary accounts are closed at the end of the period.

   2. **Purpose of budgetary accounting** -- Budgetary accounting permits organizations to **demonstrate compliance with legislatively prescribed spending limits and purposes**.

D. Encumbrance Accounting -- To ensure that the entity does not order more goods than it has the authority to purchase, an estimate of expenditures is recorded at the time an order is placed rather than waiting until the goods are received. This is known as encumbrance accounting.

E. Basis of Accounting -- The basis of accounting defines the way in which inflows and outflows of resources are measured and recognized. In governmental accounting, the basis of accounting that is used varies depending upon 1) the fund that is used to record the transaction and 2) the report that displays the transaction results. Two basis of accounting are used: **modified accrual basis** and **full accrual basis**.

   1. **Governmental fund transactions** -- The governmental funds depend on non-exchange revenues to provide the bulk of their resources. Full accrual accounting, which relies on the matching principal to determine the timing of revenue and expense recognition, is not appropriate for these types of transactions. Governmental entities modify the full accrual basis revenue and expenditure recognition rules so that their governmental funds better match the characteristics of these transactions. The resulting basis is known as the modified accrual basis, which is used to record transactions in governmental funds.

      a. A major concern for governmental entities is that they have received sufficient "financial resources" to cover their "financial expenses" ("financial resources" can be roughly translated to mean cash and near-cash equivalents). Therefore, the measurement focus for changes in resources during the period (i.e. revenues and expenditures) under modified accrual basis accounting is on *"the flow of financial resources"* : that is, on "cash" inflows and outflows.

      b. Governmental entities also need to know where they stand financially. That is, they need to know the total amount of assets available and liabilities payable at any given point in time. Thus, at the end of the period (e.g., for the balance sheet), the focus of modified accrual basis accounting is on the *"financial position"* of the organization.

2. **Proprietary fund transactions --** Proprietary funds, like for-profit businesses, incur expenses in order to generate revenues sufficient to cover the expenses and maintain the capital invested in the organization. Moreover, like for-profit businesses, most transactions of proprietary funds are exchange transactions. **Full accrual accounting** is, therefore, an appropriate basis of accounting for proprietary funds.

   a. A major concern of proprietary entities is that, over the long run, they earn a sufficient return to cover the full cost of providing goods and/or services (i.e., direct expense items such as salaries and cost of goods, as well as the cost of the capital assets used by the entity). The measurement focus of full-accrual basis accounting for changes during the period (revenues and expenses) is therefore on *"the flow of economic resources," "income determination,"* or *"capital maintenance."* "Economic resources" are broader in scope than "financial resources" as they encompass financial resources that are not immediately available (e.g., long-term investments, property, plant and equipment).

   b. Proprietary entities also need to know where they stand financially. That is, they need to know the total amount of assets available and liabilities payable at any given point in time. Thus, at the end of the period (e.g., for the balance sheet), the focus of **full accrual basis accounting** is on the *"financial position"* of the organization.

Exam Hint: Questions asking you to relate the basis of accounting to its "measurement focus" appear on almost every exam. You should memorize the following relationships:

	Measurement focus	
Basic of Accounting	**During the period**	**At the end of the period**
Modified accrual	*flow of **financial** resources*	*financial position*
Full accrual	*flow of **economic** resources*	*financial position*

F. **Financial reporting --** Governmental entities produce two distinct sets of financial statements: the **Fund statements** and the **Government-wide** (or Entity-wide) **statements**.

   1. **Fund statements --** The Fund statements include three separate sets of financial statements - one for each of the three fund categories (Governmental, Proprietary, and Fiduciary). Each of these sets of statements is prepared using the "native" basis of accounting for the fund:

      a. **Governmental funds --** Modified accrual basis;

      b. **Proprietary funds --** Full accrual basis;

      c. **Fiduciary funds --** Full accrual basis.

   2. **Government-wide statements --** The Government-wide (or Entity-wide) statements are presented for the "organization as a whole" and therefore include information from both the governmental and proprietary funds. (Note that fiduciary funds are not included as these resources are managed only on behalf of others and do not actually belong to the governmental entity.) In order to combine information from these two fund categories, they must both use the same basis of accounting. For these statements, the governmental fund transactions are converted from modified accrual basis to full accrual basis so that the **government-wide statements can be presented on a *full accrual basis.***

G. **Objective of governmental accounting**

   1. The objective of a governmental entity is the provision of services to its constituents. The objectives of governmental accounting are to:

    a. Assess the availability of current period resources to finance current period expenditures (interperiod equity);

    b. Assess the service efforts and accomplishments of the governmental entity; and

    c. Demonstrate compliance with the legal authorization to expend.

2. Interperiod equity measures the extent to which current resources are sufficient to finance current expenditures (i.e., we have a balanced budget). Interperiod equity is fundamental to public administration and is a component of accountability.

II. Fund Structure

A. Fund Categories

1. Governmental entities are organized into **three Fund Categories**. The fund category determines the basis of accounting that is used for funds within that category, whether budgetary transactions are recorded in the funds, and whether the funds can report capital assets and/or long-term debt and the financial statements that will be prepared for the funds. A fund category may use either modified accrual basis accounting or full accrual basis accounting depending on the fund's activities.

> **Note:**
> Remember the acronym **"DRIP-CEG-PIPPA"** - (**DRIP**): Debt Service Funds, Special Revenue Funds, Internal Service Funds, Permanent Funds; (**CEG**): Capital Projects Funds, Enterprise Funds, General Fund; (**PIPPA**): Pension Trust Funds, Investment Trust Funds, Private Purpose Trust Funds, Agency Funds - a mnemonic for remembering the eleven types of funds.

    a. Governmental Fund Category (modified accrual basis);

    b. Proprietary Fund Category (full accrual basis);

    c. Fiduciary Fund Category (full accrual basis).

2. **Fund Types --** Within the **three fund categories** are **eleven Fund Types**.

    a. **Governmental Funds**

        i. General Fund;

        ii. Special Revenue Funds;

        iii. Debt Service Funds;

        iv. Capital Project Funds;

        v. Permanent Funds.

    b. **Proprietary Funds**

        i. Enterprise Funds;

        ii. Internal Service Funds.

    c. **Fiduciary Funds (PIPPA)**

        i. **P**ension Trust Funds;

        ii. **I**nvestment Trust Funds;

        iii. **P**rivate Purpose Trust Funds;

        iv. **A**gency Trust Funds.

3. There is only one General Fund. All other fund types may be comprised of many individual funds.

4. **Number of funds principle --** The number of funds principle states that an organization should **use the minimum number of funds possible, consistent with**:

a. **Laws and contracts**, and

b. **Sound financial management**.

B. Governmental Fund Category

1. The five fund types in this category finance most "general government" activities (law enforcement, public safety, schools, capital projects, etc.) All governmental funds are current funds (i.e., they have only current asset and current liability accounts - no long-term items).

    a. They are **expendable funds** - they are not concerned with preserving capital. All resources that are recognized in these funds should be expended, not retained.

    b. All governmental funds use **modified accrual basis accounting**.

    c. All governmental funds can use **budgetary accounting** and **encumbrance** . (However, at least on the CPA exam, not all governmental funds use both.)

    d. **Capital assets** and **long-term debt** related to these funds are **recorded separately in off-books records**. They are not reported in the Fund statements, although they **are** included in the Government-wide statements.

> Accounting Equation: ***Current* Assets - *Current* Liabilities = *Fund Balance***

2. **Governmental Fund Types**

    a. **General Fund --** The General Fund accounts for ordinary operations of the government.

        i. Revenues typically come from taxes, licenses, fines, fees, etc.

        ii. Most **unrestricted resources** are accounted for in this fund.

        iii. Expenditures can be made for **any general government services** not specifically accounted for in another fund.

        iv. This is the **only required fund** of a governmental unit.

        v. There is **only one General Fund**.

3. **Special Revenue Funds --** Account for the proceeds of specific revenues from taxes, grants, entitlements, or other earmarked sources that are restricted or committed to expenditures for specified purposes other than debt service or major capital projects (e.g., a gasoline tax that must be spent on road maintenance, private foundation grants that must be used to provide training opportunities for disadvantaged workers).

> **Study Tip:**
> Special Revenue Funds never account for capital asset acquisition, capital asset construction, or debt service transactions on the CPA exam. CPA exam questions always assume that these transactions are recorded in the Capital Projects or Debt Service funds, respectively.

4. **Capital Projects Funds --** Account for **monies designated for acquisition or construction of significant capital items** (land, buildings, and equipment). Capital Project Funds are **short-lived**, existing only long enough to accumulate resources to acquire or construct an asset and to account for the expenditures related to the asset. After acquisition or construction, the fund is closed. Any **monies remaining** in the fund are usually **transferred to a Debt Service Fund** or, if no debt was issued to finance the project, to the General Fund.

5. **Debt Service Funds --** Account for **monies set aside to pay interest and principal** on the governmental unit's **long-term general obligation debt**. Note that the Debt Service

Fund **does not account for the liability** itself, only for the monies that are set aside to pay the principal and interest. Its function resembles that of a bond sinking fund in financial accounting.

6. **Permanent Funds** -- Account for resources received by the governmental entity with the stipulation that the principal amount remain "intact" but that earnings must be spent, for purposes that benefit the governmental entity (i.e., purchase of library books, park improvements, and cemetery maintenance). These types of funds are more generally known as **endowments**.

   a. Although the Permanent Fund receives the endowment earnings, any **expendable earnings are transferred to an appropriate governmental fund** (usually a Special Revenue Fund) to make the actual expenditure.

C. **Proprietary Fund Category**

   1. The two fund types in this category account for governmental unit activities that charge fees in exchange for goods or services. The activities accounted for in these funds are similar to those of for-profit businesses.

      a. Activities that are "self-supporting" -- that is, where **50% or more of costs are covered by fees** -- *must* **be accounted for as Proprietary Funds**. Additionally, activities in which there is *intent* to cover 50% or more of costs through fees *or* activities that would **benefit from the additional control measures provided by full accrual basis accounting** *may* be accounted for as Proprietary Funds. These activities

         i. Record and report their own capital assets and long-term debt;

         ii. Use full accrual basis accounting.

   Accounting Equation: (Current Assets +Capital Assets) - (Current Liabilities + Long-Term Liabilities) = Retained Earnings + Contributed Capital

   2. **Proprietary Fund Types**

      a. **Enterprise Funds** -- Account for activities that provide goods and services to the **general public** as well as to the governmental entity itself (i.e., utilities, transit services, golf courses, etc.) A **service fee commensurate with the benefits received** is generally charged.

      b. **Internal Service Funds** -- Account for activities that provide goods and services **only to other government agencies and departments** (i.e. motor pools, printing services, data processing services, central supplies, etc.). Fees for these services are generally paid through inter-departmental charges.

D. **Fiduciary Fund Category** -- These funds account for monies and other resources held by the governmental unit in a trustee or agent capacity. In general, fiduciary funds use full accrual accounting to record transactions.

   1. **Pension Trust Funds** -- Pension Trust Funds account for **contributions made by or on behalf of government employees to provide them with retirement income and post-retirement benefits** and for the **actual expenditures made to retirees** and terminated employees. Related transactions such as pension investment earnings and investment management expenses are recorded here as well.

   2. **Agency Funds** -- Account for monies for which the governmental unit serves as merely an agent in the process of distributing/delivering the monies to their rightful recipient; that is, when the governmental unit acts as a clearing house, collecting monies for other units and then remitting them as appropriate, usually for a small fee. These funds have only current assets and current liabilities - they do not recognize revenues or expenses.

3. **Private Purpose Trust Funds** -- Account for trust arrangements for which **other entities** (i.e., external organizations or individuals and other governmental entities) **are the beneficiaries rather than the governmental unit itself**. Private Purpose Trust Funds differ from Agency Funds in that they **often hold assets for long periods of time** (many times these funds are in the form of endowments) whereas Agency Funds hold monies only briefly before they are distributed to the proper recipient.

4. **Investment Trust Funds** -- Account for **monies received from other governmental agencies to be included in the governmental entity's Investment Pool** (Note: larger, general-purpose governments frequently provide this service to smaller agencies that lie within their jurisdiction). Earnings on the monies invested are also recorded in the Investment Trust Fund. Note that **resources belonging to the governmental entity itself** that are included in the Investment Pool are not reported in the Investment Trust Fund: **only resources from external entities are reported here**. Resources belonging to the governmental entity itself are reported in the funds that made the Investment Pool contributions.

E. **Treatment of Fixed Assets and Long-term Liabilities** -- Prior to GASB #34, account groups were used to track long-term items (fixed assets and long-term debt) associated with governmental funds. These amounts were also included in the Financial Statements on the Combined Balance Sheet. The Account Groups are not part of the GASB #34 model and are not included in the Fund Statements. They are, however, reported in Government-wide Statements.

1. In practice, many organizations may still use the two account groups to track long-term items associated with the Government Funds. These systems are well established and the information they provide is still needed, so there is little reason to abandon them.

> **Study Tip:** Even though the Account Groups are not part of the GASB #34 reporting model, it is possible that the terms may still appear as possible answers to questions and even that the examiners might ask how transactions that used to be reported in the Account Groups are now reported. Because of this, it is probably a good idea to become familiar with how these account groups were used.

2. With this in mind, the following information is of interest:

   a. **General Fixed Asset Account Group (GFAAG)** -- Used to record fixed (long-term) assets purchased by any of the governmental funds (principally the General Fund, Special Revenue Fund, and the Capital Projects Fund), as well as items donated to the governmental unit. Assets were recorded at historical cost or at FMV at the date of donation.

   b. **General Long-Term Debt Account Group (GLTDAG)** -- Used to record general obligation long-term debt of the governmental unit, including bonds, notes, and capital leases. As the debt matures (becomes current) the liability is removed from the GLTDAG and placed in a Debt Service fund for repayment.

III. **Modified Accrual Basis Accounting**

A. **A primary objective of for-profit organizations** -- is to generate a positive **net income,** which ensures that the capital invested in the organization is maintained and that there is a return to the investors. Full accrual basis accounting is designed to measure a for-profit organization's success in achieving this objective. It focuses on the matching of revenues with related expenses to determine net income.

1. Since governments have neither "investors" who provide "capital" to fund the organization nor do they raise revenues through the expending of resources (i.e., exchange transactions), the matching of revenues and expenses is not relevant, or even possible for governmental entities. Instead, the emphasis in **governmental entities** is on the **provision of services** and the **availability of resources** to provide those services.

2. Because of the differences in the objectives, full accrual basis accounting is not appropriate for governmental entities. A modification of the full accrual basis revenue and expenditure recognition rules is necessary to create a basis of accounting that is more closely aligned with their objectives. This basis of accounting is called "modified accrual basis."

B. Modified accrual basis accounting has the following characteristics

1. **Measurement Focus --** The measurement focus of modified accrual basis accounting is on the **"flow of *financial* resources,"** that is, the inflows and outflows of "expendable resources" (i.e., cash and near cash assets such as marketable securities, receivables, etc.), not on the "flow of economic resources," "income determination," and "capital maintenance" as would be the case in the full accrual basis.

2. **Revenue Recognition --** Revenues are recognized in the period in which they become "measurable and available" (not when they are "earned").

    > **Study Tip:**
    > Full accrual basis revenues are recognized when measurable and earned. The examiners frequently try to confuse candidates by including "earned" as a factor in modified accrual basis revenue recognition. **"Earned" revenue always denotes full accrual basis accounting.**

    a. The terms "measurable" and "available" have very specific meanings:

        i.   **Measurable --** the amount is known or can be reasonably estimated.

        ii. **Available --** the amount is both:

            1. Legally due

            2. Received in cash either:

                1. By the end of the fiscal period or

                2. "In time to pay for obligations of the current fiscal period" (known as the 60-day rule).

    b. **60-Day Rule --** A governmental entity may recognize monies received during the first 60 days of a new fiscal period as revenue of the old fiscal period.

        i. **Rationale --** Because many expenditures for the old fiscal period are not known and/or due until the new fiscal period (e.g., utility bills), monies received within the first 60 days of the new fiscal period are usually considered received "in time to pay for obligations of the current fiscal period."

👁 **Example:**
In Fiscal Year X Bishop County levied property taxes totaling $5,000,000. The County received payments of $4,000,000 by the end of Fiscal Year X, received $300,000 during the first 60 days of the Fiscal Year Y, received an additional $500,000 by the end of Fiscal Year Y, and received the remaining $200,000 during the first 60 days of Fiscal Year Z.

Bishop County recognizes $4,300,000 (4,000,000 + 300,000) of property tax revenue in Fiscal Year X and $700,000 (500,000 + 200,000) of property tax revenue in Fiscal Year Y.

Note: This means that most governmental revenues are recognized when received in cash, as long as they are legally due. Income taxes, sales taxes, licenses, fines, etc. are usually recognized in this manner.

Note: Although governmental entities frequently recognize revenue only when cash is received, this *is not cash basis accounting*. **Cash basis accounting is** *never* **GAAP** for governmental entities.

    c. **Revenues "Subject to Accrual" --** Revenues that are measurable and legally due prior to the receipt of cash are **normally recognized on the accrual basis**. These revenues typically result from charges that are billed to the customer/constituent by the governmental entity. Revenues that are subject to accrual include:

        i. **Property taxes**;

        ii. **Interest and penalties on delinquent taxes**;

        iii. **Investment revenue**;

        iv. **Regularly billed charges for services**;

        v. **Taxes collected by other government units but not yet remitted**.

Note: Even though revenue is recognized "up front" for these items (e.g., when the receivable is recognized), an adjusting entry is made at the end of the period to defer revenue recognition for any amounts that have not been received in cash within 60 days after the end of the fiscal period.

    d. Therefore, even though we credit Revenue when the bill is sent out, the amount of revenue actually reported on the financial statements is consistent with the modified accrual basis revenue recognition rules.

Example:
Fayette County Sheriff's Department billed residents $1,200,000 for special security services provided during the year. Of these receivables, $800,000 was paid within the fiscal period and an additional $200,000 was paid during the first 60 days of the next period.

How much revenue should Fayette County recognize when the bills for these services are sent out?

When the bills are sent out, Fayette County recognizes revenue in the full amount of the billing:

    DR: Receivables $1,200,000

        CR: Revenue $1,200,000

How much revenue is reported for these services on the financial statements?

The revenue reported on the financial statements equals the amount received in cash during the fiscal period or within the first 60 days of the next fiscal period: $1,00,000 ($800,0000 + $200,000)

How should any amounts not recognized as revenue be reported?

The remaining amount should be reported as Deferred Revenue. The following adjusting entry is made to recognize the deferral:

    DR: Revenue $200,000

        CR: Deferred Revenue $200,000

3. **Expenditure Recognition --** Expenditures, in general, are recognized on the **accrual basis**, that is, when the liability is measurable and has been incurred, **except for the following four items:**

    a. **Interest on *general long-term debt*** is not recorded until it is actually due. "Due" in this instance means **"on the due date."**

        i. ***General long-term debt* --** Refers to long-term debt incurred by governmental funds, which are funds that provide general government services. General long-term debt is reported in the GLTDAG.

        ii. ***Specific* long-term debt --** Refers to long-term debt incurred by the proprietary funds. Specific debt is reported in the proprietary funds. Interest on specific long-term debt *is accrued.*

Study Tip: Only interest on *general long-term* debt is treated in this manner. Interest on *short-term* debt (e.g., accounts payable) and interest on *specific* long-term debt are accrued. The examiners will frequently try to trick you into treating these items as if they were general long-term debt.

Example:
The City of Middleton uses a calendar fiscal year. On January 8, $3,000,000 of interest on its general obligation bonds will be due and payable to the bondholders. How much accrued interest on these bonds should be reported on its financial statements dated December 31?

No interest ($0.00) on this debt should be reported on the December 31 financial statements as interest on general, long-term debt is not reported until it is due.

Note: Only interest on *general long-term* debt is treated in this manner. Interest on *short-term* debt (e.g., accounts payable) and interest on *specific* long-term debt **are** accrued. The examiners will frequently try to trick you into treating these items as if they were general long-term debt.

---

    b. **No distinction is made between capital expenditures** (land, buildings, and equipment) **and period expenditures** (wages, rent, utilities, etc.). **All are simply reported as expenditures.**

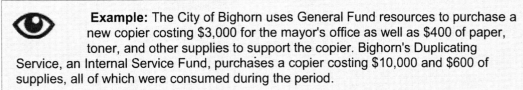

Example: The City of Bighorn uses General Fund resources to purchase a new copier costing $3,000 for the mayor's office as well as $400 of paper, toner, and other supplies to support the copier. Bighorn's Duplicating Service, an Internal Service Fund, purchases a copier costing $10,000 and $600 of supplies, all of which were consumed during the period.

The General Fund uses modified accrual basis accounting and the Internal Service Fund uses full accrual basis accounting. Bighorn reports General Fund expenditures of $3,400.

The Internal Service Fund reports $600 of expenses and reports an additional asset of $10,000.

c. **Inventoriable materials and supplies --** These may either be recognized as **expenditures either when purchased** (purchases method) **or when used** (consumption method).

> **Example:**
> Marriot County purchases $80,000 of inventoriable supplies during the year. Marriot had $40,000 of supplies on hand at the beginning of the year and $30,000 of supplies on hand at the end of the year. If Marriot uses the purchases method, it reports supplies expenditures of $80,000. If Marriot uses the consumption method, it reports supplies expenditures of $90,000 (40,000 + 80,000 - 30,000).

d. **Prepaid items --** These may be recognized as **expenditures either when purchased** (purchases method) **or when used** (consumption method). Unlike inventoriable materials, however, prepaid items are almost always expenditures in full when paid (purchases method).

> **Example:**
> At the beginning of the year, the City of Whittenville leased space in a strip mall to use for a neighborhood outreach center. Whittenville used General Fund resources to pay $36,000 in advance for the three-year lease. If Whittenville uses the purchases method, it reports lease expenditures of $36,000. If Whittenville uses the consumption method, it reports lease expenditures of $12,000 (36,000/3), the value of the lease benefits that expired during the year.

4. **Increases and decreases in net assets other than revenues and expenditures --** Funds using the modified accrual basis of accounting have a number of transactions that create increases or decreases in net assets that cannot be classified as revenues or expenditures.

   a. **Other Financing Sources (OFS) --** Increases in the net assets of a fund that do not result in an increase in the net assets of the organization as a whole.

> **Example:**
> Receipt of the **proceeds of long-term debt** and **transfers of assets from another fund** are the most common examples of OFS. Other Financing Sources are either reported with Revenues or netted against Other Financing Uses. In either event, they are **part of the net change in Fund Balance during the period.**

   b. **Other Financing Uses (OFU) --** Decreases in the net assets of a fund that do not result in a decrease in the net assets of the organization as a whole.

> **Example:**
> The transfer of assets to another fund is the most common example of an OFU. Other Financing Uses are either reported with Expenditures or netted against Other Financing Sources. In either event, they are **part of the net change in Fund Balance during the period.**

Note: The ability to distinguish Other Financing Sources and Other Financing Uses from Revenues and Expenditures is a consistent area of emphasis on the exam.

Budgetary Accounting and Encumbrance Accounting

This lesson describes typical accounting entries related to the government's budget.

After studying this lesson, you should be able to:

1. *List the accounts used to record the budget.*

2. *Prepare journal entries to record the budget.*

3. *Describe the difference between an encumbrance and an expenditure.*

4. *Prepare journal entries related to encumbrances.*

I. **Budgetary Accounting**

A. **Requirements**

1. Budgetary Accounting requires the creation of special budgetary accounts, recording of budgetary entries, and preparation of reports that compare budget amounts to actual amounts.

2. In general, only funds that use modified accrual basis of accounting use budgetary accounting. Even then, not all modified accrual basis funds use budgetary accounts. The General Fund and Special Revenue Funds are usually budgeted, Debt Service Funds are sometimes are budgeted, but Capital Projects Funds are not usually budgeted.

B. **Budgetary accounts** -- Budgetary accounts are used to record budget entries. The budgetary accounts parallel the "actual" nominal accounts found in governmental funds. The actual accounts and their normal balances are shown below:

Actual Accounts
(also known as Nominal or Temporary or Income Statement accounts)

Expenditures		**Revenues**	
DR Balance + *Increase*	- *Decrease*	- *Decrease*	CR Balance + *Increase*

Other Financing Uses*		**Other Financing Sources****	
DR Balance + *Increase*	- *Decrease*	- *Decrease*	CR Balance + *Increase*

* Examples of Other Financing Uses: Operating Transfers Out

** Examples of Other Financing Sources: Operating Transfers In, Bond Issue Proceeds

---

1. **A parallel budgetary account** is established for each of the actual revenue, expenditure, other financing source, and other financing use accounts. The budgetary accounts and their normal balances are shown below.

Budgetary Accounts
(Note: The normal balances of these accounts are opposite the normal balance of the related actual account.)

Appropriations		Estimated Revenues	
- *Close*	CR Balance + *Open; Set up*	DR Balance + *Open; Set up*	- *Close*

Estimated Other Financing Uses		Estimated Other Financing Sources	
- *Close*	CR Balance + *Open; Set up*	DR Balance + *Open; Set up*	- *Close*

Budgetary Fund Balance

Dr or CR to	**Balance Entry**

2. First, and most importantly, note that budgetary accounts have **normal balances opposite** those of their actual account counterparts. This is the most commonly tested characteristic of the budgetary accounts. You must know whether a DR or a CR is used to "set up" (increase) the budget at the beginning of the year or "close" (decrease) the budget at the end of the year for each of the four budgetary accounts.

    a. **Estimated Revenues --** Normal balance is a **DR**; the budget office established estimates for this account.

        i. **Appropriations --** Normal balance is a **CR**; the legislative body sets these **legally authorized spending limits**.

> **Note:**
> There is **not an account titled "Estimated Expenditures."** The correct title is "Appropriations."

            1. **Estimated Other Financing Sources --** Normal balance is a **DR**; this account estimates the inflow of funds that are not properly categorized as revenues (operating transfers from other funds, proceeds of bond issues, etc.)

            2. **Estimated Other Financing Uses --** Normal balance is a **CR**; this account estimates the outflow of funds which are not properly categorized as expenditures (operating transfers to other funds, etc.)

            3. **Budgetary Fund Balance --** This is an **offset account** used to balance the budgetary entry; as such, it **does not have a "normal balance"** but is **debited or credited as necessary** to make debits equal credits within the budgetary entry.

Note: The **Budgetary Fund Balance is the technically correct title** for this account and is consistently used on the CPA exam. Some textbooks, however, use **Fund Balance** as the offset account but this is **not what you will see on the CPA exam.** Moreover, for financial reporting GASB Statement No. 54 prohibits reporting reserved and unreserved categories within Fund Balance and provides five new categories within Fund Balance to be reported in fund-level financial statements. The five categories are as follows: Nonspendable, Restricted, Committed, Assigned, and Unassigned. Please refer to the lesson on Net Position and Fund Balance for a more detailed explanation of this change.

Study Tip: Budgetary accounting is always tested on the CPA exam. The questions are usually quite simple as long as the candidate remembers: The names of the budgetary accounts. Budgetary account balances are opposite their actual account counterparts. When budgetary entries are made. All of these concepts are tested on nearly every exam.

C. **Entry to record the budget --** The entry to record the budget is **made at the beginning of the year** when the budget is adopted:

> Estimated Revenues   XXX
>
>   Appropriations   XXX
>
> DR or CR Budgetary Fund Balance to balance the entry.

   1. There are usually only **two entries into the budgetary accounts:**

      a. The entry to **set up the budget** at the beginning of the year;

      b. The entry to **close the budget** at the end of the year.

   2. Mid-year entries occur only when the legislative body convenes and authorizes additional appropriations or when actual revenues are significantly different from predictions. Note that the offset account used to balance the entry is Budgetary Fund Balance.

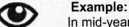 **Example:**
In mid-year, the Lawrence City Council authorized $150,000 in additional expenditures to repair damages from spring flooding. The entry to record the additional appropriation is:

> Budgetary Fund Balance   XXX
>
>   Appropriations   XXX

D. **Entry to close the budget --** If there have been no changes to the budget during the year, the entry to close the budgetary accounts at the end of the fiscal period simply reverses the original entry.

> Appropriations   XXX
>
>   Estimated Revenues   XXX
>
> DR or CR Budgetary Fund Balance to balance the entry.

1. If there have been changes to the original budget, remember that the purpose of the entry is to close (zero out) the balances in the budgetary accounts, whatever those balances may be. Always DR or CR the Budgetary Fund Balance account to balance the entry.

II. Encumbrance Accounting

A. Encumbrances represent the estimated dollar value of purchase orders outstanding

1. Using Encumbrances to Control Expenditures -- Appropriations represent legal spending limits prescribed by the entity's governing body. Appropriations are usually established for departmental units and/or for various types of expenditures (salaries, equipment, supplies, etc.). The "unexpended, unencumbered appropriation" is the remaining authorization to spend after taking into account goods still on order (encumbrances) and goods received to date (expenditures). Synonymous terms include: uncommitted appropriations, available balance, unencumbered balance, and free balance. It is calculated as:

+ Appropriations

\- Encumbrances

\- Expenditures

= Unencumbered, Unexpended Appropriation

Example:
Niles County has an Appropriation of $10,000 for computer supplies. So far this year, Niles has received and paid for $4,500 of computer supplies. An additional $2,000 of computer supplies have just been ordered. What is Niles' unencumbered, unexpended balance?

	P/O "Let"
+Appropriation	+10,000
-Encumbrances	-2,000
-Expenditures	-4,500
=Unencumbered, Unexpended Appropriation	**3,500**

The unexpended, unencumbered balance is immediately reduced by the $2,000 order to $3,500.

When the goods arrive, the encumbrance entry is liquidated (reversed) and the actual cost is recognized as an expenditure, as shown below.

+ Appropriations

\- Encumbrances

\- Expenditures

= Unencumbered, Unexpended Appropriation

Example:
Niles County has an Appropriation of $10,000 for computer supplies. So far this year, Niles has received and paid for $4,500 of computer supplies. An additional $2,000 of computer supplies have just been ordered. What is Niles' unencumbered, unexpended balance?

	P/O "Let"	Goods Received
+Appropriation	+10,000	10,000
-Encumbrances	-2,000	0
-Expenditures	-4,500	6,500
=Unencumbered, Unexpended Appropriation	3,500	3,500

a. Note that when the goods are actually received, there is no change in the Unencumbered, Unexpended Appropriation amount: the effect of the transaction has been moved forward to the point of order rather than waiting until the goods arrive.

2. **Encumbrance Accounts** -- Two additional budgetary accounts are created to record encumbrances:

Budgetary Fund Balance

Encumbrances		Assigned (or Committed) for Encumbrances	
DR Balance + PO Issued	Goods Rec'd	Goods Rec'd	CR Balance + PO Issued

3. **Encumbrances**, like Expenditures, is **a debit balance account**. It is increased (debited) when a purchase order is issued. The **Fund Balance Assigned (or Committed) for Encumbrances** is simply an **offset account** for Encumbrances. The balances in the Encumbrances and the Fund Balance Reserved for Encumbrances accounts **are always equal, but are opposite each other**. Whether "Assigned" or "Committed" is used depends on the level of authority required to make the expenditure (i.e., to encumber the amount). If the expenditure is authorized by a formal act of the government's highest decision-maker (i.e., the city council) then "Committed" should be used. On the other hand, if the expenditure is authorized by a group (i.e., finance committee) or an official (i.e., business manager) then "Assigned" should be used.

B. **Encumbrance Entries** --- (Note: in this example we assume the expenditures are authorized by a group or an official of the government and therefore "Fund Balance-Assigned" is the appropriate category).

1. When a purchase order is prepared (or "let"): the estimated amount of the purchase is recorded as an encumbrance. The entry to record the processing of a purchase order is:

Encumbrances	XXX	
Fund Balance Assigned		XXX

2. When **goods/services are received**: a two-part entry is required.

a. The **encumbrance amount is reversed** (liquidated)

b. The **actual expenditure is recognized:**

Fund Balance Assigned	XXX	
Encumbrances		XXX
Expenditures	XXX	
Vouchers Payable/Cash		XXX

C. **Differences between estimated and actual expenditures** -- When encumbered goods are received at an actual, invoiced price that differs from the estimated (encumbered) amount the encumbrance is liquidated at the original, estimated amount and the expenditure is recorded at the actual, invoiced amount. As a result of this entry, a corresponding change in the unencumbered, unexpended appropriation balance occurs.

> **Example:**
> Previously encumbered goods are received at an invoiced cost of $5,500. The estimated cost of the goods was $6,000. The entry to record the receipt of goods is as follows:
>
> | | | |
> |---|---|---|
> | Fund Balance Assigned | $6,000 | |
> | Encumbrances | | $6,000 |
> | Expenditures | $5,500 | |
> | Vouchers Payable | | $5,500 |
>
> As a result of this transaction, the balance of the unencumbered, unexpended appropriation increases by $500.

1. **At year end** -- Encumbered orders not received at fiscal year-end are generally closed out, sometimes as part of the budgetary closing entry. In addition, a portion of the Fund Balance is set aside to cover the estimated amount of orders outstanding at year-end. Depending on the level of authority by which the encumbrances were established, either Fund Balance - Committed or Fund Balance - Assigned, (both are actual Balance Sheet accounts), is used to account for these monies.

Fund Balance Assigned	XXX	
Encumbrances		XXX
Fund Balance*	XXX	
Fund Balance Assigned (or Committed)		XXX

Study Tip: In the past the CPA exam often used the following account titles interchangeably: Fund Balance; Unreserved Fund Balance; Unreserved, Undesignated Fund Balance. GASB Statement No. 54, effective for financial statement periods beginning after June 15, 2010, replaced these categories of fund balance with the following five new categories: nonspendable, restricted, committed, assigned, or unassigned.

Example:
After closing all nominal accounts except encumbrances, Morgan City had the following account balances at the end of the year:

Assets	$10,000,000
Liabilities	$7,000,000

There were $2,000,000 of purchase orders outstanding at the end of the year. There were no nonspendable, restricted, committed, or assigned amounts in the fund balance.

Currently, Morgan City's General Fund has an Unassigned, Undesignated Fund Balance of $3,000,000 ($10,000,000 assets less $7,000,000 liabilities). Since there are no nonspendable, restrictions, commitments, or assigned amounts within the fund balance, this entire amount is available for appropriation (e.g., the legislative body can decide to spend the money).

However, is that money truly available? Consider the outstanding purchase orders. They are not included in Liabilities, but they are legal obligations to purchase goods. Should the amount available for appropriation really be $1,000,000 ($3,000,000 less $2,000,000 outstanding purchase orders)?

The closing entry for the encumbrances takes note of this legal obligation:

Fund Balance Assigned for Encumbrances	$2,000,000	
Encumbrances		$2,000,000
Unassigned Fund Balance	$2,000,000	
Fund Balance - Assigned or Committed		$2,000,000

As a result of these entries, the Unassigned Fund Balance is now $1,000,000 ($10,000,000 assets less $7,000,000 liabilities less $2,000,000 outstanding purchase orders/encumbrances). The obligation for the outstanding purchase orders is seen in the Fund Balance Assigned account balance of $2,000,000.

    a.   Note that after all closing entries have been made, the balance in the Fund Balance - Assigned (or Committed) account includes the amount outstanding encumbrances at year end. According to GASB Statement No. 54, the fund-level financial statements are not separately displayed in the financial statements, but they should be disclosed in the notes to the financial statements.

D. Reversing Entries -- At the beginning of the next fiscal year: the closing entry for encumbrances is usually at least partially reversed. Because of this entry, the prior year encumbrances are then treated like any other encumbrance when the order is received.

Encumbrances - Prior Year	xxx	
Fund Balance Assigned		xxx
Fund Balance Assigned	xxx	
Unassigned Fund Balance		xxx

1. Since the fund balance and reservations of fund balance accounts are used only for financial reporting and therefore do not affect transaction processing during the year, the reversing entries may not occur. Instead, the balance in the assigned account stays in place throughout the year, and it is simply adjusted to equal the total outstanding encumbrances at the end of the year.

> **Example:**
> At the beginning of the fiscal year, Bremerton County reported $15,000,000 in its Unassigned Fund Balance and $4,000,000 in its Fund Balance Assigned (for outstanding encumbrances). The outstanding purchase orders were recognized as Encumbrances of Prior Year at the beginning of the year but the Fund Balance Assigned for Encumbrances account was not adjusted.
>
> At the end of the fiscal year, all of the orders from the prior year had been received but there were $5,000,000 of purchase orders outstanding from the current year. What entry is necessary to close the encumbrance accounts and recognize the outstanding purchase orders on the financial statements?
>
> | | | |
> |---|---|---|
> | Fund Balance Assigned | $5,000,000 | |
> | Encumbrances | | $5,000,000 |
> | Unassigned Fund Balance | $1,000,000* | |
> | Fund Balance Assigned | | $1,000,000* |
>
> * Calculation of entry for Fund Balance Assigned for Encumbrances:
>
> $5,000,000 CR desired ending balance
>
> $4,000,000 CR beginning balance
>
> $1,000,000 CR is required to achieve the ending balance

The Comprehensive Annual Financial Report and Types of Financial Statements

This lesson describes the components of the Comprehensive Annual Financial Report (CAFR) and the types of financial statements presented in it.

After studying this lesson, you should be able to:

1. *List the two government-wide financial statements.*

2. *List the types of financial statements required at the fund-level for Governmental Funds.*

3. *List the types of financial statements required at the fund-level for Proprietary Funds.*

4. *List the types of financial statements required at the fund-level for Fiduciary Funds.*

5. *List the three main sections of the CAFR.*

I. **Comprehensive Annual Financial Report (CAFR)**

    A.   **Reporting Requirements:** -- GASB specifies two levels of reporting for governmental entities: the General Purpose Financial Statements and the Comprehensive Annual Financial Report (CAFR).

        1.   **General Purpose Financial Statements (GPFS)** -- The General Purpose Financial Statements represent the minimum requirements for external reporting. The GPFS contain three principal components (all three components are discussed in more detail both below and in the GASBS #34 Reporting lesson):

> **Study Tip:**
> The items included in each of the sections of the CAFR are frequently tested on the CPA exam.

            a.   Management's Discussion and Analysis (MD&A);

            b.   Basic Financial Statements;

            c.   Required Supplementary Information (RSI).

        2.   Though the GPFS represent the minimum reporting requirements (sometimes phrased on the exam as the "minimum that can be separately released"), most medium-to-large governmental entities find it necessary to provide significantly more information in order to meet the needs of the users of the financial statements.

        3.   **Comprehensive Annual Financial Report (CAFR)** -- In order to meet the information needs of external users of the financial statements, most governmental entities produce a Comprehensive Annual Financial Report (CAFR), which is the equivalent of the annual report of a for-profit organization. GASB specifies the structure of the CAFR, which is broken up into three main sections. Each section contains several required elements:

            a.   Introductory Section;

            b.   Financial Section;

            c.   Statistical Section.

    B.   **CAFR: Introductory Section** -- The following items are usually found in the Introductory Section:

        1.   Table of contents;

2. Letter of transmittal;

3. Organizational chart;

4. GASB Certificate of Excellence for Excellence in Financial Reporting (when previously earned);

5. Other information deemed appropriate by management.

6. **Letter of Transmittal --** The letter of transmittal reviews the legal requirements for the financial reporting and examines the results presented in the financial statement.

   a. Because the Introductory Section is not usually audited, the letter of transmittal can include subjective information that would not be permitted in the statements themselves, such as interpretations of past events, predictions and expectations of future events.

   b. Information provided in the Letter of Transmittal should not duplicate information provided in the Management's Discussion and Analysis (MD&A) section. The MD&A focuses exclusively on the contents of the basic financial statements, whereas the Letter of Transmittal is broader in perspective because it interprets the financial statements in the context of the long-range economic and social environment of the governmental entity.

C. **CAFR - Financial Section --** In addition to the required financial statements, the Financial Section includes explanatory text and a number of supporting schedules. The following items are included in the Financial Section:

   1. **Auditor's Report --** This is the first item presented in the section and, in addition to providing the auditor's opinion on the fairness of the statements, specifies the scope of the audit.

      a. The Basic Financial Statements are always covered by the auditor's opinion but the accompanying information in the MD&A, the Required Supplementary Information, the combining statements, and other schedules, is *not* usually audited.

   2. **Management's Discussion and Analysis (MD&A) --** The purpose of the MD&A is to help the user assess the overall financial condition of the governmental entity and determine whether the government's position has improved or deteriorated during the period.

      a. The analysis of the MD&A is based on currently known facts and conditions. In its evaluations, forecasts or subjective information are not permitted.

      b. The information presented includes an analysis of balances and transactions in individual funds, descriptions of capital asset and long-term debt activity during the year, and an analysis of balances and transactions of individual funds.

   3. **Basic Financial Statements --** Basic Financial Statements consist of three separate items:

      a. Government-wide Statements;

      b. Fund Statements;

      c. Notes to the Financial Statements.

      d. **Government-wide Statements --** These statements present information for the government as a whole and are presented on a full accrual basis. Two statements are required:

> **Note:** GASB Statement No. 63, effective for financial statements for period beginning after December 15,2011 replaced "Net Assets" with the term "Net Position" for government-wide financial statements, proprietary fund financial statements, and fiduciary fund financial statements. Governmental fund financial statements report fund balances rather than net position.

    i. Government-wide Statement of Net Position;

    ii. Government-wide Statement of Activities;

    iii. Government-wide Statements include financial data from the Governmental and Proprietary Funds only. Fiduciary Fund financial data is *not* included in these statements.

e. Fund Statements -- Information from each of the three fund categories is presented using its native accounting basis. Each fund category has a unique set of required statements.

    i. Governmental Fund Category -- These statements are produced using modified accrual basis accounting.

        1. Balance Sheet;

        2. Statement of Revenues, **Expenditures**, and Changes in **Fund Balance**.

    ii. Proprietary Fund Category -- These statements are produced using full accrual basis accounting.

        1. Statement of Net Position;

        2. Statement of Revenues, **Expenses**, and Changes in **Net Position**;

        3. Statement of Cash Flows.

    iii. Fiduciary Fund Category -- These statements are produced using full accrual basis accounting.

        1. Statement of Fiduciary Net Position;

        2. Statement of Changes in Fiduciary Net Position.

> **Study Tip:**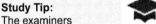
> The examiners frequently ask candidates to identify which statements are required for a fund type or category or, conversely, what funds are included in a specified statement.

f. Notes to the Financial Statements -- The GASB requires numerous disclosures in the Notes. The Notes are considered an integral part of the financial statements. Common disclosures include:

    i. Summary of significant accounting policies, including policies for:

        1. Budgetary basis of accounting;

        2. Reporting capital assets, including estimating useful lives and depreciation expense;

        3. Description of pension plans and other post-employment benefits, annual pension cost, and net pension obligation;

        4. Schedule of debt service costs to maturity;

        5. Schedule of capital assets (beginning balances, additions, deductions, ending balances);

      6. Schedule of long-term liabilities (beginning balances, additions, deductions, ending balances).

4. **Other Required Supplementary Information (RSI) --** The RSI is presented after the Basic Financial Statements and is used to display additional information other than that included in the MD&A or the Notes. The information presented in the section varies depending on the activities of the governmental entity:

    a. **Budgetary Comparison Statement --** This statement is required for *all funds subject to an annual budget.* The statement must present:

        i. Original budget (required);

        ii. Final budget ("as amended") (required);

        iii. Actual revenues and expenditures (required);

        iv. Variance (final budgeted amounts less actual amounts)(encouraged but not required).

        v. The Budgetary Comparison Statement is *presented on the budgetary basis that is used by the legislative body, which may be cash basis or near cash basis* (required when applicable).

        vi. A reconciliation between the revenues and expenditures using the GAAP basis (usually modified accrual basis) and the budgetary basis is required when the budget basis is non-GAAP.

    b. **Pension Plan Disclosures --** Actuarial information about pension plan liabilities and funding is presented in two required schedules (the specific requirements of these schedules are discussed in the Pension Trust Fund study text):

        i. Schedule of Funding Progress;

        ii. Schedule of Employer Contributions;

        iii. The schedules show historical trends by presenting information for a six-year period.

    c. **Information Related to Infrastructure Assets Accounted for Using the Modified Approach --** Governmental entities using the modified approach to calculation and reporting of depreciation expense related to infrastructure assets (streets, bridges, sidewalks, drainage systems, etc.) are required to disclose and justify their methods for determining depreciation in this section. The following information is usually presented:

        i. Description of the method used to assess condition of the assets;

        ii. Results of the most recent condition assessments;

        iii. Estimate of costs necessary to maintain the assets at the prescribed level of condition;

        iv. Comparison of actual maintenance costs to estimated costs.

5. **Combining Financial Statements and Individual Fund Financial Statements --** Although they are not specifically required by GASB, most governmental entities provide combining statements for all aggregate columns. Individual fund statements may be presented whenever the governmental entity deems it appropriate.

    a. Combining statements are used to show the individual entities included in the aggregated columns of the financial statements, for example, the "Non-Major Funds" columns found in the Fund Statements and the Component Units column in the Government-wide Statements.

D. **CAFR - Statistical Section** -- The purpose of the Statistical Section is to assist the user in evaluating the current and future performance of the governmental entity in the broader context of its social and economic environment. GASBS #44 defines five categories of information that should be presented in the Statistical Section and recommends that data be provided for a **10-year** period in order to facilitate trend evaluation.

1. **Financial Trends Information** -- Schedules in this category help the user understand how the governmental entity's financial position has changed over the past ten years. It typically displays key fund balances and key net assets category balances for this period.

2. **Revenue Capacity Information** -- This information helps the user understand the ability of the governmental entity to generate its own revenues. Information included in this section typically includes:

   a. Significant sources of revenue;

   b. Principal taxpayers;

   c. Property tax levy and collection.

3. **Debt Capacity Information** -- This section assists the user in understanding the governmental entity's obligation to service existing debt as well as its ability to finance future operations through debt. It includes information such as:

   a. Ratios of outstanding debt to personal income;

   b. Schedules of direct and overlapping debt;

   c. Legal debt limitations and debt margins;

   d. Revenues pledged to service debt.

4. **Demographics and Economic Information** -- The economic and social environment in which the governmental organization operates is presented in this section. Trend information that is frequently provided includes:

   a. Per capita income;

   b. Level of education achieved and distribution of current students across educational level;

   c. Major employers and industries;

   d. Employment and unemployment rates.

5. **Operating Information** -- The purpose of this section is to provide the user with a better understanding of the government's operations and resources. At a minimum, the following schedules of operating information should be provided:

   a. Number of government employees;

   b. Operating indicators - indicators are indicators of the demand or level of service provided, such as the number of building permits issued, number of park visits, average daily school attendance, etc.

6. **Narrative Explanations** -- The Statement requires explanatory information regarding the sources, methodologies, and assumptions used to produce each schedule and to provide narrative explanations of:

   a. The objectives of statistical section information;

   b. Unfamiliar concepts.

   c. Relationships between information in the statistical section and elsewhere in the financial report; and

   d. Atypical trends and anomalous data that users would not otherwise understand.

II. GASB #34 Financial Reporting

A. GASB Statement 34 Reporting Model -- This reporting model modifies the traditional "fund-based" statements somewhat and then adds to them two highly aggregated, entity-wide statements. This set of nine statements constitutes the "Basic Financial Statements." The Basic Financial Statements represent the minimum amount of financial information that can be taken out of the CAFR and released separately.

1. Two new sections -- Management's Discussion and Analysis (MD&A) and Required Supplementary Information (RSI) - have been added. The MD&A section includes a brief, non-technical view of the financial statements highlighting significant changes and balances, an analysis of economic conditions and outlook, and a summary of major debt and capital initiatives undertaken during the period. RSI includes comparisons of actual to budgeted results, schedules detailing infrastructure asset condition, asset condition level, and schedules relating to the basis for condition measurement. The diagram below summarizes some of these statements:

MD&A	Basic Financial Statements	RSI

Government-Wide Financial Statements	Fund-Level Financial Statements	Notes to the Financial Staements
• Statement of Net Position • Statement of Activities	**Governmental Funds** • Balance Sheet Statement of • Revenues, expenditures, and changes in Fund Balance **Proprietary Funds** • Statement of Net Position • Statement of Revenues, Expenses, and Changes in Fund Net Position • Statement of Cash Flows **Fiduciary Funds** • Statement of Net Position • Statement of Changes in Net position	

B. Government-wide Financial Statements -- The traditional fund-based statements are complemented by two highly-aggregated, government-wide statements.

1. Characteristics of government-wide statements

    a. Distinguish "governmental activities" from "business-type activities" but do **not** identify funds.

    b. The measurement focus is on "economic resources" (i.e., revenues and expenses) and thus uses full accrual based accounting.

2. Classification of funds:

Governmental Activities	Business-Type Activities	Not Reported in Government-Wide Statements
	Enterprise Fund	
General Fund Special Revenue Fund Debt Service Fund Capital Projects Fund Internal Service Fund Permanent Fund		Pension Trust Fund Agency Trust Fund Private Purpose Trust Fund
Use full-accrual basis for all funds		

3. The Account Groups are not reported in the GASB #34 model but the net assets and long-term debt from the Account Groups are included under Governmental Activities.

C. Statement of Net Position

1. Government-wide Financial Statements

	Primary Government			
	Governmental Activities	Business-Type Activities	Total	Component Units
Assets				
(listed by liquidity)	<u>xxxxx</u>	<u>xxxxx</u>	<u>xxxxx</u>	<u>xxxxx</u>
Total Assets	xxxxx	xxxxx	xxxxx	xxxxx
Liabilities				
(listed by maturity)	<u>xxxxx</u>	<u>xxxxx</u>	<u>xxxxx</u>	<u>xxxxx</u>
Total Liabilities	xxxxx	xxxxx	xxxxx	xxxxx
Net Position				
Invested in Capital Assets, net of related debt	xxxxx	xxxxx	xxxxx	xxxxx
Restricted for:				
Capital Projects	xxxxx	xxxxx	xxxxx	xxxxx
Debt Service	xxxxx	xxxxx	xxxxx	xxxxx
Community Development	xxxxx	xxxxx	xxxxx	xxxxx
Other purposes	xxxxx	xxxxx	xxxxx	xxxxx
Unrestricted	<u>xxxxx</u>	<u>xxxxx</u>	<u>xxxxx</u>	<u>xxxxx</u>
Total Net Position	xxxxx	xxxxx	xxxxx	xxxxx

2. **Assets --** These include both current and fixed assets.

    a. **Interfund payables and receivables --** among Governmental Activities funds and among Business-Type Activities funds have been eliminated;

    b. **Internal Balances --** Any remaining interfund payables and receivables between governmental-type and business-type funds are identified as **Internal Balances** under each activity type and are eliminated in the Total column.

    c. **Capital Assets --** include fixed assets previously reported in the General Fixed Assets Account Group but they must be reported net of accumulated depreciation and includes intangible assets, as provided by GASBS #51, net of amortization.

    d. **Infrastructure assets --** (roads, sidewalks, street lights, signs, and bridges) must be included as part of capital assets net of depreciation.

        i. **Modified approach --** The depreciation requirement for infrastructure assets can be waived under the following conditions:

            1. The inventory of infrastructure assets is up-to-date, information on asset condition is available, and the amount necessary to maintain and preserve the infrastructure assets is estimated.

            2. Complete condition assessments of infrastructure assets are made every three years.

    e. **Artwork and Historical Treasures --** should be capitalized at historical cost or fair value at date of donation. However, these items do not have to be depreciated.

    f. **Collections --** Special rules are available, however, for collections. Items are considered part of a collection if they are:

        i. Held for public exhibition, education, or research;

        ii. Protected and preserved;

        iii. Subject to a policy that requires proceeds from sales of collection items to be used to acquire other items for collections.

    g. **Impairments - GASBS #42 -- Accounting and Financial Reporting for Impairment of Capital Assets and for Insurance Recoveries.** This Statement requires governmental entities to recognize impairments of capital assets using criteria that mirror the requirements in financial accounting.

        i. **Recognition --** A capital asset should be considered impaired if its service utility has declined significantly and unexpectedly.

            1. The decline must be large in magnitude and the event or change in circumstance that caused the decline must be outside the normal life cycle of the capital asset. Exclusions:

                1. Events or changes that might be expected to occur during the life of the asset;

                2. Capital assets accounted for under the modified approach (GASB Statement No. 34);

                3. Impairments caused by deferred maintenance.

            2. Procedures:

                1. Indicators of impairment;

                    1. Evidence of physical damage;

   2. Change in legal or environmental factors;

   3. Technological development or evidence of obsolescence;

   4. Change in the manner or expected duration of usage of a capital asset;

   5. Construction stoppage.

2. Tests of impairment - factors to consider:

   1. Magnitude of the decline in service utility;

   2. Unexpected nature of the decline.

3. Measurement depends on whether or not the capital asset will continue to be used by the government.

   1. Assets continue to be used. The amount of the impairment is a portion of the historical cost. Use one of the following methods that best reflects the value-in-use or remaining service utility of the impaired capital asset:

      1. The restoration cost approach is typically used for impairments resulting from physical damage (e.g., fire damage to a city building). The amount of the impairment is derived from the estimated costs to restore the utility of the capital asset.

      2. The service units approach is generally used for impairments resulting from changes in legal or environmental factors or from technological development or obsolescence (e.g., new water quality standards that a water treatment plant does not meet). The amount of impairments is determined by evaluating the maximum service units or total estimated service units throughout the life of the asset before and after the event or change in circumstances.

      3. The deflated depreciated replacement cost approach is generally used for impairments resulting from a change in the manner or duration of use. The current cost for a capital asset to replace the current level of service is identified. This cost is depreciated to reflect the fact that the existing capital asset is not new and then is deflated to convert to historical cost dollars.

   2. Assets are no longer used. Impaired capital assets that will not continue to be used by the government and those impaired from construction stoppage should be reported at the lower of carrying value or fair value.

ii. **Reporting** -- Impaired capital assets should be reported at the lower of carrying value or fair value.

   1. Depending on the circumstances, the impairment loss, if significant, may be reported either as a special item or as an extraordinary item:

      1. Special items are within the control of management but are either unusual in nature or infrequent in occurrence. Special items are reported separately in the statement of activities and before extraordinary items.

      2. Extraordinary items are unusual in nature, infrequent in occurrence, and outside the control of management.

2. **Insurance Recoveries.** GASB Statement No. 42 also provides guidance on all insurance recoveries. Impairment losses are reported net of insurance recoveries. Only realized or realizable insurance recoveries should be recognized. If an insurer has admitted or acknowledged coverage, an insurance recovery is considered realizable.

iii. **Liabilities --** include both short-term and long-term liabilities and are valued using the effective *interest rate method*. This results in long-term liabilities being shown at their *present value*, rather than at their face value, which was the case when they were reported in the General Long-term Debt Account Group.

iv. **Net Position --** contains three component parts:

1. **Invested in capital assets, net of related debt --** These assets are all fixed, including infrastructure assets, and net of accumulated depreciation less the total of all general obligation long-term debt.

2. **Restricted net position --** These assets are subject to third-party restrictions governing how they may be spent (primarily the fund balances from the restricted funds - Special Revenue Fund, Debt Service Fund, Capital Projects Fund, and Permanent Fund).

3. **Unrestricted net position --** These assets may be used at any time and for any purpose. They are primarily the fund balance from the General Fund.

D. **The Statement of Activities --** This statement is developed in a functional format that highlights Program revenues and costs. The top half of the statement measures revenues and expenses by Program and categorizes the net result as either a governmental activity or a business-type activity. Net results at the program level are typically negative as much of the cost of providing these programs is financed from other sources. These other sources - General Revenues, Transfers, and Special Items - are shown in the bottom half of the statement. The overall net effect is usually to bring overall cash flows to a positive number. All reporting is on the full-accrual basis.

Government-wide Financial Statements

Statement of Activities

		Program Revenues		Net Revenue (Expense) & Changes Primary Government			
	Expenses	Charges for Services	Operating Grants	Governmental Activities	Business Activities	Total	Comp. Units
Functions							
Primary Government							
Governmental Activities							
Function #1	xxx	xxx	xxx	xxx		xxx	
Function #2	xxx	xxx	xxx	xxx		xxx	
Total Governmental Activities	xxx	xxx	xxx	xxx		xxx	
Business Type Activities:							
BTA #1	xxx	xxx	xxx		xxx	xxx	
BTA #2	xxx	xxx	xxx		xxx	xxx	

Total Business Type Activities	xxx	xxx	xxx		xxx	xxx	
Total Primary Government	xxx	xxx	xxx	xxx	xxx	xxx	xxx
Component Units	xxx	xxx		xxx			xxx
General Revenues - detailed				xxx	xxx	xxx	xxx
Contributions to permanent funds				xxx		xxx	
Special items				xxx		xxx	
Total general revenues, etc.				xxx	xxx	xxx	xxx
Change in net position				xxx	xxx	xxx	xxx
Net position - beginning				xxx	xxx	xxx	xxx
Net position - ending				xxx	xxx	xxx	xxx

1. The **functional format** is divided into Governmental Activities, Business-Type Activities, and Component Units.

2. A function's **Net Revenue (Expense)** is calculated as: the function's program revenues less the function's expenses.

   a. **Exchange revenue** is recognized on the full-accrual basis.

   b. **Nonexchange revenue** is recognized when all conditions surrounding the receipt of the monies have been met (purpose, time, reimbursement, and other contingencies).

   c. **Derived revenue** (sales taxes, income taxes, gasoline taxes, etc.) should be recognized in the same period as the underlying transaction.

   d. **Imposed nonexchange transactions** (property taxes, fines, penalties, etc.) are recognized as soon as a legally enforceable claim exists.

3. **General Revenues, special items, and transfers** are reported below the function section.

E. **Fund-based Statements** -- Although the general format and focus of the traditional "fund-based" statements remains intact, GASB Statement #34 makes several significant modifications.

   1. **Reporting** -- Formerly based on funds and fund type, reporting is now based on "major funds."

      a. A major fund is one that comprises 10% of the total assets, liabilities, revenues, or expenditures/expenses (excluding extraordinary items) for its fund category (governmental or proprietary) **and** one that comprises at least 5% of the corresponding total for all governmental and proprietary funds combined.

      b. The General Fund is always considered a major fund.

      c. Other funds may be considered major funds because of their significance to the governmental unit and/or the users of the financial statements (based on "professional judgment").

      d. Nonmajor funds are segregated by type (governmental or "business-like"), then presented in total by type in separate columns.

2. A **reconciliation** of amounts listed on the fund-based statements to amounts listed on the government-wide statements must be presented a) on the face of the fund-based financial statements or b) on a separate schedule.

3. **New Statements** -- Several new statements have been added to the list of required statements, whereas the reporting of other statements has been moved to a different section of the CAFR.

   a. Proprietary Funds and Fiduciary Funds will now present a Statement of Net Position, rather than a Balance Sheet (Governmental Funds still call their statement a Balance Sheet).

   b. Since no Fiduciary Funds will recognize revenue or expense, they produce a Statement of Changes in Net Position, rather than a Statement of Revenues and Expenses.

   c. The Statement of Revenues and Expenditures-Budget-to-Actual - essentially the budget comparison statement - has been removed from the GPFS (or, in GASB #34 terminology, the Basic Financial Statements) and is instead included with Other Required Supplementary Information.

4. **Elimination of Account Groups** -- The Account Groups have been eliminated for reporting purposes: separate reporting of fixed assets and long-term debt is terminated by GASB #34.

   a. The new "fund-based" statements do not include account group reporting.

   b. Assets and liabilities reported in the Account Groups are included in the government-wide statements only; balances are categorized as either "governmental" or "business-type" depending on their fund association.

F. **Treatment of Fiduciary Funds** -- The only statements required for fiduciary funds are a Statement of Net Position and a Statement of Changes.

   1. Although we RECORD revenues and expenses in the Trust Funds (Pension Trust, Investment Trust, and Private Purpose Trust), we DO NOT REPORT revenues and expenses for these funds in the financial statements.

      a. Because these monies do not belong to us, we cannot recognize either revenue or expense related to them.

   2. Instead, we report Additions to Net Position and Deductions from Net Position.

   3. The agency fund does not even RECORD revenues and expenses, because these funds act simply as a cash conduit;

      a. Monies in these funds belong to someone else and simply flow through the agency fund,

      b. Hence, the agency fund records and reports only assets and liabilities.

G. **Treatment of Internal Service Funds** -- Internal Service Funds are not aggregated with Enterprise Funds but are, instead, combined with the governmental funds.

H. **Change in Scope of "fixed assets"** -- GASB Statement 34 replaces the phrase "fixed assets" with "capital assets."

   1. Capital assets include infrastructure (sidewalks, street lights, roads, etc.) and easements.

      a. Inclusion of infrastructure as part of fixed assets was optional in the previous reporting model but will be required under GASB #34 for all but the smallest government entities.

      b. Implementation dates are staggered depending on the size of the entity, with the first implementation required for fiscal years beginning after June 1, 2005.

I. **Required Supplementary Information (RSI)** -- This information presents schedules and statistical data that supplement the basic financial statements. Note that the RSI is not part of the Basic Financial Statements.

    1. **Budgetary Comparison Schedules** -- include the budget as originally adopted, the final budget, and the actual results.

        a. *The basis of accounting used for this schedule **matches the basis used to develop the budget.** Note that **many** governmental entities use the **cash basis** to develop budgets.*

J. **Balance Sheet Conversion Adjustments** -- Following is a summary of the adjustments required to convert from the GASB #34 mandated fund-based balance sheets to the government-wide statement of net position. Note that, with the exception of interfund payables and receivables to Enterprise funds and the wholesale inclusion of Internal Service funds as part of governmental activities, all modifications are made to governmental funds.

    1. Add all Internal Service Fund assets and liabilities to the governmental activities balance sheet. The Internal Service Fund Net Assets are added to the Fund Balance of governmental fund.

    2. Eliminate all interfund payables/receivables except those to/from Enterprise funds.

        a. The Net payable/receivable balance to/from Enterprise funds is labeled "*internal balances.*"

    3. Add *net* general government fixed assets.

        a. Accumulated depreciation *must* be deducted from the assets.

    4. Add *net* general government long-term debt.

        a. Report using the effective interest rate method, instead of par value.

    5. Bring accruals and deferrals up-to-date according to the economic resources measurement focus (full accrual basis).

    6. Report Net Position instead of Fund Balances.

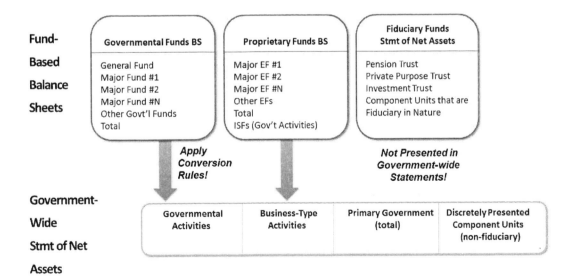

K. **Operating Statement Conversion Adjustments** -- Following is a summary of the adjustments required to convert from the GASB #34 mandated fund-based operating statements to the government-wide statement of activities. Note that, with the exception of interfund payables and receivables to Enterprise funds and the wholesale inclusion of Internal Service funds as part of governmental activities, all modifications are made to governmental funds.

1. Add all net revenue (expense) related to Internal Service Funds:

   a. Add Internal Service Funds' Net Assets to governmental funds' total Fund Balance.

2. Eliminate capital outlay expenditures and debt principal expenditures.

   a. Increase the governmental funds' total Fund Balance for these items.

3. Eliminate proceeds from issuance of GLTD and proceeds from fixed asset sales.

   a. Decrease the governmental funds' total Fund Balance for these items.

4. Adjust governmental fund interest expenditures to interest expense under the effective interest method.

   a. Includes amortization of premiums, discounts, and bond issue costs.

   b. Depending on where you are in the amortization process, this could cause the governmental funds' total Fund Balance to increase OR decrease.

5. Record gains/losses on the sale of fixed assets.

   a. Increase or decrease the total Fund Balance of governmental funds for these items, as appropriate.

6. Record depreciation expense on GFA.

   a. Decrease the governmental funds' total Fund Balance for this item.

7. Adjust revenues from modified accrual to accrual amounts.

   a. Increase or decrease the governmental funds' total Fund Balance for these items, as appropriate.

8. Convert expenditures to expenses and adjust for differences between the modified accrual and accrual bases.

   a. Increase or decrease the governmental funds' total Fund Balance for these items, as appropriate.

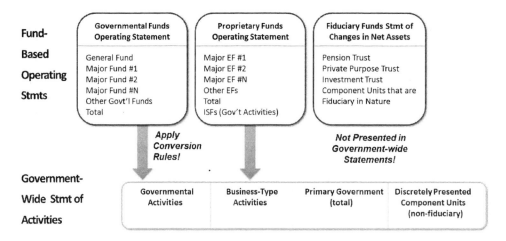

L. **Changes in the Fiduciary Fund Category** -- GASB Statement #34 made dramatic changes in the accounting and reporting of the Fiduciary Fund Category. All fiduciary funds now use the full accrual basis of accounting to record revenues and expenses. However, **none** of the fiduciary funds report revenues and expenses, since these monies do not belong to the government entity. Instead, the fiduciary funds **report Changes in Net Assets:** additions to Net Position and deduction from Net Position.

1. **Redefinition of Fiduciary Funds** -- Two of the four subfunds previously found in the pre-GASB #34 Fiduciary Fund category have been redefined and replaced. The redefinition is based primarily on whether the fund resources are held by a government in an agency or trust capacity for the government's own use or benefit or whether they are used to benefit external individuals and/or agencies.

   a. **"Old" Non-Expendable Trust Funds** -- These funds were used to account for endowments: monies given to the governmental entity for which the principal must remain in tact in perpetuity. These monies are now reported in a:

      i. **Permanent Fund** -- The earnings are used for the *benefit of the governmental entity* or to *support the government's programs*, or a

      ii. **Private-Purpose Trust Fund** -- The earnings are legally restricted so that they may be used only to benefit entities outside of the governmental entity itself.

   b. **"Old" Expendable Trust Funds** -- These funds were used to account for contributions to the governmental entity that could be expended in full. The expendable portions of the earnings on endowments were frequently moved to these funds. These monies are now reported in a:

      i. **Special Revenue Fund** -- The monies are used to support the government's own programs; that is, they are used for the *benefit of the governmental entity.*

      ii. **Private-Purpose Trust Fund** -- The monies may only be used to benefit entities outside of the governmental entity itself.

2. **Additional Fiduciary Fund** -- One completely new fund type has been added to the Fiduciary Fund Category:

   a. **Investment Trust Funds** -- These funds are used to account for monies received from other governmental entities that are pooled with reporting entity's investments. These funds account for the *external portion of the pool* **only.**

      i. Portions of the pool belonging to the reporting government should be reported in the funds that hold the equity positions in the pool.

3. **Accounting for some fund types remains the same**

   a. **Pension Trust Funds** -- Report the contributions to and distributions from the governmental entity's pension funds.

   b. **Agency funds** -- These may include only those assets that are ultimately payable to entities outside the reporting government.

      i. For example, a Property Tax Agency fund could only include those amounts due to other government entities.

      ii. Monies payable to the reporting government must be reported in the appropriate fund.

Governmental Funds

This lesson provides examples of typical accounting entries made in each type of governmental fund.

After studying this lesson, you should be able to:

1. *List the five types of government funds and describe the purpose of each.*

2. *Prepare typical entries for each type of fund.*

> **Note:** Remember the acronym **"DRIP-CEG-PIPPA"** - **(DRIP)**: **D**ebt Service Funds, Special **R**evenue Funds, **I**nternal Service Funds, **P**ermanent Funds; **(CEG)**: **C**apital Projects Funds, **E**nterprise Funds, **G**eneral Fund; **(PIPPA)**: **P**ension Trust Funds, **I**nvestment Trust Funds, **P**rivate **P**urpose Trust Funds, **A**gency Funds - a mnemonic for remembering the eleven types of funds. Governmental funds are the consonants in **"DRIP-CEG."**

I. **General Fund:**

A. **The General Fund --** Is the principal operating fund for all governmental entities. Most "general" revenues (property taxes, fines, penalties, licenses, etc.) and "general" expenditures (police, fire, city administration, etc.) are accounted for in the General Fund.

B. **General Fund Characteristics --** The General Fund is the only fund that is absolutely required in governmental accounting. There is **only one General Fund**. Like all governmental funds, the General Fund:

   1. Uses modified accrual basis accounting;

   2. Uses budgetary and encumbrance accounting;

   3. Accounts for current items only:

      a. Purchases of fixed assets are recorded in the General Fund as expenditures;

      b. Proceeds from the issuance of long-term debt are recorded in the General Fund as Other Financial Sources;

      c. Note: Although the fixed assets and the long-term debt are not recorded in the General Fund, they *are* recorded "off-books" and are included in the government-wide financial statements. These statements are discussed later in the Governmental Financial Statements section.

C. **General Fund Functions --** In addition to funding most of the current operating costs of the governmental entity, the General Fund frequently finances many other funds, such as Debt Service, Capital Projects, Enterprise, and Internal Service Funds, just to name a few -- by transferring monies to these funds. These transfers can take one of several forms:

   1. **Loans --** Monies that are transferred to another fund and are expected to be repaid are recorded either as **short-term inter-fund receivables (*Due from xxxxx fund*)** or **long-term inter-fund receivables (*Advances to xxxxx fund*)**.

👁 **Example:**
The General Fund transferred $80,000 to a newly created Capital Projects Fund to pay for project start-up expenses. The General Fund expects the Capital Projects Fund to repay the money in six months when its revenues arrive.

General Fund:
DR: **Due from** Capital Projects Fund $80,000

      CR: Cash $80,000

Capital Projects Fund:
DR: Cash $80,000

      CR: **Due to** General Fund $80,000

If the debt were not to be repaid for several years, the entry would be:

General Fund:
DR: **Advances to** Capital Projects Fund $80,000

      CR: Cash $80,000

Capital Projects Fund:
DR Cash $80,000

      CR: **Advances from** General Fund $80,000

2. **Transfers** -- Monies that are transferred to another fund and are **not** expected to be repaid are recorded as Transfers. Although the General Fund occasionally receives monies transferred-in from other funds, transfers-out from the General Fund to another fund are much more common. Transfers are usually made either to **finance another fund's on-going operations**, to **provide investment capital** to a fund (purchase fixed assets, increase working capital, etc.) or to **remove a deficit position**. These transfers are recorded by the fund providing the resources as **Other Financing Uses - Transfers-out** and by the fund receiving the resources as **Other Financing Sources - Transfers-in**.

Study Tip:
Questions on the CPA exam may refer to transfer accounts by their full title: **Other Financing Sources - Transfers-in** and **Other Financing Uses - Transfers-out** or by either part of the account title: **Transfers-in** and **Transfers-out** *or* **Other Financing Sources** or **Other Financing Uses**. Any of the three forms is equally likely to appear in a question.

D. **Common General Fund Entries**

1. **Property Taxes** -- Property taxes are one of the few governmental revenues that are "susceptible to accrual." This means that the revenues are recorded when the property taxes are levied (i.e., when bills are sent out), rather than waiting until payment is received. The standard entry to record property taxes is:

Property Taxes Receivable - Current	XXX
Est. Uncollectible Taxes - Current	XXX
Revenues (or Property Tax Revenue)	XXX

a. Notice that property tax revenue is recognized **net of the estimated uncollectible taxes**. That is, there is **no "Bad Property Tax Expense."** Note also that both the property tax levy and the related uncollectible are designated "Current."

Study Tip: Examiners sometimes test the candidates' algebraic skills along with their accounting knowledge by asking them how to calculate the amount of the property tax levy based on a specified dollar amount of revenues and given percentage of estimated uncollectible taxes.

Example:
1. Property taxes are levied in December, Year X. The taxes are not due until Year Y and are intended to finance activities in Year Y. The entry to record the tax levy is:

DR: Property Taxes Receivable - Current   XXXX

     CR: Est. Uncollectible Taxes-Current   XXXX

     CR: **Deferred** Revenues (or Deferred Property Tax Revenue)   XXXX

2. Hillborough County levies property taxes sufficient to produce revenue of $475,000. If Hillborough anticipates uncollectible taxes to equal 5% of the total levy, what is the amount of the levy?

Levy-(.05 x Levy)	= Revenue
.95 x Levy	= Revenue
.95 x Levy	= 475,000
Levy	= 475,000/.95
Levy	= 500,000

E. Accounting for Delinquent Taxes -- When taxes are not received within a specified period of time, both the receivables and the related uncollectible taxes are reclassified as delinquent.

Property Taxes Receivable - Delinquent XXX	
Est. Uncollectible Taxes - Current XXX	
Property Taxes Receivable - Current	XXX
Est. Uncollectible Taxes - Delinquent	XXX

1. **Changes in estimate of uncollectible taxes --** At the end of the period, the Estimated Uncollectible Taxes are re-evaluated and the allowance account is adjusted appropriately. Note that the offsetting entry is to Revenue. Since property tax revenues are reported net of the allowance for uncollectible taxes, a change in the estimated uncollectibles dictates that the revenue recognized from those transactions is also changed.

2. **Estimate is too low**

DR: Revenues (or Property Tax Revenue) XXX	
CR: Est. Uncollectible Taxes	XXX

3. **Estimate is too high**

DR: Est. Uncollectible Taxes	XXX
CR: Revenues (or Property Tax Revenue)	XXX

4. **End of period revenue deferral** -- Although properly tax revenue is recognized when the property tax bills are sent out (e.g., the property taxes are levied), **if the taxes are not paid during the fiscal year or in the first 60 days on the subsequent fiscal year, then revenue cannot be recognized**. At the end of the period, any revenues not received within the allowable period must be backed out and revenue recognition deferred.

> **Example:** Belmont City levies property taxes totaling $5,000,000 during the current fiscal year. Uncollectible taxes are estimated to be $50,000. When the bills are sent out, Belmont recognizes $4,950,000 in property tax revenue. During the year and in the first 60 days of the subsequent year, Belmont collects property taxes from this levy totaling $4,500,000. Belmont may only recognize the $4,500,000 as revenue during the current fiscal year. Recognition of the remaining $450,000 is deferred until the monies are actually collected by the following entry:
>
> | | | |
> |---|---|---|
> | Revenues (or Property Tax Revenues) | 450,000 | |
> | Deferred Revenues | | 450,000 |

F. **Fines and Penalties on Delinquent Taxes** -- Fines and penalties assessed by the governmental unit on unpaid taxes are handled exactly as the taxes themselves. That is, they are considered to be "susceptible to accrual" and thus revenue net of estimated uncollectible taxes and penalties is recorded when the fines are levied.

Fines and Penalties Receivable - Current	XXX	
Est. Uncollectible Fines & Penalties-Current		XXX
Revenues		XXX

G. **Revenues that are not "Susceptible to Accrual"** -- Unlike property taxes, most general fund revenues (i.e., fees for licenses and permits, charges for services, parking fines, etc.) are *not* "susceptible to accrual." These revenues are **recorded when they are received in cash**, as long as they are legally due.

Cash	XXX	
Revenues Control		XXX

1. If they are **not yet legally due, Deferred Revenues** are recognized.

> **Example:** Rintner County received an $8,000 property tax payment that was not due until the subsequent fiscal year. Rintner recognizes the receipt as Deferred Revenue, a liability account, until the taxes are due. (The account title is usually 'Taxes Received in Advance')
>
> | | | |
> |---|---|---|
> | Cash | 8,000 | |
> | Deferred Revenues | | 8,000 |

H. Long-term Debt Proceeds -- Proceeds received from bonds or other long-term debt issues are not classified as revenues but as Other Financing Sources.

Cash	XXX	
Other Financing Sources-Bond Proceeds		XXX

I. Direct Expenditures -- Not all expenditures are encumbered. Bills for services rendered, monthly billings in irregular amounts (e.g. utilities), and items purchased in a retail environment are not usually encumbered. These types of payments are often called **"direct expenditures."** They are recorded as expenditures immediately without going through the encumbrance process.

Expenditures	XXX	
Cash/Vouchers Payable		XXX

J. Capital Expenditures -- There is no difference in the entry to record payment for a fixed asset such as a computer and a period expenditure such as rent. Both **represent "outflows of financial resources" and both are recorded as expenditures**. The entry to record purchase of a new fixed asset is as follows:

Expenditures	XXX	
Cash/Vouchers Payable		XXX

II. Special Revenue Funds

Definition:
Special Revenue Funds: These funds are used to account for monies restricted or "earmarked" for specific types of general government expenditures.

A. Examples of resources usually accounted for -- Special revenue funds include entitlement monies, which must be used to improve public safety, grants to provide housing assistance to low income constituents, and taxes which must be used for specified purposes.

   1. All restricted resources can be accounted for in special revenue funds except:

      a. Monies restricted to debt service (these are accounted for in a Debt Service Fund);

      b. Monies restricted for capital projects (these are accounted for in a Capital Projects Fund);

      c. Monies that are permanently restricted (e.g., endowments - these are accounted for in a Permanent Fund).

B. Special Revenue Fund Characteristics -- The Special Revenue Fund functions like the General Fund except that it accounts only for *restricted resources*. That is, it:

   1. Uses modified accrual basis accounting;

   2. Uses budgetary and encumbrance accounting;

   3. Accounts for current items only.

C. **Special Revenue Fund Entries --** Special revenue funds receive most of their resources from:

1. Monies transferred to them from the general fund;

2. Intergovernmental transfers;

3. Voluntary grants.

D. **Transfers from the General Fund --** These receipts are always **recorded as Other Financing Sources,** *never* **as Revenues.**

DR: Cash	50,000	
CR: Other Financing Sources - Transfers-In		50,000

E. **Intergovernmental Transfers --** Intergovernmental transfers include items such as **grants, entitlements and shared revenues** which are usually distributed from larger governmental entities (i.e., the federal government) to smaller governmental entities (i.e., states, counties, cities).

1. **Grants, entitlements and shared revenues --** These are always subject to a **purpose restriction** and may also be subject to **eligibility requirements** and/or **time restrictions**. Recognition of these resources is governed by GASB #33 (However, see the note below the examples):

    a. **Eligibility requirements --** Revenue can only be **recognized when all eligibility requirements have been met.** *Most* eligibility requirements for entitlements and shared revenues are generic (e.g., they "must provide for the safety of its citizens") and can *usually* be **assumed to be met**. When there are **specific requirements that are *not* met** (e.g., they "must have provided training in CPR to all public safety officers"), **a liability is recognized** until the eligibility requirements are met.

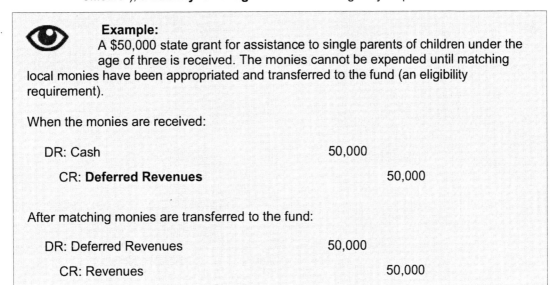

Example:
A $50,000 state grant for assistance to single parents of children under the age of three is received. The monies cannot be expended until matching local monies have been appropriated and transferred to the fund (an eligibility requirement).

When the monies are received:

DR: Cash	50,000	
CR: **Deferred Revenues**		50,000

After matching monies are transferred to the fund:

DR: Deferred Revenues	50,000	
CR: Revenues		50,000

    b. **Time requirements --** When resources **cannot be used before a specified time or event** has taken place, **revenue recognition must be deferred**.

    See the following example.

> 👁 **Example:** On February 1, the McClain School District received $500,000 in federal education entitlement monies. $200,000 of the money can be spent in the current period; the remaining $300,000 cannot be spent until September 1 of the following year.
>
> When the monies are received:
>
> | | | |
> |---|---|---|
> | DR: Cash | 500,000 | |
> | CR: Revenues | | 200,000 |
> | CR: Deferred Revenues | | 300,000 |
>
> On September 1 of the subsequent year:
>
> | | | |
> |---|---|---|
> | DR: Deferred Revenues | 300,000 | |
> | CR: Revenues | | 300,000 |

    c. **Purpose restrictions --** The existence of a **purpose restriction alone does not delay revenue recognition**. This is particularly true when the specified type of expenditure is of an ongoing nature, such as public safety, road maintenance and repair, emergency services, etc. **As long as all other eligibility requirements are met, revenue is recognized immediately**.

> 👁 **Example:** Lakeland County receives 30% of the tax collected on gasoline sales made inside the county limits. On April 10, Lakeland received $1.5M as its share of taxes collected during the first quarter. By law, these monies must be used to maintain existing roads and bridges.
>
> The requirement to use the money to maintain existing roads and bridges is **a purpose restriction, *not* an eligibility requirement**. Therefore, **revenue** related to the transaction can be **recognized immediately**.
>
> | | | |
> |---|---|---|
> | DR Cash | 1.5M | |
> | CR: Revenue | | 1.5M |

F. Voluntary Grants -- While intergovernmental revenues are usually transferred directly to the recipient government for expenditure, most voluntary grants and contracts require that, after a grant is awarded, the **recipient government makes the expenditure first** and then **bills the granting entity** for reimbursement. These types of grants are known as **expenditure-driven** or **reimbursement grants**.

    1. From a revenue recognition viewpoint, the requirement that the governmental entity must first expend resources for the purpose specified in the grant contract can be viewed as an eligibility requirement. Thus, **no revenue is recognized when the grant is awarded**. When an expenditure is made for the specified purpose, the governmental entity prepares a reimbursement request. Assuming all other eligibility requirements have been met, the governmental entity can **recognize a receivable and revenue when the reimbursement request is submitted**.

    2. Note: Recall that GASB #33, which governs revenue recognition for non-exchange transactions such as grants, entitlements, and shared revenues, is a full accrual basis standard. It defines how these revenues will be reported in the government-wide statements (which are prepared on a full accrual basis). However, since Special Revenue

Funds use modified accrual basis accounting, GASB#33 is not sufficient to determine whether revenue will be recorded in the Special Revenue Funds and reported in the fund statements. The rules governing revenue recognition under the modified accrual basis must be considered on top of the GASB #33 rules to make this determination.

Example:

1. A school board makes $20,000 of expenditures in accordance with the specifications of a federal education assistance grant. Documentation of the expenditure and a request for reimbursement is sent to the granting agency.

Expenditure is made:

DR: Expenditures	20,000	
CR: Cash		20,000

Reimbursement is requested:

DR: Grants Receivable	20,000	
CR: Revenue		20,000

2. On November 15, the Town of Live Oak was awarded an expenditure-driven grant of $50,000 by the State Parks Board. This award is appropriately accounted for in a Special Revenue Fund. In December, the Town spent $30,000 in accordance with the grant guidelines and properly billed the State Parks Board for the expenditure. Since the State Parks Board normally requires 90 days to process a reimbursement billing request, the Town does not expect to receive the $30,000 reimbursement until late in March. The Town of Live Oak uses a calendar fiscal year.

According to GASB #33, the Town should recognize revenue of $30,000 when the billing is sent to the State Parks Board. However, since the Town will not receive the reimbursement within the current fiscal period or the first 60 days of the subsequent period, modified accrual basis accounting does not permit the revenue to be recognized. Instead, revenue recognition is deferred until the subsequent period. The entry to record the billing to the State Parks Board then becomes:

DR Grants Receivable	30,000	
CR: Deferred Revenue		30,000

However, the government-wide statements will report revenue of $30,000 during the current year since full accrual basis accounting does not require cash to be received in order to recognize revenue.

III. Debt Service Funds

Definition:
Debt Service Funds: These funds are used to make interest and principal payments on general long term debt.

A. **"General" Debt** -- Debt that has been incurred by the governmental fund types. Bonds are the most common form of general obligation long-term debt but other types of long-term debt (i.e., capital leases, long-term notes payable and long-term claims and judgments against the governmental entity, etc.) are also included in this category.

B. Debt Service Funds -- Do not make payments on *short-term* liabilities or "specific debt" (revenue bonds and other long-term debt attributable to proprietary funds).

> **Note:** Debt Service Funds do not record or report the long-term debt. They only "service" the debt by making the required interest payments and principal re-payments. The long-term debt is recorded in off-books schedules until it matures (e.g., becomes due). Once the debt has matured, the debt service funds record the currently due portions of the debt. When used in reference to general long-term debt, the terms "*current*," "*due*" and, "*currently due*" **mean matured debt,** that is, debt that is on or **past the *due date*.**

> **Example:**
> The City of Mayfield uses a calendar fiscal year. On December 31, it has $100,000,000 of general obligation bonds outstanding. Of this amount, $15,000,000 will mature during the next 12 months; $5,000,000 of this amount matures on January 4.
>
> On its Fund financial statements dated December 31, Mayfield's debt service funds will not report any of this general obligation debt because none of it is currently due (e.g., "matured").
>
> On January 4 - the due date of the debt - the debt service fund will record the $5,000,000 of debt that matures on that day. The entry to recognize the liability is:
>
> DR: Expenditures-Principal $5,000,000
>   CR: Bonds Payable $5,000,000
>
> Typically, this liability will remain on the books for less than 24 hours, because the repayment checks to the bondholders are usually written on the maturity date.
>
> DR: Bonds Payable $5,000,000
>   CR: Cash $5,000,000

C. Debt Service Fund Characteristics -- Debt Service Funds **use modified accrual basis accounting** and may use budgetary accounting. Because they use modified accrual basis accounting, **interest expense** on the outstanding debt **is *not* accrued, but recorded only when it is actually *due* (i.e., *on the due date*).**

1. Debt Service Fund Entries

   a. Debt service funds include entries that:

     i. Record receipt of resources to be used to pay interest and repay principal on general obligation long-term debt;

     ii. Record investment of those resources and recognition of investment earnings;

     iii. Record liabilities related to matured interest and principal on general obligation long-term debt;

     iv. Record payment of matured interest and principal.

D. Receipt of Resources -- The majority of resources received by the debt service funds are transferred from the general fund. **These transfers are never recorded as revenue; they are always recorded as Other Financing Sources.**

Cash	XXX	
Other Financing Sources - Transfers In		XXX

1. Investment related entries -- are resources accumulated to repay the principal of bonds are usually **invested until they are needed.**

Investments	XXX	
Cash		XXX

a. Investment earnings -- are earnings recognized as **revenues.**

Cash/Interest receivable	XXX	
Interest revenue		XXX

Note: Interest revenue on the debt service fund investments, *unlike interest expense on the long-term liabilities,* **is accrued** as long as the earnings will be received in time to meet modified accrual revenue recognition criteria (e.g. within 60 days of year end, which is *usually the case.*

b. Investment management fees -- are recognized as **expenditures** in the debt service fund.

Expenditures-Management fees	XXX	
Cash		XXX

2. Recognition of matured liabilities -- Interest payable on general long-term debt is **recognized on the day that it becomes due.** It is *not* accrued.

Expenditures-Interest	XXX	
Interest Payable		XXX

3. The liability for repayment of matured portions of general long-term debt is recognized on the day that the debt matures.

Expenditures-Principal	XXX	
Bonds Payable		XXX

Note: Under modified accrual basis accounting, both the repayment of principal and payment of interest are recognized as **expenditures** (both require an outflow of financial resources). GASB requires separate reporting of each type of expenditure: **Expenditures-***Interest* and **Expenditures-***Principal.*

E. Payments to Bondholders -- If the payable has been accrued, the following entry is used to record payment to the bondholders:

Interest Payable	XXX	
Bonds Payable	XXX	
Cash		XXX

1. Often, however, the expenditure is *not* accrued but is recognized when the payment is made:

Expenditures - Interest	XXX	
Expenditures - Principal	XXX	
Cash		XXX

IV. Capital Projects Funds

Definition:
Capital Projects Funds: These funds are used to **facilitate resource accumulation** and **manage expenditures** for **major capital projects**.

A. Capital Projects Funds -- do not have to be used for all capital asset acquisition or construction. The general fund frequently finances purchases of smaller capital assets, such as computers, furniture, and vehicles. Capital projects funds are most useful for large purchases or projects in which funding from multiple sources is involved.

B. Capital Projects Fund Characteristics -- Capital Projects Funds use modified accrual basis accounting and recognized encumbrances. They may also use budgetary accounting (although they almost never do on the CPA exam).

1. Capital projects funds are "limited life funds:" they **exist for the life of the project** and are **then closed**.

2. **Surplus monies** in the fund at closing are **transferred** either to a **debt service fund** or to the **general fund**. Assets acquired or constructed through capital projects funds are reported in the Government-wide financial statements.

Note: Although the **expenditures** made to construct or acquire capital assets are recognized in the capital projects funds, the **capital asset** itself **is** *not* **recognized** in the capital projects fund. Like all governmental funds, capital asset funds cannot recognize fixed assets. This **includes "construction in progress,"** which represents the cost of an incomplete fixed asset. Assets constructed and construction in progress are **reported on the government-wide statements** at the **actual amount expended** to acquire them.

C. Capital Projects Fund Entries -- Entries in capital projects funds record:

1. **Receipt of the resources** used to finance the project;

2. **Expenditures** to construct or acquire the capital asset;

3. **Transfers of excess resources** are made when the project is complete (something that rarely happens in practice but is frequently tested on the CPA exam).

D. Receipt of Resources -- Capital projects are usually funded through a combination of bond proceeds, grants, and contributions from the general fund.

1. **Debt funding** -- If **bonds** provide funding, recognize **Another Financing Source:**

Cash	XXX
Other Financing Sources-Bond Proceeds	XXX

Note: If bonds are sold at a **premium**, the premium amount is not available for expenditure in to the capital projects fund but is transferred to a debt service fund where it can be used to repay bondholders.

Example:
Daley City issued $4 M par value bonds to finance construction of a new police headquarters. The bonds were sold for $4.1 M and the proceeds accounted for in a capital projects fund. The **premium** amount is **in excess of the amount authorized** by voters for expenditure on the project and cannot be expended in the capital projects fund. The bond covenant usually specifies that proceeds received in excess of par value must be used to repay the bond liability. Consequently, premiums are usually **transferred to** a **debt service fund**.

Record the **full amount of the proceeds** as an **Other Financing Source** in the capital projects fund.

Cash	4,100,000
Other Financing Sources-Bond Proceeds	4,100,000

Record the **transfer of the premium** to the debt service fund as an **Other Financing Use** in the **capital projects fund** and as an **Other Financing Source** in the **debt service fund**.

Capital Projects Fund:

Other Financing Use-Operating Transfer Out	100,000
Cash	100,000

Debt Service Fund:

Cash	100,000
Other Financing Source-Operating Transfer In	100,000

E. Alternative Treatment -- Capital projects funds sometimes **separate the premium from the bonds** upon receipt of the proceeds, showing only the par value of the bonds as an Other Financing Source and showing the premium as a **liability ("Due to Debt Service Fund")**. In these instances, the **debt service fund** may **recognize** the receipt of the premium as **revenue** rather than an Other Financing Source. However, most CPA exam questions do **not** *follow this approach.*

F. Grant Funding

1. If **grants** provide funding, **Revenue** is usually recognized when the grant is received. However, **depending on the terms of the grant contract**, revenue **recognition may be deferred** until eligibility requirements are met or until the monies are actually expended. The general **rules prescribed by GASB #33 govern recognition** of grant proceeds.

Cash	XXX	
Grant Revenues or Deferred Grant Revenues		XXX

2. **Transfers from other funds --** If **transfers** from the general fund or other fund provide funding, recognize the receipt as an **Other Financing Source**:

Cash	XXX	
Other Financing Sources- Transfer In		XXX

G. Expenditures -- **All amounts paid** for the acquisition or construction of a capital asset, whether for materials, labor or equipment, are recorded as **Expenditures**. Somewhat specialized entries occur, however, when construction of the asset is contracted to a private company.

1. When the **contract is signed**, an **encumbrance** is created for the entire amount of the contract. As the contractor submits **progress billings**, the **encumbrance is partially liquidated**.

> **Example:**
> **1.** Amestown signed a $2 M contract with Bowie Construction to build a new auditorium. Bowie submitted a progress billing for $200,000 when the building was 10% complete.
>
> Entry to recognize the contract:
>
> | | | |
> |---|---|---|
> | Encumbrances | 2,000,000 | |
> | Fund Balance Committed | | 2,000,000 |
>
> Entry to record the progress billing:
>
> | | | |
> |---|---|---|
> | Fund Balance Committed | 200,000 | |
> | Encumbrances | | 200,000 |
> | Expenditures | 200,000 | |
> | Contracts Payable | | 200,000 |
>
> When the progress **billing is paid**, a **portion of the payment is usually withheld**. This amount is known as a **"retained percentage"**. The retained percentage is **withheld until the project is satisfactorily completed**. If corrections need to be made and the original contractor is unable or unwilling to make the corrections, these monies are available to fund the work. Once the project has been approved any remaining money is remitted to the original contractor.
>
> **2.** Amestown's contract with Bowie Construction specified that 10% of all billings would be retained.
>
> Entry to record payment of the $200,000 progress billing already recorded.

Contracts Payable	200,000	
Retained Percentage		20,000
Cash		180,000

If **corrections are required** in order for the project to be approved and the original contractor does not elect to complete the work, the work is **paid from the Retained Percentage** account.

2. **Payments --** For additional work made from the Retained Percentage account **do *not* create any additional expenditures**.

Example:
Upon completion of the auditorium, inspection revealed that an additional $80,000 work was needed to correct deficiencies in construction. Bowie elects to forfeit that amount from its retained percentage and let another contractor complete the job.

Entry to pay the other contractor:

Retained Percentage	80,000	
Cash		80,000

H. **Transfer of Excess Resources --** After **construction is completed**, the **capital projects fund is eliminated**.

1. Any **remaining monies are transferred** to other funds. **If bonds have been used** to finance the project, the transfer is usually to the **debt service fund**.

Example:
Patterson County recently completed a new park headquarters building. The building was financed through bond issues and the construction was accounted for in a Capital Projects Fund. After all bills were paid, $30,000 cash remained in the fund.

Entry to record the transfer of the cash to the debt service fund.

Capital Projects Fund:

Other Financing Use - Transfer-out	30,000	
Cash		30,000

Debt Service Fund:

Cash	30,000	
Other Financing Source- Transfer-in		30,000

Entry to close the capital projects fund (assuming all other accounts had been closed prior to transfer of the cash to the debt service fund:

Capital Projects Fund:	
Fund Balance	30,000
Other Financing Use -Operating Transfer-Out	30,000

V. Permanent Funds

Definition:
Permanent Funds: These funds account for the principal and earnings of endowments that must be used for the benefit of governmental programs.

A. **The Endowment Principal --** This is typically received as a contribution or a bequest from a private individual or organization. By accepting the endowment, the governmental entity agrees to invest and maintain the principal intact, usually in perpetuity, and to expend the net earnings on the investment for the purposes stated in the endowment agreement. In order to be accounted for in a permanent fund, the purposes must be in support of government programs or for the benefit of the constituents in general.

Note: Most questions about permanent funds focus on whether it is appropriate to account for a contribution or bequest in a permanent fund. If the resources contributed **need** *not* **be held in perpetuity but may be expended** for the governmental purpose, they should be *not* **accounted for in a permanent fund** but would most likely be accounted for in a **special revenue fund**. If the **purpose** of the expenditures is for a **non-governmental purpose or the benefit of specific individuals** (for example, to provide an annual award to recognize an outstanding business), the resources should be accounted for in a **private purpose trust fund**.

B. **Characteristics of Permanent Funds --** Permanent funds use **modified accrual basis** accounting, but they are not usually budgeted nor do they typically use encumbrances. Although they account for the **non-expendable endowment principal** and the **expendable earnings** on the endowment, they **do** *not* **account for the related expenditures** (e.g., expenditures for the purpose(s) specified in the endowment agreement). Instead, the **net expendable earnings are transferred** to the fund responsible for the specified type of expenditure, which is usually a **special revenue fund**.

C. **Permanent Fund Entries --** Entries in permanent funds are usually limited to recognition of:

1. Receipt of the **endowment principal**;

2. Receipt of **investment earnings**;

3. **Transfer of net expendable earnings**.

D. **Receipt of Endowment Principal --** GASB #33 specifically requires that the receipt of endowment principal (a nonexchange transaction) be recognized as Revenue when received.

E. **Investment Earnings --** Investment earnings have two components: **periodic income** (i.e. interest and dividends) and **capital gains** (gains and losses on the sale of investments). Depending on the endowment agreement, these two components can receive very different accounting treatments.

1. **Interest and dividends --** Interest and dividends, net of any related expenses, are usually considered fully expendable. The **gross revenue** is recognized in the **permanent fund**.

2. Note that investment management fees and other expenditures required to maintain the endowment principal are also recognized in the permanent fund. These fees are deducted from investment earnings to determine net expendable earnings.

3. **Capital gains (and losses)** -- In the absence of specific instructions to the contrary, gains (and losses) on the sale of investments are usually considered to be adjustments to the principal. That is, they are ***not* expendable**.

F. **Transfer of Net Expendable Earnings** -- Expenditures for the purpose(s) identified in the endowment agreement are not made by the Permanent Fund. Instead, the earnings are transferred to the fund responsible for the type of expenditure specified in the agreement.

G. **Net Expendable Earnings --** Are determined by deducting management fees and other charges necessary to maintain the principal from periodic investment income (interest and dividends).

Example:
The City of Towson recently received an endowment consisting of $1,000,000 of cash and securities. The endowment agreement specified that the net earnings on the endowment were to be used to support after-school recreational activities in the city parks. During the year, the endowment received $45,000 of interest revenue and paid $2,000 in investment management fees. Expenditures totaling $20,000 were made for the purposes designated in the endowment agreement.

Entry to record receipt of endowment principal (The permanent fund is the appropriate fund in which to record the endowment as a provision of recreational activities is a governmental function that benefits the citizenry in general):

Permanent Fund:

Cash/Securities	1,0000,000	
Revenue		1,0000,000

Entry to record receipt of interest revenue:

Permanent Fund:

Cash	45,000	
Revenue-Interest		45,000

Entry to record payment of investment management fees (Permanent funds can make expenditures necessary to maintain and manage the endowment principal):

Permanent Fund:

Expenditures -investment management	2,000	
Cash		2,000

Entry to record transfer of net expendable earnings to an expendable fund (In this case, we assume a special revenue fund):

Permanent Fund:

Other Financing Uses - Transfer-out	43,000	
Cash		43,000

Special Revenue Fund:
Cash   43,000

    Other Financing Sources   43,000

Entry to record expenditure for the purpose of the endowment:

Special Revenue Fund:
Expenditures   20,000

    Cash   20,000

Proprietary Funds

This lesson describes the financial reporting for proprietary funds.

After studying this lesson, you should be able to:

1. *List the two types of proprietary funds and describe the purpose of each.*

2. *List the three types of financial statements for proprietary funds.*

Note: Remember the acronym **"DRIP-CEG-PIPPA"** - **(DRIP): D**ebt Service Funds, Special **R**evenue Funds, **I**nternal Service Funds, **P**ermanent Funds; **(CEG): C**apital Projects Funds, **E**nterprise Funds, **G**eneral Fund; **(PIPPA): P**ension Trust Funds, **I**nvestment Trust Funds, **P**rivate **P**urpose Trust Funds, **A**gency Funds - a mnemonic for remembering the eleven types of funds. Proprietary funds are the vowels in **"DRIP-CEG."**

I. **Internal Service Funds**

A. **Characteristics --** These funds use full accrual accounting since they are concerned with measuring profit and maintaining capital. Therefore, they:

1. carry their own fixed assets and long-term debt,

2. record depreciation expense;,

3. use standard accounting terminology, that is, expenses, not expenditures and net assets (replaced by "net position" by GASB #63), not fund balance.

B. **Financed --** Internal Service Funds are financed through charges to user departments (which are usually intended to recover at least 50% of operating costs) and contributions from the general fund.

C. **Receive Transfers --** Internal Service Funds most often receive transfers from the General Fund to provide capital for the initial start-up of the fund or for later expansion. These transfers are reported as Transfers (In) by the Internal Service Fund and as Other Financing Uses-Transfers (Out) by the General Fund. At year-end, the Internal Service Fund will close this amount to its Contributed Capital account.

D. **Subsidized --** The day-to-day operations of the fund may also be subsidized by transfers from the General Fund. These transfers are reported as Transfers (In) by the Internal Service Fund and as Other Financing Uses-Transfers (Out) by the General Fund. At year-end, the Internal Service Fund will close this amount to its Retained Earnings account.

See the following example.

Example:
The ABC County maintains a motor pool to provide transportation for county administrators on official business. ABC follows a practice of subsidizing 30% of the operating costs of the motor pool from General Fund resources. During the current period ABC transferred $36,000 to subsidize current operations and transferred another $80,000 to expand the motor pool by 4 vehicles. How should these transfers be reported?

General Fund:

Other Financing Uses-Operating Transfer Out	116,000	
Cash		116,000

Internal Service Fund:

Cash	116,000	
Operating Transfer In		36,000
Contributed Capital		80,000

Note: Under GASB #33, no distinctions are made between Residual Equity Transfers and Operating Transfers.

E. **Transactions --** When the Internal Service Fund charges fees to other departments for goods and services, the transactions are recorded just as they would be if the transaction was with an external business. That is, the Internal Service Fund recognizes operating revenue and the recipient fund recognizes an expenditure (or expense, as appropriate for the fund). These transactions are called Quasi-External Transactions.

1. All charges for services (i.e., revenue), which would normally result in a debit to the Accounts Receivable account, are shown as amounts "Due from (fund name):"

Due from Special Revenue Fund XXX	
Operating Revenue	XXX

2. Statement of Revenues and Expenses distinguishes *operating revenues* (charges for goods and services) from *nonoperating revenues* (interest) from *operating transfers* (regular, recurring transfers from the General Fund intended to subsidize operations)

   a. Contributions from the General Fund that are not to be repaid are recorded by crediting an equity account -- *Contributions from General Fund*;

   b. General Fund monies that are used for temporary financing needs and are expected to be repaid are accounted for by crediting *Advances from General Fund*, which is a liability account.

3. The equity section of the Balance Sheet has three principal accounts:

   a. Invested in Capital Assets, Net of Related Debt,

   b. Restricted Net Position,

   c. Unrestricted Net Position.

4. The Statement of Cash Flows has four categories (as opposed to the three categories found in for-profit statements):

    a. Operations - from the production of goods and services only (i.e., operating income, not net income); this excludes items such as interest and operating transfers,

    b. Noncapital financing - from debtor activities not clearly related to capital transactions,

    c. Capital financing - from the acquisition or disposal of capital assets or borrowing and repayment clearly related to capital activities,

    d. Investing - from gains and losses on investments and creditor activities and interest.

F. Enterprise Funds

    1. These funds account for entities that provide goods and services to the general public, such as urban transportation departments, swimming pools, electric and water utilities, etc.

    2. Accounting is the same as for Internal Service Funds.

Note: GASB Statement No. 62, *Codification of Accounting and Financial Reporting Guidance Contain in Pre-November 30, 1989 FASB and AICPA Pronouncements*, incorporates into the GASB codification guidance that was found in FASB and AICPA pronouncements. The change was necessary because the FASB Accounting Standards Codification, which supercedes the previous FASB pronouncements, would no longer be readily available to some GASB constituents. Through the issuance of GASBS #62, that guidance is now readily available within the GASB codification. In addition, GASBS #62 eliminated an election for enterprise funds and business-type activities to apply post-November 30, 1989 FASB Statements and Interpretations that do not conflict with or contradict GASB pronouncements. (November 30, 1989 was the date that the Financial Accounting Foundation reaffirmed GASB as the standard-setting body for governmental entities.)

Fiduciary Funds

This lesson describes the financial reporting for fiduciary funds.

After studying this lesson, you should be able to:

1. *List the four types of fiduciary funds and describe the purpose of each.*

2. *Describe the financial statements required for fiduciary funds.*

> **Note:** Remember the acronym **"DRIP-CEG-PIPPA"** - **(DRIP): D**ebt Service Funds, Special **R**evenue Funds, **I**nternal Service Funds, **P**ermanent Funds; **(CEG): C**apital Projects Funds, **E**nterprise Funds, **G**eneral Fund; **(PIPPA): P**ension Trust Funds, **I**nvestment Trust Funds, **P**rivate **P**urpose Trust Funds, **A**gency Funds - a mnemonic for remembering the eleven types of funds. Fiduciary funds are represented by **"PIPPA"** in the acronym.

I. Agency Funds

A. **Overview of Agency Fund Transactions** -- Governmental entities frequently act as intermediaries in the process of disbursing monies from one governmental entity to another. For example, in a federal program designed to distribute monies to cities across the country, it is common for the federal program to disburse money to the states, which are required to disburse the money to the counties within the state, which are in turn required to disburse the monies to the cities within the counties. When the intermediate entities make these disbursements according to predetermined instructions or a formula, with little or no judgment required, they are acting as Agents and appropriately account for the transactions in an Agency Fund.

1. Since the governmental entity has no claim on these resources, but merely acts as a cash conduit, it does not recognize revenues when it receives the monies or recognize expenses when it disburses the monies.

   a. Instead, it recognizes a liability when the monies are received and a reduction in liabilities when the monies are disbursed.

   b. Because the assets (usually cash) recorded in an Agency Fund are always fully offset by a related liability, Agency Funds do not have a net position: assets minus liabilities always equals zero.

   See the following example..

> **Example:** On July 13, Markson County received $800,000 from the State that is to be distributed to the school districts within the county in proportion to the number of students in each district. On July 22, Markson distributed $250,000 to the Peabody School district, $150,000 to Jim Pierce School District, and $400,000 to Central School District. Prepare the entries to record the receipt of the monies from the State and the disbursement of the monies to school districts:
>
> **Agency Fund:**
>
> DR: Cash   800,000
>
>   CR: Due to School Districts   800,000
>
> To record receipt of monies payable to the school districts
>
> DR: Due to School Districts   800,000
>
>   CR: Cash   800,000
>
> To record distribution of monies to the school districts

2. **Financial Reporting for Agency Funds --** Agency Funds, like all Fiduciary Funds, use full accrual basis accounting. Technically, also like all Fiduciary Funds, Agency Funds prepare a Statement of Net Position and a Statement of Changes in Net Position. However, since Agency Fund assets are always completely offset by liabilities, they do not report Net Position (Assets - Liabilities = 0).

   a. Because Agency Funds do not report any Net Assets, they cannot have any changes in net position and consequently do not prepare a Statement of Changes in Net Position.

B. **Tax Agency Funds --** When several governmental entities have taxing authority over a single piece of property, the governmental entities typically work together to send out a single bill to the taxpayer. The taxpayer returns a single payment to one of the taxing entities (the "collecting entity," which is typically a county), which in turn disburses the appropriate amount to each of the other taxing entities. These transactions are recorded in a Tax Agency Fund.

   1. **Five entries are commonly made in the Tax Agency Fund**

      a. **Recognizing the tax levy --** Each taxing entity records its portion of the tax levy in its general fund (or other governmental fund, as appropriate). The gross amount of the total levy across all taxing entities is recorded in the Tax Agency Fund by debiting a receivable account and crediting a generic liability account (e.g. "Due to Other Governments").

> **Example:**
> The Brower County Tax Agency fund has been established to account for the collection and distribution of the county's and the City of Thurman's property taxes. The tax levies for the year were $600,000 for the County and $400,000 for the City. It is expected that the uncollectible taxes will be $15,000 for the County and $10,000 for the City.
>
> **Agency Fund:**
>
> DR: Taxes Receivable for Other Governments   1,000,000
>
>   CR: Due to Other Governments   1,000,000
>
> To record levy of taxes (note that the full amount of the levy is recognized: *the estimated uncollectible is ignored*).

b. **Recording payments** -- When tax payments are received, the collecting entity recognizes the receipt of cash in the Tax Agency Fund and reduces the outstanding Taxes Receivable.

Example:
The previous example is continued. The County received $540,000 of tax payments.

Agency Fund:

DR: Cash	540,000	
CR: Taxes Receivable for Other Governments		540,000

To record receipt of $540,000 of tax payments.

c. **Recognizing amounts payable to specific taxing entities** -- When tax payments are received, the collecting entity determines the amounts due to each of the taxing entities according to tax rate schedules. The amount payable to each entity is recognized by creating a specific liability account for each entity and reduces the generic liability account.

Example:
The previous example is again continued. After reviewing the relevant tax rate documents, the County determined that $300,000 of the total $540,000 of tax payments belonged to the County and the remaining $240,000 belonged to the City.

Agency Fund:

DR: Due to Other Governments	540,000	
CR: Due to Brower County General Fund		300,000
CR: Due to City of Thurman		240,000

To recognize amounts due to specific taxing entities.

d. **Recognizing processing fees** -- It is usual for the collecting entity to charge a small fee, usually a percentage of the amount collected, to the other taxing entities. The fee is recognized in the Agency Fund by reducing the amounts owed to the other taxing entities and increasing the amount owed to the collecting entity. Note that revenue and expenses related to this transaction are not recognized in the Agency Fund: the individual taxing entities will recognize revenue or expense when the monies are distributed.

Example:
Suppose that, in the previous example, the County charged a 1% fee to the City to cover the administrative costs associated with collecting and disbursing the property taxes. The processing fee associated with the $240,000 of taxes due to the City of Thurman is $2,400 and is recognized by reducing the amount due to the City of Thurman and increasing the amount due to Brower County.

Agency Fund:

DR: Due to City of Thurman	2,400	
CR: Due to Brower County General Fund		2,400

e. **Disbursing the cash payments** -- Periodically (once a week, once a month), the collecting entity disburses the collections to the taxing entities. This is recorded in the Agency Fund by simply crediting cash and debiting the appropriate liability accounts.

 Example: The previous example is completed. At the end of the week the County disburses the tax payments to its General Fund and to the City of Thurmond General Fund in accordance with the individual entity liability accounts.

Agency Fund:

DR: Due to City of Thurman ($240,000 - $2,400)	237,600	
DR: Due to Brower County General Fund ($300,000 + $2,400)	302,400	
CR: Cash		540,000

To disburse tax collections to taxing entities.

2. When the taxing entity receives payment for the taxes collected on its behalf, it reduces its Property Tax Receivable account and increases its Cash account. To the extent that there is a difference between the amount of taxes actually collected and the amount disbursed to the taxing entity, the taxing entity recognizes revenues or expenditures for the difference.

 Example: In the previous example, Brower County received $302,400, which represented the tax payments collected on its behalf plus a processing fee paid by the City of Thurman. The City of Thurman received $237,600, which consisted of the tax payments collected on its behalf less the processing fee paid to Brower County. Each entity records the receipt of the payment in its General Fund as shown below:

Brower County General Fund:

DR: Cash	302,400	
CR: Property Taxes Receivable-Current		300,000
CR: Revenue - Processing Fee		2,400

To record receipt of tax payments and processing fee.

City of Thurman General Fund:

DR: Cash	237,600	
DR: Expenditures - Processing Fee	2,400	
CR: Property Taxes Receivable-Current		240,000

To record receipt of tax payments and payment of processing fee.

C. **Special Assessment Agency Funds** -- Special assessment projects are often financed with debt issues. Though the debt is to be repaid from special assessments levied on the property owners, the governmental entity usually assumes secondary liability for the debt in the event that the property owners default on their payments. Under these circumstances, the levy of the special assessment and the payments to the bondholders are accounted for in a debt service fund and the special assessment debt is included with other general long-term debt.

1. Sometimes, however, the governmental entity does not assume secondary liability for the debt and merely acts as an agent for the bondholders by collecting the special assessment levy from the property owners and remitting payments for interest and principal to the bondholders. In these cases, the levy of the special assessment and the payments to the bondholders are accounted for in an agency fund and the special assessment debt is not reported with other general long-term debt.

   a. **Five entries are commonly made in the Special Assessment Agency Fund**

      i. **Levy of the special assessment** -- After the project is completed, the special assessment is levied. The full amount of the special assessment is recorded at this time, although it is split into a current and a deferred portion. The debit for the special assessments receivable is recorded just as it would be in a debt service fund. However, instead of crediting revenues, the offsetting credit is to a liability account (usually titled "Due to Bondholders").

      Example: Mill City recently completed a street improvement project that was to be paid for in part by a special assessment of $800,000 levied on the property owners who benefited from the improvements. The special assessment is payable over 10 years, with $80,000 of the assessment becoming current each year. $800,000 of special assessment bonds, which were not secondarily backed by the City, were issued to cover the construction costs. Interest expense and principal repayments on the bonds are to be paid from the special assessment collections. The entry to record the levy of the special assessment is as follows (note that the actual liability for the bonds is not recorded as the City does not assume any liability for the bonds but merely acts as an agent in remitting payments to the bondholders).

      Special Assessment Agency Fund:

DR: Special Assessments Receivable-Current	80,000	
DR: Special Assessments Receivable-Deferred	720,000	
CR: Due to Bondholders		800,000

      To record levy of the special assessment.

      ii. **Receipt of payments from the property owners** -- In general, the entry to record payment of the currently due portion of the special assessment is straightforward: debit Cash and credit Special Assessments Receivable for the amount of the payment. Sometimes, however, the payment may also include interest and penalties for late payment. If the additional amounts have not been accrued (as is usually the case), these amounts are simply shown as being "due to the bondholders."

      Example: Mill City received $78,000 in special assessment collections. This amount represented payment of $77,000 of currently due special assessment receivables and $1,000 in interest and penalties associated with assessments that were not paid on a timely basis (the interest and penalties have not been recorded as receivables).

      Special Assessment Agency Fund:

DR: Cash	78,000	
CR: Special Assessments Receivable-Current		77,000
CR: Due to Bondholders		1,000

      To payment of special assessments.

iii. **Payment of interest and principal to bondholders --** The payment of interest and any currently due portions of principal to the bondholders is recorded by decreasing cash and decreasing the liability account "Due to Bondholders" by a corresponding amount. No expense is recognized.

Example:
At the end of the year, interest of $32,000 was due to the bondholders. In addition, $40,000 of the bond principal matured at the end of the year. The entry to record this payment to the bondholders is shown below:

Special Assessment Agency Fund:

DR: Due to Bondholders	72,000	
CR: Cash		72,000

To payment of interest and principal to bondholders.

II. Investment Trust Funds

A. **Overview of Investment Trust Fund Transactions --** In order to maximize earnings on their investments, governmental entities frequently "pool" or commingle idle cash from many funds into a single "Pooled Investment" account. Some governments also permit external governmental entities to contribute monies to the investment pool, especially if the external entities lack sufficient size and/or the expertise to manage efficiently their investments themselves. When an investment pool includes external participants, GASB requires the use of an Investment Trust Fund to record and report the interests of the external participants.

1. **Valuation of the Investment Pool Assets --** Securities held by the investment pool are reported at fair value. The pool is revalued whenever investment income is distributed to the participants and whenever a participating entity adds to or withdraws resources from the pool.

   a. Because of this, investment income is typically distributed to participants on a monthly or quarterly basis and participants can only change their investment in the pool at these points in time.

2. **Distribution of Investment Income --** Interest, dividends, and realized and unrealized gains and losses on investments are distributed to participants in the pool based on their proportionate share of the investment.

   a. Income sharing ratios are established whenever participants add to or withdraw resources from the pool. However, distribution of income does not change the income-sharing ratio since the income is distributed to all participants proportionately.

3. **Reporting Participation of External Entities --** The net interest of external entities participating in the investment pool is reported as Net Position of Investment Trust Fund.

   a. Each external entity has a separate Net Position account, which is typically listed as "Net Position Held In Trust for XXXXX."

   b. Investment pool resources related to internal participants are shown as a liability in the Investment Trust Fund.

   See the following example.

Statement of Net Position Investment Trust Fund			
Assets		**Liabilities**	
Cash	$ 1,000,000	Due to General Fund	$ 10,000,000
Investments	19,000,000	Due to Capital Projects Fund	5,000,000
Total Assets	*$20,000,000*	*Total Liabilities*	*$15,000,000*
		Net Position	
		Held in Trust for City X	$ 3,000,000
		Held in Trust for School District	2,000,000
		Total Net Position	*$5,000,000*
		Total Liabilities and Net Position	*$20,000,000*

4. **Reporting Changes in Investment --** Changes in a participant's investment in the investment pool arise from three principal sources:

   a. Contribution of resources to the investment pool - this may be the initial contribution of a new participant or an additional contribution from a current participant.

   b. Withdrawal of resources from the investment pool - the withdrawal may be a partial or complete withdrawal.

   c. Net investment earnings - here used in the broadest sense to include realized and unrealized gains and losses on the investment assets, interest revenue, and dividends - net of any management fees and transaction costs.

   d. Although the Investment Trust Fund, like the other Fiduciary Funds, uses full accrual basis accounting rules to recognize revenues and expenses, because these resources do not belong to the governmental entity, they are reported on the financial statements as "Additions" and "Deductions," respectively.

      i. Common items listed under Additions include Contributions and Investment Earnings;

      ii. Common items listed under Deductions include Withdrawals and Management Fees.

   e. Only increases and decreases in the investment assets of external pool participants are reported in the Investment Trust Fund's statements: the internal pool participants report increases and decreases in their respective funds.

      See the following example.

Statement of Changes in Net Position Investment Trust Fund

Additions:

Investment Earnings	$ 300,000
Contributions	50,000
Total additions:	350,000

Deductions:

Withdrawals	100,000
Total withdrawals:	100,000
Change in Net Position	$ 250,000
Beginning Net Position	4,750,000
Ending Net Position	$5,000,000

Note: The following entries are provided to add depth to your understanding of the purpose and use of Investment Trust Funds. However, the entries themselves are rarely tested on the CPA exam.

B. **Recognition and Distribution of Investment Income --** Although most investment pools distribute income to participants periodically, investment income, such as interest revenue, dividends, etc., accrues on a continuous basis. Therefore, as income accrues, it is first recorded in a holding account and then later distributed to the pool participants. Changes in the fair value of the pool investments are handled in a similar manner.

  1. **Common entries in Investment Trust Funds --** There are four principal entries in Investment Trust Funds.

     a. **Entry to record investment income --** When investment income is received or accrues, the appropriate asset account is debited and a holding account entitle "Undistributed Earnings on Pooled Investments" is credited.

Example:
During the quarter, the Investment Pool for Grimes County received dividends totaling $50,000 and interest totaling $120,000. At the end of the quarter, an additional $30,000 in interest had accrued. The income is placed in the holding account to await distribution as shown below:

Investment Trust Fund:

DR: Cash	170,000	
DR: Interest Receivable	30,000	
CR: Undistributed Earnings on Pooled Investments		200,000

To record investment income for the quarter.

---

     b. **Entry to record sale of securities --** When securities are sold, the gain or loss on the sale is placed in a holding account until the end of the period.

Example:
During the quarter, the securities costing $500,000 were sold for $450,000, resulting in a realized loss of $50,000. The entry to record the sale shown below:

Investment Trust Fund:

DR: Cash	450,000
DR: Undistributed Change in Fair Value of Pooled Investments	50,000
CR: Investments	500,000

To record sale of securities at a loss.

c. **Entry to record revaluation of the portfolio --** Whenever income is scheduled to be distributed to the pool participants or when participants add or withdraw resources from the investment pool, the fair value of the investment pool is determined and the change in fair value is calculated. This unrealized gain or loss is combined in the holding account with the realized gains and losses on the sale of securities for distribution to the pool participants.

Example:
At the end of the quarter, the fair value of the securities held in the investment pool was $19,350,000. The book value of the investments at the end of the quarter was $18,500,000, resulting in an unrealized gain of $850,000. This gain is recorded as shown below:

Investment Trust Fund:

DR: Investments	850,000
CR: Undistributed Change in Fair Value of Pooled Investments	850,000

To record change in fair value of the investment portfolio.

d. **Entry to record distribution of investment earnings to pool participants --** Both the Undistributed Earnings on Pooled Investments and the Undistributed Change in Fair Value of Pooled Investments are periodically distributed to the pool participants in accordance with their proportionate interest in the investment pool. Since distributions to external participants increase the net position of the Investment Trust Fund, they are recorded as revenues (additions) to the Investment Trust Fund. Distributions to internal participants, however, simply increase the liability to the internal participants recorded in the Investment Trust Fund: the internal participants will report the revenue in their fund statements.

See the following example.

Example:

At the end of the quarter, the investment earnings and change in the fair value of the investment portfolio are distributed to the participants in proportion to their interest in the pooled investment. The internal and external participants interests are as follows:

Internal Participants		Proportionate Interest
General Fund	$ 10,000,000	50%
Capital Projects Fund	5,000,000	25%

External Participants		
City X	$ 3,000,000	15%
School District	2,000,000	10%
Total Interest in Investment Pool	*$20,000,000*	*100%*

The balance in the Undistributed Earnings on Pooled Investments account of $200,000 and the balance in the Undistributed Change in Fair Value of Pooled Investments account of $800,000 are distributed as shown below:

Investment Trust Fund:

DR: Undistributed Earnings on Pooled Investments	200,000	
CR: Due to General Fund (50% x $200,000)		100,000
CR: Due to Capital Projects Fund (25% x $200,000)		50,000
CR: Additions - Investment Income (10%+15%)x $200,000)		50,000

To distribute investment earnings to investment pool participants.

Investment Trust Fund:

DR: Undistributed Change in Fair Value of Pooled Investments	800,000	
CR: Due to General Fund (50% x $800,000)		400,000
CR: Due to Capital Projects Fund (25% x $800,000)		200,000
CR: Additions - Investment Income (10%+15%)x $800,000)		200,000

To distribute realized and unrealized gains and losses on investments to participants.

2. **Recognition of investment earnings of internal participants --** Internal participants are notified when investment earnings are distributed to investment pool participants. Each internal participant makes an entry to recognize revenue in the appropriate fund and increases their Pooled Investment account to reflect the increase in the Investment Trust Fund.

See the following example.

Example:
The Investment Trust Fund notifies the internal participants of their earnings. Each fund makes an appropriate entry in their fund accounts, as shown below:

General Fund:
DR: Pooled Investments ($100,000 + $400,000)	500,000	
CR: Investment Revenue		500,000

To record quarterly earnings on pooled investments.

Capital Projects Fund:
DR: Pooled Investments ($50,000 + $200,000)	250,000	
CR: Investment Revenue		250,000

To record quarterly earnings on pooled investments.

III. Pension Trust Funds

A. **Overview of Pension Plans --** Pension plans are categorized in several different ways.

1. **Defined Contribution vs. Defined Benefit Plans --** There are two broad types of pension plans: **defined contribution** plans and **defined benefit** plans. In defined contribution plans, the employer and the employee make contributions to the plan, which are invested and earn a return. Upon retirement, the employee is entitled to the total contributions made on his or her behalf plus the accumulated earnings on those contributions, whatever they may be. Thus, while the *contributions* to these funds are defined, the *benefits* are determined by the performance of the invested assets. Because plan benefits are based on existing resources, *no actuarial calculations are necessary* to determine the plan liability or the required contribution to the plan.

   a. Defined benefit plans specify, in relative terms, the future benefits that the plan will pay out (e.g., 2/3 of the average annual salary during the last three years of employment). Actuarial calculations are necessary to establish the present dollar value of these benefits and to determine the annual contribution necessary in order to have sufficient resources available to pay retirement benefits.

      i. Pension Trust Funds account for the *nominal transactions* of both defined contribution and defined benefit plans: *no actuarial calculations* are included in the Pension Trust Fund amounts.

      ii. Defined benefit plans require the disclosure of actuarial assumptions and calculations and the inclusion of several additional schedules in the Required Supplementary Information (RSI) section of the Comprehensive Annual Financial Report (CAFR).

2. **Single employer plans vs. multiple employer plans --** "Single-employer" plans are exactly what they say. They are individual plans set up by an individual governmental employer to cover a specified class(es) of employees. A single-employer plan, however, does not necessarily mean "single-*plan*." Many governmental entities offer several different pension plans to different classes of employees (e.g., one plan for public safety personnel and another plan for administrative personnel). A governmental entity may offer several different single-employer plans.

a. Sometimes, in an effort to provide better-quality, lower-cost plans to their employees, smaller employers band together and jointly create a retirement plan that covers all of their employees. These plans are known as *multiple-employer plans*. States frequently provide a plan that is available to all the employees of any governmental entity within its jurisdiction. These plans are known as Public Employee Retirement Systems (PERS).

   i. GASB's pension reporting requirements apply to both single-employer and multiple-employer plans.

B. Reporting for Pension Trust Funds -- Pension Trust Funds account for the resources currently available in the pension plan (Statement of Plan Net Position) and for the changes in those resources during the period (Statement of Changes in Plan Net Position). All of the amounts presented in the Pension Trust Fund statements are in nominal (actual) dollar amount: *no actuarial amounts are presented*.

   1. Statement of Plan Net Position -- This statement is required for all types of pension plans. The most distinctive feature of the statement is the title of the net position section: Net Position Held in Trust for Pension Benefits.

Statement of Plan Net Position

Pension Trust Fund

Assets

Cash	$ 15,000,000
Interest Receivable	500,000
Investments	54,500,000
Total Assets	70,000,000

Liabilities

Accounts Payable	$ 500,000
Annuities Payable	1,500,000
Total Liabilities	$ 2,000,000
Net Position Held in Trust for Pension Benefits	$68,000,000

---

   2. Statement of Changes in Plan Net Position -- This statement is also prepared for both defined contribution and defined benefit plans. Note that the statement presents *Additions* and *Deductions* rather than Revenues and Expenses. This terminology reflects the fact that these resources do not belong to the governmental entity and so cannot generate revenues and expenses for the governmental entity.

   a. Additions (revenues) and Deductions (expenses) are recognized on the full accrual basis.

   b. The principal Additions (revenues) recognized in the Pension Trust Fund consist of:

   i. Contributions to the plan from the employee;

   ii. Contributions to the plan from the employer;

   iii. Investment earnings.

c. The principal Deductions (expenses) recognized in the Pension Trust Fund consist of payments to retirees, refunds to terminated employees, and investment management fees.

Note: Some CPA exam questions still ask about the amount of Revenue or Expense recognized in Fiduciary Funds. Although GASB now requires Fiduciary Funds to *report* Additions and Deductions in their financial statements, it is permissible to *record* Revenues and Expenses in the fund and simply convert them to Additions and Deductions for reporting purposes. Consequently, questions that ask about Revenue or Expense recognition in the funds can be answered without undue concern about the terminology used in the question.

Statement of Changes in Plan Net Position
Pension Trust Fund

Additions:

Contributions:

Employer	$ 1,200,000
Employee	800,000
Total Contributions:	2,000,000

Investment Income:

Interest and dividends	1,800,000
Net increase in fair value of investments	400,000
Total Investment Income:	2,200,000
Total additions	*4,200,000*

Deductions:

Retirement annuities	1,400,000
Disability benefits	400,000
Refunds to terminated employees	200,000
Administrative expenses	300,000
Total deductions	*2,300,000*

Net Increase   1,900,000

Net Position Held in Trust for Pension Benefits:

Beginning of year	*66,100,000*
End of year	*$68,000,000*

C. Accounting for Pension Trust Funds -- The transactions accounted for in pension trust funds are straightforward. The funds follow full accrual basis accounting rules when recognizing Revenues (Additions) and Expenses (Deductions) and adjust their investments to reflect market value at the end of the period. Questions on the CPA exam usually ask only whether a particular item can be recognized as a Revenue (Addition) or an Expense (Deduction) in the fund.

Example: Planerville City maintains a single-employer, defined benefit pension plan for city employees and, as required by GASB, records transactions related to the plan assets in an Pension Trust Fund. The current balances in the Pension Trust Fund are as follows:

Account	DR	CR
Cash	35,000	
Interest Receivable	5,000	
Investments	530,000	
Pension Annuities Payable		10,000
Net Position Held in Trust - Pension Benefits		560,000

During the year, the following transactions occurred:

- Planerville contributed $30,000 to the pension plan on behalf of city employees. Contributions from the employees totaled $20,000.

- Interest of $18,000 and dividends of $4,000 were received in cash during the year ($5,000 of the interest had been previously accrued). Accrued interest at year end totaled $7,000.

- Annuity payments to retirees during the year totaled $35,000, including the $10,000 that had been previously accrued. Accrued pensions payable at the end of the year totaled $15,000.

- Terminated employees requested and received refunds of their contributions totaling $5,000.

- Investment management fees of $8,000 were paid.

Pension Trust Fund:

		DR	CR
DR:	Cash	50,000	
	CR:Contributions - Employers		30,000
	CR: Contributions - Employees		20,000

To record receipt of employer and employee contributions.

		DR	CR
DR:	Cash	22,000	
	CR: Interest Receivable		5,000
	CR: Additions (Revenue): Investment Income		17,000

To record receipt of investment income.

		DR	CR
DR:	Interest Receivable	7,000	
	CR: Additions (Revenue): Investment Income		7,000

To record accrual of interest revenue.

DR: Deductions (Expenses): Retirement Annuities   25,000

DR: Pension Annuities Payable   10,000

    CR: Cash   35,000

To record payment of retirement annuities.

DR: Deductions (Expenses): Retirement Annuities   15,000

    CR: Pension Annuities Payable   15,000

To record accrual of retirement annuities.

DR: Deductions (Expenses): Refunds   5,000

    CR: Cash   5,000

To record payment of refunds to terminated employees.

DR: Deductions (Expenses): Management Fees   8,000

    CR: Cash   8,000

To record payment of refunds to terminated employees.

D. Supplemental Disclosures -- Although the Pension Trust Fund accounts for pension assets only in nominal dollars, actuarial information must be disclosed in two required schedules: the Schedule of Funding Progress and the Schedule of Employer Contributions. Both schedules are included in the Required Supplementary Information (RSI) section of the Comprehensive Annual Financial Report (CAFR).

   1. Schedule of Funding Progress -- This schedule compares the actuarial value of the plan assets to the plan's actuarial accrued liability for a six-year period. A key measure presented on the schedule is the funded ratio, which is the ratio of the actuarial value of the plan assets to the actuarial accrued liability.

      a. To provide a feeling for the magnitude of any funding deficit, the schedule also presents the dollar amount of the annual payroll covered by the pension plan and expresses the unfunded or (overfunded) actuarial accrued liability as a percentage of payroll.

Schedule of Funding Progress (in thousands)						
Actuarial Valuation Date	Actuarial Value of Assets	Actuarial Accrued Liability (AAL)	Unfunded/ (Overfunded) AAL	Funded Ratio	Covered Payroll	Unfunded/ (Overfunded) AAL as a % of Payroll
	(a)	(b)	(b-a)	(a/b)	(c)	((b-a)/c)
12/31/2007	910	1,001	91	90.9%	650	14.0%
12/31/2008	890	989	99	90.0%	670	14.8%
12/31/2009	821	967	146	84.9%	620	23.5%
12/31/2010	663	885	222	74.9%	550	40.4%
12/31/2011	666	854	188	78.0%	570	33.0%
12/31/2012	805	905	100	89.0%	600	16.7%

2. **Schedule of Employer Contributions --** This schedule presents the Annual Required Contribution (ARC) and the percentage of the required amount that was actually contributed to the plan during the period. This schedule also presents information for a six-year period.

    a. The Annual Required Contribution is an actuarially determined amount that is equal to the amount necessary to fund the pension benefits earned during the year (the normal cost) plus the amortization of any previous unfunded actuarial liability.

Schedule of Employer Contributions		
(in thousands)		
2007	36	92%
2008	32	98%
2009	38	85%
2010	36	84%
2011	35	90%
2012	33	93%

E. **Recognition of Pension Costs in the Employing Funds --** GASB Statement #27 requires that an employing fund's annual pension cost (APC) be calculated as the *actuarially determined* annual required contribution (ARC) plus or minus any adjustments arising from changes in actuarial estimates, differences between actual and required contributions to the plan, variations in plan asset performance, etc. The amount of pension costs actually recognized in the employing fund varies, however, according to the basis of accounting used by the fund.

1. **Governmental Funds --** Governmental funds recognize pension cost on the modified accrual basis: employers report the portion of the annual pension cost that has been or will be *funded with current resources of the governmental funds* as expenditures. This amount may be more or less than the current period's annual pension cost.

    a. Liability for any unfunded amount is not recorded in the fund but is maintained off-books by adding it to the Schedule of General Long-term Debt.

Example:
Largo County's offers a defined benefit pension plan to its employees. The annual pension cost for the fund for the current year is $100,000. However, the County was only able to contribute $50,000 to the pension plan. The County does not currently have plans to pay the additional $50,000 due to the pension plan.

DR: Expenditures - Pension Cost   50,000

    CR: Cash   50,000

To record pension cost. (*Note that no fund liability is accrued for the additional $50,000 that the County should have paid into the pension plan for the current year because the County has not yet committed resources to pay these costs.*)

---

2. **Proprietary Funds --** When employees are paid using proprietary fund resources, the employer's pension contributions are recognized on the full accrual basis, that is, whenever a fund liability is incurred. A fund liability is incurred whenever an enforceable claim is made against fund resources.

Example:
The above example is continued with the exception that the employees are paid using proprietary fund resources.

DR: Expenses - Pension Cost   100,000

     CR: Pension Liability   50,000

     CR: Cash   50,000

To record pension cost. (*Note that the full actuarially calculated pension cost is recognized even though the County has not yet committed resources to pay these costs: this is because full accrual basis accounting requires recognition of the full actuarially calculated liability in the period that the employee services were rendered.*)

IV. Private Purpose Trust Funds

A. Resources Managed in Trust

Definition:
Private Purpose Trust Funds: These funds are used to account for any resources managed in trust by the governmental entity, where the beneficiaries are outside of the governmental entity itself. The beneficiaries may be individuals, private organizations or businesses, or other governmental entities.

1. Individual private purpose trusts may be either expendable or non-expendable (e.g., endowments, where the principal must be retained and only the earnings may be expended).

2. Earnings from non-expendable trust funds are often transferred to another fund for the actual disbursements to be made.

3. Like Permanent Funds, capital gains and losses related to non-expendable trusts are attributed to the principal unless specifically directed to attribute elsewhere.

4. Under GASBS #52, land and other real estate held as investments are reported at fair value with the change in fair value for the period reported as investment income/loss.

Determining the Financial Reporting Entity

This lesson describes how the financial reporting entity is determined.

After studying this lesson, you should be able to:

1. *Describe a primary government.*
2. *Describe a component unit.*
3. *Describe the difference between blended presentation and discrete presentation of component unit information.*

I. **Other Entities** -- Because many governmental entities either authorize, or are otherwise associated with, a variety of other commissions, agencies, boards and special districts, a question arises as to which, if any, of these "other entities" should be included in the financial statements of the primary governmental unit. If the other entities are included, a further question concerns how their financial information should be presented. Most of these entities are legally separate organizations and enjoy some degree of financial and/or management independence.

II. **Terminology**

> **Definitions:**
> *Primary Government*: A state government, a general purpose local government (cities, counties) or a special purpose government that 1) has a separately elected governing body, 2) is legally separate and 3) is fiscally independent of other state and local governments. The Primary Government is also known as the Oversight Unit.
>
> *Component Units*: Legally separate organizations for which the primary government officials are financially accountable or for which the relationship with the primary government is such that it would be misleading or incomplete to exclude it from the primary government's financial statements.
>
> *Financial Reporting Entity*: A primary government and its component units.

III. **Deciding Whether an Entity is a Component Unit**

A. An "other entity" is a component unit if:

1. It is fiscally dependent on the Primary Government (must have authorization in order to adopt a budget, levy taxes/set rates or issue debt) **OR**

2. Its board is appointed by the Primary Government **and either** the Primary Government can impose its will on the entity (influence programs, projects, activities, level of services):

    a. **OR** significant financial burdens or benefits can be shifted from one entity to the other; (The Primary government is entitled to the other entities resources or is secondarily liable for debt issues.)

    b. **OR** the Primary Government's financial statements would be misleading without the inclusion of the other entity.

    See the following example.

Example:
What are the criteria for recognizing an independent agency as a component unit of a general-purpose governmental unit (i.e. city, county, or state)?

The component unit must be fiscally dependent on the primary government or, if not fiscally dependent, then its board must be appointed by the primary government and either the primary government can impose its will on the component unit or significant financial burdens or benefits can be shifted from one to the other.

IV. **GASBS #39 - Determining Whether Certain Organizations Are Component Units --** This Statement broadens the definition of a component unit. It requires legally separate organizations that are not fiscally dependent on the primary government, and for which the primary government is not financially accountable, to be included in the primary government's financial statements as component units if the organization raises and holds economic resources for the direct benefit of a governmental unit.

A. **Criteria --** Legally separate entities, that meet all of the following criteria, should be discretely presented as component units if:

1. The separate organization holds economic resources entirely, or almost entirely, for the direct benefit of the primary government, its component units, or its constituents.

2. The primary government is entitled to, or has the ability to otherwise access, a majority of the economic resources received or held by the separate organization.

3. The economic resources received or held by the separate organization are significant to the primary government.

Example:
The Business School alumni of Big X University establish a legally separate, not-for-profit foundation to provide scholarships to students and to establish chaired faculty positions. Although neither the Business School nor the University appoint members of the governing board of the foundation or exert any control over the foundation, all of the money raised by the foundation is channeled to the Business School, which constitutes a significant resource to the Business School and the University. Because all three requirements are met, the foundation is included as a component unit of Big X University.

V. **Presenting the Financial Information**

A. **Blending**

1. If the component unit is, in substance, a part of the primary government (i.e., a building authority established to construct facilities for the primary government) then the balances for its funds should be included with similar funds in the Primary Government.

Example:
The Component Unit's Capital Projects Fund should be added to the Primary Government's Capital Projects Funds, the Component Unit's GFAAG should be added to the Primary Government's GFAAG, etc.

2. **Exception --** An exception is made for the Component Unit's General Fund, which is considered a Special Revenue Fund for the Primary Unit.

B. Discrete Presentation

1. For all other Component Units, a special column is added to the right of the Primary Government's data. If there are multiple Component Units, their data may be aggregated into a single column and a combining statement that details the individual units is prepared.

 Example:
How and when is a component unit's financial information presented discreetly with the primary government?

All other component units (i.e., those that provide services to other than the primary government) use discrete presentation. The component unit(s) data is displayed in a separate column to the right of the primary government's information.

Nets Assets and Fund Balance

This lesson describes the equity section of each fund type.

After studying this lesson, you should be able to:

1. *List the three categories of net assets.*

2. *List the five categories of fund balance.*

3. *Describe when each category of fund balance should be used.*

I. **GASBS # 54 - Fund Balance Reporting and Governmental Fund Type Definitions**

   A. **Fund Balance and Governmental Fund Types** -- In February 2009, GASB issued Statement No, 54 entitled, "Fund Balance Reporting and Governmental Fund Type Definitions." The Statement replaces the current "reserved" and "unreserved" fund balance classifications with new classifications and it provides guidance for the types of activities that are accounted for in special revenue, capital projects, and debt service funds. The Statement became effective for financial statement periods after June 15, 2010 (i.e., for the fiscal year ending June 30, 2011) and pertains to fund balance amounts reported in fund-level financial statements for governmental fund types. You should expect questions on the fund balance categories established by GASBS # 54 on the CPA exam.

      1. **GASB Statement No. 54 Proposed Fund Balance Classifications**

         a. **Nonspendable** -- This classification is for amounts that cannot be spent because they are either not in spendable form (e.g., inventory, long-term receivables, or property held for resale) or the government is legally or contractually bound to maintain the amount (e.g., endowments in a permanent fund). However, if the proceeds from the collection of long-term receivables or from the sale of properties are restricted, committed, or assigned then these amounts should be included in the appropriate spendable fund balance category (i.e., restricted, committed, or assigned). Note also that for government-wide financial statements, amounts held in perpetuity are classified as nonexpendable in the **restricted net asset category. For fund-level financial statements , however, those amounts should be classified as nonspendable.**

         b. **Spendable** -- There are four classifications for amounts that are in spendable form (e.g., fund balance amounts associated with cash, investments, receivables).

            i. **Restricted Fund Balance** -- Amounts that are restricted to a specific purpose when constraints are placed on the use of resources that are either (1) externally imposed by creditors, grantors, contributors, or laws or regulations of other governments or (2) imposed by law through constitutional provisions or enabling legislation. Enabling legislation refers to legislation that authorizes the government to assess, levy, charge, or mandate the payment of resources and includes a legally enforceable requirement that those resources be used only for the specific purposes stipulated in the legislation. Moreover, the government can be compelled by external parties (e.g., citizens, public interest groups, or the judiciary) to use the resources created by the enabling legislation only for the purposes specified by it.

            ii. **Committed Fund Balance** -- Amounts that are committed for a specific purpose by formal action of the government's highest level of decision-making (e.g., by city council resolution). In contrast to fund balance restricted by enabling legislation, amounts in the committed fund balance category may be redeployed for other purposes by taking the same kind of formal action (e.g., resolution, ordinance, or legislation) it employed to previously commit the amounts. Moreover, constraints imposed by the governing body are not considered legally enforceable.

iii. **Assigned Fund Balance --** Amounts that are intended by the government to be used for specific purposes that are not classified as restricted or committed. Intent is usually expressed by the governing body, a committee or group (e.g., finance committee), or an official to which the governing body has delegated the authority to assign amounts for specific purposes. In contrast to committed fund balance classification, the authority for making an assignment is not required to be the government's highest decision-making authority. Moreover, constraints imposed on the use of assigned amounts are more easily removed or modified than amounts that are committed. (Note: this is the residual "catch-all" classification for spendable amounts not restricted or committed in a special revenue, capital projects, or debt service fund.) Governments should not report an assignment in the general fund for a specific purpose if the assignment would result in a deficit in unassigned fund balance in the general fund.

iv. **Unassigned Fund Balance --** The residual classification for the general fund for amounts not classified as restricted, committed, or assigned. (Note: typically, this classification is only used by the general fund with one exception: negative fund balance amounts in other governmental fund types are reported as unassigned.)

v. Comparing old and new rules on fund balance:

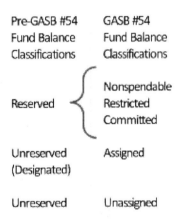

Pre-GASB #54 Fund Balance Classifications	GASB #54 Fund Balance Classifications
Reserved	Nonspendable Restricted Committed
Unreserved (Designated)	Assigned
Unreserved	Unassigned

c. **Stabilization "Rainy Day" Funds --** Many state and local governments formally and systematically set aside amounts for use in emergency situations. Stabilization amounts should be reported as a restricted or committed fund balance if they meet the criteria for being either restricted or committed. Otherwise, the amount should be reported as unassigned fund balance in the general fund.

d. **Encumbrances --** Prior to GASB Statement No. 54, encumbrances outstanding at the end of the year were shown as a reserve in the fund balance section ("Fund balance reserved for encumbrances"). Since GASB #54 removes the "reserved" classification, encumbrances should not be shown in the financial statements. If the encumbered amount has not previously been restricted, committed, or assigned it should be included within the committed or assigned fund balance depending on the level of authority used to encumber the amount. GASB states that amounts related to encumbrances should be disclosed in the notes to the financial statements.

e. **Government-wide financial statements --** The term "fund balance" is not used in government-wide financial statements. A summary reconciliation of conversion of total governmental fund balances to net assets of governmental activities in the government-wide statement of net assets must be prepared.

2. The Statement provides guidance on the types of activities accounted for in the following governmental fund types:

a. **Special revenue funds** -- Used to account for and report the proceeds of specific revenue sources that are restricted or committed to expenditure for specified purposes other than debt service or major capital projects. The "specific revenue sources" should be the foundation of the special revenue fund. Special revenue funds should not be used to account for resources held in trust for individuals, private organizations, or other governments. Restricted or committed fund balance amounts should comprise a significant portion of total fund balance. Effect: This is a "revenues-based" approach. Governments that use an "activity-based" approach (e.g., street maintenance expenditures) will need to examine whether the resources in the fund are restricted or committed amounts.

b. **Capital projects funds** -- Used to account for and report financial resources that are restricted, committed, or assigned to expenditure for the acquisition or construction of major capital facilities of the general government. Effect: These must be capital, rather than operating expenditures, in addition to nonroutine such as buildings, major building improvements, and **infrastructure assets. Non-project, routine expenditures such as buses, fire trucks, and computers should not be accounted for in a capital project fund.**

c. **Debt service funds** -- Used to account for and report financial resources that are restricted, committed, or assigned to expenditure for principal and interest payments.

II. **Net Assets**

A. "Net Assets" represent the difference between assets and liabilities in government-wide financial statements (GASB Statement No. 34) and in fund-level financial statements for proprietary fund types and fiduciary fund types. Basically, there are three categories of net assets:

1. Invested in capital assets, net of related debt – This category indicates the fund's net investment in capital assets and is calculated as the fund's gross capital assets less accumulated depreciation and less the outstanding balance of any capital asset related debt (e.g., mortgages, bonds, and other borrowings). However, the unexpended portion of capital asset related debt is not included in this net asset category.

2. Restricted net assets - At the fund level, this category indicates the amount of restricted net assets in excess of noncapital related debt and liabilities directly associated with those restricted assets. To be considered a restriction at the fund level, the constraint on the asset use must be narrower than the general limits of the activity. For example, a Water Utility Enterprise Fund does not report revenues restricted to use by the water utility as restricted net assets. According to GASB Statement No. 46, restrictions may be imposed:

a. Externally by creditors (e.g., debt covenants), grantors, contributors, or laws and regulations of other governments;

b. By constitutional provisions; or

c. By enabling legislation of the government that authorizes it to assess, levy, charge, or otherwise mandate payment of resources externally and places a legally enforceable purpose restriction on those net resources.

3. Unrestricted net assets – This category represents the remainder of the fund's net assets that does not meet the definition of the other two categories.

B. **At the Government-wide Level** -- Restricted net assets for proprietary fund types (i.e., business-type activities) in the government-wide financial statements may be larger than

(and unrestricted net assets corresponding less than) the sum of the restricted net assets used in the individual proprietary funds because the restriction on asset use is more limited in scope at the fund level than at the government-wide level. For example, assets that are restricted for water utility purposes but can be used for any legitimate purpose by the Water Utility Enterprise Fund increase unrestricted net assets in the fund level financial statements. However, the same amount is an increase in restricted net assets in the government-wide financial statements because the amounts can only be used by the water utility - they cannot be used by the parks department, street and repair maintenance, and so on.

C. Other Points --

1. Restricted net assets can never be a negative amount;

2. Although it is rare, if some assets are required to be retained in perpetuity (e.g., a permanent endowment), then two subcomponents are used - expendable and nonexpendable restricted net assets;

3. The net assets of a fiduciary fund are held in trust or in an agent capacity for specific individuals (e.g., employees and retirees), private organizations, or other governments rather than for other funds or component units of the government itself. Therefore, the net assets in a fiduciary fund are restricted net assets that are typically labeled as "Net assets held in trust."

> **Note:**
> Designations of unrestricted net assets by management indicate that the government does not intend to use those resources for the general operations of the fund. GASB **prohibits** reporting designations of net assets on the face of fund or government-wide financial statements.

4. **Note:** Recently issued GASBS # 63, "Financial Reporting of Deferred Outflows of Resources, Deferred Inflows of Resources, and Net Position," replaces "Net Assets" with "Net Position." GASBS # 63 is effective for financial statement periods beginning after 12/15/2011 (essentially for fiscal year-end 12/31/2012 and thereafter). GASBS # 63 was issued because GASB Concept Statement # 4 includes Net Position as one of five elements that make up the government-wide Statement of Financial Position. The need for the change was necessary because GASBS # 53, on derivatives, and GASBS # 60, on service concession agreements, provide for the possible reporting of deferred outflows of resources and deferred inflows of resources, which triggers the use of net position rather than net assets. Under GASBS # 63, the statement of net position can take the following form:

> Assets
> + Deferred Outflows of Resources
> - Liabilities
> - Deferred Inflows of Resources
> = Net Position

a. Similar to net assets, net position has three categories: (1) Net investment in capital assets, (2) restricted, and (3) unrestricted.

Interfund Transactions, Construction Projects, and Infrastructure

This lesson describes the types of interfund transactions and special rules related to infrastructure.

After studying this lesson, you should be able to:

1. *List the four types of interfund transactions.*

2. *Understand typical entries related to construction projects.*

3. *Describe when the "modified approach" for infrastructure can be used.*

I. **Interfund Transactions**

A. **Loans**

1. One fund transfers cash (usually) to another fund with the expectation that this amount will be repaid. The General Fund frequently loans or advances monies to an Enterprise Fund

   a. **General Fund**

Advances to Enterprise Fund *	XXX	
Cash		XXX

   b. **Enterprise Fund**

Cash	XXX	
Advances from General Fund *		XXX

   * This account title assumes that the debt is a long-term item; if it is a short-term item, the account titles are changed to Due from the Enterprise Fund (receivable) and Due to the General Fund (payable)

2. When the monies are repaid, the entries are simply reversed.

B. **Quasi-External (Interfund Sales and Purchase) Transactions** -- These transactions occur when one fund (usually an Enterprise or Internal Service fund) supplies goods/services to another fund. The transaction gives rise to a revenue entry in the fund supplying the services and an expenditure in the fund using the services.

1. For instance, if the General Fund receives copying services from the Printing and Duplication department (an Internal Service fund), the following entry is recorded:

   a. **General Fund**

Expenditures	XXX	
Due to Internal Service Fund		XXX

   b. **Internal Service Fund**

Due from General Fund	XXX	
Revenues		XXX

      c. When the amounts are paid in cash, the liability/receivable is eliminated in each of the funds.

C. Expenditure Reimbursements -- When one fund pays an expenditure on behalf of another fund and subsequently receives repayment, the expenditure is reduced in the fund that receives the repayment and increased in the fund making the repayment.

    1. For example, if the General Fund previously paid for an expenditure on behalf of a Capital Projects fund and the Capital Projects fund is now reimbursing the General Fund, the entry to record the reimbursement is:

    2. **General Fund**

Cash	XXX	
Expenditures		XXX

    3. **Capital Projects Fund**

Expenditures	XXX	
Cash		XXX

D. Residual Equity Transfers -- These are non-recurring, relatively infrequent, transfers of monies between funds, typically to establish or expand the activities of a Proprietary fund (i.e., for capital purposes), remove a deficit equity position in a Proprietary fund, or transfer a remaining balance out of a fund that is being closed. (Note: transfers from the General or Special Revenue Fund to Capital Projects or Debt Service Funds are classified as Operating Transfers, not Residual Equity Transfers!)

    1. Reporting for Residual Equity Transfers has changed in the new model.

        a. In the previous reporting model, residual equity transfers were reported as adjustments to the beginning fund balance of the transferring and receiving funds (i.e., they are not included with Revenue or Expenditure items on the operating statements).

        b. In the GASB #33 model, they are titled simply "Transfers" and are reported in the Other Financing Sources/(Uses) section of the government fund Fund-based statements and as Capital Contributions, which is a separate line item after the Net Income line of the proprietary fund Fund-based statements.

        c. The transfers of proprietary funds are closed to Capital Contributions rather than Retained Earnings.

    2. To record the transfer of remaining funds from a terminated Debt Service fund to the General Fund:

    3. **Debt Service Fund**

DR: OFU-Residual Equity Transfer to General Fund	XXX	
CR: Cash		XXX

    4. **General Fund**

DR: Cash	XXX	
CR: OFS-Residual Equity Transfer from Debt Service Fund		XXX

E. **Operating Transfers --** These are regular, routine, or recurring transfers of resources between funds to subsidize current activities. They are classified as Operating Transfers. Examples are when the General Fund transfers money to the Stores Fund (and ISF) to subsidize salary costs or when the General Fund transfers monies to a Debt Service fund to be used for the repayment of a long term liability.

1. Since these transfers do not represent revenues or expenditures for the governmental unit, they are reported as Other Financing Sources/Uses in governmental funds and as Transfers In or Out in proprietary funds (in a line(s) after Net Income).

2. The entry to record a routine transfer from the General Fund to the Debt Service Fund is shown below:

3. **General Fund**

DR: OFU - Operating Transfer to Debt Service Fund	XXX
CR: Cash	XXX

4. **Debt Service Fund**

DR: Cash	XXX
CR: OFS - Operating Transfer from General Fund	XXX

II. Entries Relating to Major Construction Projects

A. **Major Construction Projects --** When a major building project is begun, a series of entries occur that affect the Debt Service Fund and the General Fund. These entries are illustrated below.

B. **Introduction**

1. Bonds are issued to pay for the constructions (no entry required for authorization of bond issue):

a. **Capital Projects Fund**

Cash	10,000,000	
Other financing sources-Bond Proceeds		10,000,000

2. Bonds payable are shown at present value calculated using the effective interest rate method on the Government-wide financial statements.

3. Progress proceeds on the building:

a. **Capital Projects Fund**

Expenditures	5,000,000	
Cash (or Vouchers Payable)		5,000,000

4. At year end, construction in progress is included in the net fixed assets on the Government-wide financial statements in an amount equal to the expenditures incurred (do not include outstanding encumbrances):

a. **General Fixed Asset Account Group**

Construction in Progress	5,000,000	
Invest. In Fixed Assets - Capital Projects		5,000,000

5. The General Fund transfers monies to the Debt Service fund to cover interest that is now due on the debt and to provide for retirement of the bonds; the Debt Service Fund pays the interest:

   a. **General Fund**

Operating Transfer to Debt Service Fund	2,000,000	
Cash		2,000,000

   b. **Debt Service Fund**

Cash	2,000,000	
Operating Transfer from General Fund		2,000,000
Expenditures-Interest	1,000,000	
Interest Payable		1,000,000

6. The project is completed at an additional cost of 4,500,000:

   a. **Capital Projects Fund**

Expenditures	4,500,000	
Cash (or Vouchers Payable)		4,500,000

Note: The asset is reported with net fixed assets in the Government-wide financial statements.

7. The Capital Projects Fund is closed and the remaining balance is transferred to the Debt Service Fund to be used to repay the bond liability.

   See the following illustration.

a. Capital Projects Fund

Other Financing Sources	10,000,000	
Expenditures		9,500,000
Fund Balance		500,000
Residual Equity Transfer to Debt Service Fund **	500,000	
Cash		500,000
Fund Balance	500,000	
Residual Equity Transfer to Debt Service Fund **		500,000
Debt Service Fund:		
Cash	500,000	
Residual Equity Transfer from Capital Projects Fund **		500,000

** Per GASB 33 these would be reported as transfers.

Example:
The City of Mountain View approved a $3,200,000 capital project to build a city auditorium. The work was financed with a $2,500,000 bond issue, a $500,000 state grant and $200,000 of Special Revenue Fund monies. A capital projects fund named the Auditorium Fund was created to account for these transactions.

A $25,000 loan was received from the General Fund.

General Fund:		
Due from CPF	25,000	
Cash		25,000
Capital Projects Fund:		
Cash	25,000	
Due to GF		25,000

An invoice for $10,000 was received from the City's Stores Fund for supplies provided to the Street Improvement Fund. A bill for $4,000 was received from the local telephone company for the cost of moving some of its underground properties.

Stores Fund:		
Due from CPF	10,000	
Billings to Departments/Operating Revenues		10,000
Capital Projects Fund:		
Expenditures	10,000	
Due to Stores Fund		10,000
Expenditures	4,000	
Vouchers Payable		4,000

A contract was let to Reynolds Construction Company for the major portion of the project on a bid of $3,000,000. Assume that the contract was approved by the City Council and therefore this commitment will allow us to use "Fund Balance Committed" for encumbrance entries.

Capital Projects Fund:

Encumbrances	3,000,000	
Fund Balance Committed		3,000,000

The bonds were sold at 101, the grant monies were received and the Special Revenue Fund transferred its portion of the funding.

Grant:

Capital Projects Fund:

Cash	500,000	
Deferred Revenues		500,000

Transfer from Special Revenue Fund:

Special Revenue Fund:

OFU - Operating Transfers	200,000	
Cash		200,000

Capital Projects Fund:

Cash	200,000	
OFS - Operating Transfers		200,000

Bond issue:

Capital Projects Fund:

Cash	2,525,000	
OFS - Bonds Proceeds		2,500,000
Due to DSF		25,000

Debt Service Fund:

Due from CPF	25,000	
Revenues - Premium on Bonds or OFS - Premium on Bonds		25,000

Bonds payable are reported in the Government-wide financial statements at present value, which is calculated using the effective interest rate method.

The General Fund loan and the payables were paid. Additional direct expenditures of $100,000 were paid.

Capital Projects Fund:

Due to Stores Fund	10,000	
Due to General Fund	25,000	
Due to Debt Service Fund	25,000	
Vouchers Payable	4,000	
Expenditures	100,000	
Cash		164,000

General Fund:

Cash	25,000	
Due from CPF		25,000

Stores Fund:

Cash	10,000	
Due from CPF		10,000

The contractor sent in his first progress billing for $2,000,000.

Capital Projects Fund:

Fund Balance Committed	2,000,000	
Encumbrances		2,000,000
Expenditures	2,000,000	
Contracts Payable		2,000,000

The billing was paid, less a 10% retained percentage.

Capital Projects Fund:

Contracts Payable	2,000,000	
Cash		1,800,000
Contracts Payable - Retained Percentage		200,000

The accounts were closed out at year end.

Capital Projects Fund:

Deferred Revenues	500,000	
Revenues		500,000
Revenues	500,000	
OFS - Bond Proceeds	2,500,000	
OFS - Operating Transfers	200,000	
Expenditures		2,114,000
Unassigned Fund Balance	1,086,000	
Fund Balance Committed		1,000,000
Encumbrances		1,000,000
Unassigned Fund Balance	1,000,000	
Fund Balance Committed		1,000,000

Beginning of next year - reverse the encumbrance closing entry:

Encumbrances	1,000,000	
. Fund Balance Committed		1,000,000
Fund Balance Committed	1,000,000	
Unassigned Fund Balance		1,000,000

The contractor sent in his final bill for $1,000,000. The billing, less the 10% retained percentage was paid.

Capital Projects Fund:
Fund Balance Committed	1,000,000	
Encumbrances		1,000,000
Expenditures	1,000,000	
Cash		900,000
Contracts Payable - Retained Percentage		100,000

The completed building was inspected. Inspectors noted $150,000 additional work that needed to be done before the project could be approved. The contractor authorized the city to hire other contractors to complete this work. The additional work was completed and the contractors paid.

Capital Projects Fund:
Contracts Payable - Retained Percentage	150,000	
Cash		150,000

The building was approved and the remaining retained percentage was paid.

Capital Projects Fund:
Contracts Payable - Retained Percentage	150,000	
Cash		150,000

The fund was closed out.

Capital Projects Fund:
Unassigned Fund Balance	1,000,000	
Expenditures		1,000,000
Residual Equity Transfer Out **	86,000	
Cash		86,000
Unassigned Fund Balance	86,000	
Residual Equity Transfer Out **		86,000

Debt Service Fund:
Cash	86,000	
Residual Equity Transfer In **		86,000

General Long-Term Debt Account Group:
Amount Available in Debt Service Fund	86,000	
Amount to be Provided for Retirement of LT Debt		86,000

** Per GASB 33 these would be reported as transfers.

Long-term Liabilities Other Than Bonded Debt

This lesson describes the common types of long-term liabilities other than bonded debt.

After studying this lesson, you should be able to:

1. *List four common types of long-term liabilities other than bonded debt.*

2. *Describe the "general rule" at the fund level, for recognition of expenditures and liabilities.*

3. *Describe the "general rule" at the government-wide level, for recognition of expenses and liabilities.*

I. **Recognition and Reporting of Long-term Liabilities Other Than Debt in Governmental Funds**

A. **Recognize a Liability --** in the Fund-based statements only when the use of current resources is required. Governmental funds are used to account for sources, uses, and balances of expendable general government financial assets. As a result, in governmental funds:

1. Long-term assets purchased are reported as fund expenditures rather than as fixed assets; and

2. Proceeds of long-term debt are recorded as other financing sources rather than as long-term debt;

3. Long-term portions of the liability are kept off the Fund-based statements

a. only those portions of the potential liability that are likely to be paid in cash are included. For example, if sick leave does not vest to the employee then only those portions of sick leave that are reasonably expected to be paid to the employee are reported.

4. General long-term liabilities are reported in the government-wide financial statements

a. All unmatured long-term debt, except for that of proprietary funds or trust funds, is reported in the government-wide Statement of Net Assets. Matured general obligation debt, that has been recorded in or will be paid from a debt service fund, is excluded from general long-term liabilities;

b. General long-term liabilities include unmatured principal of bonds, warrants, notes, capital leases, claims and judgments, certificates of participation, compensated absences, landfill closure and postclosure care, underfunded pension plan and underfunded OPEB contributions, and other forms of general government debt. Unmatured long-term special assessment debt is also included if the government is obligated in any manner on the debt and the debt is not being serviced through an enterprise fund.

B. **Liabilities in the Government-wide Statements --** may be reported either at face value or at discounted value, depending on the circumstances.

1. If there is a "structured settlement plan" (contractual obligations to pay money on fixed or determinable dates as a means of settling a liability), then the discounted value of the plan to discharge the liability is used;

2. In the absence of a structured settlement plan, the liability is simply reported at face value.

Example:
The City of Tima Springs was assessed damages of $1,000,000 pursuant to a liability claim from a citizen who fell into an uncovered manhole. Payment of the claim is scheduled to take place over a 10-year period, with the first payment of $115,000 due in six weeks; the PV of the remaining cash flow is $465,000.

Tima would recognize the currently due portion of the settlement as an Expenditure in its Fund-based statements. The Government-wide statements would report expenses of $580,000 ($465K + $115K) and report the liability at its $465,000 PV.

Terminology

This lesson describes unique terminology and classification schemes used in governmental accounting.

After studying this lesson, you should be able to:

1. *List six expenditure classification schemes.*

2. *Distinguish between an expense and an expenditure.*

3. *List four types of nonexchange transactions.*

I. **Account Terminology and Classifications**

A. **Revenue Classifications --** Revenues of governmental funds are classified by source. The main revenue source classes are:

1. Taxes - property, sales, income, and other taxes; penalties and interest on delinquent taxes;

2. Licenses and permits - motor vehicle permits, fishing permits, building permits, alcoholic beverage licenses;

3. Intergovernmental - grants, shared revenues, and payments to other governments in lieu of taxes;

4. Charges for services - building inspection fees, copying fees, recording fees;

5. Fines and forfeits - parking fines, traffic fines;

6. Investment earnings - usually on short term investments;

7. Miscellaneous - rents and royalties, escheats. (The net assets of deceased persons who die without a will and with no known relatives revert back to the state.)

B. **Expenditure Classifications --** Most expenditures of governmental funds are authorized through appropriations. During the budgeting process, appropriations are identified not just by the type of expenditure (i.e., salaries, supplies, utilities) but also by the purpose(s) of the expenditure and its funding source. In order to show compliance with the appropriations, expenditures must also be coded to identify these characteristics.

1. **Fund --** The fund supplying the financial resources;

2. **Program or function --** The broad purpose of the expenditure (i.e., public safety, education, health, etc.);

3. **Activity --** A specific goal or objective under a program (i.e., child vaccination, low-income health care, AIDS awareness, etc.);

4. **Organizational unit --** The department or agency within the governmental entity that is responsible for managing the expenditure (i.e., Community Clinic, Emergency Services, Health Department, etc.);

5. **Character --** Identifies the period of time benefited by the expenditure:

    a. *Current expenditures* - benefit the current period only;

    b. *Capital outlay* - benefits current and future periods;

    c. *Debt service* - benefits past periods (and, potentially, current and future periods);

    d. *Intergovernmental transfers* - non-exchange (and frequently mandatory) transfers of resources from one governmental entity to another.

6. *Object* -- The 'natural' expense category, the specific purpose of the expenditures (e.g. salaries, supplies, and rent).

> **Study Tip:** 1. Of the six classifications listed, four are most frequently seen in CPA exam questions: **Fund, Program/Function, Character, and Object**.
> 2. Expenditures in the **Fund statements** for the governmental funds are reported **by character**. Expenditures in the **Government-wide statements** for the governmental funds are reported **by program/function**.

C. **Special Terminology** -- Used in Modified Accrual Basis Accounting.

   1. **Modified Accrual Basis** -- Uses alternate titles for some common accounting terms:

      a. **Expenditures, not expenses** -- Under modified accrual basis accounting, decreases in net assets are called **expenditures**, not expenses;

      b. **Fund Balance, not Retained Earnings or Owner's Equity** -- Under modified accrual basis accounting residual equity is called **Fund Balance**, not Retained Earnings or Owner's Equity;

> **Study Tip:** The examiners frequently use these two terms to indicate which type of fund is being discussed.
> If the question uses the terms **Expenditures** or **Fund Balance**, then the fund or report in question must be one of the **Governmental Funds**, as these are the only funds that use modified accrual basis accounting.
> If the question uses the terms **Expenses** or **Retained Earnings**, then the fund or report in question must be one of the **Proprietary Funds** or **Fiduciary Funds**, as these are the only funds that use full accrual basis accounting.

      c. **Vouchers Payable, not Accounts Payable** -- The term Accounts Payable may be replaced by the term Vouchers Payable in any of a governmental entity's funds. No differences in treatment are signified by the alternate terminology;

      d. **Warrants, not checks** -- The term check may be replaced by the term warrant in any of a governmental entity's funds. No differences in treatment are signified by the alternate terminology.

D. **Use of Control Accounts in Governmental Accounting**

   1. Accounts such as Revenues, Estimated Revenues, Expenditures, Appropriations, and Encumbrances frequently have the word "Control" appended to the account title. The account titles "Revenues" and "Revenues Control" refer to precisely the same account (as do "Expenditures" and "Expenditures Control", etc.).

   2. The concept of a "control" account here is the same as in financial accounting when it is used with "Accounts Receivable Control."

   3. The **control account** is a general ledger summary account that reflects the grand total balance of the subsidiary ledger accounts.

   4. For example, A/R Control represents the total dollar amount of the individual customer accounts:

Cust 1	Cust 2	Cust 3	A/R Control	
500	100	300	900	

5. In government accounting, this concept is applied to the budgetary and actual revenue and expenditure accounts: the account **"Revenue Control"** *represents the total* of the individual revenue accounts:

Rev-Taxes	Rev-Fines	Rev-Licenses	Revenue Control
600	200	300	1100

> **Note: The form of the account name does not influence the answer to the question.** A question about a revenue transaction may refer to the revenue account as "Revenue Control," "Revenue" or "Zoning Fee Revenue:" in all instances, the answer to the question would be the same.

II. GASB #33 - Accounting and Financial Reporting For Nonexchange Transactions

A. GASB #33 -- provides a comprehensive basis for recognizing nonexchange revenues such as property taxes, sales taxes, shared revenues, entitlements, and grants. It divides the revenues into four classes of transactions and defines separate recognition criteria for each class.

1. Because GASB #33 is **a full accrual basis standard** and most nonexchange revenues are recorded in governmental funds, application of the revenue recognition rules when **recording the transactions** and when **reporting them in the Fund statements** is a **two step process**:

  a. **Determine whether revenue can be recognized under GASB #33 recognition rules.** If **revenue cannot be recognized**, there is no need to go on to the second step: the transaction is **recognized as deferred revenue**;

  b. If **revenue can be recognized** under GASB #33, then we must **apply the modified accrual basis recognition standards** to determine whether revenue can be recorded in the (governmental) funds. If **revenue cannot be recognized** under modified accrual basis as well as under GASB #33, then the transaction is **recognized as deferred revenue**.

> **Note:** *These timing differences create an ongoing set of adjustments between revenue recognized in the funds and reported in the Fund statements and revenue reported in the Government-wide statements.*

2. Again, this two step process is necessary because we use a full accrual basis standard to record and report transactions in funds that use the modified accrual basis of accounting. For reporting in the **Government-wide statements**, which are presented on the full accrual basis, this two-step process is not necessary: transactions are **evaluated using only GASB #33 rules**.

> **Study Tip:** The examiners sometimes ask questions about nonexchange revenue recognition in the Government-wide statements and sometimes ask questions about nonexchange revenue recognition in the Fund statements and about when the transactions are recorded. Timing differences from revenue recognized/not recognized in prior periods may complicate these questions. It is **extremely important** to read the question carefully to **determine which basis of accounting is being used before attempting to answer the question**.

B. Nonexchange Revenue Classifications -- The following four transaction classifications are used to define and apply revenue recognition rules:

1. **Imposed nonexchange revenues --** Government assessed amounts, such as **property taxes**, fines and interest on delinquent property taxes, are billed and charged to individuals and businesses.

    a. Recognize **revenue in the period** *for which* **the taxes are levied**;

    b. Recognize an asset **(property taxes receivable) when there is an enforceable claim** or **when payment is received (cash)**.

👁 **Example:**
Property Tax Example: The City of Wellston uses a calendar fiscal year. In November, Year X, the City levied property taxes totaling $25 M to be used to finance the next fiscal year, Year Y. The taxes were due by January 31, Year Y. The City posted collections as follows:

Through December 31, Year X:	$1,5 M
Through December 31, Year Y:	$20.0 M
January 1, 2002-February 28,Year Z	$2.5 M
March 1, 2002-December 31,Year Z	$1.0 M

According to GASB #33, *all* **revenue would be recognized in Year Y** because the taxes were **levied** *for use* **in Year Y**. Note that when the **taxes are levied** in Year X, *Deferred Revenue* is credited because the revenue cannot be recognized until the following year. Therefore, the **Government-wide statements** would report:

Year X	*Deferred* Revenue	$25 M
Year Y	**Property Tax Revenue**	**$25 M**
Year Z	No revenue - all previously recognized	$0 M

In order to record the taxes in the General Fund, the requirements of modified accrual basis accounting must be considered in addition to the GASB #33 rules (i.e., revenues must be received in cash within 60 days after the end of the fiscal year). This changes the timing of the revenue recognition. Revenue is **recorded in the General Fund** and **reported in the Fund statements** as follows:

Year X	*Deferred* Revenue	$25 M
Year Y	**Property Tax Revenue** ($1.5M+$20.0M+$2.5M)	**$24 M**
Year Z	**Property Tax Revenue** (amount rec'd after 60 days)	$1 M

---

2. **Derived tax revenues --** Taxes resulting from the taxable exchange transactions of individuals and businesses. Principal examples are sales taxes and income taxes. These revenues differ from imposed revenues as the government does not know what the amount will be until it receives the tax.

    a. Recognize both assets and revenue **at the time the underlying exchange transaction takes place**.

> **Example:**
> **Sales Tax Example:** In December, Year X, merchants collected $58M in sales taxes. The merchants filed tax forms on January 31, Year Y and remitted $50M to the state. Because of a downturn in the economy, it was expected that only $5M of the remaining $8M would be collected and that $5M would not be collected until April, Year Y.
>
> The **Government-wide statements** report the net revenue in the period in which the underlying exchange transaction (e.g., the purchase of goods from the merchants) took place:
>
> **Year X: Sales Tax Revenue** ($58M-$3M estimated uncollectible)   **$55 M**
>
> **Year Y:** nothing - all revenue recognized in the prior period $0 M
>
> To record the taxes in the General Fund, we must consider the timing of the cash receipts in addition to the GASB #33 requirements. Thus, the sales taxes would be **recorded in the General Fund** and **reported in the Fund statements** as follows:
>
> **Year X: Sales Tax Revenue** ($50M rec'd within first 60 days of Year Y) **$50 M**
>
> **Year Y: Sales Tax Revenue** ($5 M rec'd after first 60 days of Year Y)   **$5 M**
>
> Notice that the total amount of revenue recognized over the two-year period is the same in the Government-wide statements as in the Fund statements. Only the timing of the recognition differs.

C. **Government-mandated nonexchange transactions --** These are intergovernmental transfers of resources including entitlements, shared revenues, and payments in lieu of taxes. Most of these resources: 1) have restrictions on how they may be used; and 2) are only available to the recipient entity if they meet specific conditions known as **"eligibility requirements."**

   1. Recognize both assets and revenue when **all eligibility requirements** have been met;

      a. Eligibility requirements include **achievement of specified objectives** and **time requirements**;

      b. *Generic* eligibility requirements **may be assumed to be met** (i.e., in order to receive highway funds, a state must have interstate highways in need of repair; even though no specific repairs may be scheduled when the monies are received, eligibility is assumed to be met because it would be unusual not to have interstate highways in need of repair).

   2. **"On-behalf of" payments --** These are , by definition, **recognized as revenue** and **as a corresponding expenditure**. (For example, state governments may make the employer portion payments for elementary and secondary schools on behalf of the school districts in order to provide equal pension benefits to teachers across the state.)

   See the following example.

Example:

Shared revenue example: A state is entitled to 40% of the federal gasoline tax collected on gas sales within its borders. The state receives these monies directly from the retailers and periodically remits 60% of the tax to the federal government. In order to be eligible to receive these monies, the drinking age in the state must be no less than 21 and the state must maintain all interstate highways within its borders at or above a specified level of condition for the entire year.

If the **drinking age in this state is below 21**, the state **may not recognize revenue**, even though it has the cash in its possession, because this **specific eligibility requirement has not been met**. This is the case both for **reporting on the Government-wide statements** and on the **Fund statements** and for **recording in the General Fund**.

If the **drinking age is 21**, the state may **recognize revenue immediately** in the **Government-wide statements** even though it has not maintained all of the interstate highways at the specified condition level for the entire year because this is a **generic eligibility requirement** and the presumption is that it will be met. **Revenue reporting in the Fund statements** and **recording in the General Fund** is dependent upon the timing of the receipt of cash.

D. **Voluntary Nonexchange Transactions Contracts** -- Entered into voluntarily by the participants which may include individuals and/or other governmental entities; this classification includes competitively awarded **grants**, cash and/or property **contributions** or **bequests**, and **endowments**; frequently **subject to use/purpose restrictions and/or eligibility requirements**;

1. Recognize both assets and revenue when **all eligibility requirements have been met**:

   a. The existence of **purpose restrictions does** *not* **affect revenue recognition**;

   b. For **reimbursement/expenditure-driven grants**, reimbursement requirements are considered to be **eligibility requirements**, so **revenue is** *not* **recognized until the expenditure is made**;

   c. **Endowments**, which could be considered to have an indefinite time restriction, are explicitly required to be **recognized as revenue upon receipt**.

Example:

Bexar City received a $100,000 grant from the Alliance for Education to be used to provide reading programs at neighborhood recreation centers. In order to receive these monies, the city must operate programs in at least three recreation centers, each with an enrollment of at least 30 children between the ages of 5 and 7. Bexar currently operates two centers with substantially more than 30 children within the required age range enrolled in programs. It plans to open a third center in two months and anticipates an enrollment of 5-7 year olds sufficient to meet the grant requirement.

When the grant monies are received, they **cannot be recognized as revenue** in either the Government-wide or Fund statements because the **specific eligibility requirements have not been met**. As soon as the third center is completed and enrollments have reached the specified level (i.e., **the eligibility requirements have been met), revenue can be recognized** in both the Government-wide and the Fund statements.

E. Other Considerations Affecting Revenue Recognition -- Resources from nonexchange transactions often have **timing restrictions** (restrictions on **when** the resources are to be used) and **purpose restrictions** (restrictions on how the resources are to be used).

1. **Time restrictions --** Resources may not be used until a **specific date or event has taken place**, and revenue must **not be recognized** until the time requirement has been met;

2. **Purpose restrictions --** When resources **must be used for specific purposes**, revenue is **recognized** *immediately;* **limitations to the availability of the resources** are shown by reporting a **reservation of fund balance (fund-based statements)** or a **restricted net asset (government-wide statements)**.

Special Items - Recent Developments

This lesson describes recent accounting standards affecting governmental entities.

After studying this lesson, you should be able to:

1. *List five types of obligating events related to pollution remediation.*

2. *Describe the conditions necessary to be met in order to capitalize internally generated assets.*

I. **Statements --** The following statements have been issued and/or implemented by GASB during the past years. Though some of these topics have been addressed in other parts of the study text, they are included in this section because, historically, the Board of Examiners tends to include questions on new statements more often than they might otherwise warrant.

II. **GASBS #49 - Accounting and Reporting for Pollution Remediation Obligations --** Many state and local governments are faced with high costs in their attempts to remediate existing pollution problems. Note, that the statement does not address costs associated with control or prevention of future pollution problems. This standard was issued November 2006 and is effective for financial statement periods beginning after December 15, 2007.

A. **Liability Recognition Triggers --** The government must recognize a liability for pollution remediation if the cost can be reasonably estimated and one of the following five events occurs:

1. **Pollution poses an imminent danger** to the public or environment and a government has little or no discretion to avoid fixing the problem.

2. The government has **violated a pollution prevention-related permit or license.**

3. **The government has been identified by a regulator** (i.e., the Environmental Protection Agency (EPA)) as being responsible (or potentially responsible) for cleaning up pollution, or for paying all or some of the cost of the clean up.

4. **An outcome (or likely outcome) of a lawsuit** will compel the governmental entity to address a pollution problem.

5. **The government begins to clean up pollution** or conducts related remediation activities (or the government legally obligates itself to do so).

B. **Expense or Expenditure Recognition --** Recognition of the expense varies with the fund responsible for the cleanup costs.

1. **Government-wide Financial Statements and Proprietary Fund Statements --** Report expenses as the liability related to the pollution remediation is accrued. As the work is preformed and payments are made, the liability is reduced.

2. **Governmental Fund Statements --** Report expenditures when the payment for the cleanup is made.

C. **Capitalization of Pollution Remediation Costs --** Not every pollution remediation is recognized as an expense. Pollution remediation costs can instead be capitalized when they are used for the following:

1. Prepare property for sale in **anticipation of a sale**;

2. Prepare property for use when the **property was acquired with known or suspected pollution that was expected to be remediated**;

3. Perform pollution remediation that **restores a pollution-caused decline in service utility, which was previously recognized as an asset impairment**;

    4. Acquire property, plant, and equipment that has a **future alternative use other than remediation efforts.**

III. Other Postemployment Benefits -- The GASB has recently issued several statements covering the reporting and disclosure of Other Postemployment Benefits - that is, retirement benefits such as health insurance, life insurance, long-term disability insurance, etc. - and the disclosure requirements for both pensions and other postemployment benefits. The measurement and disclosure requirements of the Statements are related, and disclosure requirements are coordinated to avoid duplication when an OPEB plan is included as a trust or agency fund in an employer's financial report.

  A. GASBS #43 - Financial Reporting for Postemployment Benefit Plans;

  B. GASBS #45 -Accounting and Financial Reporting for Employers for Postemployment Benefit;

  C. GASBS #50 - Pension Disclosures: An Amendment of GASB Statements No. 25 and No. 27 - Issued May 2007 and effective for periods beginning after June 15, 2007.

  D. Financial Reporting for Postemployment Benefit Plans -- This Statement prescribes reporting requirements for postemployment benefits that mirrors the reporting requirements for pensions.

    1. Two financial statements are required to report the current financial information about plan assets:

      a. Statement of Plan Net Assets;

      b. Statement of Changes in Plan Net Assets.

    2. Two schedules are required to provide actuarially determined historical trend information about the status of the plan:

      a. Schedule of Funding Progress;

      b. Schedule of Employer Contributions.

> **Study Tip:**
> Because all three of these related statements have recently been implemented it is highly likely that accounting for OPEB will be regularly tested on the exam for the next several years. Recognition and reporting requirements for OPEB are basically the same as requirements for pensions: these requirements are discussed in detail in the Study Text for Pension Trust Funds.

  E. Reporting Postemployment Benefit Costs for Employers -- This Statement establishes standards for the measurement, recognition, and display of OPEB expense/expenditures and related liabilities (assets) and note disclosures. Prior to the issue of this Statement, most organizations recognized OPEB on a pay-as-you-go basis. The Statement requires organizations to recognize the cost of these benefits during the period that they are earned. In general, reporting for OPEB follows reporting requirements for pension benefits. That is:

    1. Annual OPEB cost is equal to the employer's annual required contribution to the plan (ARC) - which is an actuarially computed value.

      a. The Government-wide Statements and the Proprietary Fund Statements both report the OPEB cost as an expense of the current period.

      b. The Governmental Fund Statements report only the amount actually contributed as a current period expenditure.

    2. The Net OPEB obligation is equal to the cumulative difference between the annual OPEB cost and the employer's contributions to the plan.

      a. Retroactive application of these measurement requirements is *not* required; therefore, the OPEB liability at the beginning of implementation of the Statement will be zero.

  F. Reporting Pension and OPEB Plan Status -- Note disclosures and RSI requirements for pensions and OPEB are very similar after the implementation of GASBS # 50.

1. **Notes to the Financial Statements** -- The actuarial methods and assumptions used in the most recent actuarial valuation should be disclosed in the notes, rather than in the RSI. The funded status of the plan should be disclosed in the notes but should reference the more complete information contained in the Schedule of Funding Progress in the RSI.

2. **Required Supplementary Information** -- When actuarial values are used to calculate the Annual Required Contribution (ARC) to the plan, as is the case for virtually all defined benefit pension plans and OPEB, a Schedule of Funding Progress should be presented in the RSI along with a Schedule of Employer Contributions. Both schedules use actuarial calculations to determine the value of the plan assets, as well as the plan liability. The actuarial valuation is required every two years for plans with a total membership of 200 or more and every three years for plans with less than 200 members. (See the Pension Trust study text for details relating to these schedules.)

IV. **GASBS #51 - Accounting and Financial Reporting for Intangible Assets** -- GASBS #51 was issued to resolve inconsistencies that had developed in accounting and financial reporting for intangible assets. The types of intangible assets held by governments include the following: water rights, timber rights, patents, trademarks, computer software, and easements. Easements are mentioned in GASBS #34 (paragraph 19) as a type of capital asset, and it is this reference that is considered the source of the inconsistencies in accounting for intangible assets observed in practice. Issued June 2007 and effective for financial statement periods beginning after June 15, 2009.

A. **Characteristics of Intangible Assets** -- An intangible asset is an asset that possess all of the following characteristics:

1. **Lack of physical substance** -- The asset may be contained in, or on an item of, physical substance (e.g., software on a computer disc) or closely associated with another item that has physical substance (e.g., the underlying land in the case of a right-of-way). These modes of containment and associated items are not considered when determining whether an asset lacks physical substance.

2. **Nonfinancial nature** -- The asset is not in monetary form nor does it represent a claim or rights to assets in monetary form.

3. **Initial useful life** extending beyond a single reporting period.

B. **Exceptions** -- The provisions of GASBS #51 do not apply to the following intangible assets:

1. Those acquired or created for the purpose of obtaining income or profit - which should follow guidance for investments;

2. Assets resulted from capital lease transactions reported by lessees;

3. Goodwill created through combination.

C. **Recognition** -- An intangible asset should be recognized in the statement of net assets, if it is identifiable. One of the following two conditions must be met for intangible assets to be considered identifiable:

1. The asset is separable. It is capable of being separated or divided from the government and sold, transferred, licensed, rented, or exchanged;

2. The asset arises from contractual or other legal rights.

D. **Internally Generated Intangible Assets** -- Internally generated intangible assets are capitalized only when all three of the following conditions are met. Outlays prior to meeting the three conditions should be expensed as incurred.

1. The project is expected to provide an intangible asset upon completion of the project.

2. Technical or technological feasibility for completion of the project is demonstrated so that the intangible asset will provide its expected service capability.

3. The intention, ability, and presence of effort to complete or continue development of the intangible asset is demonstrated.

E. **Internally Generated Computer Software --** Activities involved in developing and installing internally generated computer software can be grouped into three stages:

   1. Preliminary project stage: Activities include the conceptual formulation and evaluation of alternatives, the determination of the needed technology, and the final selection of alternatives. Treatment: expense.

   2. Application development stage: Activities include design, software configuration and interfaces, coding, hardware installation, and testing. Treatment: Capitalize.

   3. Post-implementation/operation stage: Activities include application training and software maintenance. Treatment: expense.

   4. Activities in the preliminary project stage and the post-implementation/operation stage should be expensed. Outlays in the application development stage should be capitalized; however, the following two criteria must be met in order to capitalize application development stage activities:

      a. The activities in the preliminary project stage are completed;

      b. There is an ongoing authorization and commitment to funding.

F. **Modification of Computer Software --** Additional criteria must be met to capitalize outlays associated with an internally generated modification of computer software that is already in operation. One of the following criteria must be met:

   1. An increase in the functionality of the computer software;

   2. An increase in the efficiency of the computer software;

   3. An extension of the estimated useful life of the software.

G. **Amortization --** The amortization period should not exceed the period of service capacity provided in contractual or legal rights. Renewal periods related to such rights may be considered if there is evidence that the government will seek to achieve the renewal and that the outlays associated with the renewal are nominal in relation to the level of service capacity expected to be obtained by the renewal. An intangible with an indefinite useful life should not be amortized (e.g., a permanent right-of-way easement).

H. **Effective Date --** Financial statements for periods beginning after June 15, 2009. Applied retroactively by restating financial statements for all prior periods presented. If the actual historical cost of an intangible asset is not known, the government should report the estimated historical cost for intangible assets acquired after June 30, 1980.

V. **GASBS #52 - Land and Other Real Estate Held as Investments by Endowments --** Prior to this standard, permanent and term endowments reported land and other real estate held as investments at their historical cost. This statement requires that endowments report their land and other real estate investments at fair value. Changes in fair value should be reported as investment income. Effective date is used for financial statement periods beginning after June 15, 2008.

VI. **GASBS #53 - Accounting and Financial Reporting for Derivative Instruments: --** The key provision of this statement is that derivative instruments, with the exception of synthetic guaranteed investment contracts, are reported at fair value. Issued June 2008 and effective for financial statement periods beginning after June 15, 2009. The table below describes how changes in the fair value of derivative instruments are reported:

	Purpose of Derivative Instrument	
	Investment	Hedging
Reporting of change in the fair value of the derivative instrument	Investment Revenue-Loss	Deferred Charge or Credit
Reported in:	Statement of Activities	Statement of Net Assets-Balance Sheet

A. GASBS #53 limits the use of the deferred recognition approach to those it describes as effective hedges. In essence, a hedge is considered effective when a change in the fair value of the hedging derivative is offset by the change in the fair value of the underlying hedged item. The standard provides three methods to evaluate the effectiveness of a hedge:

1. **Consistent Critical Terms Method --** If the critical terms of the hedgeable item and the derivative instrument are the same, or very similar, the changes in cash flows or fair values of the derivative instrument will substantially offset the changes in the cash flows or fair values of the hedgeable item.

2. **Quantitative Methods**

   a. **Dollar-offset method --** This method evaluates effectiveness by comparing the expected cash flows or fair values of the derivative instrument with the changes in the expected cash flows or fair values of the hedgeable item. If the changes of either the hedgeable item or the derivative instrument divided by the other falls in the range of 80 to 125 percent, these changes substantially offset and the derivative instrument is considered to be an effective hedge. For example, if the actual results are such that the change in fair value of the derivative instrument is a decrease of $100 and the fair value of the hedgeable item increased by 110, the dollar-offset percentage is 110/100, which is 110 percent, or 100/110, which is 91 percent. In either case, the hedging derivative instrument is determined to be effective.

   b. **Regression analysis method --** This method evaluates effectiveness by considering the statistical relationship between the cash flows or fair values of the derivative instrument and the hedgeable item. The changes in cash flows or fair values of the derivative instrument substantially offset the changes in the cash flows or fair value of the hedgeable item, if all of the following criteria are met:

      i.   The R-squared of the regression analysis is at least 0.80;

      ii. The F-statistic calculated for the regression model demonstrates that the model is significant using a 95 percent confidence level;

      iii. The regression coefficient for the slope is between -1.25 and - 0.80.

3. **Synthetic Instrument Method --** Sometimes, a government will combine an interest-bearing hedgeable item with a derivative instrument to create a third synthetic instrument. This method is limited to cash flow hedges in which the hedgeable items are interest bearing and carry a variable rate. Under this method, the derivative instrument is effective if the actual synthetic rate is substantially fixed. The hedge is considered substantially fixed if the actual synthetic rate is within 90 percent to 111 percent of the fixed rate. For example, if an interest-rate swap's fixed payment rate is 7.00 percent, an actual synthetic instrument rate that falls within a range between 6.30 percent (90 percent of 7.00 percent) and 7.77 percent (111 percent of 7.00 percent) is considered to be substantially fixed and, therefore, the derivative instrument is considered effective.

B. Changes in the fair value of derivative instruments, that do not qualify as effective using one the methods described above, are reported in the Statement of Activities.

VII. GASBS # 55 - The Hierarchy of Generally Accepted Accounting Principles for State and Local Governments

A. The purpose of Statement No. 55 is to move the relevant parts of the AICPA Statement on Auditing Standards No. 69, "*The Meaning of* Present Fairly in Conformity with Generally Accepted Accounting Principles," to the GASB codification. Issued and effective March 2009. The GAAP hierarchy for all state and local governmental entities is categorized in descending order of authority as follows:

1. Officially established accounting principles - Governmental Accounting Standards Board (GASB) Statements and Interpretations.

2. GASB Technical Bulletins and, if specifically made applicable to state and local entities by the AICPA and cleared by GASB, AICPA Industry Audit and Accounting Guides, and AICPA Statements of Position.

3. AICPA Practice Bulletins, if specifically made applicable to state and local entities and cleared by GASB, as well as consensus positions of a group of accountants organized by GASB that attempt to reach consensus positions on accounting issues applicable to state and local governmental entities.

4. Implementation guides (Q&As) published by the GASB staff, as well as practices that are widely recognized in state and local government. If the accounting treatment for a transaction or other event is not specified by a pronouncement or established practice described in categories (a)-(d), a governmental entity may consider other accounting literature. Other accounting literature includes: GASB Concept Statements, pronouncements referred to in categories (a)-(d) not specifically made application by GASB, and other pronouncements issued by FASB, FASAB, AICPA, IPSAB, and accounting textbooks, handbooks, and articles.

VIII. GASBS # 56 - Codification of Accounting and Financial Reporting Guidance Contained in the AICPA Statements on Auditing Standards -- Issued and effective March 2009.

A. This Statement adds accounting guidance in the AICPA auditing literature to the GASB codification in three areas:

1. **Related Party Transactions** -- State and local governments are required to disclose related party transactions and should recognize the substance of the transaction rather than its legal form.

2. **Subsequent Events** -- Two types of subsequent events are described in the Statement. Recognized events consist of those events that provide additional evidence with respect to conditions that existed at the date of the statement of net assets and require adjustments to the financial statements. **Nonrecognized** events consist of events that provide evidence with respect to conditions that did not exist at the date of the statement of net assets. These events should not result in adjustment of the financial statements, but they may be disclosed in the notes of the financial statements.

3. **Going Concern Considerations** -- The Statement requires financial statement preparers to evaluate whether there is a substantial doubt about a government's ability to continue as a going concern for 12 months beyond the financial statement date (or shortly thereafter, which GASB describes as "an additional three months"). Indicators of substantial doubt include:

a. Negative trends (e.g., recurring budget deficits);

b. Other indicators of financial difficulties (e.g., loan default);

c. Internal matters (e.g., work stoppages);

d. External matters (e.g., legal proceedings).

4. If the evaluation determines that there is substantial doubt about a governmental entity's ability to continue as a going concern, then the notes to the financial statements should include the following disclosures:

   a. Pertinent conditions and events giving rise to the assessment that a substantial doubt exists about the ability of the entity to continue as a going concern;

   b. The possible effects of such conditions and events;

   c. Government officials' evaluation of the significance of those conditions and events;

   d. Possible discontinuance of operations;

   e. Government officials' plans;

   f. Information about the recoverability or classification of recorded assets amounts or the amounts or classification of liabilities.

IX. **GASB Concept Statement No. 5 - Service Efforts and Accomplishments Reporting --** An Amendment of GASB Concepts Statement No. 2.

   A. **Service Efforts and Accomplishments (SEA) --** Issued November 2008.

      1. CS-5 amends CS-2 by stating that SEA reporting is voluntary and that it will provide guidelines (i.e., suggestions) only. Essentially CS-5 states that it is beyond the scope of the GASB to mandate SEA reporting practices. Instead, GASB provides conceptual guidance regarding the reporting of SEA performance information. CS-5 identifies the following three elements of SEA performance measures:

         a. Measures of service efforts - input measures (e.g., number of work hours devoted to road maintenance);

         b. Measures of service accomplishments - output and outcome measures (number of miles of road repaired);

         c. Measures that relate service efforts to service accomplishments - efficiency measures and cost-outcome measures (labor cost per mile of road resurfaced)..

      2. CS-5 also identifies related information that provides a context for understanding SEA performance measures. Related quantitative and narrative information that can help provide a context for users to understand reported SEA performance measures fall into the following five categories:

         a. Comparison information - to previous years, to established targets, progress toward goals, to generally accepted norms and standards, to comparable entities and jurisdictions;

         b. Unintended effects - significant indirect consequences (positive or negative);

         c. Demand for services - changes in the demand for services and effect of other programs competing for the same resources;

         d. Factors that influence results - external and internal factors that affect results;

         e. Narrative information - explanations for the level of SEA performance, unintended effects, actions taken.

Alphabetical Index